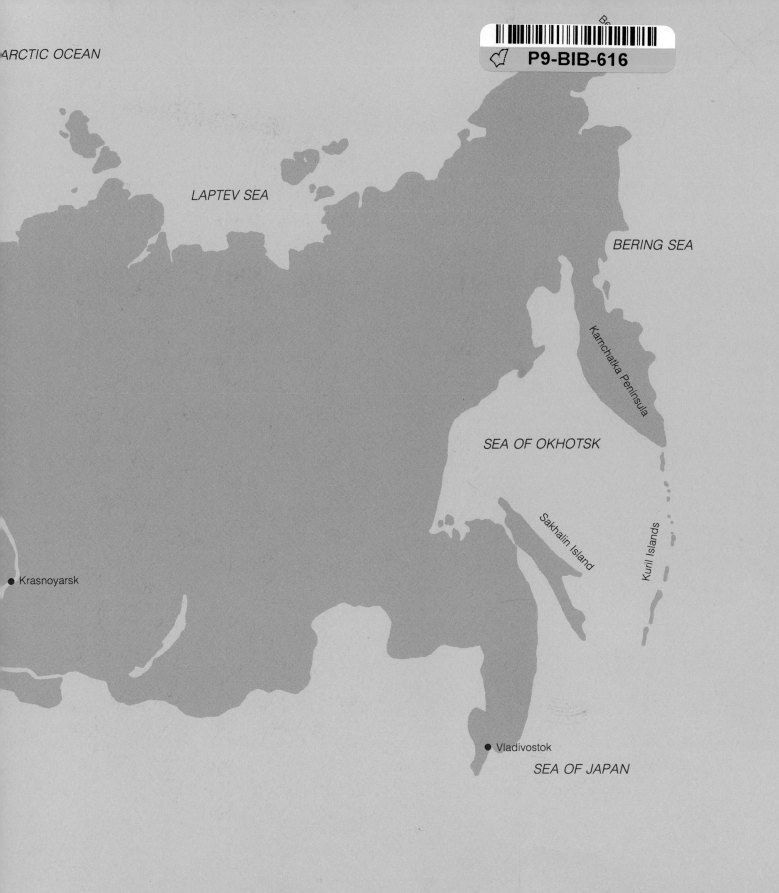

ARCTIC OCEAN

LAPTEV SEA

BERING SEA

Kamchatka Peninsula

SEA OF OKHOTSK

Sakhalin Island

Kuril Islands

● Krasnoyarsk

● Vladivostok

SEA OF JAPAN

# Guide to the Soviet Navy

# Guide to the Soviet Navy

THIRD EDITION

## By Norman Polmar

Naval Institute Press
Annapolis, Maryland

Second printing, 1983

*Library of Congress Cataloging in Publication Data*
Polmar, Norman.
  Guide to the Soviet navy.

  Second ed. by S. Breyer and N. Polmar.
  Bibliography: p.
  Includes indexes.
  1. Soviet Union. Voenno-morskoĭ flot.   I.  Breyer,
Siegfried. Guide to the Soviet navy.   I. Title.
VA573.P598   1983        359.3′0947        83-11431
ISBN 0-87021-239-7

Printed in the United States of America

Dedicated to the memory of
Captains Donald Macintyre and Stephen W. Roskill
naval officers, historians, and friends.

Anyone who would study the Soviet Navy would do well to keep in mind the words of those who have known Russia and the Soviet Union firsthand.

> Talking about Russia one always imagines that one is talking about a country like the others; in reality, this is not so at all.
>
> Peter Chaadaev, leading figure of Moscow society during the Crimean War

> I cannot forecast to you the action of Russia. It is a riddle wrapped in a mystery inside an enigma; but perhaps there is a key. That key is Russian national interest.
>
> Winston Churchill

> There are no experts on the Soviet Union; only varying degrees of ignorance.
>
> Ambassador Charles E. (Chip) Bohlen American Ambassador to the USSR (1952–1957)

# Contents

# Preface

The Soviet Navy is today in a period of change from a sea-denial navy to one that will—in several key respects—look much like the U.S. Navy. The most dramatic indication of this is the construction of large-deck aircraft carriers, probably nuclear propelled. However, those ships are probably not intended to fight the U.S. fleet on the high seas, but to provide control of the air and sea in support of Soviet direct or indirect intervention in the Third World.

At the same time, the development of the Oscar-class submarine and the Blackjack strike aircraft will help to defeat U.S. surface naval forces that may attempt to counter such Soviet actions in the Third World as well as to deny U.S. forces access to the sea approaches of the Soviet Union. In addition to this growth in weapons and platforms there has been significant Soviet development of the command, control, reconnaissance, and communications systems for directing worldwide Soviet naval operations.

This third edition of the *Guide to the Soviet Navy* describes the Soviet Navy of the mid-1980s as it embarks on a new phase of development. The most obvious indications of this new phase are the generation of warships to emerge from Soviet shipyards in the past decade. These include the aircraft carriers of the KIEV class, the nuclear-powered missile cruiser KIROV, the Krasina-class antiship cruiser, the SOVREMENNYY and UDALOY destroyer classes, several new nuclear and diesel-electric submarine classes, advanced amphibious and auxiliary ships, and numerous lesser naval units as well as accompanying naval aircraft. These latest Soviet efforts are detailed in this edition of *Guide to the Soviet Navy*. Also included are the organization of the Soviet Navy, its aircraft, personnel, shipyards, bases and ports, and other features.

In the mid-1980s the Soviet Union has the world's largest fleet in numbers of warships (see figure 1-1). In terms of displacement this fleet is second only to that of the United States. However, the U.S. tonnage advantage is due primarily to the relatively few U.S.

large aircraft carriers and amphibious helicopter carriers. Current trends in Soviet naval construction could lead to Soviet equality in tonnage by about the year 2000. This will be almost certainly true if the current long-range shipbuilding program developed by U.S. Secretary of the Navy John Lehman is not brought to fruition.

Direct comparisons of Soviet and U.S. fleets are useful, but cannot be considered absolute indicators of relative strength. The two superpowers construct different types of ships, with different political considerations, and for different missions that require different tactics. Indeed, the most significant "lesson" that might be drawn from this volume is that the Soviet and U.S. navies are different, and thus, direct comparisons are of limited value and could be misleading.

Added to the comparisons of U.S. and Soviet fleets must be some consideration of the increasing complexity of modern navies. Admiral of the Fleet of the Soviet Union S.G. Gorshkov, the long-serving Commander in Chief of the Soviet Union, has written that:

> The qualitative transformations which have taken place in naval forces have also changed the approach to evaluating the relative might of navies and their combat groupings: we have had to cease comparing the number of warships of one type or another and their total displacement (or the number of guns in a salvo or the weight of this salvo), and turn to a more complex, but also more correct appraisal of the striking and defensive power of ships, based on a mathematical analysis of their capabilities and qualitative characteristics.[1]

The Soviets have led the U.S. Navy in the deployment (although not necessarily the development) of ocean surveillance satellites, cruise and ballistic missiles, vertical-launch missile systems, gas-turbine ship propulsion, advanced nuclear-propelled submarines,

[1]S.G. Gorshkov, "Navies in War and Peace," *Morskoy Sbornik*, No. 2, 1972, p. 20.

and Vertical Take-Off and Landing (VTOL) aircraft. However, here too comparisons can be misleading because of the Soviet procurement philosophy of producing "adequate" rather than the "best" equipment. There is said to be a plaque in the office of Admiral Gorshkov that declares "Better is the Enemy of Good Enough." This attitude recognizes the limitations of Soviet manpower (scope of education, limited service duration for enlisted men) and the overall state of the Soviet industry (long-term planning, quality-control problems, etc.).

Another qualitative measure of evaluating the modern Soviet Navy is to review the trends in the Soviet Navy's forward operations and the scale of their naval exercises. The scope of operations during the past two decades has definitely been enlarged from coastal activities to a modern, capable "blue-water" fleet.

In addition, the Soviet Union has a large and modern merchant fleet; the world's largest research fleet, with more ships than all of the Western nations combined; and the world's largest fishing fleet, harvesting more food from the sea than any nation except Japan. Along with the Soviet Navy, these other fleets represent a massive and unprecedented peacetime investment in the use of the sea.

While the ships, submarines, aircraft, and even the manpower of the Soviet Navy can be counted and "measured" by the West with reasonable accuracy, the question of fleet effectiveness is more difficult to ascertain. There are several methods of approaching this issue. One method is based on information obtained from recent interviews with immigrants from the Soviet Union, including defectors from the armed forces. Virtually all are strongly anti-Soviet and have given the Soviet armed forces very poor marks with respect to how well they could fight. In contrast, the former Soviet naval personnel among them, while few in number, tend to give the Soviet Navy uniformly high marks.

Their assessment results largely from the fact that navies operate in peace much as they do in war. A high level of competence is necessary merely to ensure the safe operation of ships and aircraft, whether in conflict or in peacetime operations. Armies, by comparison, do not require similar levels of competence for peacetime operations.

This does not and should not imply that the Soviets are "ten feet tall." Indeed, the Soviet Navy and the other military services suffer from the labor and quality control problems and shortages that plague their society as a whole. There have also been significant accidents and losses in the Soviet fleet, most notably the November-class nuclear submarine that sank off the coast of Spain in 1970 and the Kashin-class destroyer that caught fire and blew up in the Black Sea in 1974.

Most statements about the respective capabilities of the U.S. and Soviet Navies tend toward extremes. Objective and balanced conclusions or statements are difficult to obtain. This seems especially true for the senior officers of both navies, who tend to polarize their positions (e.g., "our submarines have *never* been detected in the open ocean" or "their capabilities are improving rapidly and will soon threaten our. . . ."). A more realistic approach may have been put forth by Admiral Elmo R. Zumwalt, who as U.S. Chief of Naval Operations (1970–1974) stated that given their respective missions and capabilities, the Soviet Navy could probably perform its wartime missions more successfully than could the U.S. Navy.

The ship data in this volume are derived from a variety of official Western sources and other published material. Of particular value have been *Combat Fleets of the World* by Jean Labayle Couhat, published every second year in an English-language edition prepared by A.D. Baker III, and *Weyer's Warships of the World* by Gerhard Albrecht, also published in alternate years in English. (These books are originally published as *Flottes de Combat* and *Weyers Flotten Taschenbuch*, respectively.)

Additional sources are noted in the text and in the reading list (appendix C) at the end of the book. A number of Soviet sources have been used, both in English and in Russian. The latter have included *Sovetskaya Voyennaya Entsiklopediya (Soviet Military Encyclopedia), Krasnaya Zvezda* (Red Star), *Morskoy Sbornik* (Naval Digest), and *Sudostroeniye* (Shipbuilding). A careful reading of these and other Soviet publications reveals a relatively accurate picture of Soviet doctrinal, strategic, and tactical thought. Some analysts, however, view with skepticism material drawn from unclassified sources. Still, as one analyst has observed, "It is important to bear in mind that Soviet military doctrine is not a set of carefully contrived external propaganda poses, but an important body of functional operating principles for internal consumption by the Soviet military. Since the Soviet military leadership can scarcely afford to lie to its own officer corps about its strategic intentions and objectives merely to deceive the West, and since the size and complexity of the Soviet political-military infrastructure preclude the communication of policy guidance solely through secret channels, it should only stand to reason that the bulk of declared Soviet military doctrine reflects a reasonably faithful image of actual Soviet strategic thinking."[2]

A considerable amount of information on Soviet naval matters is available from U.S. government sources, especially the state-

[2]Benjamin A. Lambert, "The Sources of Soviet Military Doctrine" in F.B. Horton III, ed., *Comparative Defense Policy* (Baltimore, Md.: Johns Hopkins University Press, 1979), p. 214.

ments and hearings of the appearances of U.S. defense officials before various congressional committees. While here too some propaganda is evident, a large amount of information is available. Significantly, there are also major differences in the data provided by U.S. officials. For example, in the 1983 statement on Military Posture by the Joint Chiefs of Staff the displacement of the Soviet cruiser KIROV is given at 28,000 tons, while the Secretary of Defense report *Soviet Military Power* published at the same time lists the KIROV at 23,000 tons, and the latter document lists the new Krasina-class cruiser at both 12,500 tons and 13,000 tons. The larger KIROV displacement, used in this edition of *Guide to the Soviet Navy*, agrees with the estimates of the U.S. Defense Intelligence Agency.

As implied in this book's epigraph, he who would seek to describe Russian naval activities—under tsars and commissars—does so at great peril. Several of the persons cited below have sought to help my understanding of this subject. Regardless, I must take full responsibility for any errors of fact and understanding that have survived their guidance and my editor's red pencil.

Many individuals have provided assistance on this project, providing technical assistance and allowing me to benefit from their analyses and writings, especially Captain Thomas A. Brooks, USN, assistant chief of staff for intelligence, Atlantic Fleet; Dr. Norman Friedman and Dr. Milan Vego, naval analysts and authors; and Mr. Fred Rainbow, managing editor of the Naval Institute *Proceedings*.

I am also grateful for the assistance of Mr. Joel B. Bloom, naval analyst; Rear Admiral E.A. Burkhalter of the Intelligence Community Staff; Mr. Robert A. Carlisle of the Office of U.S. Navy Information and his assistants Miss Evelyn Jutte and Domingo Cruz; Mr. John Jedrlinic, merchant marine analyst; Lieutenant Colonel Donald Keith, USA (Retired), editor; Captain William H.J. Manthorpe, Jr., USN (Retired), former assistant U.S. naval attaché in Moscow; Professor Michael MccGwire, naval analyst and former Royal Navy officer; Mr. Steve Roberts of the Central Intelligence Agency; Mr. Frank Uhlig, Jr., editor, Naval War College *Review*; and Commander Bruce Valley, USN, of the Secretary of the Navy's staff.

The Royal Navy and Royal Air Force have provided a number of the photographs used in this volume through the efforts of Captain John Collins, RN, Captain Ian Sutherland, RN, and Mr. F.E. Dodman. Photographs have also been provided by Mr. Khoji Ishiwata, editor of *Ships of the World*, Professor Jürgen Rohwer, editor of *Marine-Rundschau*, Captain Uwe Rohwer of the West German Navy, Mr. A.D. Baker, the Royal Swedish Air Force, and the Royal Australian Air Force.

The analyses and writings of several students of the Soviet Navy have been most helpful in this project, especially those of Mr. Kenneth Brower; Master Chief Sonar Technician James Bussert, USN (Retired); Captain James Kehoe, USN (Retired); Mr. John Malone; and Mr. Raymond A. Robinson.

Finally, I have drawn upon writings of Dr. Nicholas G. Shadrin, a former Soviet naval officer, and conversations with Dr. Shadrin and several Soviet naval officers have aided in my efforts to understand the modern Soviet Navy.

This book could not have been written without the support of Mr. Thomas F. Epley, director of the Naval Institute Press; the efforts of Mesdames Carol Swartz, Patty Maddocks, and Misses Beverly Baum and Susan Sweeney of the staff of the Naval Institute; and Mr. Jan Snouck-Hurgronje who originally invited me to participate in this project.

*Guide to the Soviet Navy* is planned for publication on a periodic basis. Correspondence relating to this book should be addressed to the author in care of the Naval Institute Press, Annapolis, Maryland 21402.

\* \* \*

This volume continues the series begun by Siegfried Breyer, first published in German in 1964. This was followed by a second edition, co-authored by Breyer and myself, published in English.

NORMAN POLMAR
Alexandria, Virginia
October, 1983

# Guide to the Soviet Navy

# 1
# State of the Fleet

The Soviet Navy of the mid-1980s is engaged in a massive modernization program. This is characterized most dramatically by the simultaneous construction of the nuclear-powered missile cruisers of the KIROV class and three other classes of major surface missile combatants, the completion of the last of four KIEV-class aircraft carriers, and the keel laying of a nuclear-powered aircraft carrier. These and other surface ship and submarine projects mark the largest naval construction effort undertaken in the Soviet Union since the death of Josef Stalin in March of 1953.

Perhaps even more significant than the actual ships, this phase of Soviet naval development may well be part of a synthesis of Soviet military capability and foreign policy goals. Soviet leaders have long sought military capabilities to support an aggressive foreign policy in the postwar period to deter actions by the West in the Third World and to provide military support for socialist societies and Soviet "adventurism" in the Third World. Professor Roman Kolkowicz, a long-time observer of the Soviet political-military scene, has written: "The Brezhnev regime has succeeded where previous Soviet leaders have failed: Soviet strategic and conventional military power is now equal to that of the West; Soviet strategic doctrines are now global in scope. Soviet foreign policy is now globally oriented."[1]

The modern Navy is obviously a principal military means for supporting political-strategic aims of the Soviet state. The Navy's strategic missile submarines are a principal component of the Soviet nuclear warfighting capabilities and provide an "umbrella" for Soviet political-military actions at lower levels. The current Soviet naval programs represent the fourth major phase of Soviet naval development since the end of World War II. These postwar phases are significant because (1) the Soviet Navy has changed "direction" or policy four times since 1945 and (2) the United States and other major Western nations have generally been slow to react to these Soviet shifts. The analyses of these phases and the weapons involved could be indicative of the trends that have led to the latest phase of Soviet use of the sea as well as to future developments.[2] The following is a simplified description of these phases.

Phase I: From 1945 to about 1955 the Soviet Union undertook the construction of a large, conventional surface fleet, with supporting submarines, at the personal instigation of Stalin. With Communist-inspired civil wars beginning in Greece and Yugoslavia, the government of Turkey being threatened by the USSR, with Soviet troops in northern Iran, and the promise of free access to the world's oceans by Churchill,[3] it appeared that a rejuvenated Soviet fleet might soon have free access to the Mediterranean Sea and Indian Ocean as well as to the North Atlantic and Pacific.

The highest possible priorities were given to the rebuilding of the shipyards at Leningrad and those at Nikolayev and elsewhere along the Black Sea coast. At the same time, the Soviets appropriated German naval technology and machinery and brought German technicians back to the USSR to infuse their talents into the Soviet Navy. Several ships were also taken, including the unfinished carrier GRAF ZEPPELIN that later sank in the Baltic, a few other surface units, and at least ten submarines, half of them the highly advanced Type XXI U-boats.

By 1950 the keels were laid down for new classes of cruisers, destroyers, submarines, and other ships. Plans were being drawn up for a class of battle cruisers (STALINGRAD class) and even light aircraft carriers. This fleet was to control the seas adjacent to the Soviet Union and prevent an Allied assault from the sea. These programs were abruptly cancelled or reduced severely when Stalin died in March of 1953. The remnants of this large shipbuilding effort are the surviving SVERDLOV-class 6-inch gun cruisers, the older SKORYY and Kotlin destroyers, and the remaining Whiskey, Zulu, Romeo, and Quebec diesel submarines.

---

opposed by most of the U.S. Navy's leadership, was not a change in doctrine, but a strategic adjunct to the carrier programs. However, the development and wide deployment of the Harpoon and Tomahawk cruise missiles—"distributive firepower"—may mark the start of a new U.S. naval doctrine. Some senior U.S. aviation and submarine officers also opposed the development of cruise missiles.

[3]". . . it was my policy to welcome Russia as a Great Power on the sea. I wished to see Russian ships sailing across the oceans of the world. Russia had been like a giant with his nostrils pinched by the narrow exits from the Baltic and Black Sea. . . . I said that I personally would support . . . giving Russia access to the Mediterranean. I repeated that I welcomed Russia's appearance on the oceans, and this referred not only to the Dardanelles, but also to the Kiel Canal, which should have a regime like the Suez Canal, and to the warm waters of the Pacific." Winston S. Churchill, *Triumph and Tragedy* (Boston, Mass.: Houghton Mifflin, 1953), p. 542.

[1]Roman Kolkowicz, "The Military and Soviet Foreign Policy," *The Journal of Strategic Studies*, vol. 4, no. 4, December 1981, pp. 337–55.

[2]U.S. naval doctrine has not significantly changed since 1945, still being based on the same carrier task force concepts developed in 1943–1945 for the war against Japan. The Polaris submarine missile program, which was initially

Phase II: From 1955 to 1961, Stalin's successor, Nikita Khrushchev, sought to reduce the size and cost of the huge Soviet military machine, especially the Navy. He once described cruisers and other large warships as useful only for carrying political leaders on state visits. Stalin's massive shipbuilding program was cut back severely. When the head of the Navy, Admiral N.G. Kuznetsov, architect of Stalin's postwar program, protested the reductions, he was fired (and reduced in rank). The new commander in chief (CinC) who took office in January 1956, was 46-year-old S.G. Gorshkov, previously the Black Sea Fleet commander.

Admiral Gorshkov was directed to dispose of the big ships and to build cheaper naval systems, with emphasis on missiles, aircraft, and submarines. The principal targets of these systems would be the U.S. aircraft carriers, whose nuclear strike aircraft could threaten the Soviet homeland.[4]

During the 1950s the Soviet Navy developed nuclear torpedoes for the purpose of attacking U.S. coastal cities as well as submarine-launched strategic ballistic and cruise missiles.[5] The development of nuclear weapons, ballistic and cruise missiles, and other technological advances in the Soviet armed forces in this period are described by the Soviets as a "revolution" in military affairs. The new weapons also meant that the Soviet naval forces could, for the first time, effectively compete with the Western fleets. According to one prominent Soviet theorist, Admiral S.E. Zakharov:

> The creation in the USSR of a submarine-aviation nuclear missile navy has for the first time in history deprived the English and Americans of their naval superiority. Our submarine and naval aviation, should the aggressors choose to unleash a war, are capable of carrying out devastating strikes against enemy ground targets and ships in any region, as required. . . .[6]

Still, at about the time of the establishment of the Strategic Rocket Forces (SRF) as a separate military service in late 1959, *strategic* naval weapon efforts were slowed and possibly terminated. Addressing the new defense policies that included the establishment of the SRF, Khrushchev stated on 14 January 1960 that like the Air Forces, the Navy had lost its former significance. He then added that, "the submarine fleet is acquiring great importance, whereas surface ships can no longer play the role they played in the last [war]."

Phase III: From 1961 to the present the Soviet Navy has faced more complex and challenging problems. The Kennedy administration, which took office in January 1961, accelerated the Polaris Submarine-Launched Ballistic Missile (SLBM) and Minuteman ICBM programs, increased conventional warfare forces, including the fleet, and took other steps to counter the Soviet Union at all levels of confrontation. The Cuban missile crisis of October 1962 further demonstrated American strategic and naval capabilities and options.

[4]Nuclear strike was the primary mission of U.S. aircraft carriers from 1951 until about 1962.

[5]In the 1950s the U.S. Navy deployed the Regulus strategic cruise missile, which was operational until 1964. The equivalent Soviet system, the SS-N-3 Shaddock, was not discarded, but adopted for the anti-ship as well as land-attack role and continues in service. See chapter 24.

[6]Admiral S.E. Zakharov, *Istoriya Voyenno-Morskogo Iskusstva* [A History of the Art of Naval Warfare] (Moscow: Military Publishing House, 1969), p. 102 (of U.S. Joint Publications Research Service translation of 29 January 1971).

Oliver Cromwell, seventeenth century British political leader, declared that a "man-of-war is the best ambassador." The Soviet Navy of the Brezhnev-Gorshkov era has certainly understood his meaning, and this Kashin-class destroyer and her young, clean-cut sailors visiting a Middle Eastern port demonstrate Soviet interest and military capability in that part of the world.

These events led Khrushchev and his successors, Alexei Kosygin and Leonid Brezhnev, both of whom had naval ties, to support a major buildup of Soviet naval forces. Admiral Gorshkov, who had scrapped the obsolete battleships, cruisers, and lesser ships, was now able to begin building large numbers of advanced-technology ships and submarines, while also building up Soviet Naval Aviation (SNA) and reestablishing a marine corps—Naval Infantry in the Soviet vernacular. And soon after, the Navy was again given the strategic attack mission that it may have lost with the establishment of the Strategic Rocket Forces. The Delta-class strategic missile submarine was apparently approved as early as 1961, with its long-range missile permitting it to be employed as a strategic withhold or strategic reserve weapon.

The fleet that Gorshkov built in the 1960s and 1970s seems to have centered on three primary missions:

- Anti-Submarine Warfare (ASW) to counter the Western strategic missile submarines.
- Strategic missile submarines, in reality "mobile ICBMs" that could form a strategic reserve as well as a strategic war-fighting force.
- Conventional surface and air forces, in large part to protect the strategic missile submarines and to provide "combat stability" by supporting attack submarines.

Today it is obvious that the Soviet Navy's leadership is confident that it has the weapons and tactics to counter the relatively few U.S. aircraft carriers operating in forward areas. Increasingly, the graceful, heavily armed warships that emerged from Soviet yards in the 1960s and 1970s were primarily built to serve in the pro-*Soviet* submarine role, especially to protect Soviet strategic missile submarines. Although ships and aircraft are not always employed in the roles for which they were intended, the above role appears to have been the purpose for which they were built.

**TABLE 1–1. NAVAL ORDER OF BATTLE, MID-1983**

| | Soviet Union | | | | | United States |
|---|---|---|---|---|---|---|
| | Northern Fleet | Baltic Fleet | Black Sea Fleet‡ | Pacific Fleet | Total | |
| **Submarines—Nuclear** | | | | | | |
| Modern strategic missile | | | | | 62 | 34 |
| SSBN Typhoon class | 1 | — | — | — | | |
| SSBN Delta class | 22 | — | — | 14 | | |
| SSBN Yankee class | 15 | — | — | 10 | | |
| SSBN Hotel | 4 | — | — | — | 4 | |
| SSGN cruise missile | † | † | † | † | 50 | } 91 |
| SSN torpedo attack | † | † | † | † | 70 | |
| **Submarines—Diesel-electric** | | | | | | |
| SSB Golf class | 1 | 6 | 1 | 7 | 15 | — |
| SSG cruise missile | † | † | † | † | 20 | — |
| SS torpedo attack | † | † | † | † | 150 | 4 |
| Special purpose | † | † | † | † | ~10 | 3 |
| Total submarines | 184 | 34 | 25 | 122 | 380 | 132 |
| Aircraft Carriers | — | — | 2 | 1 | 3 | 13 |
| Helicopter Carriers | — | — | 2 | — | 2 | 12 |
| Battleships | — | — | — | — | — | 1 |
| Cruisers | 10 | 3 | 10 | 13 | 36 | 28 |
| Destroyers | 18 | 9 | 17 | 20 | 64 | 71 (5) |
| Frigates | 48 | 32 | 46 | 50 | 176 | 87 (4) |
| Missile Corvettes | † | † | † | † | 25 | 5 |
| Missile/Patrol/Torpedo Craft | † | † | † | † | 255 | — |
| Fleet Minesweepers | 30 | 35 | 40 | 40 | 145 | 3 (22) |
| Amphibious Ships | 10 | 26 | 25 | 22 | 83 | 49 (4) |
| **Naval Aviation** | | | | | | |
| Carrier-Based Aircraft | | | | | 100+ | ~1,100+ |
| Land-Based Strike Aircraft | | | | | 400 | — |
| Land-Based Patrol/ASW/Reconnaissance Aircraft | | | | | 380 | ~400 |
| All Other Naval Aircraft (including U.S. Naval Air Reserve) | | | | | 680 | ~4,060 |

*Most U.S. Navy SSNs can launch cruise missiles (Harpoon and Tomahawk).
†Exact disposition unknown.
‡Includes Caspian Sea Flotilla.
   U.S. numbers in parentheses indicate additional ships manned by composite active-duty and naval reserve crews.

Phase IV: The Soviet Union is now engaged in a fourth phase of postwar naval development. The approval for several of the current naval programs was probably given by the Soviet government around 1965, at the start of a five-year planning cycle. In 1970 the first of the KIEV-class VTOL aircraft carriers was laid down, followed at regular intervals by three sister ships. A short time later work was started on the KIROV-class nuclear cruisers and three other classes of missile-armed cruisers and destroyers, the IVAN ROGOV-class amphibious ships, and then the large nuclear-powered aircraft carrier.

The surface warships are the most dramatic evidence of this new phase of Soviet naval development. Less visible are improved submarine classes and large replenishment and other support ships.[7] Related to these "platforms" is the continued emphasis by the Soviet Navy on surveillance, intelligence collection, and command systems. These increases have been both qualitative and quantitative.

Admiral Gorshkov, in his series of articles that appeared in the official journal *Morskoy Sbornik* during 1972–1973, espoused a new mission for the Soviet Navy: The projection of Soviet military power overseas in the context that in the future only naval forces would be able to guarantee Soviet state interests in the Third World. These countries are already vital to the West for markets and resources, and are taking on increasing significance for the Soviet Union.

Thus, the Soviet Navy appears to be moving toward a long-range capability of confronting Western or Third World forces at several levels of crisis or combat, including the ability to fight a conventional as well as a nuclear war at sea. However, Party Chairman Brezhnev passed away in November 1982. Brezhnev's successor, former KGB chief Yuri Andropov, will probably not have the strong feelings for the Navy that his predecessor had, and Gorshkov's successor will probably not have the great influence with the Soviet military and political leadership that Gorshkov has enjoyed. But the momentum for a continued naval buildup is strong, and the rigidly structured economy of the USSR prevents radical changes in defense programs. Above all, the Soviet leadership certainly understands the importance of Soviet use of the seas for that nation's political, economic, and military activities.

[7]However, the high-speed, deep-diving nuclear submarine Alfa apparently dates from decisions of the late 1950s; see chapter 10.

# 2

# Glossary of Terms

| | |
|---|---|
| AA | Anti-Aircraft |
| AA-( ) | NATO designation for Soviet Air-to-Air missile |
| AAW | Anti-Air Warfare |
| ACW | Anti-Carrier Warfare |
| AGI | intelligence collection ship |
| AS-( ) | NATO designation for Soviet Air-to-Surface missile |
| ASW | Anti-Submarine Warfare |
| beam | extreme width of hull |
| $C^3$ | Command, Control, and Communications |
| CBR | Chemical-Biological-Radiological (warfare) |
| CinC | Commander in Chief |
| DP | Dual-Purpose (for use against surface and air targets) |
| draft | maximum draft at full load, including fixed projections below keel, if any (e.g., sonar dome) |
| ehp | equivalent horsepower |
| ECM | Electronic Countermeasures |
| ELINT | Electronic Intelligence |
| EW | Electronic Warfare |
| full load | ship displacement complete and ready for sea in all respects, including all fuels, munitions, and provisions as well as aircraft |
| GFCS | Gunfire Control System |
| GRT | Gross Register Tons |
| HF | High-Frequency |
| HF/DF | High-Frequency Direction-Finding |
| hp | horsepower |
| IGE | In Ground Effect (hover) |
| ihp | indicated horsepower |
| kgst | kilograms of static thrust |
| lbst | pounds static thrust |
| length | length overall |
| light | ship displacement without crew, fuel, munitions, or provisions, and without aircraft |
| LRA | Long-Range Aviation (Soviet strategic air arm) |
| MAD | Magnetic Anomaly Detector |
| MOD | Ministry of Defense |
| MPA | Main Political Administration of the Army and Navy |
| NATO | North Atlantic Treaty Organization |
| n.mile | nautical mile (1.15 statute miles) |
| OGE | Out of Ground Effect (hover) |
| REC | Radio Electronic Combat |
| SA-N-( ) | NATO designation for Soviet Surface-to-Air Naval missile |
| shp | shaft horsepower |
| SIGINT | Signal Intelligence |
| SLBM | Submarine-Launched Ballistic Missile |
| SNA | Soviet Naval Aviation |
| SP | Single-Purpose (suitable for surface targets only) |
| SRF | Strategic Rocket Forces |
| SS | torpedo attack submarine (diesel) |
| SS-N-( ) | NATO designation for Soviet Surface-to-Surface Naval missile |
| SSAG | auxiliary submarine (diesel) |
| SSB | ballistic missile submarine (diesel) |
| SSBN | ballistic missile submarine (nuclear) |
| SSG | guided (cruise) missile submarine (diesel) |
| SSGN | guided (cruise) missile submarine (nuclear) |
| SSN | torpedo attack submarine (nuclear) |
| SSQ | $C^3$ submarine (diesel) |
| SSR | radar picket submarine (diesel) |
| SST | target-training submarine (diesel) |
| standard | ship displacement complete and ready for sea with all munitions, provisions, and aircraft, but without fuels |
| STOL | Short Take-Off and Landing aircraft |
| SUW-N-( ) | NATO designation for Soviet Surface-to-Underwater Naval missile |
| TE | Turbo-Electric |
| 3-D | three-dimensional (radar) |
| VDL | Video Data Link |
| VDS | Variable Depth Sonar |
| VLS | Vertical Launch System |
| VSTOL | Vertical/Short Take-Off and Landing aircraft |
| VTOL | Vertical Take-Off and Landing aircraft |
| wl | waterline |

# 3

# Soviet Ship Designations

The general arrangement of ships in this volume by generic type (e.g., cruisers, destroyers, frigates) is based on the U.S. Navy's ship classification scheme.[1] However, because of the major differences in U.S. and Soviet warship designs and roles, this volume does not use U.S. Navy ship type designations (CG, CGN, DD, DDG, etc.). The similarity of submarine types does make it feasible to use U.S. submarine designations, as SS, SSN, SSG, and SSGN.

During the post–World War II period the Western intelligence services developed two principal schemes for identifying Soviet naval ships:

(1) Submarines were assigned code letter designations; generally the phonetic word for the letter is used, as Alfa, Bravo, Charlie, and Delta. Major variations within the class are indicated by roman numerals, as Charlie I and Charlie II. The principal exception to this scheme is the Western use of the Soviet term Typhoon (*Tayfun*).

There has been no order for assigning the submarine code letters, the first having been Whiskey. Because of the massive Soviet submarine construction effort, in early 1983 only four letters were unused: Mike, Sierra, Uniform, and X-ray. (Uniform had been used briefly for the Victor II submarine.)

(2) Surface warships have been given K-series code names from the mid-1950s onward, as Kara, Kresta, Kynda. Again, roman numerals indicate principal class variants, as Kresta I and Kresta II. Since the late 1960s most new Soviet surface combatant classes have been generally identified by their Soviet names, as MOSKVA, KIEV, and KIROV. Lesser Soviet naval ships have been assigned NATO code names in the following categories:

- small combatants: insects
- mine warfare: diminutives of names
- amphibious ships: amphibious creatures and shipyards (e.g., Polnocny class constructed in the Polnocny yard in Poland)
- auxiliaries: various, including trees, fruits, and vegetables

The Soviet Navy's designations for its ships are listed below (table 3-1). In addition, the Soviets use a "ship rank" (*rang korablya*) classifica-

tion scheme based on the ship's purpose, firepower, displacement, and crew size. The seniority of the ship's commanding officers, the status of their crews, and their logistic support are based on this ranking. There are four ranks:

1st Rank: nuclear-powered submarines, ASW cruisers (i.e., KIEV, MOSKVA), guided missile cruisers.

2nd Rank: large and medium diesel submarines, large guided missile and ASW ships, destroyers.

3rd Rank: small ASW ships, escort ships, medium amphibious warfare ships, ocean minesweepers, missile craft.

4th Rank: ASW patrol boats, motor torpedo boats, gunboats, landing craft, coastal and harbor minesweepers.

Under Soviet naval regulations, first and second rank ships hoist the jack simultaneously with the naval ensign when not under way; the third and fourth rank ships do not fly a jack.

**TABLE 3-1. SOVIET SHIP TYPE DESIGNATIONS**

| | Russian Terminology | English Translation |
|---|---|---|
| AK | *Artilleriyskiy Kater* | Artillery Cutter |
| BDK | *Bol'shoy Desantnyy Korabl'* | Large Landing Ship |
| BPK | *Bol'shoy Protivolodochnyy Korabl'* | Large Anti-Submarine Ship |
| BRK | *Bol'shoy Raketnyy Korabl'* | Large Missile Ship |
| BT | *Bazovyy Tral'shchik* | Base Minesweeper |
| DK | *Desantnyy Korabl'* | Landing Ship |
| DKVP | *Desantnyy Korabl' Na Vozdushnoy Podushke* | Air-Cushion Landing Ship |
| EHOS | *Ekspeditsionnoye Okeanograficheskoye Sudno* | Expeditionary Oceanographic Vessel |
| EM | *Eskadrennyy Minonosets* | Destroyer |
| GKS | *Gidroakusticheskoye Kontrol'noye Sudno* | Hydroacoustic Monitoring Vessel |
| GS | *Gidrograficheskoye Sudno* | Hydrographic Vessel |
| KIL | *Kilektor* | Lift Ship |
| KR | *Kreyser* | Cruiser |
| KRZ | *Korabl' Razvedyvatel'nyy* | Intelligence Ship |
| KS | *Kabel'noye Sudno* | Cable Vessel |
| KSV | *Korabl' Svyazey* | Communications Ship |
| KTs | *Kontrol'naya Tsel'* | Controlled Target |
| KVN | *Korabl' Vozdushnogo Nablyudeniya* | Radar Surveillance Ship |
| LDK | *Ledokol* | Icebreaker |
| MB | *Morskoy Buksir* | Seagoing Tug |

---

[1]A detailed discussion of Soviet ship types is given in Arthur D. Baker III, "Soviet Ship Types," Naval Institute *Proceedings*, November 1980, pp. 111–17, December 1980, pp. 115–20, and October 1982, pp. 168–74. Also see Lieutenant Commander Charles E. Adams, USN, and A.D. Baker III, "Soviet Naval Ship Names," *Proceedings*, July 1979, pp. 113–19; and Commander Tyrone G. Martin, USN, "What's in a Name?" *Proceedings*, July 1974, pp. 117–18.

**TABLE 3-1.   SOVIET SHIP TYPE DESIGNATIONS** (Cont.)

|      | Russian Terminology | English Translation |
|------|---------------------|---------------------|
| MPK | *Malyy Protivolodochnyy Korabl´* | Small Anti-Submarine Ship |
| MRK | *Malyy Raketnyy Korabl´* | Small Missile Ship |
| MT | *Morskoy Tral´shchik* | Seagoing Minesweeper |
| MVT | *Morskoy Vodnyy Tanker* | Seagoing Water Tanker |
| OS | *Opitnoye Sudno* | Experimental Vessel |
| PB | *Plavuchaya Baza* | Floating Base |
| PKA | *Protivolodochnyy Kater* | Anti-Submarine Cutter |
| PKR | *Protivolodochnyy Kreyser* | Anti-Submarine Cruiser |
| PL | *Podvodnaya Lodka* | Submarine |
| PLA | *Podvodnaya Lodka Atomnaya* | Submarine (nuclear) |
| PLARB | *Podvodnaya Lodka Atomnaya Raketnaya Ballisticheskaya* | Ballistic Missile Submarine (nuclear) |
| PLARK | *Podvodnaya Lodka Atomnaya Raketnaya Krylataya* | Cruise Missile Submarine (nuclear) |
| PLRB | *Podvodnaya Lodka Raketnaya Ballisticheskaya* | Ballistic Missile Submarine |
| PLRK | *Podvodnaya Lodka Raketnaya Krylataya* | Cruise Missile Submarine |
| PSKR | *Pogranichniy Storozhevoy Korabl´* | Border Patrol Ship |
| RKA | *Raketnyy Kater* | Missile Cutter |
| RKR | *Raketnyy Kreyser* | Missile Cruiser |
| SB | *Spasatel´nyy Buksir* | Rescue Tug |
| SBR | *Sudno Bol´shogo Razmagnichivanya* | Large Deperming Vessel |
| SDK | *Srednyy Desantnyy Korabl´* | Medium Landing Ship |
| SKR | *Storozhevoy Korabl´* | Patrol Ship |
| SR | *Sudno Razmagnichivanya* | Deperming Vessel |
| SS | *Spasatel´noye Sudno* | Salvage Vessel |
| SSV | *Sudno Svyazyy* | Communications Vessel |
| TAKR | *Takticheskoye Avianosnyy Kreyser* | Tactical Aircraft Carrying Cruiser |
| TKA | *Torpednyy Kater* | Torpedo Cutter |
| US | *Uchebnoye Sudno* | Training Vessel |
| VT | *Voyennyy Tanker* | Military Tanker |
| VTR | *Voyennyy Transport* | Military Transport |
| ZM | *Zagraditel´ Minnyy* | Minelayer |

Soviet nuclear attack submarines or PLA were initially developed for the anti-ship/anti-carrier role in contrast to American SSNs that are intended primarily for hunting Soviet undersea craft. However, U.S. officials believe that the Victor SSNs, as this Victor III transiting the Straits of Malacca, were developed for the ASW role. (1982, U.S. Navy)

# 4

# Organization and Command

## SOVIET NATIONAL COMMAND

The national command structure of the Soviet Union consists of three major organizations: (1) the Defense Council, (2) the Main Military Council, and (3) the General Staff.

The Defense Council (*Sovyet Oborony*) is the highest Soviet military-economic-political planning body, responsible for planning and preparing the country for war. Chaired by the General Secretary of the Communist Party (formerly Leonid Brezhnev and now Yuri Andropov), the council consists of selected members of the Politburo, including the Minister of Defense, the chairmen of the Committee for State Security (*Komitet Gosudarstvennoi Bezopasnosti*—KGB), Council of Ministers, GOSPLAN (the national economic planning agency), and the Chief of the General Staff. Others who would probably join the Defense Council in wartime (see below) include the commander of Warsaw Pact Forces and the Party Secretary for Defense Industry.[1]

In wartime this body would become the State Committee of Defense (GKO), essentially a war cabinet with oversight of all aspects of the nation at war. At such time the General Secretary would assume the function of Supreme Commander in Chief of the armed forces. (Brezhnev held the rank of Marshal of the Soviet Union.[2])

The Main Military Council or Collegium of the Ministry of Defense (*Kollegiya Ministerstva Oborony*) is responsible to the Defense Council for military strategy and operations, including training and readiness. The Minister of Defense heads this council. The members of the council include the General Secretary of the Communist Party, the ten deputy ministers of defense—including the five service chiefs—and certain other senior defense officials. In wartime the council would become the headquarters of the Supreme High Command or *Stavka*, which would exercise direct control of the Soviet armed forces, either through the General Staff or directly through the commanders in chief.[3]

The General Staff is the executive agency for the Main Military Council in peacetime and for the wartime *Stavka*. It is charged with basic military planning for all of the services. Together the *Stavka* and General Staff form the Supreme High Command (VGK). The Soviet General Staff was formally established in 1935 and evolved into its present form in 1942.

In many respects the various Soviet operating forces are directed by the Ministry of Defense in peacetime and by the *Stavka* in wartime through the General Staff. The Soviet General Staff differs significantly

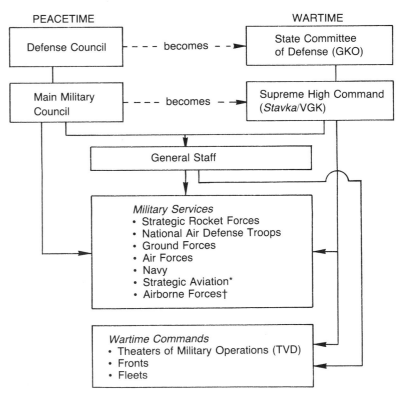

Figure 4–1. High Command

*Strategic aviation is administratively part of the Air Forces, but operationally is directly under the General Staff.

†Airborne Forces are administratively part of the Ground Forces, but operationally are directly under the General Staff.

[1]The Chief of the Military Industrial Commission or VPK.
[2]This is the penultimate Soviet military rank. Stalin took the rank of Generalissimo in 1945.
[3]*Stavka* was a tsarist term. Stalin established the first Soviet *Stavka* when the Germans invaded Russia in June 1941. During World War II the *Stavka* consisted of about 20 general officers. (At the end of the tsarist regime in 1917 there were about 250 senior officers and officials in the *Stavka*.)

from the U.S. Joint Chiefs of Staff (JCS). The latter is a representative body of the U.S. armed forces, having a working staff composed of officers from the various services, generally individuals with no specialized staff training. The Soviet agency is a professional planning staff, comprised mostly of "army" officers, with key positions held only by officers who have graduated from the two-year course at the Voroshilov General Staff Academy, the highest professional military school in the nation.

Although dominated by ground ("army") officers, since 1972 a senior naval officer has served as a deputy chief of the General Staff. Admiral of the Fleet Semen M. Lobov, who had served as CinC of the Northern Fleet from 1964 to 1972, was the first naval officer so assigned. Lobov was succeeded on the General Staff in 1978 by Admiral Nikolay N. Amel'ko, who had been CinC of the Pacific Fleet from 1962 to 1969, when he became a deputy CinC of the Soviet Navy, a position he held until 1978. The assignment of senior naval officers with major fleet command experience demonstrated the increasing importance of naval matters in Soviet military planning. Several naval officers hold lesser positions on the General Staff.

## MINISTRY OF DEFENSE

The Ministry of Defense (MOD) serves as an administrative entity for the five armed services and several defense agencies. In their normal order of precedence, the five armed services are: Strategic Rocket Forces, Troops of National Air Defense, Ground Forces, Air Forces, and Navy. The commanders in chief of the five services also serve as deputies to the Minister of Defense.

There are additional deputy ministers of defense, several of whom head specialized and support agencies. All of these deputy minister positions are held by active-duty officers. The Minister of Defense, Dmitri F. Ustinov, is a civilian ordnance specialist and industrial administrator. He had been head of armament production in the Soviet Union since June 1941 and afterwards held a succession of senior positions in the defense industry and economic planning.[4] Ustinov held the rank of engineer-colonel general before being appointed defense minister in April 1976, when he was awarded the rank of General of the Army. On 30 July of that year the rank of Marshal of the Soviet Union was conferred upon him. His political positions culminated in his becoming a candidate member of the Politburo from 1966 and a full member in 1976.

*History.* The current Soviet defense structure is based on the reorganization of 1953, when the Ministry of Defense was established to direct the military services. During the next few years the other services and most other components of the current MOD were established in their current form. (The National Air Defense Forces—PVO-*Strany*—gained

---

[4]Ustinov was People's Commissar for Armaments from 1941–1946, Minister for Armaments 1946–1953, and Minister of Defense Industry 1953–1957.

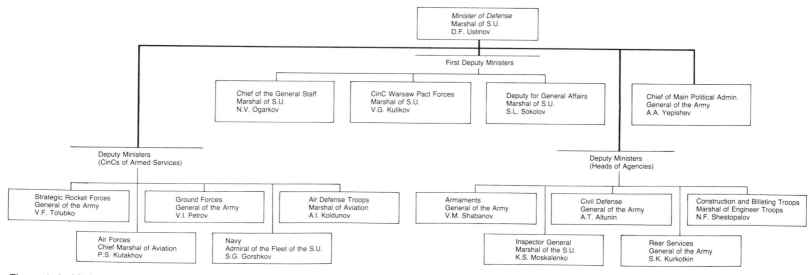

Figure 4–2. Ministry of Defense

the status of a separate service in 1948 and was reorganized as the Troops of National Air Defense about 1980, incorporating the air defense troops of the Ground Forces; the Strategic Rocket Forces became a separate service in 1959).

The phrase *Army and Navy* is still widely used by the Soviet leadership to indicate the military services. For example, the military political directorate is called the Main Political Administration of the Army and Navy. However, on a practical and operational basis, the current MOD organization has five separate military services. The first Minister of Defense under the 1953 reorganization was Marshal Nikolai Bulganin, a political officer with very limited military experience. He was succeeded in 1955 by Marshal Georgi Zhukov, the leading Soviet military hero of World War II. Zhukov was the successful architect of the defenses of Leningrad and Moscow and of the battle of Stalingrad (now Volgograd). The latter battle is considered the turning point in the 1941–1945 war against Germany. Zhukov, the first professional soldier to head the Soviet defense establishment, was immensely popular in the Soviet Union. As Minister of

Defense he was the first soldier to hold full membership in the ruling Presidium (as the Politburo was then called). Still, in 1957 the Soviet political leadership under Nikita Khrushchev ousted Zhukov from office because of fears that he was gaining too much power.

His place was taken by another professional soldier, Marshal Rodion Malinovsky, who had been closely associated with Khrushchev during World War II. Malinovsky died in 1967 and the top defense post was given to still another professional soldier, Marshal Andrei Grechko. He too was given membership in the Politburo, but only with candidate (non-voting) status. After Grechko's death in 1976 the position of Minister of Defense went to Ustinov, already a full member of the Politburo and head of the defense industry.

As previously noted, a senior admiral has served as a deputy chief of the General Staff since 1972. Additionally, Admiral A.I. Sorokin has served as 1st Deputy Chief of the Main Political Administration (MPA) since late 1981. He is believed to be the first naval officer to hold that

The Soviet national command is oriented toward war, with an extensive peacetime staff and C³ activities that could rapidly shift to a combat environment. Typical of the Soviet emphasis on extensive, redundant, and survivable command and control facilities has been the conversion of Golf-class submarines to serve in this role, as the craft shown here—with several of her crew sunbathing atop the sail. (1978)

position, making him a prime candidate for the highly important position of head of the MPA, a post held for two decades by Army General A.A. Yepishev. Admiral Sorokin has served in the MPA since 1976 as one of several lesser deputy chiefs.

Also in 1981, Admiral of the Fleet G.M. Yegorov stepped down as Chief of the Main Naval Staff, a most important position that he had occupied since 1977. He became chairman of the Central Committee of DOSAAF, the national paramilitary training organization (see chapter 9). This position has probably not been held before by a naval officer and thus may give the Navy added prestige and influence. (However, some Western analysts feel his move may actually have been a demotion, resulting from the grounding of a Soviet submarine in Swedish waters in November 1981.)

Two other admirals hold major non-Navy positions: Admiral V.V. Mikhaylin, former commander of the Baltic Fleet, is a deputy CinC of the Warsaw Pact military forces, and Admiral V.P. Maslov, former commander of the Pacific Fleet, is the Warsaw Pact liaison to the East German Navy.

### THEATERS OF OPERATIONS (*TEATRII VOYENNYKH DEYSTVIY*)

Soviet military activities in wartime would be conducted in up to nine Theaters of Military Operations (TVD), which are geographic divisions to facilitate the unified direction of military operations. These are similar in concept to U.S. unified military commands, which direct all military activities within an area. However, the Soviets do not normally have commanders in chief and staffs assigned to these TVDs in peacetime.

The TVD concept—as an intermediate level between the *Stavka* and the fronts (i.e., army groups)—was used briefly and ineffectively early in the European war. More significantly, in March 1945 a theater command was established in the Far East in preparation for Soviet entry into the war against Japan.[5] This High Command of Soviet Forces in the Far East was "invested with broad authority for direction of combat operation" and had "a relatively autonomous character." The distance from Moscow to the new war zone and the communication limitations over that distance led to the formation of this TVD, which directed three ground fronts, three air armies, the Pacific Fleet, and the Amur Flotilla in the war against the Japanese. Soviet experience with the theater command concept was limited. The success of the admittedly brief but complex and large-area campaign in the Far East has provided Soviet military leaders with a model for future theater command structures.

Currently there appears to be planning for military operations in five continental Eurasian TVDs and four naval or maritime TVDs. The naval TVDs are the Atlantic, Pacific, Indian, and Northern-Arctic ocean regions. It seems likely that these would be under a naval commander in wartime, while naval operations in "seas" such as the Baltic and Black Sea would be part of the continental Eurasian TVDs. Reportedly, a Far Eastern TVD was activated in 1979, probably to formalize the command relationships, communications links, and logistics network for a possible future conflict in that important region.

In wartime, headquarters would be established in some or all of the other TVDs as required to direct and coordinate combat and support operations. The continental TVDs would direct the fronts (groupings of ground forces), the supporting air and naval units, and the Military Districts within the area. (The Soviet Union is divided into 16 Military Districts, which include most military units, installations, and activities of the armed forces within the area. All of the units of the Ground Forces within Soviet borders are assigned to Military Districts.)

### NAVAL FORCES (*VOYENNO-MORSKOY FLOT*)

The Navy became subordinate to the Ministry of Defense established in 1953. A separate People's Commissariat (ministry) for the Navy had existed briefly in 1918, and then from December 1937 through World War II. In February 1946, when the decisions were being made to initiate a major fleet building program, the Navy was integrated into the People's Commissariat for the Armed Forces, whose title was changed on 15 March of that year to Ministry for the Armed Forces. Four years later, in February 1950, this unified ministry was divided into a War Ministry and a Navy Ministry, again placing the Navy high command in a position of parity with the Army. Finally, the supra-level MOD was established in 1953, with the Navy once again becoming a subordinate service.

The Commander in Chief of the Soviet Navy is the equivalent of the U.S. Chief of Naval Operations as well as the Secretary of the Navy. The CinC directs operations afloat and ashore primarily through four fleet commands, plus several task force (*eskadra*) groupings. There is evidence that the day-to-day operational control of Soviet strategic missile submarines is vested with the Soviet General Staff as is control of the Soviet strategic air arm.

In contrast to Western standards, Soviet military and naval officers frequently remain in their positions for long periods of time. Admiral of the Fleet of the Soviet Union Sergei Gorshkov has held the dual position of a deputy minister and naval CinC since January 1956.[6] His tenure has now spanned 13 U.S. Secretaries of the Navy and eight Chiefs of Naval Operations. Several other senior Soviet naval officers have had lengthy assignments, although in recent years tours of about four or five years have been more typical for the senior positions in the fleets.

*History.* Gorshkov's immediate predecessor, Admiral of the Fleet of the Soviet Union Nikolai G. Kuznetsov, served as head of the Navy from April 1939 to January 1947, and again from July 1951 to January 1956. He first became CinC at the age of 37. Initially, Kuznetsov's title was People's Commissar of the Navy. At the start of the Great Patriotic War (the Soviet term for the 1941–1945 conflict in Europe), the fleets were subordinated to Army front commanders. In December 1943, Kuznetsov proposed that the fleets be assigned to Navy headquarters for operational control because of the large-scale operations planned in coastal areas and the increasing significance of independent naval operations. Accordingly, on 31 March 1944 the fleets, with the exception of the Baltic Fleet, were placed directly under the command of Kuznetsov, who at the time was designated as the Commander in Chief of Naval

---

[5] In February 1945 the Allies had agreed that the USSR would enter the war against Japan three months after the end of the war in Europe, i.e., August 1945.

[6] The longest-serving U.S. Chief of Naval Operations since that position was established in 1915 has been Admiral Arleigh Burke, who served as CNO from August 1955 to August 1961.

From left to right: Josef Stalin (U.S. Army); Leonid Brezhnev (Sovfoto); Dmitri Ustinov (Sovfoto); Nikolai Kuznetsov (U.S. Army); Sergei Gorshkov (U.S. Navy).

Forces. (At a later date, when the Baltic was opened for Soviet naval operations, the Baltic Fleet was transferred from the Leningrad Front to the CinC Naval Forces.) Kuznetsov was made a member of the *Stavka* in 1945 and command of all fleets and flotillas then emanated directly from the General Headquarters through him.

Kuznetsov's 12 years of command were interrupted in 1946 when he was accused of giving information about captured German torpedoes to the British, the wartime ally of the Soviet Union. He was reduced to the rank of rear admiral, replaced as CinC by Admiral Ivan Yumashev, and "exiled" to the Soviet Pacific Fleet.

Kuznetsov was returned to command of the Navy in 1951 with the rank of vice admiral. (He was later promoted to Admiral of the Fleet of the Soviet Union; see chapter 9.) Apparently Stalin brought him back to the Moscow post to resume direction of the building of a major surface fleet. Subsequently, Kuznetsov's continued demands for large, conventional warships after Stalin's death in 1953 caused Khrushchev to appoint Gorshkov to replace him as commander in chief of the Navy. This second fall of Kuznetsov in 1955–1956 is vividly described in Khrushchev's memoirs, as is Gorshkov's rise to CinC.[7] Kuznetsov was demoted to vice admiral and was retired. (When he died in 1974, the Soviet press called him a "prominent military figure" and declared his "glowing memory . . . will remain in our hearts forever"; the most senior Soviet officials signed his obituary.)

Khrushchev, according to his memoirs, had known Gorshkov slightly in World War II. He accepted Gorshkov mainly on the recommendation of Marshal Malinovsky. Malinovsky was one of Khrushchev's favorites among the military leadership and would be appointed the Minister of Defense in 1957.

Gorshkov (born 1910) attended the Frunze Higher Naval School in Leningrad (1927–1931), after which he served in surface ships in the

Black Sea Fleet and then the Pacific Flotilla, rising to command a destroyer in 1938 at age 28. The early promotion was possible, in part, because of Stalin's purges of the Soviet military, which caused the death or imprisonment of several thousand officers. The following year Gorshkov commanded a destroyer brigade in the Black Sea, after which he attended the course for senior officers at the Voroshilov Naval Academy (i.e., war college), and was then promoted to rear admiral after war broke out in 1941. He served with distinction in the Black Sea and, especially, as commander of the flotilla in the Sea of Azov and later on the Danube. After the war he commanded a squadron in the Black Sea, was then chief of staff of the fleet, and finally commander in chief from 1951 until mid-1955 when he was named first deputy CinC of the Navy in preparation for becoming CinC, and also made a deputy minister of defense on 5 January 1956. Gorshkov is the only naval officer who is a full member of the Central Committee, a political position he has held since 1961. (Twenty-two other officers of the armed forces are full members of the Central Committee of the Communist Party of the Soviet Union.)

There were some indications when this volume went to press that Admiral Gorshkov would retire as Commander in Chief, in part because the ascendancy of Andropov meant an end of the support he had enjoyed from Khrushchev and then from Kosygin and Brezhnev, with patronage being a key factor in the success of Soviet officials. For the past decade Gorshkov's First Deputy CinC, N. I. Smirnov, had been looked upon as his logical successor. But Smirnov's age (born 1917) and other factors indicate he will not be Gorshkov's successor. Another prominent candidate was Yegorov (born 1918), whose experience as Chief of the Main Naval Staff and commander of the Northern Fleet gave him excellent credentials, although his age was a negative factor. However, his reassignment as chairman of DOSAAF in late 1981 has apparently removed him as a potential CinC.

Thus, the most likely candidate to succeed Gorshkov appears to be Vladimir N. Chernavin, holding the key position of Chief of Main Naval Staff (since 1981) and, like Smirnov, a First Deputy CinC. Previously,

[7] N.S. Khrushchev, *Khrushchev Remembers* (Boston: Little, Brown & Co., 1974), pp. 18–34.

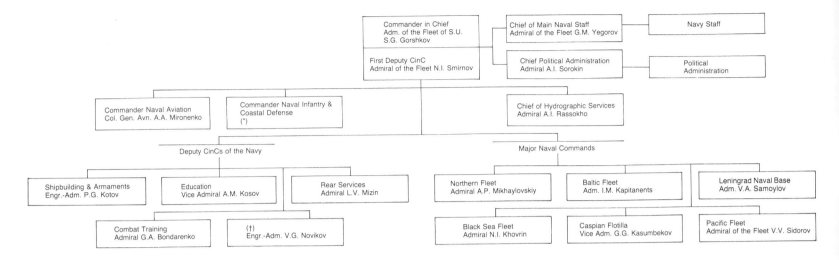

†Specific duties not known.

Figure 4–3. Navy Organization

from 1977 to 1981, he was CinC of the Northern Fleet and before that had served under Gorshkov at naval headquarters. He is a submariner and younger than Smirnov and Yegorov (born 1928).

None of the current fleet commanders appear to be viable candidates for the CinC position.

The basic organization of the Soviet Navy is shown in figure 4-3. The headquarters is a highly centralized organization with several deputy commanders in chief supporting the CinC. Current operations and long-range planning are the province of the Main Naval Staff, under a chief of staff who probably ranks after the first deputy CinC within naval headquarters. The deputy CinCs appear to have specific responsibilities and supporting organizations, but not all have been publicly identified. The Soviet Navy does not appear to have deputy CinCs for warfare areas or "platforms," like the U.S. Navy's Deputy Chiefs of Naval Operations for air, surface, and submarine matters.

Although technically not a deputy CinC, the head of the Navy's political administration has the stature of one. The Military Council of the Navy consists of the CinC, 1st Deputy CinC, the Chief of Main Naval Staff, the head of the political administration, and possibly some of the other deputy CinCs. The council appears to be an advisory body to the Commander in Chief, providing a senior forum for discussions of major policy issues, especially those that transcend political and specialized areas.

The senior officers within Soviet naval headquarters also include the Commander of Naval Aviation, Commander of Naval Infantry and Coastal Defense, and Chief of Hydrographic Services.

## MARITIME BORDER TROOPS

There are two military services in the Soviet Union that are not part of the Ministry of Defense. These are the approximately 175,000 border guards of the Committee for State Security (KGB) and the 175,000 interior troops of the Ministry of Internal Affairs (*Ministerstvo Vnutrennikh Del*—MVD). These troops of both services are organized into combat formations with combat vehicles, heavy weapons, helicopters, and light fixed-wing aircraft. The KGB troops include a coastal patrol force designated as Maritime Border Troops.

The Maritime Border Troops are responsible for coastal security—protecting Soviet maritime borders against penetration by foreign agents or paramilitary forces, and preventing Soviet citizens from leaving by water without proper authorization. The force operates small patrol craft in most if not all of the nine border districts as well as icebreakers, corvettes, and supply ships in coastal waters. The strength of the Maritime Border Troops is not available in published literature.

The Border Troops have an army-style organization with Vice Admiral N.N. Dalmatov holding the position of a deputy CinC for maritime forces. His staff maintains close liaison with naval headquarters, and apparently there are joint seamanship training and small craft procurement programs. These troops have Navy-style uniforms, the officers having green shoulder boards bearing their insignia of rank, and enlisted men wearing green cap ribbons inscribed with the words "Naval Forces of the Border Troops."

# 5

# Fleets and Flotillas

The current Soviet naval organization consists of four fleets and one flotilla. The Caspian Flotilla is the only survivor of the 12 lake, sea, and river flotillas that existed in the Soviet Navy during World War II. In peacetime the fleets are administrative as well as tactical organizations. In addition to the four fleets and the Caspian Flotilla, the Soviet Navy lists the Red Banner Leningrad Naval Base as a major command, hence it is included in this chapter.

The headquarters of each fleet and the Caspian Flotilla is similar to that of naval headquarters. The operating forces of the fleets are organized into *eskadra*(s), brigades, and divisions, with each fleet having its own naval aviation, naval infantry, and coastal defense components. The *eskadra*—literally squadron—can be a semi-independent command, as the Fifth *Eskadra* in the Mediterranean, commanded by a vice admiral. There are other commands at this level, with the Soviet Indian Ocean naval force possibly being an *eskadra* command.

## NORTHERN FLEET

The Red Banner Northern Fleet is the second largest, and in several respects the most important, Soviet fleet.[1] Based mainly in the Kola Peninsula and White Sea areas, the Northern Fleet has more direct access to the Atlantic than the Baltic and Black Sea fleets and is thus responsible for wartime operations in the Atlantic and Arctic regions. In addition, the Northern Fleet normally provides submarines for operations in the Mediterranean Sea because of the Montreux Convention, which imposes restrictions on submarine transits between the Black Sea and the Mediterranean.

Russia's longest and most inhospitable coast is in the Arctic region. The waters are largely icebound every winter except for a 70-mile stretch of the Kola Peninsula, which includes the major ports of Pechenga and Murmansk. The region is subjected to long winter nights; in the Murmansk area the sun does not rise above the horizon from mid-November to mid-January.

*History.* At the beginning of the reign of Peter the Great, the father of modern Russia as well as the Russian Navy, the northern region was the country's only access to the sea.[2] Although Peter soon undertook campaigns to gain access to the Baltic and Black seas, the Arctic coast remained vital to Russian trade. During World War I ports on the northern coast provided the route for Allied aid to the tsarist regimes, and then for the landings of U.S. and British troops during the Civil War (1918–1921). The first major Soviet naval units to be assigned to the region were the patrol ships SMERCH and URAGAN, and the submarines DEKABRIST (D-1) and NARODOVOLETS (D-2), which transited the Baltic-White Sea Canal from Kronshtadt to Murmansk in the summer of 1933. This was the start of the Northern Naval Flotilla. Reinforcements of ships and submarines followed, and in September 1935 a flight of MBR-2 flying boats was transferred to the Kola Gulf to begin naval air operations in the north.

The flotilla was reorganized as the Northern Fleet on 11 May 1937. At the start of the Great Patriotic War the fleet had 15 submarines, 8 destroyers, 7 patrol ships, and numerous lesser craft, plus 116 naval aircraft. It was thus the smallest of the four fleets when the Soviet Union entered World War II. (Naval forces in the White Sea area were organized as the separate White Sea Flotilla in August 1941.) The Northern Fleet participated in extensive combat operations against German naval forces off northern Norway and Finland. The Arctic operating area was important to the United States and Britain for convoys carrying war material to the Soviet Union.

---

[2]Peter I was born in 1672. He became tsar under a regency at age ten, sharing the throne with a weak-minded older brother, Ivan V. Upon the latter's death in 1689 Peter then ruled alone as tsar until his own death in 1725.

A contemporary French diplomat, de Campredon, cited Peter's military accomplishments in these words: ". . . through inconceivable labour and patience, he has managed to form some excellent military and naval officers, a body of splendid soldiers, an army of more than 100,000 regular troops, and a fleet of sixty vessels, including twenty of the line. Russia, whose very name was scarcely known, has now become the object of attention of the greater number of powers of Europe, who solicit its friendship."

The above is quoted from British military historian Christopher Duffy's excellent *Russia's Military Way to the West,* subtitled "Origins and Nature of Russian Military Power 1700 1825 (London: Routledge & Kegan Paul, 1981), p. 40. Duffy also notes, "The Russian navy was possibly the proudest of Peter's creations. . . ." (p. 36).

---

[1]The Order of Red Banner has been awarded to various Soviet units and activities for exemplary service in wartime. The Baltic Fleet was cited for its role in the Revolution of 1917, and all four fleets and the Caspian Flotilla were cited for the Great Patriotic War (1941–1945). The Baltic Fleet is formally referred to as the Twice-Honored Red Banner Baltic Fleet.

In the initial postwar period the Northern Fleet was considered of secondary importance to the fleets in the Baltic and Black Seas. This situation changed in the late 1950s when, under Admiral Gorshkov's direction, the naval forces that would operate in the Atlantic during wartime were shifted to the Northern Fleet where they would have more direct access to the open sea.

Today the Northern Fleet has approximately 50 percent of the Soviet Navy's submarines, 25 percent of the surface warships (frigates and larger units), 25 percent of the naval aircraft, and 25 percent of the naval personnel. The Pacific Fleet is slightly larger in all categories except submarines. The Northern and Pacific Fleets share the Navy's nuclear submarines and ballistic missile submarines (except for six Golf-class SSBs assigned to the Baltic Fleet).

Beyond operations in the Atlantic, the Northern Fleet probably has the responsibility for amphibious operations, should they be undertaken, against Norway, Iceland, and the North Sea approaches to the Danish straits. Periodically Northern Fleet amphibious ships have transited into the Baltic for multi-fleet amphibious exercises.

Under the command of Admiral A.P. Mikhaylovskiy, who has held the position since 1981, the Northern Fleet headquarters is located at Murmansk. Generally the commander of the Northern Fleet has been senior to the other fleet commanders, although when this edition of *Guide to the Soviet Navy* went to press the Pacific Fleet was commanded by an admiral of the fleet, and the Northern, Baltic, and Black Sea Fleets by admirals. A former nuclear-powered-submarine commander, Mikhaylovskiy previously served as commander of the sprawling Leningrad naval base and training complex. Before the Leningrad command, which he held as a vice admiral (promoted to admiral in 1980), he served in the Northern Fleet as a rear admiral. He was a delegate to the 26th Communist Party Congress in 1981, and that same year he was elected a candidate member of the Central Committee.

The fighting forces of the Soviet Navy are assigned to four fleets. Elements of the three European fleets often join forces, as in the Mediterranean where the Fifth *Eskadra* consists primarily of surface ships supported by land-based air from the Black Sea Fleet and submarines from the Northern Fleet. This photograph of the Kythira anchorage shows a Sᴠᴇʀᴅʟᴏᴠ-class cruiser, five destroyers, two missile corvettes, and five support ships. (1973, U.S. Navy)

The Northern and Pacific Fleets share the Soviet Navy's nuclear-propelled strategic missile submarines such as this Delta III, observed operating in the Barents Sea. The missile ranges of the newer Soviet SSBNs alleviate the need for them to pass out into the Atlantic and Pacific oceans to target American cities. (1982)

His predecessor as CinC of the Northern Fleet, Admiral V.N. Chernavin, had held that post from 1977 to 1981, when he was named to the important post of Chief of the Main Naval Staff.

## BALTIC FLEET

The Twice-Honored Red Banner Baltic Fleet was the principal Russian naval force for most of the period from the time of Peter the Great until the early tenure of Admiral Gorshkov as CinC of the Soviet Navy. Because the Baltic Fleet's access to the open sea is through waters controlled by NATO navies (Denmark, Norway, and West Germany), Admiral Gorshkov directed a redeployment of naval forces. As a result, those air, surface, and submarine forces with wartime assignments in the Atlantic were shifted to the Northern Fleet.

The Soviet naval forces in the Baltic are intended almost exclusively for operations in that area. The major exceptions are those ships undergoing trials and training relative to the huge Leningrad shipbuilding complex and training facilities. Thus, the principal missions of the Baltic Fleet in wartime appear to be supporting army operations and conducting landing and other naval operations to gain control of the Danish straits. Amphibious operations and certain other Soviet naval activities would be supported by the East German and Polish navies. At the same time, the Soviet and other Pact forces would seek to deny use of the Baltic to the NATO navies.

In 1980 and again in 1981 a task group of Soviet, East German, and Polish ships passed out of the Baltic through the Danish straits and conducted exercises in the North Sea. These exercises may have been the harbinger of Warsaw Pact naval missions beyond the Baltic. Such a shift could be largely political, i.e., a counter to the long-established NATO multi-national naval maneuvers in the Atlantic or the recent extension of West German naval operational areas to the North Sea.

The Baltic is of major importance to the Soviet Union as a commercial shipping route from the Western Russian industrial region to European and world ports. In addition, Leningrad is the transshipment point for the express container route from Japan across the USSR by train and then by ship to Atlantic nations. From a military viewpoint the Baltic forms the northern flank of the Central Front, while the Soviet shipyards on the Baltic are vital to the Soviet fleet in a prolonged conflict.

Much of the northern Baltic, including the Gulf of Finland where Leningrad is located, the Gulf of Riga, and the Gulf of Bothnia are frozen over during the winter months. The low clouds in the autumn and winter months limit air operations in the region.

*History.* Russian influence in the Baltic area dates to 1703, when Peter the Great established a city in the marshes of the Neva River where it enters the Gulf of Finland. Naming this city St. Petersburg and making it the capital of Russia, he sought to bring Western influence to the country, and envisioned St. Petersburg as a "window on the west." (The city's German-sounding name was changed to Petrograd in 1914, on the eve of World War I, and later on to Leningrad after V.I. Lenin's death in 1924.) Subsequently, in 1721 forces under Peter, relying heavily on assistance from British and other foreign naval specialists, defeated the Swedes in a series of battles in the Gulf of Finland. These victories established Russia as a Baltic power and a principal European state. Russian activity and interests in the region grew rapidly under Peter's successors. The Baltic was a major theater of combat between German and Russian naval forces in World War I. During the Communist Revolution that erupted in October 1917 against the Kerensky government, sailors from the Baltic Fleet were in the forefront of the revolutionaries. Blank rounds fired by the cruiser AVRORA, which was moored in the Neva River and had disobeyed government orders to sail, signaled the start of the Communist assault on the Winter Palace (Hermitage), site of the government that had replaced the tsarist regime in Russia.

Although sailors had helped spark the Revolution in 1917, by 1921 many were disillusioned with Lenin's form of dictatorship. In February they rioted in the city and seized control of the island naval base of Kronshtadt in the Gulf of Riga. The Gulf was frozen and the island was taken after a series of bloody assaults across the ice by Communist

The Soviets have kept several non-nuclear ballistic missile submarines in the Baltic for several years to provide a theater strike capability. Here one of these Golf II-class SSBs steams through the Danish straits accompanied by the U.S. frigate PHARRIS (FF 1094). Recently the Soviets have shifted non-nuclear cruise missile submarines to the Baltic. (1978, U.S. Navy, Colin Fritz)

In another passage through the Baltic, this Danish warship is escorting a Soviet Polnocny-C landing ship out of Denmark's territorial waters. The Soviet Baltic Fleet as well as the navies of East Germany and Poland have major amphibious forces, apparently to support ground operations along the coast and in time of war to seize the island of Bornholm and possibly the Danish straits.

forces. Several hundred sailors and the workers who allied with them were executed or exiled to Siberia. The Baltic in 1918–1920 was also the scene of extensive British naval operations against the Communists, including highly successful torpedo boat attacks against anchored Russian battleships.

Between the two world wars Leningrad became the industrial and training center of the Soviet Navy. At the outbreak of conflict in June 1941, the Baltic Fleet was the largest of the Soviet naval forces, consisting of 2 battleships, 4 cruisers, 21 destroyers, 65 submarines, and numerous lesser craft, all supported by 656 naval aircraft. German naval forces almost immediately gained control of the Baltic as German armies pushed north and east from Poland, eventually encircling Leningrad (and being stopped almost within sight of Moscow). Pro-German Finland assisted in the war against the USSR.

The Germans laid anti-submarine minefields and nets across the entrance to the Gulf of Finland to stop Soviet submarines from operating

in the Baltic. These measures, plus German naval forces and the winter ice, limited the effectiveness of the Baltic Fleet. During the three-year siege of Leningrad the large-caliber guns of the battleships and cruisers trapped in the port were used to provide fire support for Soviet ground forces.

After the war Leningrad's shipyards and other naval facilities were rebuilt as part of Stalin's fleet rehabilitation. The Baltic Fleet was the nation's largest in the immediate postwar period. However, by the late 1950s Admiral Gorshkov was transferring most of the oceangoing forces to the Northern Fleet where they would have more direct access to the Atlantic in wartime.

Today the Baltic Fleet consists primarily of combat forces intended for wartime control of the area and for amphibious assaults against West German or Danish positions, to support Soviet ground operations, or to seize control of vital waterways (with the Danish island of Bornholm being

The protected cruiser AVRORA, as now preserved at Leningrad. Launched at the New Admiralty yard in 1900, her crew ignored orders from the Russian Provisional Government in October 1917 to take the ship to sea. Moored in the Neva River at the time, blank shots from her forward gun were taken as a signal for the Bolsheviks to seize power in Leningrad. (1972, John Burcham)

considered a prime target of Warsaw Pact amphibious assault). The Baltic Fleet is currently assigned 9 percent of the Soviet Navy's submarines, 17 percent of the surface warships (frigate and larger), 19 percent of the Navy's aircraft, and about 23 percent of the Navy's personnel. The Baltic Fleet's naval air arm includes a regiment of Su-17 Fitter-C/D aircraft, the only land-based aircraft of the fighter-bomber type flown by the Soviet Navy from about 1960 to the early 1980s.

The disproportionate share of personnel is due to the large numbers of officers and enlisted men in various schools in the area, and who are assigned to surface ships and submarines under construction in the several Baltic shipyards. The Leningrad schools and other activities are considered a separate command from the Baltic Fleet by the Soviets, but the division of personnel is not readily known in the West (see below).

The operational submarines normally assigned to the Baltic Fleet are all diesel-electric craft, although nuclear submarines are present for training as well as trials, overhaul, and modernization. During September-October 1976 six Golf II ballistic missile submarines (SSB) were shifted from the Northern Fleet to the Baltic to provide a sea-based theater nuclear strike capability. Periodically one of these submarines travels out of the Baltic and back to the Northern Fleet area for missile test firings.

In 1982, at least four diesel-powered Juliett cruise missile submarines (SSG), each armed with four Shaddock missiles, shifted from the Northern Fleet to the Baltic. Although generally considered as anti-ship

weapons, the geography and NATO forces in the Baltic make it obvious that these missiles—like the SS-N-5 Serb ballistic missiles in the Golf SSBs—are for theater strike.

While the Baltic Fleet is intended principally for Baltic operations, its diesel-electric attack submarines do conduct periodic training patrols in the North Sea and in waters to the west of Great Britain.

Cruisers (two Kresta II, one Kresta I, and one SVERDLOV) and destroyers are normally the largest warships in the Baltic. However, during the Zapad (West) '81 exercise during September 1981 the aircraft carrier KIEV and the helicopter carrier LENINGRAD operated in the Baltic, the first time such ships had operated in that sea. The large amphibious ship IVAN ROGOV, which had recently returned from the Pacific, was also among the 60 Soviet naval units that conducted the exercise, the largest peacetime maneuvers ever held in the Baltic. During Zapad '81 Soviet amphibious ships and merchant ships landed some 6,000 marines (Naval Infantry) and ground troops along the coast, a short distance from the Polish border. The landings were conducted by the Baltic Fleet's Naval Infantry regiment and subunits of the "Proletarian-Moscow-Minsk" Guards Motorized Rifle Division, stationed in Leningrad.

The troops were carried in nine Alligator-class LSTs and Ropucha-class LSTs from the Northern and Black Sea Fleets as well as from the Baltic Fleet, in addition to the IVAN ROGOV and five roll-on/roll-off merchant ships. Air-cushion landing craft, Mi-24 Hind helicopters, T-72 tanks, and other advanced equipment were used in the landings.

The landing near Baltiysk on the Lithuanian coast was the site of several previous exercises, but being only 15 miles (24 km) from the Polish border it took on special significance in view of the unrest in Poland at the time. Official Soviet statements cited more than 100,000 troops participating in the Baltic coast exercises. Zapad '81 was observed by Defense Minister Ustinov and ministers from the Warsaw Pact nations,

This highly stylized painting shows Bolshevik leader Leon Trotsky handing orders to sailors from the AVRORA. Although the Bolsheviks relied on many former tsarist naval officers, paintings and other documentation of the Revolution invariably show enlisted men—members of the proletariat from which the Reds sought their strength. (Naval Museum, Leningrad)

Cuba, Mongolia, and Vietnam. However, no ships from other Warsaw Pact navies participated in the amphibious exercises.

The Baltic Fleet is under the command of Admiral I.M. Kapitanets, whose headquarters is located at Baltiysk (formerly Pillau) near the Lithuanian port of Kaliningrad (formerly Koenigsberg). Kapitanets, a delegate to the 26th Party Congress (1981), was appointed to command the Baltic Fleet in February 1981, having previously served as first deputy CinC in the grade of vice admiral. His predecessor, Admiral V.V. Sidorov, had held the post for two and one-half years before being reassigned as CinC of the Pacific Fleet.

## LENINGRAD NAVAL BASE

The Red Banner Leningrad Naval Base is considered a major command, on the level with the fleet commands. The Leningrad area consists of a number of schools and other training facilities (see chapter 9) as well as shipyards (see chapter 28). The city also contains the Central Naval Museum (housed in the imposing stock exchange building of the tsarist era) and the Central Naval Library, with its collection of about one million volumes.

Admiral V. A. Samoylov is believed to have been commandant of the Leningrad Naval Base since 1982.

## BLACK SEA FLEET

The Red Banner Black Sea Fleet is responsible for operations in the Black Sea and, more significantly, it provides surface warships and aircraft for operations in the Mediterranean Sea as the Fifth *Eskadra* (task force). However, the Black Sea Fleet does not provide submarines for Mediterranean operations. As already noted, the submarine deployments to the Mediterranean are provided by the Northern Fleet. Because of the significance of Black Sea-Mediterranean operations, this fleet has a greater proportion of large warships than the Baltic Fleet, although—unlike the Baltic Fleet's operational area—the Black Sea is essentially a "Soviet lake" with Turkey the only potentially hostile nation bordering the sea.

Black Sea ports are second only to those of the Baltic in handling Soviet maritime imports and exports. As in the Baltic, there are major shipyards located along the Black Sea coast. Despite its relatively southern location, some Black Sea ports, including the leading port of Odessa, are frozen in for about six weeks of the year as is the smaller Sea of Azov, which is immediately north of the Black Sea. In general, the Black Sea climate is the best in the Soviet Union, with many resorts located along the coast, including several for naval personnel. The good flying weather is a major reason why the Navy's air training center is located in the area.

*History.* Russian naval activities on the Black Sea are traced to 1783, when ships from the Sea of Azov visited the village of Akhtiar (renamed Sevastopol the following year). Subsequent Russian interest in the area led to a series of wars with Turkey during the late eighteenth and nineteenth centuries, with British and French naval forces at times being allied with those of Turkey. The Russians were highly innovative in tactics and weapons during their battles with the Turks, introducing rifled shells

among other developments. During this period shipbuilding became a major activity along the Black Sea coast, especially at Nikolayev.

Like their comrades in the Baltic, many sailors of the Black Sea Fleet were at the forefront of revolutionary fervor at the start of this century, and in the abortive revolts of 1905 there was a much-publicized mutiny aboard the battleship POTEMKIN (an event made immortal in Sergei Eisenstein's classic film of 1925).[3] During the Russian revolution of 1917 and the subsequent Civil War, the British and French landed troops on the Black Sea coast to support the anti-Red forces in the area. After the success of the Communists and the withdrawal of foreign fleets, the remnants of the Black Sea Fleet fled to North Africa, where they were interned.

In May of 1920 the newly established Bolshevik regime organized the Naval Forces of the Black Sea and Sea of Azov. These forces were redesignated as the Black Sea Fleet on 11 January 1935. During the 1930s the Black Sea region regained its importance in the shipbuilding and maritime industries. At the outbreak of the Great Patriotic War in June 1941, the Black Sea Fleet was the nation's second largest, with 1 battleship, 6 cruisers, 3 destroyer leaders, 14 destroyers, and 47 submarines, with 625 land-based aircraft. During the early stages of the German invasion of the Soviet Union in 1941, enemy troops assaulted the Ukraine. German land-based aircraft were the primary threat to Soviet ships supporting the Red Army. The Germans pushed through the Ukraine and along the Black Sea coast, finally being stopped at Novorossiysk in late 1942. The Soviet fleet then supported the counteroffensive, which ended in triumph. Several naval flotillas were established in the Black Sea area by the Soviet high command during the war, among them the Azov and Danube flotillas. Both flotillas saw extensive combat under the command of then-Rear Admiral Gorshkov. Also, Party Chairman Brezhnev saw action with the Black Sea Fleet as political officer in the 18th Army during an amphibious landing.

After the war the shipyards in the Black Sea region were rapidly rehabilitated to help rebuild the Soviet fleet. The formation of NATO in 1949 with Turkey and Greece successfully resisting Communist takeover seemed to deny the Black Sea Fleet easy access to the Mediterranean through the Turkish Straits. Still, in 1958 the Soviets first deployed naval forces into the Mediterranean. These were submarines that in 1960 were based, with a tender, at Vlore (Valona), Albania. The following year, as a by-product of the Sino-Soviet dispute, the Soviets were forced to abandon Vlore, leaving behind two Whiskey-class submarines seized by the Albanians. The loss of this base pointed up the limitation of Soviet naval logistics, and Soviet combatant forces were not again deployed on a sustained basis to the Mediterranean until 1964.

From the mid-1960s onward Soviet naval forces have operated continuously in the Mediterranean, with surface ships and aircraft coming from the Black Sea Fleet and submarines from the Northern Fleet. By the early 1970s the Soviets had an average daily strength of 50 or more naval units in the Mediterranean on a regular basis. This force, the Fifth *Eskadra*, reached a peak strength of some 60 surface ships and 25 sub-

[3]More properly the KNIAZ POTEMKIN TAVRICHESKI. After the mutiny she was renamed PANTELIMON and from May 1917 the BORETZ ZA SVOBODU.

On a quiet Mediterranean day the helicopter carrier MOSKVA prepares to fuel from a naval tanker that is already fueling a Mirka-class light frigate, while another Mirka waits her turn. Leisurely replenishments were the rule in Soviet naval operations until the advent of the KIEV-class carriers led to development of high-tempo UNREP practices similar to those of the U.S. Navy. (1969, U.S. Navy)

marines during the October 1973 confrontation with the United States in the Yom Kippur war in the Middle East.[4] Efforts to obtain support bases for the Soviet Mediterranean squadron have centered on Egypt (until they were ejected in 1973) and Syria. The typical composition of the Fifth *Eskadra* is:

| | | |
|---|---|---|
| 6 to 8 | torpedo attack submarines |
| 1 or 2 | cruise missile attack submarines |
| 1 or 2 | missile cruisers |
| 6 to 8 | destroyers and frigates |
| 1 to 3 | minesweepers |
| 1 to 3 | amphibious ships |
| 15 to 20 | auxiliary ships |
| 5 or 6 | survey, research, and intelligence collection ships |

Soviet combat operations in the Black Sea and Mediterranean would be supported by land-based naval aircraft from bases in the Crimea. In addition, cruiser–helicopter carriers of the MOSKVA class are based in the Black Sea and operate regularly in the Mediterranean as do the KIEV-class aircraft carriers when they are in the Black Sea area. The Black Sea Fleet also has the largest cruiser-destroyer force of any of the Soviet

[4]The Soviet force consisted of 5 cruisers, 14 destroyers, 6 escort ships, 2 Nanuchka-class missile ships, 8 amphibious ships, 36 intelligence collection and auxiliary ships, and about 25 submarines. Most if not all of the surface ships were from the Black Sea Fleet; all of the submarines were from the Northern Fleet. At that time the U.S. Sixth Fleet in the Mediterranean had some 60 ships, but that force's 3 aircraft carriers provided a superior *surface* striking force.

fleets. In total, the Black Sea Fleet has 27 percent of the Navy's major combatants (frigates and above) but only 7 percent of the Navy's submarines (with no nuclear or ballistic missile units). Including the Caspian Flotilla, the Black Sea Fleet has 25 percent of the Navy's aircraft and 22 percent of the personnel.

The Black Sea Fleet is commanded by Admiral N.I. Khovrin, who has held that position since 1974, before which he served in the Pacific Fleet. His headquarters are at Sevastopol´. When this volume went to press he was the longest serving of the four Soviet fleet commanders. Khovrin was a delegate to both the 25th (1976) and 26th (1981) Communist Party Congresses.

### CASPIAN SEA FLOTILLA

The small Red Banner Caspian Sea Flotilla is primarily a small patrol force operating in the world's largest inland sea, which is shared with Iran. Under Peter the Great the Russian forces fortified portions of the Caspian coast and built a fleet that gained the ports of Baku and Derbend by treaty. Subsequently, Baku was lost only to be recaptured from Persia in 1816. Later treaties gave the Russians exclusive right to have warships on the sea, although Persia continued to hold the southern coast and Iran continues to operate patrol boats in this area.

Russian and Soviet naval operations on the Caspian continued with the construction of a canal from the Black Sea permitting the rapid transfer of ships up to destroyer size between the two bodies of water. Although naval activity on the Caspian is limited, there is considerable shipping with most of the cargo being oil and grain. Offshore oil wells in the Caspian contribute significantly to the Soviet Union's ability now to produce more oil per day than any other nation.

The Caspian Sea Flotilla is commanded by Vice Admiral G.G. Kasumbekov, who has his headquarters at Baku. He has been the Caspian CinC since 1977.

## PACIFIC FLEET

The largest of the four Soviet fleets and the one with the largest operating area is the Red Banner Pacific Fleet. Whereas the three European fleets are oriented against the United States and other NATO forces, the Pacific Fleet has wartime responsibilities against the People's Republic of China as well as the United States and its allies (South Korea, Japan, and possibly other nations, depending upon the wartime scenario). The peacetime responsibilities of the Pacific Fleet include operations throughout the broad Pacific as well as providing most of the ships that carry out deployments in the Indian Ocean.

There has been a significant buildup of the Pacific Fleet during the past few years because of the unsettled political situation in Southeast Asia, the Soviet invasion of Afghanistan in 1979, the turmoil in the Persian Gulf region, and the continued unrest along the eastern coast of Africa. The principal mission of the Pacific Fleet, of course, is defending the Soviet Siberian coast, second only to the Arctic coast in length. In general, the Soviet Pacific coast provides more direct access to the open

oceans than do those of the European coasts. The major port complex of Vladivostok opens into the Sea of Japan with four major straits giving egress into the Pacific. The Soviets control one exit (Kuril Strait), and another separates Japan and the Russian-held island of Sakhalin (La Pérouse), while the two other exits are controlled by Japan and Japan and South Korea (Tsugaru and Korean Straits, respectively). Their blockade by the West is unlikely except in the most extreme circumstances because of the dependence of Japan and Korea on maritime trade. The second major naval port in the Far East is Petropavlovsk on the coast of desolate Kamchatka. Most of the Pacific Fleet's submarines are based there, with direct access to the Pacific Ocean.

From an economic viewpoint the Soviet Siberian coast has several ports vital to Soviet trade. These ports move cargo to and from European Russia (reducing the load on the severely limited trans-Siberian railway). They facilitate the economic and politically lucrative trade with the Third World nations of western South America, Southeast Asia, India, the Middle East, and eastern Africa.

*History.* Russians reached the Pacific coast of Siberia in significant numbers in the mid-seventeenth century, founding the towns of Anadyr´ and Okhotsk in 1649. The area grew in importance at a rapid pace, largely because of trade with China and then with Japan. Commodore Matthew Calbraith Perry, commander of the U.S. East India Squadron, forced the opening of Japan in 1853–1854 to preempt a Russian squadron in the area and prevent the tsar's officers from reaping the benefits of a treaty with Japan. From an organizational viewpoint, a Russian Okhotsk Flotilla was formed in 1731, being reorganized and renamed the Siberian Naval Flotilla in 1856. In addition to the flotilla, the 1st Pacific Squadron was established. At the start of the 1904–1905 war with Japan the Russian Navy had 7 of its 15 modern battleships based at Port Arthur (compared to the Japanese Navy's six modern battleships then in commission).

The Russo-Japanese war of 1904–1905 was a disaster for the Pacific Squadron as well as for a reinforcing fleet sent from the Baltic and Black Sea. The Japanese triumph at the Battle of Tsushima on 27 May 1905 destroyed Russian naval power in the Pacific and established Japan as a world power. After the war the Russian Navy in the Far East consisted of the weakened Siberian and Amur flotillas. The Revolution of 1917 was followed by Japanese and American troops landing at Vladivostok to support anti-Communist forces and to help the removal of a Czech army in central Russia that the Allies wished to transport to the European theater to rejoin the battle against Germany. The Japanese left Siberia in 1922, after which the Soviets formed the Vladivostok ship detachment and the Amur Naval Flotilla in the Far East. These organizations were disbanded in 1926, with the ships and craft being assigned to the border guards and the new Far Eastern Naval Flotilla. The naval units were organized as the Naval Forces of the Far East in April 1932, and as Soviet forces in the area increased, on 11 January 1935 the title Pacific Fleet was assigned.

Pacific Fleet aircraft were involved in the late 1930s fighting with Japan in Manchuria, with ships moving troops and material and evacuating the wounded. When the Great Patriotic War began in Europe in June 1941 the Pacific Fleet consisted of 14 destroyers, 91 submarines, numer-

The Soviet Pacific Fleet has had extensive opportunities to observe U.S. naval activities, especially during the Vietnam War. U.S. carrier operations in the Gulf of Tonkin were regularly under surveillance, as seen here with the AGI Gidrofon observing the Coral Sea (CV 43) and her screening ships during a refueling operation. Note the extensive antenna arrays on the Gidrofon. (1969, U.S. Navy)

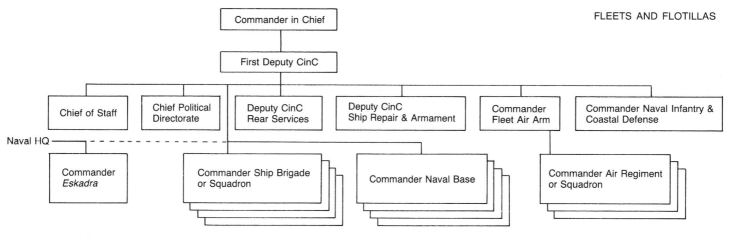

Figure 5–1. Fleet Organization

ous lesser craft, and some 500 aircraft. These units were essentially idle during the war with 147,000 men from the fleet being sent to fight as ground troops in the European theater.

When the Soviet Union attacked Japan in August 1945, the Pacific Fleet had 2 cruisers, 13 destroyers, 78 submarines, plus other ships and craft, and 1,500 aircraft. During operations against Manchuria and Korea in the final days of the war, the fleet attacked Japanese shipping and supported ground operations with air attacks and logistic support. Several amphibious landings, largely unopposed, were made at ports along the coasts of Korea, Sakhalin, and the Kuril Islands. Some were undertaken in conjunction with parachute landings.

In January 1947 the Pacific Fleet was divided into the Fifth Fleet (headquarters at Vladivostok) and the Seventh Fleet (headquarters at Sovetskaya Gavan´). They were reunited into a single Pacific Fleet in 1953. Significant long-range operations of the Pacific Fleet began in 1959 when a SVERDLOV-class cruiser and two destroyers visited Djakarta, Indonesia. This was the harbinger of Soviet naval assistance to the Sukarno government in Indonesia. It included the transfer of a SVERDLOV, a dozen Whiskey-class submarines, eight destroyers, eight escort ships, a dozen Komar-type missile craft, and other naval material. (Sukarno's fall from power in 1965 ended Russian influence in the island nation.) Soviet naval operations expanded in the Pacific during the 1960s and spread into the Indian Ocean, with ship and missile transfers to the Indian Navy contributing to that force's startling success against Pakistan in the 1971 war between the two nations.

The Soviet Pacific Fleet observed the U.S. operations in the Vietnam War with great interest. Soviet intelligence collection ships—AGIs—periodically operated in the Gulf of Tonkin, with one AGI usually on station off Guam to observe the U.S. Polaris submarine base and detect B-52 bomber missions taking off from the island. Warnings of these raids against Communist forces in Vietnam were broadcast moments after the planes took off. Soviet naval ship visits to Communist Vietnam began in March 1979, calling at the northern port of Haiphong and the southern ports of Da Nang and Cam Ranh Bay. Bear-D naval reconnaissance aircraft began flights from Da Nang in April 1972, flying missions over the South China Sea, including flights over U.S. naval ships. Reportedly, the

Soviets also began improvements to facilities at Kompong Som in Cambodia.

During the 1970s the Pacific Fleet began receiving first-line units at about the same time as the Soviet European fleets. This was highlighted by the transfer of the MINSK, the second of the KIEV-class aircraft carriers, to the Pacific in June 1979. The carrier was accompanied by the IVAN ROGOV, the largest amphibious ship in the Soviet Navy. Four guided missile cruisers (one Kresta I, one Kresta II, and two Karas) plus several lesser surface warships and submarines also joined the Pacific Fleet from 1978 to 1980.

During her transit from the Black Sea, around Africa, across the Indian Ocean, through the Straits of Malacca, and up to Vladivostok, the MINSK and accompanying ships visited numerous Third World ports. Especially significant were the six-day visit to Luanda (Angola), a five-day stopover at Maputo—helping to demonstrate Soviet support for Mozambique vis-a-vis Rhodesia and South Africa—and an eight-day visit to Aden (South Yemen), which included air and amphibious demonstrations. While providing some increase in the Soviet Pacific Fleet's military capability, in some respects the MINSK transit had even more important political significance.

In the early 1980s, the Pacific Fleet has one-third of the Soviet submarine force (including almost half of the SSBN force), 30 percent of the major surface warships (frigate and larger), and the largest of the fleet air arms with some 30 percent of the total SNA aircraft. Some 28 percent of the Navy's manpower is assigned to the fleet.

Admiral of the Fleet V.V. Sidorov commands the Pacific Fleet from his headquarters in Vladivostok. He took the CinC position after Admiral Ye.N. Spiridonov and several other senior Pacific Fleet officers were killed in an air crash in European Russia on 7 February 1981. (Spiridonov had held the fleet command for less than a year and a half before his death.) Sidorov was CinC of the Baltic Fleet when ordered to take command of the Pacific Fleet on short notice; he had commanded the Baltic Fleet since July 1978. A surface warfare specialist, he had earlier served as chief of staff of the Pacific Fleet. As a fleet admiral he is the highest ranking of the four fleet commanders. He was a delegate to the 26th Communist Party Congress in 1981 and was elected as a candidate member of the Central Committee that same year.

# 6

# Naval Aviation

Soviet Naval Aviation (*Aviatsiya Voyenno-Morskogo Flota*) is the world's second largest naval air arm and operates more combat aircraft than any European NATO air force. This air arm is undergoing significant modernization, and several aspects of Soviet Naval Aviation—referred to as SNA in the West—demonstrate imagination and originality in the opinion of several Western analysts, including the dean of Soviet military watchers, Professor John Erickson.[1]

*History.* Dating back to the end of the nineteenth century there has been a strong interest in aviation by Russian naval officers. During World War I the Russian Navy flew a large number of aircraft, with some floatplanes based aboard merchant ships. The naval air arm was rebuilt as part of the fleet programs of the 1930s, with 1,445 aircraft reported in naval service at the start of the Great Patriotic War, albeit mostly outdated types. Naval aircraft flew missions in support of maritime operations, but also carried out other missions on a regular basis as directed by ground and area commanders. A few "strategic" missions were flown by the Navy, as on the night of 7–8 August 1941, when five Navy Il-4 bombers flew from Estonia to make a token and ineffective raid on Berlin.

Soviet naval aircraft flew exclusively from land bases during the war. In the late 1930s there had been an effort to obtain plans and components for aircraft carriers in the United States, but this did not come to fruition (see chapter 10).

According to Soviet sources, at the end of the war there were 1,500 aircraft assigned to the Pacific Fleet alone. This testifies to the importance accorded to air support of naval operations. Most of these planes were of indigenous design and manufacture; however, 185 were the ubiquitous PBY/PBN Catalina flying boats, transferred to Russia in 1942–1943. They were followed by licensed production for the Soviet Navy with the designation GST. The Soviet aircraft industry profited from the spoils of war as German technology, machinery, and aircraft engineers were brought back to the Soviet Union. In addition, the unfinished German aircraft carrier GRAF ZEPPELIN was loaded with booty and taken in tow across the Baltic for Leningrad. However, she sank in rough seas, her heavy load causing her demise. Stalin's fleet rebuilding program initiated in the late 1940s apparently included aircraft carriers, but none was ever laid down.

Even after the halt of Stalin's shipbuilding program in 1953, Khrushchev, his successor, wrote in his memoirs: "Aircraft carriers, of course, are the second most effective weapon in a modern navy (after submarines). I'll admit I felt a nagging desire to have some in our own navy, but we couldn't afford to build them. They were simply beyond our means."[2]

Rather, the postwar Soviet naval air arm concentrated on land-based aircraft. By the late 1950s land-based bomber aircraft were being armed with air-to-surface missiles for use against enemy ships. The first such weapon was designated AS-1 Kennel by Western intelligence. It resembled a scaled-down MiG-15 turbojet fighter and was credited with being able to deliver a high-explosive warhead against surface ships or ground targets some 63 miles (100 km) from the launching bomber. These weapons were initially carried by Tu-4 Bull piston-engine bombers, the Soviet copy of the American B-29 Superfortress. Subsequently, the Kennel and other anti-ship missiles were carried by the Tu-16 Badger turbojet bomber.

Soviet Naval Aviation reached a peak strength of several thousand aircraft in the late 1950s, with large numbers of land-based strike aircraft supported by fighter aircraft, which could also be employed to protect naval installations from American carrier strikes. About 1960 SNA was stripped of its fighters, which were assigned to the National Air Defense

[2]Nikita S. Khrushchev, *Khrushchev Remembers—The Last Testament* (Boston Little, Brown & Co., 1974), p. 31.

The first aircraft carrier to fly the hammer-and-sickle was the German aircraft carrier GRAF ZEPPELIN. Launched in 1938, the carrier was never completed and looked like this near the end of the war. She was scuttled at Stettin on 25 April 1945. Salved by the Soviets, she sank at sea in the Baltic, off Rügen on 15 August 1947 according to some reports. (1945, Courtesy *Bibliothek fur Zeitgeschichte Archiv*)

[1]John Erickson in foreword to Alexander Boyd, *The Soviet Air Force Since 1918* (London: Macdonald and Jane's, 1977), p. xix, n.

A Badger-D streaks low over the British carrier ARK ROYAL during a NATO naval exercise in 1971. The Soviet Navy flies several hundred bomber-type aircraft in the strike, reconnaissance, electronic warfare, and tanker roles. The missile-armed Badgers are being supplemented in the strike role by the Backfire bomber and, in the 1980s, will probably be joined by the new Blackjack. (British Ministry of Defence)

Forces. This reduced the Navy to about 750 aircraft. Later the Soviet strategic air arm transferred most if not all of its missile-armed Badger medium bombers to the Navy for the anti-ship role. (The only missile-armed bombers retained by strategic aviation at the time were the long-range Bears.) By the mid-1960s SNA had some 400 Tu-16 Badger medium bombers and 100 older Il-28 Beagle torpedo bombers. The remaining 250 naval aircraft were patrol, ASW, transport, and utility aircraft, including some helicopters. From that nadir the naval air arm has been built up until today SNA has some 1,500 aircraft. Most of these are land based, but with a small, significant number of ship-based fighter-attack aircraft and helicopters.

## COMMAND, ORGANIZATION, AND STRENGTH

The overall commander of Soviet Naval Aviation, on the staff of the Commander in Chief of the Navy in Moscow, is currently Colonel-General of Aviation A.A. Mironenko, who took that post in 1975. A career naval aviator, he previously commanded naval aviation in the Black Sea from 1956 until 1972 (16 years!). Afterwards he served as Chief of Staff for SNA until assuming his current position.

Within each of the four fleets there is a naval air force commander with the rank of lieutenant-general of aviation. The senior staff of SNA and each fleet air force includes a first deputy, chief of staff, chief of political department, and senior engineer.

The current SNA strength of about 1,500 aircraft represents a net increase of over 250 planes during the last five years, with more than 100 of those being Backfire anti-ship strike aircraft. An estimated 63,000 officers and enlisted men are assigned to SNA, representing 14 percent of the Navy's total personnel. A possible indication of the complexity of modern SNA aircraft may be seen in the 35 percent increase in personnel assigned to the naval air arm during the past decade with only a 25 percent increase in aircraft. (SNA strength in 1972 was estimated by Western intelligence at approximately 40,000 personnel and 1,100 aircraft.)

Each of the four fleets has its own naval air force. There is a naval air commander at each fleet headquarters with the appropriate staff to direct the operations of assigned aircraft. The composition of the various fleet air arms varies with geography and mission. For example, anti-ship strike aircraft and patrol/ASW aircraft are assigned to each fleet. The long-range Tu-20 Bear-D reconnaissance aircraft are found only in the Northern and Pacific Fleets, where their great range provides large-area search capabilities. The Baltic Fleet, apparently because of the short distances involved and the nature of the Western threat in the Baltic, has about 40 land-based fighters of the Su-17 Fitter-C/D type.

The KIEV class aircraft carriers are assigned to the Northern, Black Sea, and Pacific Fleets, bringing to those operating areas their complements of Yak-36 Forger VTOL aircraft and Ka-25 Hormone helicopters. Both of the MOSKVA-class helicopter ships, with Ka-25 Hormones embarked, are in the Black Sea Fleet. Several classes of cruisers carry Hormone-A ASW helicopters or Hormone-B missile-targeting helicopters, with some Hormone-C utility variants also being seen aboard ship. The Hormone's successor, the Helix, was first seen at sea in 1981 aboard the ASW destroyer UDALOY.

A major limitation of SNA has been the lack of forward-deployed aircraft to support air operations beyond the Soviet Eurasian landmass. This situation is being partially corrected by the construction of the KIEV and later classes of aircraft carriers. Also, from 1970 on the Soviet Union has had significant overseas air bases available. The first major overseas air operation took place during the *Okean* multi-ocean exercises of April 1970 when a pair of Bear-D naval reconnaissance aircraft took off from a Northern Fleet base, flew down the Norwegian Sea, over Soviet ships operating in the Iceland-Faeroes gap area, and then continued south to land in Cuba. This nonstop flight of more than 5,000 miles marked the first time that Bear aircraft had landed outside of Soviet bloc countries.[3] After a few days the Bears returned to their home base. In late April another pair of Bear-D aircraft flew into Cuba and a third pair made the flight in May 1970, establishing a regular pattern for such operations. There were an average of five such flights per year until 1981, normally with two Bears in each flight (with four making the trip in September 1972 and three in July of 1973). Since 1981 the presence of Bears in Cuba has been virtually continuous. These flights provide long-range navigation training and area familiarization for the aircraft crews, with the Bears also conducting surveillance and Electronic Intelligence (ELINT) collection along the coast of North America and over U.S. ships they overfly.

In 1973 pairs of Bear aircraft began calls at Conakry, Guinea. On several occasions Bears in Cuba and Bears in Conakry appear to have carried out coordinated reconnaissance of the South and Central Atlantic. Subsequently, in 1977, the Bears ceased flying out of Conakry.

---

[3]The previous July a Soviet surface ship–submarine group had operated in the Caribbean, probably the first visit of a Russian squadron to the Western Hemisphere since the American Civil War. A similar force entered the Caribbean at the end of the *Okean* exercises in late April 1970.

The pattern also changed when during 1977 the Bear-D flights began to call at Luanda, Angola, with the flights then crossing the Atlantic between Cuba and Angola. In the Mediterranean, Soviet aircraft were observed on airfields in Libya (including the former Wheelus U.S. Air Force Base) from the early 1970s, with SNA aircraft beginning operational deployments in 1981. Naval aircraft have also flown on an operational basis from Egypt (until 1973) and Syria. SNA operations over the Indian Ocean generally originate from bases in the Crimea with overflights of Iran. During the 1970s a major base complex was available to the Soviets at Berbera in Somalia, but they were soon evicted from that country and began using a base in Ethiopia instead. Naval aircraft also use Aden (South Yemen).

A quartet of Forger-A fighter-attack aircraft rest on the flight deck of the VTOL aircraft carrier KIEV. Soviet Naval Aviation is undergoing a major modernization effort as well as an expansion in numbers of aircraft and aircraft-carrying ships. The four KIEV-class carriers are expected to be followed by a larger, nuclear-propelled "flattop." (1980, U.S. Navy)

The movement of Soviet troops to Afghanistan in late 1979 opened the possibility of SNA forward bases in that country at some future date, increasing operational capabilities over the Indian Ocean. In the Pacific, long-range flights from bases in Siberia have been supplemented since April 1974 by Bear operations from the former U.S. air bases at Da Nang and Cam Ranh Bay in Vietnam. With the major exception of Badger, Cub, and Mail operations from Egypt, these forward-base operations have been largely by Bear and May reconnaissance/patrol aircraft. Nevertheless, they demonstrate a potential for using such bases to extend the range of naval strike aircraft. (The Soviets had built a missile assembly and checkout facility at Berbera, Somalia, that could have supported naval strike aircraft.)

## STRIKE AIRCRAFT

Soviet Naval Aviation's anti-ship strike role developed in the 1950s to counter American aircraft carriers, which were, at the time, justified primarily for the nuclear strike mission.[4] Sometimes called Anti-Carrier Warfare (ACW) by the U.S. Navy, anti-ship strike continues to be a high-priority Soviet mission.

Soviet doctrine apparently calls for coordinated strikes by missile-armed aircraft and submarines, possibly with surface ships participating in the attack if they can be brought within range of the target at the proper time and place. An anti-ship missile strike would include not only bomber aircraft with stand-off missiles, but possibly reconnaissance and targeting aircraft, tanker aircraft to extend the range of the strike planes, and Electronic Countermeasure (ECM) aircraft to help degrade defensive radars.

The principal aircraft employed in the anti-ship role is the Tu-16 Badger, a twin-turbojet medium bomber that first entered Soviet service in 1954. (See chapter 24 for detailed characteristics of SNA aircraft.) Some 275 Badger-C and -G aircraft are in SNA, each capable of carrying two AS-2 Kipper or AS-5 Kelt missiles with ranges up to about 135 miles (220 km). These planes may also be capable of delivering the newer AS-6 Kingfish. Regiments of strike Badgers are assigned to all four Soviet fleets.

The Tu-22M Backfire, with two turbojet engines and variable-sweep wings, has been in SNA service since late 1974. This aircraft has been the subject of considerable controversy in the United States because of its possible use in the strategic attack role against North American targets. However, the fact that from the start of deliveries of the Backfire one-half of the planes have gone directly into SNA regiments tends to indicate that the half that have gone to the Soviet strategic air arm are theater and not strategic aircraft. If they were intended for the strategic role, the strategic air arm would undoubtedly have been given more of the early Backfire production run to replace the aging Tu-20 Bear and Mya-4 Bison long-range bombers assigned to the strategic strike role.

The Backfire's high speed (Mach 2 high altitude dash), long range (2,875/4,625-km radius), and ability to carry one or two of the AS-4 Kitchen missiles and possibly the new AS-6, make it a most potent

weapon. In the anti-carrier role, Backfires flying from bases in the Kola Peninsula could attack shipping in the North Atlantic through an arc intersecting Gibraltar to the coast of Labrador. In the Pacific, Backfires from Petropavlovsk bases could reach the Philippine Sea and westernmost Hawaiian islands. In-flight refueling could significantly extend these ranges. Backfires from bases in the Crimea could reach throughout the Mediterranean.

While the Backfire is generally addressed in the context of an anti-ship missile carrier, most if not all of the naval Backfires that have been reported with missiles have been seen carrying only one AS-4. This could imply a trade-off of missiles for more range. Alternatively, a new missile may be in development for the Backfire. Additionally, SNA may plan to use the Backfire as a penetrating minelayer as well as missile carrier. In the latter role the aircraft would seek to reach the approaches to key West European ports to sow aerial mines in order to deny use of the ports to NATO forces. (The U.S. Navy had developed the turbojet P6M Seamaster flying boat in the late 1950s primarily as an aerial minelayer.)

The initial Backfire regiments were assigned to the Baltic and Black Sea Fleets, with the first Backfire regiment in the Pacific Fleet being established in 1980. By early 1982 some 100 Backfires had been delivered to SNA; two regiments were reported in the Baltic Fleet and one each in the Black Sea and Pacific Fleets. Production continues at a rate of 2½ aircraft per month, indicating that the Navy could gain about 15 to 18 aircraft, or almost one strike regiment per year.

The number of bomber-type aircraft in SNA has increased by some 50 aircraft over the past five years, indicating that the older Badgers are not being replaced by Backfires at a one-for-one rate, but rather the strike force is being increased as well as qualitatively improved.

Another high-performance bomber, given the NATO code name Blackjack, is expected to enter Soviet service in 1986–1987, with a significant number of the aircraft probably going to naval aviation. Indeed, the design of the aircraft may well have been based to a major extent on

**TABLE 6-1.   SOVIET NAVAL AIRCRAFT, LATE 1982**

| Type | Aircraft | Strength |
|---|---|---|
| Missile Strike | Backfire-B | |
| | Badger-C/G | |
| Bomber | Badger-A | 400 |
| | Blinder-A | |
| Fighter/Attack | Fitter-C/D | |
| | Forger-A/B | 80 |
| Reconnaissance/EW | Badger-D/E/F/H/J/K | |
| | Bear-D | 180 |
| | Blinder-C | |
| Tanker | Badger-A | 80 |
| Anti-Submarine | Bear-F | |
| | Mail | 200 |
| | May | |
| ASW Helicopter | Haze-A | |
| | Helix | 250 |
| | Hormone-A | |
| Utility/Transport/Training | (various)* | 375 |
| Total (rounded) | | 1,560 |

*Includes some Coot/Cub transports configured for ECM and ELINT missions, etc.

---

[4] U.S. aircraft carriers were withdrawn from this primary role about 1962 as U.S. land-based and sea-based ballistic missiles became available in large numbers.

This Backfire-B strike aircraft, armed with an AS-4 Kitchen missile under her fuselage, on a training mission over the Baltic Sea. SNA continuously carries out reconnaissance and exercise strike flights over regional waters as well as ocean areas, demonstrating the increasing range and combat capabilities of Soviet naval air (Swedish Air Force)

SNA requirements. The aircraft has variable-sweep wings and a range estimated by some sources as over 7,440 miles (12,000 km). This Tupolev aircraft was originally designated RAM-P in the West, "RAM" derived from the plane having been observed at the Ramenskoye aircraft test facility near Moscow.

In addition to the Blackjack, there is at least one other long-range bomber under development in the Soviet Union. This aircraft, assigned the bureau designation Tu-160, is reported to be a bomber version of the Tu-144, the fixed-wing Supersonic Transport (SST) that entered Soviet commercial service late in 1975. This aircraft, assigned the NATO code name Charger, has reportedly reached a speed of Mach 2.4. A total of 13 commercial aircraft were built, including prototypes. A bomber version would have been extensively redesigned and would be a reversal of the usual practice of adopting commercial variants from military aircraft. Regardless of whether the Tu-160 is a true bomber adaptation of the Tu-144 and no matter what its exact status is, the Tupolev bureau is unquestionably continuing to design advanced bomber aircraft, and they probably have features for naval use.

Beyond the missile-armed strike aircraft, SNA still operates a small number of Badger-A and Tu-22 Blinder-A bombers that carry free-fall bombs. These aircraft would probably be used against ground targets in support of amphibious operations or would support ground forces in combat. These could also be employed in reconnaissance and tanker roles.

The other bomber-type aircraft in SNA are employed to support the strike aircraft: Eighty Badger-A tankers are flown by SNA to refuel strike

aircraft, and almost that many Badger aircraft are employed in the ECM and reconnaissance roles. The ECM mission calls for some aircraft to accompany the strike planes in close formation and others to stand off from the ships being attacked to jam or confuse defensive radars. These planes have powerful on-board radar jammers and can drop chaff. The built-in ECM capabilities of the Backfire apparently permit that aircraft to operate independent of specialized jammer escort planes.

### FIGHTER-ATTACK AIRCRAFT

The Baltic Fleet's air arm has been assigned a regiment of about 40 Fitter-C/D fighter-ground attack aircraft since the 1970s. These aircraft have variable-sweep wings and can carry almost 8,000 pounds (3,632 kg) of ordnance and can reach Mach 2 + speeds when "clean." These planes appear to have anti-shipping or amphibious support roles, if not both. In the early 1980s; a Fitter unit was established in the Pacific Fleet.

The KIEV-class aircraft carriers operate the Yak-36 Forger Vertical Take-Off and Landing (VTOL) aircraft in the fighter and attack roles. Two variants have been observed at sea, the single-seat A and the two-seat B. With only four of these ships being constructed, the total Forger inventory will be about 50 aircraft aboard ship.

The KIEVs are expected to be succeeded by a larger carrier class capable of handling conventional fixed-wing aircraft (employing ship-

Forger and Hormone aircraft at rest aboard a KIEV-class VTOL carrier.

A Forger comes aboard the VTOL carrier MINSK. Although the KIEV-class ships are inferior in aviation capabilities to U.S. aircraft carriers, they do represent a highly capable "first-generation" carrier. In addition, they have potent self-defense and anti-ship weapons. The MINSK—like most other Soviet ships—has periodically changed pendant numbers. (1980, U.S. Navy)

board catapults and arresting wires). The available material does not indicate a specific aircraft for this role. The 20 August 1979 issue of *Aviation Week* magazine reported that U.S. reconnaissance satellites had photographed catapult and arresting gear tests in the Soviet Union with what appeared to be a modified MiG-27. Assigned the NATO designation Flogger-D, this is a high-performance ground-attack aircraft. A single-seat aircraft, it has a six-barrel 23-mm Gatling-type gun, and under the fuselage and on the wings, seven positions for external stores—fuel tanks, bombs, air-to-surface missiles, or air-to-air missiles. The MiG-27 has a maximum take-off weight estimated at 44,310 pounds (20,100 kg), an estimated Mach 0.95 speed at sea level, and a speed of Mach 1.75 at altitude.

The first of the larger carriers will not be operational until the late 1980s, and the Soviet aircraft industry could certainly adapt or produce one or more fighter-type aircraft for shipboard use before that date.

### RECONNAISSANCE AND TARGETING AIRCRAFT

Several specialized reconnaissance aircraft are flown by SNA. The fixed-wing aircraft are Badger-D, -E, and later variants used for photographic and electronic reconnaissance, plus large Bear-D aircraft. The Badgers can be identified by camera ports or electronic pods under their wings and "blisters" or electronic domes on their fuselage. Soviet An-12 transport aircraft have been configured to electronic roles in the -B and -C configuration as has the Il-18 in the Coot-A variant. The Cub-C, sometimes in civil *Aeroflot* markings, has periodically overflown U.S. naval forces. These flights—by naval and civil aircraft—are under Navy subordination.

But the most remarkable Soviet aircraft in many respects is the giant Bear. This graceful-looking aircraft has large, swept-back wings and four turboprop engines turning contra-rotating propellers. The Bear-D has an unrefueled range of some 7,800 n. miles (14,500 km) and is fitted for in-flight refueling! This aircraft, with a prominent under-fuselage radome (NATO designation Big Bulge), makes radar and electronic sweeps of ocean areas and can relay target information via Video Data Link (VDL)

to missile-armed surface ships and submarines. All of the approximately 45 Bear-D aircraft appear to be assigned to the Northern and Pacific Fleets.

A final naval reconnaissance and targeting aircraft is the Hormone-B helicopter. This ship-based aircraft, operational since 1967, is carried in several guided missile cruisers plus the KIEV-class carriers to provide over-the-horizon targeting for the SS-N-3 and SS-N-12 anti-ship missiles. Only about two dozen of these helicopters are in service.

### ANTI-SUBMARINE AIRCRAFT

At this time SNA flies almost 100 Be-12 Mail flying boats, 50 Il-38 May aircraft, and 50 of the Bear-F variants in the maritime patrol/ASW role. The Mail—dubbed *Chaika* (seagull) by the Soviets—and the Japanese *Shin Meiwa* are the only flying boats remaining in first-line naval service. The flying boats are assigned to all four fleets, while the giant Bear-F aircraft are in the Northern and Pacific Fleets.

The May, redesigned from the Il-18 Coot commercial transport, first appeared in its naval configuration about 1970. Relatively few were built compared to its U.S. Navy counterpart, the P-3 Orion, which continues in production with over 500 having been delivered to the U.S. and allied services. From the available information it is not clear whether May production was limited because SNA was not satisfied with the plane or whether a more capable ASW platform is being developed (or planned). Some Western analysts have speculated that the May simply could not carry sufficient sonobuoys and torpedoes for the long-endurance ASW mission. The Bear-F aircraft, still in production some 30 years after the first flight of this aircraft type, is an extensively redesigned aircraft configured for the ASW role.

The An-12 Cub is being used as a test platform for ASW systems. Little has appeared in the Western press about this variant of the four-turboprop An-12, which is widely used by the Soviet armed forces as a transport and ELINT aircraft. (See photo, chapter 24.)

Helicopters are employed extensively for ASW, the Hormone-A being carried in cruiser classes as well as in the MOSKVA and KIEV aviation ships for that purpose. About 150 Hormone-A helicopters are in service, having become operational about 1967. Production stopped a few years ago, and an improved Kamov-designed helicopter designated Helix in the West is entering service in the ASW role.

Also relatively new to SNA is the larger, land-based Mi-14 Haze, an amphibious derivative of the Mi-8 Hip transport helicopter. The Haze is too large for shipboard use, being unable to fit on the elevators of the MOSKVA and KIEV classes. Rather, it was developed to replace the out-dated Mi-4 Hound for shore-based ASW operations, and over 100 appear to have been delivered.

### SUPPORT AND TRAINING AIRCRAFT

Beyond the operational aircraft described above, SNA has some 320 transport, training, and utility aircraft. These service the fleets and Navy headquarters in Moscow and also provide specialized naval aviation training. The Soviet Air Forces provides most flight training for naval aviators. There is the Levanskiy SNA school complex at Nikolayev in the Black Sea Fleet area for specialized naval training.

During the past few years Soviet amphibious exercises have included the use of Mi-6 Hook and Mi-8 Hip helicopters to carry Naval Infantry. However, their use in amphibious landings is limited mainly to shore-to-shore operations, since into the early 1980s only the ships of the IVAN ROGOV class have a viable helicopter capability. (There has been no evidence of the carriers of the KIEV or MOSKVA classes embarking marines for amphibious landings.)

Finally, during the 1974 mine-clearing operation by the Soviet Navy at the southern end of the Suez Canal, the helicopter ship LENINGRAD operated Hip-C helicopters in the minesweeping role. The number of helicopters in that configuration is not known nor if they are permanently assigned to that role.

### STRATEGIC AVIATION

The Soviet Air Forces have a mission to support maritime operations, the most significant contribution being the strategic air arm (formerly designated Long-Range Aviation or *Aviatsiya Dalnovo Deistviya*). The strategic air arm's missile strike aircraft have been observed practicing in the anti-ship role. There are almost 700 strike aircraft consisting of some 100 Bear, 45 Mya-4 Bison, about 85 Backfire-B, 320 Badger, and 140 Blinder aircraft. Some of the Bears carry the AS-3 Kangaroo stand-off missile, the remainder as well as the Bisons carrying gravity bombs. Most of the other aircraft carry stand-off missiles, including anti-ship weapons as well as bombs. Coupled with the Badger and Bison reconnaissance aircraft and aerial tankers, the Soviet strategic air arm can provide a powerful augmentation to naval aviation. There is evidence that the strategic air arm is increasingly conducting maritime reconnaissance and strike exercises, with production of a missile-armed Bear (-G variant ?) continuing.

The hermaphrodite cruiser-helicopter carriers MOSKVA (shown here) and LENINGRAD failed as anti-Polaris weapons, but the ships did provide the Soviet Navy with valuable experience in the problems of operating ship-based aircraft. (Sovfoto)

# 7

# Naval Infantry and Coastal Missile-Artillery Force

The Soviet Navy has two ground-combat arms, the Naval Infantry, which corresponds in many respects to the U.S. Marine Corps and Royal Marines, and the Coastal Missile-Artillery Force, which protects key points from seaborne assault. The two arms are administratively combined into a single organization (see below). Components of these two arms are assigned to all of the fleets.

## NAVAL INFANTRY (*MORSKAYA PEKHOTA*)

The principal roles of the Naval Infantry are to gain control of territory adjacent to important straits and other waterways, to support ground forces by flanking operations, and to conduct raids against enemy coastal positions.

The relatively small size of the Soviet "marines" when compared to the U.S. Marine Corps, their distribution among the four Soviet fleets, and the limited capacity of the amphibious ships would tend to prevent their being employed in large-scale landings, in the manner planned by the U.S. Marine Corps. The Soviet Navy's leadership has carefully stated that the Naval Infantry is not intended to be employed in the American style. For example, Vice Admiral K.A. Stalbo, Soviet naval historian and theorist, has written:

> The experience of our Navy in landing naval forces during the Great Patriotic War [1941–1945] attests to the fact that in those years the Soviet school of the art of the amphibious landing of troops was built up and was crystallized in the course of battle, having developed along its own path, which differs considerably from the paths taken by the naval art of the foreign navies, primarily the U.S. Navy.[1]

*History.* In 1705 Peter the Great activated the first naval infantry regiment for his newly created fleet on the Baltic. The regiment had a total of 45 officers and 1,320 soldiers, organized in two battalions of five companies each. The creation of the regiment is considered the birth date of the Russian marine force (officially celebrated on 16 November). One of the first victories of the Russian marines came a year later when they captured the Swedish boat ESPERN in a boarding fight. And begin-

ning in 1707, the marines were used repeatedly in landings along the coast of Sweden and offshore islands.

Russian marines subsequently fought at sea and ashore, with a significant number being in the Russian fleets that periodically operated in the Mediterranean. They helped capture the city of Navarino in 1770 and the fortress of Beirut in 1773, and several islands in the Ionian Sea and the fortress of Corfu in 1798–1800. The number of marines in the fleet was rarely large, the exceptions being during the Crimean War (1853–1856) and the Russo-Japanese War (1904–1905) when sailors from immobilized or sunken ships were formed up to fight as naval infantry. In World War I a specially formed regiment of marines made several amphibious landings in the Baltic, with as many as 2,000 participating in some of the operations. Smaller landings were carried out in the Black Sea. Plans were under way to organize a marine division and then a corps, probably for assaults on the Turkish straits, when the October Revolution erupted in 1917.

During the Revolution and the Civil War that followed many Russian sailors served ashore, but they could hardly be considered marines although they apparently participated in some river crossings and coastal operations while under fire. No Soviet marine units appear to have been organized after the Revolution until 1939, when the 1st Separate Naval Infantry Brigade was established in the Baltic Fleet and used in the war with Finland (1939–1940). By mid-1941, when the Soviet Union entered World War II, there were 25 individual naval rifle brigades and 12 naval artillery brigades.

As the war continued, a total of 40 brigades, 6 independent regiments, and several separate battalions of naval troops were formed. They varied in composition, with most having organic artillery units and two of the Baltic Fleet's brigades having tank battalians. (These two brigades, the 2nd and 5th, fought as ground troops and were not used in landing operations.) When the war ended there were almost 500,000 sailors fighting ashore, some in what were called Naval Rifle units and some in army units, while the troops with the fleet were still called Naval Infantry. There were significant amphibious operations during the conflict. Approximately 100,000 naval infantrymen who remained under fleet and flotilla control were used to defend naval bases and islands as well as to carry out amphibious landings with army troops.

The Soviet Navy conducted 114 amphibious landings during World War II, some quite small—essentially raids of platoon size. But four of the

---

[1]Rear Admiral K.A. Stalbo, "The Naval Art in the Landings of the Great Patriotic War," *Morskoy Sbornik*, no. 3, 1970, pp. 23–30. Subsequently promoted to vice admiral, Stalbo is a doctor of naval sciences, an honored scientist, and a state prize laureate.

An Alligator LST unloads BRDM-2 reconnaissance cars during a landing exercise of Black Sea Fleet marines. A pair of Polnocny landing ships are maneuvering offshore. The Soviets still prefer to conduct landings in this manner or with amphibious vehicles, although the Naval Infantry increasingly employs air-cushion vehicle landing craft and helicopters in exercises. (1978, Sovfoto)

landings, two at Kerch´-Feodosiya and one at Novorossiysk on the Black Sea, and one at Moon Sound in the Baltic, each involved several thousand troops. According to Soviet sources, of the 114 landings, 61 were planned and organized in less than 24 hours! In all, the Navy landed some 330,000 troops during the war, soldiers as well as marines.[2] Most of the landings were short-range operations, across straits, bays, and rivers, and several were made in coordination with parachute landings, especially those against the Korean coast in August 1945.

Several important Soviet officials were associated with amphibious operations during the war. Admiral Gorshkov directed landings in the Black Sea-Azov-Danube campaigns; the late Leonid Brezhnev was a political officer with the 18th Army during landings on the Black Sea coast, where he received a minor wound; and Marshal V.F. Margelov, commander of Soviet airborne forces from 1954 to 1974, served in the Naval Infantry during the war. (Margelov changed the uniform of airborne troops to include the blue-and-white-striped tee shirt of the Navy as a symbol of the specialized nature of paratroopers, who could also "cross seas" for the assault.)

After the war the Naval Infantry was disbanded for almost two decades. However, Soviet observations of U.S. and British marines in the postwar period, and the Soviets' own analyses of their requirements as naval operations expanded, led to the decision to reinstitute a marine force. The Soviets publicly acknowledged the existence of Naval Infantry units on 24 July 1964, when, in conjunction with the traditional Navy Day, a front-page pictorial in the military newspaper *Krasnaya Zvezda* (Red Star) showed marines coming ashore in amphibious personnel carriers. It was announced that these newly formed units conducted amphibious maneuvers during joint operations with other Warsaw Pact forces. Naval Infantry—about 500 marines from the Baltic Fleet—participated in the Moscow parade on 7 November 1967 commemorating the October Revolution, the first time such a body was seen on parade in Red Square since World War II.

[2]Stalbo, op. cit.

## COMMAND AND ORGANIZATION[3]

Naval Infantry and the Coastal Missile-Artillery Force appear to be directed by a major general on the staff of the Commander in Chief of the Navy. His rank is relatively low compared to other branch and department chiefs at naval headquarters.

Soviet Naval Infantry currently consists of an estimated 12,000 officers and enlisted men.[4] Within each of the four fleets there is a naval infantry force based on the regimental structure. There is one regiment with the Northern Fleet (based at Pechenga, near Murmansk); one regiment with the Baltic Fleet (Baltiysk); one regiment with the Black Sea Fleet (Sevastopol´); and two regiments are with the Pacific Fleet (Vladivostok).

Each regiment has some 2,000 officers and enlisted men. They are "combined arms" units, as shown in figure 7-1. The naval infantry regiments, like units of the Soviet Ground Forces, are organized on a triangular basis, with each regiment having three infantry battalions plus various combat support units. There is also a tank battalion organic to each regiment as well as artillery units. Command and support functions for the regiment are provided by several small companies (about the size of U.S. platoons).

*Infantry Battalions.* Each of the three infantry battalions has some 400 men, organized primarily into three infantry companies of about 100 men each (see figure 7-2). Transportation for the battalion is provided by 34 armored, amphibious assault vehicles of the BTR-60PA or PB type. The availability of these combat vehicles marks a significant difference in

[3]The organization charts in this chapter are based on Lieutenant Colonel Louis N. Buffardi, U.S. Army, "The Soviet Naval Infantry" (Washington, D.C.: Defense Intelligence Agency, April 1980).

[4]The current U.S. Marine Corps strength is approximately 194,500; the Soviet Naval Infantry is the second largest marine force, with Britain's Royal Marines numbering approximately 8,000 troops.

Soviet marines come ashore in BTR-60P amphibious personnel carriers. Few of these vehicles remain in service with first-line units. They can carry 14 troops in addition to a crew of two. The later BTR-60PB accommodates only eight troops, but has turret-mounted 14.5-mm and 7.62-mm guns and overhead armor protection (the BTR-60P has an open top). (Sovfoto)

U.S. and Soviet marines, as American units have no armored vehicles that are designed to carry troops in combat once ashore.

Each battalion also has a mortar platoon, with three 82-mm or 120-mm mortars, and an anti-tank platoon with AT-3 Sagger or AT-5 Spigot guided missiles.[5]

(The BTR-60PB is an amphibious/armored personnel carrier. It is a wheeled vehicle with a loaded weight of 21,000 lbs/9.45 mt, and carries a

[5]SA for Surface-to-Air missiles and AT for Anti-Tank missiles are Western designations; all others used here are Soviet nomenclature.

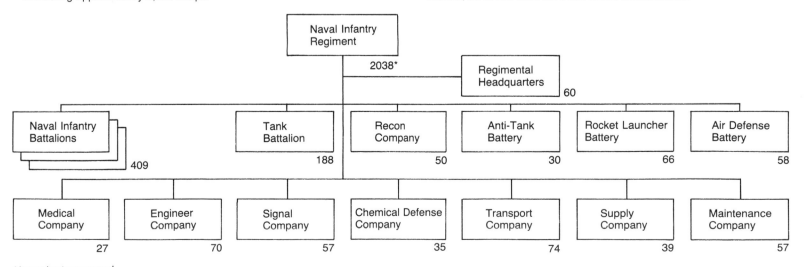

*Approximate personnel.

Figure 7-1. Naval Infantry Regiment

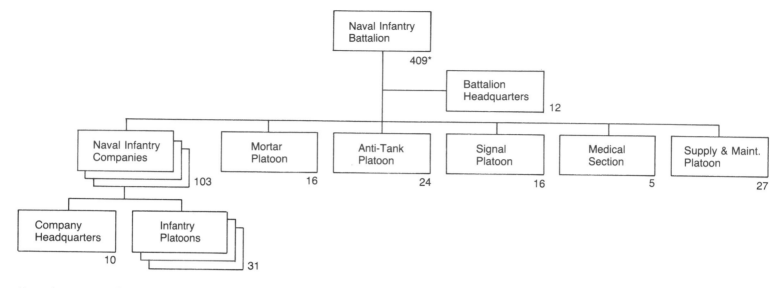

*Approximate personnel.

Figure 7–2.  Naval Infantry Battalion

crew of two plus 12 troops. A turret with one 14.5-mm and one 7.62-mm machine gun is mounted, with some vehicles fitted to carry SA-7 Grail anti-aircraft missiles or AT-3/5 anti-tank missiles. The BTR-60PA is an earlier version.)

*Tank Battalion.*  The tank battalion has one medium tank company, with 10 T-54/55 tanks, and three light tank companies, each with 10 of the amphibious PT-76 light tanks.

(The T-54 medium tank entered service in 1959, with the improved T-55 version operational from about 1961. The tank weighs 80,000 lbs/36 mt loaded, and has a 100-mm main gun. Diesel-powered, it can ford water 18 feet/5.5 m deep with a snorkel that can be rapidly installed by the crew. The PT-76 is a fully amphibious light tank that weighs 31,000 lbs/14 mt; a 76-mm gun is fitted.)

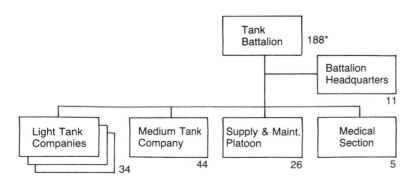

*Approximate personnel.

Figure 7–3.  Tank Battalion

*Reconnaissance Company.*  The regiment's reconnaissance company has three PT-76 light tanks and nine BRDM-2 reconnaissance vehicles.

(The BRDM-2 is a wheeled amphibious personnel carrier weighing 15,400 lbs/9.9 mt loaded, which carries four men with protection against small arms. A 14.5-mm and a 7.62-mm machine gun are mounted in a rotating turret.)

T-54/55 medium tanks come ashore from Polnocny-class landing ships during a Baltic amphibious exercise. Soviet Naval Infantry—like other elements of the Soviet armed forces—regularly exercise in a simulated CBR environment. Naval Infantry regiments each have a chemical defense "company" of some 35 marines. They are charged with detecting CBR agents and decontaminating men and equipment.

The Soviets are increasingly employing air-cushion landing craft, especially the large Aist shown here in *Zapad* 81, to bring troops ashore. The Aist is the world's largest military ACV, able to carry two medium tanks or two personnel carriers, with a maximum speed of approximately 70 knots. (TASS via UPI)

*Rocket Launcher Battery.* The regiment's artillery component consists of rocket launcher, anti-tank, and air defense batteries. The rocket battery has six BM-21 multiple rocket launchers, descendants of the infamous "Stalin's organ" of World War II.

(The BM-21 is a truck-mounted, 40-tube, 122-mm rocket launcher. Range is about 22,500 yards/20,500 m and manual reload time is ten minutes.)

*Air-Defense Battery.* AA defense of the regiment is provided by this battery, consisting of one platoon armed with four ZSU-23-4 Shilka, self-propelled, quad 23-mm guns, and one platoon equipped with SA-9 Gaskin guided missiles on four BRDM-2 armored vehicles.

(The ZSU-23-4 is a potent short-range anti-aircraft weapon, with integral fire control radar, mounted on a tank chassis. The rate of fire is about 200 rounds per minute per barrel. The SA-9 is carried and fired from a canister, four of which are mounted atop the BRDM-2. It is an infrared-homing missile, with a maximum range of some 8,800 yds/8,000 m. In addition to these vehicle weapons, there are 27 SA-7 Grail man-portable rocket launchers in a regiment.)

*Anti-Tank Battery.* This unit has six multiple-rail AT-3 Sagger or AT-5 guided missile systems mounted on BRDM-2 vehicles. (There are also several SPG-9 73-mm recoilless rifles and AT-3 man-carried guided missiles in the regiment.)

*Engineer Company.* These troops are used primarily to clear underwater and land obstacles in the assault area. K-61 amphibious cargo vehicles are used by these engineers, but they also land in advance of the assault waves by BTR-60P vehicles, helicopters, and high-speed boats.

## PERSONNEL

The Naval Infantry has distinctive fatigue uniforms, consisting of black coveralls with the distinctive blue-and-white-striped tee shirt visible at the open neck and a circular anchor insignia on the left sleeve. The marines also wear a black beret with an anchor insignia on the left side and a red star in front. The enlisted dress uniform is almost the same as for the rest of the Navy, with some differences in cut and color.

Military rather than naval ranks are used by the Naval Infantry (and Coastal Missile-Artillery Force). As noted above, the senior naval infantry officer is a major general (one star) with colonels commanding the regiments and lieutenant colonels or majors commanding the battalions. Naval Infantry officers are graduates of higher military schools rather than higher naval schools, with a number of officers known to be graduates of the Baku Higher Combined Arms Command School.

## DOCTRINE AND TACTICS

Naval Infantry units are used to strike at hostile shores, coming ashore from amphibious ships (see chapter 19). These troops are landed from the amphibious ships primarily by amphibious personnel carriers, supported by amphibious tanks. Troop-carrying helicopters and Air-Cushion Vehicle (ACV) landing craft are also used, but these can be carried in only a few naval and merchant ships, and the personnel carriers are the main way that troops are brought ashore. All Soviet amphibious ships, including the new Ivan Rogov, the first with a docking well for carrying ACV landing craft, have bow ramps to permit unloading heavy vehicles and

### TABLE 7–1.  NAVAL INFANTRY WEAPONS AND VEHICLES

| | Tanks | | Armored Vehicles | | Self-Propelled Weapons | |
|---|---|---|---|---|---|---|
| | T-54/55 | PT-76 | BTR-60P | BRDM | ZSU-23-4 | BM-21 RL |
| Regimental Headquarters | | | 4 | | | |
| Infantry Bns (3) | | | 3 × 34 | | | |
| Tank Bn | 10 | 31 | 3 | | | |
| Recon Co | | 3 | | 9 | | |
| Anti-Tank Bty | | | | 6* | | |
| Rocket Bty | | | | | | 6 |
| Air Defense Bty | | | | 4† | 4 | |
| Signal Co | | | 2 | | | |
| Chem. Def. Co | | | | 3 | | |
| Total Regiment | 10 | 34 | 111 | 22 | 4 | 6 |

*Fitted with anti-tank missiles.
†Fitted with anti-aircraft missiles.

supplies onto causeways or directly onto the beach if the gradient conditions permit.

The accompanying diagram (figure 7-4) shows a typical assault plan for a reinforced battalion of naval infantry.

Under Soviet amphibious doctrine the assault echelon consists of the most mobile landing forces, using amphibious tanks and amphibious tractors. These are unloaded from amphibious ships directly into the water and then they "swim" ashore. As air-cushion landing craft become increasingly available, they will be used to bring the assault echelon, including tanks, ashore faster than the amphibious tractors, and from amphibious ships standing farther offshore. The follow-up echelons are then landed by the amphibious ships coming up to the shore and "beach-

Soviet marines, BTR-60PB amphibious personnel carriers, and equipment are crowded on the deck of an Alligator-class LST during an exercise. Some BTR-60PBs carry anti-aircraft or anti-tank missiles.

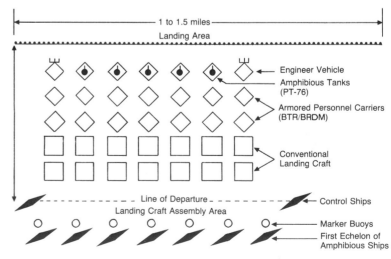

Figure 7–4. Assault Plan for Landing a Reinforced Naval Infantry Battalion

One of the Pacific Fleet's Naval Infantry regiments is assembled at snow-covered Vladivostok. The marines in the foreground are holding banners while several in the center have cameras, as a ceremony is about to take place. Although small by American standards, the Soviet Naval Infantry is half-again as large as Britain's Royal Marines and much more versatile and better equipped. (Sovfoto)

ing," if the depth of water permits. If the water depth is insufficient, the follow-up echelons are brought ashore in landing craft and ships' boats.

During the past few years troop-carrying helicopters have begun to be employed in amphibious assault exercises. Some of these, of the Mi-8 Hip type, have been observed with Soviet Naval Aviation markings. (The IVAN ROGOV is also the first Soviet amphibious ship with a helicopter hangar; a few of the smaller Polnocny-class landing ships have helicopter platforms, but no hangar or support facilities.)

Most Soviet articles and manuals addressing amphibious tactics point out that naval gunfire support and close air support will be provided in landing operations. The SVERDLOV-class cruisers, with up to 12 6-inch guns, are employed in this role. Mine countermeasure craft and special units to deal with obstacles in the beach approaches and on the beach

are also considered in amphibious planning. Indeed, the Soviet Navy's leadership has stated that the modern amphibious landing is the most complex type of military operation.

Shortly after the Naval Infantry branch was reestablished, marine units began periodic deployments aboard amphibious ships. There have been troop-carrying "amphibs" in the Mediterranean on a periodic basis since the mid-1960s. The first amphib deployment to the Indian Ocean (from the Pacific Fleet) took place in 1968, and subsequently, beginning in 1970, amphibious ships with marines on board have been observed on deployments off the western coast of Africa (Angola). The periodic amphibious landings in the fleet areas have been supplemented by larger landings in the *Okean* '70 and '75 exercises, as well as by a landing by Naval Infantry on the coast of Syria and the practice amphibious assault

Soviet marine regiments are based on the "combined arms" concept, somewhat similar to U.S. Marine task organizations, but on a permanent basis. For example, the Soviet marine regiment has integral anti-aircraft capabilities with man- and vehicle-carried SA-7 Grail missiles and the ZSU-23-4 Shilka self-propelled AA gun. Each of the four 23-mm barrels fires 200 rounds per minute.

near the Polish border (*Zapad* '81), both in 1981. (See chapter 9/Fleet Training and Exercises.)

In most exercises the initial assault by marines is followed by ground forces being landed, coming ashore from amphibious ships or merchant ships. Motorized rifle battalions have been seen in this role. Also, the Soviets appear to plan to use airborne troops from the eight Soviet airborne divisions in coordination with amphibious forces. This mode of assault was employed in the landings by Soviet forces along the coast of North Korea in August of 1945.

### COASTAL MISSILE-ARTILLERY FORCE

The Soviet Navy's Coastal Missile-Artillery Force has received far less publicity than the Naval Infantry. There are some 8,000 men currently assigned to coastal defense, a reduction of about 10,000 since the early 1970s. This drop may presage a phasing out of this component of the armed forces, with increased warship and naval aircraft capabilities making the contribution of the Coastal Missile-Artillery Force to the defense of the homeland marginal.

Before the cutback in strength, the Coastal Missile-Artillery Force was reported to consist of three missile battalions with the Northern Fleet, six battalions in the Baltic Fleet, and five battalions each in the Black Sea and Pacific Fleet. It is not publicly known how many battalions are organized at this time.

The missile battalions are believed to be armed with the SS-C-1b Sepal anti-ship missile, with a range of at least 250 n.miles (460 km). This is a land-launched version of the SS-N-3/12 Shaddock weapon. The 15 to 18 missiles in each Sepal battalion are carried on eight-wheeled, transporter-launcher vehicles. This provides a high degree of mobility, even over rough terrain, with road speeds up to 50 mph (80 km/h). (The smaller Samlet anti-ship missile, previously used for coastal defense, has been phased out of Soviet service.)

Coastal defense guns are also used by the Coastal Missile-Artillery Force. The older weapons have been discarded; the more modern guns reported in service include an advanced M-46 130-mm gun with a range of approximately 22 miles (35 km), using fixed ammunition. There may also be a few anti-aircraft gun and missile units in the Coastal Missile-Artillery Force.

In addition, coastal defense exercises are periodically conducted by the Ground Forces. Again, motorized rifle battalions are most often cited in accounts of these coastal defense maneuvers, although there has been some mention in the Soviet press of mountain infantry battalions being employed in this role.

# 8

# Missions and Tactics

The principal mission of the Soviet Navy—as well as of the other armed services—is the defense of the homeland.[1] This has led to a tactical style that tends to pervade all naval missions. Similarly, although the Navy has gone through a series of radical changes in organization and leadership as well as some changes in mission, the consistency of tactical style in the Soviet Navy is remarkable.

It would appear in 1983—as it did 50 years earlier—that the basic tactical concept of the Soviet Navy is to attack any hostile ship attempting to approach within striking range of the Soviet land mass or sensitive sea-air space. The concepts of concentration of force and of all-arms strike that were developed during the post-Revolution decade also remain in force today. These concepts, of course, have been transmuted very considerably, so that the attack may now be mounted far from the Soviet coast and the target may now be a U.S. strategic missile submarine rather than a hostile battleship approaching the coast. However, the similarities and the consequences remain.

Profound differences between Soviet and Western naval "style" have important analytical consequences. Soviet warships with characteristics somewhat similar to Western types often have very different roles and should not be counted as analogous to those Western ships. Perhaps the most significant point here is that the fundamental Soviet mission has been, and remains, the defense of the homeland, with the perimeter of that defense continuously expanding outward.

In the early 1960s, strategic strike by submarines was added as a primary Soviet naval mission. In turn, the defense of those missile submarines and, with deployment of the SS-N-8 missile in Delta SSBNs, the "sanctuaries" within which missile submarines might operate became an additional mission. This defensive mission—"pro-submarine" operations— is alien to American naval thought. U.S. attack submarines as well as strategic missile submarines operate independently, depending upon stealth and communications silence for their survivability and hence their effectiveness.

The Soviets think differently. This is due in significant part to geography. Soviet attack submarines must reach the open seas through straits or "choke points" where they could be vulnerable to interdiction. But there is also an historical precedent.

Admiral Gorshkov has written of the U-boat campaign in the Atlantic during World War II that "despite the exceptional threat to submarines by ASW forces, the German naval command did not conduct a single operation or other specially organized combat actions directed at destroying these forces, which doubtlessly reduced the intensity of the [German U-boat] communications battle."[2] And one of the main reasons why the U-boats did not achieve victory "was that the submarines did not receive support from other forces, and above all from the Air Force, which would have been able both to carry out the reconnaissance for the submarines and destroy ASW forces. . . ."[3]

Also, there appears to be no strain of Soviet naval thought parallel to Western concepts of sea control. This is true on both the mission and tactical levels. From a mission viewpoint, the Soviet Navy under Gorshkov has rejected the Mahanist theories which, although generally quoted without having been actually read, form the basis of U.S. naval thought. Admiral Gorshkov has written, "The Mahan theory of 'control of the sea,' considered indisputable, according to which only a general engagement of major line forces could lead to victory. . . . did not at all take into account not only the near-future prospects, but even the notable trends in the development of naval technology."[4]

Rather, Gorshkov prefers a Russian naval strategist and historian, Rear Admiral V.A. Belli, who wrote:

> To achieve superiority of forces over the enemy in the main sector and to pin him down in the secondary sectors at the time of the operation means to achieve *control of the sea* in a theater or a sector of a theater, i.e., to create such a situation that the enemy will be paralyzed or constrained in his operations, or weakened and thereby hampered from interfering with our execution of a given operation . . . .[5] [Gorshkov's emphasis]

[1]This chapter is based in part on research by Dr. Norman Friedman for the Hudson Institute discussion paper "Soviet Naval Tactics" (20 May 1982).

[2]Admiral Gorshkov, *Red Star Rising at Sea* (Annapolis, Md.: Naval Institute Press, 1974), p. 100. This is a compilation of translations of the 11 articles authored by Admiral Gorshkov that originally appeared in *Morskoy Sbornik* [Naval Digest] in 1972–1973. These unprecedented articles by the serving head of a navy were reprinted in the Naval Institute *Proceedings* during 1974. The articles were revised and reprinted in book form, again under Gorshkov's byline, as *Morskaya moshch gosudarstva* [The Sea Power of the State] (Moscow: Voenizdat, 1976), and in English by the Naval Institute Press in 1979.

[3]Ibid., p. 103.

[4]Ibid., p. 40.

[5]Ibid., p. 71. Rear Admiral Belli, at the time a Captain 2nd Rank, made the statement in his synopses-theses "Theoretical Principles of Conducting Operations" at the Naval Academy (i.e., Soviet naval war college), 1938.

Defense of the Soviet homeland continues to be the principal mission of the Soviet armed forces, and the Soviet Navy has placed considerable emphasis on ASW—tactical and strategic—during the past two decades. One of the latest manifestations of this emphasis is the ASW destroyer UDALOY, shown here with her stern sonar housing being opened.

In reality, Mahan's concepts had little practical application to the USSR during the 1920s and 1930s because of the lack of capital ships and the limited nature of Soviet maritime activities. By the 1950s the availability of radar, effective communications, long-range aircraft, advanced submarines, guided missiles, and even nuclear weapons for the war at sea made Mahan's concepts even more questionable. Coupled with geographic considerations and other factors applicable to considerations of the USSR and the Soviet fleet, these technology factors have given Mahan little if any relevance to the Soviet Navy of the Gorshkov era.

On a tactical level of sea control, the Soviets certainly wish to protect their own coastal shipping and their ocean-going units from Western naval attack. But in general the Soviets appear to view the sea in wartime as a "jungle," with all or most warships at sea subject to rapid destruction. Recent decisions to build relatively large and expensive surface combatants, such as aircraft carriers and the nuclear-powered battle cruiser

The Soviet Navy has increasingly been used as "ambassadors" to Third World nations, demonstrating Soviet political support, the ability to project Soviet military power, countering Western political-military activities, and serving as training cruises for Soviet seamen. Here, from left, a Kildin, Kynda, and Kashin visit Cuba in the summer of 1969. (Sovfoto)

"Friendly visits" to Third World ports by Soviet ships often include Red sailors going ashore to play soccer or provide entertainment with bands and dancers. Here bandsmen wait to participate in Ethiopian Navy Day celebrations at Massawa. (1972, U.S. Navy, John Gorman)

KIROV, may cause a rethinking of this tactical issue, but most of the current Soviet fleet reflects earlier tactical concepts.

Indeed, the development of these ships fits more with a new Soviet naval mission, first espoused during the 1960s when Soviet naval forces began regular, and in some cases sustained, deployments in non-contiguous seas—the Mediterranean, Caribbean, and Indian Ocean, and most recently the eastern Pacific. These are missions of "political presence" and "force projection" in the Third World. To again quote Admiral Gorshkov, speaking of forward operations in peacetime:

> Friendly visits by Soviet seamen offer the opportunity to the peoples of the countries visited to see for themselves the creativity of socialist principles in our country, the genuine parity of the peoples of the Soviet Union and their high cultural level. In our ships they see the achievements of Soviet science, technology and industry. Soviet mariners, from rating to admiral, bring to the peoples of other countries the truth about our socialist country, our Soviet ideology and culture and our Soviet way of life.[6]

Only polemics? Unlikely. The Soviet Union, with approximate strategic and conventional weapons "parity" with the United States, is seeking to gain advances in the Third World and, as Oliver Cromwell remarked, "A man-of-war is the best ambassador." Now the Soviets have gone a step further than sending sailors as ambassadors. In a less-publicized exposition on naval cruises, Admiral Gorshkov has been more pointed:

> Further growth in the power of our navy will be characterized by an intensification of its international mission. While appearing within our armed forces as an imposing factor in regard to restraining imperialist aggression and ventures, at the same time the Soviet Navy is a consolidator of international relations. . . .[7]

For several years the Soviet Union has used proxy troops in Africa, the Middle East, and Southeast Asia, all armed with Soviet weapons and sometimes directed by Soviet advisors.

The naval and merchant fleets now being built will permit—in Western terms—"force projection" into the Third World. According to Gorshkov, "The Soviet navy, in the policy of our Party and state, acts as a factor for stabilizing the situation in different areas of the world, promoting the strengthening of peace and friendship between the peoples and restraining the aggressive strivings of the imperialist states."[8] Thus, new missions have been added to the Soviet Navy. In probable order of development, the Soviet Navy's missions are:

| | |
|---|---|
| early 1950s | Coastal Defense/Anti-Amphibious* |
| 1950s | Anti-Carrier* |
| | Anti-Western Sea Lanes* |
| 1960s | Anti-Polaris* |
| | Strategic Strike |
| | Pro-SSBN |
| 1970s | Forward Deployments for Political Considerations |

[6]Admiral Gorshkov, *The Sea Power of the State* (Annapolis, Md.: Naval Institute Press, 1979), p. 252.
[7]Admiral Gorshkov, "Naval Cruises Play Role in Training, International Relations," *Bloknot Agitatora*, no. 8, April 1973, pp. 3–6.
[8]Gorshkov, *The Sea Power of the State*, p. 277.

Forward deployments by Soviet naval forces can reduce Western political-military options because of the possibility of escalation of a Soviet-U.S. confrontation. Here a Kynda-class cruiser steams with a U.S. carrier task group in the Mediterranean in late 1969. A Soviet AGI steams off the starboard bow of the carrier, the JOHN F. KENNEDY (CV 67). (1969, U.S. Navy)

| 1980s | Force Projection |
| | Support to Third World |

The asterisks indicate those missions that are extensions of the defense of the homeland.

## TACTICS

Given defense of the homeland as the primary Soviet tactical concept, the primary naval operation becomes the destruction of enemy warships as they attempt to enter the defensive area. This, in turn, requires a combination of (1) reconnaissance and surveillance, to detect the intruder, (2) command and control, to bring superior forces to attack at the proper time and location, and (3) effective strikes against the target ship or group of ships. These elements have been developed to a high degree by the Soviet Navy.

*History.* The development of contemporary Soviet doctrine and tactics dates from the problems faced immediately after the Revolution and Civil War. The new socialist state had no significant capital ships nor the industrial base to build an effective fleet. At the same time, threats from the sea were a major concern, as Britain, France, Japan, and the United States had used their navies to support anti-Bolshevik forces during the Russian Civil War.

Soviet naval forces were only gradually built up, and then in the context of a military program that emphasized ground and air forces. Once Soviet industrialization had begun in earnest, it was far easier to build light craft and then small warships. Although former tsarist officers continued to call for a battle fleet as a prerequisite for effective naval defense, a "young school" (*molodaia shkola*) of Soviet naval theorists attempted to turn this weakness into a tactical strength by a combination of limiting the naval mission and at the same time enforcing combined-arms operations.

The debate was considerable. V.I. Zov, the naval commissar from 1924–1926, personally criticized the members of the "old school." In an address at the Naval Academy (i.e., war college) in 1925 he declared:

> You speak of aircraft carriers and of the construction of new types of ships . . . at the same time completely ignoring the economic situation of our country and corresponding conditions of our technical means, completely ignoring the fact that perhaps tomorrow or the day after we will be called on to fight. And with what shall we fight? We will fight with those ships and personnel that we have already.[9]

Thus, the concept of sea control in the Western sense was largely abandoned. In its place came pure coastal defense, with the advantages to be gained by tight coordination of the forces that could be afforded: coastal guns, land-based aircraft, light craft, and mines. Submarines and offshore pickets—designated *Storozhevoy Korabl´* (SKR) or "guard ship" by the Soviets—were, it appears, seen primarily as a means of detecting enemy ships entering the guarded area.

Stalin did begin to build a conventional, blue-water surface fleet in the late 1930s. By that time the heavy industry base had been built up, and Soviet support of the Republicans in the Spanish Civil War of 1936–1938 and the limited campaign against Japan in 1937 demonstrated the need for major naval forces to support Soviet foreign policy. The Second World War halted Stalin's fleet-building program, but he sought to do the same again after the war.

What seems remarkable in retrospect is that there appears to have been no development of tactics for blue-water operations, even with the few large ships that were available. For example, the Soviets spent little if any effort in developing anti-submarine tactics for the screening of large ships, even when the SVERDLOV-class cruisers became available in the early 1950s. Rather, the destroyers built in that period were armed and exercised primarily in the anti-ship role, not ASW or even air defense.

Similarly, not until the *Okean* exercises of 1975 did the Soviets demonstrate a major interest in escorting oceangoing convoys and amphibious groups. Previous naval escort activities appear to have been oriented either to coastal operations or to simulating Western tactics.

In the prewar period the Soviets had employed submarines, guard ships, and land-based aircraft to detect intruders in Soviet territorial areas. They reported to a central commander ashore who could maintain a plot of the combat area and coordinate the attack. This type of command and control led directly to the present Soviet command structure and the Soviet Ocean Surveillance System (SOSS in Western terminology), which seeks to make available to a fleet commander a full picture of the potential battle area.

The SOSS has a much greater range than pre–World War II capabilities, but the concept is largely the same. Even before the war the Soviets had used shore-based radio direction finders to complement the submarines, guard ships, and reconnaissance aircraft. At the end of the war they captured superior High-Frequency Direction-Finding (HF/DF) technology from the Germans. As the area of concern extended outward from the USSR, surveillance technology became increasingly important, until today it has extended to a worldwide system (see below).

An important concept in centralized targeting by Soviet forces is the "circle of uncertainty." Target data are generally fleeting: an enemy ship or force is at a specific point for a brief period. Its movement after that may be random and may well be unknown. In this situation there is an expanding circle of uncertainty around the original datum in which the target may be found. The longer the delay in reaching the target area, the larger the circle and the more difficult the subsequent search and reacquisition.

The Soviets have often emphasized high speed in their attack platforms as well as in their missiles precisely because of this problem. There is a very great difference in the circle of uncertainty at, for example, 200 miles (320 km) by a Mach 2 missile compared to a Mach 0.8 cruise missile, and the need for the high speed (with all its design penalties) testifies to continued reliance on centralized targeting and an attempt to avoid the need for mid-course guidance, which may be difficult or impossible in a combat environment.

Rigid, centralized tactical control has several advantages. First, in earlier periods it enhanced political control of military units, which for many years appeared to come before military effectiveness in priority. Second, a centralized commander could, at least in theory, make the most effective use of the weapons available. Initially, small attack craft, submarines, and land-based aircraft were the main striking force of the Soviet Navy; individually they would not be effective against capital ships, but under centralized control their potential effectiveness was enhanced considerably. Centralized control also permitted a reduction in the search and targeting requirements for the individual units (radar, sonar), allowing more units to be provided for a given cost.

Soviet naval tactics have thus become statistical in character; an alternative description, to use the Soviet term, is "scientific" in contrast to traditional naval tactics. The combination of centrally collected intelligence and centrally controlled attack forces continues as the basis of Soviet practice, although a trend toward some decentralization has become apparent in the past few years. In virtually every tactical context, the attack is delivered simultaneously, often along several different axes in an effort to overwhelm the defenses of the target ship or group of ships. Also, the strike is delivered at almost maximum weapon range. Increased stand-off weapon range permits attacks to be made sooner than if the attacking ships or aircraft had to close with the target; facilitates strikes by several ships or aircraft; and helps preserve the firing platform from enemy defenses.

The longer weapon range also contributes to another key Soviet tactical concept, that of surprise or, in Gorshkov's words, "the battle for the first salvo." This concept is a favorite topic of Soviet tactical discussions. One Soviet military writer recently used this definition:

[9]Quoted in Commander Robert W. Herrick, U.S. Navy (Ret.), *Soviet Naval Strategy* (Annapolis, Md.: U.S. Naval Institute, 1967), p. 10; the Zov speech was printed in the May 1925 issue of *Morskoy Sbornik*.

Surprise is one of the most important principles of military art. This principle consists in choosing the time, means and methods of combat actions allowing to deliver a surprise blow at the enemy and thus to a certain extent to paralyse his will to resist. Surprise gives the possibility to achieve maximum result with the minimum spending of manpower, equipment and time.[10]

Addressing this concept, Admiral Gorshkov has written:

"the battle for the first salvo"—is taking on a special meaning in naval battle under present-day conditions (conditions including the possible employment of combat means of colossal power [nuclear weapons]). Delay in the employment of weapons in a naval battle or operation inevitably will be fraught with the most serious and even fatal consequences, regardless of where the fleet is located, at sea or in port.[11]

These combat concepts are applicable to almost all phases of Soviet naval tactics. In airborne strikes the missile-carrying aircraft must fly high enough for the lead plane to acquire the intended target with its own missile-control radar. All aircraft in a wave then lock their missiles onto the target, and all launch together in an effort to overwhelm the defenses. In some situations the bombers may also attack from several directions, either simultaneously or in series, and there could even be coordinated flights from different bases. (The strike aircraft do not make the initial detection of the target. Rather, they are launched toward the predetermined datum, under centralized control.)

Surface torpedo and missile boat tactics are analogous to those of bombers. Attacks are controlled either from a shore position or from a larger surface ship, such as a destroyer. The small torpedo or missile craft are merely attack platforms acting under the directions of a central commander.

Missile and torpedo boat groups often operate together, generally with one grouping of missile boats and two of torpedo boats. At times these craft also attack in coordination with gunboats, destroyers, coastal missile-artillery batteries, and land-based aircraft. Soviet doctrine indicates that the Osa-type missile craft will attack by groups, with each Osa firing a two-missile salvo at ranges of 10 to 13 n.miles (18 to 24 km), or about one-half maximum missile range. Similarly, the torpedo boats will launch two-torpedo salvos after closing to a range of about three n.miles (5.5 km).[12]

With respect to submarines, at least through the 1950s Soviet submarines acting in the coastal defense role were closely controlled by commanders ashore. This was a continuation of prewar Soviet practices.

In a related manner, the Soviets appear to have developed the "flying torpedoes"—anti-ship missiles—to provide these submarines with greater stand-off range against intruders. Note that these submarines are best employed with off-board sensors and centralized control to coordinate strikes. While these more recent submarine weapons and tactics

were developed for "defensive" purposes, they are obviously intended for the anti-carrier role in that the Soviets continue to consider U.S. aircraft carriers as a nuclear threat to their homeland.

(The older, surface-launched SS-N-3 submarine missile was developed for strategic attack against the United States; however, in the tactical role it is conceptually similar to the later SS-N-7 and SS-N-9 submarine-missile systems, being best served by sensors other than those on the submarines, i.e., "off-board" sensors such as satellites and aircraft, and centralized command.)

### ANTI-SUBMARINE WARFARE[13]

Contemporary Soviet ASW has developed along similar tactical concepts. At least into the 1970s most ASW forces were organized into brigades controlled by commanders ashore. In search-and-attack operations, all of the ships defending an area would transmit their sonar data to a shore-based computer that would assign them attack courses and speeds, and thus determine the appropriate point for attack. Finally, the computers went to sea aboard cruisers and destroyers, which were designated *Bol´shoy Protivolodochnyy Korabl´* (BPK) or large anti-submarine ship. These ships became command ships for ASW groups.

Systematic airborne ASW tactics were developed in the late 1960s as new ASW aircraft became operational, beginning with the Il-38 May. The tactics were analogous with air anti-ship tactics: the land-based ASW aircraft would fly out to a datum, release sonobuoys to reacquire and localize the target, and then attack. Limitations in the technique included the short range of Soviet sonobuoys, meaning that aircraft could rarely reacquire the target. Nor could the Il-38 carry enough weapons to achieve the "saturation" effect of surface ships firing anti-submarine rockets.

The later and larger land-cased Bear-F aircraft may have been developed to overcome this limitation. The turboprop bomber carries large numbers of sonobuoys to reacquire and hold contact on a submarine and also carries a large weapons payload.

Whereas the U.S. Navy considers its nuclear-powered attack submarines (SSN) as primarily anti-submarine platforms, the first Soviet SSN class (November) appears to have been intended for other purposes. The high-performance Alfa SSN, designed shortly afterwards, may have been originally intended as an anti-submarine craft, with the high speed for rapidly closing to within torpedo range of intruders. The Victor-class SSNs (completed from 1967 onward) are generally considered ASW craft in the Western sense, i.e., for trailing enemy submarines and possibly serving in anti-submarine barriers. The Soviets also use diesel-electric attack submarines in this role.

Soviet submarines have been observed in ASW exercises with surface warships and aircraft. While the U.S. Navy has put forward the concept that the high-speed LOS ANGELES (SSN 688)-class submarines provide direct support for surface ships, the Soviets have employed this tactic for a much longer period. The SSN, in coordination with surface

[10]Colonel B. Frolov, Ph.D. Candidate of Sciences (History), "Surprise," *Soviet Military Review*, no. 9, 1980, pp. 27–29.

[11]Admiral Gorshkov, *Red Star Rising*, pp. 131–32.

[12]A detailed description of missile and torpedo boat tactics is found in Milan Vego, "Tactical Employment of Soviet FPBs," Naval Institute *Proceedings*, June 1980, pp. 95–98, and July 1980, pp. 106–11.

[13]Extensive discussions of Soviet ASW, mainly from the hardware perspective, are in N. Polmar, "Thinking About Soviet ASW," Naval Institute *Proceedings*, May 1976, pp. 108–29; and N. Polmar, "Soviet ASW—Highly Capable or Irrelevant?" *International Defense Review*, 5/1979, pp. 721–29.

strategic missile submarines. With the advent of the Delta-class SSBN, which could target the United States from Soviet home waters, a new tactical problem evolved. This meant that Soviet missile submarines from the Northern Fleet would no longer have to transit through narrow, and hence potentially dangerous, passages into the Atlantic. Instead, "sanctuaries" would be established in home waters where the missile submarines would be safe from American SSNs—defended by a combination of surface ships, submarines, and land-based aircraft. The KIEV-class aircraft carriers may have been justified from a political viewpoint in full or in part for this role. Also, the redesignation of the Krivak-class "frigates" from large ASW ships (BPK) to guard ships (SKR) may have reflected the Soviet view that the ASW designation applies to components of submarine hunter-killer groups rather than ASW pickets.

The development of the MOSKVA-class helicopter carriers in the early 1960s was in line with the above-described ASW tactics, to bring many attack units (helicopters) into an area to attack a U.S. Polaris submarine initially detected by long-range, surface ship sonar or possibly by other means. This concept was abandoned, the MOSKVA class being halted at two ships because of the increasing range of Polaris missiles and the large number of submarines.

Nevertheless, the MOSKVAS and their Hormone-A anti-submarine helicopters did provide the Soviet fleet with its first experience with ship-based aircraft while taking to sea a significant ASW capability. The experience with the MOSKVAS was essential to the development of the subsequent KIEV-class aircraft carriers.

Also in 1967, the first Kresta I missile cruiser went to sea, carrying a single Hormone-B helicopter for missile targeting. This was the first Soviet surface combatant (other than the helicopter ship MOSKVA) to have a full helicopter support capability. The ship design was refined into an ASW ship, the Kresta II, which appeared in 1970; it carried a Hormone-A ASW helicopter, demonstrating a significant advance in Soviet ASW doctrine for surface forces.

The Soviets have shown considerable interest in helicopter ASW, operating helicopters in this role from ashore as well as afloat as their principal means of attacking submarines at "medium" ranges, i.e., 30–40 n.miles (55–74 km). The Soviet enthusiasm for helicopters is evidenced in the Mi-14 Haze, developed from the widely used Mi-8 Hip specifically for land-based operation, and in the multiple helicopter capacities of the new surface combatants KIROV and UDALOY. Writing on ASW tactics, a Soviet specialist explained the enthusiasm:

> The participation of helicopters in the search for submarines . . . not only widens the field of "visibility" of the warship carrying it but also substantially increases the ship's capability for conducting protracted tracking of a detected enemy. [Also] it increases the reliability of the employment of ASW weapons. And if it presents no great problem to a submarine to avoid a surface ship, the situation changes radically when a shipborne helicopter comes into the picture. Having a significantly greater speed than a submarine, [the helicopter] puts the submarine in a far more difficult situation. . . .[14]

[14]Captain 1/Rank N. Vo´yunenko, Doctor of Naval Science, "Concerning Some Trends in the Development of Naval Tactics," *Morskoy Sbornik*, no. 10, October 1975, pp. 21–26.

The MOSKVA (shown here) and LENINGRAD have two helicopter hangars built into the after portion of their superstructure, another unusual feature of these ships. Their design, intended for the anti-Polaris mission, was unique among contemporary warships.

ASW ships or aircraft, provides a deep, relatively quiet sonar platform. Once a target submarine is detected, the Soviet SSN would probably withdraw to be out of danger in the ensuing surface or air attack.

All three ASW platforms—aircraft, surface ships, and submarines—can be employed to help Soviet submarines "break out" through NATO ASW barriers and also to "defend the homeland" against Western

The U.S. Navy has identified five potential categories of Soviet submarine methods: acoustics, thermohydrodynamics, magnetics, chemical contaminants, and direct observables. Sonars and sonobuoys used by the Soviets are addressed—albeit briefly—in chapter 26. There are periodic reports of Soviet emphasis on the other, nonacoustic means of submarine detection. The systems used for nonacoustic detection other than magnetic are not readily observed and identified. While some of the ASW tactics employed by the Soviet Navy are obviously oriented toward acoustics as the principal means of detection, some maneuvers that cannot be readily explained, or at least differ significantly from Western activities, could be related to nonacoustic ASW.

## TACTICAL NUCLEAR AND CHEMICAL WARFARE[15]

Any discussion of Soviet tactics must include theater/tactical nuclear weapons and chemical weapons, which appear to be fully integrated into all levels of Soviet naval forces and planning. The Soviet Navy is armed with a variety of nuclear weapons and regularly conducts offensive and defensive exercises.[16] While there is less information available publicly concerning the potential use of chemical weapons by the Soviet Navy, the massive chemical warfare capability of Soviet Ground Forces, the apparent use of Soviet-provided chemical agents in Afghanistan, Cambodia, and Yemen, and the Soviet Navy's extensive CBR defense training all indicate a significant capability in this field as well. (There are also indications of continued Soviet activity in the biological warfare area, but information here is severely limited and there is some overlap between chemical and biological agents.)

The Soviet armed forces began developing their nuclear doctrine in the mid-1950s after the death of Stalin. Previously, Stalin had believed that the geographic expanse and manpower reserves of the USSR would more than compensate for Western superiority in nuclear weapons. Although he did authorize the development of nuclear weapons, his reluctant attitude inhibited military leaders from realistically considering how to use them or even how to defend themselves against them.

The initial Soviet nuclear doctrine postulated that any war with the West would inevitably escalate to a strategic nuclear exchange. This concept was quite in line with the Khrushchev defense policies, which sought to reduce large (expensive) conventional forces in favor of a minimal strategic force, primarily ICBMs, and "unconventional" efforts against the West—e.g., wars of national liberation and foreign trade.

In the post-Khrushchev period this attitude has been modified con-

Soviet sailors perform simulated decontamination of an SA-N-1 missile launcher aboard a warship. The Soviet Navy continuously practices nuclear-chemical warfare activities—both offensive and defensive. This preoccupation with CBR defense is also shown in Soviet ship design and construction. Similar attitudes prevail in Soviet air and ground forces. (1972, Sovfoto)

siderably. Writing in *Krasnaya Zvezda*, the daily newspaper of the Ministry of Defense, a Soviet general officer in 1976 warned that a conventional conflict in Europe "carries with it the constant danger of being escalated into a nuclear war."[17] This appears to be the central theme of contemporary Soviet views on theater/tactical nuclear weapons: (1) war in Europe is the principal factor in Soviet nonstrategic planning, and (2) there is a distinct danger of escalation of conventional conflict to nuclear conflict. But the same article also implies that should a NATO conflict reach a nuclear phase, it need *not* necessarily reach an all-out, intercontinental nuclear exchange between the Soviet Union and the United States.[18]

An American analysis of Soviet military writings in this field concludes:

> One of the striking aspects of Soviet military literature is the heavy emphasis given to nuclear war fighting and the minute detail with which certain of its combat aspects are addressed. This is particularly true in those writings dealing with the ground-air campaign in the continental land theatre, but it also carries over into the Soviet naval professional literature. The net impression is that the Soviet military has faced up to the reality of nuclear warfare, focused on it in their military schools and academies, and at least worked out the theory of how it should be fought and won. There is abundant evidence that the Soviets have designed and structured their forces in accordance with their theoretical writings, giving the impression that these writings have rationalized concepts which were later incorporated into doctrine.[19]

---

[15]There has been minimal discussion in the U.S. Navy of the subjects of nuclear and chemical war at sea on either an official or unofficial basis. One of the few published articles on this subject by a U.S. naval officer is Captain Linton F. Brooks, U.S. Navy, "Tactical Nuclear Weapons: The Forgotten Facet of Naval Weapons," Naval Institute *Proceedings*, January 1980, pp. 28–33. This article draws heavily on research of the BDM Corporation, published in part as "The Soviet Navy Declaratory Doctrine for Theater Nuclear Warfare" (Washington, D.C.: Defense Nuclear Agency, 30 September 1977), hereinafter referred to as BDM. Also see Lieutenant Commander T. Wood Parker, U.S. Navy, "Theater Nuclear Warfare and the U.S. Navy," Naval War College *Review*, January–February 1982, pp. 3–16.

[16]See chapter 25 for a list of Soviet naval weapons believed to have nuclear warheads.

[17]BDM, op. cit., p. 10.
[18]Ibid., p. 13.
[19]Ibid., pp. 21–22.

This attitude is reflected in the Soviet Navy by the relatively large number and variety of tactical nuclear weapons in the fleet. These include "offensive" anti-ship weapons and "defensive" anti-aircraft and anti-submarine weapons, apparently deployed in ships ranging in size from the Nanuchka and Tarantul classes of missile corvettes to the large KIEV-class aircraft carriers. Tactical nuclear weapons of various types are also carried in Soviet attack/cruise-missile submarines and aircraft.

Nuclear weapons appear to provide two major offensive advantages over conventional weapons in war at sea. First, whereas multiple hits with conventional weapons would probably be required to destroy a cruiser or carrier, a single nuclear weapon, of even small size, would suffice. Second, a defense against nuclear weapons would require a 100 percent effectiveness, since a single penetrating missile or "leaker" could destroy the target.

In the anti-air warfare role the nuclear weapon, from the Soviet perspective, would deter concentrated U.S. air attacks against ships, while in ASW operations a nuclear weapon could compensate for the target submarine's area of uncertainty or the limited effectiveness of conventional weapons. Another consideration is the potential use of high-altitude bursts of nuclear weapons to create Electro-Magnetic Pulse (EMP) effects that could seriously degrade electronic and optical systems of ships and aircraft over large ocean areas. Underwater nuclear bursts could similarly degrade sonar effectiveness, creating a condition over certain acoustic frequencies known as "blue out." Soviet writings demonstrate a familiarity with all of these aspects of nuclear weapons.

A final advantage of employing nuclear weapons is that a commander can use *all* of the weapons at his disposal, conventional as well as nuclear. The reverse is not so. A conventional-only attack denies a commander the use of a significant number of weapons—those with nuclear warheads.

Soviet naval readiness for nuclear warfare also includes significant defensive measures. The design of Soviet warships incorporates CBR defensive measures. Warships of all size down to the small Osa missile craft have protective "citadels," which are areas that can be sealed to provide a safe, controlled atmosphere, with overpressure to keep out contaminants. Naval ships are also provided with periscopes and other equipment for conning from sealed bridges, with CBR washdown devices, and other features to facilitate survival in a nuclear or chemical environment.[20] Observations of Soviet ships also indicate some hardening features, such as protection of radar wave guides (cables) from the EMP effects of nuclear explosions as well as from blast damage.

A third area indicative of Soviet preparedness for nuclear conflict is training and fleet exercises. Soviet naval personnel carry out CBR defense training on a regular basis, and nuclear defensive and offensive maneuvers are a regular part of fleet exercises.

Thus, Soviet naval weapons, warship configuration, and training and exercises point to a major capability for fighting a theater/tactical nuclear conflict at sea. Almost all of these defensive features apply equally to the chemical warfare capability of the Soviet Navy. Again, the Soviet Ground Forces have a considerable chemical warfare capability in terms of munitions and protective measures. An official U.S. government evaluation states:

> The armed forces of the Soviet Union in particular and the Warsaw Pact forces in general are better equipped, structured and trained than any other military force in the world to conduct offensive and defensive chemical warfare operations. Their capabilities are steadily improving.
>
> The Soviets have deployed a variety of modern agents and multiple delivery systems, and have the tactical doctrine for large-scale employment of chemical weapons. A significant portion of all Soviet delivery systems—including missile and rocket systems, aerial bombs and artillery—are chemical-weapon capable. Warsaw Pact forces are well-trained, organized and equipped for offensive CW [Chemical Warfare] operations.
>
> In Soviet military doctrine, toxic chemicals are associated primarily with theater warfare. The basic principle is to achieve surprise by using massive quantities of chemical agents against unprotected troops or against equipment or on terrain to deny its use.[21]

Chemical munitions can inflict considerably more casualties per weapon than can conventional, high-explosive munitions. This means that chemical weapons offer the opportunity of very high effectiveness per hit without escalation to the nuclear weapons threshold.

The Soviet Navy can be considered prepared for the use of theater/tactical nuclear weapons and chemical weapons, while the U.S. Navy's surface forces are highly vulnerable to their use.

## OCEAN SURVEILLANCE AND INTELLIGENCE

All Soviet naval operations are centrally controlled, a concept that demands that the commander of a fleet or force or theater (TVD) have all possible information on the disposition and status of his own forces and enemy forces. The Soviet Ocean Surveillance System (SOSS) makes use of a variety of means for surveillance and reconnaissance, among them the Navy's operating forces (aircraft, surface ships, and submarines) and specialized collection activities to provide this information.

The principal intelligence-collection components of SOSS are: aircraft, radio intercept, satellites, surface ships, and "spies."

*Aircraft.* The Soviet Navy employs specially configured An-12 Cub, Il-18 Coot, Tu-16 Badger, and Tu-20 Bear aircraft for reconnaissance and surveillance.

The most notable aircraft are the long-range, four-turboprop Bear-D aircraft, which conduct radar and ELINT reconnaissance missions and have the ability to transmit radarscope data to missile-launching platforms through a Video Data Link (VDL). Although the approximately 45 Bear-D aircraft in service would be highly vulnerable in wartime, their range (enhanced by in-flight refueling and overseas basing) makes them an invaluable component of SOSS during "peacetime" and crisis periods.

---

[20]The only U.S. surface warship configured to operate in a nuclear-chemical environment was the destroyer HERBERT J. THOMAS (DD 833), which was modified in 1963–1964 and discarded in 1974 (transferred to Taiwan).

[21]Secretary of Defense Caspar W. Weinberger, "Soviet Military Power" (Washington, D.C.: Department of Defense, n.d. [1981]), pp. 37–38.

The Tu-16 Badger flies in Soviet naval markings in several reconnaissance configurations, again using radar and ELINT collection systems. While lacking the Bear's range, these aircraft can also be refueled in flight and have a higher speed. (These reconnaissance aircraft are separate from the Badger electronic countermeasure aircraft that support strikes against surface forces.)

Reconnaissance-ELINT variants of the An-12 Cub and Il-18 Coot civilian and military transports are also employed in seeking out surface naval forces, mainly for the purpose of collecting data on electromagnetic emissions from Western ships.

*Radio Intercept.*  The Soviets operated a network of land-based radio intercept stations prior to World War II. After the conflict, employing captured German technology the Soviets built an elaborate High-Frequency Direction-Finding (HF/DF) network given the code name "Krug" (German for "ring" or "circle").

This system along the land and sea borders of the USSR seeks to intercept transmissions from surface ships and submarines and to triangulate their positions. Some overseas HF/DF stations have also been established, notably in Egypt during the period of close cooperation between the armed forces of the two nations (1956 to 1973) and in Cuba. The Soviets provided the Egyptians with special equipment and personnel to help intercept and monitor the communications of the U.S. Sixth Fleet in the Mediterranean.

*Satellites.* The Soviets employ three types of satellites for ocean surveillance: ELINT or electronic intercept "ferreting" vehicles that can detect and "lock on" electronic signals from ships, providing location and, possibly from radar signals, information on the type of ship; Radar Ocean Reconnaissance Satellite (RORSAT) vehicles that use active radar to detect ships; and photographic satellites.

While specific details of these satellites are lacking in the unclassified literature, it is evident that there are several operating modes. Sometimes the satellites are operated in pairs of one or both types, to enhance coverage or to permit the passive ELINT satellite to "key" the RORSAT to areas of interest. These satellites use battery and solar energy as power sources, with some using nuclear power.[22]

These and other satellites are in extensive use by the Soviet armed forces for tactical and strategic (e.g., early warning) reconnaissance and surveillance. The Soviets apparently employed reconnaissance satellites to keep track of the 1973 war in the Middle East. Four reconnaissance satellites were orbited during a 12-day period in early October, apparently related to the Arab-Israeli conflict that erupted on 6 October 1973. Similarly, the Soviets increased their satellite collection during the Iranian and Afghan crises that began in 1979, in 1980 when Iraq invaded Iran, and during the Anglo-Argentine war in the South Atlantic and the massive Israeli invasion of Lebanon, which occurred in 1982. With respect to the last period, beginning 2 April 1982, the day Argentina seized the Falklands, the Soviet Union orbited a record number of reconnaissance and strategic early warning satellites. At least eight of the strategic warning satellites were put up through early June (the Israelis invaded Lebanon in early June).[23] One reconnaissance satellite was kept in orbit for 50 days, a Soviet record at the time.

[22]The nuclear-powered RORSAT with the Soviet designation Cosmos 954 malfunctioned in January 1978, going into an uncontrolled reentry and spreading radioactive debris over Northern Canada. The Soviets resumed orbiting nuclear-powered ocean surveillance satellites in April 1980 at the rate of two or more per year. Radioactive portions of another nuclear surveillance satellite, the COSMOS 1402, began breaking up in December 1982 and crashed into the Indian Ocean in January 1983.

[23]The early warning satellites used infrared sensors to detect the launch of U.S. ballistic missiles. Nine of these strategic warning vehicles were launched; one failed to achieve orbit, and the radios of a second failed. The nine, at angles of

The ubiquitous AGI at sea. These ships, increasingly larger and more capable, operate in important waterways, off Western test ranges and bases, and near U.S. and NATO exercises, quietly gleaning various types of intelligence. This AGI reveals the ex-survey ship/buoy-tender lines of the Moma class, but with a variety of ELINT/SIGINT antennas fitted amidships.

The USSR employs a variety of means to gather technical and operational intelligence on U.S. naval forces. The more overt means have included this Kashin-class destroyer steaming alongside the U.S. carrier FRANKLIN D. ROOSEVELT (CV 42) as the flattop conducted flight operations in the Mediterranean. These maneuvers during a crisis period could also provide targeting for Soviet strike forces. (1971, U.S. Navy)

The Soviets have also orbited photographic satellites, but details of their ability to track warships have not been addressed in public forums.

The anti-satellite program of the U.S. Department of Defense has Soviet ocean surveillance satellites as their primary target. According to a U.S. defense official, "The principal motivation for our ASAT [Anti-Satellite] program is to put us in a position to negate Soviet satellites that control Soviet weapon systems that could attack our fleet."[24]

The Soviet Navy also makes use of satellites for communication and navigation purposes.

*Surface Ships.* More than 50 specialized "intelligence collectors," designated AGI by Western intelligence, are in Soviet naval service.[25] While they are sometimes depicted in the press as disguised fishing trawlers, the Soviet AGIs are naval units, readily identified by their naval ensign and electronic antennas, and are manned by naval personnel. The latest and largest AGI class is also armed, while most earlier AGIs have been backfitted with the SA-7 Grail heat-seeking missile (see chapter 20).

Soviet AGI-type ships normally keep watch off the U.S. strategic

submarine base at Holy Loch, Scotland, and off the southeastern coast of the United States—a position that permits surveillance of the submarine base at Charleston, S.C., or Kings Bay, Ga., or the missile activity off Cape Kennedy, Fla. AGIs also operate in important international waterways, such as the Strait of Gibraltar, the Sicilian Straits, and the Strait of Hormuz. And AGIs regularly keep watch on U.S. and other NATO exercises.

Of course, Soviet warships also conduct surveillance of Western forces, with those Soviet ships engaged in close trailing operations referred to as "tattletales."

Beyond naval ships, SOSS can also be expected to make use of information obtained from the state-owned and centrally controlled merchant and fishing fleets, and from the large Soviet research ocean fleets. The last consist of ships and aircraft engaged in academic oceanographic and polar research, as well as in support of the nation's civilian and military space and atmospheric research programs.

*"Spies."* The Soviet national intelligence service, the KGB, and the military intelligence organization, the GRU, also gather information on Western naval movements and activities. Their activities appear to range from placing agents in Western defense organizations to simply reading newspapers and magazines that discuss naval deployments, exercises, and port visits.

There has been periodic evidence that the Soviet intelligence has succeeded in placing high-level agents in Western defense organizations or subverting employees, some with special knowledge of naval matters. These have included Bernard Michell and William Martin, who defected from the U.S. National Security Agency; George Blake, a Soviet agent in British intelligence; Gordon Lonsdale, John Vassall, and Harry Houghton, who were involved with British naval intelligence and weapons research; and, most recently, long-term employee Arthur Prime of the super-sensitive Government Communications Headquarters in Cheltenham, England.

The information garnered by the various components of SOSS are collected and correlated at command centers in the four fleet headquarters and at naval headquarters in Moscow. These command centers have hardened, highly survivable communications facilities associated with them, with alternate emergency facilities ready to serve as a backup, to ensure a rapid intake of intelligence data and rapid directions to fleet and tactical commanders. Although Soviet tactics are highly dependent upon communications, once hostilities start it is possible that Soviet forces may be *less dependent* on command direction than are Western naval forces because of the Soviets' rigid doctrine and tactics.[26]

In addition to these fixed facilities, the command ship–cruisers ADMIRAL SENYAVIN and ZHDANOV and the KIROV-class battle cruisers probably are fitted with sufficient C³ systems to process and employ the products of SOSS.

For the Soviet naval forces to carry out successfully their assigned missions, these products are essential.

40° to the earth, would have provided continuous observation of ICBM silos in the United States. Still, seven such satellites simultaneously in orbit were a record number.

[24]Testimony of Dr. Seymour Zeiberg, Deputy Under Secretary of Defense (Research and Engineering) for strategic and space systems before the Committee on Armed Services, House of Representatives, 27 March 1979.

[25]The U.S. Navy discarded its passive intelligence-collection ships after the capture of the PUEBLO (AGER 2) by North Korea in 1968 and the accidental Israeli attack on the LIBERTY (AGTR 5) during the 1973 Middle East war.

[26]For a more detailed description of Soviet C³ systems and concepts, see N. Polmar, "Soviet C³," *Air Force Magazine*, June 1980, pp. 58–66.

## ELECTRONIC WARFARE

The Soviet Navy's own reliance on "real-time" transmission of reconnaissance and targeting data, the Soviet need for effective C[3], and the comprehensive Soviet understanding of the potential vulnerabilities of U.S. military C[3] activities have led to extensive emphasis on Electronic Warfare (EW). The Soviet term for offensive and defensive EW is *radioelectronnaya bor'ba* (Radio Electronic Combat or REC), and it includes detection of hostile electronic transmissions, as noted above, but also the neutralization or destruction of the electronic threat and the protection of Soviet systems.

Offensive EW includes the jamming and spoofing as well as the destruction of hostile communication centers and radars; to do this a variety of systems are used—from Soviet shore installations as well as from airplanes, surface ships, and possibly submarines. One U.S. Navy communications security specialist has speculated that the Soviet Golf-class submarines, converted to special communications craft (SSQ), "may have a REC mission in addition to, if not in place of, their postulated C[3] function. What could be more perfect than a jamming/deception platform that you would probably not detect until it started transmitting? Even then, given the confusion that even a partially successful IFF [Identification Friend or Foe] spoofing, pulse jamming, deceptive repeating or intrusion incident generates, the submarine would probably remain undetected, especially if the source could not be seen on radar."[27]

Several Soviet publications have stressed the need to strike Western C[3] installations at the onset of a conflict. While public Soviet discussions in this area of naval warfare are limited, an official U.S. Army evaluation of Soviet REC estimates that the goal of this activity is to destroy or disrupt at least 50 percent of an enemy's command, control, and weapon direction systems by either jamming or disruptive fires.[28] In addition to missile and gunfire (and the potential use of nuclear weapons in the EMP mode), Soviet techniques employed in offensive EW are: radar jamming by barrage and spot "noise," chaff, and decoys; electronic jamming of command guidance systems by pulse and simulation techniques; and radio communications noise jamming of AM and FM signals.

A variety of defensive EW techniques have also been discussed, stressing Communications Security (COMSEC) and Electronic Counter Countermeasures (ECCM). For example, although the Soviets must ensure effective radio communications, radio operators will change power, modulation, and antenna direction as well as frequencies to the extent possible. In addition to the command ships and submarines mentioned earlier in this chapter, the Soviet naval communications achieve a high degree of survivability through redundant paths for multiple transmission of the same message, use of reliable (if slow) methods such as manual morse, and hardened communication centers ashore. In the Soviet tradition, naval headquarters and the fleet command centers, and probably naval communication stations all have several echelons of fully equipped backup facilities.

Radar operators will similarly change frequency, power, polarization, and modulation to reduce vulnerability. And, of course, the Soviets stress Emission Control (EMCON) with all electronic and communication equipment. Finally, the Soviets employ anti-radar "camouflage" when possible with such techniques as creating false targets or blending into the terrain and background.

The West has had limited examples of Soviet REC effectiveness, especially during the Soviet invasion of Czechoslovakia in 1969 and the Egyptian crossing of the Suez Canal in the 1973 Yom Kippur War.

[27]Lieutenant Commander Guy Thomas, U.S. Navy, "Soviet Radio Electronic Combat and the US Navy," *Naval War College Review*, July–August 1982, pp. 16–24. This is an excellent discussion of Soviet REC. Also see Dr. Norman Friedman, "C[3] War at Sea," U.S. Naval Institute *Proceedings*, May 1977, pp. 124–41, and N. Polmar, "Soviet C[3]," op. cit.

[28]Department of the Army, *Soviet Army Operations* (Arlington, Va.: U.S. Army Intelligence and Threat Analysis Center, 1978), p. 5–81.

The Soviets have long used submarine tenders, like the Don-class FEDOR VIDYAYEV, as flagships for deployed squadrons or *eskadras* as well as to support submarines. The conversion of two SVERDLOV-class cruisers to command ships, as well as the facilities available in the new KIROV-class cruisers, reduce the use of these ships in the flagship role. (1982, U.S. Navy)

# 9

# Personnel and Training

The Soviet Navy today has approximately 452,000 officers and enlisted men on active duty, some 311,000 less than the U.S. naval services, which have some 569,000 in the Navy and 194,500 in the Marine Corps.[1]

The Soviet Navy's personnel are allocated approximately as follows (percentages rounded):[2]

| | | |
|---|---|---|
| Afloat | 188,000 | (42%) |
| Naval Aviation | 63,000 | (14%) |
| Naval Infantry | 13,000 | (3%) |
| Coastal Defense | 8,000 | (2%) |
| Training | 57,000 | (13%) |
| Shore Support | 123,000 | (27%) |

There has been a significant increase in Soviet naval manpower during the past few years. There had been a sharp reduction in naval personnel during the early 1970s, with Western intelligence reporting a Navy strength of 470,000 at the start of the decade, but only 427,000 about five years later. The major reductions in that period were 10,000 from coastal defense forces and 45,000 from shore support activities. In the same period there was a significant increase in the naval air arm, with Soviet Naval Aviation going from about 40,000 to 50,000 men. From the mid-1970's strength the Navy's manpower has increased by some 16,000 men—most going to afloat assignments and naval aviation, and lesser numbers to the naval infantry and training establishment. The size of the shore establishment is estimated to have further declined (from 175,000 in 1972, to 130,000 in 1977, and 123,000 in 1982).

## MILITARY SERVICE

The Soviet Union's Law on Universal Military Service applies to the Soviet naval service as well. This law, last revised in 1981, states that all male citizens of the Soviet Union must perform two years of military service at age 18 and provides for their conscription. But Navy shipboard personnel and men conscripted for the Strategic Rocket Forces must serve for three years. The 1967 law reduced general conscription from three years and shipboard duty from four years, apparently because there was an abundance of draft-age men. The conscription pool is based on an 18-year-old population that has generally completed the Soviet Union's required 10-year secondary school system. (The State provides free education at all levels, including institutions of higher learning; instruction in minority languages as well as Russian; coeducation at all levels; and a uniform course of study. According to Soviet statements, over 90 percent of the men entering Soviet naval service have completed secondary education, although there are some indications that the actual percentage may be lower.)

Draft deferments are provided for family, medical, or educational reasons. Exemptions are more difficult to obtain, generally being given to men with a physical disability or a serious criminal record, to married men with two or more children, and to men who are the sole support of parents or siblings. The extent to which deferments and exemptions are granted because a man's skills are needed in the civilian sector is not clear.

Soviet conscription provides for call-ups twice a year, in May–June and in November–December, with about 450,000 men drafted for all of the armed services in each call-up. Conscription, reserve programs, and other support activities for all of the armed services are directed by the 16 Military Districts that encompass the Soviet Union.

Service in the Soviet Ground Forces (i.e., army) is extremely arduous and spartan. The Navy and the other services are thus often preferred despite the longer term and the possible long cruises. Those men with physical or psychological conditions not sufficient to exempt them from military service are assigned to duties usually performed in Western navies by civilians, such as cargo handling and facility maintenance.

Enlisted men can be held beyond their official two- or three-year period for up to six months of additional service. Those men who wish to reenlist are usually placed in the warrant (*michman*)[3] program. Very few are allowed to remain on active duty as enlisted men beyond their initial service, in part because of the requirement to take in large numbers of conscripts on a continuous basis. The number of men remaining as petty officers has been estimated by Western sources to be as low as 1 or 2 percent. These are generally men who do not have the qualifications to enter the *michman* program.

Men who have completed their obligatory service and certain in-

[1] This chapter is based in part on the research of Dr. Milan Vego and on the BDM Corporation analysis "The Soviet Naval Personnel Series" (1978), in which the author of this book participated.

[2] All personnel figures are as estimated by Western intelligence; changing methods of estimating may account for differences of as much as 10 to 15 percent over a period of time.

[3] Adopted from the English term *midshipman*.

The lookers are being looked at in this view of the bridge watch of a Soviet warship passing close aboard a U.S. warship. Under Admiral Gorshkov's direction, Soviet sailors have worked harder and sailed farther than ever before in peacetime. There are still problems, but these men have earned awards for excellence in air defense/AAW (larger star) and AAW missiles/radar.

dividuals who have received exemptions are required to serve in the reserves up to age 50. All reservists are subject to periodic recalls to active duty for a total of up to two years of service, the exact amount of time and the assignment being decided largely by the Military District and varying with the category of reservist. There is evidence that the reserve program is hindered by resentment to the recalls and other requirements, and by active personnel who make only limited use of reservists who are recalled.

The law also provides for the conscription of women from age 19 to 40 who are trained in medical and other specialties. Women are not normally drafted, and very few serve in the Navy in a professional role. Most women in naval service appear to serve in administrative, com-

There are relatively few women in Soviet naval service, and none is believed to serve aboard ship. These young ladies are cited as being outstanding in political and military training.

munications, supply, and medical roles. The use of women in the Soviet armed forces is limited also by the high percentage employed in the civilian sector as well as by the cultural and religious problems related to Asian and minority women working outside of their homes or villages. (Women served extensively in the Soviet army and air forces during World War II, with many seeing extensive combat. In the postwar period there have been several women test pilots and one woman cosmonaut.)

Another problem related to military service is the decline in the birth rate of the large Russian and Ukrainian portions of the Soviet population and hence the increase in the number of conscripts from Asian and minority groups who lack upbringing in a technical environment and who speak Russian very poorly (and in some cases not at all). This problem is becoming more acute. A U.S. defense analyst has observed, "From the standpoint of socialization and education, however, those same young men who are least desirable from a narrowly military perspective are also those most in need of the socialization and vocational training offered by the military experience."[4] Significantly, the Soviets do not allow the need to use such personnel in the military to threaten combat effectiveness or the political stability of units. Specific minorities who lack language or technical competence, and certain other groups who may be politically questionable, are not allowed to serve in sensitive positions (e.g., assignments with communications, intelligence, nuclear weapons) or certain front-line units.

In the long view the Soviets can solve this minority problem by selective personnel assignments (an option not fully available to U.S. personnel managers), reduction of the number of legal deferments, extending naval service for all conscripts by six months as allowed under the existing law, or a change in the law affecting length of service. However,

[4]Dr. Ellen Jones, "Soviet Military Manpower: Prospects in the 1980s," *Strategic Review*, Fall 1981, pp. 65–75; also see her "Minorities in the Soviet Armed Forces," *Comparative Strategy*, vol. III, no. 4 (1982), pp. 285–318.

extreme care must be taken that any actions to help the military manpower situation do not adversely affect the civilian sector, which has shortages in some technical disciplines.

## PRESERVICE TRAINING

The reduction of required service in the 1967 law coupled with the basic Soviet concept of political indoctrination for all citizens has led to a comprehensive premilitary training program. Closely related are military sports and political activities.

There is military-patriotic training at all levels and in numerous aspects of Soviet life, often depicting the struggle between the Soviet Union and the Western world. Official Soviet literature is inundated with such statements as, "School children . . . must know the real danger which imperialism poses to mankind. The work done in a school by way of military-patriotic indoctrination must prepare students in practical ways to overcome difficulties during times of possible severe trials."[5]

From this basis, the Soviet Union has developed an intensive program of preconscription military training. It begins at the preschool level with cartoon comics depicting military heroes and continues throughout the required ten years of school and the year between completion of public school and being called up into the armed forces. History books emphasize the importance of the military in Russian history, the children visit war memorials and military museums, and retired military persons visit schools for presentations and talks. There are part-time, voluntary, paramilitary training programs for children as young as age ten.

[5]N.P. Aksenova, "On the Effectiveness of Military-Patriotic Indoctrination of School Children," *Sovetskaya Pedagogika*, February 1972, pp. 46–51.

Preservice military training in the USSR begins on a voluntary basis with the start of primary school, and there are required programs for male students in high school and between graduation and being conscripted. While shortcomings exist in these programs, they still provide some training—quite valuable in some areas—and contribute to the "military environment" of the Soviet society.

Civil defense training begins in the second grade and continues throughout the educational career of most Soviet youth. (The Soviet civil defense program is under the direction of a military officer and is a part of the Ministry of Defense.) During the last two years of school, all male students in the 9th and 10th grades (normally ages 16 and 17) participate in a compulsory premilitary training program of 140 formal hours. Courses are given in military history, the wearing and care of uniforms, small arms (with live munitions, including hand grenades), and radio and radar operation. Field exercises of several days' duration are also conducted as part of the program.

In the year between leaving high school and being called into active service, the young men participate in a part-time military program with courses in driving, vehicle maintenance, and communications. Although training does not always prepare men for the branch of service they will enter, those who will go into the airborne forces are often given preliminary parachute training; prospective submariners may receive a submarine familiarization course, and those who are to go into Navy diving work participate in the following program. "During their period of training at the Naval Club, the future divers learn a great deal and acquire many practical skills. They must be able to read drawings and schematics; draw sketches and measure underwater structures; and carry out rigging, assembly, repair and construction work while submerged. They must possess a good knowledge of the principles for conducting photographic, movie-making and television work, while submerged."[6] These training programs are for young men in school, working in factories or on the farms prior to induction. Soviet press statements indicate that one conscript in three has a technical specialty before entering active service.

The various preservice paramilitary activities are conducted by the Little Octobrists (ages 6–9), Young Pioneers (ages 10–15), the *Komsomol* (Communist Youth League, ages 14 and up), and DOSAAF (Voluntary Society for Cooperation with the Army, Aviation, and Fleet). The programs are conducted through the Military Districts, with all groups participating in war games as a part of the yearly round of activities, obviously tailored to the members' age and level of training. The Young Pioneers participate in *zarnitsa* or "summer lightning" games. Introduced in 1967, these games include familiarization with army weapons, including firing dummy ammunition, CBR defense, first aid, drill, and reconnaissance tasks.

The premilitary training programs vary in their degree of success, in part because of different attitudes and approaches within the separate Military Districts. With respect to civil defense, the general public attitude is not serious and there are major material deficiencies, in part because of general shortages and poor organization and management—traditional Russian problems. In the physical training programs the administrators tend to be overindulgent and inconsistent, often passing young men who should fail or who are marginal in order to fulfill the program's preestablished norms. With respect to actual preinduction military training, there is a wide range of quality. There are reports of inadequately prepared instruction, overworked instructors, significant

absenteeism, lack of equipment, and improper facilities. However, there is evidence of major efforts to upgrade the areas in which there are failings, and the overall programs must be considered successful in that they provide the draftee with some knowledge of the military before he enters active service. As periodically noted in the Soviet press, these premilitary programs do result in the average Soviet man being far different from his Western counterpart when he is called into active service at the age of 18.

The most significant program from a viewpoint of military training is DOSAAF, which is credited with some 336,000 units that provide preconscription training to some one-third of the young men entering the Soviet armed forces. DOSAAF is looked at as only one step removed from active military service. The seriousness of this program is evidenced by the assignment of a senior officer to head the organization, currently Admiral of the Fleet G.M. Yegorov, formerly CinC of the Northern Fleet and Chief of the Main Naval Staff.

## ENLISTED MEN

The Soviet Navy is a conscript navy with some three-quarters of the 452,000 men serving two or three years. The Soviet sailor is called to active duty for three years, except that some who will serve only ashore are conscripted for two years. (The reduction of one year in each category from the previous requirement went into effect in 1968). Once on active duty, most conscripts will undergo an initial Navy training program that can vary from four or five weeks to as long as six months; some, with previous DOSAAF or technical training, may go directly to fleet assignments, and a few go directly into the *michman* program.

Each of the four fleets conducts its own basic training and assigns the enlisted men. "Boot camp" of four or five weeks is devoted mostly to close-order drill, small arms, regulations and traditions of the service, individual CBR defense, and, of course, the ubiquitous physical training and political indoctrination. Upon completion of this brief recruit training, the conscript takes the formal military oath and becomes a full-fledged member of the Soviet Navy. At this point those sailors destined for menial or support jobs ashore—because of physical or political reliability problems or lack of aptitude—or who have previously acquired technical skills (from DOSAAF or other programs) go on to their permanent duty stations.

Those men slated for duty afloat or who require more technical schooling attend specialist training, which is normally five months' duration. Men going to nuclear submarines receive nuclear crew training in addition to their specialty course. The fleet is confronted with a paradox: The reduction in first-term service to three years reduces the time available for training, while the complexities of modern equipment and operations require that personnel be more highly qualified than previously. One result is more intensive on-the-job training (OJT in the Western vernacular) and making more use of preservice military training. During his active service the typical sailor will only work on one piece of equipment at one duty station, permitting the Navy to make maximum use of the time he is available.

The Soviet sailor is increasingly encouraged to expand his knowledge beyond his narrow specialty. However, he is still narrowly trained by U.S.

[6]Engineer-Captain 1st Rank Ye. Shikanov, "Conquerors of the Depths," *Voennyie Znaniia*, February 1973, pp. 36–37.

**TABLE 9–1.   ENLISTED RANKS**

| Naval Rank | Military Rank |
|---|---|
| Chief Petty Officer (*Glavnyy Starshina*) | Senior Sergeant |
| Petty Officer 1st Class (*Starshina Vtoroy Stati*) | Sergeant |
| Petty Officer 2nd Class (*Starshina Vtoroy Stati*) | Corporal |
| Senior Seaman (*Starshiy Matros*) | Private First Class |
| Seaman (*Matros*) | Private |

standards. Stability in the assignment of officers to ships and stations and the emphasis on specialist qualifications make up for this lack of versatility in the conscript.

Conscripts begin service with the rank of seaman (*matros*). The majority of seamen can expect to be promoted one grade, to senior seamen, by the time they have completed their three years of service. A first-term seaman may be promoted to petty officer second class and possibly even first-class if his billet calls for that rank and he can pass the qualification tests, or if he is able to attend additional specialized training. The billet availability seems to be the key factor. Although there is a

procedure for enlisted men to extend their service for two years, and hence become eligible for first class or chief petty officer status, few take this option, preferring instead to remain in the Navy in the warrant rank if they can qualify, or leaving the Navy and taking their technical knowledge to industry.

First-term servicemen live a spartan life compared to Western sailors; pay is low, food is simple, alcoholic beverages are forbidden, and there is little, or in some cases no, off-base liberty. However, an annual leave is given to visit home, and on base or aboard ship there is a variety of social and cultural activities. In general, naval life is less harsh and less demanding than in the Ground Forces. The families of first-term servicemen

(1975, U.S. Navy)

(1976)

(1973, U.S. Navy, Harold D. Phillips)

Soviet sailors have few recreational activities, ashore or afloat. Physical fitness—always stressed in the Soviet armed forces—and recreation are combined in crewing, a frequent pastime for Soviet sailors, as these men from a SAM Kotlin anchored in the Mediterranean demonstrate. More fortunate were sailors from the Kashin that visited Portsmouth, England, one of whom made friends with this young lady at a soccer game, and these sailors from another SAM Kotlin visiting Massawa, Ethiopia.

have special privileges, such as having work found for their wives and being exempt from the tax on married citizens with few or no children. Family housing assistance and guarantees of post-service employment also help the servicemen. Of course, he may learn a technical skill while in the Navy that could be in great demand by the civilian economy when he leaves the Navy.

During his shipboard service the first-term sailor undergoes a year of training and specialist qualification. This training year is a constant and carefully planned program in which the serviceman becomes integrated first with his ship or unit, then with small formations, and, finally, with fleet exercises.

Specialist qualification, which is independent of rank, is awarded on the basis of examinations in a man's skill area. A man who qualifies as a specialist receives extra pay although qualification may be withdrawn for disciplinary reasons. Enlisted specialist badges indicating 1st, 2nd, and 3rd class and master specialist, are worn on dress uniforms. (The experience required for the master specialist is too extensive for a first-term conscript to acquire.) The number of men in a crew who have specialist qualifications contribute to the standing of the ship or unit in the Navy-wide socialist competition.

Socialist competition within the Navy provides for the entire crew of a ship, unit, or base to strive for specialist qualification. This system of officially recognized rivalry originated in the civilian economy and is now an integral part of military training. It relies on moral incentives, honorary awards, and exhortations to stimulate servicemen and units to improve their skills, operational performance, discipline, and even political education. It involves meeting or exceeding "norms" in almost every facet of naval activity from the quality of food served in the messes to the accuracy of missile firings. (To some extent it is reminiscent of the intensive competition in the U.S. Navy for battle efficiency "E" awards in the 1920s and 1930s, when everything legally permissible was encouraged to gain a ship or squadron a coveted "E.")

During one recent competition the crew of the nuclear submarine 60 LET VELIKOGO OKTYABRYA "analyzed the results of the previous training year and in endeavoring to reinforce the achieved successes, approved new socialist obligations."[7] The submarine crew's new socialist obligations included:

- To reduce by 15 percent the time required for bringing the equipment, weapons and the ship as a whole into a state of combat readiness . . .
- To see to it that 75 percent of the departments and services are outstanding
- To have each crew member become a class specialist, 20 percent of the sailors should have the qualifications of master, and 70 percent 1st and 2nd class. The number of 1st class missile troops and sonar operators should be increased by 50 percent.

The submariners' pledges for the coming year included cultural and political promises as well as proposals for military achievement, including "to have a permanent amateur artistic collective and on the long voyages to systematically organize amateur artistic concerts," and "to constantly

study the military, revolutionary and labor traditions of the Communist Party, the Soviet people and their Armed Forces, and the experience of political indoctrination as generalized by Comrade L.I. Brezhnev in his books. . . ."

A report of the achievement of the Krivak-class frigate BODRYY, commended as the first ship in the fleet in the mid-1970s, cited that the crew "overfilled their Socialist commitments: 92 percent of their men have become class specialists, and one-third of them have mastered a related specialty. Aboard the ship eight out of ten men have been declared by their CO to be outstanding in combat and political training."[8] The article on the BODRYY's achievements also noted that the commanding officer "showed himself to be a fighting, tactically competent CO, an outstanding mariner, and a skillful educator and pedagogue."

Aboard ships and in other units the commanding officer is directly responsible for conducting the competition on a day-to-day basis. In organizing, publicizing, and running the competition, he is assisted primarily by his political officer and, to a lesser degree, by Communist Party and Komsomol members aboard his ship. There is a standard scoring scheme for socialist competition, with ships and units having high scores being rewarded and publicized while "laggards" are exposed to public censure, and pressure is brought to force them to improve. Failure to achieve "norms" can bring even stronger penalties. One ship—identified only as "X" in the Soviet military press—failed to fulfill certain commitments. The "defects" in the ship were examined, and as a result, during late 1980 the ship's commanding officer, V. Churikov (no rank was given), was relieved of his post and reassigned with a demotion, while officers (again no rank given) V. Volk, V. Dmitriyevskiy, L. Seregin, and others were made "answerable to the party."

Enlisted men who achieve outstanding individual ratings are rewarded with decorations, are publicized, and are given additional home leave. Petty officers and warrant officers whose sub-units have achieved excellent results may be promoted or given preference in admission to higher naval schools that would graduate them as commissioned officers. Another form of award for outstanding performance is to notify an enlisted man's former place of employment of his exemplary performance, a significant action because many sailors will return to their previous job when they leave the Navy. Departments, ships, and units that are cited by the fleet command as the year's best get to fly a special pennant or banner, and their officers can expect such an achievement to help advance their careers.

Since the rewards for success and penalties for failure are greatest for career warrant officers and commissioned officers, there is some falsification or exaggeration of achievements. The most serious competition is sometimes between officers, and this can lead to friction and tension. Thus, the greatest positive results of socialist competition are probably at the individual and sub-unit level, where skills can be increased in return for direct and important personal benefits.

Again, only a few sailors remain on active duty in an enlisted status beyond the required conscription period (although extensions add up to six months to the required two or three years). Most sailors are discharged into the reserves, in which they serve up to age 50.

[7]"New Scope for the Socialist Competition/High Dependability for the Ocean Watch," Krasnaya Zvezda, 23 November 1978, p. 1.

[8]"Large ASW Ship Bodryy Lauded," Krasnaya Zvezda, 1 December 1974, p. 1.

## WARRANT RANKS

The warrant rank or *michman* was first introduced in the Russian Navy in 1716 and was used almost continuously until 1917 as the initial officer grade, corresponding to 2nd lieutenant in the army. The Soviet government reintroduced the rank of *michman* in the Navy on 30 November 1940 as the highest rank for petty officers (*starshinii*).

The status of warrant rank in the Soviet armed forces (*praporshchik* in the other military services) was changed to a separate category on 1 January 1972. The program is open to qualified enlisted men under age 35. Most have completed a term of service as a conscript, but some with sufficient prior training are recruited directly from boot camp and some are former servicemen who have returned to active duty from the reserves. The reason for establishing warrant ranks at this level appears to have been the need for more career enlisted men, especially those with technical experience. Previously there was no formal program for training enlisted men after their first term of service. The importance and success of the *michmanii* program was indicated when, in early 1981, the senior warrant rank (*starshi michman*) was established in the Navy, to be conferred on men who have served as warrant officers for five years or more, with at least one year in positions normally staffed by officers or senior warrant officers.

After their appointment, the *michmanii* attend specialized, generally technical schools for one or two years, after which they usually go to an operational unit for their commitment of five years of post-training service. Subsequent multi-year enlistments are then possible until retirement age is reached.

Aboard ship the *michmanii* are assigned to each division, normally as the deputies to junior officers with direct command authority over petty officers and seamen. For example, an unmodified Kashin-class missile destroyer has a peacetime complement of approximately 20 officers, 20 *michmanii*, and just over 200 enlisted men. When possible, aboard ship and at naval bases the *michmanii* have a separate mess. Along with having a distinctive uniform, special privileges, and higher pay than enlisted men, the *michmanii* represent the most technically competent group within the Soviet Navy.

## OFFICERS

Soviet naval officers belong to an elite group that enjoys numerous privileges and opportunities while having a key role in Soviet defense and political strategies. The principal sources for the approximately 2,000 officers who are commissioned in the Soviet Navy every year are:

Higher Naval Schools    85%
Civilian Higher Schools    5%
Technical Institutes    10%

However, many naval officers begin their "career" at the age of 15 when they enter the Nakhimov secondary school in Leningrad.[9] Originally four schools were established in 1944 for the sons of deceased naval officers. Three of the schools have been disestablished and from the mid-1960s the remaining Nakhimov school in Leningrad has served as an officer "prep" school for specially chosen young men, generally the sons, nephews, or other relatives of naval officers and Communist Party officials. These students are accepted at Nakhimov for the last two years of secondary school, as preparation for Higher Naval Schools.

At the Nakhimov school the cadets receive academic, military, and political training. Upon graduation from the Nakhimov schools the young men join graduates of other secondary schools and a select number of enlisted men in attending one of 11 Higher Naval Schools, the equivalent of the U.S. Naval Academy:[10]

M.V. Frunze Higher Naval School (Leningrad)
Kaliningrad Higher Naval School (Kaliningrad) (Leningrad)
S.M. Kirov Caspian Higher Naval School (Baku) (Leningrad)
S.O. Makarov Pacific Higher Naval School (Vladivostok)
P.S. Nakhimov Black Sea Higher Naval School (Sevastopol´)
F.E. Dzerzhinskiy Higher Naval Engineering School (Leningrad)
Sevastopol´ Higher Naval Engineering School (Sevastopol´)
V.I. Lenin Higher Naval Engineering School (Pushkin, near Leningrad)
A.S. Popov Higher Naval School of Radio-Electronics (Petrodvorets, near Leningrad)
Leninsky Komsomol Higher Naval School of Submarine Warfare (Leningrad)
Kiev Higher Naval Political School (Kiev)

The first five of these schools educate surface line officers with the Frunze school being the most prestigious, tracing its heritage to naval cadet training that began in St. Petersburg in 1752. Two Higher Naval Schools are dedicated to line engineering, and one each to shore engineering, radio-electronics, submarine warfare, and political affairs. All of the schools have a five-year course of instruction except for the political school, which has a four-year curriculum. These Higher Naval Schools provide a highly specialized education. The first two years are devoted primarily to basic, naval-related subjects and undergraduate studies. The remaining three years emphasize areas of specialization with the result that Soviet naval officers are more technically educated and more specialized than their Western counterparts. Most naval officers will spend their entire career in the specialized field in which they were instructed at the higher naval school.

Practical training includes long-range cruises in warships and special training ships, after which the cadets receive a "distant cruise" badge. Physical fitness is stressed at sea and ashore. An article describing the Popov Higher Naval Radio-Electronics School states that, "At the school they have a fine sports palace with a swimming pool, open sports area, and a firing range. Almost all of the students have sports ratings. In the past five years alone they have prepared here more than 20 masters of sports and hundreds of first-class sportsmen. Many students have often become champions and prize-winners of the armed forces, Leningrad, RSFSR [Russian Soviet Federated Socialist Republic] and USSR."[11]

---

[9]Vice Admiral Povel Stepanovich Nakhimov won a major victory over a Turkish fleet at Sinope in 1853; his name is also given to a higher naval school and a cruiser.

[10]There are approximately 140 higher military schools in the Soviet Union that provide officer education for the armed forces; there are four such schools in the United States—the Naval, Military, Air Force, and Coast Guard Academies.

[11]Captain 1st Rank (Reserve) V. Nikolayev, "Named for A.S. Popov," *Voyennyye Znaniya*, no. 5, 1978, pp. 18–19.

Soviet naval officers, as this rear admiral, are among the elite of Soviet society. Most of a line officer's time will be spent aboard ships, with periodic schooling and only occasional shore duty. Long shipboard assignments are compensated for, in part, by individual Soviet ships spending less time at sea than their U.S. counterparts. (U.S. Navy)

Motivation is also stressed during an officer's education. The following comment by a ship's political officer illustrates this attitude: "Motivation comes first, the technology can come later . . . without motivation, technology is worthless." This motivation carries over to an officer's use of technology: "There is, first of all, the ship commanding officer's personal responsibility to the Motherland and the people for his use of the latest weapons and equipment. However, the responsibility is not limited to his service duties of controlling the ship and weapons. This responsibility is also determined by his role in training and educating his subordinates, in inculcating in them a high sense of duty to their Motherland."[12]

Graduates of Higher Naval Schools are awarded an academic degree similar to the American baccalaureate and are commissioned as officers,

[12]Rear Admiral G. Kostev (Assistant Professor), "The Ship's CO," *Soviet Military Review*, no. 8, 1979, pp. 16–17.

in most instances as junior lieutenants. After graduation the new officers generally go on to their duty stations. The opportunity to proceed immediately to advanced education is available only to exceptional graduates. However, more than half the Soviet naval officers will receive postgraduate education at a later stage of their careers, a significant number achieving a level roughly equivalent to a doctorate in the West.

The other major sources for the education of Soviet naval officers are civilian higher schools (i.e., colleges) and technical institutes. These are generally four- and two-year establishments, respectively. There are reserve training programs at some of these schools, with the instructional staff consisting of active service, reserve and retired officers, and civilians.

Upon commissioning, the new officers are generally sent to sea and spend their initial four to six years in a specific shipboard department (see below). During this period the young officer seeks to attain qualification in his specialty area and will seek to move up to assistant commander (department head). Most officers will move up in a specialist area. Failure to serve in an executive or command position does not limit promotion and upward career movement. For example, a navigation specialist can serve as a ship, division, brigade, and fleet navigator, being promoted even while serving in the same position if his performance merits it. This policy sometimes results in rank inversion and at times officers of superior rank will work for more-qualified juniors.

Soviet ships have up to seven "command" and four "staff" departments. The command departments, designated BCh for *Boevayie Chasti* and headed by assistant commanders of the ship, are BCh-1 navigation, BCh-2 missile and/or gunnery, BCh-3 mine and torpedo, BCh-4 operations, BCh-5 engineering, BCh-6 air, and BCh-7 command and control. The four staff departments are S.1-R electronics, S.1-Kh chemical, S.1.M medical, and S.1-S supply. An officer who goes aboard ship will probably serve in the same department during his entire time aboard that ship, and when he goes to another ship he will usually be in the same department as well.

Most graduates of Higher Naval Schools are assigned to cruisers, destroyers, and frigates, with graduates of the Leninsky Komsomol submarine school going to submarines. Graduates of the Dzerzhinskiy and Pushkin schools are assigned to BCh-5 departments in submarines. Some outstanding graduates are immediately assigned as department heads, executive officers, and after brief service and additional training, even commanding officers of small combatants. These latter officers generally have an edge in subsequent promotion and major command assignments.

Aboard the larger ships the outstanding department heads compete for the position of executive officer, with the BCh-1 generally having the edge. By tradition, the executive officer of a ship usually becomes her commanding officer. The commanding officer often selects, or at least approves, the selecton of the executive officer (called assistant commander or *starpom* in the Soviet lexicon). The commanders of major warships (frigates and larger) range from captain-lieutenants to captains 1st rank, with some strategic missile submarines identified as having a rear admiral as commanding officer. From the mid-1970s onward there have been several "deep" selections for commanding officer, captain-lieutenants serving as commanders of several Krivak ASW ships and Kashin guided missile destroyers. These officers have nine years or less of commissioned service and some are under 30 years of age. This is approximately two ranks lower than frigate and destroyer commanders in the U.S. Navy. (There has been a similar reduction of unit commander ages in the Soviet Ground Forces, where there are regimental commanders as young as 32 and division commanders only 38 years old.) However, as discussed below, "flag specialists" may ride these ships for some time, observing and guiding the officer before he is fully designated a commanding officer in the Western sense.

Although young officers given such major assignments may not gain the staff experience of their Western counterparts, the use of general and naval staffs by the Soviet Union alleviates the need for all officers to be rotated through as many positions ashore as their Western counterparts. This, in turn, permits the "line" officers to have more fleet experience.

There are classes for prospective executive and commanding officers, but little has been published about them. Before he is formally selected, an officer must undergo a series of practical examinations in various naval areas, which are administered by the staff officers of the command to which the ship is attached. He must also have an interview with the division or other senior commander. The examinations are rigorous, with some candidates failing. (At least one officer with previous command experience is known to have failed the examinations.)

After being selected as a ship commander, an officer undergoes a lengthy process to qualify for "independent command." During this process the division commander or a "flag specialist" with previous command experience will frequently ride the ship and observe the newly appointed CO. The rider may countermand or modify orders, as he deems appropriate. Thus the new CO is taken through the annual evolution of exercises and training, and sometimes makes operational deployments with a flag specialist on his bridge before he is fully certified for command at sea. This practice, alien to most Western navies, partially explains the young age and junior rank of some Soviet commanding officers.

The fleet commanders in chief and ship and unit commanders have a major voice in officer promotion and assignment, much more so than their counterparts in the U.S. Navy. Advancement through captain 3rd rank is reported to be essentially automatic in the Soviet Navy. Selection to captain 2nd rank and above is apparently done by the Main Naval Staff. Those officers failing this selection generally remain on active duty until age 45.

Postgraduate education/training is generally a requirement for promotion to senior naval rank, with most officers being required to take competitive examinations for entry to advanced educational programs. Exceptions include outstanding graduates from Higher Naval Schools, who are exempt from some portions of the examinations. The entrance examinations for a military academy may be taken up to three times.

Candidates for flag rank generally attend the Naval Academy in Leningrad, named in 1976 for the late Marshal Grechko (formerly the Order of Lenin Naval Academy).[13] This Leningrad institution, founded in 1828, is similar in concept to the U.S. Naval War College, but attendance confers more prestige and is more significant to an officer's promotion than is the American institution.[14] At this time line officers up to age 38 and engineering officers up to age 35 are being accepted for resident graduate study, while officers are accepted for nonresident correspondence courses up to age 40. Candidates are required to pass entrance examinations in specialized areas and in a foreign language.

In addition to its advanced academic curriculum, the Naval Academy conducts studies and analyses for naval headquarters and helps to develop strategy and tactics for the Navy. Potential flag officers may attend the prestigious Voroshilov General Staff Academy in Moscow, where broad strategic, economic, and policy issues are addressed. The Voroshilov school has a two-year course (compared to the one-year course at the similar U.S. National War College and the Industrial College of the Armed Forces).

All of the Higher Naval Schools offer graduate courses, both in residence and by correspondence, the length of courses varying from 12 to 18 months. Correspondence students are exempt from certain duties in order to study. There are some naval postgraduate institutions, in particular the Krylov institution (currently part of the Grechko Naval Academy), a technical school that has no counterpart in the United States except perhaps the civilian Massachusetts Institute of Technology (MIT), and the Naval Officers Technical School at Kronshtadt near Leningrad. In addition, naval officers receive specialized advanced education and training at the numerous schools operated by other services.

The Soviet military academies and higher military schools are commanded by general or flag officers. The Grechko Naval Academy is commanded by Admiral V.S. Sysoyev, a former commander of the Black Sea Fleet who holds a doctorate in military science. (The U.S. Naval War College is commanded by a rear admiral.)

Those naval officers who fail promotion to the next higher rank may be retired. However, there is considerable flexibility in the system, because officers can be promoted while in the same position. There are published retirement ages: active service for all junior officers currently lasts at least until they reach age 40; for captain 2nd and 3rd rank the retirement age is 45; for captain 1st rank age 50; for rear admiral and vice admiral age 55; and for admiral and admiral of the fleet age 60. There are numerous exceptions, the most notable one being Admiral Gorshkov, Commander in Chief of the Navy, born in 1910, who remained on active duty when this volume went to press.

Upon retirement officers are transferred to the reserve where they serve up to ten years. These officers are subject to annual call-up, but this happens infrequently.

---

[13]The full name of this institution is Naval Order of Lenin, Ushakov and October Revolution Academy *imeni* [named for] Marshal of the Soviet Union A. A. Grechko. The Academy includes the Krylov Institute. The Krylov school, the top naval engineering institution in the USSR, was an independent activity from 1945 to 1960 (the A. N. Krylov Naval Academy of Shipbuilding and Armaments).

[14]There are believed to be 18 military academies in the Soviet Union; there are nine approximately equivalent schools in the United States; the Naval, Air, Army, and National War Colleges, the Industrial College of the Armed Forces, the Armed Forces Staff College, the Army and Air Force command and staff colleges, and the Naval Postgraduate School.

## OFFICER RANKS

Line officers of the Soviet Navy have traditional naval ranks, with seven grades of commissioned rank below flag ranks compared to six in the U.S. Navy. This rank structure reflects the early German naval influence on the Russian Navy. Exact comparisons with U.S. ranks are difficult. For example, a Soviet captain 1st rank has the broad sleeve stripe of a commodore in Western navies yet still wears the shoulder insignia of a colonel, his nominal army equivalent. The issue is further complicated because the Soviet military services do not have a brigadier rank; their one-star military rank is major general.

*History.* The military rank of admiral was introduced into the Russian Navy by Peter the Great in 1699, and the grades of rear (*kontr*), vice (*vitse*), and full admiral were used over the years with minor variations. The admiral grades fell into disuse at the start of the Soviet regime.

TABLE 9–2.  OFFICER AND WARRANT RANKS

| Soviet Navy | Soviet Military and Specialized Naval Branches | Approximate U.S. Navy Rank |
|---|---|---|
| **Officer Ranks** | | |
| Admiral of the Fleet of the Soviet Union (*Admiral Flota Sovyetskoga Soyuza*) | Marshal of the Soviet Union | Fleet Admiral |
| (none) | Chief Marshal Chief Marshal of Aviation | (none) |
| Admiral of the Fleet (*Admiral Flota*) | Marshal | Admiral |
| Admiral (*Admiral*) | General of the Army Colonel General | Admiral |
| Vice Admiral (*Vitse Admiral*) | General Lieutenant | Vice Admiral |
| Rear Admiral (*Kontr Admiral*) | General Major | Rear Admiral |
| (none) | (none) | Commodore |
| Captain 1st Rank (*Kapitan Pervogo Ranga*) | Colonel | Captain |
| Captain 2nd Rank (*Kapitan Vtorogo Ranga*) | Lieutenant Colonel | Commander |
| Captain 3rd Rank (*Kapitan Tretyego Ranga*) | Major | Lieutenant Commander |
| Captain Lieutenant (*Kapitan Leytenant*) | Captain | Lieutenant |
| Senior Lieutenant (*Starshiy Leytenant*) | Senior Lieutenant | Lieutenant (j.g.) |
| Lieutenant (*Leytenant*) | Lieutenant | Ensign |
| Junior Lieutenant (*Mladshiy Leytenant*) | Junior Lieutenant | Ensign |
| **Warrant Ranks** | | |
| Senior Warrant | Senior Ensign | Chief Petty Officer or Warrant Officer |
| Warrant | Ensign | Chief Petty Officer or Warrant Officer |

Position titles were used for senior naval officers until late 1935 when the ranks of *flagman* (flag-officer) 1st and 2nd grade were introduced. "Admiral" was still not acceptable to the Communist regime; at that time, the term "general" was also avoided in the Red Army, but five army officers were named Marshal of the Soviet Union in 1935. The various grades of general and admiral were belatedly introduced in the Soviet armed forces on 7 May 1940, with seven Soviet naval officers being given admiral rank at that time: N.G. Kuznetsov, the chief of naval forces, and I.S. Isakov and L.M. Galler, both at naval headquarters, were made admirals; the commanders of the Baltic and Pacific Fleets became vice admirals; and the commanders of the Northern and Black Sea Fleets became rear admirals. S.F. Zhavoronkov, head of naval aviation, became a lieutenant general (two stars) at the same time. Many more flag officers were appointed during the war. The senior political officers assigned to the armed forces were given appropriate general or admiral ranks in December 1942.

The rank of admiral of the fleet (*admiral flota*) was also introduced in the Soviet Union on 7 May 1940. It was abolished on 3 March 1955 with the introduction of the rank of Fleet Admiral of the Soviet Union, but was reestablished on 28 April 1962 and corresponds to the military ranks of general of the army and marshal of an arm or service.

Admiral of the Fleet of the Soviet Union (*Admiral Flota Sovetskogo Soyuza*) is the highest rank of the Soviet Navy and corresponds to the rank of Marshal of the Soviet Union. It was introduced on 3 March 1955 and on that date was awarded to Isakov, the leading Soviet theorist of the 1930s, and Kuznetsov, who headed Stalin's fleet buildups of the late 1930s and early 1950s.

Admiral Gorshkov was a full admiral (since 1954) when he became Commander in Chief of the Soviet Navy in January 1956. He was subsequently promoted to admiral of the fleet on 28 April 1962 and was awarded the rank of Admiral of the Fleet of the Soviet Union on 28 October 1967, the third officer to receive this highest Soviet naval rank.

In the Soviet Navy the rear, vice, and full admirals have insignia similar to their Western counterparts and in most instances hold comparable positions. The flag rank issue becomes confused because the Soviet Navy has four admirals of the fleet on active duty, a rank not now held by officers serving in Western navies. The admirals currently in this grade are the first deputy CinC of the Navy; the CinC of the Pacific Fleet; the former first deputy CinC of the Navy, who is now assigned to the Ministry of Defense; and the former chief of the Main Naval Staff, now head of the DOSAAF organization. (See Appendix A.)

The grades of captain 1st, 2nd, and 3rd rank (*ranga*) existed in the Russian Navy from 1713 to 1732, and again from 1751 to 1917, and in the Soviet Navy since 22 September 1935. Traditionally, these officers held the rank corresponding to the rank of the ship they commanded (*ranga korablya*). Thus, a captain 2nd rank would normally command a second-rank ship (see chapter 3 for current Soviet naval ship ranks).

An *approximate* comparison of Soviet military and naval ranks with U.S. ranks is provided in table 9-2. Recent commanders of the four Soviet fleets have held the ranks of admiral of the fleet, admiral, or vice admiral, while in the U.S. Navy the area fleet commanders are admirals (Atlantic and Pacific Fleets) and the numbered fleet commanders are vice admirals (Second, Third, Sixth, Seventh). In both navies the officer in charge

**TABLE 9–3.  OFFICER CAREER ASSIGNMENTS**

| Years of Service | Rank | Typical Assignments |
|---|---|---|
| 19 to 25 | Captain 1st Rank | Military Academy of the General Staff |
| | | Brigade Commander (small combatants) |
| | | Division Commander (destroyers/cruisers) |
| | | Fleet Navigator |
| | | CO strategic missile submarine |
| | | CO KIEV (aircraft carrier) |
| | | CO KIROV (cruiser) |
| | | CO SVERDLOV (cruiser) |
| 14 to 21 | Captain 2nd Rank | Naval Academy |
| | | Higher Naval School (instructor) |
| | | Division Commander (small combatants) |
| | | CO KIEV (aircraft carrier) |
| | | CO MOSKVA (helicopter carrier) |
| | | CO SVERDLOV (cruiser) |
| | | CO Kara (cruiser) |
| | | CO Kresta II (cruiser) |
| | | CO Kynda (cruiser) |
| | | CO destroyer |
| | | CO large landing ship |
| 9 to 16 | Captain 3rd Rank | Postgraduate Studies |
| | | CO submarine (diesel) |
| | | CO Kara (cruiser) |
| | | CO Kresta II (cruiser) |
| | | CO destroyer |
| | | CO Krivak (frigate) |
| | | CO large landing ship |
| | | CO fleet minesweeper |
| | | CO submarine tender |
| | | XO surface combatant |
| | | Department Head, surface combatant |
| 5 to 12 | Captain Lieutenant | Naval base or headquarters |
| | | CO Krivak (frigate) |
| | | CO minesweeper |
| | | CO small missile combatant |
| | | XO destroyer |
| | | XO frigate |
| | | Department Head, submarine |
| 2 to 8 | Senior Lieutenant | CO small combatant |
| | | XO small combatant |
| 0 to 5 | Lieutenant | XO small combatant |
| 0 to 2 | Junior Lieutenant | sea duty |

**TABLE 9–4.  SOVIET VERSUS U.S. NAVAL OFFICERS**

| | Soviet Union | United States |
|---|---|---|
| Pre-military Training | Extensive | None |
| Political Indoctrination | Extensive | None |
| Scope of Education | Specialized | General |
| Sources | Higher Naval Schools 85% | Naval Academy 10% |
| | Other Institutions 15% | NROTC 11% |
| | | College & OCS 79% |
| Shipboard Assignment | Very Specialized | Semi-Specialized |
| Technical Work | Hands-on | Managerial |
| Rotation | 4 to 6 years | 2 to 3 years |
| Shore Duty | Minimal | Extensive |

SVERDLOV, Kara, and Kresta II classes are mostly commanded by captains 2nd rank while ships of their size in the U.S. Navy would have captains as commanding officers. At least one Kara-class cruiser is commanded by a captain 3rd rank. And some commanding officers of SSBNs have retained their commands after being promoted to rear admiral.

Senior instructors of the Soviet Navy have their rank prefixed with the term *professor* (professor) and engineering officers have the prefix *inzhener* (engineer).

The specialized branches of the Soviet Navy include Naval Aviation, Naval Infantry (marines), Coastal Missile-Artillery Force, Medical Service, and Rear Services. All have distinctive uniforms and military ranks, separate schools, and other institutional trappings. These services are fully integrated into naval organizations in the same manner, for example, as U.S. Navy medical personnel are assigned to Marine Corps units and the Fleet Marine Forces are components of the U.S. Atlantic and Pacific Fleet commands.

## FLEET TRAINING AND EXERCISES

According to Admiral Gorshkov, ". . . our fleets conduct strenuous training the year round. In classrooms, on gunnery ranges and in simulators, on ships and in units (*chasti*), our seamen gain sound knowledge and the ability to handle machinery and systems and intricate weapons."

"Ocean cruises and distant voyages serve as the highest stage of this training."[16]

Combat training in the Soviet Navy is highly centralized and conducted in accordance with a detailed annual, monthly, weekly, and daily plan. The importance of combat training and of having continuity of training is evidenced by the Navy having a Deputy CinC for Combat Training with the rank of full admiral. Admiral G.A. Bondarenko has held this position since 1973. (The Deputy CinC for Educational Institutions and the Chief of the Navy's Personnel Directorate are vice admirals; see appendix A.)

Shipboard training encompasses a wide range of activities. Because of the large number of draftees the Navy must accept twice a year, a very detailed plan is worked out for the training cycles of each type of ship. In

of "hardware"—the Chief of Naval Material (U.S.) and Deputy CinC for Shipbuilding and Armaments (Soviet)—are full admirals. Thus, it seems reasonable to equate a Soviet admiral with the U.S. flag officer wearing the same insignia.[15]

Direct comparisons of lower officer ranks are also difficult. For example, the commanding officers of some Soviet warships hold a similar rank to their American counterparts. However, cruisers of the MOSKVA,

[15] In the U.S. Navy the rank of commodore was abolished for peacetime service in 1899. Subsequently, the rank was used only in wartime, although the commander of any grouping of ships up to the rank of captain was accorded the *title* of commodore while in command. The rank of commodore was reinstituted in the U.S. Navy as a peacetime rank in 1981.

[16] Admiral Gorshkov, "Ocean Cruises—School of Combat Training," in Rear Admiral N.I. Shablikov, et. al., *Okean—Manevry Voyenno-Morskogo Flota SSR* [Okean—Maneuvers of the USSR Navy] (Moscow: Military Publishing House, 1970), p. 11.

the first phase the crew engages in both theoretical and practical training in classrooms and simulators ashore, and aboard ships in port.

After review by the ship's squadron or division staffs, the ship moves to the second, at-sea phase of the training cycle. This includes steaming exercises and live firings of all (conventional) weapons. Again, there is an examination at the end of the phase.

The third phase consists of small numbers of ships operating together, carrying out formation steaming and multi-ship exercises. After approval by higher command, the ships move into the fourth phase, in which larger groupings of ships conduct exercises. The duration of the phases and the specific evolutions vary with the type of ship. Also, the phase can be determined by the percentage of new crewmen on board.

After Admiral Gorshkov took command of the Soviet Navy in early 1956, there was an increase in emphasis on at-sea training. By the 1960s Soviet ships and squadrons were ranging farther from their home ports than at any time since the Russo-Japanese War of 1904–1905. Sustained deployments, which were in large part training exercises, began in mid-1964. The average of about five Soviet naval units in the Mediterranean that year increased steadily. For probably the first time since the abortive effort to establish a submarine base in Albania in 1961, a submarine tender in company with several surface warships and submarines entered Mediterranean ports in 1966, visiting Egypt and Algeria. That same year a Soviet destroyer visited Massawa, Ethiopia, beginning regular Soviet naval operations in the Indian Ocean. (In January 1967, Admiral Gorshkov was present for a destroyer's visit to Massawa.)

More formal fleet training and exercises were conducted in Soviet coastal waters and seas. In July 1968 a joint command and staff exercise code-named *Sever*—Russian for "north"—was held in the North Atlantic

The modern Soviet sailor will often travel far and wide as the Navy undertakes sustained, long-range deployments in many ocean areas. But the seas adjacent to the USSR are not ignored, as extensive exercises and port visits are conducted by ships such as the SAM Kotlin Nastochivyy in the Baltic. Here she stands by for official visitors during a call at Copenhagen. (1976)

and in the Baltic, Norwegian, and Barents seas. East German and Polish ships joined with Soviet units in this first major naval exercise of Warsaw Pact nations—the largest Soviet naval exercise to that time. *Sever* included "eastern" and "western" fleets simulating Soviet and NATO naval groups meeting in combat, and also convoy escort, anti-submarine, and amphibious operations, with land-based naval aircraft participating. On 16 July a simulated Western amphibious force, under a Polish naval officer, carried out landings in the Baltic. Polish troops came ashore first, followed by Soviet naval infantry and then East German troops. The following day another amphibious group, under Soviet command, conducted a major landing on the Rybachiy Peninsula in the Barents Sea. Apparently only Soviet troops were brought ashore in this second, larger landing.

Two years after *Sever*, the Soviet Navy alone undertook operation *Okean* (Ocean), the largest naval exercises to be held by any navy since World War II. *Okean '70* was conducted during April and May 1970, with some 200 surface ships and submarines, plus hundreds of land-based aircraft, participating. Exercises were conducted in the Atlantic and Pacific regions including the Barents, Norwegian, Baltic, Mediterranean, and Philippine Seas, and the Sea of Japan. In the main operating areas they followed the same exercise sequence of: (1) deployment of forces, (2) anti-submarine warfare, (3) anti-carrier warfare, and (4) amphibious landing. In the anti-carrier phase, simulated air strikes were flown against Soviet task groups in the Atlantic and Pacific. Executed according to a preplanned schedule, the SNA Badgers struck at the simulated NATO carrier groups in the North Atlantic and North Pacific within a few minutes of each other—a remarkable achievement in planning and execution. Surface missile ships and submarines also simulated attacks against the carrier groups.

Interestingly, there were several Soviet surface ships and submarines in the Indian Ocean during *Okean '70*, including a Kynda-class missile cruiser. However, the Soviets did not consider that area, nor the visit of a Soviet task group to Cuba that immediately followed, part of the exercise. (During the height of *Okean*, two pairs of naval Bear-D reconnaissance aircraft flew from a Northern Fleet base nonstop to Cuba. The first two Bear-Ds conducted reconnaissance of Soviet surface forces in the North Atlantic late on 21 April, the day before the simulated attacks against the Western carrier group.)

*Okean '70* had several purposes. Marshal Grechko, the Minister of Defense, who observed the landings on Rybachiy Peninsula with other Soviet and Warsaw Pact officials, declared: "The *Okean* maneuvers were evidence of the increased naval might of our socialist state, an index of the fact that our Navy has become so great and so strong that it is capable of executing missions in defense of our state interests over the broad expanses of the World Ocean."[17] *Okean* was thus a "report" to the Soviet government and people of the capabilities of the Soviet Navy. It came, along with a large exercise of Soviet Ground Forces, at the end of a five-year defense-economic program.

For the Soviet Navy, the *Okean* exercises were conducted "to test and make further improvements in the combat training level of our naval forces and in staff operational readiness"[18]—the ultimate training exercises.

Finally, coming at the 100th anniversary of Lenin's birth, *Okean* also had a psychological purpose, demonstrating that the Soviet Navy was a full component of the Communist system.

Five years later, in April 1975, there was a similar multi-ocean exercise dubbed *Vesna* by the Soviets and *Okean '75* in the West. Again there was a series of evolutions in the Atlantic and Pacific regions, involving some 200 naval ships and submarines, plus numerous aircraft. Also, major convoy defense exercises were conducted in the Barents Sea and Sea of Japan. These were possibly to evaluate Soviet convoy-defense as well as anti-convoy tactics. Significantly, the cruiser-helicopter ships MOSKVA and LENINGRAD, which had major roles five years earlier, were not at sea during *Okean '75*. Several overseas bases were used in this exercise, with Bear-D reconnaissance aircraft using an airfield in Guinea, Il-38 May ASW aircraft and An-12 Cub recce/ELINT aircraft flying from Somalia, and An-12 Cubs using the airfield at Aden. (Bear-D aircraft also operated over the Indian Ocean, flying from bases in the Soviet Union.)

After *Okean '70* and '75 the Soviet Navy continued annual large-scale exercises, part of the fourth phase of the regular training cycle. The carrier KIEV joined in these exercises for the first time in 1976 as did other new ships. A major *Okean*-style exercise was expected to occur in the spring of 1980, as had taken place at the conclusion of the previous Soviet five-year plans. During the year there were several small exercises, and there was a significant Soviet naval presence in the Indian Ocean as well as in the Mediterranean. But there was no *Okean '80*.

Some of the reasons for this may have been: the great potential danger of a superpower confrontation because of the high state of U.S. military readiness; U.S. operations in the Indian ocean due to the Iranian hostage situation; and the fear of further antagonizing the West after the Soviet invasion of Afghanistan in 1979. However, one senior U.S. intelligence officer has noted that by that time the Soviet Navy had demonstrated its ability to conduct multi-ocean exercises, and that an *Okean* would not be worth the time and expense. More likely, *Okean '80* did not occur for a combination of these reasons.

But the Soviet fleet was not idle. In July 1981 there was a large amphibious exercise in the eastern Mediterranean, a joint Soviet-Syrian exercise in which 1,000 Soviet marines were landed. Also that summer, a combined Soviet-Polish-East German naval maneuver was held in the Baltic, and the massive, all-Soviet *Zapad '81* landing was carried out that fall in the eastern Baltic (see chapter 5/Baltic).

These maneuvers and exercises were particularly significant because of their location and timing. They demonstrated that the combat training of the Soviet Navy had reached the point of being directly related to world events and, in view of the situation in the Middle East and in Poland in 1981, with world crises.

## POLITICAL ACTIVITIES

The military establishment is in many respects the most powerful segment of the Soviet society, with probably more influence on the society

---

[17]Marshal of the Soviet Union A.A. Grechko, "Always be Prepared to Defend the Socialist Fatherland," in Shablikov, et al., p. 7.

[18]Gorshkov, op. cit., p. 12.

than the educational, agricultural, or even industrial sectors. Because of this, the military has always been carefully watched and controlled by the Communist Party. However, during the past few years there is increasing evidence that the party now feels that the military establishment has become fully integrated with respect to ideals and goals. Over 90 percent of all naval officers are believed to be members of the Communist Party or *Komsomol*—probably a higher percentage than in the other armed services. For a naval officer to obtain command or hold other important or sensitive positions, party membership is essential.

*History.* Traditionally the Communist Party has maintained close watch and control over the military establishment. Although sailors were in the forefront of the ill-fated 1906 revolution as well as the Great October Revolution of 1917. But the discontent of the Baltic sailors led to riots, and there followed a long period of distrust of the political reliability of the fleet.

The loyalty of former tsarist officers was also a problem for the new Communist regime. Because of the lack of command experience and technical knowledge among the Bolsheviks, these officers were essential to the military units. The result was the assignment of military commissars (*voyenkomi*) to each ship and unit, to ensure that all orders by commanding officers were politically as well as militarily correct. At each subunit there were political instructors or *politruks* to indoctrinate soldiers and sailors daily in party tenets. (However, some former tsarist officers, especially I.S. Isakov and L.M. Galler, served in the most senior positions of the Soviet Navy.)

In June 1924, the new head of the armed forces, M.V. Frunze, abolished the dual-command system in favor of "unity of command" (*yedino-*

Political indoctrination and education also inundate every level of Soviet society, including the armed forces. Every ship, organization, and base has regular political activities, especially lectures. But there appears to be no conflict between the political and naval officers—all serve the same goals of the Soviet state.

*nachalye*), in which the commanding officer no longer needed to have all orders countersigned by the political officer. This scheme took several years to institute fully. In each unit, however, there was a political assistant to the commander, this assistant being independent from the commander in virtually all respects.

The situation changed again in the late 1930s with Stalin's massive purges of the Soviet political and government leadership, which spread to the military establishment in 1937. Political commissars were reintroduced in June of that year, and "military councils" were established at all command levels, generally consisting of the commander, chief of staff, and political commissar. Decisions were made in the name of the council, with all three (or sometimes more) officers signing such orders—and sharing responsibility for them. In June 1940 as war approached, the concept of unity of command was again introduced, only to be abolished a year later when Germany invaded the Soviet Union and the dual-command system was reinstituted.

By the fall of 1942, when the German armies had been fought to a halt, and Stalin was satisfied with the political reliability of most Soviet officers, he again ordered unity of command. But the October 1942 policy established an assistant commander for political affairs, in essence the system that continues today. These political officers were given military ranks in December 1942. Still, the power of the political officer was, and is, considerable.

In general, there was distrust, if not actual hatred, for the political officers on the part of many "naval" officers. Navy chief Kuznetsov discussed military matters with the chief political officer of the Navy, I.V. Rogov, "cautiously." Rogov was known as "Ivan the Terrible" in the fleet, his nickname a reference to the savage tsar of the sixteenth century who, partially mad, murdered his son. Another view of the Soviet Navy's political officers comes from a discussion of operations in the Baltic during the war:

> It very frequently happened that when a Russian vessel was sunk the survivors, fearing their commissar, refused to be taken on board, and would not give up their resistance until the commissar had been shot. . . . This is how it was, for example, on 14 September 1943 when six survivors were sighted after a [Soviet] PT boat went down in the Baltic Sea. As the German boat approached, the commissar shot two of his people floating in the water, and the other three could not be taken aboard until after the commissar was shot dead.
>
> When [the] large transport *Josef Stalin*, which had around 4,000 men on board, was stranded in the Gulf of Finland, the Russian survivors hanged their commissar.[19]

After the war the concept of one-man control continued, with political officers serving as an assistant or deputy commander at every level of command. The current Soviet policy has been stated in the following words by the head of the Main Political Administration of the Army and Navy:

> One essential condition for the establishment and maintenance of stable order in all units is strict observance of the Leninist principle of

[19]Captain Erwin M. Rau, Federal German Navy, "Russia and the Baltic Sea: 1920–1970," *Naval War College Review*, September 1970, pp. 23–30.

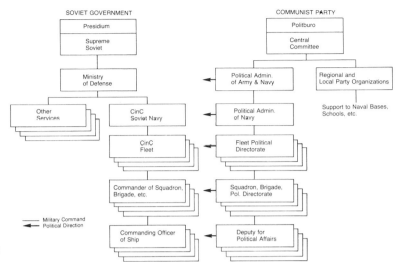

Figure 9–1. Naval Political Organization

one-man command. In the Army and Navy it is more necessary than anywhere else to ensure the strictest unity of action of large masses of people, their subordination to the will of one man. As evidenced by the one-half century of the Soviet Armed Forces, one-man command is the most effective method of troop control, particularly in a combat situation. It ensures really efficient, centralised and reliable direction of operations, achievement of victory in war and the necessary level of fighting efficiency and combat readiness in peacetime.

One-man command plays an especially big role today, when the Army and Navy are armed with nuclear weapons and other up-to-date combat means. . . .[20]

Political activities within the Soviet armed forces are directed by the Main Political Administration (MPA), established in its present form in 1946. The MPA is also a department of the Central Committee of the Communist Party, making it responsible to the Party leadership outside of the military chain of command. Under the MPA, political administrations are established within each service. As indicated in figure 9-1, under the MPA each service has a political directorate. The Chief of the Navy's Political Directorate is a senior flag officer, whose rank is at the level of Deputy CinC of the Navy. (Brezhnev, as a civilian, was head of the Navy's political directorate in the early 1950s.) The Navy directorate supervises political officers assigned to the fleets and specialized branches of the Navy, as well as in all units and ships.

Within each naval command (ashore and afloat) there is a political officer (*zampolit*) who serves as an assistant commander but additionally has his own chain of command up to the Navy's Political Directorate. His duties aboard ship are diverse: he directs the ideological indoctrination of the crew; monitors the political reliability of the officers and enlisted men; ensures that party directives are carried out; enforces discipline; and acts as both "chaplain" and social worker for the crew. Under the direction of the commanding officer, he is responsible for the morale of the crew.

The political officer directs the crew's political education, with regular formal sessions for the enlisted men and meetings for officers on a periodic basis. Beyond these meetings there are continual "agitation and propaganda" activities, as described in a recent Soviet book:

Agitation and propaganda work is designed to instill in the personnel profound conviction in communist ideals, Soviet patriotism, proletarian internationals, uncompromising hatred for the enemies of communism, to strengthen their ideological staunchness and resistance to bourgeois influence in whatever form. An uncompromising struggle is being daily waged against hostile ideology and the aggressive essence and schemes of imperialism are unmasked.

The basic methods of agitation and propaganda work conducted in the Soviet Navy include:
—printed agitation and propaganda through books, pamphlets, leaflets, magazines and newspapers;
—oral agitation and propaganda through lectures, periodic reports, talks and consultations;
—poster agitation.[21]

Thus, the *zampolit* has a direct and integrated role in the operations and life of a ship. If a ship or unit performs well, the political officer will share credit with the commanding officer and his other assistants; if it does poorly, the political officer as well as the commanding officer will suffer. Also, according to a U.S. Navy evaluation, "In recent years . . . there has been a trend toward giving the political officer practical naval experience as a line officer prior to his entry into the political field."

The overlap of the naval and political areas reflects the current high degree of confidence of the Communist Party leaders in the reliability and loyalty of the armed forces. This is to be expected after more than 60 years of Communist rule and achievements. The last significant challenge to Party control over the military came in the early 1950s when Marshal Zhukov attempted to limit the influence of political officers over military decision making. However, since the unsettled period that followed Stalin's death (in 1953) and the resulting "revolution" in military affairs, the political-military situation has settled down, and the political officers are in most cases considered a part of the service "team." This

[20]General of the Army A.A. Yepishev, *Some Aspects of Party-Political Work in the Soviet Armed Forces* (Moscow: Progress Publishers, 1975), pp. 197–98.

[21]Admiral V.M. Grishanov, ed., *Man and Sea Warfare* (Moscow: Progress Publishers, 1978), p. 30.

has resulted in significant "cross-fertilization" between the line and political officers, with some political officers eventually being given ship commands.

Despite this integration of the *zampolit* into the "regular navy," the political officer retains his separate and direct line of communication to his political superiors up to the MPA and the party leadership.

Navy political officers are trained at the Kiev Higher Naval Political School, one of several similar schools set up in 1967 for the different services. The four-year curriculum at the Kiev school stresses the political aspects of the armed forces, with emphasis on agitation and education in the fleet. Some naval line training is provided, but the newly commissioned political officers clearly do not have the same level of training as do graduates of the ten other Higher Naval Schools. After service in the fleet and ashore, senior political officers receive graduate-level instruction at the Lenin Military Political Academy in Moscow.

The relationship between the professional naval officer and the party's other means of controlling the military—the Committee for State Security or KGB—is less than cordial. The KGB, as noted in chapter 4, includes the Border Troops whose maritime units are responsible for the security of the Soviet Union's long coastline. There are other special KGB troops that may deal with the Navy, such as the communications security units that operate and protect radio and teletype links for the Soviet leadership.

The KGB is charged with counterespionage against internal and foreign enemies. Most of the public knowledge of KGB activities within the armed forces comes from Soviet defectors, and they have been almost exclusively associated with the Ground Forces. Reportedly, the Third Directorate of the KGB is responsible for counterintelligence within the armed forces, and there are officers from this directorate assigned to all branches of the armed forces. They generally wear standard military uniforms, but are readily known as KGB officers and report only through the KGB chain of command. Within the Navy, uniformed KGB officers are assigned to large surface ships. Covert KGB officers are assigned throughout the Navy and operate a network of "informers."

Within the units (or ships) the KGB officers recruit men to report directly to them. According to one KGB defector, a former captain assigned to a motorized rifle regiment in East Germany, he was instructed that "When recruiting informers, you must not only convince them but also compel them to work for us. The KGB has enough power for that."[22] And,

> The KGB had the rights and the power needed. If it was an officer [wanted as an informer], then his career could be threatened (without KGB approval no officer can be sent to a military academy or get promotion). With regular [enlisted] servicemen it was even simpler; they could just be dismissed from the army. Any Soviet citizen's life, too, could be threatened; he could be barred from an institute or from work in any undertaking, or be forbidden to travel abroad.[23]

While the political officers can be considered as part of the Navy and contributing to the performance of ships and units, the KGB officers can only be regarded with distrust and resentment.

Despite the unity of the Communist Party and the armed forces in their goals, there is still some political unrest. Indeed, there is some evidence of this throughout the Soviet Union, mostly related to the privileges of party leaders at all levels and to the nation's continued economic problems. On rare occasions this political unrest surfaces. Probably the most dramatic example of the post-Stalin period occurred at the Baltic port of Riga on the night of 7–8 November 1975, as members of the crew of the Krivak-class frigate STOROZHEVOY mutinied. The poor morale of the crew had been cited in the Soviet press, for which the ship's political officer had been criticized.

During the night the political officer, named Captain 3rd Rank V.M. Sablin, and several crew members locked most of the other officers in their spaces and got the ship under way. Shortly after the ship successfully escaped from Riga, heading for the Swedish island of Gotland some 200 miles (320 km) to the west, the alarm was given, possibly by one of the officers escaping from his cabin and reaching the radio room.

Aircraft were dispatched to locate the ship, and nine warships in Riga weighed anchor to join the hunt. It was reported that Admiral Gorshkov himself ordered the ship sunk rather than allow her to reach Swedish waters. The STOROZHEVOY was found and after ignoring signals from reconnaissance aircraft, the bombers were dispatched. According to French reports, the planes actually attacked the ship, inflicting damage and killing and wounding about 50 crewmen before the mutineers surrendered. Other reports say the ship received only superficial damage with no casualties.

Regardless, the STOROZHEVOY was recaptured. The ringleaders of the mutiny are believed to have been executed or imprisoned. After a conspicuous cruise in the Baltic just outside of Swedish territorial waters, as if to demonstrate the loyalty of the crew, the ship is reported to have been transferred to the Pacific Fleet.

No other overt instances of unrest in the Soviet Navy in the recent past are known. Indeed, among the Navy's officers, who are increasingly part of the elite of the Soviet Union, the opposite attitude appears to be true. A postscript to the STOROZHEVOY mutiny comes from a Swedish military officer:

> Those who think this shows weakness are a little stupid. There is not a point of weakness. This demonstrates a will and a skill in making decisions. It shows the Russians are strong enough to do what is necessary.[24]

## PAY AND BENEFITS

There are two basic types of compensation paid to Soviet naval personnel: minimal pay to conscripts and a relatively high pay to career servicemen, most of whom are warrant officers and commissioned officers.

The lowest ranking conscript, the seaman or *matros*, receives 3 rubles 80 kopecks per month[25] while a senior seaman, depending upon his assignment, receives between 5 rubles 20 kopecks and 6 rubles 80 kopecks per month basic allowance. An additional supplement is paid for specialist qualification, 1 ruble for third class, 2 rubles 50 kopecks for

---

[22]Aleksei Myagkov, *Inside the KGB* (New York: Ballantine Books, 1981), p. 82.
[23] Ibid.

[24]Bernard D. Nossiter, "Soviet Mutiny Ended Swiftly," *The Washington Post*, 7 June, 1976, p. 18.
[25]The official exchange rate is approximately 1 ruble = $1.40.

Low pay and severe restrictions on free-time activities for Soviet enlisted men lead to the encouragement of musical and other do-it-yourself recreation. These sailors have organized a jazz band to play American jazz—highly popular in the USSR—as well as Russian music. (Soviet Navy)

second class, and 5 rubles if the sailor qualifies as a specialist first class. Petty officers and some senior seamen earn 10 to 20 rubles per month plus specialist pay if they are in certain specified billets. In addition, an extra three rubles per month are paid for sea duty during a sailor's first two years of service, and six rubles per month in the third year—as apparent compensation for serving longer than men in other services. Thus, a conscript who becomes head of a subunit could earn as much as 30 rubles per month during his last year of service, still much less than the average Soviet worker in industry. Further, the additional money does not appear to compensate for the added responsibility and work of being the head of a subunit.

Sailors are provided with food, minimal clothing, and limited medical care. Free recreation and cultural activities are provided, often interrelated and stressing political themes. Specific recreation activities stressed in the Navy include choir singing, do-it-yourself hobbies such as painting and handicrafts, and amateur acting. Discussions and reading are encouraged, with ship and station libraries stocked especially with books "dealing with political subjects, books on military history, the memoirs by outstanding military leaders, literature on the navies and armies of capitalist countries as well as books of fiction are all popular with Soviet navymen. While at sea during a prolonged cruise the men particularly appreciate magazines, satirical and comic publications."[26]

The sailor who is promoted to warrant rank can earn some 200 to 240 rubles per month, well above the average Soviet worker's income.

Pay for commissioned officers is relatively high and a major incentive for a naval career. Officer pay is based on position, rank, length of service, and proficiency, with substantial supplements for sea duty, sub-

[26]Admiral Grishanov, op. cit., p. 174.

marine duty, assignment to remote areas (Northern and Pacific Fleet regions), and education. The most significant component of this pay package is position pay. There is also longevity pay, an increase for every five years of service. This amount is based on rank and position pay, with service in remote areas counting more than service in other areas.

A junior lieutenant beginning service earns approximately 140 to 160 rubles per month, the equivalent of the average Soviet wage. After about five years of service his earnings, as senior lieutenant, could be 115 rubles for his assignment, 80 rubles for rank, 45 rubles for sea duty, and 210 rubles—tax free—for assignment to the Northern Fleet area, a total of 450 rubles per month. Despite having to pay significant taxes and (if a member) dues to the Communist Party, his pay would be significant by Soviet standards, the equivalent to the manager of a factory with more than 6,000 employees. Captains and flag officers earn from 500 to 2,000 rubles per month and, as noted below, have considerable nonmonetary benefits, as befits the elite of a society.

Soviet sailors who are able to make foreign port visits in the West are often impressed by the quality and variety of goods available, as well as by their relatively high prices. But they are told that the cost in the West for such goods includes a high crime rate, high unemployment, and exploitation of workers, especially minorities. (1975, U.S. Navy)

While regulations prescribe housing standards for servicemen, in some cases they are known to be substandard, especially for conscripts. (However, the same situation exists in the U.S. armed forces.) The daily food ration in the Soviet Navy is stipulated at providing 3,000 to 4,000 calories, with the highest allocation going to nuclear submarine crews. There are reportedly 40 special diets for Soviet servicemen, especially developed for men in the arctic and tropical climates (aboard ship or ashore), aviators, submariners, etc. The quality is reported to vary widely, with limited variety and some shortages reported. In part as a supplement, military cafes, post exchanges, and mobile stores at many bases provide "luxury" food items such as fresh fruit and vegetables in addition to staples.

These benefits are supplemented by certain social services in the Soviet Union. A childless wife of a sailor or warrant officer is exempt from paying the income tax levied on other childless workers. If there are children they are provided with day care or kindergarten places, a benefit worth about 400 rubles per year. Special efforts are made to find housing and work for wives, and to help integrate them in new surroundings as the Navy seeks to move families to base areas or home ports if the sailor is assigned to a ship. And when the conscript leaves the Navy, efforts are made to ensure that he is employed.

Still, embezzlement, poor quality, poor service, and poor management reduce the value of many of the benefits and services intended for conscripts. But because the Soviet armed forces have a high priority in the Soviet society, major efforts are under way to remedy these problems. Nevertheless, these problems reflect the overall conditions of the Soviet state.

The situation with respect to nonmonetary benefits is much better for officers. The housing, goods, and services are of relatively high quality. Senior officers, like officials of the Communist Party and important foreigners, have the use of special shops to purchase otherwise unavailable foods and goods, including imported products. Soviet naval officers are normally given 30 days of paid leave per year; senior officers and those who are assigned to remote areas or perform arduous duty receive 45 days per year. Special arrangements facilitate their travel, and recreation and vacation centers are available for them, including villas for senior officers on the Black Sea coast, the Soviet riviera. As one young Russian woman is said to have told an American officer, "A Soviet officer is a hell of a catch."[27]

[27]Colonel Donald L. Clark, USAF (Ret.), "Who Are Those Guys?" *Air University Review*, May–June 1979, pp. 47–65.

Helicopter crewmen race across the flight deck of the Minsk as the aircraft carrier rides at anchor at a Far Eastern port. There are major personnel problems within the Sovied armed forces, but for a number of reasons the quality of Soviet naval personnel appears high. (Sovfoto)

# 10

# Fleet Development

The massive fleet building program initiated by Stalin after World War II was intended to provide a fleet to secure the seas adjacent to the USSR, to prevent an amphibious assault against Soviet territory, and to support possible moves by the Red Army into bordering states.

As soon as the major shipyards could resume work, the unfinished hulls of the prewar and wartime programs were rushed to completion. These were principally the light cruisers of the CHAPAYEV class and various destroyers, submarines, and lesser craft. The unfinished hulls of the battleships and battle cruisers laid down in 1938–1940 were scrapped. (See chapter 28.)

Simultaneous with the rejuvenation of the shipyards, the various ship design bureaus were rehabilitated, and plans were prepared for a new generation of Soviet warships. These would become the first phase of the postwar development of the Soviet fleet.

## PHASE I: STALIN PERIOD

These postwar ships would be based largely on existing designs, with some updating from captured German drawings, equipment, and ships, plus assistance from former German technicians brought to the Soviet Union. By the late 1940s the keels for the first of these new designs were being laid down. Professor Michael MccGwire, a former British intelligence officer, has calculated that under Stalin's direction a 20-year shipbuilding plan was developed. Although the credible data are limited, MccGwire has postulated the number of ships that were to have been completed by about 1967. His estimates and data from other sources are shown in table 10-1.

Stalin's program would have produced a massive, albeit highly conventional, fleet. The Soviets began building the only postwar capital ships to be started by any nation—the STALINGRAD class. The lead ship of some 35,000 to 37,000 tons (standard) displacement was laid down at Nikolayev on the Black Sea in early 1949. Two years later, when Admiral Kuznetsov was reappointed to head the Navy in July 1951, he told the fleet's senior officers that the future of the Navy was bright and that in the near future the construction of aircraft carriers would begin.

But of particular concern to NATO military planners in the immediate postwar period was the specter of some 1,200 Soviet submarines that could be operational by the late 1970s. The medium-range Whiskey had been designed before the war ended, but the design was modified to take

**TABLE 10–1.  POSTULATED SHIPBUILDING PLAN, 1946–1967**

| Type | Class | Lead Ship Completion | Total Planned | Actually Built |
|---|---|---|---|---|
| Aircraft Carriers | (new design) | 1956? | 4+ | — |
| Battle Cruisers | STALINGRAD | 1955? | 4+ | — |
| Light Cruisers | CHAPAYEV | 1949 | 5 | 5 |
| Light Cruisers | SVERDLOV | 1952 | 24 | 14 |
| Cruisers | (new design) | 1958 | 16 | — |
| Destroyers | SKORYY | 1950 | 80 | 72 |
| Destroyers | Tallinn | 1955 | 12 | 1 |
| Destroyers | Kotlin | 1955 | 36 | 39* |
| Destroyers | (new design) | 1958 | 80+ | — |
| Submarines | Whiskey | 1952 | 336 | 231 |
| Submarines | Zulu | 1952 | 36 | 26 |
| Submarines | Quebec | 1955 | 96+ | 30 |
| Submarines | (new designs) | 1958 | 720+ | — |

*Includes 12 ships completed with SS-N-1 missile (Kildin and Krupnyy classes).

advantage of some German wartime developments. The ocean-going Zulu demonstrated more German influence, several features being adopted from the highly advanced Type XXI U-boat. The Zulu's successor, the Foxtrot (operational from 1958) was even further developed, and became widely used by the Soviet Navy, as well as by several Third World navies, during the 1960s and 1970s.

The follow-on medium-range Soviet submarine, the Romeo (operational from 1958) also incorporated German technology, while the smaller Quebec, a coastal submarine, would have a closed-cycle power plant to permit use of diesel engines underwater to charge batteries without the need to raise a snorkel breathing tube. This system also had German origins.[1]

In the event, Stalin's death in March 1953 brought this ambitious program to almost a complete halt. Within days stop-work orders were sent out to some yards, and several major revisions were made in the shipbuilding program during the 1953–1955 period. Five of the CHAPAYEV-class cruisers, which had been started before the war, were

[1] After World War II the U.S. and Royal Navies experimented with closed-cycle diesel plants based on the German Walther concept. The British built two experimental submarines with this propulsion system, HMS EXPLORER and HMS EXCALIBUR. The only U.S. craft built with such a system was the midget submarine X-1.

The recent Soviet emphasis on surface combatants in the Soviet Union resulted in four cruiser-destroyer classes being under construction simultaneously. The latest design to emerge is the Krasina (formerly designated Black-Com-1). The cruiser is intended primarily for the anti-ship role with a battery of 16 SS-N-12 Shaddock-type missile tubes forward and facilities for a targeting helicopter aft. In comparison, in the early 1980s the U.S. Navy had only one cruiser-destroyer class under construction, the TICONDEROGA (CG 47) class, fitted with the Aegis air-defense system. (Siegfried Breyer)

The development of the Soviet fleet during the past two decades has emphasized advanced surface warships and, more lately, aircraft carriers as well as naval aircraft. But submarine development has not been ignored. The single Papa SSGN—illustrated here—was the prototype for the new, highly capable Oscar-class submarines.

completed. Only 14 of the planned 24 light cruisers of the SVERDLOV class were finished, as were only relatively few of the planned destroyers and submarines. The battle cruiser STALINGRAD was about 60 percent complete in 1953; the ship was launched and expended in missile tests. Neither the second battle cruiser, believed to have been named MOSKVA or IZMAIL, was laid down, nor were any of the aircraft carriers.

But of great significance for the future Soviet fleet, Stalin's ambitious program did provide the industrial and design base for building a large navy.

## PHASE II: KHRUSHCHEV PERIOD[2]

Khrushchev and his colleagues who inherited the mantle of Stalin moved rapidly to cut back the naval rebuilding effort. There was little opposition to the reductions. Early in his tenure as Party Secretary and hence head of the ruling Politburo, Khrushchev reassigned several of the recently rebuilt and new shipyards to the construction of merchant ships.

[2]See "The Navy" in Nikita Khrushchev, *Khrushchev Remembers—The Last Testament*, (Boston: Little, Brown & Co.) pp. 19–34.

Several Whiskey-class submarines of the Stalin period remain in Soviet service. Although obsolescent, they are useful for training and regional operations, and apparently are still employed in reconnaissance activities, as was the boat that grounded near a sensitive Swedish naval base in November 1981. Soviet submarines stopped wearing pendant numbers in the late 1960s.

He then urged the Navy to seek more innovative weapons in place of large surface warships—low-cost, high-firepower ships that could counter Western naval forces. Khrushchev would later write quite candidly how he would have liked to build large ships: "I'll admit I felt a nagging desire to have some [aircraft carriers] in our own navy, but we couldn't afford to build them. They were simply beyond our means. Besides, with a strong submarine force, we felt able to sink the American carriers if it came to war. In other words, submarines represented an effective defensive capability as well as reliable means of launching a missile counter attack."[3]

Admiral Kuznetsov, the Commander in Chief, continued to demand the construction of a large, conventional surface fleet and argued against Khrushchev. Finally, Kuznetsov was fired; Admiral Gorshkov officially succeeded him as CinC in January 1956.

Khrushchev directed Gorshkov to scrap the battleships and cruisers and to build a fleet of smaller, missile-armed ships and submarines that could defend the USSR against Western naval-amphibious attacks. Of particular concern to the Soviet leadership were the American aircraft carriers, which could launch nuclear-armed strike aircraft against the USSR.

This period of Soviet naval development is described as a "revolution" in military affairs. Within the next few years Gorshkov disposed of the outdated battleships and older cruisers and initiated or accelerated the advanced weapon programs. Soviet shipyards produced swarms of the Komar and then Osa missile boats, armed with the short-range SS-N-2 Styx missile, and several destroyers were completed with the 100-n.mile (185-km) SS-N-1 Scrubber/Strela anti-ship missile.

The more-capable SS-N-3 Shaddock missile, originally developed for strategic attack from submarines, went to sea in the Kynda-class missile cruisers. Called rocket cruisers (*raketnyy kreysers*) by the Soviets, these ships demonstrated the progress made by Admiral Gorshkov in "selling" new surface ships to the Soviet leadership. Preparations were also put forward for building a still-larger Shaddock missile cruiser.

During this phase of fleet development the Soviet Navy also put to sea a strategic strike force. Diesel-electric submarines were first armed with nuclear torpedoes to strike American coastal cities. More significant, and more practical, the Soviets, again building on German technology, developed both guided (cruise) and ballistic missiles for launching from submarines against land targets. The SS-N-3 Shaddock cruise missile was surface launched, with a land-attack range of more than 400 n.miles (735 km) carrying a nuclear warhead.

Initially, Whiskey-class submarines were converted to fire the Shaddock, first the single-cylinder type, then the twin cylinder type, and finally the "long-bin" design, which had four tubes fitted in an enlarged conning tower. Reportedly, 72 of the Whiskey long-bin conversions were planned (only seven were actually completed as were six of the earlier conversions). Subsequently, new-construction Shaddock submarines were begun—the Juliett diesel (SSG) and Echo I/II nuclear (SSGN) classes.

Almost simultaneously the Soviets developed submarine-launched ballistic missiles, the first to enter service being the SS-N-4 Sark, a surface-launched weapon with a range of some 300 n.miles (645 km). Several Zulu-class diesel submarines were converted to carry two of these missiles, followed by the new-construction Golf diesel (SSB) and Hotel nuclear (SSBN) classes.

Thus, for both categories of weapons the Soviets simultaneously built both diesel and nuclear submarines. Further, the SSGN and SSBN designs were developed at the same time as the first Soviet nuclear

[3]Ibid., p. 31.

submarine design, the torpedo-armed November class.[4] This large and multiple-design nuclear submarine program demonstrated (1) early Soviet belief in the effectiveness of nuclear submarines, (2) the decision to put large numbers of missile-armed submarines to sea as rapidly as possible, (3) the desire to use all available building capacity, and (4) possibly the limited availability of nuclear reactor plants. The size of the Soviet nuclear submarine program can also be seen when by 1970 the USSR surpassed the United States in numbers of nuclear submarines built, shortly after the completion of the massive U.S. Polaris SSBN construction program. Although the capability of the Sark missile in the Soviet SSB/SSBNs was severely limited, especially when compared to the U.S. Polaris that would follow shortly, the Soviet Navy did deploy a Submarine-Launched Ballistic Missile (SLBM) before the United States.

This strategic submarine effort of the Soviet Navy was stopped short of its apparent goals. The establishment of the Strategic Rocket Forces (SRF) as a separate service in late 1959 caused a cutback in, or possibly even termination of, the SSB/SSBN programs. Only eight Hotel SSBNs were completed along with 23 of the Golf SSBs, and plans for more advanced ballistic missile submarines were shelved.[5] The Shaddock-armed submarines were shifted to the anti-carrier role.

Under both tsars and commissars Russia had demonstrated a major interest in submarines. While the Soviets failed in this period to build the 1,200 submarines reportedly planned under Stalin, a large number of undersea craft were produced. The medium-range Whiskey-class diesel boats were mass-produced at four yards, and when the last was completed in 1957, an estimated 231 had been built. In one year alone 90 had been launched, an ominous indication of Soviet industrial capacity just a decade after World War II had ended.

While the Whiskey program was under way, the larger Zulu diesel attack boat and the Quebec coastal submarine were being built, albeit in smaller numbers. The Quebec's closed-cycle plant was not successful, with several accidents occurring. The submarines were modified to operate as conventional diesel-electric craft, and served into the 1970s. Counting some older boats of wartime design, this massive submarine effort provided a peak force of some 475 submarines in 1958, after which there was a decline as the older craft were retired at a faster rate than new construction.

There was one other significant submarine development initiated in this period—the Alfa SSN. This advanced-technology undersea craft was begun in the late 1950s, even before the first Soviet nuclear submarine had gone to sea. There are three possible explanations for the development of the Alfa. First, the Alfa may have been intended as a high-speed "interceptor," to dart out from base upon warning of an enemy warship approaching the coast. Another explanation may be found in the American press of the time, which estimated (incorrectly) that the U.S. submarine SKIPJACK (SSN 585), launched in 1958, had a top speed of 45 knots. Finally, the Alfa may be the result of a Soviet multi-

[4]A recent, more detailed discussion of Soviet nuclear submarine development is found in N. Polmar, "Soviet Nuclear Submarines," Naval Institute *Proceedings*, July 1981, pp. 31–39.
[5]Components for an additional Golf SSB were transferred to Communist China and assembled there.

Khrushchev sought to employ cheap substitutes for large warships, among them small missile craft. He thus encouraged the development of weapons like the Styx that could be employed from inexpensive platforms. These two well-publicized photos show a Styx being lowered into a launch tube and an Osa I firing one of her four anti-ship missiles.

Khrushchev—probably spurred on by Admiral Gorshkov—accepted the need for extending the range of Soviet sea defenses, and by the late 1950s construction began of the Kynda-class ships, armed with Shaddock anti-ship missiles. The eight large missile tubes, although in many respects awkward, provided more protection and some advantages over the U.S. Navy's scheme for handling the similar Regulus missile.

(1962, U.S. Navy)

(1962, Soviet Navy)

The Soviet emphasis on submarines dates from the tsarist era, and innovative designs have continued to emerge from the nation's shipyards. The Golf SSB was the world's first ballistic missile submarine, while the first November SSN was completed in 1958, a surprisingly short time after the USS NAUTILUS (SSN 571), the world's first nuclear ship. The lower photo shows the November-class submarine LENINSKIY KOMSOMOLETS at the North Pole in 1962.

track approach to the development of nuclear propulsion. If this theory is correct, one development effort produced the pressurized-water reactor used in the Hotel, Echo, and November (HEN) classes, while a separate program led to the liquid-metal reactor of the Alfa.[6]

**PHASE III: REACTING TO U.S. THREATS**

Khrushchev's plan to reduce the size of the Soviet Union's conventional armed forces in favor of a limited nuclear striking force (operated by SRF) and to "fight" the West in the Third World, fell apart when John F. Kennedy became president of the United States in January 1961. Kennedy, elected in a campaign that publicized a "missile gap" because of the Soviet Sputnik and missile test successes, began a buildup of U.S. strategic and conventional military forces. He accelerated the development of the Polaris SLBM and Minuteman ICBM, increased the number of naval ships in commission, and built up forces to fight Soviet-sponsored insurgents in the Third World—most notably the Army's Special Forces.

The U.S. strategic buildup was most dramatic, as the Polaris and Minuteman programs were given the highest priorities. This situation created consternation in the Kremlin and led to major reconsiderations of defense planning. The recently decided Soviet defense policies emphasizing ICBMs were found wanting, as was Soviet missile development, which was encountering technical problems. Several revisions in defense planning were initiated, and in a move to overcome shortfalls in the ICBM program, Khrushchev ordered medium-range missiles and nuclear-capable strike aircraft to be secretly based in Cuba. The ensuing Cuban missile crisis of October 1962 demonstrated that (1) the United

[6]A similar two-track effort had been undertaken in the United States, with the liquid-metal project being cancelled after technical problems, although the project offered the promise of higher reactor power. This plant, using liquid sodium as the heat-exchange medium, went to sea from 1957–1958 in the USS SEAWOLF (SSN 575).

States was willing to use conventional military force against the Soviets in the Western Hemisphere, (2) the U.S. strategic offensive weapons could overwhelm those of the USSR, and (3) the Soviet Navy was unable to support an overseas adventure.

Even while the Soviet missiles and bombers were still being withdrawn from Cuba, Deputy Foreign Minister V.V. Kuznetsov told an American official, "we will live up to this agreement, but we will never be caught like that again." Soviet military programs were accelerated, long-range plans were revised, and in March 1963 there was a top-level realignment of the country's economic management—just three months after a long-planned reorganization had occurred. A new Supreme Economic Council was set up, headed by Dmitri Ustinov, long-time head of armament production (see chapter 4/Ministry of Defense). This appointment gave military planning clear priority in the national economy after Khrushchev's earlier attempts at a more-balanced approach. Within the defense establishment, in the aftermath of Cuba a new chief of the Soviet General Staff was named in early 1963 and there were indications that Khrushchev, age 71, might soon retire. (He did so in October 1964.)

The events of 1961–1963 had considerable effect on the Soviet Navy. The significance of the Navy within the armed forces was enhanced, for naval forces could help to counter the U.S. Navy's Polaris submarines, could help to redress the "missile gap" that existed in favor of the United States, and might make future incursions into the Third World more successful.

As new naval programs were put in hand, during 1962–1964 Admiral Gorshkov changed his senior deputies, the men who would direct the

Although SSBNs were initiated in the Khrushchev regime, the Soviet Union achieved superiority over the West in the number of strategic missile submarines as well as SLBMs under Brezhnev. The Yankee was the first modern Soviet SSBN, with series production almost reaching the U.S. Polaris building rate of the 1960s—but without the cutback in other submarine types as occurred in the United States. This Yankee has a hatch open revealing the retractable Cod Eye-B celestial sight.

third phase of postwar Soviet naval development. V.A. Kasatonov became first deputy CinC of the Navy (he had earlier succeeded Gorshkov in command of the Black Sea Fleet); N.D. Sergeyev became Chief of the Main Naval Staff; V.M. Grishanov became head of the Navy's political administration; and I.I. Borzov became commander of Soviet Naval Aviation. And in 1965, P.G. Kotov became the deputy CinC for shipbuilding and armaments. Both Borzov and Kotov moved up from the first deputy position of their respective offices; thus, they had already worked closely with Gorshkov in formulating future fleet development.

With respect to actual programs, the construction of Kynda-class missile cruisers was halted first after only four units were built; plans for a larger Shaddock-armed ship for the anti-carrier role were abandoned. The anti-carrier effort would be left mainly to missile-armed aircraft and cruise missile submarines. The Kyndas were replaced on the building ways at the Zhdanov shipyard in Leningrad by the interim Kresta I class, which mounted only half of the Kynda's missile battery. However, the Kresta I had improved anti-aircraft and helicopter capabilities. After only four of these ships were built, the matured Kresta II design appeared.

The Kresta II is an anti-submarine ship, with long-range ASW missiles (SS-N-14) replacing the Shaddock anti-ship missiles. At the same time, the Nikolayev south yard in the Black Sea area was producing the Moskva-class hermaphrodite missile cruiser-ASW helicopter carriers. These ships, the first true aviation ships to be built in the USSR, were intended to counter the U.S. Polaris submarines in regional seas adjacent to the Soviet Union.

The Moskva was completed in 1967 and her sister ship Leningrad was finished the following year. But they were incapable of coping with the Polaris submarines, for by that time the U.S. Navy had 41 strategic missile submarines, at least half of which were always at sea. Also, the Polaris A-3 missile, which became operational in 1964, had a range of 2,500 n.miles (4,600 km), reducing the potential effectiveness of the Moskva with her short-range ASW helicopters.

The Kresta II and subsequent Kara ASW ships could effectively serve as command ships for ASW forces seeking to protect Soviet submarines from Western anti-submarine forces, especially U.S. nuclear attack submarines. The pro-submarine mission seems to have been the rationale for several major Soviet programs of this period.

And the Soviets continued to produce large numbers of submarines. The production of earlier types—nuclear and diesel—was continued. Three new, major classes of nuclear submarines were begun in the early 1960s, the second generation of such craft. The Echo I/II cruise missile submarines, which launched their Shaddock missiles from the surface, were followed into service by the more-advanced Charlie-class SSGN. The Charlie is armed with eight, short-range (30 n.mile/55 km) cruise missiles, but these can be fired while the submarine remains completely submerged.

The same reactor plant used in the Charlie also propels the Victor torpedo-attack submarine (SSN). The Victor is believed to have been developed specifically for the anti-submarine role, as have essentially all U.S. Navy SSNs. With a maximum speed in excess of 30 knots, the Victor was the world's fastest operational submarine when it entered service in 1967.

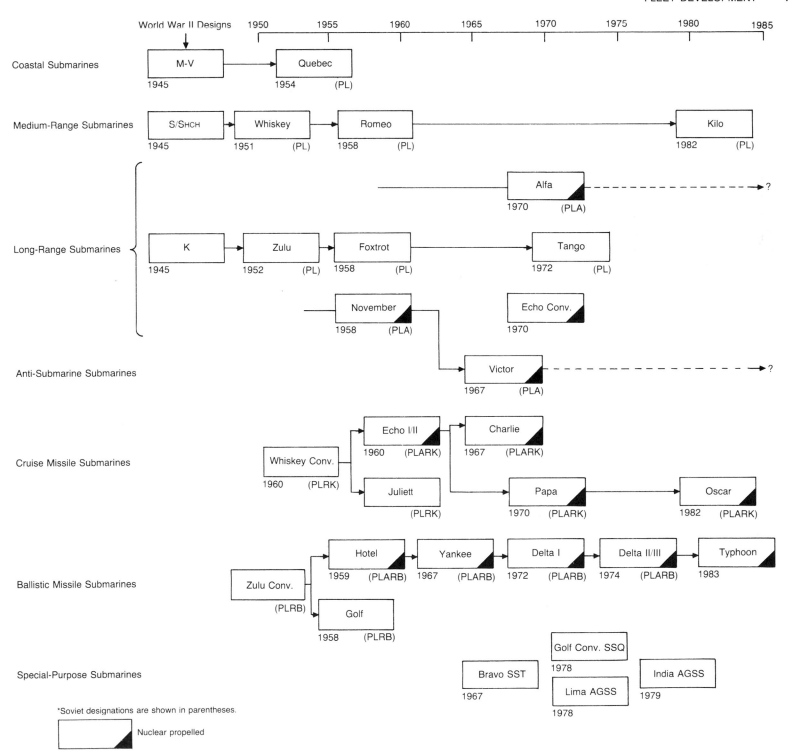

Figure 10–1*. Submarine Development

A third submarine employing the same reactor plant is the Yankee strategic missile submarine. As noted above, Soviet SSBN development slowed or was possibly halted completely with the 1959 defense decisions. However, with the U.S. strategic buildup, the Cuban fiasco, and problems in ICBM development, the Soviet SSBN program was given new life. The immediate result was a new submarine design closely resembling the U.S. Polaris submarines, which NATO gave the confusing code name Yankee. Armed with 16 missiles in two rows of internal tubes abaft the sail structure, the Yankee design shows evidence of having been hastily completed and ordered into construction with the highest priorities. Production was undertaken at two yards, Severodvinsk in the Arctic and Komsomol´sk in the Far East.

The first Yankee SSBN was completed in 1967, the year the 41st and last U.S. Polaris submarine was completed. Yankee production reached a peak of ten units in 1970, after which it slowed as the yards prepared for the follow-on Delta SSBN. The later submarines, which began to enter service in 1972, were the world's largest submarines built up to that time.

More significant than its size, the Delta SSBN carried a very long range missile, initially the SS-N-8 with a range of more than 4,000 n.miles (7,360km). This meant that Delta submarines could remain in Soviet coastal waters in the Barents Sea and Sea of Okhotsk while targeting virtually the entire United States. This capability would invalidate Western ASW concepts, which called for intercepting Soviet SSBNs (as well as attack submarines) as they transited from their base or patrol areas to missile-launching positions.

Additional torpedo-attack and cruise missile submarine classes were laid down during the early 1960s, continuing the Soviet policy of not only large numbers of submarines, but also the development of multiple classes. The Papa of this period is a one-of-a-kind cruise missile submarine, larger and faster than the Charlie SSGN. And at this time construction began on the first Alfa SSN.

Diesel submarine construction continued in Soviet yards. The U.S. Navy abandoned the construction of diesel combat submarines in the late 1950s. The Soviets apparently believed that diesel submarines could undertake some missions as effectively or more so than nuclear submarines. It is also possible that Soviet industry simply could not produce the number of reactor plants needed for an all-nuclear undersea force.

The long-range Whiskey and Romeo diesel submarines have been followed by the further improved Tango-class SS (operational in 1972), which continues in production. The medium-range Whiskey and Romeo diesel submarines have been followed by the Kilo-class SS, the first of which probably entered service in 1982. Also built in this period were the four Bravo-class submarines, which are specialized target-training craft (SST). These serve to both train submarine personnel and serve as targets for ASW forces, while having some combat capability.

Thus, the Soviet Navy continued to put its emphasis on submarines, although production slowed in the late 1950s as the nuclear programs were instituted, and again in the late 1960s as the shipyards geared up to again produce new classes. Only seven submarines were completed in 1971: five Yankee SSBNs, one Charlie SSGN, and one Victor SSN. This was the smallest number of submarines built in any year since 1945. (In 1970 an estimated 19 submarines were completed, all but one nuclear powered.)

During this third phase of postwar Soviet naval development the Naval Infantry ("marines") were reactivated (see chapter 7). Construction was begun of specialized ships to carry and land these troops—the Polnocny LSMs at the shipyard of that name in Gdansk, Poland, and the Alligator LST at Kaliningrad.

Finally, sustained deployments were beginning in the Mediterranean and Indian Oceans, and the periodic visits of warships to the Gulf of Mexico–Caribbean area and to African ports created new requirements for at-sea replenishment ships. Previously, almost all fuel and supplies transferred to Soviet warships on the high seas came from merchant ships. However, starting with the fuel munitions ship BORIS CHILIKIN (completed in 1971) the Soviets have increasingly used specialized Underway Replenishment (UNREP) ships, an often overlooked but vital component of fleet development. The six CHILIKIN-class ships were followed by the single large BEREZENIA, comparable in many respects to the U.S. Navy's most advanced AOE/AOR ships. These ships, along with the large number of other support and replenishment ships constructed in the postwar era, have enhanced the efficiency and range of operations of the Soviet fleet.

## PHASE IV: TODAY

In 1970, after observing a major Soviet military exercise, Party Chairman L.I. Brezhnev declared, "No question of any importance in the world can be solved without our participation, without taking into account our economic and military might." Whereas Stalin had avoided involvement in the Third World, and Khrushchev's "adventurism" had too often failed,

The MINSK, being watched here by the crew of a U.S. cruiser in the East China Sea, and her sister carriers of the KIEV class represent a major commitment by the Soviet government to naval construction. The KIEVs are significantly larger and more complex than any previous Soviet naval ships, requiring a significant amount of industrial capability and other resources. (1979, U.S. Navy)

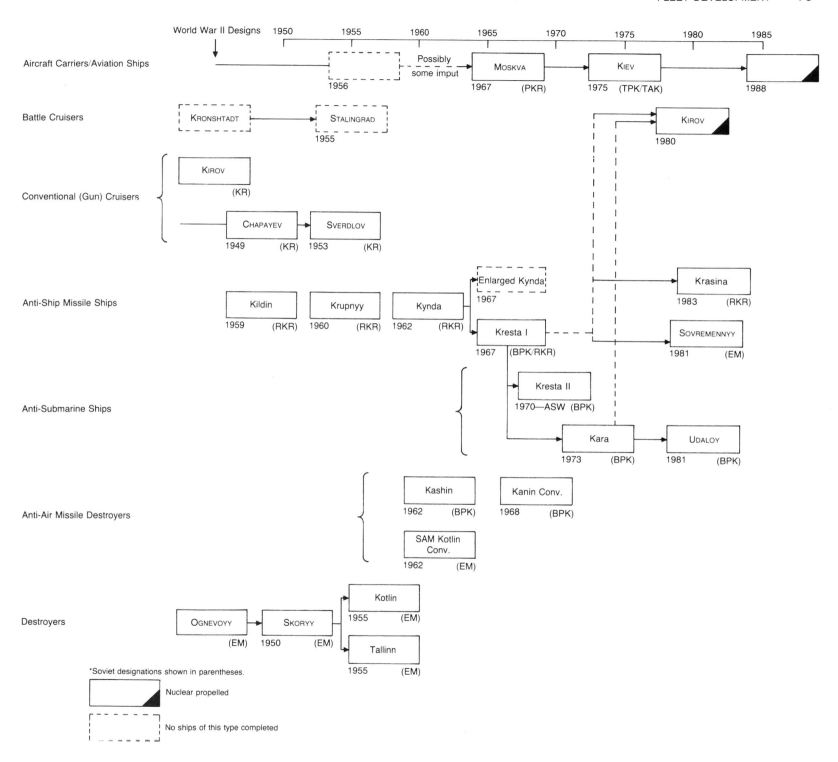

Figure 10–2*.  Surface Warship Development

Of course, the Soviet Navy continues to emphasize submarines, "attack" and strategic types, nuclear and conventional types. At left is a Foxtrot SS and at right its successor, the Tango. Design and construction of diesel-electric submarines continues, the Foxtrot still being built for foreign customers, and the Tango and new Kilo for Soviet naval use.

Brezhnev seems determined that the Soviet Union have an active role in the Third World. The USSR supports emerging and established socialist states and carries out other Soviet goals in these countries, including efforts to counter Western influence and activity.

Aden, Angola, Cuba, Egypt, El Salvador, Ethiopia, Iraq, Libya, Nicaragua, Somalia, Syria, Vietnam, and Yemen have all become recipients of Soviet attention during the Brezhnev era. In some cases Soviet troops have been present (as in Cuba and Egypt); more often, proxy troops (especially Cubans, but often with East German, Vietnamese, or Soviet advisors) have been used, and Soviet merchant ships carrying weapons and supplies are always in evidence. Increasingly, Soviet naval ships have also been present.

Admiral Gorshkov strongly supports this role (see chapter 8). By 1970, when Brezhnev made the statement cited above, decisions had already been made to construct still another generation of Soviet warships—led by the first aircraft carriers to be built by the Soviet regime and the first nuclear-propelled surface warships.

By late 1971 the U.S. reconnaissance satellites overflying the USSR brought back evidence of an aircraft carrier under construction at the Nikolayev south yard, where the Moskva and her sister ship Leningrad were constructed. The following December the ship was launched, revealing the largest naval unit yet built in the Soviet Union. Named Kiev, the 38,000-ton ship is a true aircraft carrier, with an angled flight deck that

is linked to the hangar deck through two aircraft lifts. The ship has a large starboard island structure. But there the similarity to Western aircraft carriers ends.

Forward and around the island the Kiev is fitted with heavy batteries of anti-aircraft, anti-submarine, and anti-surface weapons, plus Gatling-type, rapid-fire guns for close-in defense against cruise missiles. The anti-ship weapons are the SS-N-12, an improved version of the Shaddock with a range of some 300 n.miles (555 km).[7] Also, the Kiev lacks the catapults and arresting wires of Western carriers that permit the operation of conventional aircraft. Instead, the Kiev carries an air group of some 35 Yak-36 Forger VTOL aircraft and Ka-25 Hormone helicopters. The Forger, a transonic fighter-attack aircraft, was the second vertical-operation aircraft to go to sea, the first having been the Anglo-American Harrier.

The decisions to build the Kiev and her sister carriers seem to have been taken at the Politburo level around 1965. The decision to build aircraft carriers had to have been made at the highest level of government because of the costs in facilities, materials, and people.

A factor in those decisions was the mission for these carriers. The fact

[7]The Kiev was the first aircraft carrier of any nation to be provided with significant anti-ship weapons since the U.S. carriers Lexington (CV 2) and Saratoga (CV 3) beached their 8-inch (203-mm) guns in 1940–1941.

that the KIEV is limited to a relatively small number of aircraft, of inferior types when compared to U.S. carrier aircraft, strongly indicates that the Soviet carriers were not intended to counter Western carriers. Rather, two other roles appear more probable. First, the Soviet "pro-submarine" mission—that is, supporting and protecting Soviet submarines, especially SSBNs—has been cited by Western analysts as an obvious rationale for the ship. Looked at in isolation, this has some validity. However, the subsequent construction of larger carrier-type ships, the anti-ship weapons mounted in the KIEV, and the lack of a fixed-wing ASW aircraft reduce the credibility of the pro-submarine mission.

A more likely factor was the increasing Soviet activities in the Third World. By the late 1960s the U.S. Department of Defense had announced the decision to reduce the American carrier force to 12 ships, and the Royal Navy as well as other NATO fleets were giving up conventional aircraft carriers. At the same time, the airfields available to the United States in the Third World were declining. As a result, one or more KIEV-type ships in the right place at the right time could have considerable influence in combat or crisis situations.

Shortly after the lines of the KIEV became visible in satellite photography, there were indications that another large warship was being built at the Baltic shipyard in Leningrad. Although the Baltic yard had not constructed warships since the SVERDLOV program, the yard was building the nuclear-powered ARKTIKA-class icebreakers. The new Baltic ship was the KIROV, a nuclear-powered missile cruiser. At some 28,000 tons, the KIROV is the largest warship except for aircraft carriers built by any nation since World War II. Here again, the KIROV demonstrates a highly innovative design. The ship has vertical-launch anti-aircraft (SA-N-6) and anti-ship (SS-N-19) missiles, the latter giving the KIROV, like the KIEV, a stand-off strike weapon. In addition, the KIROV carries anti-submarine and close-in defense weapons, as well as several helicopters.

The role of the KIROV has also perplexed Western naval analysts. Most suggest that the KIROV class is intended to serve in a surface action group—that is, with cruisers and destroyers—or as a major carrier escort ship. In the opinion of the author of this volume, the weapons, helicopter capability, and $C^3$ facilities make the KIROV superfluous to a task group with a KIEV-type carrier. The KIROV may have been developed as a screening ship for the nuclear carrier, with the latter delayed because of the need to use the same building dock that was constructing the four KIEV-class carriers. However, at this writing it seems likely that the new nuclear carrier will have the same design concept as the KIEV and MOSKVA—heavily laden with weapons and electronics. Further, at the risk of "mirror imaging" the American task force concept, a KIROV built to screen a carrier would have more anti-aircraft weapons and less anti-ship capability than the KIROV.

Rather, the KIROV will more likely be employed as the core of a surface action group, operating in Third World areas where the ability of the United States to project tactical air power from carriers or land bases is limited.

The KIROV was but the harbinger of a Soviet surface nuclear program. The KIEV has been followed by three sister ships at the Nikolayev south shipyard. Even as the fourth unit was being built, the graving dock where construction took place was being lengthened and components were being assembled in the yard for a larger, nuclear-powered carrier. The

new ship was laid down shortly after the fourth KIEV was launched in 1982.

Simultaneous with these "capital ships," the Soviets initiated three other cruiser-destroyer classes, the UDALOY, an ASW destroyer, the SOVREMENNYY, an anti-ship destroyer, and a cruiser given the NATO code name Krasina, apparently a successor to the KARA but with a large SS-N-12 missile battery. With four yards engaged in building these four cruiser-destroyer classes, this is the largest surface combatant effort undertaken in the USSR since the Stalin era.

In this fourth phase of postwar fleet development, the Soviets have continued submarine construction with a record of ten classes probably being in production in the early 1980s:

| | | | |
|---|---|---|---|
| SSBN | Typhoon | SSN | Alfa |
| SSBN | Delta III | SSN | Victor III |
| SSGN | Oscar | SS | Kilo |
| SSN | new design (Severodvinsk) | SS | Tango |
| SSN | new design (Sudomekh) | SS | Foxtrot (foreign users) |

The last Charlie II had been launched at Gor'kiy in 1980, but at least two new SSN classes were under construction, plus conversions of the older Yankee SSBNs. Party Chairman Brezhnev revealed to President Gerald Ford at their November 1974 meeting in Vladivostok that the USSR was building a giant strategic missile submarine, the *Tayfun*. Brezhnev claimed the new SSBN was a response to the U.S. Trident program.

Built at Severodvinsk, the first Typhoon SSBN was launched in 1980. At some 25,000-ton submerged displacement, she is half again the size of the U.S. Trident missile submarines, the first of which was completed in 1982, earlier than the Soviet giant.

Similarly, the Oscar SSGN, displacing about 13,000 tons submerged, is about half again the size of the America LOS ANGELES (SSN 688)-class attack submarines. The Oscar presents a new level of threat to Western naval planners, being armed with 24 SS-N-19 anti-ship missiles or three times the number of missiles carried by the earlier Echo-II and Charlie SSGN classes. Further, the SS-N-19 combines the best features of the Echo-II missiles (long range) and the Charlie missiles (underwater launch).

After her long gestation period, series production was undertaken of the Alfa SSN. Simultaneously, construction of the Charlie SSGN and Victor SSN classes continued as well as that of the Tango and the new Kilo diesel attack submarines. Two new SSN classes, possibly with a torpedo tube-launched cruise missile capability, were also being built in the early 1980s, with at least one probably a titanium-hull successor to the high-speed, deep-diving Alfa. These boats are being built at Severodvinsk and Sudomekh.

In this fourth phase of Soviet fleet development, amphibious and auxiliary ship construction has continued. Construction of over-the-beach LST and LSM classes continued into the 1970s, and in 1978 the first of at least two IVAN ROGOV-class ships was completed. The ROGOV is a multi-purpose amphibious ship, the first Soviet unit with a docking well for carrying air-cushion vehicles, and the first with a helicopter landing area and hangar. Coupled with the continued Soviet merchant ship construction, these "amphibs" provide a steady increase in the ability of the USSR to move troops and equipment by sea and to mount amphibious assaults.

## INSTITUTIONAL FACTORS[8]

Friedrich Engels, who with Karl Marx wrote the *Communist Manifesto* (1847), the blueprint for the Bolshevik movement in Russia, addressed the relationship of warships to the countries that produce them: "A modern warship is not merely a product of major industry, but at the same time is a sample of it. . . ."[9] The modern warships of the Soviet Navy are the product of numerous institutional factors of the USSR. These factors include:

*National Leadership.* The leadership of the USSR is very stable by Western standards. In the postwar period, major military and industrial decisions have been vested mainly in the Chairman of the Communist Party and in the Politburo.

During the long period of Stalin's leadership (1922–1953) there were innumerable occasions when he personally made design and procurement decisions. Admiral Kuznetsov wrote ". . . without Stalin no one ventured to decide the large questions concerning the navy."[10] British historian Albert Seaton addressed Stalin's decision making:

> Soviet writers are agreed that Stalin took a personal and directing role in the development of army equipment. Indeed, according to [Marshal G.K.] Zhukov, no single pattern of armament could be adopted or discarded without Stalin's approval. . . .

And,

> [Colonel-General K.A.] Vershinin said in 1948 that Stalin alone made the final decisions in aircraft development, and this is supported by the air[craft] designer Yakovlev's account. . . .[11]

For the subsequent Khrushchev period (1955–1964) we have the late Party Chairman's own words to describe his decision making. After learning that the United States was placing ICBMs in underground silos, he took action:

> I summoned the people responsible and said, "Now look what's happened! The Americans have begun to dig the ballistic missile shafts which I proposed a long time ago. Let's get started on this program right away."

Khrushchev continued, describing how he personally inquired about digging techniques and equipment, and how he was "proud of my role in originating the idea and later seeing [that] the conversion [to underground ICBM silos] was begun."[12]

Decision making by senior Soviets with respect to specific weapons continues in the Brezhnev era. However, it acquired a different aspect after 1965 when Ustinov was made a candidate member of the Politburo. His background in armament development and then his becoming a full Politburo member and Minister of Defense in 1976 imply that defense policy and hardware can be discussed more freely in the Politburo, without the need to call in outside experts.

Decision making at the Politburo level coupled with the stability of the leadership of the USSR tend to ensure that policy and hardware decisions by national leaders will be carried out. In the post-Khrushchev period there appears to have been less "interference" with naval programs from a technical viewpoint. This is probably due in large part to the relationship of Brezhnev, the late Prime Minister Kosygin, and Politburo member Romanov with the Navy's leadership. Still, the increasing forward operations of the Navy and the related political implications probably make naval activities a periodic subject of Politburo discussions.

The stability of Soviet leadership—military as well as political—is amazing by Western standards. Brezhnev was Party Chairman from 1964 to 1982, Ustinov the Minister of Defense since 1976, and Marshal of the Soviet Union N.V. Ogarkov the Chief of the General Staff since 1977. Admiral Gorshkov has been the head of the Navy since 1956, the current head of the Air Forces has held that post since 1969, the head of SRF since 1972, the head of Air Defense Troops since 1978, and the head of the Ground Forces since 1980. Most of these men served in a first deputy position before assuming the senior position. This longevity suggests that projects that win top-level approval will be pursued, but those projects rejected by the leadership must wait long periods until there is a change in administration.

*Long-Range Planning.* The Soviet Union has longer range planning in the defense and industrial sectors than Western nations. The entire Soviet economy is based on long-term, integrated planning. Whereas the United States has a five-year defense plan that is "extended" annually to add the "next" year, the Soviet five-year plan is for a finite period. Thus, while American leaders can repeatedly postpone difficult decisions or projects until the later years of the five-year program, the Soviet scheme provides for a specific period and end-of-plan accounting.

In addition, the Soviet planning cycle is tied in with all aspects of society, including all military services and other defense agencies. Hence, a long-range naval construction effort would be linked to steel production, transportation, coal matters, commercial shipbuilding, and so forth.

*Employment Policies.* Full employment is a basic goal of the Soviet state. The Soviet constitution guarantees the right to work. Thus, in the eyes of the Soviet leadership, the admission of unemployment would indicate the failure of this guarantee. Accordingly, once a factory or product line is established, it is difficult to close it down without major political implications. This may, in part, explain the continued production of outdated and even obsolete hardware. The Tupolev-designed Bear aircraft is an example of the very long Soviet production runs, it having been in production from 1954 into the 1980s.

There is also significant worker stability because Soviet citizens are

[8]This section is in part adopted from the author's report "Factors That Have Influenced the Soviet Navy—Potential Lessons for Aegis Shipbuilding" (30 April 1981), prepared for the U.S. Navy's Aegis shipbuilding project manager. Also see Arthur J. Alexander, *Decision-Making in Soviet Weapons Procurement* (London: International Institute for Strategic Studies, 1978; Adelphi Papers No. 147 and 148); Alexander Boyd, *The Soviet Air Force* (London: Macdonald and Jane's, 1977); and Colonel Oleg Penkovskiy, *The Penkovskiy Papers* (New York: Doubleday, 1965).

[9]F. Engels, *Izbrannyye Voyennyye Proizvedeniye* [Selected Military Works] (Moscow: Voyenizdat, 1957), p. 17.

[10]Admiral Kuznetsov, "On the Eve," *Oktyabr´*, no. 9, 1965, pp. 158–89; also see no. 8, 1965, pp. 161–202 and no. 11, 1965, pp. 134–71.

[11]Albert Seaton, *Stalin as Military Commander* (New York: Praeger, 1976), pp. 87–89.

[12]Khrushchev, op. cit., p. 49.

generally not permitted to change jobs in critical industries without authorization.

*Copying Technology.* The Soviets appear to be willing, able, and anxious to copy Western technology. There are several classic examples of the Soviets doing this, from allies and enemies alike. At the end of World War II the Soviets carted off much of Eastern Europe's surviving industrial facilities as well as German technology, scientists, and technicians. In the same manner, American equipment was copied, including radars on U.S. ships transferred to the Soviet Navy and the B-29 heavy bombers that landed in Siberia and were interned after bombing raids against Japan.

The Soviets continue to seek Western technology by overt and covert means. The covert activities by the KGB and GRU (military intelligence) seek information on virtually all Western military and industrial activities. The results of these efforts regularly appear in Soviet systems. The Soviets are thus able to take advantage of Western developments while saving Soviet industrial and research resources that would have otherwise been invested in those areas.

Overt collection methods include the outright purchase of material and also information from the virtually limitless Western press. In the naval-maritime area, the Soviets have purchased numerous merchant and fishing ships from the West as well as marine engines, computers, and electronics.

*Production Rates.*[13] The Soviets have always stressed quantities of military equipment. Despite the ravages of war from 1941 to 1945, by the end of the conflict some 40,000 aircraft per year were being produced in the USSR. About 80 percent of these were single-engine fighter and ground-attack aircraft, mostly of wooden construction. It was still a major achievement when one considers the worker problems, shortages of materials, the severe weather conditions, and the fact that most of the plants building aircraft and engines had been removed from European Russia and reestablished in the Urals early in the war.

After the war there were significant shifts in the types and numbers of aircraft produced, but the level of effort remained high. For example, in 1950 the Soviet aircraft industry produced about 4,000 MiG-15 turbojet fighters, 1,000 turbojet bombers, and several hundred Tu-4 Bull four-engine piston bombers, and a number of other aircraft. While these totaled significantly less than the number of aircraft produced five years earlier, the effort was probably similar in terms of man-hours and resources required. This relatively high production rate continues. For example, in 1980, the last year for which comparative data are available, the USSR produced more than four times the number of military aircraft as the United States (see table 10–2).

Similarly, the Soviet Union has continued a high rate of ship construction, naval and commercial. In 1955 Soviet shipyards launched an estimated 81 submarines, the peak of the Stalin production effort; in 1980 those yards launched 12 submarines, eight of them nuclear propelled units. Of the 1955 launchings, 62 were of the Whiskey class with a

**TABLE 10–2. AIRCRAFT PRODUCTION, 1980***

| Aircraft Type | Soviet Union | United States |
|---|---|---|
| Bombers | 25 | — |
| Fighter/Fighter-Bomber/Attack | 1,300 | 390 |
| Electronic/Early Warning | — | 19 |
| Patrol/Anti-Submarine | 10 | 12 |
| Transport | 350 | 14 |
| Trainer | 225 | 60 |
| Helicopter | 750 | 146 |
| Utility | 100 | 6 |
| Total | 2,760 | 647 |

*Estimated 1980 production for USSR; 1980 (fiscal 1981) procurement authorized for United States.

1,050-ton (standard) displacement. These were diesel-electric craft, armed only with torpedoes. The 1980 submarines included the first Typhoon SSBN with a standard displacement of perhaps 20,000 tons, the rough equivalent of 19 Whiskey-class submarines, and the first Oscar SSGN of about 10,000 tons standard displacement, equal in tonnage to more than nine Whiskeys. This displacement ratio provides a very rough approximation of the resources involved.

Also, beyond being larger, the newer submarines have mostly nuclear propulsion, more complex electronics, more advanced weapons, and other features that demonstrate the continuation of a high level of effort in this category of industrial endeavor.

*Quantity versus Quality.* The Soviet Union is a land of quantity versus quality. Numbers are important and, indeed, are the means by which much of the Soviet military-industrial complex is graded. A given factory or industry is generally rated on the basis of numbers of units produced; quality is a secondary consideration. The grades thus given become the basis for promotions, pay increases, bonuses, and special privileges.

The "numbers mentality" results in the USSR having more equipment of certain types than can be used by the active military establishment. This provides equipment for the reserves as well as ready equipment to replace combat losses and for foreign transfer. As an example, after the 1973 war in the Middle East the Soviet Union was able to rapidly provide several hundred tanks to Egypt and Syria to replace their losses.

This approach to producing large numbers of units has also led to the practice of replacing rather than repairing damaged equipment and platforms at the unit or organizational level. This, in turn, reduces the maintenance requirements in Soviet units, always a problem with the short-term draftees that comprise the vast majority of the Soviet armed forces. At the same time, this emphasis on the production of "things" that can be easily counted, such as tanks and aircraft, sometimes leads to component shortfalls, that is, "things" that cannot be as easily counted and are thus shorted in favor of producing more of what can be counted against "norms" and quotas.

*Component Similarity.* Soviet design agencies and industry seek to provide similar components for successive generations of systems and platforms. Components appear to change only for specific reasons, such as product improvement or availability because of production line

[13]This material is based on research by Dr. Norman Friedman for the Hudson Institute discussion paper "Soviet Mobilization" (8 November 1977).

changes. Accordingly, some components and systems have a long service life over successive classes of platforms.

There are obvious advantages to this scheme in terms of production costs, maintenance, spares, training, and personnel assignment. However, when there are limited production facilities or other problems with widely used components, there are bottlenecks. This appears to be the current situation with respect to integrated circuits; too many Soviet military (and possibly civil) systems are in need of advanced circuitry, and too few production facilities are available.

*Component Availability.* Related to the issue of component similarity there are limited selections of components available, at least by Western standards. A design bureau cannot simply look through catalogues or phone up component producers to obtain minor but critical components for new systems. The Soviet industrial system limits the numbers and variety of equipment produced; relatively few components or systems are developed "on speculation"—that is, developed because they *may* be used or even needed.

As a result, new systems tend to make use of existing components, or for prototype systems the laboratory or factory may produce the components on an individual basis. While this is highly inefficient by Western standards, it may be the only way in which a Soviet producer can obtain a key component within required time constraints.

*Innovation.* The Soviets military-industrial environment both encourages and retards innovation. It encourages innovation because the various design bureaus, with one or more specializing in the development of different weapons and platforms, are continually producing new designs. These may or may not be put into production, but that is irrelevant to the purpose of these bureaus.

However, for all of the reasons cited above, innovation in the weapons and platforms being produced is difficult, and hence it should be avoided when possible. The limitations on innovation are acceptable to the armed forces because of manpower limitations on using and supporting new and more complex equipment.

This is not to imply that innovation is opposed in principle. Rather, that change must contribute to force or unit effectiveness and at not too great a cost. To again quote the plaque alleged to be in Admiral Gorshkov's office, "Better is the Enemy of Good Enough."

These institutional factors all affect Soviet fleet development.

## MAINTENANCE AND SUPPORT

The maintenance and support of equipment in the fleet have been traditional problems for the Soviet Navy, in part because of the Soviet economic practice of producing "units" rather than spare parts, problems with workmanship and quality control, and personnel limitations.

Estimates by the West of the success of the Soviet Navy in maintaining and supporting military equipment vary considerably. Undoubtedly,

some of the more critical comments are based on the appearance of some Soviet ships. Flaking paint and rust stains are sometimes used as the criteria for such judgments; another criterion sometimes used is the time at sea of individual Soviet ships compared with American units, as well as the Soviet practice of towing ships to or from deployment areas. But observing appearances and operating modes may not be an entirely accurate means of measuring actual maintenance levels and the resulting readiness.

For example, the Soviets seem to place less emphasis on the appearance of their ships—except during port visits—than does the U.S. Navy. Rather, the Soviet emphasis seems to be on keeping the equipment working. This has been a traditional attitude. For example, Rear Admiral Kemp Tolley, when assistant naval attaché in Moscow during World War II, recorded the following in his diary about the crews that brought U.S. and British ships around North Cape to Soviet Arctic ports:

> Our people found the Russian sailorman can be a complex fellow. By nature slovenly, they kept their ordnance, engineering, and most mechanical equipment clean, plentifully greased and operative. Not energetic, they were physically capable of great hardship. They were "heavy handed" in operating, maintenance and repairing of equipment; wasteful of spare parts, tools and supplies. Mechanical sense was crude, jumping to conclusions child-like that they knew-it-all, to the hazard of the inanimate gear they were working on.

This attitude, coupled with the conservative design of their equipment—built with the level of technical competence of the sailor in mind—indicates that the equipment the Soviets have in their ships is kept in working order. At the same time, the operating mode of the Soviet fleet tends to conserve equipment and other resources whenever possible. In February 1982, the U.S. Chief of Naval Operations told a congressional committee that

> . . . the Soviet concept of material readiness stresses conservation of resources by limiting the use of military equipment in peacetime. They apparently believe that limited use is the best way to ensure that equipment will be ready on short notice during a crisis. That is one reason the Soviets normally keep a smaller percentage of their forces deployed than we do, and why Soviet deployed forces generally maintain lower operational tempos.

Still, the Soviet Navy does suffer from the general maintenance and support problems that plague all aspects of Soviet society. Throughout the society there are too often examples of poor workmanship, insufficient quality control, shortages of parts, and lack of competent personnel or incentives to do the job properly. The only mitigation is that within the Soviet society the armed forces have the highest priorities for men and material (after certain party-related activities), and during the past two decades the Navy has received the "cream" of those resources.

Thus, the for at least the near-term the Soviet Navy appears capable of maintaining and supporting the fleet that has been developed since World War II.

The destroyer PROVORNYY as configured to test the SA-N-7 missile system (launcher is abaft the second pair of gas turbine exhaust stacks, under canvas) and the Top Steer radar (after mast). Soviet naval development is continuous, with new weapons and electronic systems being introduced on a regular basis.

In arctic ice during her maiden voyage, the nuclear icebreaker SIBIR' is ostensibly a civilian ship. The arming of the lead ship of the class for her sea trials and the construction of the KIROV-class battle cruisers in the Baltic Shipyard demonstrate the close relationship between Soviet naval and commercial ship development. (Sovfoto)

The anti-ship destroyer SOVREMENNYY displays her clean lines in this view. The ability of the Soviet Navy to simultaneously design and construct four classes of modern cruisers and destroyers demonstrates the strength of the nation's shipbuilding industry and the degree of resources now being allocated to naval developments.

# 11

# Submarines

The Soviet Navy has the world's largest submarine force with approximately 380 submarines in active service as of mid-1983, almost half of them nuclear propelled. About 100 additional submarines are believed to be in reserve, some or all of which may have been cannibalized for spare parts.

In March of 1983, the U.S. Secretary of Defense reported: "In the near future, a new [Soviet] attack submarine will begin series production at two shipyards. This class will have significantly more capability than the older Victor III." This new submarine may be of an improved Alfa-class design (see page 105).

The submarines believed to be currently in active status are shown in table 11−1.

Designations: Soviet submarine type designations are explained in chapter 3.

Names: Soviet submarine classes have been assigned letter designations by the U.S.-NATO intelligence community; the phonetic word for the letter is generally used. The exception is the Typhoon, which is the Soviet term for the craft (Russian *Tayfun*).

The assignment of the code name "Yankee" to the first modern Soviet SSBN class has caused confusion with the public and, at times, within Western defense establishments. The term "Russian Yankee" is sometimes used in an effort to reduce confusion.

Performance: Performance data for the newer submarines is estimated. Diesel-electric submarine range is on diesel engines.

TABLE 11−1.  ACTIVE SUBMARINES

| Type | Class | Number* | Notes |
|---|---|---|---|
| SSBN | Typhoon | 4 | in production |
| SSBN | Delta I/II/III | 36 | in production |
| SSBN | Yankee I/II | 25 | |
| SSBN | Hotel II/III/IV | 5 | others in reserve |
| SSB | Golf II/III/IV | 15 | others in reserve |
| SSGN | Oscar | 2 | in production |
| SSGN | Papa | 1 | |
| SSGN | Charlie I/II | 19 | |
| SSGN | Echo II | 29 | |
| SSG | Juliett | 16 | |
| SSG | Whiskey Long Bin | 4 | training duties |
| SSN | Alfa | ~7 | in production |
| SSN | Victor I/II/III | 38 | in production |
| SSGN/SSN | Yankee | ~9† | converted SSBN |
| SSN | Echo I | 5 | converted SSGN |
| SSN | November | 12 | others in reserve |
| SS | Kilo | 2 | in production |
| SS | Tango | ~15 | in production |
| SS | Foxtrot | 55 | in production for foreign users |
| SS | Romeo | 12 | |
| SS | Quebec | ? | |
| SS | Zulu IV | 8 | |
| SS | Whiskey | 57 | others in reserve |
| SSR | Whiskey Canvas Bag | 1 | |
| AGSS | India | 2 | |
| AGSS | Lima | 1 | |
| SST | Bravo | 4 | |
| SSQ | Golf | 3 | converted SSB |

\* The larger numbers are approximate and rounded.
† These submarines are not all operational; see class listings.

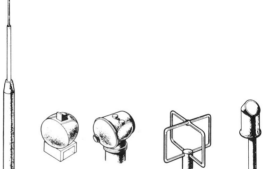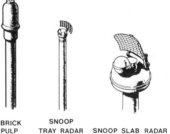

HF MAST   COD EYE 'A'   COD EYE 'B'   QUAD LOOP ANTENNA   DUSTBIN   GOLF BALL   BRICK PULP   SNOOP TRAY RADAR   SNOOP SLAB RADAR   STOP LIGHT ESM   PUNCH BOWL RADOME   PERT SPRING   PARK LAMP DF LOOP

Submarine masts (Courtesy Royal Navy)

The Oscar-class SSGN—in series production at Severodvinsk—is the world's largest "attack" submarine. The artist's concept shows one of these undersea craft being fitted out; note the retractable bow diving planes, elongated sail structure, and missile tube openings along the amidships hull. The closeup photo shows the Oscar's sail structure breaking through the water. (U.S. Department of Defense)

b

### 1 + NUCLEAR-PROPELLED BALLISTIC MISSILE SUBMARINES (SSBN): TYPHOON

| Name | Laid Down | Launched | Completed |
|---|---|---|---|
| . . . . . . | 1975 | Aug 1980 | 1983 |

| | |
|---|---|
| Builders: | Severodvinsk |
| Displacement: | 25,000 tons submerged |
| Length: | 561 ft (170.0 m) |
| Beam: | 76 ft (23.0 m) |
| Draft: | |
| Propulsion: | steam turbines: 2 shafts |
| Reactors: | 2 |
| Speed: | approx. 30 knots submerged |
| Complement: | |
| Missiles: | 20 SS-N-20 SLBM |
| ASW weapons: | torpedoes |
| Torpedoes: | . . . 21-in (533-mm) torpedo tubes (bow) |
| Radars: | |
| Sonars: | low frequency |

The Typhoon is the largest undersea craft yet constructed, being almost half-again as large as the U.S. Trident strategic missile submarines of the OHIO (SSBN 726) class, which displace 18,700 tons submerged. The above dates for the lead unit, based on published material, indicate a relatively long construction period for a Soviet submarine, possibly due to the complexity of this class. The lead submarine began sea trials in mid-1981.

Additional submarines of this class are under construction, at least one of which had been launched by the beginning of 1983.

Design: The Typhoon design differs considerably from previous SSBN designs; the missile tubes are fitted *forward* of the sail structure, which is aft of center. The submarine may be intended for operations in the Arctic ice pack, with its high-rise hull and stub sail structure permitting it to break through the ice for missile launch.

Two separate submarine pressure hulls are fitted side-by-side within an outer hull, with the missile compartment between the main pressure hulls. Forward diving planes are mounted on the bow where they can be retracted (possibly to prevent ice damage), as compared to the previous Delta and Yankee classes, which have sail-mounted diving planes.

Designation: Soviet PLARB type.

Engineering: Like all previous Soviet SSBNs, these submarines have twin propeller shafts (all Western SSBNs are single-shaft submarines). These submarines have two complete reactor plants.

A U.S. Department of Defense artist's impression of the Soviet Typhoon submarine. Note the position of the 20 missile tubes *forward* of the short, squat sail structure, the height of the hull structure, and the unusual stern configuration. This configuration may be intended to facilitate the submarine operating in the Arctic and surfacing through the ice pack to launch missiles.

**14 + NUCLEAR-PROPELLED BALLISTIC MISSILE SUBMARINES (SSBN): DELTA III/IV**

| Name | Completed |
|---|---|
| . . . . . . (2 units) | 1975 |
| . . . . . . (4 units) | 1976 |
| . . . . . . (2 units) | 1977 |
| . . . . . . (2 units) | 1978 |
| . . . . . . (4 units) | 1979–1982 |

| | |
|---|---|
| Builders: | Severodvinsk |
| Displacement: | 10,500 tons surface |
| | 13,250 tons submerged |
| Length: | 511 ft 6 in (155.0 m) |
| Beam: | 39 ft 6 in (12.0 m) |
| Draft: | 28 ft 9 in (8.7 m) |
| Propulsion: | steam turbines; 50,000 shp 2 shafts |

| | |
|---|---|
| Reactors: | 1 pressurized-water type |
| Speed: | approx. 23–24 knots |
| Complement: | approx. 120 |
| Missiles: | 16 SS-N-18 SLBM |
| ASW weapons: | torpedoes |
| Torpedoes: | 6 21-in (533-mm) torpedo tubes (bow) |
| Radars: | Snoop Tray |
| Sonars: | low frequency |

These are similar to the previous Delta-class submarines, but are capable of carrying 16 of the improved SS-N-18 missiles. Construction of this class is expected to end in the near future. One unit is believed to be named 60 Let Oktyabrskiy Velikiy.

Design: The "hump" or turtle back" structure abaft the sail is higher than in previous classes to permit carrying the longer SS-N-18 SLBMs.

Designation: Soviet PLARB type.

Delta III SSBN, showing the long, high "turtle back" aft of the sail that houses 16 SLBMs.

Delta III-class SSBN

**4 NUCLEAR-PROPELLED BALLISTIC MISSILE SUBMARINES (SSBN): DELTA II**

| Name | Completed |
|------|-----------|
| . . . . . . | 1974–1975 |

| | |
|------|------|
| Builders: | Severodvinsk |
| Displacement: | 10,000 tons surface |
| | 12,750 tons submerged |
| Length: | 511 ft 6 in (155 m) |
| Beam: | 36 ft 6 in (12 m) |
| Draft: | 29 ft (8.8 m) |
| Propulsion: | steam turbines; 50,000 shp; 2 shafts |
| Reactors: | 1 pressurized-water type |
| Speed: | approx. 24 knots submerged |

| | |
|------|------|
| Complement: | approx. 120 |
| Missiles: | 16 SS-N-8 SLBM |
| ASW weapons: | torpedoes |
| Torpedoes: | 6 21-in (533-mm) torpedo tubes (bow) |
| Radars: | Snoop Tray |
| Sonars: | low frequency |

These are Delta I-class submarines lengthened to accommodate four additional SS-N-8 missiles for a total of 16, the number carried in contemporary U.S., British, and French SSBNs.

Designation: Soviet PLARB type.

Delta II at high surface speed. The starboard, sail-mounted diving plane is just visible. The Yankee and later SSBNs were the first Soviet submarines with sail-mounted diving planes.

**18 NUCLEAR-PROPELLED BALLISTIC MISSILE SUBMARINES (SSBN): DELTA I**

| Name | Completed |
|------|-----------|
| . . . . . . (1 unit) | 1972 |
| . . . . . . (4 units) | 1973 |
| . . . . . . (6 units) | 1974 |
| . . . . . . (2 units) | 1975 |
| . . . . . . (2 units) | 1976 |
| . . . . . . (3 units) | 1977 |

| | |
|------|------|
| Builders: | Komsomol'sk |
| | Severodvinsk |
| Displacement: | 9,000 tons surface |
| | 11,750 tons submerged |
| Length: | 462 ft (140.0 m) |
| Beam: | 39 ft 6 in (12.0 m) |
| Draft: | 28 ft 9 in (8.7 m) |
| Propulsion: | steam turbines; 50,000 shp; 2 shafts |
| Reactors: | 1 pressurized-water type |
| Speed: | approx. 25 knots submerged |

| | |
|------|------|
| Complement: | approx. 120 |
| Missiles: | 12 SS-N-8 SLBM |
| ASW weapons: | torpedoes |
| Torpedoes: | 6 21-in (533-mm) torpedo tubes (bow) |
| Radars: | Snoop Tray |
| Sonars: | low frequency |

The Delta is an enlargement of its predecessor, the Yankee SSBN, intended to launch the larger SS-N-8 ballistic missile. The Delta I was the world's largest undersea craft yet built when the first unit was completed in 1972. The subsequent Delta II and III designs were further enlarged to accommodate 16 missiles vice the 12 in the Delta I.

Designation: Soviet PLARB type.

Propulsion: The Delta SSBNs have the same reactor plant used in the previous Yankee SSBN class and similar to that of the Charlie SSGN and Victor SSN classes.

A Delta I on the surface with naval ensign flying and Pert Spring antenna, high-frequency mast, and one periscope raised. (1979)

Delta I-class SSBN

**25 NUCLEAR-PROPELLED BALLISTIC MISSILE SUBMARINES (SSBN): YANKEE I/II**

| Name | Completed |
|---|---|
| . . . . . . (10 units) | 1970 |
| . . . . . . ( 5 units) | 1971 |
| . . . . . . (10 units) | 1972–1974 |

| | |
|---|---|
| Builders: | Komsomol'sk |
| | Severodvinsk |
| Displacement: | 8,000 tons surface |
| | 9,600 tons submerged |
| Length: | 429 ft (130.0 m) |
| Beam: | 39 ft 6 in (12.0 m) |
| Draft: | 29 ft (3.3 m) |
| Propulsion: | steam turbines; 50,000 shp; 2 shafts |
| Reactors: | 1 pressurized-water type |
| Speed: | approx. 27 knots submerged |
| Complement: | approx. 120 |
| Missiles: | Yankee I class 16 SS-N-6 SLBM |
| | Yankee II class 12 SS-N-17 SLBM |
| ASW weapons: | torpedoes |
| Torpedoes: | 6 21-in (533-mm) torpedo tubes (bow) |
| Radars: | Snoop Tray |
| Sonars: | low frequency |

The Yankee was the first "modern" Soviet SSBN class, being very similar to the earlier U.S. and British Polaris designs, whose initial units were completed in 1960 and 1967, respectively. Thirty-four Yankee SSBNs were completed from 1967 to 1974. Subsequently, under the terms of the missile submarine limitations in the SALT I agreement with the United States, the Soviets have been deactivating the missile tubes in these submarines; nine submarines have thus been removed from the ballistic missile role through 1982 and are listed separately in this volume as attack submarines (SSGN/SSN).

The above completion dates are for the latter 25 units of the class, based on the assumption that the Soviets have been deleting the oldest submarines first in the shift from the SSBN to SSN role. The construction rate of this class reached a peak of 10 submarines completed in 1970 (8 at Severodvinsk and 2 at Komsomol'sk), compared to a U.S. maximum annual rate of 13 for Polaris SSBNs.

Conversion: One Yankee SSBN has been modified to carry the enlarged, advanced-technology SS-N-17 missile. Note that the number of missile tubes was reduced from 16 to 12.

Design: These were the first Soviet submarines to have sail-mounted diving planes vice bow planes. The Yankees have a smaller rise to the top of the hull abaft the sail over the missile tubes, than in the Delta class. Some Yankees have an angled edge at the forward base of their sail for a sonar installation.

Designation: Soviet PLARB type.

Engineering: The Yankee uses a reactor plant similar to that of the Charlie SSGN and Victor SSN. This plant is estimated to generate 50,000 shp compared to 15,000 shp for the S5W reactor plant in the U.S. Polaris-Poseidon submarines. Accordingly, the Soviet SSBNs are much faster than their Western counterparts. However, Soviet nuclear submarine machinery is reported to have significantly higher noise levels.

Closeup of Yankee sail structure; note angled forward base and opened sail hatches that reveal various antennas.

Yankee-class SSBN

Yankee-class SSBN

Yankee-class SSBN

Overhead view of Yankee SSBN. Note rounded bow sonar installation.

### 1 NUCLEAR-PROPELLED BALLISTIC MISSILE SUBMARINE (SSBN): HOTEL III

| Name | Conversion Completed |
| --- | --- |
| . . . . . . | 1965 |

| | |
| --- | --- |
| Builders: | Severodvinsk |
| Displacement: | 5,500 tons surface |
| | 6,400 tons submerged |
| Length: | 429 ft (130.0 m) |
| Beam: | 29 ft 9 in (9.0 m) |
| Draft: | 23 ft (7.0 m) |
| Propulsion: | steam turbines; 30,000 shp; 2 shafts |
| Reactors: | 1 pressurized-water type |
| Speed: | approx. 20 knots surface |
| | approx. 25 knots submerged |
| Complement: | approx. 80 |
| Missiles: | 3 SS-N-8 SLBM |
| ASW weapons: | torpedoes |
| Torpedoes: | 6 21-in (533-mm) torpedo tubes (bow) |
| | 2 16-in (406-mm) torpedo tubes (stern) |
| Radars: | Snoop Tray |
| Sonars: | medium frequency |

One Hotel II submarine was converted in the early 1960s as test ship for the SS-N-8 missile (for the Yankee SSBN). The submarine was lengthened almost 50 feet (15.2 m) to accommodate the larger missiles and associated equipment. This submarine is based in the Northern Fleet.

### 4 NUCLEAR-PROPELLED BALLISTIC MISSILE SUBMARINES (SSBN): HOTEL II

| Name | Completed | Conversion Completed |
| --- | --- | --- |
| . . . . . . | 1959–1962 | 1962–1967 |

| | |
| --- | --- |
| Builders: | Komsomol'sk |
| | Severodvinsk |
| Displacement: | 5,000 tons surface |
| | 6,000 tons submerged |
| Length: | 379 ft 6 in (115.0 m) |
| Beam: | 29 ft 9 in (9.0 m) |
| Draft: | 23 ft (7.0 m) |
| Propulsion: | steam turbines; 30,000 shp; 2 shafts |
| Reactors: | 1 pressurized-water type |
| Speed: | approx. 20 knots surface |
| | approx. 25 knots submerged |
| Complement: | approx. 80 |
| Missiles: | 3 SS-N-5 SLBM |
| ASW weapons: | torpedoes |
| Torpedoes: | 6 21-in (533-mm) torpedo tubes (bow) |
| | 2 16-in (406-mm) torpedo tubes (stern) |
| Radars: | Snoop Tray |
| Sonars: | medium frequency |

The Soviet Navy constructed eight of these SSBNs, further production being halted because of the changes in strategic forces policy in 1959–1961 and the subsequent development of the more capable Yankee SSBN.

One Hotel II has been converted to the Hotel III configuration as test ship for the SS-N-8 missile; one Hotel I was decommissioned in the early 1980s and apparently stricken. Two other units of the Hotel II configuration are being decommissioned or converted. One unit is named KRASNOGVARDETS (Red Guardsman).

Conversion: All eight submarines originally fitted with the surface-launch SS-N-4 missile (designated Hotel I). Seven were refitted with the underwater-launch, longer-range SS-N-5 missile, including one unit apparently completed as Hotel II.

Design: This design was unique to the Soviet Navy, being similar to the Golf SSB design, but nuclear propelled. The missile tubes are fitted in the sail structure, penetrating the submarine pressure hull.

Designation: Soviet PLARB type.

Engineering: The Hotel Class is fitted with the same reactor plant installed in the Echo SSGN and November SSN classes.

Hotel II sail structure with radar mast, radio antennas, and one periscope raised. (U.S. Navy, 1972)

A Hotel II SSBN at high speed. The pendant number on the sails of Soviet submarines changed periodically, as with surface ships, until the 1970s when display of these numbers stopped.

A Hotel II on the surface in the North Atlantic, some 600 n.miles northeast of Newfoundland. At the time, the submarine had machinery problems and was later towed to the Soviet Union. The bow diving planes are retracted into the hull; note the bow sonar installation (lighter colors). (U.S. Navy, 1972)

## (1) BALLISTIC MISSILE SUBMARINE (SSB): GOLF IV

| Name |
|------|
| . . . . . . |

| | |
|---|---|
| Builders: | (see Golf II listing) |
| Displacement: | 3,000 tons surface |
| | 3,400 tons submerged |
| Length: | 389 ft 4 in (118.0 m) |
| Beam: | 28 ft (8.5 m) |
| Draft: | 21 ft 9 in (6.6 m) |
| Propulsion: | diesel electric; 6,000 bhp diesels/5,300 shp electric motors; |
| | 3 shafts |
| Speed: | 17 knots surface |
| | 12 knots submerged |
| Range: | 9,000 n.miles at 5 knots |
| Complement: | approx. 90 |
| Missiles: | 6 SS-N-6 SLBM |
| ASW weapons: | torpedoes |
| Torpedoes: | 10 21-in (533-mm) torpedo tubes (6 bow; 4 stern) |
| Radars: | Snoop Tray |
| Sonars: | medium frequency |

One Golf I submarine was converted to this configuration about 1970 to serve as a test ship for the SS-N-6 missile. During the conversion the submarine was lengthened about 60 feet (18 m). The ship has probably been decommissioned.

Designation: Soviet PLRB type.

## 1 BALLISTIC MISSILE SUBMARINE (SSB): GOLF III

| Name |
|------|
| . . . . . . |

| | |
|---|---|
| Builders: | (See Golf II listing) |
| Displacement: | 2,900 tons surface |
| | 3,300 tons submerged |
| Length: | 363 ft (110 m) |
| Beam: | 28 ft (8.5 m) |
| Draft: | 21 ft 9 in (6.6 m) |
| Propulsion: | diesel-electric; 6,000 bhp diesels/5,300 shp electric motors; |
| | 3 shafts |
| Speed: | 17 knots surface |
| | 12 knots submerged |
| Range: | 9,000 n.miles at 5 knots |
| Complement: | approx. 90 |
| Missiles: | 6 SS-N-8 SLBM |
| ASW weapons: | torpedoes |
| Torpedoes: | 10 21-in (533-mm) torpedo tubes (6 bow; 2 stern) |
| Radars: | Snoop Tray |
| Sonars: | medium frequency |

One Golf I was converted to serve as a test ship for the SS-N-8 missile, being lengthened some 33 feet (10 m). This unit has been reported being dismantled in 1982–1983 to keep within the SALT I submarine missile limitations.

Designation: Soviet PLRB type.

## 14 BALLISTIC MISSILE SUBMARINES (SSB): GOLF II AND V

| Name | Completed |
|------|-----------|
| . . . . . (2 units) | 1958 |
| . . . . . (8 units) | 1959 |
| . . . . . (5 units) | 1960 |
| . . . . . (7 units) | 1961 |
| . . . . . (1 unit) | 1962 |

| | |
|---|---|
| Builders: | Komsomol'sk (7 units) |
| | Severodvinsk (16 units) |
| Displacement: | 2,300 tons surface |
| | 2,700 tons submerged |
| Length: | 330 ft (100.0 m) |
| Beam: | 28 ft (8.5 m) |
| Draft: | 21 ft 9 in (6.6 m) |
| Propulsion: | diesel-electric; 6,000 bhp diesels/5,300 shp electric motors; |
| | 3 shafts |
| Speed: | 17 knots surface |
| | 12–14 knots submerged |
| Range: | 9,000 n.miles at 5 knots |
| Complement: | approx. 85 |
| Missiles: | 3 SS-N-5 SLBM in Golf II |
| ASW weapons: | 1 SS-N-20 SLBN in Golf V |
| Torpedoes: | torpedoes |
| Radars: | 10 21-in (533-mm) torpedo tubes (6 bow; 4 stern) |
| Sonars: | Snoop Tray |
| | medium frequency |

A Golf II in the North Atlantic. Note the communications mast on the starboard side of the sail structure and the housing aft for a communications buoy.

These are mostly Golf I-class submarines that were converted from 1965 on to the Golf II configuration with the installation of the underwater-launch SS-N-5 missile. One Golf II has had her three missile tubes removed and one missile tube for the SS-N-20 missile installed in their place; she was redesignated Golf V. The submarine is now in the Black Sea.

A total of 23 Golf-class submarines were built, 22 being completed as Golf I and possibly one as a Golf II. The above dates and shipyards reflect the entire class. Of these, 13 were converted to Golf II, one each to Golf III and IV, and three have been modified to special communications configurations (SSQ). One additional Golf was lost at sea in the mid-Pacific in 1968 with her entire crew; portions of that submarine were raised in 1974 by the U.S. Central Intelligence Agency. Thus, three remain in essentially the original Golf I SSB configuration (see below).

The plans and some components of an additional Golf SSB were given to China and assembled there, the submarine being launched in 1964.

Of the 12 remaining Golf II submarines, 6 are based in the Baltic and 6 in the Pacific.

Designation: Soviet PLRB type.

Golf II-class SSB

One of the Soviet Navy's Golf II submarines in the Baltic Sea off the coast of Denmark. (U.S. Navy, 1978)

Golf II SSB with communications buoy housing aft of sail structure. The circles on the deck indicate hatches and rescue/emergency communication buoys.

## 4 BALLISTIC MISSILE SUBMARINES (SSB): GOLF I

| | |
|---|---|
| Builders: | (see Golf II listing) |
| Displacement: | 2,300 tons surface |
| | 2,700 tons submerged |
| Length: | 330 ft (100.0 m) |
| Beam: | 28 ft (8.5 m) |
| Draft: | 21 ft 9 in (6.6 m) |
| Propulsion: | diesel electric; 6,000 bhp diesels/5,300 shp electric motors; 3 shafts |
| Speed: | 17 knots surface |
| | 12–14 knots submerged |
| Range: | 9,000 n.miles at 5 knots |
| Complement: | approx. 85 |

| | |
|---|---|
| Missiles: | 3 SS-N-4 SLBM |
| ASW weapons: | torpedoes |
| Torpedoes: | 10 21-in (533-mm) torpedo tubes (6 bow; 4 stern) |
| Radars: | Snoop Tray |
| Sonars: | medium frequency |

These are the survivors of the Golf SSBN class in the original configuration. All are believed to have been retired from the SSB role by the early 1980s. One of these units may be in the process of conversion to a communications submarine (SSQ).

Designation: Soviet PLRB type.

This dated but classic photograph of a Golf I SSB clearly shows the submarine's lines, with two men standing atop the sail structure indicating the craft's size. (U.S. Navy, 1962)

Golf I SSB with the hatch of one SS-N-4 tube in the open position and various antennas and masts partially raised. (U.S. Navy, 1962)

## 2 + NUCLEAR-PROPELLED GUIDED MISSILE SUBMARINES (SSGN): OSCAR

| Name | Launched | Completed |
|------|----------|-----------|
| . . . . . . | Apr 1980 | 1982 |

| | |
|------|------|
| Builders: | Severodvinsk |
| Displacement: | approx. 10,000 tons surface |
| | approx. 14,000 tons submerged |
| Length: | 472 ft (143.0 m) |
| Beam: | 57 ft 9 in (17.5 m) |
| Draft: | |
| Propulsion: | steam turbines: 2 shafts |
| Reactors: | 1 |
| Speed: | approx. 30 knots submerged |
| Complement: | |
| Missiles: | 24 SS-N-19 anti-ship |
| ASW weapons: | torpedoes |
| | SS-N-15 |
| Torpedoes: | . . . 21-in (533-mm) torpedo tubes |
| Radars: | new variant of Snoop Series |
| Sonars: | low frequency |

The Oscar is a very large "attack"-type submarine, carrying three times the number of anti-ship missiles than the previous Charlie SSGN. The 24 missile tubes are in two rows of 12, fixed in elevation at an angle of approximately 40°. The missiles are launched while the submarine is submerged.

Additional units are believed to be under construction.

Designation: Soviet PLARK type.

## 1 NUCLEAR-PROPELLED GUIDED MISSILE SUBMARINE (SSGN): PAPA

| Name | Completed |
|------|-----------|
| . . . . . . | 1970 |

| | |
|------|------|
| Builders: | Gor'kiy |
| Displacement: | 6,700 tons surface |
| | 7,500 tons submerged |
| Length: | 359 ft 9 in (109 m) |
| Beam: | 36 ft 6 in (12.0 m) |
| Draft: | 28 ft (8.5 m) |
| Propulsion: | steam turbines; 2 shafts |
| Reactors: | 1 |
| Speed: | approx. 35–40 knots submerged |
| | (see below) |
| Complement: | approx. 85 |
| Missiles: | 10 SS-N-9 anti-ship |
| ASW weapons: | torpedoes |
| | SS-N-15 |
| Torpedoes: | 8 21-in (533-mm) torpedo tubes (bow) |
| Radars: | |
| Sonars: | low frequency |

Only a single Papa-class SSGN has been built, apparently as a prototype for advanced SSGN concepts. The Papa is considerably larger and carries more missiles and longer-range weapons than in the Charlie submarines.

The larger size may be related to an advanced power plant, with some reports indicating a speed almost as high as that of the Alfa. A U.S. official has described the Papa's speed as "remarkable" and indicated that the submarine's horsepower could be as high as 60,000.

Designation: Soviet PLARK type.

Papa SSGN under way at high surface speed in Barents Sea. Note the "notched" upper rudder configuration. (U.S. Navy, 1982)

Stern view of Papa SSGN in Barents Sea. (U.S. Navy, 1982)

Sail structure of a Papa-class SSGN.

The single Papa-class submarine displaying the submarine's unusual lines. The Papa has a very high submerged speed, carries a large missile battery, and apparently served as prototype for advanced SSGN concepts, some of which were incorporated in the subsequent Oscar class. (Ministry of Defence)

**7 NUCLEAR-PROPELLED GUIDED MISSILE SUBMARINES (SSGN): CHARLIE II**

| Name | Completed |
|------|-----------|
| . . . . . . (1 unit) | 1973 |
| . . . . . . (1 unit) | 1974 |
| . . . . . . (1 unit) | 1977 |
| . . . . . . (1 unit) | 1979 |
| . . . . . . (1 unit) | 1980 |
| . . . . . . (1 unit) | 1981 |
| . . . . . . (1 unit) | 1982 |

| | |
|---|---|
| Builders: | Gor'kiy |
| Displacement: | 4,300 tons surface |
| | 5,100 tons submerged |
| Length: | 340 ft (103.0 m) |
| Beam: | 33 ft (10.0 m) |
| Draft: | 26 ft 4 in (8.0 m) |
| Propulsion: | steam turbines; 30,000 shp; 1 shaft |
| Reactors: | 1 pressurized water |

| | |
|---|---|
| Speed: | approx. 26 knots submerged |
| Complement: | approx. 85 |
| Missiles: | 8 SS-N-7 or SS-N-9 |
| ASW weapons: | torpedoes |
| | SS-N-15 |
| Torpedoes: | 6 21-in (533-mm) torpedo tubes (bow) |
| Radars: | Snoop Tray |
| Sonars: | low frequency |

These are improved versions of the original Charlie SSGN, lengthened forward of the sail structure by 26⅓ ft (8 m) to accommodate improved weapons and electronic capabilities. The Charlie II can fire the SS-N-7 or longer-ranger SS-N-9. These submarines were built at about half the rate of the Charlie I class; construction ended, with the last unit being launched in 1980.

Designation: Soviet PLARK type.

Charlie II-class SSGN (1979)

Charlie II-class SSGN

## 12 NUCLEAR-PROPELLED GUIDED MISSILE SUBMARINES (SSGN): CHARLIE I

| Name | Completed |
|------|-----------|
| . . . . . (1 unit) | 1967 |
| . . . . . (2 units) | 1968 |
| . . . . . (1 unit) | 1969 |
| . . . . . (3 units) | 1970 |
| . . . . . (2 units) | 1972 |
| . . . . . (3 units) | 1973 |

| | |
|---|---|
| Builders: | Gor'kiy |
| Displacement: | 4,000 tons surface |
| | 4,900 tons submerged |
| Length: | 313 ft 6 in (95.0 m) |
| Beam: | 33 ft (10.0 m) |
| Draft: | 26 ft 4 in (8.0 m) |
| Propulsion: | steam turbines; 30,000 shp; 1 shaft |
| Reactors: | 1 pressurized-water |
| Speed: | approx. 27 knots |
| Complement: | approx. 80 |

| | |
|---|---|
| Missiles: | 8 SS-N-7 anti-ship |
| ASW weapons: | torpedoes |
| | SS-N-15 |
| Torpedoes: | 6 21-in (533-mm) torpedo tubes (bow) |
| Radars: | Snoop Tray |
| Sonars: | low frequency |

These submarines have shorter-range missiles than the previous Echo SSGN, but have the significant advantage of underwater missile launch. The above completion dates are based on the average of two submarines per year.

Design: The missile tubes are housed in the bow, external to the pressure hull, angled upward, four on each side, with large outer doors. The tubes cannot be reloaded from within the submarine.

Designation: Soviet PLARK type.

Engineering: The Charlie SSGN reactor plant is similar to that in the Victor SSN and Yankee-Delta SSBN classes, but with less horsepower and only one shaft.

Charlie I-class SSGN (1982)

A Charlie I cruise missile submarine on the surface while transiting the South China Sea en route to her new home port in the Far East. Forward of the sail structure are the outline of the retracted diving planes and the hatches for the four SS-N-7 missile tubes on the starboard side of the bow.

Charlie I SSGN sail showing (left to right) periscope, HF antenna, VHF antenna (partially hidden), Park Lamp direction-finding loop, Snoop Tray radar antenna, and Brick Pulp ESM antenna. (Ministry of Defence)

Charlie I-class SSGN

**29 NUCLEAR-PROPELLED GUIDED MISSILE SUBMARINES (SSGN): ECHO II**

| Name | Completed |
|------|-----------|
| . . . . . . (2 units) | 1962 |
| . . . . . . (4 units) | 1963 |
| . . . . . . (7 units) | 1964 |
| . . . . . . (7 units) | 1965 |
| . . . . . . (6 units) | 1966 |
| . . . . . . (3 units) | 1967 |

| | |
|---|---|
| Builders: | Komsomol'sk |
| | Severodvinsk |
| Displacement: | 5,000 tons surface |
| | 6,000 tons submerged |
| Length: | 379 ft 5 in (115.0 m) |
| Beam: | 29 ft 9 in (9.0 m) |
| Draft: | 24 ft 9 in (7.5 m) |
| Propulsion: | steam turbines; 25,000 shp; 2 shafts |
| Reactors: | 1 pressurized water |
| Speed: | approx. 20 knots surface |
| | approx. 23 knots submerged |
| Complement: | approx. 90 |
| Missiles: | 8 SS-N-3a Shaddock or SS-N-12 anti-ship |
| ASW weapons: | torpedoes |
| Torpedoes: | 6 21-in (533-mm) torpedo tubes (bow) |
| | 4 16-in (406-mm) torpedo tubes (stern) |
| Radars: | Front Door |
| | Front Piece |
| | Snoop Slab |
| Sonars: | low frequency |

These were the Soviet Navy's primary anti-carrier submarines during the 1960s and 1970s. They are the definitive Shaddock-armed SSGNs, evolving from the Echo I and Juliett submarine designs. These submarines are being modified to fire the improved SS-N-12.

The Echo II SSGNs were built in about equal numbers by the Komsomol'sk and Severodvinsk yards. (All of five Echo I-class SSGNs were built at Komsomol'sk.)

Class: The Echo I class was a different design. The five SSGNs of that class were subsequently converted as SSNs.

Design: These submarines have their large missile tubes mounted in pairs above the pressure hull. For firing, the submarine surfaces and the paired tubes are elevated. The forward section of the sail structure rotates 180° to reveal the Front-series missile guidance radars.

Designation: Soviet PLARK type.

Engineering: The reactor plant is similar to that of the Hotel SSBN and November SSN classes.

Echo II SSGN with two pairs of SS-N-3 Shaddock missile tubes in elevated (firing) position. (U.S. Navy)

Echo II SSGN with openings for missile blast exhaust visible behind paired tubes; the radio antenna at the after end of the sail structure folds down. (U.S. Navy)

Echo II-class SSGN

A closeup of an Echo II SSGN in the North Atlantic. The broad face of the sail structure covers the Front Door radar used for guiding the SS-N-3/12 anti-ship missiles; note also the open spaces abaft the paired missile tubes and the recessed opening abaft the sail for the HF radio mast, seen here in the fully extended position. (Ministry of Defence)

Echo II SSGN with forward edge of sail structure rotated to expose Front Door radar. (Ministry of Defence)

## 16 GUIDED MISSILE SUBMARINES (SSG): JULIETT

| Name | Completed |
| --- | --- |
| . . . . . (1 unit) | 1961 |
| . . . . . (2 units) | 1962 |
| . . . . . (2 units) | 1963 |
| . . . . . (2 units) | 1964 |
| . . . . . (2 units) | 1965 |
| . . . . . (2 units) | 1966 |
| . . . . . (2 units) | 1967 |
| . . . . . (2 units) | 1968 |
| . . . . . (1 unit) | 1969 |

| | |
| --- | --- |
| Builders: | Gor'kiy |
| Displacement: | 3,000 tons surface |
| | 3,750 tons submerged |
| Length: | 297 ft (90.0 m) |
| Beam: | 33 ft (10.0 m) |
| Draft: | 23 ft (7.0 m) |
| Propulsion: | diesel-electric; diesel motors 7,000 bhp/electric motors 5,000 shp; 2 shafts |
| Speed: | 16 knots surface |
| | 8 knots submerged |
| Range: | 9,000 n.miles at 7 knots |
| Complement: | approx. 80 |
| Missiles: | 4 SS-N-3a Shaddock anti-ship |
| ASW weapons: | torpedoes |
| Torpedoes: | 6 21-in (533-mm) torpedo tubes (bow) |
| | 4 16-in (406-mm) torpedo tubes (stern) |
| Radars: | Front Door |
| | Front Piece |
| | Snoop Slab |
| Sonars: | low frequency |

These submarines remain in front-line service. Note that their period of construction overlaps the nuclear-powered Echo II SSGNs and the improved Charlie SSGNs. These submarines were divided about evenly between the Northern and Pacific Fleets until 1982 when at least four were assigned to the Baltic Fleet.

Design: The Shaddock missile tubes are paired, above the pressure hull; they elevate for firing. The Front Door/Front Piece guidance radar is built into the forward edge of the sail structure and opens by rotating 180°.

Designation: Soviet PLRK type.

Juliett-class SSG

A Juliett SSG on the surface off the coast of Spain in 1972 with a score of officers and enlisted men atop her sail. The bow sonar installation is clearly visible as well as the openings abaft the two pairs of SS-N-3 Shaddock launch tubes. The Juliett has a relatively long sail structure with a snorkel exhaust faired into the after end. Julietts from the Northern Fleet regularly deploy to the Mediterranean Sea. (U.S. Navy, 1972)

## 4 GUIDED MISSILE SUBMARINES (SSG): WHISKEY LONG BIN

| Name | Conversion Completed |
|---|---|
| . . . . . . | 1962–1965 |

| | |
|---|---|
| Builders: | Baltic Shipyard, Leningrad |
| Displacement: | 1,200 tons surface |
| | 1,500 tons submerged |
| Length: | 274 ft (83.0 m) |
| Beam: | 20 ft 2 in (6.1 m) |
| Draft: | 16 ft 6 in (5.0 m) |
| Propulsion: | diesel-electric; diesel engines 4,000 bhp/electric motors 2,700 shp; 2 shafts |
| Speed: | 13.5 knots surface |
| | 8 knots submerged |
| Range: | 6,000 n.miles at 5 knots |
| Complement: | approx. 60–65 |
| Missiles: | 4 SS-N-3a Shaddock anti-ship |
| ASW weapons: | torpedoes |
| Torpedoes: | 4 21-in (533-mm) torpedo tubes (bow) |
| Radars: | Snoop Tray |
| Sonars: | medium frequency |

These are the survivors of seven Whiskey-class submarines converted to the so-called "Long Bin" configuration. The conversions were completed between 1962 and 1967 (additional conversions were cancelled). The two remaining submarines are probably employed in training.

Class: See Whiskey-class attack submarines (SS) for class notes. The six earlier Whiskey-SSG conversions (five "Twin Cylinder" and one "Single Cylinder") have been discarded.

Conversion: In conversion to missile configurations, these submarines were lengthened about 26 ft 4 in (8 m) and fitted with four Shaddock missiles tubes in the sail structure, fixed at an elevation of about 15°. The large, broad sail structure led to the name "long bin." Stern torpedo tubes removed.

Designation: Soviet PLRK type.

Whiskey Long Bin SSG during a naval review with a Kynda missile cruiser in the background.

A Whiskey Long Bin SSG at sea in the North Atlantic with a periscope and HF radio mast in the raised position. The four Shaddock tubes are in pairs, staggered one above the other, inclined at a fixed vertical angle within the enlarged sail structure. (Royal Navy, 1978)

Whiskey Long Bin SSG observed at high surface speed in the North Atlantic. (Royal Navy, 1978)

Alfa-class SSN

### . . . NUCLEAR-PROPELLED ATTACK SUBMARINES (SSN): IMPROVED ALFA

The long gestation period of the Alfa-class SSN and the traditional Soviet submarine design and construction practices indicate that an advanced nuclear attack submarine based on the Alfa propulsion technology is under construction, being built at either the Sudomekh-Admiralty complex in Leningrad or at Severodvinsk or both yards. Both yards are building new SSNS.

### 7 + NUCLEAR-PROPELLED ATTACK SUBMARINES (SSN): ALFA

| Name | Completed | Notes |
| --- | --- | --- |
| ....... (1 unit) | 1969 | Stricken |
| ....... (7 + units) | 1978 | |

| | |
| --- | --- |
| Builders: | Sudomekh Shipyard, Leningrad |
| Displacement: | Severodvinsk(?) |
| | 2,800 tons surface |
| | 3,680 tons submerged |
| Length: | 267 ft (81.0 m) |
| Beam: | 31 ft 4 in (9.5 m) |
| Draft: | 23 ft (7.0 m) |
| Propulsion: | steam turbines; 24,000 shp; 1 shaft |
| Reactors: | 1 liquid-metal type |
| Speed: | 42–45 knots submerged |
| Complement: | approx. 45 |
| ASW weapons: | torpedoes |
| | SS-N-15; 2 tubes(?) |
| | possibly SS-N-16; 2 tubes(?) |
| Torpedoes: | 6 21-in (533-mm) torpedo tubes (bow) |
| Radars: | Snoop Series |
| Sonars: | low frequency |

The Alfa was the world's fastest and deepest diving submarine when this volume went to press. The submarine incorporates a number of innovations, including a high power-to-weight reactor plant, a titanium hull, and extensive automation. The genesis of the Alfa was in the late 1950s (see chapter 10).

The first Alfa was initially completed in 1969 and underwent lengthy trials in the Baltic and Northern Fleet areas. Major problems were encountered with the lead ship, which has since been cut up and discarded. The second hull became operational in 1978. Series production was begun in the early 1970s.

Design: The Alfa is the world's only submarine known to have a titanium hull, providing considerable strength while being lighter than a steel-hulled craft. A very high degree of automation is provided in the engineering spaces, which may be unmanned while the submarine is under way. An operating depth of at least 2,000 feet (606 meters) is reported, significantly deeper than any other combat submarine. The U.S. research submarine DOLPHIN (AGSS 555) has a reported operating depth at least as great, but is an unarmed submarine test platform.

Designation: Soviet PLA type.

Engineering: The Alfa has an advanced reactor that uses a liquid metal, such as sodium rather than a pressurized-water type, as the heat-exchange medium between the reactor and the steam system. Acoustic data on the first Alfa SSNs indicated that the radiated noise levels at lesser speeds were generally similar to that of other Soviet SSNs, indicating a net improvement in view of the higher power of the Alfa reactor plant.

The very low manning levels in the Alfa indicate a high degree of automation in the propulsion system.

Alfa SSN sail showing (from left to right) Park Lamp DF loop, HF radio mast, radome mast, search and attack periscopes.

Alfa SSN. Note "notched" tail fin and minimal hull seen while on surface. Into 1983 the Alfa and Victor III SSN were being built at a combined rate of three submarines per year.

### 15 + NUCLEAR-PROPELLED ATTACK SUBMARINES (SSN): VICTOR III

| Name | Completed |
|------|-----------|
| . . . . . . | 1978 – |

| | |
|------|------|
| Builders: | Admiralty Shipyard, Leningrad |
| | Komsomol'sk |
| Displacement: | 4,600 tons surface |
| | 5,800 tons submerged |
| Length: | 349 ft 9 in (106.0 m) |
| Beam: | 52 ft 9 in (16.0 m) |
| Draft: | 23 ft (7.0 m) |
| Propulsion: | steam turbines; 30,000 shp; 1 shafts |
| Reactors: | 1 pressurized-water type |
| Speed: | approx. 29 knots submerged |
| Complement: | approx. 85 |
| ASW weapons: | torpedoes |
| | SS–N–15 } {2 tubes(?)} |
| | SS–N–16 |
| Torpedoes: | 8 21-in (533-mm) torpedo tubes (bow) |
| Radars: | Snoop Tray |
| Sonars: | low frequency |

These are further improvements of the Victor SSN, with the additional hull space forward of the sail structure probably being for an improved weapons capability. Construction of this class is continuing at Komsomol'sk. The towed sonar array pod was previously thought to house a communications antenna.

Designation: Soviet PLA type.

A dead-astern view of a Victor III making high speed on the surface. The pod atop the upper rudder apparently houses a towed sonar array. The streamlined hull form and sail are evident in this view taken in the Straits of Malacca. (1982).

Victor III SSN, showing small sail structure (compared to SSGN/SSBN designs) and tear-shaped pod structure atop tail fin.

Victor III-class SSN

## 7 NUCLEAR-PROPELLED ATTACK SUBMARINES (SSGN): VICTOR II

| Name | Completed |
| --- | --- |
| . . . . . . (1 unit) | 1972 |
| . . . . . . (1 unit) | 1974 |
| . . . . . . (1 unit) | 1975 |
| . . . . . . (2 units) | 1976 |
| . . . . . . (1 unit) | 1977 |
| . . . . . . (1 unit) | 1978 |

| | |
| --- | --- |
| Builders: | Admiralty Shipyard, Leningrad |
| Displacement: | 4,500 tons surface |
| | 5,700 tons submerged |
| Length: | 330 ft (100.0 m) |
| Beam: | 33 ft (10.0 m) |
| Draft: | 23 ft (7.0 m) |
| Propulsion: | steam turbines; 30,000 shp; 1 shaft |
| Reactors: | 1 pressurized-water type |
| Speed: | 28 knots submerged |
| Complement: | approx. 80 |
| ASW weapons: | torpedoes |
| | SS–N–15 |
| | SS–N–16  {2 tubes(?)} |
| Torpedoes: | 8 21-in (533-mm) torpedo tubes (bow) |
| Radar: | Snoop Tray |
| Sonar: | low frequency |

These are improved Victor-class SSNs.

Designation: Soviet PLA type. This variant was initially given the NATO code name Uniform; changed to Victor II.

Victor II-class SSN

Victor II-class SSN

## 16 NUCLEAR-PROPELLED ATTACK SUBMARINES (SSN): VICTOR I

| Name | Completed |
|---|---|
| . . . . . (2 units) | 1967 |
| . . . . . (1 unit) | 1968 |
| . . . . . (2 units) | 1969 |
| . . . . . (3 units) | 1970 |
| . . . . . (1 unit) | 1971 |
| . . . . . (3 units) | 1972 |
| . . . . . (2 units) | 1973 |
| . . . . . (2 units) | 1974 |

| | |
|---|---|
| Builders: | Admiralty Shipyard, Leningrad |
| Displacement: | 4,300 tons surface |
| | 5,100 tons submerged |
| Length: | 313 ft 6 in (95.0 m) |
| Beam: | 33 ft (10.0 m) |
| Draft: | 23 ft (7.0 m) |
| Propulsion: | steam turbines; 30,000 shp; 1 shaft (see notes) |
| Reactors: | 1 pressurized-water type |
| Speed: | 30–32 knots |
| Complement: | approx. 80 |
| ASW weapons: | torpedoes |
| | SS-N-15 |
| Torpedoes: | 8 21-in (533-mm) torpedo tubes (bow) |
| Radar: | Snoop Tray |
| Sonar: | low frequency |

These are advanced attack submarines, built to the tear-drop hull design for high underwater speeds. One unit is named 50 LET SSR (50 Years of the USSR).

Designation: Soviet PLA type.

Engineering: The Victor SSN reactor plant is the same as is fitted in the Charlie SSGN and is similar to the Yankee-Delta SSBN plants.

Two small, two-bladed propellers are fitted on the stern planes for slow-speed operation in all of the Victor classes.

Victor I SSN with bow diving planes extended.

Victor I SSN on surface in South China Sea while en route to assignment with the Pacific Fleet. Her sail is crowded with men sunbathing, a favorite Soviet pastime while ashore or afloat. The Victor is generally considered to be the first Soviet submarine designed specifically for the anti-submarine role, the principal mission of the U.S. Navy's SSNs. (U.S. Navy, 1974)

### 5 NUCLEAR-PROPELLED ATTACK SUBMARINES (SSN): ECHO (formerly SSGN)

| Name | Completed | Conversion Completed |
|---|---|---|
| . . . . . . (2 units) | 1960 | |
| . . . . . . (2 units) | 1961 | 1970–1974 |
| . . . . . . (1 unit) | 1962 | |

| | |
|---|---|
| Builders: | Komsomol'sk |
| Displacement: | 4,500 tons surface |
| | 5,500 tons submerged |
| Length: | 363 ft (110.0 m) |
| Beam: | 29 ft 9 in (9.0 m) |
| Draft: | 24 ft 9 in (7.5 m) |
| Propulsion: | steam turbines; 25,000 shp; 2 shafts |
| Reactors | 1 pressurized-water type |
| Speed: | 20 knots surface |
| | 25 knots submerged |
| Complement: | approx. 75 |
| ASW weapons: | torpedoes |
| | SS-N-15(?) |
| Torpedoes: | 6 21-in (533-mm) torpedo tubes (bow) |
| | 4 16-in (406-mm) torpedo tubes (stern) |
| Radars: | Snoop Tray |
| Sonars: | medium frequency |

Five Echo I SSGNs were built with an armament of six SS-N-3 Shaddock missiles. They lacked the radar suite and certain other features of the Juliett SSG and Echo II SSGN classes. All five are assigned to the Pacific Fleet.

Conversion: Conversions to attack configuration began in 1968, with all five units modified at Komsomol'sk.

Designation: Soviet PLA type.

### 9 NUCLEAR-PROPELLED ATTACK SUBMARINES (SSN/SSGN) YANKEE

| Name | Completed |
|---|---|
| . . . . . . (1 unit) | 1967 |
| . . . . . . (3 units) | 1968 |
| . . . . . . (5 units) | 1969 |

These are converted Yankee SSBNs with their SS-N-6 missile tubes inoperative and possibly removed. Into 1983 they were all inactive, but they are expected to be modified and employed in the SSN role. The above completion dates are based on the first nine Yankee submarines.

At least one unit has emerged from the yard in a cruise missile configuration.

Designations: Soviet PLA type.

Echo SSN at high speed. The hull has been plated over and streamlined with removal of the six Shaddock tubes, giving the submarine improved underwater performance. A full SSN sonar suite is provided. The radio mast, shown here in the raised position, is lowered into deck recess when submerging. (The suffix Roman numeral I is generally not used for this class since conversion to SSN.)

## 12 NUCLEAR-PROPELLED SUBMARINES (SSN): NOVEMBER

| Name | Completed |
|------|-----------|
| Leninskiy Komsomolets | 1958 |
| . . . . . . (12 units) | 1959–1964 |

| | |
|---|---|
| Builders: | Severodvinsk |
| Displacement: | 4,500 tons surface |
| | 5,300 tons submerged |
| Length: | 363 ft (110.0 m) |
| Beam: | 29 ft 9 in (9.0 m) |
| Draft: | 25 ft 4 in (7.7 m) |
| Propulsion: | steam turbines; 30,000 shp; 2 shafts |
| Reactors: | 1 pressurized-water type |
| Speed: | 30 knots submerged |
| Complement: | approx. 80 |
| ASW weapons: | torpedoes |
| Torpedoes: | 8 21-in (533-mm) torpedo tubes (bow) |
| | 4 16-in (406-mm) torpedo tubes (stern) |
| Radars: | Snoop Tray |
| Sonars: | medium frequency |

November SSN leaving an Arctic port with her crew mustered on deck. The uppermost torpedo tube openings are just below the lighter-colored bow sonar dome. (Soviet Navy)

These were the Soviet Navy's first nuclear submarines. The Leninskiy Komsomolets was commissioned on 8 Apr 1958; she was the first Soviet submarine to reach the geographic North Pole (1962). Fifteen submarines of this class were built; one was lost (see below), and two are in reserve. Additional units can be expected to be decommissioned in the near future.

Class: One submarine of this class sank off the Atlantic coast of Spain in April 1970. (No personnel are believed to have been lost.)

Designation: Soviet PLA type.

Engineering: The November's reactor plant is similar to that of the Echo II SSGN and Hotel SSBN classes.

November SSN sail structure with mast-mounted radome raised.

November SSN. Note the submarine's relatively conventional lines and the large amount of the hull seen above the surface compared to later Soviet SSN/SSGN classes. The Hotel-Echo-November reactor plants are similar, i.e., Soviet first-generation.

## 2 + ATTACK SUBMARINES (SS): KILO

| Name | Launched | Completed |
|---|---|---|
| . . . . . . | Sep 1980 | 1982(?) |

Builders:        Komsomol'sk
Displacement:    2,500 tons surface
                 3,200 tons submerged
Length:          221 ft (67.0 m)
Beam:            29 ft 9 in (9.0 m)
Draft:
Propulsion:      diesel-electric; 2 shafts
Speed:

Range:
Complement:
ASW weapons:     torpedoes
Torpedoes:       . . . 21-in (533-mm) torpedo tubes (bow)
Radars:
Sonars:          low frequency

The Kilo is a medium-range submarine, apparently the replacement for the Whiskey and Romeo classes. At least one additional unit had been launched by early 1983.

Designation: Soviet PL type.

This is probably the lead Kilo-class submarine, photographed during a high-speed surface run in the northern Sea of Japan. She has an advanced hull form and streamlined sail structure. (1982)

Kilo-class SS; the forward and aft escape hatches are highlighted to assist rescue operations, and the top of a rescue communications buoy is visible just ahead of the after hatch. (1982)

**15 + ATTACK SUBMARINES (SS): TANGO**

| Name | Completed |
|------|-----------|
| . . . . . . | 1972– |

| | |
|------|------|
| Builders: | Gor'kiy |
| Displacement: | 3,000 tons surface |
| | 3,700 tons submerged |
| Length: | 302 ft (91.5 m) |
| Beam: | 29 ft 9 in (9.0 m) |
| Draft: | 23 ft (7.0 m) |
| Propulsion: | diesel-electric; diesel engines 6,000 bhp/electric motors |
| | 6,000 shp; 3 shafts |
| Speed: | 20 knots surface |
| | 16 knots submerged |
| Range: | |
| Complement: | approx. 70 |
| ASW weapons: | torpedoes |
| Torpedoes: | 6 21-in (533-mm) torpedo tubes (6 bow) |
| Radars: | Snoop Tray |
| Sonars: | low frequency |

Tango-class SS (Ministry of Defence)

These are long-range attack submarines, the successor to the Foxtrot-class SS in Soviet service. Construction continues.

Design: These submarines have significantly more pressure-hull volume than the Foxtrot class, the increased space providing more battery capacity.

Designation: Soviet PL type.

Tango-class SS (Royal Air Force, 1981)

Tango SS at high surface speed. The Tango's bow sonar dome is not painted in a lighter color as in similar Foxtrot and other Soviet submarines. This submarine was photographed in the Western Mediterranean. (Ministry of Defence, 1981)

## 55 ATTACK SUBMARINES (SS): FOXTROT

| Name | Completed |
|---|---|
| CHELYABINSKIY KOMSOMOLETS | |
| KOMSOMOLETS KAZAKHSTANA | |
| KUIBISHEVSKIY KOMSOMOLETS | |
| MAGNITOGORSKIY KOMSOMOLETS | 1958–1967 |
| PSKOVSKIY KOMSOMOLETS | 1971–(?) |
| UL'YANOVSKIY KOMSOMOLETS | |
| VLADIMIRSKIY KOMSOMOLETS | |
| YAROSLAVSKIY KOMSOMOLETS | |
| . . . . . . (52 units) | |

| | |
|---|---|
| Builders: | Sudomekh Shipyard, Leningrad |
| Displacement: | 1,950 tons surface |
| | 2,400 tons submerged |
| Length: | 302 ft (91.5 m) |
| Beam: | 24 ft 9 in (7.5 m) |
| Draft: | 19 ft 9 in (6.0 m) |
| Propulsion: | diesel-electric; diesel engines 6,000 bhp/electric motors 5,300 shp; 3 shafts |
| Speed: | 16 knots surface |
| | 15.5 knots submerged |
| Range: | 11,000 n.miles at 8 knots |
| Complement: | 75–80 |
| ASW weapons: | torpedoes |
| Torpedoes: | 6 21-in (533-mm) torpedo tubes (bow) |
| | 4 16-in (406-mm) torpedo tubes (stern) |
| Radars: | Snoop Tray |
| Sonars: | medium frequency Herkules/Feniks |

These are highly capable long-range submarines, an improved version of the Zulu class.

Class: Sixty-two units are believed to have been built for the Soviet Navy, with 45 delivered through 1967, followed by a second group after a four-year hiatus. Two Foxtrot submarines have been used for oceanographic research with the names SATURN and SIRIUS; in 1983 a unit was sighted with the name REGUL (i.e., "RIGEL").

At least 14 additional Foxtrots have been built for foreign transfer, with 2 going to Cuba, 8 to India, and 5 to Libya through late 1982 (with probably a sixth to follow).

Designation: Soviet PL type.

Engineering: Submerged (non-snorkel) endurance is estimated at more than seven days at very slow speed.

Names: Class names that are known honor *komsomol* (young communist) groups within cities.

The differences in hull configuration of the Foxtrot (left) and Tango (right) submarine designs are readily evident in this photo of the undersea craft being serviced by an Oskol "floating workshop" (*plavuchaya masterskaya*). This is the PM 24, with her twin 25-mm gun mounts aft and a twin 57-mm gun mount forward.

A Foxtrot attack submarine on the surface in the Mediterranean with the U.S. destroyer JONAS INGRAM (DD 938) keeping watch. The submarine's radio mast and a whip antenna are raised, while the larger antenna mast is folded to the deck abaft the sail. The "step" at the after end of the sail is the snorkel exhaust. (U.S. Navy, 1973)

Closeup of Foxtrot SS sail structure with Snoop Tray radar raised. The upper row of "windows" open to the inner bridge level, while the lower row are sonar antennas. The bridge watch is wearing foul-weather gear. (1982)

Foxtrot-class SS (Soviet Navy)

Foxtrot-class SS (1982)

## 12 ATTACK SUBMARINES (SS): ROMEO

| Name | Completed |
|------|-----------|
| . . . . . . | 1958–1962 |

| | |
|------|-----------|
| Builders: | Gor'kiy |
| Displacement: | 1,330 tons surface |
| | 1,700 tons submerged |
| Length: | 254 ft (77.0 m) |
| Beam: | 22 ft (6.7 m) |
| Draft: | 16 ft 2 in (4.9 m) |
| Propulsion: | diesel-electric; diesel engines 4,000 bhp/electric motors 3,000 shp; 2 shafts |
| Speed: | 15.5 knots surface |
| | 13 knots submerged |
| Range: | 7,000 n.miles at 5 knots |
| Complement: | approx. 55 |
| ASW weapons: | torpedoes |
| Torpedoes: | 8 21-in (533-mm) torpedo tubes (6 bow; 2 stern) |
| Radars: | Snoop Plate |
| Sonars: | medium frequency Tamir |

The Romeo is a medium-range submarine, a much-improved successor to the Whiskey.

Class: Twenty submarines of this class were built at Gor'kiy, of which two have been transferred to Bulgaria and six to Egypt. One unit report-edly planned for transfer to Algeria was retained by the Soviet Navy. Construction of this design has also been undertaken in China and North Korea; two of the Chinese-built craft were transferred to Egypt in 1982.

Designation: Soviet PL type.

Romeo sail structure with (left to right) radio antenna, Quad Loop DF antenna, Snoop Tray radar, and two periscopes in raised position. The Romeo is easily identified by the faired extension to the periscope housings. (1974)

Romeo SS on the surface with guard rails rigged. The small amount of deck structure showing indicates that the boat is rigged for diving.

Romeo-class SS at high surface speed. Note the earlier, overhang configuration of the forward edge of the sail structure.

## ? ATTACK SUBMARINES (SS): QUEBEC

| Name | Completed |
| --- | --- |
| . . . . . | 1954–1957 |

| | |
| --- | --- |
| Builders: | Sudomekh Shipyard, Leningrad |
| Displacement: | 400 tons surface |
| | 540 tons submerged |
| Length: | 184 ft 9 in (56.0 m) |
| Beam: | 16 ft 9 in (5.1 m) |
| Draft: | 12 ft 6 in (3.8 m) |
| Propulsion: | diesel-electric; diesel engines 3,000 bhp/electric motors |
| | 2,200 shp; 3 shafts |
| Speed: | 18 knots surface |
| | 16 knots submerged |
| Range: | |
| Complement: | 30 |

| | |
| --- | --- |
| ASW weapons: | torpedoes |
| Torpedoes: | 4 21-in (533-mm) torpedo tubes (bow) |
| Radars: | Snoop Plate |
| Sonars: | medium frequency Tamir/Feniks |

All of the survivors of 30 ships of this class have apparently been decommissioned. Four ships were reported in active service as late as 1982, probably as training ships. Some units may be retained in reserve.

Class: Thirty units built.

Designation: Soviet PL type.

Engineering: Designed to have a closed-cycle Kreislauf diesel system that permitted underwater use of the diesel to charge batteries without the use of snorkel. The system was not successful, with several accidents occurring. Subsequently fitted with conventional diesel-electric system.

Quebec-class SS

## 8 ATTACK SUBMARINES (SS): ZULU IV

| Name | Completed |
| --- | --- |
| . . . . . | 1952–1955 |

| | |
| --- | --- |
| Builders: | Severodvinsk |
| | Sudomekh |
| Displacement: | 1,900 tons surface |
| | 2,350 tons submerged |
| Length: | 297 ft (90.0 m) |
| Beam: | 24 ft 9 in (7.5 m) |
| Draft: | 19 ft 9 in (6.0 m) |
| Propulsion: | diesel-electric; diesel engines 6,000 bhp; electric motors |
| | 5,300 shp; 3 shafts |
| Speed: | 18 knots surface |
| | 16 knots submerged |
| Range: | 9,500 n.miles at 8 knots |
| Complement: | approx. 70 |
| Guns: | (removed) |
| ASW weapons: | torpedoes |
| Torpedoes: | 10 21-in (533-mm) torpedo tubes (6 bow; 4 stern) |
| Radars: | Snoop Plate |
| Sonars: | medium frequency Herkules/Feniks |

The first Soviet long-range submarines of postwar design, the Zulu also provided the platform for the world's first ballistic missile submarine. Most of the surviving units are believed to be in reserve or employed in research and other special activities.

Class: A total of 26 Zulu-class submarines were built. Several were converted in the 1950s to ballistic missile submarines, being fitted with two tubes for the SS-N-4 SLBM (redesignated Zulu V); subsequently scrapped. Two others served as oceanographic research ships, renamed LIRA and VEGA. A third may have been employed in that role with the name ORION.

Design: This class incorporates several German design features. As built (Zulu I to III configuration), this class had deck guns and no snorkel. All updated to Zulu IV standards (guns removed, snorkel fitted, and other improvements).

Designation: Soviet PL type.

The Zulu IV class was built in relatively small numbers compared to the Foxtrot and, especially, the Whiskey classes. However, they have proved effective, long-range patrol submarines. The advanced hull form is based on the German Type XXI design, which also influenced postwar U.S. attack submarine design. (Ministry of Defence, 1979)

Zulu IV-class SS

## 57 ATTACK SUBMARINES (SS): WHISKEY

| Name | Completed |
|---|---|
| . . . . . . | 1951–1957 |

| | |
|---|---|
| Builders: | Baltic Shipyard, Leningrad |
| | Gor'kiy |
| | Komsomol'sk |
| | Marti, Nikolayev (south) |
| Displacement: | 1,050 tons surface |
| | 1,350 tons submerged |
| Length: | 247 ft 6 in (75.0 m) |
| Beam: | 20 ft 9 in (6.3 m) |
| Draft: | 15 ft 9 in (4.8 m) |
| Propulsion: | diesel-electric; diesel engines 4,000 bhp/electric motors |
| | 2,500 shp; 2 shafts |
| Speed: | 17 knots surface |
| | 13.5 knots submerged |
| Range: | 6,000 n.miles at 5 knots |
| Complement: | 50–55 |
| Guns: | (removed) |
| ASW weapons: | torpedoes |
| Torpedoes: | 6 21-in (533-mm) torpedo tubes (4 bow; 2 stern) |
| Radars: | Snoop Plate |
| Sonars: | medium frequency Tamir |

This was the first Soviet postwar submarine, built in larger numbers than any other submarine class in peacetime and still widely used. Of the surviving units, some 45 are in various degrees of active status and about 15 more are in operational reserve; others may be in a lesser stage of preservation. Some active units are apparently employed in research-experimental roles.

A Baltic Fleet unit is known to be named PSKOVSKIY KOMSOMOLETS.

Class: Four Soviet yards produced 236 Whiskey-class submarines before the program was abruptly halted. Thirteen were converted to various missile configurations to carry the SS-N-3 Shaddock missile (SSG); 4 or 5 to radar picket configurations (SSR); and 2 to fisheries research ships (renamed SEVERYANKA and SLAVYANKA).

At least 39 Whiskey-class submarines are believed to have been transferred to foreign navies—4 to Albania, 2 to Bulgaria, 6 to China, 1 to Cuba, 7 to Egypt, 12 to Indonesia, 2 to North Korea, and 5 to Poland. The Cuban unit was transferred in 1979 as a nonoperational training and battery-charging craft. Additional units have been built in China.

These submarines normally carry 12 reload torpedoes in addition to those in the tubes for a total loadout of 18 torpedoes.

Design: The class was designed during World War II, but some German features were incorporated. Units built to the Whiskey I, II, and IV designs had light anti-aircraft guns; most were subsequently modified to the definitive Whiskey V configuration.

Designations: Soviet PL type.

Whiskey SS sail structure. The antenna forward of the Quad Loop is the Stop Light ESM. (1982)

One of the 236 Whiskey-class submarines on the surface. Although production of the Whiskey was prematurely halted, it remains the largest submarine class built since World War II. Note the distinctive sail configuration with the snorkel exhaust and fixed Quad Loop DF antenna.

A Whiskey traveling at high speed on the surface in the Sea of Japan. This craft was fitted with several experimental sonar antennas forward when this photograph was taken in 1969. (U.S. Navy)

## 1 RADAR PICKET SUBMARINE (SSR): WHISKEY CANVAS BAG

| Name | Conversion Completed |
|------|---------------------|
| . . . . . . | 1958–1963 |

Four or five Whiskey-class attack submarines were converted to a radar picket configuration during the period indicated above. Character-

istics approximately as SS configuration, but with stern torpedo tubes removed and electronic equipment fitted, including air-search radar with the NATO code name Boat Sail. The designation "Canvas Bag" is derived from the covering sometimes seen over the Boat Sail radar.

One SSR has reverted to SS status in an apparent experimental role, and two or three have been scrapped.

Whiskey Canvas Bag SSR with elongated sail structure.

Whiskey Canvas Bag radar picket (SSR) submarine with the Boat Sail radar. When submerging, the radar folds in half and is often covered with a canvas bag, leading to the NATO code name. Visible just forward of the radar are the Stop Light and Quad Loop antennas.

## 2 AUXILIARY SUBMARINES (AGSS): INDIA

| Name | Completed |
|---|---|
| . . . . . . (1 unit) | 1979 |
| . . . . . . (1 unit) | 1980 |

| | |
|---|---|
| Builders: | Komsomol'sk |
| Displacement: | 3,200 tons surface |
| | 4,000 tons submerged |
| Length: | 349 ft 9 in (106.0 m) |
| Beam: | 33 ft (l0.0 m) |
| Draft: | |
| Propulsion: | diesel-electric; 2 shafts |
| Speed: | |
| Range: | |
| Complement: | |
| ASW weapons: | torpedoes |
| Torpedoes: | possibly . . . 21-in (533-mm) torpedo tubes (bow) |
| Radars: | |
| Sonars: | medium frequency |

These submarines are specially configured for salvage and rescue operations, with facilities for carrying two small submersibles. One unit is assigned to the Pacific Fleet and one to the Northern Fleet, the latter transiting via the Arctic route in 1980.

Design: These submarines were designed from the outset for the salvage and rescue role. Their hulls are configured for high surface speed, probably to permit them to deploy rapidly to operational areas. Two submersibles are carried semirecessed in tandem deck wells abaft the sail structure. There is probably direct access from the submersibles to the submarine while submerged (as in the U.S. Navy's DSRV rescue submersibles) to facilitate clandestine and under-ice operations. It is assumed that they are fitted with bow torpedo tubes.

The Northern Fleet's India-class salvage and rescue submarine, under way in the Barents Sea, with her two submersibles in their "nests." Note the large deck casing and the sail-mounted diving planes. (U.S. Navy, 1982)

India-class salvage and rescue submarine on the surface, while transiting to the Soviet Northern Fleet via the Arctic route as evidenced by the ice guard fitted over the bow and the two deck openings for submersibles being plated over. (1980)

India AGSS on the surface with two salvage-rescue submersibles in their "nests" in the deck casing abaft the sail. They can be entered directly from the submarine while submerged. The India is believed to be the only Soviet diesel submarine with sail-mounted diving planes. (1982)

A salvage-rescue submersible. The craft is similar in concept to the U.S. Navy's Deep Submergence Rescue Vehicles (DSRV), two of which have been built and can be carried and supported by most U.S. and British submarines. (1982)

### 1 AUXILIARY SUBMARINE (AGSS): LIMA

| Name | Completed |
|------|-----------|
| . . . . . . | 1978 |

| | |
|------|------|
| Builders: | Sudomekh Shipyard, Leningrad |
| Displacement: | 2,000 tons surface |
| | 2,400 tons submerged |
| Length: | 280 ft 6 in (85.0 m) |
| Beam: | 31 ft 4 in (9.5 m) |
| Draft: | 24 ft 4 in (7.4 m) |
| Propulsion: | diesel-electric |
| Speed: | |
| Range: | |
| Complement: | |
| ASW weapons: | |
| Torpedoes: | |
| Radars: | |
| Sonars: | |

Only one submarine of this type has been reported; she is believed to be operating in the Black Sea area.

The exact purpose and characteristics of this submarine are unknown. The hull length-to-beam ratio is relatively small, there is a large flatdeck area, the sail structure is set well amidships, and there is a fixed radar mast.

## 4 TARGET TRAINING SUBMARINES (SST): BRAVO

| Name | Completed |
|---|---|
| . . . . . . (1 unit) | 1967 |
| . . . . . . (2 units) | 1968 |
| . . . . . . (1 unit) | 1970 |

| | |
|---|---|
| Builders: | Komsomol'sk |
| Displacement: | 2,400 tons surface |
| | 2,900 tons submerged |
| Length: | 241 ft (73.0 m) |
| Beam: | 32 ft 4 in (9.8 m) |
| Draft: | 24 ft (7.3 m) |
| Propulsion: | diesel-electric; 1 shaft |
| Speed: | 14 knots surface |
| | 16 knots submerged |
| Range: | |
| Complement: | approx. 65 |
| ASW weapons: | torpedoes (?) |
| Torpedoes: | 6 21-in (533-mm) torpedo tubes (bow) (?) |
| Radars: | Snoop Tray |
| Sonars: | |

These are specialized target training submarines for ASW forces. They are similar in concept to the USS MACKEREL (SST 1) and MARLIN (SST 2) built in the 1950s. The Soviet boats may also have a training role and, in wartime, could be employed operationally.

Design: The torpedo tubes may not be fitted. The submarines are specially configured to permit their use as "hard" targets for ASW practice torpedoes.

Bravo-class SST

Bravo-class SST (1975)

The Bravo is a unique submarine class in contemporary navies, having been developed specifically as target submarines. The "hump" abaft the sail is apparently a "padded" area for the impact of dummy homing torpedoes. All four of the class were built in the Far East, but units have subsequently been transferred to the Northern and Baltic Fleets.

**3 COMMUNICATIONS SUBMARINES (SSQ): GOLF (former SSB)**

| Name | Conversion Completed |
|------|---------------------|
| . . . . . . | 1978 |

These are Golf I-class submarines converted to serve as command and communication ships or possibly electronic jamming platforms (see chapter 8). This concept was discussed for the U.S. nuclear submarine TRITON (SSRN 586), but was never carried out. One modified Golf is assigned to the Northern Fleet and two to the Pacific Fleet. An additional Golf I may be undergoing conversion to an SSQ.

The three tubes for the SS-N-4 missiles have been removed and special electronic equipment fitted, including a sail extension to house a communications antenna buoy and several radio antennas. See Golf-class SSB listing for basic characteristics.

Golf SSQ (1979)

Golf SSB converted to the communications role (SSQ), with extensive radio gear added, a communications buoy housing abaft the sail structure, and numerous antennas added. The cone-shaped antenna raised from the sail has the NATO designation Pert Spring. (1978)

# 12

# Aircraft Carriers

Tbilisi

4 3. NUCLEAR-PROPELLED AIRCRAFT CARRIER

| Name | Builder | Laid down | Launch | Complete | Status |
|------|---------|-----------|--------|----------|--------|
| ① Tbilisi | Black Sea Shipyard, Nikolayev (south) | 1983 | (1986–1987) | ~~(1988–1989)~~ | ~~Building~~ Trials |

② Riga (1990) ③ Ulyanovsk (1995) ④ (1996)

Preparations for the construction of this ship were first observed by Western intelligence, apparently by U.S. reconnaissance satellites, late in 1979. This indicates that a decision was taken to construct the ship in the five-year economic-defense plan that began in 1976. Completion can be expected before the end of the 1986–1990 five-year plan. She is being constructed in the same building dock as the KIEV-class carriers;

the dock was enlarged after the fourth ship of the earlier class was started.

Design: It is estimated that the ship will displace some 60,000 to 70,000 tons at full-load displacement. She is expected to have catapults and arresting wires for the operation of conventional fixed-wing aircraft. Aircraft capacity is expected to be 60–70.

The Soviet Union's first true aircraft carrier, the KIEV. The ship has classic aircraft carrier lines, but with several unusual features, such as the large island structure laden with antennas and the massive AAW/ASW/anti-surface weapon batteries forward. In this view there are four Ka-25 Hormone helicopters, with folded rotor blades, on the flight deck.

4

3 + 1 AIRCRAFT CARRIERS: "KIEV" CLASS

| Name | Builder | Laid down | Launched | Completed | Status |
|------|---------|-----------|----------|-----------|--------|
| KIEV | Black Sea Shipyard, Nikolayev (south) | Sep 1970 | Dec 1972 | May 1975 | **Northern** |
| MINSK | Black Sea Shipyard, Nikolayev (south) | Dec 1973 | May 1975 | Feb 1978 | **Pacific** |
| NOVOROSSIYSK | Black Sea Shipyard, Nikolayev (south) | Oct 1975 | Dec 1978 | 1981 | ~~Black Sea~~ *Pacific* |
| ~~KHARKOV~~ *Baku* | Black Sea Shipyard, Nikolayev (south) | 1978 | 1982 | (1984) | ~~Building~~ *Northern* |

| | |
|---|---|
| Displacement: | 32,000 tons standard |
| | 37,000–38,000 tons full load |
| Length: | 901 ft (273.0 m) overall |
| | 823 ft 4 in (249.5 m) waterline |
| Beam: | 108 ft (32.7 m) |
| Extreme width: | 155 ft 9 in (47.2 m) |
| Draft: | 27 ft (8.2 m) |
| Propulsion: | steam turbines; 140,000 shp; 4 shafts |
| Boilers: | |
| Speed: | 32 knots |
| Range: | 4,000 n.miles at 31 knots |
| | 13,500 n.miles at 18 knots |
| Complement: | approx. 1,700 |
| Aircraft: | approx. 36 { 12 Yak-36 Forger VTOL / up to 24 Ka-25 Hormone helicopters |
| Missiles: | 2 twin SA-N-3 Goblet launchers (72) |
| | 2 twin SA-N-4 launchers (40) |
| | 8 SS-N-12 Shaddock tubes (8 + 16 reloads) |
| Guns: | 4 76.2-mm/60-cal AA (2 twin) |
| | 8 30-mm close-in (8 × 1 multibarrel) |
| ASW weapons: | 1 twin SUW-N-1 missile launcher |
| | 2 RBU-6000 rocket launchers |
| | torpedoes |
| Torpedoes: | 10 21-in (533-mm) torpedo tubes (2 quin) |
| Radars: | 4 Bass Tilt (fire control) |
| | 2 Don-2 (navigation) |
| | 1 Don Kay (navigation) |
| | 2 Head Lights (fire control) |
| | 2 Owl Screech (fire control) |
| | 2 Pop Group (fire control) |
| | 1 Trap Door (fire control) |
| | 1 Top Sail (3-D air search) |
| | 1 Top Steer (3-D air search) |
| | 1 Top Knot (air control) |
| Sonars: | low frequency (hull mounted, bistatic) |
| | medium frequency (variable depth) |
| EW systems: | Bell Clout |
| | Bell Bash |
| | Bell Thump |
| | Rum Tub |
| | Side Globe |
| | Top Hat-A/B |

These ships are the first Soviet aircraft carriers to be built, having a full flight deck and a hull designed from the outset as a carrier. Two previous Soviet carrier programs, of the late 1930s and early 1950s, were cancelled early on. Construction of this class was probably approved in the five-year plan that began in 1966.

Aircraft: On her initial (1975) deployment to the Mediterranean, the KIEV operated 25 aircraft—9 Yak-36 Forger-A and 1 Yak-36 Forger-B VTOL aircraft plus 14 Ka-25 Hormone-A and 1 Ka-25 Hormone-B helicopters. All could be carried on the hangar deck. Maximum hangar capacity is estimated at 30 to 35 aircraft. (U.S. aircraft carriers stow less than half of their embarked aircraft in the hangar.)

Designation: The Soviet Navy originally classified the KIEV as a

heavy anti-submarine cruiser (*tyazholyi protivolodchyi kreyser*). However, by the early 1980s the ship was being referred to as a tactical aircraft-carrying cruiser (*takticheskoye avionosnyy kreyser*) with some senior Soviet naval officers referring to the ships as anti-submarine carriers or simply aircraft carriers.

NATO assigned the code name Kurile to this class before the Soviet name KIEV became known. Subsequently the name KIEV was adopted for reporting purposes.

Design: This class has a very large island structure on the starboard side and an angled flight deck, canted at about 4.5° to port from the centerline. No catapults or arresting wires are fitted. Unlike U.S. aircraft carriers, the KIEV has a full missile cruiser's armament of anti-air, anti-ship, and anti-submarine weapons. Most of these are fitted forward, depriving the ship of significant forward flight deck area. Portions of the flight deck are covered with blast-resistant (refractory) tile for VTOL aircraft operation.

The hull design features long, low lines, with boat stowage cut into the after hull. Aft, the ship has a freeboard of only some 42 ft 6 in (12.9 m) compared to more than 60 ft (18.2 m) for large U.S. carriers. The KIEV's stern counter has an opening for VDS and a reinforced panel to resist exhaust blast as aircraft hover immediately astern while transitioning from conventional to vertical landing flight configuration.

There are two relatively small aircraft elevators, one alongside the island and one immediately abaft the island—63 ft 4 in × 34 ft 2 in (19.2 m × 10.35 m) and 61 ft × 15 ft 6 in (18.5 × 4.7 m), respectively. There are also four weapon elevators that service the flight deck, one forward of the forward aircraft elevator, and three on the starboard side, abaft the island.

The full waterplane hull design of the KIEVs (common to Soviet warships) and active fin stabilization provide the ship with considerable stability.

Missiles: The KIEV and older Kynda cruiser classes are the only Soviet ships fitted with reloads for surface-to-surface missiles. The large SS-N-12 missiles are stowed in a below-deck magazine and carried to the launch tubes by an athwartships elevator. Sixteen reloads are stowed in the magazine, giving the ship a total of 24 Shaddock-type missiles.

Names: These ships are named for major Soviet cities, all of which experienced major combat in World War II.

Operational: The KIEV made her first operational deployment to the Mediterranean in July 1976. She subsequently transferred to the Northern Fleet that August, being assigned to that fleet until late December 1977, when she returned to the Mediterranean-Black Sea area. The ship appears to be permanently based in the Murmansk area, but returns to the Nikolayev yards for overhaul/upkeep.

The MINSK transited to the Pacific Fleet in 1979, steaming around the Cape of Good Hope and across the Indian Ocean; her home port is Vladivostok.

Island structure of the KIEV with (from left to right) antennas for Owl Screech, Don-2, Head Lights, Top Sail, Side Globe (EW domes on side of superstructure), Top Knot, Top Steer, Head Lights, and Owl Screech. (1976)

The MINSK under way in the South China Sea while transiting to the Pacific Fleet. The KIEV-class ships have a low freeboard compared to U.S. aircraft carriers. The large, dark shape at left is a blast/spray deflector, while the opening for the ship's VDS is under the ship's name. (U.S. Navy, 1979)

KIEV-class aircraft carrier

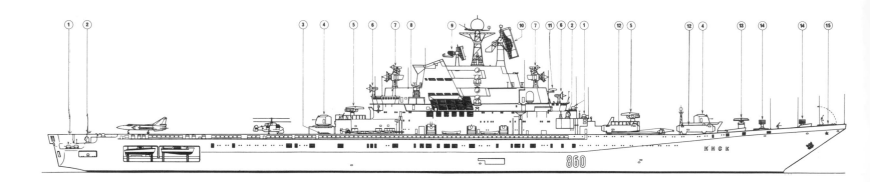

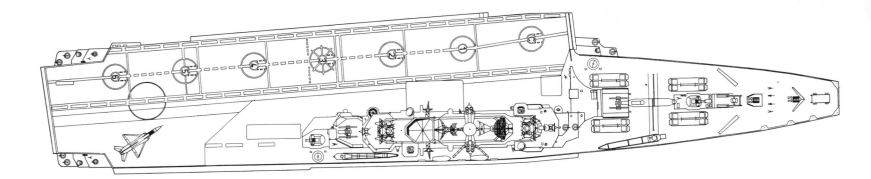

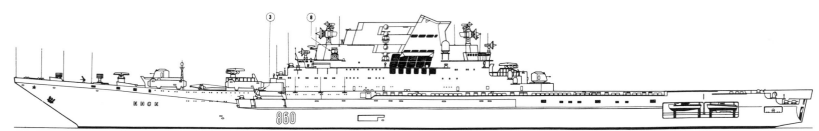

1. 30-mm Gatling guns 2. Bass Tilt radar 3. SA-N-4 launcher (retracted) 4. twin 76.2-mm AA gun mount 5. SA-N-3 launcher 6. Owl Screech radar 7. Head Lights radar 8. Pop Group radar 9. Top Steer radar 10. Top Sail radar 11. Don-2 radar 12. SS-N-12 missile tubes 13. SUW-N-1 launcher 14. RBU-6000 launchers (H. Simoni)

The carrier MINSK showing tiled flight deck area and heavy armament mounted on bow. There are two Gatling guns at the forward edge of the angled deck, two more forward of the island, and two on each of the stern quarters. (1980)

MINSK with aircraft elevator abaft the island lowered to hangar deck. (Ministry of Defence)

**2 HELICOPTER CARRIERS: "MOSKVA" CLASS**

| Name | Builder | Laid down | Launched | Completed | Status |
|---|---|---|---|---|---|
| MOSKVA | Black Sea Shipyard, Nikolayev (south) | 1962 | 1964 | July 1967 | **Black Sea** |
| LENINGRAD | Black Sea Shipyard, Nikolayev (south) | 1964 | 1966 | 1968 | **Black Sea** |

| | |
|---|---|
| Displacement: | 14,500 tons standard |
| | 17,000–18,000 tons full load |
| Length: | 623 ft 6 in (189.0 m) overall |
| Beam: | 85 ft 9 in (26.0 m) |
| Extreme width: | 112.5 ft (34.1 m) |
| Draft: | 25 ft 5 in (7.7 m) |
| Propulsion: | steam turbines; 100,000 shp; 2 shafts |
| Boilers: | 4 |
| Speed: | 31 knots |
| Range: | 4,500 n.miles at 29 knots |
| | 14,000 n.miles at 12 knots |
| Complement: | approx. 850 |
| Helicopters: | 14 Ka-25 Hormone helicopters |
| Missiles: | 2 twin SA-N-3 Goblet launchers (44) |
| Guns: | 4 57-mm/80-cal AA (2 twin) |
| ASW weapons: | 1 twin SUW-N-1 missile launcher |
| | 2 RBU-6000 rocket launchers |
| Torpedoes: | (removed) |
| Radars: | 3 Don-2 (navigation) |
| | 2 Head Lights (fire control) |
| | 1 Head Net-C (3-D air search) |
| | 2 Muff Cob (fire control) |
| | 1 Top Sail (3-D air search) |
| Sonars: | low frequency (hull mounted) |
| | medium frequency (variable depth) |
| EW systems: | Bell series |
| | Side Globe |
| | Top Hat |

These are hybrid helicopter carriers and missile cruisers. They were developed to counter Western strategic missile submarines, but the program was aborted after two ships because of the expanding capabilities of missile submarines. Both ships are based in the Black Sea and periodically deploy to the Mediterranean; they have also operated in the Atlantic, and the LENINGRAD in the northwest Indian Ocean region and Baltic Sea.

The MOSKVA was trials ship for the Yak-36 Forger in 1973–1974.

Design: These ships are missile cruisers forward with a clear, open flight deck abaft the superstructure. That structure is "stepped" forward to support missile launchers and radars, with a smooth after face. A small hangar is located between the stack uptakes in the superstructure. Two elevators connect the flight deck to the hangar deck. The flight deck is approximately 284 × 112 ft (86 × 34.0 m).

The MOSKVA class introduced the SA-N-3 missile system and the Top Sail and Head Lights radars to Soviet warships.

Designation: Soviet PKR type.

Names: These ships are named for the country's two traditional capital cities.

Torpedoes: Two five-tube 21-in (533-mm) rotating banks of torpedo tubes were cut into the sides of the ships as built (immediately behind the accommodation ladders). They have been removed.

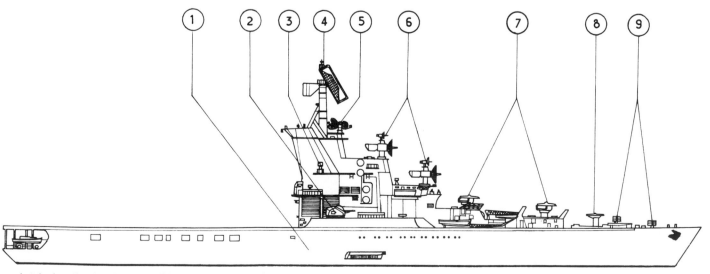

1. former torpedo tube location 2. twin 57-mm AA gun mount 3. Muff Cob radar 4. Top Sail radar 5. Head Net-C radar 6. Head Lights radar 7. SA-N-3 launchers 8. SUW-N-1 launcher 9. RBU·6000 rocket launchers (H. Simoni)

LENINGRAD at sea with both helicopter elevators lowered to the hangar deck. Forward, the MOSKVAS are heavily armed AAW/ASW missile cruisers. Although these ships were not suitable for the envisioned anti-SSBN mission, they were probably invaluable in providing the Soviet Navy with experience in operating large numbers of aircraft at sea.

The LENINGRAD at anchor with an Mi-8 Hip helicopter on her flight deck. The ship operated these helicopters to sweep mines in the Straits of Gubal to reopen the southern end of the Suez Canal in 1973. Note the shadow of the flight deck overhang aft and the plated-over torpedo tube bay abaft the accommodation ladder. (French Navy)

Moskva-class aircraft carrier

The Leningrad off the coast of Scotland with three Ka-25 Hormone helicopters on her flight deck. Both of her elevators are lowered, and the doors of one of the hangars beneath the funnel are open. There is an aircraft control station on the after face of the funnel; also note the VDS fitted beneath the after end of the flight deck, with boats stowed on both sides. (Royal Navy, 1980)

The Moskva island structure showing (from left to right) antennas for Top Sail, Head Net-C, Side Globe (EW domes on side of superstructure), and two Head Lights (trained aft). There is a twin 57-mm AA mounting at the 01 level, beneath the Top Sail antenna. (U.S. Navy, 1968)

# 13

# Cruisers

**1 + 2 GUIDED MISSILE CRUISERS: Krasina (ex-Black-Com-1)** _SLAVA._

| Name | Builders | Laid down | Launched | Completed | Status |
|------|----------|-----------|----------|-----------|--------|
| SLAVA | 61 Kommuna Shipyard, Nikolayev (north) | 1976 | 1979 | 1983 | **Black Sea** |
| . . . . . | 61 Kommuna Shipyard, Nikolayev (north) | 1978 | 1980 | 1983 | Building |
| . . . . . | 61 Kommuna Shipyard, Nikolayev (north) | 1979 | 1981 | 1984 | Building |

| | | | |
|---|---|---|---|
| Displacement: | 12,500 tons full load | | . . . Palm Frond (navigation)(?) |
| Length: | 617 ft (187 m) | | 2 Pop Group (fire control) |
| Beam: | | | 1 Top Dome (fire control) |
| Draft: | | | 1 Top Sail (3-D air search) |
| Propulsion: | gas turbines; 2 shafts | | 1 Top Steer (3-D air search) |
| Speed: | 30 + knots | Sonars: | low frequency (bow mounted) |
| Range: | | | |
| Complement: | | | |
| Helicopters: | 1 or 2 Ka-25 Hormone-B | | |
| Missiles: | 16 SS-N-12 anti-ship tubes | | |
| | 8 vertical SA-N-6 launchers (64) | | |
| Guns: | 2 130-mm/70-cal DP (twin) | | |
| | 8 30-mm close-in (8 × 1 multibarrel) | | |
| ASW weapons: | 1 twin SS-N-14 missile launcher (?) torpedoes | | |
| Radars: | 4 Bass Tile (fire control) | | |
| | 2 Eye Bowl (fire control)(?) | | |
| | 1 Kite Screech (fire control) | | |

These ships are primarily anti-ship cruisers. There have been reports that eight ships of this class will be built, but a smaller number of ships is more probable.

Designation: Soviet designation will probably be RKR. The NATO designation has been Black-Com-1 pending public knowledge of the lead ship's actual name. Subsequently the NATO code name Krasina was assigned.

Guns: See SOVREMENNYY-class destroyers (page 158) for additional gun notes.

**2 + 1 NUCLEAR-PROPELLED GUIDED MISSILE CRUISERS: "KIROV" CLASS[1]**

| Name | Builder | Laid down | Launched | Completed | Status |
|------|---------|-----------|----------|-----------|--------|
| KIROV | Baltic Shipyard, Leningrad | 1973 | Dec 1977 | Sep 1980 | **Northern** |
| FRUNZE KALININ | Baltic Shipyard, Leningrad | Jan 1978 | June 1981 | 1983 | Black Sea |
| | Baltic Shipyard, Leningrad | 1983 | | | Building |

| | | | |
|---|---|---|---|
| Displacement: | approx. 28,000 tons full load | Torpedoes: | 8 21-in (533-mm) torpedo tubes (2 quad) |
| Length: | 818 ft 4 in (248.0 m) | Radars: | 4 Bass Tilt (fire control) |
| Beam: | 92 ft 5 in (28.0 m) | | 2 Eye Bowl (fire control) |
| Draft: | 29 ft (8.8 m) | | 1 Kite Screech (fire control) |
| Propulsion: | steam turbines; 150,000 shp; 2 shafts | | 3 Palm Frond (navigation) |
| Reactors: | 2 pressurized-water type | | 2 Pop Group (fire control) |
| Boilers: | (oil-fired boilers for superheat) | | 2 Top Dome (fire control) |
| Speed: | approx. 32 knots | | 1 Top Pair (3-D air search) |
| Range: | | | 1 Top Steer (3-D air search) |
| Complement: | approx. 800 | Sonars: | low frequency (bow mounted) |
| Helicopters: | 3 to 5 Ka-25 Hormone-A/B | | low frequency (variable depth) |
| Missiles: | 2 twin SA-N-4 launchers (40) | EW systems: | Bell-series |
| | 12 vertical SA-N-6 launchers (96) | | Rum Tub |
| | 20 SS-N-19 anti-ship | | Side Globe |
| Guns: | 2 100-mm/70 cal DP (2 single) | | |
| | 8 30-mm close-in (8 × 1 multibarrel) | | |
| ASW weapons: | 1 twin SS-N-14 missile launcher | | |
| | 1 RBU-6000 rocket launcher | | |
| | 2 RBU-1000 rocket launchers | | |
| | torpedoes | | |

[1]A series of excellent discussions of recent Soviet cruiser and destroyer designs has been written by Captain James Kehoe, USN (Ret.) and Mr. Kenneth Brower for the Naval Institute _Proceedings_, and by Mr. John Jordan for the British journal _Defence_. These articles provide a useful assessment of the more recent Soviet classes. Also see, Commander Don East, USN, "Their Sovremennyy," _Proceedings_, July 1983, pp. 112–16.

The KIROV is the largest warship built by any nation since World War II except for aircraft carriers. The lead ship went to sea on trials in the Baltic Sea in May 1980.

Armament: The KIROV has two vertical-launch missile systems: the SA-N-6 weapons are in 12 below-deck rotary launchers and the 20 SS-N-19 weapons in single-launch tubes, angled forward at approximately 45°. The SS-N-14 system has the first reloadable launcher for this missile in Soviet ships.

There are reports that the second ship has provisions for a laser close-in weapon system for defense against anti-ship missiles. Reportedly, the system could be operational by 1984.

Class: Two ships of this class were built at the Baltic yard, coming in a production sequence between two ARKTIKA nuclear icebreakers and a series of nuclear barge-carrying merchant ships. However, while the latter were under construction the yard also began building the third ARKTIKA-class ship, indicating that facilities are available for simultaneous construction of two classes of nuclear ships at the yard (see chapter 28). A third KIROV was begun about 1983.

Design: The ship has a huge superstructure, with numerous radars, EW antennas, and weapons evident despite the SA-N-6 and SS-N-19 systems being out of sight within the hull. Note also that these missiles are forward, leaving the after portion of the hull available for machinery and the helicopter hangar.

Helicopters are lowered to the hangar by an elevator that fits flush with the deck, immediately forward of the landing area. The stern has large doors for the VDS.

Extensive command and control facilities are provided.

Designation: Soviet RKR type. The term "battle cruiser" has been widely used in the West and seems appropriate in view of the ship's size, hull lines, and fire power.[2]

Engineering: The KIROV class is also unique in being the only warship with a combination nuclear and steam propulsion plant. There are two reactors that are coupled with oil-fired superheaters (boilers) that further boost the heat of the steam to increase power for high-speed operations.

The ARKTIKA nuclear icebreakers constructed at the Admiralty Shipyard have a two-reactor plant producing an estimated 75,000 shp. Assuming the KIROVs use the same basic reactor, an all-nuclear propulsion system in the cruisers would have required four reactors.

Names: The KIROV is named for S.M. Kirov (1888–1934), a leading Bolshevik revolutionary. The name was subsequently given to the lead ship of the only heavy cruiser class built by the Soviets (completed 1938 and stricken in the late 1970s).

---

[2]The term *battle cruiser* evolved during the DREADNOUGHT era, denoting a ship with a battleship's firepower and more speed, with some sacrifice in armor. HMS HOOD was the last battle cruiser completed by any nation (1923); the Soviets have twice begun the construction of battle cruisers, the KRONSHTADT and STALINGRAD classes, but none was ever finished. The U.S. Navy also never completed any battle cruisers, although the "large cruisers" GUAM (CB 2) and ALASKA (CB 1), both completed in 1944, were in some respects conceptually similar to battle cruisers. Some German warships of the World War II era have been described as battle cruisers but were in reality fast battleships.

KIROV superstructure showing antennas (from left to right) for Top Dome, Top Steer, modified Vee Cone (communications antennas), Round House (aircraft navigation), Top Pair, and Round House, with Side Globe (EW domes) on side of superstructure. (U.S. Navy, 1981)

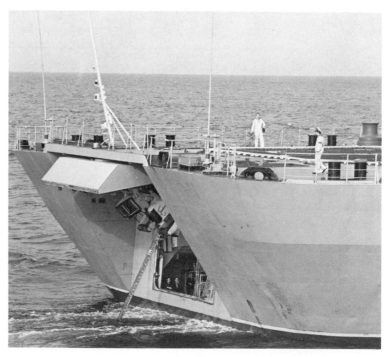

Stern counter of KIROV with door to sonar compartment raised and VDS deployed. (Royal Navy, 1980)

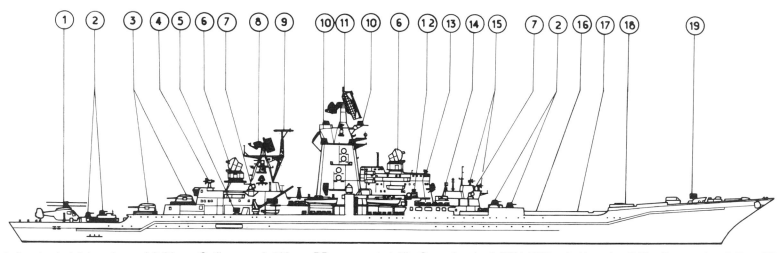

1. helicopter deck (above hangar) 2. 30-mm Gatling guns 3. 100-mm DP gun mounts 4. Kite Screech radar 5. RBU-1000 rocket launcher 6. Top Dome radars 7. Bass Tilt radar 8. Top Steer radar 9. Vee Tube HF antenna 10. Round House helicopter control system 11. Top Pair 12. Pop Group radar 13. Palm Frond radar 14. SA-N-4 launcher (retracted) 15. Eye Bowl radars 16. SS-N-19 vertical launch system 17. SA-N-6 vertical launch system 18. SS-N-14 missile tubes 19. RBU-6000 rocket launcher (H. Simoni)

KIROV (1980)

The KIROV heels to port while on her sea trials in October 1980. Her imposing size and lines are reminiscent of World War II-era capital ships. Soviet ships—especially combatants—generally wear a distinctive pendant number for trials and shakedown and subsequently another number during service. The latter changes periodically with some assignment by types indicated; these should not be confused with the use of hull numbers in the U.S. Navy.

SA-N-6 and SS-N-19 launcher arrangement in KIROV. The SA-N-6 launchers are combination vertical launch/rotary magazine systems. (Courtesy *Ships of the World*)

KIROV (Royal Navy, 1980)

KIROV (Ministry of Defence, 1980)

## 7 GUIDED MISSILE CRUISERS: KARA CLASS

| Name | Builder | Laid down | Launched | Completed | Status |
|---|---|---|---|---|---|
| NIKOLAYEV | 61 Kommuna Shipyard, Nikolayev (north) | 1969 | 1971 | 1973 | **Black Sea** |
| OCHAKOV | 61 Kommuna Shipyard, Nikolayev (north) | 1970 | 1972 | 1975 | **Black Sea** |
| KERCH' | 61 Kommuna Shipyard, Nikolayev (north) | 1971 | 1973 | 1976 | **Black Sea** |
| AZOV | 61 Kommuna Shipyard, Nikolayev (north) | 1972 | 1974 | 1977 | **Black Sea** |
| PETROPAVLOVSK | 61 Kommuna Shipyard, Nikolayev (north) | 1973 | 1975 | 1978 | **Pacific** |
| TASHKENT | 61 Kommuna Shipyard, Nikolayev (north) | 1975 | 1976 | 1979 | **Pacific** |
| TALLINN | 61 Kommuna Shipyard, Nikolayev (north) | 1976 | 1977 | 1980 | **Pacific** |

| | | | |
|---|---|---|---|
| Displacement: | 8,200 tons standard | Torpedoes: | 10 21-in (533-mm) torpedo tubes (2 quin) |
| | 9,700 tons full load | Radars: | 2 Bass Tilt (fire control) |
| Length: | 571 ft (173.0 m) | | 1 Don-2 or Palm Frond (navigation) |
| Beam: | 61 ft 4 in (18.6 m) | | 2 Don Kay (navigation) |
| Draft: | 22 ft 2 in (6.7 m) | | 2 Head Lights (fire control) except 1 in Azov plus 1 Top Dome |
| Propulsion: | 4 gas turbines; 120,000 shp; 2 shafts | | 1 Head Net-C (3-D air search) |
| Speed: | 34 knots | | 2 Owl Screech (fire control) |
| Range: | 3,000 n.miles at 32 knots | | 2 Pop Group (fire control) |
| | 8,800 n.miles at 15 knots | | 1 Top Sail (3-D air search) |
| Complement: | approx. 525 | Sonars: | low frequency (bow mounted) |
| Helicopters: | 1 Ka-25 Hormone-A | | medium frequency (variable depth) |
| Missiles: | 2 twin SA-N-3 Goblet launchers (72), except 1 in Azov plus 1 vertical SA-N-6 launcher | EW systems: | Bell Clout |
| | 2 twin SA-N-4 launchers (40) | | Bell Slam |
| Guns: | 4 76.2-mm/60-cal AA (2 twin) | | Bell Tap |
| | 4 30-mm close-in (4 × 1 multibarrel) | | Side Globe |
| ASW weapons: | 2 quad SS-N-14 launchers | | (see notes) |
| | 2 RBU-6000 rocket launchers | | |
| | 2 RBU-1000 rocket launchers; deleted from PETROPAVLOVSK | | |
| | torpedoes | | |

These are large, graceful ships, a refinement of the Kresta II design with major anti-air and anti-submarine capabilities. They were built almost simultaneously with the Kresta II class at the Zhdanov shipyard.

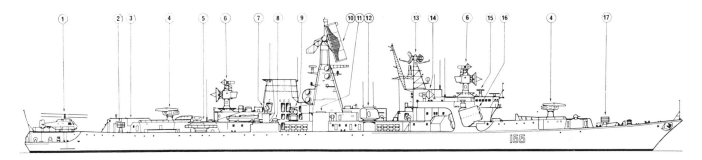

1. helicopter deck 2. RBU-1000 rocket launcher 3. helicopter hangar 4. SA-N-3 launchers 5. 533-mm torpedo tubes 6. Head Lights radars 7. Bass Tilt radar 8. 30-mm Gatling guns 9. Pop Group radar 10. Top Sail radar 11. SA-N-4 launcher (retracted) 12. twin 76.2-mm AA gun mount 13. Head Net-C radar 14. Owl Screech radar 15. Don Kay radar 16. SS-N-14 missile tubes 17. RBU-6000 rocket launcher (H. Simoni)

Armament: While ostensibly armed with only AAW and ASW missiles, both the SA-N-3 and SS-N-14 have an anti-ship capability.

The Azov has been fitted as the test ship for the SA-N-6 vertical-launch AAW system; a launcher has replaced the after SA-N-3 system, and the Top Dome missile control radar has been fitted in place of the after Head Lights. (The Azov's Top Dome is different from those in the Kirov, apparently indicating a prototype installation.)

Design: These ships are significantly larger than the Kresta II class, have a heavier gun armament, are fitted with extensive command-and-control facilities, and are all gas-turbine propelled. Their sizable superstructure is dominated by the large, low gas-turbine funnel. The helicopter hangar, just forward of the landing area, is partially recessed below the flight deck. To stow the helicopter, the hangar's roof hatch and rear doors open, and the helicopter is pushed in and then lowered by elevator to the hangar deck.

Designation: Soviet BPK class.

Electronics: The Nikolayev and Ochakov carry the same EW suite as the Kresta II-class ships. The Kerch´ and later ships have the Rum Tub Electronic Surveillance Measure (ESM) antennas in place of the Bell Slam and Bell Tap of the earlier ships. The Petropavlovsk has a drum-shaped Round House TACAN (Tactical Air Navigation) antenna on either side of the helicopter hangar, requiring the deletion of the RBU-1000 rocket launchers.

Engineering: The Kara class is the world's largest warship design with all-gas-turbine propulsion.

Names: These ships are named for port cities of the USSR except for inland Tashkent.

Operational: The Petropavlovsk and Tashkent transited to the Pacific in the spring of 1979 in company with the Minsk. The Tallinn shifted to the Pacific at a later date. The Azov has not been sighted outside of the Black Sea.

Stern view of Petropavlovsk with helicopter hangar door open. (1979)

The Kara-class missile cruiser Tashkent; she and the Petropavlovsk transferred to the Pacific Fleet in 1979.

This overhead view of the Kara-class missile cruiser PETROPAVLOVSK shows the prominent twin 76.2-mm gun mountings and the large gas turbine exhaust funnel. The ship has twin Round House aircraft control systems outboard of the stern hangar in place of the RBU-1000 rocket launchers found in most or all other units. A Ka-25 Hormone rests on the fantail. (U.S. Navy, 1980)

The Kara-class cruiser NIKOLAYEV in the western Mediterranean in 1981.

**10 GUIDED MISSILE CRUISERS: KRESTA II CLASS**

| Name | Builder | Laid down | Launched | Completed | Status |
|------|---------|-----------|----------|-----------|--------|
| KRONSHTADT | Zhdanov Shipyard, Leningrad | 1966 | 1967 | 1970 | **Northern** |
| ADMIRAL ISAKOV | Zhdanov Shipyard, Leningrad | 1967 | 1968 | 1971 | **Northern** |
| ADMIRAL NAKHIMOV | Zhdanov Shipyard, Leningrad | 1968 | 1969 | 1972 | **Baltic** |
| ADMIRAL MAKAROV | Zhdanov Shipyard, Leningrad | 1969 | 1970 | 1973 | **Northern** |
| MARSHAL VOROSHILOV | Zhdanov Shipyard, Leningrad | 1970 | 1971 | 1973 | **Pacific** |
| ADMIRAL OKTYABRSKIY | Zhdanov Shipyard, Leningrad | 1970 | 1972 | 1974 | **Pacific** |
| ADMIRAL ISACHENKOV | Zhdanov Shipyard, Leningrad | 1971 | 1973 | 1975 | **Baltic** |
| MARSHAL TIMOSHENKO | Zhdanov Shipyard, Leningrad | 1972 | 1974 | 1976 | **Northern** |
| VASILIY CHAPAYEV | Zhdanov Shipyard, Leningrad | 1973 | 1975 | 1977 | **Pacific** |
| ADMIRAL YUMASHEV | Zhdanov Shipyard, Leningrad | 1974 | 1976 | 1978 | **Northern** |

| | | | |
|--|--|--|--|
| Displacement: | 6,000 tons standard | EW systems: | Bell Clout |
| | 7,700 tons full load | | Bell Slam |
| Length: | 524 ft 6 in (159.0 m) | | Bell Tap |
| Beam: | 56 ft (17.0 m) | | Side Globe |
| Draft: | 19 ft 9 in (6.0 m) | | |
| Propulsion: | steam turbines; 100,000 shp; 2 shafts | | |
| Boilers: | 4 | | |
| Speed: | 35 knots | | |
| Range: | 2,400 n.miles at 32 knots | | |
| | 10,500 n.miles at 14 knots | | |
| Complement: | approx. 380 | | |
| Helicopters: | 1 Ka-25 Hormone | | |
| Missiles: | 2 twin SA-N-3 Goblet launchers (72) | | |
| Guns: | 4 57-mm/80-cal AA (2 twin) | | |
| | 4 30-mm close-in (4 × 1 multibarrel) | | |
| ASW weapons: | 2 quad SS-N-14 launchers | | |
| | 2 RBU-6000 rocket launchers | | |
| | 2 RBU-1000 rocket launchers | | |
| | torpedoes | | |
| Torpedoes: | 10 21-in (533-mm) torpedo tubes (2 quin) | | |
| Radars: | 2 Bass Tilt (fire control) in ADMIRAL MARKAROV and later ships | | |
| | 2 Don-2 (navigation) | | |
| | 2 Don Kay (navigation) | | |
| | 2 Head Lights (fire control) | | |
| | 1 Head Net-C (3-D air search) | | |
| | 2 Muff Cob (fire control) | | |
| Sonars: | medium frequency (bow mounted) | | |

These are large ASW/AAW ships, similar to the Kresta I design but with improved missiles and electronics, including the SS-N-14 anti-submarine system in place of the earlier ship's four SS-N-3 Shaddock anti-ship missiles.

Design:  These ships have essentially the same hull and arrangement as the interim Kresta I design. Significant changes are provided over the previous class in missiles and electronics, the most prominent feature being the large Top Sail radar antenna surmounting the superstructure pyramid and the Head Lights fire control radars for the SA-N-3 missile systems. (The SA-N-3 has an anti-ship capability, as does the SS-N-14.) The helicopter is hangared in the same manner as in the Kara class.

The ships are fitted with fin stabilizers.

Designation:  Soviet BPK type.

Names: Most of these ships are named for Soviet military and naval commanders. V.I. Chapayev (1887–1919) was a Bolshevik military commander; he was previously honored by the light cruiser CHAPAYEV (completed in 1949 and discarded in the late 1970s).

MARSHAL VOROSHILOV (1974)

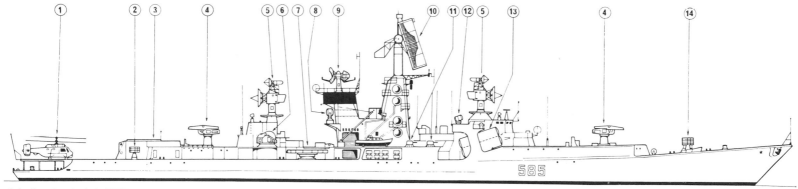

1. helicopter deck 2. RBU-1000 rocket launcher 3. helicopter hangar 4. SA-N-3 launchers 5. Head Lights radars 6. twin 57-mm AA gun mounts 7. 533-mm torpedo tubes 8. Muff Cob radar 9. Head Net-C radar 10. Top Sail radar 11. 30-mm Gatling guns 12. Bass Tilt radar 13. SS-N-14 missile tubes 14. RBU-6000 rocket launcher (H. Simoni)

Closed helicopter hangar on Kresta II (note wind sock and helicopter control station on port side of hangar). (U.S. Navy, 1971)

Open helicopter hangar on ADMIRAL ISACHENKOV with Ka-25 Hormone on fantail, rotors spread. (Royal Navy, 1975)

Kresta II-class missile cruiser.

Marshal Timoshenko with hangar doors open. (U.S. Navy, 1982)

Kresta II missile cruisers showing (from left to right) antennas for Head Lamps, Muff Cob (mounted on funnel), Head Net-C, Top Sail, Bass Tilt (above rear of SS-N-14 tubes), and Head Lamps with Side Globe domes on superstructure. (1978)

**4 GUIDED MISSILE CRUISERS: KRESTA I CLASS**

| Name | Shipyard | Laid down | Launched | Completed | Status |
|------|----------|-----------|----------|-----------|--------|
| Admiral Zozulya | Zhdanov Shipyard, Leningrad | Sep 1964 | 1965–1966 | 1967 | **Northern** |
| Vladivostok | Zhdanov Shipyard, Leningrad | 1965 | 1967 | 1968 | **Pacific** |
| Vitse Admiral Drozd | Zhdanov Shipyard, Leningrad | 1965 | 1967 | 1968 | **Baltic** |
| Sevastopol' | Zhdanov Shipyard, Leningrad | 1966 | 1968 | 1969 | **Pacific** |

| | |
|---|---|
| Displacement: | 6,000 tons standard |
| | 7,600 tons full load |
| Length: | 513 ft 2 in (155.5 m) |
| Beam: | 56 ft (17.0 m) |
| Draft: | 19 ft 9 in (6.0 m) |
| Propulsion: | steam turbines; 100,000 shp; 2 shafts |
| Boilers: | 4 |
| Speed: | 35 knots |
| Range: | 2,400 n.miles at 32 knots |
| | 10,500 n.miles at 14 knots |
| Complement: | approx. 380 |
| Helicopters: | 1 Ka-25 Hormone-B |
| Missiles: | 2 twin SA-N-1 Goa launchers (44) |
| | 2 twin SS-N-3 Shaddock launchers |
| Guns: | 4 57-mm/80-cal AA (2 twin) |
| | 4 30-mm close-in (1 × 8 multibarrel) in Vitse Admiral Drozd |
| ASW weapons: | 2 RBU-6000 rocket launchers |
| | 2 RBU-1000 rocket launchers |
| | torpedoes |
| Torpedoes: | 10 21-in (533-mm) torpedo tubes (quin) |
| Radars: | 2 Bass Tilt (fire control) in Vitse Admiral Drozd |
| | 1 Big Net (air search) |
| | 2 Don-2 (navigation) |
| | 1 Head Net-C (3-D air search) |
| | 2 Muff Cob (fire control) |
| | 2 Peel Group (fire control) |
| | 2 Plinth Net (surface search) |
| | 1 Scoop Pair (fire control) |
| Sonars: | Hercules medium frequency (hull mounted) |
| EW systems: | Bell Clout |
| | Bell Slam |
| | Bell Tap |
| | Side Globe |

These ships are an interim design, carrying the Shaddock anti-ship missiles but apparently intended for other weapon systems (see Kresta II listing). The lead ship began trials in the Baltic Sea in February 1967.

Aircraft: One Hormone-B is embarked to provide over-the-horizon targeting/guidance for the Shaddock missiles.

Design: These ships are considerably larger than the previous Kynda series and have a different hull form. They also have two surface-to-air missile systems and are the first Soviet surface combatants with a helicopter hangar. No mine rails are fitted, as in the previous postwar cruiser and destroyer classes.

Compared to the Kynda-class rocket cruisers (RKR), the Kresta I design has one-half the number of Shaddock launch tubes and one-fourth the total missiles. The Kresta missile tubes are mounted under cantilevered bridge wings; they cannot be trained, but are elevated to a firing position.

Designation: Originally designated BPK; changed to RKR in 1977–1978, reflecting the primary armament of anti-ship missiles.

Modifications: These ships have been modified during their service. The Vitse Admiral Drozd was modified from 1973–1975 with a two-deck structure installed between the bridge and radar pyramid, where four 30-mm close-in weapons (Gatling guns) are fitted along with the Bass Tilt fire-control radars. The Sevastopol' received a similar deckhouse in 1980, but the Gatling guns and radars had not been observed when this volume went to press.

Names: The names of these ships honor two Soviet flag officers and two major port cities.

The Vitse Admiral Drozd, one of three missile cruisers assigned to the Baltic Fleet when this edition went to press. The Kresta I class has a low stern and lacks the Top Sail radar of later cruiser designs. The class appears to have been an interim step as the Soviet Navy shifted from an emphasis on anti-carrier warfare to ASW weapons in its missile cruisers. (1976)

A Kresta I photographed in the Mediterranean. This class does not normally deploy to that area. Note the Scoop Pair fire-control radar for the SS-N-3 Shaddock missiles mounted on the front of the pyramid structure. (U.S. Navy, 1969)

A Pacific Fleet Kresta I in the eastern Pacific with part of her crew mustered on the helicopter deck. (Canadian Forces, 1971)

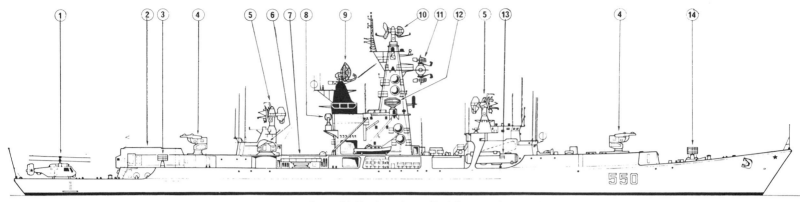

1. helicopter deck 2. helicopter hangar 3. RBU-1000 rocket launcher 4. SA-N-1 launcher 5. Peel Group radars 6. twin 57-mm AA mount 7. 533-mm torpedo tubes 8. Muff Cob radar 9. Big Net radar 10. Head Net-C radar 11. Scoop Pair radar 12. Plinth Net radar 13. SS-N-3 missile tubes 14. RBU-6000 rocket launcher (H. Simoni)

A Pacific Fleet Kresta I at anchor with other Soviet units in Hawaiian waters. The superstructure of this class is dominated by a huge, central pyramid supporting various radar antennas. (U.S. Navy, 1971)

## 4 GUIDED MISSILE CRUISERS: KYNDA CLASS

| Name | Builder | Laid down | Launched | Completed | Status |
|---|---|---|---|---|---|
| GROZNYY | Zhdanov Shipyard, Leningrad | June 1959 | Apr 1961 | June 1962 | **Black Sea** |
| ADMIRAL FOKIN | Zhdanov Shipyard, Leningrad | 1960 | Nov 1961 | Aug 1963 | **Pacific** |
| ADMIRAL GOLOVKO | Zhdanov Shipyard, Leningrad | 1961 | 1963 | July 1964 | **Black Sea** |
| VARYAG | Zhdanov Shipyard, Leningrad | 1962 | 1964 | Feb 1965 | **Pacific** |

| | |
|---|---|
| Displacement: | 4,400 tons standard |
| | 5,500 tons full load |
| Length: | 467 ft 7 in (141.7 m) |
| Beam: | 52 ft 2 in (15.8 m) |
| Draft: | 17 ft 6 in (5.3 m) |
| Propulsion: | steam turbines; 100,000 shp; 2 shafts |
| Boilers: | 4 |
| Speed: | 36 knots |
| Range: | 2,000 n.miles at 34 knots |
| | 7,000 n.miles at 14.5 knots |
| Complement: | approx. 375 |
| Helicopters: | (no hangar) |
| Missiles: | 1 twin SA-N-1 Goa launcher (24) |
| | 2 quad SS-N-3 Shaddock launchers (8 + 8 reloads) |
| Guns: | 4 76.2-mm/60-cal AA (2 twin) |
| | 4 30-mm close-in (4 × 1 multibarrel) in VARYAG |
| ASW weapons: | 2 RBU-6000 rocket launchers |
| | torpedoes |
| Torpedoes: | 6 21-in (533-mm) torpedo tubes (2 triple) |
| Mines: | no rails fitted |
| Radars: | 2 Bass Tilt in VARYAG |
| | 2 Don-2 (navigation) |
| | 2 Head Net-A or -C (air search) |
| | 1 Owl Screech (fire control) |
| | 1 Peel Group (fire control) |
| | 2 Plinth Net (surface search) except none in ADMIRAL GOLOVKO |
| | 2 Scoop Pair (fire control) |
| Sonars: | Herkules high frequency (hull mounted) |
| EW systems: | Bell Clout |
| | Bell Slam |
| | Bell Tap |
| | Top Hat |

These were among the first of the modern Soviet warships resulting from the defense decisions made in the mid-1950s. Additional ships were probably planned, but cancelled, including a larger Shaddock missile cruiser.

Design: The Kynda-class cruisers are only slightly longer than the Krupnyy and Kildin destroyer classes, but have traditional cruiser lines and significantly more firepower. These ships introduced the imposing pyramid structures to Soviet ships to support radar and EW antennas. They are the only ships with pyramids and twin funnels. The large Shaddock tubes are mounted in four-tube banks forward and amidships. They swing outboard and elevate to fire. Eight reload missiles are in magazines in the superstructure behind the launchers. However, reloading the Shaddock tubes is a slow and awkward process.

No helicopter hangar or maintenance facilities are provided. There is a landing area for a Hormone-B for over-the-horizon missile targeting.

Mine rails are fitted.

Designation: Soviet RKR type. The U.S. Navy originally listed these ships and subsequent Soviet RKR/BPK ships as "guided missile frigates" (DLG) until the 1975 reclassification of U.S. frigates to destroyers or cruisers. At that time the Soviet RKR/BPK classes were designated as cruisers by Western intelligence.

Modifications: VARYAG fitted with Gatling guns and Bass Tilt radars in 1981.

Built with two Head Net-A radars; some ships subsequently refitted: the ADMIRAL FOKIN has one Head Net-A and one Head Net-C, and the VARYAG has two Head Net-C radars. Plinth Net added after completion.

Names: Two ships remember Soviet flag officers (A.G. Golovko having commanded the Northern Fleet 1940–1946 and the Baltic Fleet 1952–1956 and V.A. Fokin the Pacific Fleet 1958–1962). The GROZNYY and VARYAG are traditional Russian warship names ("Terrible" for Tsar Ivan and "Varangian" or Norseman, respectively).

A Kynda-class missile cruiser in Hawaiian waters. (U.S. Navy, 1974)

The Kynda was the first class of the modern Soviet missile cruisers. The class has a balanced SS-N-3 Shaddock battery, with four tubes forward and four aft, with eight reloads in the superstructure adjacent to the tubes. The SA-N-1 Goa launcher forward is balanced by the two 76.2-mm twin gun mounts aft. There is no helicopter platform. (U.S. Navy, 1968)

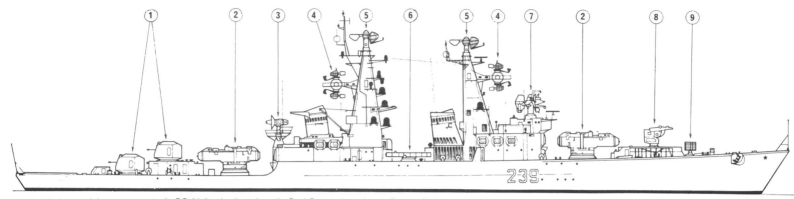

1. twin 76.2-mm AA gun mounts 2. SS-N-3 missile tubes 3. Owl Screech radar 4. Scoop Pair radars 5. Head Net-A radars 6. 533-mm torpedo tubes 7. Peel Group radar 8. SA-N-1 launcher 9. RBU-6000 rocket launcher (H. Simoni)

The VARYAG, one of two Kyndas in the Pacific Fleet. This ship has been extensively modified, with two Gatling gun systems fitted on each side abaft the forward mast, two Bass Tilt gun control systems, and additional structures have been added amidships. However, she still has empty electronic platforms on her after mast. (1981)

A Kynda missile cruiser's superstructure with antennas (from left to right) for Owl Screech, Scoop Pair (on after mast), Head Net-A (atop both masts), Scoop Pair (on forward mast), and Peel Group. Electronic suites and air-search radars vary among the four ships of the class.

Modified superstructure of VARYAG. (1981)

## 1 GUIDED MISSILE CRUISER: CONVERTED "SVERDLOV" CLASS

| Name | Builder | Laid down | Launched | Completed | Conversion Completed | Status |
|------|---------|-----------|----------|-----------|----------------------|--------|
| DZERZHINSKIY | Marti, Nikolayev (south) | May 1949 | 1951 | Nov 1952 | 1962 | **Black Sea** |

| | |
|---|---|
| Displacement: | 12,900 tons standard |
| | 17,000 tons full load |
| Length: | 660 ft (200.0 m) waterline |
| | 693 ft (210.0 m) overall |
| Beam: | 72 ft 6 in (22.0 m) |
| Draft: | 23 ft 9 in (7.2 m) |
| Propulsion: | steam turbines; 110,000 shp; 2 shafts |
| Boilers: | 6 |
| Speed: | 32.5 knots |
| Range: | 2,500 n.miles at 32 knots |
| | 10,200 n.miles at 13.5 knots |
| Complement: | approx. 1,050 |
| Helicopters: | no facilities |
| Missiles: | 1 twin SA-N-3 Guideline launcher (10) |
| Guns: | 9 152-mm/57-cal SP (4 triple) |
| | 12 100-mm/50-cal DP (6 twin) |
| | 16 37-mm/60-cal AA (8 twin) |
| ASW weapons: | none |
| Torpedoes: | removed |
| Mines: | rails for approx. 200 |
| Radars: | 1 Big Net (air search) |
| | 6 Egg Cup (fire control) |
| | 1 Fan Song−E (fire control) |
| | 1 Low Sieve (air search) |
| | 1 Neptune (navigation) |
| | 1 Slim Net (air search) |
| | 2 Sun Visor (fire control) |
| | 1 Top Bow (fire control) |
| Sonars: | none |
| EW systems: | |

The DZERZHINSKIY was completed as a standard SVERDLOV-class light cruiser and converted to a guided missile ship in 1961−1962. Only one ship was converted to this configuration. The DZERZHINSKIY is probably in reduced commission and is not believed to have deployed into the Mediterranean for several years. (One of her last foreign port visits was to Istanbul, flying the flag of Commander, Black Sea Fleet, in November 1978.) See SVERDLOV-class light cruisers for additional notes.

Conversion: The ship's No. 3 turret of three 152-mm guns was removed for installation of the SA-N-2 system. A small pedestal was installed between the after funnel and the missile launcher for the Fan Song-E radar antenna. The SA-N-2 system is not believed to have ever been fully operational.

Designation: Soviet KR (*kreyser*) type.

Modifications: The High Lune radar was removed in 1976.

Names: F.E. Dzerzhinskiy (1877−1926) was a Communist agitator and founder of the secret police (*Cheka*).

This closeup of the DZERZHINSKIY shows the High Lune height-finding radar that was mounted abaft the forward funnel until 1976. A Big Net radar is fitted to the after tripod mast with a Fan Song-E missile control radar abaft the second funnel. (U.S. Navy, 1967)

The DZERZHINSKIY was the only SVERDLOV-class light cruiser converted to an anti-aircraft missile configuration. The ship's SA-N-2 Guideline missile system has never been fully operational. The SA-N-2 launcher dominates the superstructure, replacing the triple 152-mm gun turret in the "X" position. Assigned to the Black Sea Fleet, the ship has not deployed to the Mediterranean during the past few years.

**2 COMMAND CRUISERS: CONVERTED "SVERDLOV" CLASS**

| Name | Builder | Laid down | Launched | Completed | Conversion Completed | Status |
|---|---|---|---|---|---|---|
| Admiral Senyavin | Baltic Works, Leningrad | May 1951 | Sep 1952 | July 1954 | 1972 | **Pacific** |
| Zhdanov | Baltic Works, Leningrad | Oct 1949 | Dec 1950 | Jan 1952 | 1972 | **Black Sea** |

| | | | | |
|---|---|---|---|---|
| Displacement: | 12,900 tons standard | | Guns: | 6 152-mm/57-cal SP (4 triple) (9 guns in Zhdanov) |
| | 17,000 tons full load | | | 12 100-mm/50-cal DP (6 twin) |
| Length: | 660 ft (200.0 m) waterline | | | 16 37-mm/60-cal AA (8 twin) |
| | 693 ft (210.0 m) overall | | | 16 30-mm/60-cal AA (8 twin) (8 guns in Zhdanov) |
| Beam: | 72 ft 6 in (22.0 m) | | ASW weapons: | none |
| Draft: | 23 ft 9 in (7.2 m) | | Torpedoes: | removed |
| Propulsion: | steam turbines; 110,000 shp; 2 shafts | | Mines: | rails removed |
| Boilers: | 6 | | Radars: | 4 Drum Tilt (2 in Zhdanov) |
| Speed: | 32.5 knots | | | 6 Egg Cup (fire control) |
| Range: | 2,500 n.miles at 32 knots | | | 1 Pop Group (fire control) |
| | 10,200 n.miles at 13.5 knots | | | 1 Sun Visor (fire control) |
| Complement: | approx. 1,000 | | | 2 Top Bow (fire control) |
| Helicopters: | 1 Ka-25 Hormone-C in Admiral Senyavin | | | 1 Top Trough (air search) |
| Missiles: | 1 twin SA-N-4 launcher (20) | | Sonars: | none |
| | | | EW systems: | |

The Admiral Senyavin as configured as a command ship. Assigned to the Black Sea Fleet, she differs slightly from the Zhdanov in the Pacific Fleet. The command ships have a third mast to support Vee Cone communications antennas; both now have large, satellite communication radomes abaft the second funnel (as seen here). The Zhdanov retains an after triple 152-mm gun turret. (U.S. Navy, 1982)

Zhdanov command cruiser

These ships were standard SVERDLOV-class light cruisers that were extensively converted for the command ship role in 1971–1972. Both ships are in commission. See SVERDLOV-class light cruisers for additional notes.

Conversion: The different configurations of these ships probably represent the requirements of the fleet commanders for their respective operating areas. Most obvious, the ADMIRAL SENYAVIN has a large helicopter hangar aft (requiring removal of all after 152-mm guns). Both ships have been fitted with extensive command and communications facilities. A third mast, abaft the second funnel, carries satellite communications antennas, and an after superstructure has been built, with the SA-N-4 missile system and 30-mm guns installed for close-in defense. The ZHDANOV, without hangar, does have a helicopter landing area aft and an aircraft control position at the after end of the superstructure. Their mine rails and torpedo tubes have been removed.

Designation: Soviet KU (command ship) type.

Names: The ADMIRAL SENYAVIN honors a family of five distinguished eighteenth century Russian naval officers. A.A. Zhdanov (1896–1948) was a leading Soviet official with major responsibilities in the development of the Soviet Navy.

ZHDANOV with Top Trough radar antenna atop second mast and Vee Cone communications antennas on second mast; the circular hatch on after superstructure covers an SA-N-4 missile launcher. (French Navy, 1973)

ZHDANOV (prior to installation of satellite communication radomes)

## 9 LIGHT CRUISERS: "SVERDLOV" CLASS

| Name | Builder | Laid down | Launched | Completed | Status |
|------|---------|-----------|----------|-----------|--------|
| ADMIRAL LAZAREV | Baltic Works, Leningrad | May 1950 | Oct 1951 | Nov 1952 | **Pacific** |
| ADMIRAL USHAKOV | Baltic Works, Leningrad | July 1950 | May 1952 | Aug 1953 | **Black Sea** |
| ALEKSANDR NEVSKIY | Marti, Leningrad (Admiralty) | Mar 1950 | June 1951 | 1952 | **Northern** |
| ALEKSANDR SUVOROV | Marti, Leningrad (Admiralty) | Oct 1950 | June 1952 | 1953 | **Pacific** |
| DMITRIY POZHARSKIY | Baltic Works, leningrad | Sep 1951 | Apr 1953 | 1953 | **Pacific** |
| MIKHAIL KUTUZOV | Marti, Nikolayev (south) | 1950 | May 1954 | 1953 | **Black Sea** |
| MURMANSK | Severodvinsk | 1952 | 1955 | 1955 | **Northern** |
| OKTYABRSKAYA REVOLUTSIYA | Severodvinsk | 1951 | 1954 | Sep 1954 | **Baltic** |
| SVERDLOV | Baltic Works, Leningrad | July 1949 | July 1950 | 1951 | **Baltic** |

| | |
|---|---|
| Displacement: | 12,900 tons standard |
| | 17,000 tons full load |
| Length: | 660 ft (200.0 m) waterline |
| | 693 ft (210.0 m) overall |
| Beam: | 72 ft 6 in (22.0 m) |
| Draft: | 23 ft 9 in (7.2 m) |
| Propulsion: | steam turbines; 110,000 shp; 2 shafts |
| Boilers: | 6 |
| Speed: | 32.5 knots |
| Range: | 2,500 n.miles at 32 knots |
| | 10,200 n.miles at 13.5 knots |
| Complement: | approx. 1,000 |
| Helicopters: | no facilities |
| Guns: | 12 152-mm/57-cal SP (4 triple) |
| | 12 100-mm/50-cal DP (6 twin) |
| | 32 37-mm/60-cal AA (16 twin) (28 in ships with 30-mm guns) |
| | 16 30-mm/60-cal close-in (8 twin) in ADMIRAL USHAKOV, |
| | ALEXANDR SUVOROV, OKTYABRSKAYA REVOLUTSIYA |
| ASW weapons: | none |
| Torpedoes: | removed |
| Mines: | rails for approx. 200 |
| Radars: | 1 Big Net or Top Trough (air search) |
| | 1 Don-2 or Neptune (navigation) |
| | 4 Drum Tilt (fire control) in ships with 30-mm guns |
| | 8 Egg Cup (fire control) |
| | 1 High Sieve or Low Sieve (air search) |
| | 1 Knife Rest (air search) in some ships |
| | 1 Slim Net (air search) |
| | 2 Sun Visor (fire control) |
| | 2 Top Bow (fire control) |
| Sonars: | none |
| EW systems: | Watch Dog |

These are the last conventional, all-gun cruisers in commission with any navy. The only ship in commission with larger guns when this volume went to press was the U.S. battleship NEW JERSEY (BB 62) with a 16-inch (406-mm) main battery.

All nine ships are listed as being in commission by Western intelligence, although the exact status of the ships varies, with some in reduced commission. The OKTYABRSKAYA REVOLUTSIYA is considered a gunnery training ship. They all periodically serve as fleet flagships. Several of these ships can be expected to be decommissioned in the near future.

Class: Twenty-four of these ships were planned in the post–World War II construction program. Only 20 ships were laid down, 14 being completed between 1951 and 1955 as light cruisers. Three additional hulls were launched but not finished.

ALEKSANDR SUVOROV in Philippine Sea (U.S. Navy, 1970)

The ADMIRAL NAKHIMOV and DZERZHINSKIY were converted to missile ships; the former was a test ship for the SS-N-1 Scrubber/Strela missile and did not operate beyond the Black Sea before being scrapped about 1961; the DZERZHINSKIY, fitted with the SA-N-2 Guideline, is listed separately. Two additional ships, the ADMIRAL SENYAVIN and ZHDANOV, were converted to command ships and are listed separately.

The ORDZONIKIDZE was transferred to Indonesia in October 1962 (renamed IRIAN); she was scrapped in Taiwan in 1972.

Design: These are large, graceful-looking ships, with classic World War II era lines. Their design reveals the strong, prewar influence of Italian designers on Soviet warships; also, the USSR obtained the Italian cruiser DUCA D'AOSTA and the German cruiser NÜRNBERG after the war and used some of their features in these ships. There is a prominent, free-standing conning tower forward, separate funnels, and two tripod masts immediately forward of the funnels. The SVERDLOV's long forecastle extends to the after gun turrets. Tracks for between 140 and 250 mines (depending upon type) are fitted on the after deck. A stern anchor is fitted in addition to the bow anchors.

Designation: Soviet KR type.

Modifications: The radars on these ships have been modified significantly during their service lives. Three ships have had 30-mm close-in guns fitted on an enlarged superstructure in the area of their forward mast and funnel.

Names: The OKTYABRSKAYA REVOLUTSIYA was originally named MOLOTOVSK; she was renamed in 1957, after completion, with the political demise of Foreign Minister V.M. Molotov. The other ships honor Russian naval and military heroes, the port city of Murmansk, and Russian revolutionary Ya.M. Sverdlov (1885–1919).

Torpedoes: As built, these ships had ten 21-in (533-mm) torpedo tubes mounted in two banks on the main deck, outboard of the motor launch stowage. They were removed from all ships by the early 1960s.

OKTYABRSKAYA REVOLUTSIYA with Knife Rest radar antenna behind the after Long Ears gun director. (Ministry of Defence)

ADMIRAL USHAKOV in Mediterranean Sea (U.S. Navy, 1973)

ADMIRAL USHAKOV showing Top Trough radar atop second mast, Round Top gun director with Sun Visor radar (between funnels), and Long Ears gun director atop conning tower; an Egg Cup-A fire control radar is visible on the 152-mm turret and an Egg Cup-B on the 100-mm turrets. (Dr. Giorgio Arra, 1973)

The DMITRY POZHARSKI with 100-mm guns at full elevation. The ship has a Big Net radar mounted on the after tripod mast and a Spoon Rest radar mounted abaft the after Long Ears gun director. An anchor is fitted in the stern counter. (1975)

# 14

# Destroyers

**2 + GUIDED MISSILE DESTROYERS: "UDALOY" CLASS**

| Name | Builder | Laid down | Launched | Completed |
|------|---------|-----------|----------|-----------|
| Udaloy | Kaliningrad | 1978 | 1980 | 1981 |
| Vitse Admiral Kulakov | Zhdanov Shipyard, Leningrad | 1978 | 1980 | 1981 |
| . . . . . | Kaliningrad | 1979 | | |
| . . . . . | Zhdanov Shipyard, Leningrad | 1979 | | |

| | | | | |
|---|---|---|---|---|
| Displacement: | 6,200–6,700 tons standard | | ASW weapons: | 2 quad SS-N-14 launchers |
| | 7,900 tons full load | | | 2 RBU-6000 rocket launchers |
| Length: | 531 ft 3 in (161.0 m) | | | torpedoes |
| Beam: | 62 ft 6 in (19.0 m) | | Torpedoes: | 8 21-in (533-mm) torpedo tubes (2 quad) |
| Draft: | 19 ft 9 in (6.0 m) | | Mines: | rails fitted |
| Propulsion: | 4 gas turbines; 100,000–120,000 shp; 2 shafts | | Radars: | 2 Bass Tilt (fire control) |
| Speed: | approx. 33-35 knots | | | 2 Eye Bowl (fire control) |
| Range: | approx. 2,400 n.miles at 32 knots | | | 1 Kite Screech (fire control) |
| | approx. 10,500 n.miles at 14 knots | | | 3 Palm Frond (navigation) |
| Complement: | approx. 300 | | | 2 Strut Pair (surface search) |
| Helicopters: | 2 Ka-27 Helix-A | | Sonars: | low frequency (bow mounted) |
| Missiles: | 8 vertical SA-N. . . launchers | | | low frequency (variable depth) |
| Guns: | 2 100-mm/70-cal DP (2 single) | | EW systems: | Bell Shroud |
| | 4 30-mm close-in (2 twin) | | | Bell Squat |
| | | | | (space provided for additional systems) |

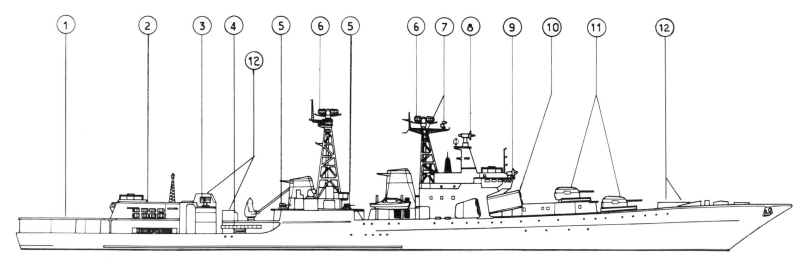

1. helicopter deck (above VDS) 2. twin helicopter hangars 3. RBU-6000 4. 533-mm torpedo tubes 5. 30-mm Gatling gun 6. Strut Pair radar 7. Palm Frond radar 8. Kite Screech radar 9. Eye Bowl radar 10. SS-N-14 missile tubes 11. 100-mm DP gun mounts 12. SA-N-. . . vertical launch systems (H. Simoni)

These are large anti-submarine destroyers, similar in concept to the U.S. Navy's Spruance (DD 963) class. Series production is under way at two shipyards. The lead ship began trials in the Baltic Sea in August 1980. The first two ships are assigned to the Northern Fleet.

Design: These ships have a long, low superstructure with their quad SS-N-14 launchers under a cantilevered extension to the bridge structure, as in the Kresta II and Kara classes. Forward of the guns and between the second lattice mast and helicopter hangar are provisions for a total of eight vertical-launch missile systems with an estimated capacity of 48 to 64 weapons. The hangar has separate bays to accommodate two helicopters, which are lowered into them by elevators similar to the arrangement in the Kara and Kresta II classes. A variable-depth sonar is fitted in the stern counter, similar to that in the Kirov class.

Designation: Soviet BPK type. This class was designated Bal-Com-3 (Baltic Combatant) by NATO intelligence pending disclosure of the lead ship's name.

Guns: Fitted with the same main gun battery as the Krivak-II-class frigates, but with the turrets installed forward.

Names: Udaloy means "courageous"; Vice Admiral N.M. Kulakov was a Soviet naval political officer during World War II.

Vitse Admiral Kulakov (1982)

The overhead view of the ASW destroyer Udaloy shows the two 100-mm guns mounted forward, the four gas turbine funnels, and the large helicopter area aft. The new vertical-launch missile systems are forward of the guns and between the after mast and hangars. Twin helicopter hangars are fitted aft. (U.S. Navy, Capt. J. W. Kehoe, 1981)

UDALOY (U.S. Navy, 1981)

Forward mast of VITSE ADMIRAL KULAKOV showing Kite Screech on pedestal, Palm Fronds on mast arms, and Strut Pair atop mast. (1982)

A Helix helicopter sits on the stern of the UDALOY with the doors to the port hangar open. There is a position atop the hangars for an additional helicopter control/homing radar. Note the control station between the hangars, radar and wind sock on the starboard side, and door covering VDS compartment.

The VITSE ADMIRAL KULAKOV bridge showing the No. 2 100-mm gun mount, the two SS-N-14 quad ASW missile launchers, and two Eye Bowl missile guidance radars atop the bridge. (1982)

**2 + ? GUIDED MISSILE DESTROYERS: "SOVREMENNYY" CLASS**

| Name | Builder | Laid down | Launched | Completed |
|------|---------|-----------|----------|-----------|
| SOVREMENNYY | Zhdanov Shipyard, Leningrad | 1976 | Nov 1978 | 1981 |
| OTCHAYANNYY | Zhdanov Shipyard, Leningrad | 1977 | Aug 1980 | 1982 |
| . . . . . . | Zhdanov Shipyard, Leningrad | 1978 | 1981 | |
| . . . . . . | Zhdanov Shipyard, Leningrad | 1979 | | |

| | |
|---|---|
| Displacement: | 6,200 tons standard |
| | 7,800 tons full load |
| Length: | 524 ft 6 in (159.0 m) |
| Beam: | 56 ft (17.0 m) |
| Draft: | 20 ft 2 in (6.1 m) |
| Propulsion: | 2 steam turbines; 100,000–110,000 shp; 2 shafts |
| Boilers: | 4 |
| Speed: | 35 knots |
| Range: | 2,400 n.miles at 32 knots |
| | 10,500 n.miles at 14 knots |
| Complement: | approx. 350 |
| Helicopters: | 1 Ka-25 Hormone-B |
| Missiles: | 2 quad SS-N-9 anti-ship tubes |
| | 2 single SA-N-7 launchers |
| Guns: | 4 130-mm/70-cal DP (2 twin) |
| | 4 30-mm close-in (4 × 1 multibarrel) |
| ASW weapons: | 2 RBU-1000 rocket launchers |
| | torpedoes |
| Torpedoes: | 4 21-in (533-mm) torpedo tubes (2 twin) |
| Mines: | rails fitted |
| Radars: | 1 Band Stand (fire control) |
| | 2 Bass Tilt (fire control) |
| | 1 Kite Screech (fire control) |
| | 3 Palm Frond (navigation) |
| | 1 Top Steer (3-D air search) |
| | 6 Front Dome (fire control) |
| Sonars: | medium frequency (bow mounted) |
| EW systems: | Bell Shroud |
| | Bell Squat |

This destroyer class is intended for anti-ship operations. Minimal ASW weapons and sensors are provided. With the UDALOY class, they have succeeded the Kresta II cruisers in series production at the Zhdanov yard. The SOVREMENNYY began sea trials in the Baltic in August 1980; she is assigned to the Northern Fleet.

Design: This class is similar in size to the UDALOY, but with very different hull form, propulsion, weapons, and sensors. The quad surface-to-surface missile launchers are mounted slightly forward of the bridge structure; the main gun armament is divided fore and aft (the UDALOY has guns forward); pressure-fired steam propulsion is provided (vice the UDALOY's gas turbines); and there is a telescoping helicopter hangar adjacent to the landing area to accommodate a single Ka-25 Hormone-B helicopter for over-the-horizon targeting. This is the first Soviet surface combatant with the landing area amidships instead of at the stern, and the first to use the telescoping hangar.

Minimal ASW armament is fitted, and while the ship does have a bow sonar dome, it is significantly smaller than that in the UDALOY and other recent BPK classes. However, like the UDALOY, mine rails are provided.

Designation: Soviet EM (*destroyer*) type. These ships were originally designated Bal-Com-2 by Western intelligence.

Engineering: The return to steam propulsion in the SOVREMENNYY was somewhat surprising in view of the use of gas turbines in the previous Kara class and the contemporary UDALOY. The estimated range of the two destroyer classes is the same.

Guns: The 130-mm guns are of a new, fully automatic, water-cooled type. They are the largest guns installed in any new-construction ship by any navy since the SVERDLOV cruisers built in the 1950s.[1] The same guns are also mounted in the Krasina cruiser.

[1]The U.S. Navy mounted a single 8-in (203-mm)/55-cal in the destroyer HULL (DD 945) from 1975 to 1979; proposals to install this Major Caliber Light-Weight Gun (MCLWG) in a strike cruiser (CSGN) or in destroyers of the SPRUANCE class did not come to fruition. The U.S. Navy also proposed building an amphibious fire support ship to carry large-caliber guns, but this design was cancelled as was the CSGN.

The SOVREMENNYY with "balanced" gun and missile armament—twin 130-mm turret and SA-N-7 launcher forward and aft and large anti-ship missiles beside the bridge. This class also can be distinguished from the UDALOY by the mast/radar arrangement and single funnel. (U.S. Navy, 1982)

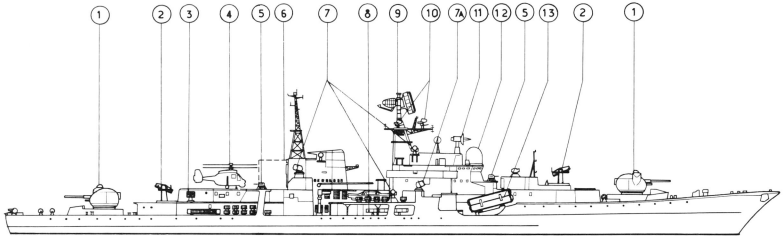

1. 130-mm DP gun mounts 2. SA-N-7 launchers 3. RBU-1000 rocket launcher 4. helicopter deck 5. 30-mm Gatling gun 6. telescoping hangar 7. Front Dome radars 7A. Bass Tilt radar 8. 533-mm torpedo tubes 9. Top Steer radar 10. Palm Frond radar 11. Kite Screech radar 12. Band Stand radar 13. improved SS-N-9 missile tubes (H. Simoni)

SOVREMENNYY

The SOVREMENNYY. Note the helicopter landing area and the expandable hangar.

## 6 GUIDED MISSILE DESTROYERS: MODIFIED KASHIN CLASS

| Name | Builder | Completed | Conversion Completed |
|------|---------|-----------|----------------------|
| OGNEVOY | Z | | |
| SLAVNYY | Z | | |
| SDERZHANDOYY | N | 1963–1971 | 1973–1980 |
| SMELYY | N | | |
| SMYSHLENNYY | N | | |
| STROYNYY | N | | |

| | |
|---|---|
| Builders: | N = 61 Kommuna Shipyard, Nikolayev (north) |
| | Z = Zhdanov Shipyard, Leningrad |
| Displacement: | 3,950 tons standard |
| | 4,500 tons full load |
| Length: | 485 ft (147.0 m) |
| Beam: | 52 ft 2 in (15.8 m) |
| Draft: | 15 ft 10 in (4.8 m) |
| Propulsion: | 4 gas turbines: 96,000 shp; 2 shafts |
| Speed: | 37–38 knots |
| Range: | 1,500 n.miles at 36 knots |
| | 4,000 n.miles at 20 knots |
| Complement: | approx. 280–330 |
| Helicopters: | (no hangars) |
| Missiles: | 2 twin SA-N-1 Goa launchers (44) |
| | 4 single SS-N-2c Styx anti-ship launchers |
| Guns: | 4 76.2-mm/60-cal AA (2 twin) |
| | 4 30-mm close-in (4 × 1 multibarrel) |
| ASW weapons: | 2 RBU-6000 rocket launchers |
| | torpedoes |
| Torpedoes: | 5 21-in (533-mm) torpedo tubes (1 quin) |
| Mines: | rails removed |
| Radars: | 2 Bass Tilt (fire control) |
| | 1 Big Net (3-D air search) |
| | 2 Don Kay (navigation) |
| | 1 Head Net-C (3-D air search) except 2 Head Net-A in OGNEVOY |
| | 2 Owl Screech (fire control) |
| | 2 Peel Group (fire control) |
| Sonars: | medium frequency (hull mounted) |
| | medium frequency (variable depth) |
| EW systems: | Bell Shroud |
| | Bell Squat |
| | (space provided for additional system) |

These are Kashin-class destroyers modified with improved electronics and installation of four rear-firing, improved Styx missiles. In addition to the SS-N-2c missiles, the SA-N-1 system has an anti-ship capability. See Kashin-class listing for additional details.

Of the 19 surviving ships of the Kashin and modified Kashin classes, 3 are assigned to the Northern Fleet, 3 to the Baltic Fleet, 9 to the Black Sea Fleet, and 4 to the Pacific Fleet.

Conversion: Conversions were completed between 1973 and 1980 with the SDERZHANNYY probably having been completed to this configuration. The hull was lengthened by approximately 6 feet 6 in (2.0 m), a stern VDS installation being provided under the raised helicopter deck. Improved hull-mounted sonar was also fitted. Rapid-fire Gatling guns were provided in place of two RBU-1000 rocket launchers that were previously mounted. Improved air-search radars are provided in all but OGNEVOY. The field of fire of the after 76.2-mm gun mount is severely restricted by the VDS housing and helicopter platform. There is no hangar.

Designation: Soviet BPK type.

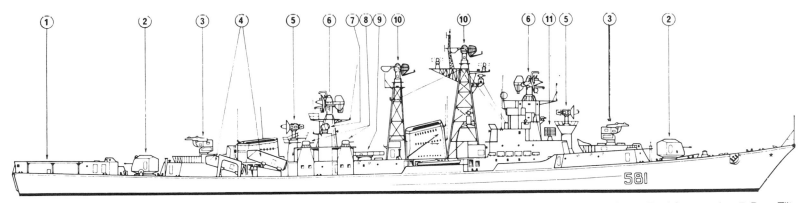

1. helicopter deck (above VDS) 2. twin 76.2-mm AA gun mounts 3. SA-N-1 launchers 4. SS-N-2c missile tubes 5. Owl Screech radars 6. Peel Group radars 7. Bass Tilt radars 8. 30-mm Gatling guns 9. 533-mm torpedo tubes 10. Head Net-A radars 11. RBU-6000 rocket launcher (H. Simoni)

SLAVNYY (Ministry of Defence)

Modified Kashin (U.S. Navy, PH2 J.C. Brown, 1980)

## 13 GUIDED MISSILE DESTROYERS: KASHIN CLASS

| Name | Builder | Completed |
|------|---------|-----------|
| KOMSOMOLETS UKRAINYY | N | |
| KRASNYY KAVKAZ | N | |
| KRASNYY KRYM | N | |
| OBRAZTSOVYY | Z | |
| ODARENNYY | Z | 1963–1971 |
| PROVORNYY | Z | |
| RESHITELNYY | N | |
| SKORYY | N | |
| SMETLIVVY | N | |
| SOOBRAZITELNYY | N | |
| SPOSOBNYY | N | |
| STEREGUSHCHIY | Z | |
| STROGIY | N | |

Builders:     N = 61 Kommuna Shipyard, Nikolayev (north)
                 Z = Zhdanov Shipyard, Leningrad
Displacement:    3,750 tons standard
                 4,500 tons full load
Length:           475 ft 2 in (144.0 m)
Beam:             52 ft 2 in (15.8 m)
Draft:              15 ft 10 in (4.8 m)
Propulsion:      4 gas turbines; 96,000 shp; 2 shafts

Speed:             37–38 knots
Range:             1,500 n.miles at 36 knots
                 4,000 n.miles at 20 knots
Complement:    approx. 280–330
Helicopters:     (no hangar)
Missiles:        2 twin SA-N-1 Goa launchers (44) except 1 single SA-N-7
                 launcher in PROVORNYY
Guns:             4 76.2-mm/60-cal AA (2 twin)
ASW weapons:   2 RBU-6000 rocket launchers
                 2 RBU-1000 rocket launchers
                 torpedoes
Torpedoes:       5 21-in (533-mm) torpedo tubes (1 quin)
Mines:           rails for approx. 20
Radars:         1 Big Net and 1 Head Net-C (3-D air search)
                 or 2 Head Net-A
                 or 2 Head Net-C
                 or 1 Head Net-C in PROVORNYY
                 2 or 3 Don-2 (navigation)
                 2 Owl Screech (fire control)
                 2 Peel Group (fire control)
                 1 Top Steer (3-D air search) in PROVORNYY
                 8 Front Dome (fire control) in PROVORNYY
Sonars:         high frequency (hull mounted)
EW systems:    Watch Dog

Kashin-class guided missile destroyer with Big Net radar (U.S. Navy, 1971)

The Kashins were the world's first major warships with all-gas-turbine propulsion. These are multipurpose destroyers. The OBRAZTSOVYY visited Portsmouth, England, in June 1976, the first visit of a Soviet warship to the United Kingdom in 20 years.

Class: Twenty ships were built to this class for the Soviet Navy, and subsequently three modified ships (Kashin II) were built for the Indian Navy (completed 1980–1982). One Soviet ship, the OTVAZHNYY, was lost to an internal fire and explosion in the Black Sea on 31 August 1974. According to press reports, at least 200 crewmen were killed.

Six ships have been extensively modified and are listed separately. The PROVORNYY was converted to a test ship for the SA-N-7 missile system (see below).

Conversion: The PROVORNYY was converted in the mid-1970s, becoming operational in late 1981 as an SA-N-7 test ship. Both SA-N-1 systems and associated Peel Group radars were removed. A single SA-N-7 launcher was mounted aft and provisions made for fitting two similar systems forward. Radars also modified. Her guns, torpedo tubes,

and ASW weapons were retained. The PROVORNYY operates in the Black Sea.

Design: These are large, graceful flush-deck destroyers, with a low superstructure topped by four large funnels for gas turbine exhaust, two radar-topped lattice masts, and four smaller radar towers. There is a helicopter landing area aft (with enclosed control station) but no hangar.

In the first Kashin completed, all four funnels were the same height. Apparently, problems were encountered with the flow of exhaust gases. In subsequent ships the forward pair of funnels were heightened about 1.5 meters.

Designation: Originally BKR (large missile ship); changed to BPK in early 1960s.

Names: Most Kashin-class ships have "adjective" names, as OBRAZTSOVYY (exemplary) and ODARYENNYY (gifted). The exceptions are KOMSOMOLETS UKRAINY (Ukrainian Young Communists), KRASNYY KAVKAZ (Red Caucasus), and KRASNYY KRYM (Red Crimea).

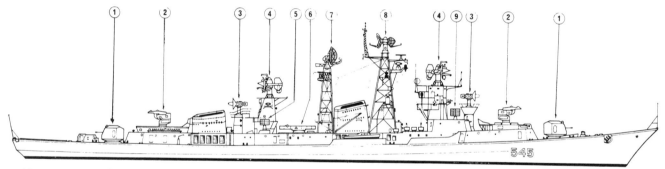

1. twin 76.2-mm AA gun mounts 2. SA-N-1 launchers 3. Owl Screech radars 4. Peel Group radars 5. RBU-1000 rocket launcher 6. 533-mm torpedo tubes 7. Big Net radar 8. Head Net-C radar 9. RBU-6000 rocket launcher (H. Simoni)

The PROVORNYY at sea with her new, solid-structure second mast carrying a Top Steer radar antenna. The ship has two missile directors above the RBU-6000 rocket launchers on the bridge, two on each mast, and two adjacent to the after pair of funnels. Photos of details are in chapter 26. (*Bibliothek fur Zeitgeschichfe*)

RESHITELNYY with Big Net radar

Kashin superstructure showing Head Net-A radar antennas atop both masts, Peel Group radar atop bridge, and Owl Screech radar at far right (adjacent to RBU-6000 rocket launchers). (Dr. Giorgio Arra, 1973)

The PROVORNYY's SA-N-7 launcher under cover. (Courtesy Bibliothek fur Zeitgeschichfe)

The PROVORNYY, trials ship for SA-N-7 missile system, with one launcher installed between after funnels and 76.2-mm gun mount and provision for two more launchers forward of the bridge. The ship has eight missile directors and retains her original gun and torpedo armament, giving her a significant combat capability for a trials ship. (U.S. Navy, 1982)

## 8 GUIDED MISSILE DESTROYERS: KANIN CLASS

| Name | Completed | Conversion Completed |
|------|-----------|---------------------|
| BOIKIY | | |
| DERZKIY | | |
| GNEVNYY | | |
| GORDYY | 1960–1962 | 1968–1977 |
| GREMYASHCHIY | | |
| UPORNYY | | |
| ZHGUCHIY | | |
| ZORKIY | | |

| | |
|------|------|
| Builders: | 61 Kommuna Shipyard, Nikolayev (north) |
| | Severodvinsk |
| | Zhdanov Shipyard, Leningrad |
| Displacement: | 3,700 tons standard |
| | 4,750 tons full load |
| Length: | 458 ft 9 in (139.0 m) |
| Beam: | 49 ft 5 in (15.0 m) |
| Draft: | 16 ft 6 in (5.0 m) |
| Propulsion: | steam turbines; 80,000 shp; 2 shafts |
| Boilers: | 4 |
| Speed: | 35 knots |
| Range: | 1,100 n.miles at 32 knots |
| | 4,500 n.miles at 15 knots |
| Complement: | approx. 300–350 |
| Helicopters: | (no hangar) |
| Missiles: | 1 twin SA-N-1 Goa launcher (22) |
| Guns: | 8 57-mm/70-cal AA (2 quad) |
| | 8 30-mm/60-cal close-in (4 twin) |
| ASW weapons: | 3 RBU-6000 rocket launchers |
| | torpedoes |
| Torpedoes: | 10 21-in (533-mm) torpedo tubes (2 quin) |
| Mines: | no rails fitted |
| Radars: | 2 Don Kay (navigation) |
| | 2 Drum Tilt (fire control) |
| | 1 Hawk Screech (fire control) |
| | 1 Head Net-C (3-D air search) |
| | 1 Peel Group (fire control) |

| | |
|------|------|
| Sonars: | medium frequency (bow mounted) |
| EW systems: | Bell-series |
| | Top Hat |

These are AAW/ASW destroyers converted from surface-to-surface missile ships. Five of the ships are in the Northern Fleet and three in the Pacific Fleet.

The BOIKIY and ZHGUCHY visited Boston, Massachusetts, in May 1975 in celebration of the 30th anniversary of the end of World War II. They were the first Soviet warships to visit the United States since the war.

Conversion: These ships are converted Krupnyy-class missile destroyers (two SS-N-1 launchers), which were based on the Kotlin-class design. For their present configuration, the forward SS-N-1 launcher was replaced by a second quad 57-mm mount and an RBU-6000; the after SS-N-1 launcher and quad 57-mm gun mount were deleted and the after section of the ship reconfigured for the SA-N-1 system and a larger helicopter deck. The superstructure was modified and additional electronics and twin 30-mm guns fitted, the latter in place of two amidships 57-mm mounts. (Gun armament as Krupnyy was 16 57-mm weapons.) Torpedo armament increased (from six tubes) and electronics upgraded. The conversions were completed between 1968 and 1977.

All converted at Zhdanov except for the GNEVNYY and GORDYY, which were converted at Vladivostok.

Design: This class has the lightest gun armament in terms of weapon size of any contemporary destroyers.

Designation: Soviet BPK type.

Names: These ships have "adjective" names.

A Kanin-class guided missile destroyer. These ships have the lightest main gun battery of any destroyer in service today—eight 57-mm AA guns in quad mounts (plus eight 30-mm guns in twin mounts for close-in defense against cruise missiles). However, their heavy torpedo battery, ASW rocket launchers, and limited helicopter capability in addition to the SA-N-1 launcher make them versatile ships.

The BOIKIY entering Boston (U.S. Navy, 1975)

Kanin-class guided missile destroyer (Ministry of Defence)

## 3 GUIDED MISSILE DESTROYERS: MODIFIED KILDIN CLASS

| Name | Builder | Completed | Conversion Completed |
|------|---------|-----------|---------------------|
| BEDOVYY | N | | |
| NEULOVIMYY | Z | 1959–1960 | 1973–1975 |
| PROZORLIVYY | Z | | |

| | |
|---|---|
| Builders: | N = 61 Kommuna Shipyard, Nikolayev (north) |
| | Z = Zhdanov Shipyard, Leningrad |
| Displacement: | 2,800 tons standard |
| | 3,500 tons full load |
| Length: | 417 ft 6 in (126.5 m) |
| Beam: | 43 ft (13.0 m) |
| Draft: | 15 ft 2 in (4.6 m) |
| Propulsion: | steam turbines; 72,000 shp; 2 shafts |
| Boilers: | 4 |
| Speed: | 38 knots |
| Range: | 1,000 n.miles at 32 knots |
| | 3,600 n.miles at 18 knots |
| Complement: | approx. 300 |
| Helicopters: | (no facilities) |
| Missiles: | 4 single SS-N-2c Styx anti-ship launchers |
| Guns: | 4 76.2-mm/60-cal AA (2 twin) |
| | 16 57-mm/70-cal AA (4 quad) except 16 45-mm/85-cal (4 quad) in BEDOVYY |

| | |
|---|---|
| ASW weapons: | 2 RBU-2500 rocket launchers |
| | torpedoes |
| Torpedoes: | 4 21-in (533-mm) torpedo tubes (2 twin) |
| Radars: | 1 Don-2 (navigation) |
| | 2 Hawk Screech (fire control) |
| | 1 Head Net-C (3-D air search) except Strut Pair in BEDOVYY |
| | 1 Owl Screech (fire control) |
| Sonars: | 1 Herkules or Pegas medium frequency (hull mounted) |
| EW systems: | Watch Dog |

The three modified Kildin-class ships have had their single SS-N-1 (aft) launcher replaced by twin 76.2-mm gun mounts and four SS-N-2c anti-ship missiles.

Class: Four ships were redesigned during construction from Kotlin-class destroyers to the world's first missile destroyers. Subsequently, three ships were modified by removing their SS-N-1 launcher; they rejoined the fleet in 1973–1975. The fourth Kildin, the NEUDERZHIMYY, was not converted (see page 169).

Conversion: All three ships converted at Nikolayev north.

Designation: Soviet BRK type.

Electronics: Strut Pair 3-D radar fitted in BEDOVYY in mid-1970s.

The NEULOVIMYY following her extensive conversion from a surface-to-surface missile ship, with two 76.2-mm twin gun mounts replacing the SS-N-1 missile system. She retains her original quad 57-mm mounts forward and abaft the forward funnel, a total of 16 of those weapons. Four aft-firing SS-N-2c Styx missiles are fitted as in the modified Kashin class.

**1 GUIDED MISSILE DESTROYER: KILDIN CLASS**

| Name | Completed |
| --- | --- |
| NEUDERZHIMYY | 1958 |

Builder:          Komsomol'sk

The sole survivor of the four Kildin-class destroyers, the NEUDERZHIMYY is in essentially her original configuration with a single SS-N-1 launcher aft supplemented by 16 57-mm AA guns. Basic characteristics as the modified Kildin class.

The ship is in the Pacific Fleet and unlikely to be modified because of her age.

A Kildin in essentially original configuration. One ship of this type remains in Soviet service, the lone survivor of four Kildin (one SS-N-1 launcher) and eight Krupnyy (two SS-N-1 launchers) missile destroyers. Note arrangement of 57-mm guns forward and amidships plus ASW armament of two RBU-2500s and four 533-mm torpedo tubes.

## 8 GUIDED MISSILE DESTROYERS: SAM KOTLIN CLASS

| Name | Completed | Conversion Completed |
|------|-----------|----------------------|
| BRAVYY | | 1962 |
| NAKHODCHIVYY | | |
| NASTOCHIVYY | | |
| NESOKRUSHIMYY* | 1954–1959 | 1966–1972 |
| SKROMNYY | | |
| SKRYTNYY* | | |
| SOZNATEL'NYY* | | |
| VOZBUZHDENNYY* | | |

| | |
|------|------|
| Builders: | Komsomol'sk |
| | 61 Kommuna Shipyard, Nikolayev (north) |
| | Zhdanov Shipyard, Leningrad |
| Displacement: | 2,700 tons standard |
| | 3,500 tons full load |
| Length: | 412 ft 6 in (125.0 m) |
| Beam: | 43 ft (13.0 m) |
| Draft: | 15 ft 2 in (4.6 m) |
| Propulsion: | steam turbines; 72,000 shp; 2 shafts |
| Boilers: | 4 |
| Speed: | 38 knots |
| Range: | 1,000 n.miles at 34 knots |
| | 3,600 n.miles at 18 knots |
| Complement: | |
| Helicopters: | (no facilities) |
| Missiles: | 1 twin SA-N-1 Goa launcher (22) |
| Guns: | 2 130-mm/58-cal DP (1 twin) |
| | 4 45-mm/85-cal AA (1 quad) except BRAVYY 12 45-mm (3 quad) |
| | 8 30-mm/60-cal close-in (4 twin) in 4 ships(*) |

| | |
|------|------|
| ASW weapons: | 2 RBU-6000 rocket launchers except BRAVYY, SKROMNYY |
| | 2 RBU-2500 |
| | torpedoes |
| Torpedoes: | 5 21-in (533-mm) torpedo tubes (1 quin) |
| Mines: | rails removed |
| Radars: | 1 or 2 Don-2 (navigation) |
| | 2 Drum Tilt in 4 ships(*) |
| | 1 Egg Cup (fire control) except NASTOCHIVYY |
| | 1 Hawk Screech (fire control) |
| | 1 Head Net-C (3-D air search) |
| | 1 Peel Group (fire control) |
| | 1 Sun Visor (fire control) |
| Sonars: | Herkules or Pegas high-frequency (hull mounted) |
| EW systems: | Watch Dog |

These are AAW destroyers with a heavier gun battery than the later Kildin-class ships. Two ships serve in the Northern Fleet, 1 in the Baltic Fleet, 3 in the Black Sea Fleet, and 2 in the Pacific Fleet.

Class: Nine ships were converted from standard Kotlin-class destroyers to this SAM configuration. The SPRAVEDLIVYY was transferred to Poland in 1970.

Conversion: The Kotlin's after twin 130-mm gun mount and half the torpedo battery were removed. An SA-N-1 missile system and associated radars were fitted as well as improved electronics and ASW weapons.

The BRAVYY was the first converted; she was employed as the SA-N-1 trials ship. Details of the ships differ.

Designation: Soviet EM type.

The prototype of the SAM Kotlin conversions was the BRAVYY, completed in 1962. The pedestal for her Peel Group missile control radar and after funnel differ from the eight later conversions completed 1966–1972 (one of which was transferred to Poland). Unlike the later Kanin conversions, the SAM Kotlins have 130-mm DP guns forward in addition to quad AA guns amidships. (U.S. Navy, 1975)

A later SAM Kotlin-class guided missile destroyer conversion

The NASTOCHIVYY showing (from left to right) Hawk Screech, Sun Visor on Wasp Head director, two Don-2 (on tripod mast), Head Net-C, and Peel Group antennas. (1976)

## 18 DESTROYERS: KOTLIN CLASS

| Name | Name | Name | Completed |
|---|---|---|---|
| Besslednyy | Moskovskiy | Svetlyy | |
| Blagorodnyy* | Komsomolets* | Veskiy | |
| Blestyashchiy* | Naporistiy* | Vdokhnovennyy* | |
| Burlivyy* | Plamennyy* | Vozmushchyennyy | 1954–1958 |
| Byvalyy* | Speshnyy | Vyderzhannyy* | |
| Dal'nevotochnyy | Spokoynyy | Vyzyvayushchiy* | |
| Komsomolets | Svedushchiy* | | |

| | |
|---|---|
| Builders: | 61 Kommuna Shipyard, Nikolayev (north) |
| | Komsomol'sk |
| | Zhdanov Shipyard, Leningrad |
| Displacement: | 2,600 tons standard |
| | 3,500 tons full load |
| Length: | 417 ft 6 in (126.5 m) |
| Beam: | 43 ft (13.0 m) |
| Draft: | 15 ft 2 in (4.6 m) |
| Propulsion: | steam turbines; 72,000 shp; 2 shafts |
| Boilers: | 4 |
| Speed: | 38 knots |
| Range: | 1,000 n.miles at 34 knots |
| | 3,600 n.miles at 18 knots |
| Complement: | approx. 335 |
| Helicopters: | no facilities |
| Missiles: | none |
| Guns: | 4 130-mm/58-cal DP (2 twin) |
| | 16 45-mm/85-cal AA (4 quad) |
| | 4 25-mm/60-cal AA (2 twin) except 8 guns (4 twin) in modified ships(*) |
| ASW weapons: | 6 BMB-2 depth-charge projects in unmodified ships |
| | 2 depth-charge racks in unmodified ships |
| | 2 RBU-600 rocket launchers in modified ships(*) except 2 RBU-6000 rocket launchers in Moskovskiy Komsomolets |
| | torpedoes |
| Torpedoes: | 10 21-in (533-mm) torpedo tubes (2 quin) except 5 tubes (1 quin) in modified ships(*) |
| Mines: | rails fitted for approx. 55 mines |
| Radars: | 2 Don-2 or 1 Neptune (navigation) |
| | 2 Egg Cup (fire control) |
| | 2 Hawk Screech (fire control) |
| | 1 Post Lamp or Top Bow (fire control) |
| | 1 Sun Visor (fire control) |

| | |
|---|---|
| Sonars: | Herkules high-frequency (hull mounted) |
| | medium frequency (variable depth) in Moskovskiy Komsomolets |
| EW systems: | Watch Dog |

These are graceful, flush-deck destroyers. Eleven ships have been modified (*) and are considered as a sub-class. Other Kotlins have been partially and fully converted to missile configurations (see below). All of these ships are believed to be in active service.

The Soviet class name is reported as Plamennyy.

Class: Twenty-seven Kotlin-class ships of a planned 36 were completed between 1954 and 1961. Nine of these ships were subsequently converted to the SAM Kotlin configuration (armed with SA-N-1). Another four of these hulls were completed as Kildin (SS-N-1) missile destroyers, and eight new ships of this basic design were built as Krupnyy (SS-N-1) missile destroyers. The latter ships were later converted again, to the Kanin configuration (SA-N-1 system).

Design: These were the world's last destroyers to be built to classic World War II destroyer lines, mounting heavy DP and light AA gun batteries, with a large torpedo battery, high speed, and minimal ASW weapons and sensors.

Designation: Soviet EM type.

Engineering: These were the first of the Soviet Navy's very high speed surface combatants, being faster than any non-Soviet cruisers or destroyers of post–World War II construction.

Modification: Eleven ships were modified between 1960 and 1962, having their after bank of torpedo tubes replaced by a deckhouse and improvements in ASW weapons. The Moskovskiy Komsomolets was further modified, being fitted with two RBU-6000 launchers forward, and in 1978 a variable-depth sonar was provided. The Svetlyy has been fitted with a helicopter platform aft.

Names: Most of these ships have "adjective" names with two ships being named for city komsomols. The Western class name Kotlin is derived from the ships being first seen off Kotlin Island (Kronshtadt) in the Gulf of Riga.

A modified Kotlin-class destroyer off the island of Crete in the Mediterranean; note built up structure abaft second funnel in place of second bank of torpedo tubes. (U.S. Navy, 1973)

The Moskovskiy Komsomolets is the only Kotlin-class destroyer fitted with variable-depth sonar. In this view the ship's after guns are at maximum elevation.

The Svetlyy is believed to be the only Kotlin-class destroyer fitted with a helicopter platform. Her depth charges have been removed, making her ten 533-mm torpedo tubes her only ASW armament.

A Kotlin-class destroyer en route from her home port in the Soviet Far East to the Indian Ocean. (U.S. Navy, 1974)

## ~20 DESTROYERS: "SKORYY" CLASS

| Name | Name | Name | Completed |
|------|------|------|-----------|
| BEZUDERZHNYY | SMOTRYASHY | STREMITELNY | |
| OGNENNYY* | SOLIDNY | SUROVY | |
| OSTOROZHNY* | SOKRUSHITELNYY | SVOBODNY | 1949–1954 |
| OTVETSTVENNYY* | SOVERSHENNYY | VDUMCHIVY | |
| OZHESTOCHENNYY | STATNY | VNIMATELNY | |
| OZHIVLENNY | STEPENNY | VRAZUMITELNY | |
| SERDITY | STOYKY | | |

| | |
|---|---|
| Builders: | 61 Kommuna Shipyard, Nikolayev (north) |
| | Komsomol'sk |
| | Zhdanov Shipyard, Leningrad |
| Displacement: | 2,600 tons standard |
| | 3,180 tons full load |
| Length: | 400 ft (121.2 m) |
| Beam: | 39 ft 6 in (12.0 m) |
| Draft: | 14 ft 10 in (4.5 m) |
| Propulsion: | steam turbines; 60,000 shp; 2 shafts |
| Boilers: | 4 |
| Speed: | 33 knots |
| Range: | 850 n.miles at 30 knots |
| | 3,500 n.miles at 14 knots |
| Complement: | approx. 220 |
| Helicopters: | no facilities |
| Guns: | |
| *standard* | 4 130-mm/50-cal SP (2 twin) |
| | 2 85-mm/50-cal AA (1 twin) |
| | 7 or 8 37-mm/60-cal AA (7 single or 4 twin) |
| | 4 or 6 20-mm AA (2 or 3 twin) (see notes) |
| *modified* | 5 57-mm/70-cal AA (5 single) |
| ASW weapons: | |
| *standard* | 2 depth-charge projectors |
| | 2 depth-charge racks |
| | torpedoes |
| *modified* | 2 RBU-2500 rocket launchers |
| | 2 depth-charge racks |
| | torpedoes |
| Torpedoes: | 10 21-in (533-mm) torpedo tubes (2 quin) except 5 tubes (quin) in modified ships(*) |

| | | |
|---|---|---|
| Mines: | rails fitted for approx. 50 mines | |
| Radars: | | |
| | *standard* | 1 Cross Bird (air search) |
| | | 1 or 2 Don-2 (navigation) |
| | | 1 Half Bow or Post Lamp or Top Bow (fire control) |
| | | 1 High Sieve (air search) |
| | *modified* | 1 or 2 Don-2 (navigation) |
| | | 2 Hawk Screech (fire control) |
| | | 1 Slim Net (air search) |
| Sonars: | 1 Pegas high-frequency | |
| EW systems: | Watch Dog | |

These were the first Soviet destroyers constructed after World War II. The above names are estimated to be the approximately 20 surviving units, of which 12 are believed to be active with the remainder in reserve. Their military value is very limited.

Class: Seventy-two destroyers of this class were built. Six were transferred to Egypt, 7 to Indonesia, and 2 to Poland.

Design: This design was based on the prewar OGNEVOY class, the first ship of that class having been laid down in 1939 but not completed until 1943. The SKORYY design incorporated some features from German ships and had improved seakeeping, increased torpedo armament, and more AA guns compared to the OGNEVOY class.

Designation: Soviet EM type.

Guns: In the early 1970s those ships with eight 37-mm weapons were provided with 25-mm AA guns. The main battery lacks sufficient elevation for dual-purpose use.

Modification: A modernization program began in 1958, but in the event only eight ships were updated, probably because of the expense involved and because the yard capacity was needed for new construction. The principal change was the upgrading of radar, construction of a deckhouse in place of the forward torpedo bank, and installation of modern 57-mm guns in place of earlier AA armament.

Names: These ships have "adjective" names. The lead ship SKORYY (speedy) has been stricken, with that name now carried by a Kashin-class destroyer.

A standard SKORYY-class destroyer with ten torpedo tubes. The SKORYY was the last "broken-deck" destroyer built in the Soviet Union until the SOVREMENNYY and UDALOY classes. (The one-of-a-kind Tallinn-class destroyer NEUSTRASHIMYY, completed in 1955, was a flush-deck ship.)

Modified SKORYY-class destroyer

# 15

# Frigates

## 1 ANTI-SUBMARINE FRIGATE: KONI CLASS

| Name | Completed |
|------|-----------|
| Timofey Ul'yantsev | 1976 |

| | |
|---|---|
| Builders: | Zelenodolsk |
| Displacement: | 1,900 tons full load |
| Length: | 320 ft (97.0 m) |
| Beam: | 42 ft 3 in (12.8 m) |
| Draft: | 13 ft 10 in (4.2 m) |
| Propulsion: | CODAG: 2 diesels 15,000 bhp/ 1 gas turbine 15,000 shp; 3 shafts |
| Speed: | 27 knots |
| Range: | 1,800 n.miles at 14 knots |
| Complement: | approx. 110 |
| Helicopters: | no facilities |
| Missiles: | 1 twin SA-N-4 launcher (20) |
| Guns: | 4 76.2-mm/60-cal AA (2 twin) |
| | 4 30-mm/65-cal close-in (2 twin) |
| ASW weapons: | 2 RBU-6000 rocket launchers |
| | 2 depth-charge racks |
| Torpedoes: | none |
| Mines: | rails for 20 mines |
| Radars: | 1 Don-2 (navigation) |
| | 1 Drum Tilt (fire control) |
| | 1 Hawk Screech (fire control) |
| | 1 Pop Group (fire control) |
| | 1 Strut Curve (air search) |
| Sonars: | medium frequency (hull mounted) |
| EW systems: | Watch Dog |

The Koni is a coastal ASW ship, apparently developed specifically for foreign transfer.[1] Only one ship appears to be in Soviet service for demonstration and crew training roles. Construction continues at about one unit per year.

[1] The term *frigate* in the contemporary context is used by Western navies. The Soviet ships in this chapter have the designations patrol ship (SKR—*Storozhevoy Korabl'*) and small ASW ship (MPK—*Malyy Protivolodochnyy Korabl'*); they are roughly equivalent in size and capability to Western frigates, Western intelligence generally listing all but the Krivaks as "light" frigates (i.e., FFL).

The Koni-class frigate ROSTOCK, subsequently transferred to East Germany, wearing her original pendant number and flying the Soviet ensign aft. Production of these ships continue for foreign transfer at the rate of about one per year, with a single Koni retained by the Soviet Navy in the Black Sea, apparently for training foreign crews.

The ASW sensors and weapons are both short range and intended for shallow depths (e.g., they lack variable-depth sonar and torpedo tubes, which are unsuitable for shallow-water attacks), and the ship is both speed and range limited.

Class: Two ships of this class have been transferred to East Germany (1978–1979), one to Yugoslavia (1980), one to Cuba (1981), and two to Algeria (1980, 1982). The Koni is the largest surface warship ever to fly the Algerian and Cuban colors.

Design: The design follows Soviet small combatant lines, with the Koni having similar lines to the smaller Grisha. (The Grisha has only a two-step bridge structure and no gun mount forward.)

The ship has a "split" superstructure, with the space between possibly having been intended for tubes in some roles (as mounted in the Grisha classes). There are two depth-charge racks aft as well as provisions for minelaying and minesweeping.

Designation: Soviet SKR type.

Engineering: Combination Diesel And Gas turbine (CODAG) propulsion with a total horsepower output of 30,000 to three propellers.

Closeup of Koni-class superstructure showing (from left to right) twin RBU-6000 rocket launchers, Hawk Screech radar, direction-finding loop, Don-2 just above yardarm, Strut Curve atop mast, and Drum Tilt (partially obscured).

Koni-class frigate (1981)

## 32 + GUIDED MISSILE FRIGATES: KRIVAK I/II CLASSES

| Name | Name | Name | Completed |
|------|------|------|-----------|
| *Krivak I* | | | |
| Bditel'nyy | Druzhnyy | Razyashchiy | |
| Bezukoriznennyy | Ladnyy | Retivyy | 1970– |
| Bezzevetniy | Leningradskiy Komsomolets | Sil'nyy | |
| Bodryy | Letuchiy | Storozhevoy | |
| Deyatel'nyy | Pylkiy | Svirepyy | |
| Doblestnyy | Pytlivyy | Zadornyy | 1976– |
| Dostoynyy | Razumnyy | Zharkyy | |
| | | . . . . . . | |
| *Krivak II* | | | |
| Bessmennyy | Neukrotimyy | Rezkiy | |
| Gordelivyy | Pitlivyy | Rezvyy | |
| Gromkiy | Razitel'nyy | R'yanyy | |
| Grozyashchiy | Revnosttnyy | . . . . . . | |

| | |
|---|---|
| Builders: | Kaliningrad (Krivak I/II) |
| | Kamysh-Burun Shipyard, Kerch' (Krivak I) |
| | Zhdanov Shipyard, Leningrad (Krivak I) |
| Displacement: | 3,800 tons full load |
| Length: | 407 ft 6 in (123.5 m) |
| Beam: | 46 ft 6 in (14.1 m) |
| Draft: | 15 ft 2 in (4.6 m) |
| Propulsion: | 2 gas turbines (24,200 hp) + 2 boost gas turbines (48,600 hp); total output 48,600 shp; 2 shafts |
| Speed: | 32 knots |
| Range: | 1,600 n.miles at 31 knots |
| | 4,600 n.miles at 20 knots |
| Complement: | approx. 200 |
| Helicopters: | no facilities |
| Missiles: | 2 twin SA-N-4 launchers (40) |
| Guns: | 4 76.2-mm/60-cal AA (2 twin) in Krivak I |
| | 2 100-mm/70-cal DP (2 single) in Krivak II |
| ASW weapons: | 1 quad SS-N-14 launcher |
| | 2 RBU-6000 rocket launchers |
| | torpedoes |
| Torpedoes: | 8 21-in (533-mm) torpedo tubes (2 quad) |
| Mines: | rails for 20 mines |

| | |
|---|---|
| Radars: | 1 Don-2 or Spin Trough (navigation) |
| | 1 Don Kay or Palm Frond (navigation) |
| | 2 Eye Bowl (fire control) |
| | 1 Head Net-C (3-D air search) |
| | 1 Kite Screech (fire control) in Krivak II |
| | 1 Owl Screech (fire control) in Krivak I |
| | 2 Pop group (fire control) |
| Sonars: | medium frequency (bow mounted) |
| | medium frequency (variable depth) |
| EW systems: | Bell Shroud |
| | Bell Squat |

These are low-lying, graceful ASW ships, but have relatively short range and lack helicopter facilities. The first ships became operational in 1970, being built at two shipyards. Subsequently, construction began at Kerch´. The principal difference in the Krivak II class is the main gun battery. Construction of both types continues at the rate of two or three ships per year.

As of mid-1982 there were 7 Krivaks assigned to the Northern Fleet, 7 to the Baltic Fleet, 6 to the Black Sea Fleet, and 10 to the Pacific Fleet. Others were on trials and fitting out.

Class: The simultaneous and continuing construction of this class at three shipyards indicates that a very large number are planned. This will probably become the largest class of surface combatants (frigate and larger) built in the USSR since the Stalin programs.

Design: These are among the most heavily armed frigates afloat, their SA-N-4 systems, large torpedo battery, and gun battery making them relatively versatile ships. However, by Western standards the lack of helicopter facilities limits their ASW effectiveness in some situations.

The Krivak II has larger caliber guns and the improved Owl Screech gun FCS. Also, the sonar housing is larger in the later ships.

Designation: Soviet SKR or patrol ship type. Originally, the Soviet designation was BPK or large ASW ship; it was changed in 1977–1978, probably a reflection of the ship's limited range.

Western intelligence originally classified these ships as destroyers, in part based on the estimate that the large missile launchers were for an SS-N-10 anti-ship weapon. In 1978 the Krivak was reclassified as a frigate.

Names: These ships have "adjective" or "trait" names.

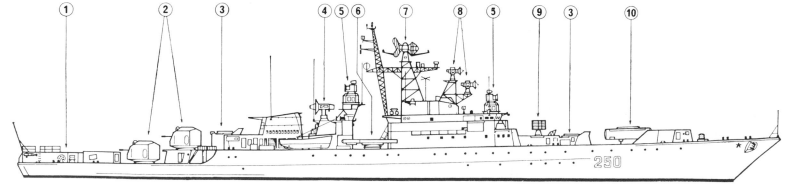

1. VDS housing 2. twin 76.2-mm AA gun mounts 3. SA-N-4 missile launchers (retracted) 4. Owl Screech radar 5. Pop Group radars 6. 533-mm torpedo tubes. 7. Head Net-C radar 8. Eye Bowl radars 9. RBU-6000 rocket launcher 10. SS-N-14 missile tubes (H. Simoni)

The Krivak I-class frigate BODRYY steaming through the English Channel. Note her long, low superstructure with unique arrangement of quad SS-N-14 launcher forward, reminiscent of the Kynda's much larger quad SS-N-3 Shaddock launchers. The Krivak and other Soviet ASW frigates lack the helicopter capabilities of their Western counterparts. (U.S. Navy, 1975)

Krivak II-class frigate GROMKIY (U.S. Navy, 1980)

Krivak I-class ASW frigate; note VDS housing, roller openings in stern for mine rails, and towed torpedo decoys in racks on fantail. (1977)

## ~45 ANTI-SUBMARINE FRIGATES: GRISHA I/II/III CLASSES

| Name | Completed |
|---|---|
| . . . . . . (~22 units Grisha III type) | 1975– |
| 7 units Grisha II type (see "Names" below) | 1974–1976 |
| . . . . . . (16 units Grisha I type) | 1968–1974 |

| | |
|---|---|
| Builders: | Khabarovsk |
| | Kamysh-Burun |
| | Zelenodolsk |
| Displacement: | 950 tons standard |
| | 1,200 tons full load |
| Length: | 236 ft 3 in (71.6 m) |
| Beam: | 32 ft 4 in (9.8 m) |
| Draft: | 12 ft 3 in (3.7 m) |
| Propulsion: | CODAG: 4 diesels 16,000 bhp/ 1 gas turbine 15,000 shp; 3 shafts |
| Speed: | 30 knots |
| Range: | 950 n.miles at 27 knots |
| | 4,500 n.miles at 10 knots |
| Complement: | approx. 60 |
| Helicopters: | no facilities |
| Missiles: | *Grisha I/III*  1 twin SA-N-4 launcher (20) |
| Guns: | *Grisha I/III*  2 57-mm/80-cal AA (1 twin) |
| | *Grisha II*  4 57-mm/80-cal AA (2 twin) |
| | *Grisha III*  1 30-mm close-in (multibarrel) |
| ASW weapons: | 2 RBU-6000 rocket launchers |
| | 2 depth-charge racks (see notes) |
| | torpedoes |
| Torpedoes: | 4 21-in (533-mm) torpedo tubes (2 twin) |
| Mines: | rails for 18 mines |
| Radars: | 1 Don-2 (navigation) |
| | 1 Muff Cob (fire control) except Bass Tilt in Grisha III |
| | 1 Pop Group (fire control) deleted from Grisha II |
| | 1 Strut Curve (air search) |
| Sonars: | medium frequency (hull mounted) |
| EW systems: | Watch Dog |

These are small ASW frigates with minor differences in armament (see below). The 16 similar ships of the Grisha I and the 20-plus ships of the Grisha III type are operated by the Navy. The seven ships of the Grisha II design—with an additional 57-mm gun mount in place of the SA-N-4 launcher—are operated by the KGB Maritime Border Troops, the largest warships operated by that organization. Several KGB-manned icebreakers are heavily armed (see chapter 20). Names are known only for the KGB's Grisha II ships.

Construction of the Grisha III type continues.

Design: The various Grisha mods have a heavy ASW armament coupled with a heavy self-defense armament. The Grisha I type has a retractable SA-N-4 launcher forward and a twin 57-mm gun aft. In the Grisha II a second 57-mm twin mount is fitted forward in place of the missile launcher. The Grisha III returns to the original weapons arrangement, but there is an enlarged deck structure aft with an improved Bass Tilt director and a single 30-mm Gatling gun.

Racks for 12 depth charges can be fitted to the after end of the mine rails.

These ships have a layout similar to the larger Koni class, but with only two "steps" forward on the superstructure. The Grishas also have a solid mast structure similar to the Koni, in contrast to the lattice masts of the earlier Mirkas and Petyas.

Designation: The Grisha I and III series are Soviet MPK type, while the KGB-operated Grisha II type are PSKR. Western intelligence designates the Grishas and other Soviet light frigates, as well as other small combatants, with personal nicknames, *Grisha* translating to "Greg."

Names: Soviet names are known for six of the seven Grisha II KGB ships: AMETIST, BRILLIANT, IZUMRUD, RUBIN, SAFFIR, and ZHEMCHUG. One of the Grisha IIIs may be named ORLOVSKIY KOMSOMOLETS.

Stern view of Grisha III with offset Bass Tilt radar for aft-mounted twin 57-mm AA gun mount and single 30-mm Gatling gun. Stern openings are for mine rails or depth-charge racks.

Grisha III-class frigate

Grisha II frigate with twin 57-mm gun mounts forward and aft. These ships are manned by the KGB border forces. They retain two RBU-6000 rocket launchers forward and four 533-mm torpedo tubes amidships as well as mine rails and depth-charge racks. In this view the racks are fitted over the mine rails. (U.S. Navy)

A Grisha I at high speed. A retractable SA-N-4 missile launcher is fitted in the bow, forward of the RBU-6000 rocket launchers. (Ministry of Defence, 1975)

**18 ANTI-SUBMARINE FRIGATES: MIRKA I/II CLASSES**

| Name | Completed |
|---|---|
| . . . . . . (9 units Mirka II type) | 1965–1966 |
| . . . . . . (9 units Mirka I type) | 1964–1965 |

| | |
|---|---|
| Builders: | Kaliningrad |
| Displacement: | 950 tons standard |
| | 1,150 tons full load |
| Length: | 272 ft (82.4 m) |
| Beam: | 30 ft 4 in (9.2 m) |
| Draft: | 9 ft 7 in (2.9 m) |
| Propulsion: | CODAG: 2 diesels 12,000 bhp/2 gas turbines 30,000 shp; 2 shafts |
| Speed: | 32 knots |
| Range: | 500 n.miles at 30 knots |
| | 4,800 n.miles at 10 knots |
| Complement: | approx. 100 |
| Helicopters: | no facilities |
| Guns: | 4 76.2-mm/60-cal AA (2 twin) |
| ASW weapons: | *Mirka I*    4 RBU-6000 rocket launchers |
| | 1 depth-charge rack |
| | torpedoes |
| | *Mirka II*    2 RBU-6000 rocket launchers |
| | torpedoes |
| Torpedoes: | *Mirka I*    5 16-in (406-mm) torpedo tubes (1 quin) |
| | *Mirka II*    10 16-in (406-mm) torpedo tubes (2 quin) |
| Mines: | no rails fitted |

| | |
|---|---|
| Radars: | 1 Don-2 (navigation) |
| | 1 Hawk Screech (fire control) |
| | 1 Slim Net (air search) except Strut Curve in some Mirka IIs |
| Sonars: | 1 Herkules or Pegas high frequency (hull mounted) |
| | 1 helicopter dipping sonar in Mirka II |
| EW systems: | Watch Dog |

A small number of these light frigates were built simultaneously with the larger Petya series construction. Nine ships were modernized to the Mirka II configuration, with a helicopter-type dipping sonar installed in a new stern structure. The name of the lead ship of this type is believed to be GANGUTETS.

Design:  These ships are generally similar to the Petya series, but with two shafts, each driven by a gas turbine and diesel compared to the triple-shaft Petya in which the gas turbines drive the outer shafts and the diesel the central shaft. The turbines were placed all the way aft, preventing the fitting of mine rails.

The classes can be readily distinguished by the Petya's mast being adjacent to the bridge structure and the Mirka's mast standing separate amidships. The Petya has a short, squat funnel amidships while the Mirka has large air intakes at the stern and exhaust ports in the stern transom.

Designation: Soviet SKR type. NATO name *Mirka* translates to the Russian nickname for Vladimir.

Mirka I-class frigate with single bank of five 406-mm torpedo tubes abaft the mast. In addition to the two RBU-6000 rocket launchers forward of the bridge, a second pair (covered with tarpaulins) are next to the first air intake for the gas turbines. The ship is at anchor with the men on her deck, wearing shorts, apparently awaiting swim call.

Mirka I in port showing Hawk Screech radar above open bridge, Slim Net radar atop mast, and second set of RBU-6000 rocket launchers abaft the second twin 76.2-mm gun mount. (1976)

A Mirka II with a bank of five 406-mm torpedo tubes immediately aft of the bridge and a second bank abaft the mast. The Mirka's mast is freestanding, while the mast in the Petya-class frigates is immediately behind the bridge. In this view the Mirka II's port RBU-6000 rocket launcher is in the vertical position for automatic reloading. (Ministry of Defence)

Closeup of stern of Mirka I-class frigate (1975)

A Petya II with coverings over the RBU-6000 rocket launchers on bridge and two banks of torpedo tubes. (U.S. Navy)

## 26 ANTI-SUBMARINE FRIGATES: PETYA II CLASS

| Name | Completed |
|------|-----------|
| . . . . . . | 1964–1969 |

| | |
|------|-----------|
| Builders: | Kaliningrad |
| | Komsomol'sk |
| Displacement: | 950 tons standard |
| | 1,160 tons full load |
| Length: | 270 ft (81.8 m) |
| Beam: | 30 ft 4 ln (9.2 m) |
| Draft: | 9 ft 7 in (2.9 m) |
| Propulsion: | CODAG: 1 diesel 6,000 bhp/2 gas turbines 30,000 shp; 3 shafts |
| Speed: | 32 knots |
| Range: | 450 n.miles at 29 knots |
| | 4,900 n.miles at 10 knots |
| Complement: | approx. 80–90 |
| Helicopters: | no facilities |
| Guns: | 4 76.2-mm/60-cal AA (2 twin) |
| ASW weapons: | 2 RBU-6000 rocket launchers |
| | 2 depth-charge racks; removed from modified Petya II |
| | torpedoes |
| Torpedoes: | 10 16-in (406-mm) torpedo tubes (2 quin) except 5 tubes in modified Petya II |
| Mines: | rails for 22 mines |
| Radars: | 1 Don-2 (navigation) |
| | 1 Strut Curve (air search) |
| | 1 Hawk Screech (fire control) |
| Sonars: | Herkules high frequency (hull mounted) |
| | helicopter dipping sonar in modified Petya II |
| EW systems: | Watch Dog |

The Petya II light ASW frigate is an improved version of the original Petya, having the more-capable RBU-6000 rocket launchers with automatic reloading. A single Petya II was modified with a small VDS at the stern, the sonar housing permitting retention of the mine/depth-charge capability.

See Petya I listing for additional class notes.

Class: In addition to units built for the Soviet Navy, modified export versions were constructed for India (10), Syria (2), and Vietnam (4).

Designation: Soviet SKR type.

Torpedoes: The second bank of ASW torpedo tubes was fitted on the stern of these ships, replacing the two after RBU-2500s of the Petya I design.

Petya II in rough waters of the Philippine Sea. Both 76.2-mm twin gun mounts and Hawk Screech radar are trained to starboard. (U.S. Navy, 1970)

## 19 ANTI-SUBMARINE FRIGATES: PETYA I CLASS

| Name | Completed |
|------|-----------|
| . . . . . . | 1961–1965 |

| | |
|------|------|
| Builders: | Kaliningrad |
| | Komsomol'sk |
| Displacement: | 950 tons standard |
| | 1,160 tons full load |
| Length: | 270 ft (81.8 m) |
| Beam: | 30 ft 4 in (9.2 m) |
| Draft: | 9 ft 7 in (2.9 m) |
| Propulsion: | CODAG: 1 diesel 6,000 bhp/2 gas turbines 30,000 shp; 3 shafts |
| Speed: | 32 knots |
| Range: | 450 n.miles at 29 knots |
| | 4,900 n.miles at 10 knots |
| Complement: | approx. 80–90 |
| Helicopters: | no facilities |
| Guns: | 4 76.2-mm/60-cal AA (2 twin) reduced to 2 guns in some modified ships |
| ASW weapons: | |
| *standard* | 4 RBU-2500 rocket launchers |
| | 2 depth-charge racks |
| | torpedoes |
| *modified* | 2 RBU-2500 rocket launchers |
| | 1 depth-charge rack |
| | torpedoes |
| Torpedoes: | 5 16-in (406-mm) torpedo tubes (1 quin) |
| Mines: | rails for 22 mines; removed from modified ships |
| Radars: | 1 Don-2 (navigation) |
| | 1 Strut Curve (air search) |
| | 1 Hawk Screech (fire control) |
| Sonars: | Herkules high frequency (hull mounted) |
| | helicopter dipping sonar in modified Petya I |
| EW systems: | Watch Dog |

The Petya was produced in larger numbers than the similar Mirka class, indicating a more successful design. The initial Petya I series has been modified into at least four different configurations (see below).

Class: Twenty-four ships of this design were built for Soviet service.

Designation: Soviet SKR type. The NATO *Petya* translates in Russian to "Pete."

Engineering: These were the first large Soviet warships to have gas turbine propulsion.

Modification: The ten "modified" ships have a raised stern deckhouse containing a large variable depth sonar. Some ships with this arrangement have their after 76.2-mm twin mount and mine rails removed.

One unit has been fitted with a large VDS but has raised stern; one ship has a deckhouse abaft the stack with a complex towing and cable-handling array; one ship has a small, box-like structure at her stern.

Bridge of Petya I-class frigate with Hawk Screech, two Don-2 antennas (above direction-finding loop), and Slim Net atop mast. (1977)

Petya-I class frigate with Slim Net radar and four RBU-2500 rocket launchers (U.S. Navy 1979)

Modified Petya I-class frigate. (1979)

Petya I-class frigate with Slim Net radar. (U.S. Navy)

Modified Petya I-class frigate with VDS lowered. (1973)

Petya I-class frigate with Strut Curve radar and four RBU-2500 rocket launchers (U.S. Navy)

## 37 ANTI-SUBMARINE FRIGATES: RIGA CLASS

| Name | Name | Name | Completed |
|---|---|---|---|
| Astrakhan'skiy Kom. | Kobchik | Pantera | |
| Arkhangel'skiy Kom. | Komsomolets Gruziy | Rys Rosomakha | |
| Bars | Komsomolets Litviy | Shakal | |
| Barsuk | Krasnodarskiy Kom. | Tigr | 1952–1958 |
| Bobr | Kunitsa | Turman | |
| Buyvol | Leopard | Volk | |
| Byk | Lev | Voron | |
| Gepard | Lisa | Yaguar | |
| Giena | Medved | . . . . . . (11 units) | |

| | |
|---|---|
| Builders: | Kaliningrad |
| | Komsomol'sk |
| | Nikolayev |
| Displacement: | 1,260 tons standard |
| | 1,510 tons full load |
| Length: | 300 ft 4 in (91.0 m) |
| Beam: | 33 ft 8 in (10.2 m) |
| Draft: | 10 ft 7 in (3.2 m) |
| Propulsion: | steam turbines; 20,000 shp; 2 shafts |
| Boilers: | 2 |
| Speed: | 30 knots |
| Range: | 550 n.miles at 28 knots |
| | 2,000 n.miles at 13 knots |
| Complement: | approx. 175 |
| Helicopters: | no facilities |
| Guns: | 3 100-mm/56-cal DP (3 single) |
| | 4 37-mm/60-cal AA (2 twin) |
| | 4 25-mm/60-cal AA (2 twin) |

| | |
|---|---|
| ASW weapons: | 2 RBU-2500 rocket launchers; deleted in ships with ECM mod |
| | 2 depth-charge racks |
| | torpedoes |
| Torpedoes: | 2 or 3 21-in (533-mm) torpedo tubes (1 twin or triple) |
| Mines: | rails for 28 mines |
| Radars: | 1 Don-2 or Neptune (navigation) |
| | 1 Hawk Screech (fire control) in 1 ship |
| | 1 Slim Net (air search) |
| | 1 Sun Visor (fire control) |
| Sonars: | Herkules or Pegas high frequency (hull mounted) |
| EW systems: | Watch Dog |
| | Bell series in ships with ECM mod |

An estimated sixty-six Rigas were built, 58 for the Soviet Navy plus eight ships going directly to foreign navies. In addition to the 37 ships reported in active service, there are another 11 ships believed laid up in reserve.

Class: Ships of this class have been transferred to Bulgaria (2), East Germany (5), Finland (2), and Indonesia (8). (Eight ships are believed to have been built for foreign use, with the other transfers being ex-Soviet ships.) A modified Riga design was constructed in China.

Designation: Soviet SKR type. Riga is a NATO code name.

Electronics: Some ships have been modified with a Bell Series ECM system installed on a short mast fitted aft. These ships also have their two RBU-2500 launchers deleted and an enlarged cowling fitted to their funnel.

Riga-class frigate showing Slim Net antenna atop mast and Wasp Head gunfire control director with Sun Visor radar (aimed at camera). (U.S. Navy, 1970)

Riga-class frigate (1982)

Riga-class frigate

# 16

# Corvettes

**2 + GUIDED MISSILE CORVETTES: TARANTUL I/II CLASSES**

| Name | Completed |
|---|---|
| . . . . . | 1979 – |

| | |
|---|---|
| Builders: | Petrovskiy Shipyard, Leningrad |
| Displacement: | 480 tons standard |
| | 540 tons full load |
| Length: | 186 ft 6 in (56.5 m) |
| Beam: | 34 ft 8 in (10.5 m) |
| Draft: | 8 ft 3 in (2.5 m) |
| Propulsion: | CODAG: 1 diesel/2 gas turbines; 3 shafts |
| Speed: | 36 – 38 knots |
| Range: | |
| Complement: | approx. 50 |
| Missiles: | 2 twin SS-N-2c Styx anti-ship launchers |
| | 1 quad SA-N-5 Grail launcher (16) |
| Guns: | 1 76.2-mm/60-cal DP |
| | 2 30-mm close-in (2 multibarrel) |
| ASW weapons: | none |
| Torpedoes: | none |
| Mines: | none |
| Radars: | 1 Band Stand (fire control) in 1 ship |
| | 1 Bass Tilt (fire control) in 1 ship |
| | 1 Spin Trough (air search) |
| | 1 . . . . . . (targeting) |
| Sonars: | none |
| EW systems: | . . . . . . (passive) |

A Tarantul-class missile corvette at high speed in the Baltic. She is very heavily armed and carries an extensive array of electronics. The twin gas-turbine exhaust ports in the stern are open in this shot.

This class may have been developed for export. The Tarantul II has the Nanuchka's Band Stand radome in place of the Bass Tilt and a different air intake/gas exhaust vent arrangement.

## 20 + GUIDED MISSILE CORVETTES: NANUCHKA I/III CLASSES

| Name | Name | Name | Completed |
|---|---|---|---|
| Burun | Shkval | Tsiklon | |
| Grad | Shtorm | Zub' | 1969–1976 |
| Maduga | Tayfun | . . . . . (8 units) | |
| . . . . . (4 + units Nanuchka III type) | | | 1977– |

| | |
|---|---|
| Builders: | Petrovskiy Shipyard, Leningrad |
| Displacement: | 780 tons standard |
| | 770 tons full load |
| Length: | 195 ft 8 in (59.3 m) |
| Beam: | 41 ft 7 in (12.6 m) |
| Draft: | 7 ft 11 in (2.4 m) |
| Propulsion: | 3 diesels (M-504); 30,000 bhp; 3 shafts |
| Speed: | 32 knots |
| Range: | 900 n.miles at 30.5 knots |
| | 2,500 n.miles at 12 knots |
| Complement: | approx. 60 |
| Missiles: | 2 triple SS-N-9 anti-ship launchers |
| | 1 twin SA-N-4 anti-aircraft launcher (20) |
| Guns: | *Nanuchka I*    2 57-mm/80-cal AA (1 twin) |
| | *Nanuchka III*    1 76.2-mm/60-cal DP |
| | 1 30-mm close-in (multibarrel) |
| ASW weapons: | none |
| Torpedoes: | none |
| Mines: | none |

| | | |
|---|---|---|
| Radars: | *Nanuchka I* | 1 Band Stand (fire control) |
| | | 1 Muff Cob (fire control) |
| | | 1 Peel Pair (air search) |
| | | 1 Pop Group (fire control) |
| | *Nanuchka III* | 1 Band Stand (fire control) |
| | | 1 Bass Tilt (fire control) |
| | | 1 Peel Pair (air search) |
| Sonars: | none | |
| EW systems: | . . . . . (passive) | |

These are heavily armed coastal missile ships. They appear to be successors to the Komar/Osa coastal missile craft, but with a more-powerful missile battery and an air-defense capability. Construction of the Nanuchka III class, with improved gun/fire control systems, continues, as does that of the Nanuchka II export variant.

Class:  The Nanuchka II is an export version similar to the Nanuchka I, but with four SS-N-2c Styx missiles in place of the SS-N-9. Three ships of this type have been transferred to Algeria (1980–1982), three to India (1976–1978), and probably four to Libya (1981–      ).

Design:  These ships are reported to be poor sea boats.

Designation:  Soviet MRK type. The NATO designation *Nanuchka* is a child's name.

Names:  The known names are Russian words for meteorological phenomena.

The Nanuchka III has a single-barrel 76.2-mm DP mount aft plus a 30-mm Gatling gun in place of the twin 57-mm gun mount of the earlier Nanuchkas and a different bridge/Band Stand radar arrangement. These ships have a considerable amount of electronics for their size. (1981)

A Nanuchka I-class missile corvette in the Mediterranean. Note the blast shield abaft the SS-N-9 missile tubes and the twin 57-mm AA mount aft. (U.S. Navy, 1982)

A Nanuchka II-class missile corvette at high speed in the Baltic. These later units have a larger superstructure in addition to the armament changes. These ships are reportedly poor sea boats in heavy weather. Their firepower is impressive for a small combatant, although the U.S. Navy's Harpoon missile permits small craft to easily carry eight 60-mile anti-ship missiles, albeit with warheads about half the size of the SS-N-9. (West German Navy)

### 3 + ANTI-SUBMARINE CORVETTES: PAUK CLASS

| Name | Completed |
|---|---|
| . . . . . . | 1979– |

| | |
|---|---|
| Builders: | |
| Displacement: | 480 tons standard |
| | 530 tons full load |
| Length: | 189 ft 9 in (57.5 m) |
| Beam: | 34 ft 8 in (10.5 m) |
| Draft: | 8 ft 3 in (2.5 m) |
| Propulsion: | 2 diesels; 20,000 bhp; 2 shafts |
| Speed: | 28–34 knots |
| Range: | |
| Complement: | approx. 40 |
| Missiles: | 1 quad SA-N-5 Grail launcher (16) |
| Guns: | 1 76.2-mm/60-cal AA |
| | 1 30-mm close-in (multibarrel) |
| ASW weapons: | 2 RBU-1200 rocket launchers |
| | 2 depth-charge racks |
| | torpedoes |
| Torpedoes: | 4 16-in (406-mm) torpedo tubes (4 single) |
| Mines: | none |
| Radars: | 1 Bass Tilt (fire control) |
| | 1 Spin Trough (air search) |
| | 1 . . . . . . (search) |
| Sonars: | medium frequency (hull mounted) |
| | medium frequency (dipping) |
| EW systems: | . . . . . . (passive) |

Pauk-class ASW corvette. (1980)

The large, circular structure on the stern of the Pauk houses the craft's dipping sonar. (1982)

These ASW ships have the same hull as the Tarantul missile corvettes, but have ASW weapons and sensors fitted and all-diesel propulsion. The lead ship is reported to have entered the Baltic in early 1979. This may be the successor to the Poti class.

Designation: Soviet MPK type.

The Pauk-class ASW corvette has the same hull as the Tarantul missile corvette but with all-diesel propulsion and the SS-N-2c Styx missiles deleted. A large housing for dipping sonar projects from the stern and four 406-mm torpedo tubes are fitted in addition to gun armament. (1980)

## 62 ANTI-SUBMARINE CORVETTES: POTI CLASS

| Name | Completed |
|------|-----------|
| . . . . . . | 1961–1970 |

| | |
|---|---|
| Builders: | Khaborovsk |
| | Zelenodolsk |
| Displacement: | 500 tons standard |
| | 580 tons full load |
| Length: | 196 ft (59.4 m) |
| Beam: | 26 ft (7.9 m) |
| Draft: | 6 ft 7 in (2.0 m) |
| Propulsion: | CODAG: 2 diesels (M503A) 8,000 bhp/2 gas turbines 40,000 shp; |
| | 2 shafts |
| Speed: | 38 knots |
| Range: | 520 n.miles at 37 knots |
| | 4,500 n.miles at 10 knots |
| Complement: | approx. 50 |
| Missiles: | none |
| Guns: | 2 57-mm/80-cal AA (1 twin); see notes |
| ASW weapons: | 2 RBU-6000 rocket launchers |
| | torpedoes |
| Torpedoes: | 2 or 4 16-in (406-mm) torpedo tubes (2 or 4 single) |
| Mines: | none |
| Radars: | 1 Don-2 (navigation) |
| | 1 Muff Cob (fire control) |
| | 1 Strut Curve (air search) |
| Sonars: | Herkules high frequency (hull mounted) |
| | . . . . . . (dipping sonar) |
| EW systems: | Watch Dog |

About 70 of these ASW ships were built for Soviet service, with most surviving.

Class: Three of these ships were transferred to Bulgaria (1975) and three to Romania (1970).

Design: The early ships were built with an open 57-mm/70-cal twin mount, two RBU-2500 rocket launchers, and two torpedo tubes. Most have been upgraded. The fixed torpedo tubes are angled out some 15° from the centerline.

Designation: Soviet MPK type.

Electronics: The dipping sonar is the same used in the Hormone-A helicopter.

A Poti-class ASW corvette with the gas turbine air intakes at the stern covered over with tarpaulins and the gas turbine exhaust ports in the stern counter closed.

Poti-class ASW corvette

Poti-class ASW corvette with amidships twin 57-mm AA mount at high elevation.

---

**17 PATROL CORVETTES: T-58 CLASS (Ex-Minesweepers)**

| Name | Name | Completed |
|---|---|---|
| Dzerzhinskiy | Malakhit | |
| Kaliningrad Komsomolets | Sovietskiy Pogranichnik | 1957–1961 |
| Komsomolets Latviy | . . . . . . (12 units) | |

| | |
|---|---|
| Builders: | |
| Displacement: | 725 tons standard |
| | 860 tons full load |
| Length: | 231 ft (70.0 m) |
| Beam: | 30 ft (9.1 m) |
| Draft: | 8 ft 3 in (2.5 m) |
| Propulsion: | 2 diesels; 4,000 bhp; 2 shafts |
| Speed: | 17 knots |
| Range: | 2,500 n.miles at 13.5 knots |
| Complement: | |
| Missiles: | none |
| Guns: | 4 57-mm/70-cal AA (2 twin) |
| ASW weapons: | 2 RBU-1200 rocket launchers |
| | 2 depth-charge racks |
| Torpedoes: | none |
| Mines: | rails for 18 mines |
| Radars: | 1 Don-2 (navigation) |
| | 1 Muff Cob (fire control) |
| | 1 Spin Trough (air search) |
| Sonars: | high frequency (hull mounted) |
| EW systems: | Watch Dog |

These are former T-58 minesweepers reassigned from 1975 on to ASW/patrol roles. Several are operated by the KGB Maritime Border Troops.

Class: One unit of this configuration has been transferred to Guinea (1979) and one to South Yemen (1978).

Designation: Soviet SKR type in naval service and PSKR in KGB service.

T-58 minesweeper employed as a gunboat/corvette. (1978)

A T-58 minesweeper employed as a gunboat/corvette.

---

**1 + RADAR SURVEILLANCE SHIPS: T-58 CLASS (Ex-Minesweepers)**

| Name | Completed | Conversion Completed |
|---|---|---|
| . . . . . . | 1957–1961 | 1979– |

| | |
|---|---|
| Builders: | |
| Displacement: | 725 tons standard |
| | 860 tons full load |
| Length: | 231 ft (70.0 m) |
| Beam: | 30 ft (9.1 m) |
| Draft: | 8 ft 3 in (2.5 m) |
| Propulsion: | 2 diesels; 4,000 bhp; 2 shafts |
| Speed: | 17 knots |
| Range: | 2,500 n.miles at 13.5 knots |
| Complement: | |
| Missiles: | 2 quad SA-N-5 Grail launchers |
| Guns: | 2 57-mm/70-cal AA (1 twin) |
| | 4 30-mm/65-cal AA (2 twin) |

| | |
|---|---|
| ASW weapons: | 2 depth-charge racks |
| Torpedoes: | none |
| Mines: | none |
| Radars: | 1 Big Net (air search) |
| | 1 Muff Cob (fire control) |
| | 1 Spin Trough (air search) |
| | 1 Strut Curve (air search) |
| Sonars: | none |
| EW systems: | |

One T-58 fleet minesweeper was converted to a radar picket ship at the Izhora Shipyard, Leningrad, being completed in 1979. More conversions are anticipated.

Designation: Soviet KVN type.

A T-58 rebuilt for the radar surveillance role with enlarged superstructures forward and aft and a small deckhouse on the stern. Note the 30-mm guns mounted on the after deckhouse. Details of the after radar masts differ on the two ships whose photographs are available (pendants 335 and 374).

**6 RADAR SURVEILLANCE SHIPS: T-43 CLASS (Ex-Minesweepers)**

| Name | Completed |
|---|---|
| . . . . . . | 1952–1954 |

| | |
|---|---|
| Builders: | Leningrad Kerch |
| Displacement: | 500 tons standard |
| | 570 tons full load |
| Length: | 191 ft 4 in (58.0 m) |
| Beam: | 28 ft 4 in (8.6 m) |
| Draft: | 7 ft 7 in (2.3 m) |
| Propulsion: | 2 diesels (9D); 2,200 bhp; 2 shafts |
| Speed: | 15 knots |
| Range: | 2,800 n.miles at 14 knots |
| | 5,300 n.miles at 8 knots |
| Complement: | approx. 75–80 |
| Missiles: | none |
| Guns: | 4 37-mm/60-cal AA (2 twin) |
| | 2 25-mm/60-cal AA (1 twin) in ships with Big Net radar |
| ASW weapons: | 2 depth-charge mortars |
| Torpedoes: | none |
| Mines: | rails for 14 mines |
| Radars: | 1 Big Net or 2 Knife Rest (air search) |
| | 1 Don series (navigation) |
| Sonars: | none |
| EW systems: | Watch Dog |

These are radar picket versions of the T-43 minesweeper design. They are expected to be disposed of in the near future, probably being replaced by T-58 conversions.

Class: From about 1958 on 20 T-43 minesweepers were converted to radar picket ships.

Design: The early conversions were fitted with two Knife Rest radars, one fitted to the lattice mast atop the bridge and the second to a pole mast in place of the deleted 37-mm gun mount. In addition, a third mast was fitted at the forward edge of the funnel.

Later conversions have the larger Big Net radar fitted on a heavy, four-legged support between the funnel and the 37-mm gun mount.

Designation: Soviet KVN type.

T-43 minesweeper converted to radar picket and refitted with two Knife Rest air-search radar antennas, one fitted atop the bridge and one abaft the funnel. A third mast was added forward of the funnel. The primary armament of four 37-mm AA guns in twin mounts was retained. (1974)

T-43 minesweeper of later series converted to radar picket and fitted with a Big Net air-search radar antenna installed abaft the funnel. The four 37-mm AA guns were retained as well as a twin 25-mm AA mount abaft the Big Net support. These ships were intended to protect Soviet air/water areas, much the same as the U.S. Navy operated YAGR/AGR and DER radar pickets in the 1950s and 1960s. (U.S. Navy)

# 17

# Missile, Patrol, and Torpedo Craft

## 8 + HYDROFOIL GUIDED MISSILE CRAFT: MATKA CLASS

| | |
|---|---|
| Completed: | 1978– |
| Builders: | Izhora Shipyard, Leningrad |
| Displacement: | 225 tons standard |
| | 260 tons full load |
| Length: | 130 ft 8 in (39.6 m) |
| Beam: | 25 ft (7.6 m) hull |
| | 41 ft 3 in (12.5 m) over foils |
| Draft: | 6 ft 3 in (1.9 m) hullborne |
| Propulsion: | 3 diesels (M504); 15,000 bhp; 3 shafts |
| Speed: | 40 knots foilborne |
| Range: | 420 n.miles at 35 knots |
| | 820 n.miles at 25 knots |
| Complement: | approx. 30 |
| Missiles: | 2 single SS-N-2c Styx anti-ship launchers |
| Guns: | 1 76.2-mm/60-cal DP |
| | 1 30-mm close-in (multibarrel) |
| ASW weapons: | none |
| Torpedoes: | none |
| Mines: | none |
| Radars: | 1 Bass Tilt (fire control) |
| | 1 Cheese Cake (fire control) |
| | 1 . . . . . . (search) |
| Sonars: | none |
| EW systems: | |

The Matka is a missile-armed version of the Turya-class hydrofoil torpedo boat, with a larger superstructure (to accommodate more complex missile system) and a different gun arrangement. Construction continues at a slow rate.

Design: This class is derived from the Osa hull arrangement, with hydrofoils fitted forward. At high speeds the craft's stern planes on the water surface.

Designation: Soviet TKA type.

A Matka-class missile boat at high speed on foils; note the new targeting radar (in place of Square Tie) and the fully automatic 76.2-mm gun mount.

Matka-class missile craft (Courtesy *Ships of the World*)

A Matka missile boat hullborne. The Styx missile tubes are fitted aft compared to the amidships position on the Sarancha. (West German Navy)

## 1 HYDROFOIL GUIDED MISSILE CRAFT: SARANCHA CLASS

| | |
|---|---|
| Completed: | 1977 |
| Builders: | Petrovskiy Shipyard, Leningrad |
| Displacement: | 320 tons full load |
| Length: | 149 ft 2 in (45.2 m) hull |
| | 176 ft 11 in (53.6 m) over foils |
| Beam: | 33 ft 8 in (10.2 m) hull |
| | 77 ft 6 in (23.5 m) over foils |
| Draft: | 8 ft 7 in (2.6 m) hullborne |
| | 24 ft (7.3 m) foilborne |
| Propulsion: | 2 gas turbines; 20,000 shp; 4 shafts |
| Speed: | 58 knots |
| Range: | |
| Complement: | |
| Missiles: | 2 twin SS-N-9 anti-ship launchers |
| | 1 twin SA-N-4 launcher (20) |
| Guns: | 1 30-mm close-in (multibarrel) |
| ASW weapons: | none |
| Torpedoes: | none |
| Mines: | none |
| Radars: | 1 Band Stand (fire control) |
| | 1 Bass Tilt (fire control) |
| | 1 Pop Group (fire control) |
| Sonars: | none |
| EW systems: | IFF only |

Only a single unit of this highly complex design has been constructed.

Engineering: Two propellers are fitted to each of two pods mounted on the after foils.

The Sarancha missile boat at speed on foils. In addition to the hydrofoil craft operated by the Navy and KGB Maritime Border Troops, there are about one thousand civilian hydrofoils in operation on rivers, lakes, and coastal waters.

## ~40 GUIDED MISSILE CRAFT: OSA II CLASS

| | |
|---|---|
| Completed: | 1966–1970 |
| Builders: | Petrovskiy Shipyard, Leningrad |
| | and other yards |
| Displacement: | 215 tons standard |
| | 240 tons full load |
| Length: | 127 ft 5 in (38.6 m) |
| Beam: | 25 ft (7.6 m) |
| Draft: | 6 ft 7 in (2.0 m) |
| Propulsion: | 3 diesels (M504); 15,000 bhp; 3 shafts |
| Speed: | 35 knots |
| Range: | 500 n.miles at 34 knots |
| | 750 n.miles at 25 knots |
| Complement: | approx. 30 |
| Missiles: | 4 single SS-N-2b/c Styx anti-ship launchers |
| | 1 SA-N-5 launcher (hand held) in some units |
| Guns: | 4 30-mm/65-cal close-in (2 twin) |
| ASW weapons: | none |
| Torpedoes: | none |
| Mines: | none |
| Radars: | 1 Drum Tilt (fire control) |
| | 1 Square Tie (fire control) |
| Sonars: | none |
| EW systems: | IFF only |

The Osa II is an improved version of the basic Osa I design, capable of carrying the improved SS-N-2c missile.

Class: An estimated 114 units of this type were built with more than 60 being transferred to Warsaw Pact and Third World navies—Algeria, Bulgaria, Cuba, Egypt, Ethiopia, Finland, Iraq, Libya, Morocco, Somalia, Syria, Tunisia, and South Yemen.

Design: These craft can be distinguished from the Osa I type by their circular, ribbed missile tubes. At least one unit has been observed with a deckhouse between the bridge and Drum Tilt radar. See Osa I listing for additional notes.

Designation: Soviet RKA type.

Names: Soviet names believed to apply to this class are: AMURKIY KOMSOMOLETS, KIROVSKIY KOM., TAMBOVSKIY KOM., and KRONSHTADTSKIY KOM.

A stern view of a Sarancha at high speed. The Sarancha has twice as many Styx tubes as the smaller Matka and an SA-N-4 launcher (in place of the smaller craft's 76.2-mm gun).

Osa II missile craft, shown under tow to a foreign navy. Note the "ribbed" SS-N-2 Styx launch tubes, twin 30-mm mounts forward and aft, and Drum Tilt radar on pedestal between after tubes. Even these small craft have extensive CBR protective systems including a "citadel" that can be closed with an overpressure to keep out contaminents.

An Osa II missile craft at high speed

An Osa II alongside a tug. The pedestal supporting the Drum Tilt radar differs within the class. (1980)

## ~65 GUIDED MISSILE CRAFT: OSA I CLASS

| | |
|---|---|
| Completed: | 1959–1966 |
| Builders: | Petrovskiy Shipyard, Leningrad and other yards |
| Displacement: | 175 tons standard |
| | 215 tons full load |
| Length: | 127 ft 5 in (38.6 m) |
| Beam: | 25 ft (7.6 m) |
| Draft: | 6 ft (1.8 m) |
| Propulsion: | 3 diesels (M503A); 12,000 bhp; 3 shafts |
| Speed: | 35 knots |
| Range: | 500 n.miles at 34 knots |
| | 750 n.miles at 25 knots |
| Complement: | approx. 30 |
| Missiles: | 4 single SS-N-2a/b Styx anti-ship launchers |
| Guns: | 4 30-mm/65-cal close-in (2 twin) |
| ASW weapons: | none |
| Torpedoes: | none |
| Mines: | none |
| Radars: | 1 Drum Tilt (fire control) |
| | 1 Square Tie (fire control) |
| Sonars: | none |
| EW systems: | IFF only |

These are steel-hulled missile boats, developed to succeed the wood-hulled, two-missile Komar type.

Class:  An estimated 175 units of this type were built in the USSR and a reported 96 have been built in China. Over 100 of the Soviet-built units have been transferred to Warsaw Pact and Third World navies — Algeria, Bulgaria, China, Cuba, Egypt, East Germany, India, Iraq, North Korea, Poland, Romania, Sudan, Syria, and Yugoslavia.

Some of the earlier Osas have been discarded from Soviet service, a number being converted to target craft. All of the earlier Komar boats have been discarded from Soviet service.

Design:  The Osa has an all-welded-steel hull with a superstructure of fabricated steel and aluminum alloy. A "citadel" control station is provided for operation in a CBR environment. These craft have four Styx missile launchers, twice the number in the preceding Komar class. The launchers are fixed; the two after launchers, elevated to approximately 15°, fire over the forward launchers, which are elevated to about 12°. The mounting of the Drum Tilt gunfire control radar varies. The Matka, Mol, Stenka, and Turya classes have the basic Osa hull (the Mol being a torpedo boat developed for export).

Designation: Soviet RKA type. The NATO name *Osa* is Russian for "Wasp" (*Komar* was "Mosquito").

An Osa I in Egyptian service (U.S. Navy, 1974)

An Osa I in East German colors making high speed

## ~30 HYDROFOIL TORPEDO CRAFT: TURYA CLASS

| | |
|---|---|
| Completed: | 1972–1979 |
| Builders: | Petrovskiy Shipyard, Leningrad |
| Displacement: | 205 tons standard |
| | 240 tons full load |
| Length: | 127 ft 5 in (38.6 m) |
| Beam: | 25 ft (7.6 m) |
| | 41 ft 3 in (12.5 m) over foils |
| Draft: | 6 ft (1.8 m) hullborne |
| | 13 ft 2 in (4.0 m) foilborne |
| Propulsion: | 3 diesels (M504); 15,000 bhp; 3 shafts |
| Speed: | 40 knots |
| Range: | 420 n.miles at 35 knots |
| | 820 n.miles at 25 knots |
| Complement: | approx. 25 |
| Missiles: | none |
| Guns: | 2 57-mm/80-cal AA (1 twin) |
| | 2 25-mm/60-cal AA (1 twin) |
| ASW weapons: | torpedoes |
| Torpedoes: | 4 21-in (533-mm) torpedo tubes (4 single) |
| Mines: | none |
| Radars: | 1 Muff Cob (fire control) |
| | 1 Pot Drum (fire control) |
| Sonars: | dipping sonar |
| EW systems: | IFF only |

These are high-speed coastal ASW and attack craft.

Class: Six units of this class were transferred to Cuba.

Design: The Turya uses a modified Osa II hull and propulsion plant.

The forward foils are fixed and the craft's stern planes on the water at high speed. The stern is trimmed by an adjustable flap with twin supports protruding from the stern transom. Later units are reported to have semiretractable foils to facilitate berthing. The torpedo tubes are fixed on deck, two on each side; the twin 57-mm mount dominates the after portion of the ship.

Designation: Soviet TK type.

Electronics: The Hormone-A helicopter dipping sonar is fitted on the starboard quarter. (Not provided in units transferred to Cuba.)

Turya hydrofoil torpedo craft at high speed with bow raised on foil

A Turya torpedo craft at high speed with twin 57-mm gun mount trained to starboard. The craft has a fixed foil forward and at high speeds the stern water planes. (Sovfoto)

Baltic Fleet sailors race to their Turya torpedo craft during an exercise. Most units have Hormone-type dipping sonar fitted in canister housing on starboard quarter. The craft have no mine rails or depth charges, relying on their four 406-mm torpedo tubes for ASW weapons. (Sovfoto)

## 30 HYDROFOIL TORPEDO CRAFT: SHERSHEN CLASS

| | |
|---|---|
| Completed: | 1959–1970 |
| Builders: | |
| Displacement: | 150 tons standard |
| | 170 tons full load |
| Length: | 114 ft 6 in (34.7 m) |
| Beam: | 22 ft 1 in (6.7 m) |
| Draft: | 5 ft (1.5 m) |
| Propulsion: | 3 diesels (M503A); 12,000 bhp; 3 shafts |
| Speed: | 45 knots |
| Range: | 460 n.miles at 42 knots |
| | 850 n.miles at 30 knots |
| Complement: | approx. 15 |
| Missiles: | none |
| Guns: | 4 30-mm/65-cal close-in (2 twin) |
| ASW weapons: | 2 depth-charge racks |
| | torpedoes |
| Torpedoes: | 4 21-in (533-mm) torpedo tubes (4 single) |
| Mines: | rails for 6 mines |
| Radars: | 1 Drum Tilt (fire control) |
| | 1 Pot Drum (fire control) |
| Sonars: | none |
| EW systems: | IFF only |

These are high-speed torpedo boats, now being withdrawn from Soviet service.

Class: About 80 of the craft are believed to have been built in the USSR with another 12 assembled in Yugoslavia. Units of this class (some in a patrol configuration without torpedo tubes) have been transferred to Angola, Bulgaria, Cape Verde Islands, Egypt, East Germany, Guinea, North Korea, Vietnam, and Yugoslavia.

Design: The Shershen hull is similar to the Osa I, but slightly smaller, with the Osa I propulsion plant. The payload flexibility of the Shershen is demonstrated by the Yugoslav units carrying, instead of depth charges, four KMD-1000 or eight KMD-500 Soviet-designed mines and some Egyptian units having their torpedo tubes replaced by two BM-21, eight-tube multiple rocket launchers.

Designation: Soviet TKA type.

A Shershen torpedo craft in East German service, the WILHELM FLORIN

### 1 HYDROFOIL PATROL CRAFT: BABOCHKA CLASS

| | |
|---|---|
| Completed: | 1978 |
| Builders: | |
| Displacement: | 400 tons full load |
| Length: | 165 ft (50.0 m) |
| Beam: | 33 ft 8 in (10.2 m) hull |
| | 52 ft 10 in (16.0 m) over foils |
| Draft: | |
| Propulsion: | CODOG: 2 diesels/3 gas turbines approx 30,000 shp; 3 shafts |
| Speed: | 45 + knots |
| Range: | |
| Complement: | |
| Missiles: | none |
| Guns: | 2 30-mm close-in (2 multibarrel) |
| ASW weapons: | torpedoes |
| Torpedoes: | 8 16-in (406-mm) torpedo tubes (2 quad) |
| Mines: | none |
| Radars: | 1 Bass Tilt (fire control) |
| | 1 Don-2 (navigation) |
| | 1 . . . . . . (search) |
| Sonars: | none |
| EW systems: | |

The Babochka-class hydrofoil patrol craft making slow speed. The two "nests" of four ASW torpedo tubes are on the main deck, just forward of the pendant number "292." One 30-mm Gatling gun is on the bow and the second amidships, atop the deckhouse.

This is a prototype ASW craft, only one unit being built. It is the largest Soviet military hydrofoil, being significantly larger than the U.S. PEGASUS (PHM 1) class. The torpedo tubes are forward of the deckhouse, in two banks of four tubes.

A Mol-class torpedo boat under tow en route from the USSR to Somalia. This design is a modification of the Shershen class, with units having been transferred to Ethiopia (2), Somalia (4), and Sri Lanka (1). Some do not have torpedo tubes installed.

## 30 + INSHORE PATROL CRAFT: ZHUK CLASS

| | |
|---|---|
| Completed: | 1975– |
| Builders: | |
| Displacement: | 50 tons full load |
| Length: | 75 ft 7 in (22.9 m) |
| Beam: | 16 ft 2 in (4.9 m) |
| Draft: | 5 ft (1.5 m) |
| Propulsion: | 2 diesels (M50); 2,400 bhp; 2 shafts |
| Speed: | 30 knots |
| Range: | |
| Complement: | approx. 28 |
| Missiles: | none |
| Guns: | 2 or 4 14.5-mm machine guns (1 or 2 twin) |
| ASW weapons: | none |
| Torpedoes: | none |
| Mines: | none |
| Radars: | 1 Spin Trough (search) |
| Sonars: | none |
| EW systems: | |

These patrol craft have been built in large numbers for Soviet and foreign use. Most and possibly all of the Soviet units are manned by KGB Border Troops.

Class: Units of this class have been transferred to several foreign nations, including Iraq, Vietnam, and South Yemen.

Guns: One MG mount is fitted aft; units with two gun mounts have one forward of the bridge.

## 1 PATROL GUNBOAT: SLEPEN CLASS

| | |
|---|---|
| Completed: | ~1969 |
| Builders: | Petrovskiy Shipyard, Leningrad |
| Displacement: | 205 tons standard |
| | 230 tons full load |
| Length: | 128 ft 8 in (39.0 m) |
| Beam: | 25 ft 5 in (7.7 m) |
| Draft: | 6 ft (1.8 m) |
| Propulsion: | 3 diesels (M504); 15,000 bhp; 3 shafts |
| Speed: | 36 knots |
| Range: | |
| Complement: | approx. 30 |
| Missiles: | none |
| Guns: | 1 76.2-mm/60-cal DP |
| | 1 30-mm close-in (multibarrel) |
| ASW weapons: | none |
| Torpedoes: | none |
| Mines: | none |
| Radars: | 1 Bass Tilt (fire control) |
| | 1 Don-2 (navigation) |
| Sonars: | none |
| EW systems: | IFF only |

This is the Soviet Navy's only high-speed gunboat. The craft may be employed as a trials ship for small combatant systems.

Design: Similar to the Matka design, but without foils or missiles.

Guns: As built, the ship had a twin 57-mm gun mount forward; it was replaced by the single 76.2-mm gun in 1975.

## ~100 PATROL CRAFT: STENKA CLASS

| | |
|---|---|
| Completed: | 1967– |
| Builders: | Petrovskiy Shipyard, Leningrad (and other yards) |
| Displacement: | 170 tons standard |
| | 210 tons full load |
| Length: | 130 ft 4 in (39.5 m) |
| Beam: | 25 ft (7.6 m) |
| Draft: | 6 ft (1.8 m) |
| Propulsion: | 3 diesels (M503A); 12,000 bhp; 3 shafts |
| Speed: | 35 knots |
| Range: | 550 n.miles at 34 knots |
| | 820 n.miles at 25 knots |
| Complement: | approx. 22 |
| Missiles: | none |
| Guns: | 4 30-mm/65-cal AA (2 twin) |
| ASW weapons: | 2 depth-charge racks |
| | torpedoes |
| Torpedoes: | 4 16-in (406-mm) torpedo tubes (4 single) |
| Mines: | none |
| Radars: | 1 Drum Tilt (fire control) |
| | 1 Pop Drum or . . . . . . (search) |
| Sonars: | dipping sonar |
| EW systems: | IFF only |

These are patrol craft operated by the KGB Maritime Border Troops.

Design: Derivatives of the Osa design. The torpedo tubes are deleted in some units, and a new search-navigation radar is fitted in recent units in place of the Pot Drum. Twelve depth charges are carried.

Designation: Soviet PKR type.

Electronics: Fitted with a Hormone-A helicopter dipping sonar.

A Stenka-class patrol craft off the Far Eastern port of Nakhodka. Most and possibly all of these craft in Soviet service are manned by KGB Border Troops. A motor launch is carried in davits on the starboard side. This unit has depth-charge racks aft (covered over). (Khoji Ishiwata, 1976)

Stenka-class patrol craft (note boat davits)

Pchela-class patrol craft. Note twin 14.5-mm machine gun mount forward of the bridge; the after mount is not visible in the craft's stern clutter.

## 20 HYDROFOIL PATROL CRAFT: PCHELA CLASS

| | |
|---|---|
| Completed: | 1964–1965 |
| Builders: | |
| Displacement: | 75 tons full load |
| Length: | 88 ft 6 in (26.8 m) |
| Beam: | 19 ft 10 in (6.0 m) hull |
| | 26 ft 9 in (8.1 m) over foils |
| Draft: | 4 ft 3 in (1.3 m) hullborne |
| | 9 ft 3 in (2.8 m) foilborne |
| Propulsion: | 2 diesels; 6,000 bhp; 2 shafts |
| Speed: | 42 knots |
| Range: | 450 n.miles at 35 knots |
| Complement: | approx. 12 |
| Missiles: | none |
| Guns: | 4 14.5-mm machine guns (2 twin) |
| ASW weapons: | 2 depth-charge racks |
| Torpedoes: | none |
| Mines: | none |
| Radars: | 1 Pot Drum (search) |
| Sonars: | dipping sonar in some units |
| EW systems: | . . . . . . (passive) |

These craft are all operated by KGB Maritime Border Troops. A few units have Hormone-A dipping sonar. The MG are aircraft-type mountings.

Design: The Pchela has a partially submerged V-shaped foil forward and a fully submerged foil aft.

Designation: Soviet PSKR type.

The stern of a Pchela-class patrol craft showing the after twin 14.5-mm gun mount (covered with a tarpaulin) and the gun-aiming position at the after end of the craft's deckhouse.

## ~30 ANTI-SUBMARINE CRAFT: S.O.-1 CLASS

| | |
|---|---|
| Completed: | 1957–1964 |
| Builders: | Petrovskiy Shipyard, Leningrad |
| | Zelenodolsk |
| Displacement: | 190 tons standard |
| | 215 tons full load |
| Length: | 138 ft 7 in (42.0 m) |
| Beam: | 20 ft 2 in (6.1 m) |
| Draft: | 6 ft 3 in (1.9 m) |
| Propulsion: | 3 diesels; 7,500 bhp; 3 shafts |
| Speed: | 28 knots |
| Range: | 340 n.miles at 28 knots |
| | 1,900 n.miles at 7 knots |
| Complement: | approx. 30 |
| Missiles: | none |
| Guns: | 2 or 4 25-mm/60-cal AA (1 or 2 twin) |
| ASW weapons: | 4 RBU-1200 rocket launchers |
| | 2 depth-charge racks |
| | torpedoes in some units (see below) |
| Torpedoes: | 2 16-in (406-mm) torpedo tubes (2 single) in ships with 2 guns |
| Mines: | rails for 10 mines |
| Radars: | 1 Pot Head (fire control) |
| Sonars: | Tamir high frequency (hull mounted) |
| | dipping sonar in some units |
| EW systems: | IFF only |

These are outdated coastal ASW craft, now being discarded from Soviet service. Some are operated by the KGB Maritime Border Troops.

Class: Just over 100 units of this class were built for Soviet service and additional units were built for export. They have been transferred to Algeria, Bulgaria, China, Cuba, Egypt, East Germany, Iraq, North Korea, Vietnam, and South Yemen.

Design: They are reported to be poor sea boats. The last few were completed with the two fixed torpedo tubes in place of the after gun mount. All of the rocket launchers are forward. The depth-charge racks carry only six charges each.

Electronics: Hormone-A helicopter dipping sonar has been fitted in some units.

Bow section of S.O.-1 patrol craft showing four RBU-1200 rocket launchers on bow. Depth charges are carried aft, and some units have been fitted with two 406-mm ASW torpedo tubes aft, replacing the twin 25-mm gun mounting. (1977)

Stern of S.O.-1 showing after twin 25-mm AA gun mount and depth charges, plus stern configuration for minelaying with rails outboard of the depth-charge racks. (1977)

S.O.-1-class patrol craft

### ~30 INSHORE PATROL CRAFT: POLUCHAT I CLASS

| | |
|---|---|
| Completed: | 1953–1956 |
| Builders: | |
| Displacement: | 90 tons full load |
| Length: | 97 ft 8 in (29.6 m) |
| Beam: | 19 ft 2 in (5.8 m) |
| Draft: | 5 ft (1.5 m) |
| Propulsion: | 2 diesels (M50); 2,400 bhp; 2 shafts |
| Speed: | 18 knots |
| Range: | 450 n.miles at 17 knots |
| | 900 n.miles at 10 knots |
| Complement: | approx. 20 |
| Missiles: | none |
| Guns: | 2 14.5-mm machine guns (1 twin) |
| ASW weapons: | none |
| Torpedoes: | none |
| Mines: | none |
| Radars: | . . . . . . (short-range navigation) |
| Sonars: | none |
| EW systems: | |

The Poluchat is a modification of the standard Soviet torpedo retriever craft with the stern ramp decked over, a small boat carried aft, and a twin machine gun fitted. Most if not all Soviet units are operated by KGB Maritime Border Troops.

Class: Patrol craft of this type have been transferred to Angola, Guinea, Iraq, Somalia, and South Yemen.

A Poluchat I-class torpedo retriever; the patrol variant of this craft is similar. A small navigation radar and radio direction finder are mounted forward of the open bridge.

### 5 RIVERINE PATROL CRAFT: YAS CLASS

This is a new type of patrol craft observed in the Pacific area.

### ~85 RIVER GUNBOATS: SHMEL CLASS

| | |
|---|---|
| Completed: | 1967–1974 |
| Builders: | |
| Displacement: | 60 tons full load |
| Length: | 93 ft 4 in (28.3 m) |
| Beam: | 15 ft 2 in (4.6 m) |
| Draft: | 3 ft (0.9 m) |
| Propulsion: | 2 diesels (M50); 2,400 bhp; 2 shafts |
| Speed: | 22 knots |
| Range: | 240 n.miles at 20 knots |
| | 600 n.miles at 10 knots |
| Complement: | approx. 15 |
| Missiles: | 1 18-tube 122-mm rocket launcher |
| Guns: | 1 76.2-mm/48-cal SP |
| | 2 25-mm/60-cal AA machine guns (1 twin) |
| | 5 7.62-mm machine guns (5 single; see notes) |
| ASW weapons: | none |
| Torpedoes: | none |
| Mines: | 8 mines can be carried |
| Radars: | none |
| Sonars: | none |
| EW systems: | none |

These are heavily armed river craft, similar in concept to the French and U.S. riverine monitors of the Indochina-Vietnam wars. They patrol the several Soviet rivers that border on foreign states.

Design: These are very shallow draft craft. A 76.2-mm weapon is a tank turret with one 7.62-mm MG coaxially mounted. The other 7.62-mm MGs are hand-held and fired through ports in the open-top deckhouse. The rocket launcher—mounted abaft the deckhouse—is deleted in some units.

Designation: Soviet AKA type.

A Shmel river patrol gunboat with its tank-turret 76.2-mm gun forward and an open twin 25-mm AA gun mount aft.

Close-up of Shmel river gunboat with multiple-tube rocket launcher

# 18

# Mine Warfare Ships and Craft

One of three Alesha-class specialized minelayers built for the Soviet Navy in the late 1960s. Most Soviet surface warships can also lay mines; however, in combat situations bomber-type aircraft and submarines can be expected to serve as the principal minelaying platforms. (1969)

## 3 MINELAYERS: ALESHA CLASS

| Name | Name | Name | Completed |
|------|------|------|-----------|
| PRIPET | . . . . . . | . . . . . . | 1967–1969 |

| | |
|---|---|
| Builders: | |
| Displacement: | 2,900 tons standard |
| | 3,500 tons full load |
| Length: | 320 ft (97.0 m) |
| Beam: | 46 ft 2 in (14.0 m) |
| Draft: | 17 ft 10 in (5.4 m) |
| Propulsion: | 4 diesels; 8,000 bhp; 2 shafts |
| Speed: | 17 knots |
| Range: | 4,000 n.miles at 16 knots |
| | 8,500 n.miles at 8 knots |
| Complement: | approx. 190 |
| Helicopters: | no facilities |
| Guns: | 4 57-mm/70-cal AA (1 quad) |
| ASW weapons: | none |
| Mines: | rails for approx. 300 |
| Radars: | 1 Don-2 (navigation) |
| | 1 Muff Cob (fire control) |
| | 1 Strut Curve (air search) |
| Sonars: | none |
| EW systems: | IFF only |

These are mine support ships, similar in concept to the now-discarded U.S. Navy MCS types. The Soviet ships can serve as minelayers, net layers, minesweeper tenders, and mine operation command/control ships.

Design: Mine rails are fitted from the superstructure aft, with a stern ramp over which mines can be laid or large objects hauled aboard. Two cranes are fitted forward and two amidships, with the arrangements of the forward cranes differing.

Designation: Soviet ZM type. NATO code names for Soviet mine warfare ships and craft are Russian names for children, as *Alesha*, *Natya*, and *Yurka* ("Georgie").

Stern view of an Alesha-class minesweeper.

## FEW MINEHUNTERS: NATYA II CLASS

| Name | Completed |
|------|-----------|
| . . . . . . | 1981– |

| | |
|---|---|
| Builders: | |
| Displacement: | 650 tons standard |
| | 750 tons full load |
| Length: | 201 ft 4 in (61.0 m) |
| Beam: | 32 ft 4 in (9.8 m) |
| Draft: | 10 ft (3.0 m) |
| Propulsion: | 2 diesels; 5,000 bhp; 2 shafts |
| Speed: | 17 knots |
| Range: | 1,800 n.miles at 16 knots |
| | 5,200 n.miles at 10 knots |
| Complement: | |
| Guns: | 4 30-mm/65-cal close-in (2 twin) |
| ASW weapons: | none |
| Mines: | none |
| Radars: | 1 Don-2 (navigation) |
| | 1 Drum Tilt (fire control) |
| Sonars: | minehunting high frequency |
| EW systems: | IFF only |

Natya I-class fleet minesweeper. These ships and the smaller Yurka class have a distinctive mast-mounted Drum Tilt fire control radar for their twin 30-mm close-in gun mounts. Most Soviet minesweepers can also lay mines, and the Natyas have in addition a limited ASW capability.

These are minehunter versions of the Natya-class fleet minesweepers. They can be distinguished from the minesweeper variant by the long deckhouse aft in place of the sweep gear and the deletion of ASW armament and 25-mm guns. Construction continues.

Designation: Soviet MT type.

**30 + FLEET MINESWEEPERS: NATYA I CLASS**

| Name | Name | Name | Completed |
|------|------|------|-----------|
| ADMIRAL PERSHIN | SEMEN ROSHAL' | TURBINIST | |
| DMITRIY LYSOV | SNAYPER | ZENITCHIK | 1969– |
| KONTRADMIRAL HOROSHKIN | SVYAZIST | . . . . . . (~22 units) | |

| | |
|---|---|
| Builders: | |
| Displacement: | 650 tons standard |
| | 750 tons full load |
| Length: | 201 ft 4 in (61.0 m) |
| Beam: | 32 ft 4 in (9.8 m) |
| Draft: | 10 ft (3.0 m) |
| Propulsion: | 2 diesels; 5,000 bhp; 2 shafts |
| Speed: | 17 knots |
| Range: | 1,800 n.miles at 16 knots |
| | 5,200 n.miles at 10 knots |
| Complement: | approx. 50 |
| Guns: | 4 30-mm/65-cal close-in (2 twin) |
| | 4 25-mm/60-cal AA (2 twin) |
| ASW weapons: | 2 RBU-1200 rocket launchers |
| Mines: | can carry 10 mines |
| Radars: | 1 Don-2 (navigation) |
| | 1 Drum Tilt (fire control) |
| Sonars: | Tamir minehunting high frequency |
| EW systems: | IFF only |

These are fleet minesweepers with a limited ASW capability and self-defense armament, permitting them to serve as anti-submarine escorts. Construction continues.

Class: Six ships of this class have been built for India and two for Libya.

Design: These ships have aluminum-alloy hulls. Early ships have fixed davits aft for handling sweeping gear; the davits are articulated in later units. There is a stern ramp to facilitate handling sweep gear. The twin 25-mm guns are "hidden" in the topside clutter, with one mount on the port side just forward of the funnel and the other on the starboard side, abaft the funnel and just behind the launch.

Designation: Soviet MT type.

Bow section of Natya I (1977)

Stern of Natya I with old-style davits. The Natya with pendant No. 903 has the newer style. (1977)

A Natya I at sea; the twin 30-mm mounts are visible forward and amidships; the RBU-1200 ASW rocket launchers are just abaft the bow 30-mm mount, and the twin 25-mm gun mounts are just forward of the funnel on the port side and just aft (behind the motor launch) on the starboard side. (U.S. Navy, 1982)

## ~45 FLEET MINESWEEPERS: YURKA CLASS

| Name | Name | Name | Completed |
|------|------|------|-----------|
| Evgeniy Nikonov | Gafel' | . . . . . . (~43 units) | 1962–1970(?) |

| | |
|---|---|
| Builders: | Izhora |
| Displacement: | approx. 450 tons standard |
| | 540 tons full load |
| Length: | 170 ft (51.5 m) |
| Beam: | 29 ft (8.8 m) |
| Draft: | 8 ft 7 in (2.6 m) |
| Propulsion: | 2 diesels: 4,000 bhp; 2 shafts |
| Speed: | 16 knots |
| Range: | 2,000 n.miles at 14 knots |
| | 3,200 n.miles at 10 knots |
| Complement: | approx. 45 |
| Guns: | 4 30-mm/65-cal close-in (2 twin) |
| ASW weapons: | none |
| Mines: | can carry 16 mines |
| Radars: | 1 Don-2 (navigation) |
| | 1 Drum Tilt (fire control) |
| Sonars: | Tamir minehunting high frequency |
| EW systems: | IFF only |

These are smaller than the succeeding Natya class, without the later ships' ASW weapons.

Class: Ships of this class have been transferred to Bulgaria, Egypt, and Vietnam.

Yurka-class fleet minesweeper. Note the funnel shape.

Design: Aluminum-alloy hulls. This is a similar design to the Natya class, but without the stern ramp. The Yurka's broad funnel indicates a side-by-side arrangement of the diesel engines. The classes are easily distinguished when viewed from the side by the Natya's larger funnel.

Designation: Soviet MT type.

Yurka-class fleet minesweeper

## 40 FLEET MINESWEEPERS: T-43 CLASS

| Name | Name | Name | Completed |
|------|------|------|-----------|
| Ivan Fioletov | Kom. Kalmykiy | Sakalinskiy Kom. | |
| Kom. Byelorussiy | Lamine Sadjikaba | Stephan Saumyan | 1949–1957 |
| Kom. Estoniy | Mezhadiy Azizbakov | . . . . . . (30 units) | |
| Kontradmiral Yurokovkiy | Nikolay Markin | | |

| | | |
|---|---|---|
| Builders: | Leningrad | |
| | Kerch' | |
| Displacement: | early units | 570 tons full load |
| | later units | 590 tons full load |
| Length: | early units | 191 ft 4 in (58.0 m) |
| | later units | 198 ft (60.0 m) |
| Beam: | 28 ft 5 in (8.6 m) | |
| Draft: | 7 ft 7 in (2.3 m) | |
| Propulsion: | 2 diesels (9D); 2,200 bhp, 2 shafts | |
| Speed: | 15 knots | |
| Range: | 2,000 n.miles at 14 knots | |
| | 3,200 n.miles at 10 knots | |
| Complement: | | |
| Guns: | Navy | 4 37-mm/60-cal AA (2 twin) |
| | | 4 25-mm/60-cal AA or 4 or 8 14.5-mm machine guns (all twin mountings) |
| | KGB | 4 37-mm/60-cal AA (2 twin) or 2 45-mm/85-cal AA (2 single) |
| | | 4 25-mm/60-cal AA or 4 or 8 14.5-mm machine guns (all twin mountings) |
| ASW weapons: | 2 depth-charge mortars | |
| Mines: | can carry 16 mines | |
| Radars: | 1 Ball End (fire control) | |
| | 1 Don-2 (navigation) or Spin Trough (search) | |
| Sonars: | Tamir high frequency | |
| EW systems: | IFF only | |

The T-43 class was the Soviet Navy's first postwar minesweeper design. Over 200 units were built, many of which were later modified for auxiliary roles as well as for radar picket ships (see chapter 16). Several T-43s have gone to other navies, and several are operated by the KGB Maritime Border Troops. The remaining units in Soviet service will probably be discarded in the near future.

Class: More than 200 ships of this class were built. Ships have been transferred to Albania, Algeria, Bulgaria, China, Egypt, Indonesia, Iraq, Poland, and Syria.

Design: Steel-hulled ships. The early ships had a shorter hull and a "flat face" bridge structure; later units were two meters longer with a stepped bridge and a broader stern. Some KGB units have modified armament.

Designation: Soviet designations are MT in the minesweeping role and PSKR in the border patrol role.

A T-43 riding at anchor off Crete. The tripod mast, platform forward of bridge (for two 12.7-mm twin MG mounts), and other configuration differences identify a ship of the later T-43 series. (1967, U.S. Navy)

A T-43 fleet minesweeper under way with guns and mine cable reel under tarpaulins (U.S. Navy, 1965)

---

## ~35 COASTAL MINESWEEPERS: SONYA CLASS

| Name | Completed |
|------|-----------|
| KOMSOMOLETS KIRGIZIY . . . . . . (~35 units) | 1973– |

| | |
|------|------|
| Builders: | Izhora |
| Displacement: | 350 tons standard |
| | 450 tons full load |
| Length: | 161 ft (48.8 m) |
| Beam: | 29 ft (8.8 m) |
| Draft: | 7 ft (2.1 m) |
| Propulsion: | 2 diesels; 2,400 bhp; 2 shafts |
| Speed: | 15 knots |
| Range: | 1,600 n.miles at 14 knots |
| | 3,000 n.miles at 10 knots |

| | |
|------|------|
| Complement: | approx. 43 |
| Guns: | 2 30-mm/65-cal close-in (1 twin) |
| | 2 25-mm/60-cal AA (1 twin) |
| ASW weapons: | none |
| Mines: | none |
| Radars: | 1 Spin Trough (search) |
| Sonars: | |
| EW systems: | IFF only |

These are modern coastal minesweepers with wooden hulls sheathed in fiberglass. Construction is probably continuing. Two units were transferred to Cuba (1980).

Designation: Soviet BT type.

Sonya-class coastal minesweeper

Sonya-class coastal minesweeper

## 2 COASTAL MINESWEEPERS: ZHENYA CLASS

| Name | Completed |
|---|---|
| . . . . . . | 1970 |

| | |
|---|---|
| Builders: | Izhora |
| Displacement: | 220 tons standard |
| | 290 tons full load |
| Length: | 140 ft (42.4 m) |
| Beam: | 26 ft (7.9 m) |
| Draft: | 6 ft (1.8 m) |
| Propulsion: | 2 diesels; 2,400 bhp; 2 shafts |
| Speed: | 16 knots |
| Range: | 1,400 n.miles at 14.5 knots |
| | 2,400 n.miles at 10 knots |

| | |
|---|---|
| Complement: | approx. 40 |
| Guns: | 2 30-mm/65-cal close-in (1 twin) |
| ASW weapons: | none |
| Mines: | none |
| Radars: | 1 Spin Trough (search) |
| Sonars: | |
| EW systems: | |

These were prototypes for an advanced coastal minesweeper, but series construction was deferred, apparently in favor of producing the Sonya design.

Design: fiberglass (plastic) hulls.
Designation: Soviet BT type.

Zhenya-class coastal minesweeper

Zhenya-class coastal minesweeper

## ~70 COASTAL MINESWEEPERS: VANYA I/II CLASSES

| Name | Completed |
|---|---|
| . . . . . . | 1960–1973 |

| | |
|---|---|
| Builders: | Izhora |
| Displacement: | 200 tons standard |
| | *Vanya I*    250 tons full load |
| | *Vanya II*    260 tons full load |
| Length: | *Vanya I*    132 ft 8 in (40.2 m) |
| | *Vanya II*    136 ft (41.2 m) |
| Beam: | 26 ft (7.9 m) |
| Draft: | 5 ft 7 in (1.7 m) |
| Propulsion: | 2 diesels; 2,200 bhp; 2 shafts |
| Speed: | 16 knots |
| Range: | 1,400 n.miles at 14 knots |
| | 2,400 n.miles at 10 knots |
| Complement: | approx. 30 |
| Guns: | 2 30-mm/65-cal close-in (1 twin) |
| ASW weapons: | none |
| Mines: | can carry 12 mines |
| Radars: | 1 Don-2 (navigation) |
| Sonars: | |
| EW systems: | IFF only |

A large class of coastal minesweepers, at least one of which has been reconfigured as a minehunter.

Class: Four of these units were transferred to Bulgaria.

Design: Wooden-hulled ships. The modified or Vanya II type are slightly larger, having a more extensive fantail work area; they can be identified by the larger diesel generator exhaust pipe amidships.

Designation: Soviet BT type.

Modification: At least one unit was refitted as a minehunter in 1974 with two 25-mm guns (single mounts) in place of the 30-mm mount, a Don Kay radar in place of the Don-2, a small mast fitted amidships, sweep gear removed, and other changes.

Vanya-class coastal minesweeper

Vanya-class coastal minesweeper

## 8 COASTAL MINESWEEPERS: SASHA CLASS

| Name | Completed |
|---|---|
| . . . . . . | 1954–1959 |

| | |
|---|---|
| Builders: | |
| Displacement: | 250 tons standard |
| | 280 tons full load |
| Length: | 148 ft 10 in (45.1 m) |
| Beam: | 20 ft 6 in (6.2 m) |
| Draft: | 6 ft (1.8 m) |
| Propulsion: | 2 diesels; 2,200 bhp; 2 vertical cycloidal propellers |
| Speed: | 19 knots |
| Range: | 1,300 n.miles at 18.5 knots |
| | 2,100 n.miles at 12 knots |
| Complement: | approx. 25 |
| Guns: | 1 45-mm/85-cal AA or 57-mm/70-cal AA |
| | 4 25-mm/60-cal AA (2 twin) |
| ASW weapons: | none |
| Mines: | can carry 12 mines |
| Radars: | 1 Ball End (fire control) |
| Sonars: | |
| EW systems: | IFF only |

The last of a class of coastal sweepers also employed as patrol boats. They will probably be retired in the near future. They have steel hulls.

Designation: Soviet RT type.

Sasna-class coastal minesweeper

## ~40 INSHORE MINESWEEPERS: YEVGENYA CLASS

| | |
|---|---|
| Completed: | 1970– |
| Builders: | |
| Displacement: | 70 tons standard |
| | 90 tons full load |
| Length: | 86 ft 6 in (26.2 m) |
| Beam: | 20 ft 2 in (6.1 m) |
| Draft: | 5 ft (1.5 m) |
| Propulsion: | 2 diesels; 600 bhp; 2 shafts |
| Speed: | 11 knots |
| Range: | 300 n.miles at 10 knots |
| Complement: | approx. 10 |
| Guns: | 2 14.5-mm machine guns (1 twin) |
| ASW weapons: | none |
| Mines: | none |
| Radars: | 1 Spin Trough (search) |
| Sonars: | |
| EW systems: | IFF only |

Fiberglass-hulled craft, several of which have been transferred abroad. Some export versions have a twin 25-mm AA gun mounting. Designation: Soviet RT type.

Yevgenya-class inshore minesweeper

## 3 SPECIAL MINESWEEPERS: ANDRYUSHA CLASS

| | |
|---|---|
| Completed: | 1975–1976 |
| Builders: | |
| Displacement: | 320 tons standard |
| | 360 tons full load |
| Length: | 148 ft 2 in (44.9 m) |
| Beam: | 27 ft (8.2 m) |
| Draft: | 10 ft (3.0 m) |
| Propulsion: | 2 diesels; 2,200 bhp; 2 shafts |
| Speed: | 15 knots |
| Range: | |
| Complement: | approx. 40 |
| Guns: | none |
| ASW weapons: | none |
| Mines: | none |
| Radars: | 1 Spin Trough (search) |
| Sonars: | |
| EW systems: | IFF only |

These minesweepers have nonmagnetic wooden or fiberglass hulls with large cable ducts along their sides, indicating a probable magnetic-sweep capability.

## 5 MINESWEEPING BOATS: OLYA CLASS

| | |
|---|---|
| Completed: | 1976– |
| Builders: | |
| Displacement: | 50 tons standard |
| | 70 tons full load |
| Length: | 84 ft 2 in (25.5 m) |
| Beam: | 14 ft 10 in (4.5 m) |
| Draft: | 4 ft 8 in (1.4 m) |
| Propulsion: | 2 diesels; 600 bhp; 2 shafts |
| Speed: | 15 knots |
| Range: | |
| Complement: | approx. 15 |
| Guns: | 2 25-mm/60-cal AA |
| ASW weapons: | none |
| Mines: | none |
| Radars: | 1 Spin Trough (search) |
| Sonars: | none |
| EW systems: | none |

## ~45 MINESWEEPING BOATS: K-8 CLASS

| | |
|---|---|
| Completed: | 1953–1959 |
| Builders: | Polnocny Shipyard, Gdansk |
| Displacement: | 19.4 tons standard |
| | 26 tons full load |
| Length: | 51 ft (17.0 m) |
| Beam: | 10 ft 11 in (3.3 m) |
| Draft: | 2 ft 8 in (0.8 m) |
| Propulsion: | 2 diesels (3D6); 300 bhp; 2 shafts |
| Speed: | 12 knots |
| Range: | 300 n.miles at 12 knots |
| Complement: | approx. 6 |
| Guns: | 2 14.5-mm machine guns (1 twin) |
| ASW weapons: | none |
| Mines: | none |
| Radars: | none |
| Sonars: | none |
| EW systems: | none |

Outdated, wooden-hulled sweeps; being replaced by the Yevgenya class. A large number served in the Polish Navy.

## 10 MINESWEEPING DRONES: ILYUSHA CLASS

| | |
|---|---|
| Completed: | 1970– |
| Builders: | |
| Displacement: | 50 tons standard, |
| | 70 tons full load |
| Length: | 80 ft 6 in (24.4 m) |
| Beam: | 16 ft 2 in (4.9 m) |
| Draft: | 4 ft 7 in (1.4 m) |
| Propulsion: | 1 diesel; 450 bhp; 1 shaft |
| Speed: | 12 knots |
| Range: | |
| Complement: | (see notes) |
| Guns: | none |
| ASW weapons: | none |
| Mines: | none |
| Radars: | none |
| Sonars: | none |
| EW systems: | none |

K-8-class minesweeping boat

These appear to be radio-controlled minesweeping craft, similar to the smaller MSD-type operated by the U.S. Navy in the Vietnam War. They can be manned for self-transit for short distances.

Soviet "force projection" capabilities—a Western term—are shared by the Soviet Navy and merchant fleet, with the latter having a large number of modern ships capable of carrying troops, vehicles, and military equipment. But the Soviet merchant fleet also provides logistics support to Soviet naval ships, such as the 18,400-deadweight-ton tanker INTERNATIONAL seen here refueling a Ropucha-class landing ship. (1982, U.S. Navy)

# 19

# Amphibious Warfare Ships

## 1 + 1 HELICOPTER/DOCK LANDING SHIPS: "IVAN ROGOV" CLASS[1]

| Name | Completed |
|------|-----------|
| IVAN ROGOV | 1978 |
| ALEKSANDR NIKOLAYEV | (1983) |

| | |
|---|---|
| Builders: | Kaliningrad |
| Displacement: | 13,000 tons full load |
| Length: | 521 ft 5 in (158.0 m) |
| Beam: | 79 ft 2 in (24.0 m) |
| Draft: | 27 ft (8.2 m) |
| Propulsion: | 2 gas turbines; 20,000 shp; 2 shafts |
| Speed: | 23 knots |
| Range: | 8,000 n.miles at 20 knots |
| | 12,500 n.miles at 14 knots |
| Complement: | approx. 200 |
| Troops:[2] | approx. 550 |
| Helicopters: | 4 Ka-25 Hormone-C |
| Missiles/Rockets: | 1 twin SA-N-4 launcher (20) |
| | 1 40-tube 122-mm barrage rocket launcher |
| Guns: | 2 76.2-mm/60-cal AA (1 twin) |
| | 4 30-mm close-in (4 multibarrel) |

| | |
|---|---|
| Radars: | 2 Bass Tilt (fire control) |
| | 2 Don Kay (navigation) |
| | 1 Head Net-C (air search) |
| | 1 Owl Screech (fire control) |
| | 1 Pop Group (fire control) |
| EW systems: | Bell Shroud |
| | Bell Squat |

These are the largest and most versatile amphibious ships yet constructed for the Soviet Navy. Each ship can embark a Naval Infantry battalion, including its vehicles and equipment.

The lead ship was transferred to the Pacific Fleet in 1979 (with the aircraft carrier MINSK); she returned to the Baltic in the fall of 1981 for the *Zapad* amphibious exercises and has remained with that fleet.

Class: Only two ships have been observed; the lead ship was launched in 1978 and the second in 1982, a very slow construction rate.

[1] Detailed discussions of recent Soviet amphibious ship developments are in John Jordan, "*Ivan Rogov*—The New Soviet LPD," *Defence* [England], March 1980, pp. 198–200, and May 1980, pp. 341–45.
[2] Troop capacity is the number for whom berths are provided; a much larger number could be carried in all classes of amphibious ships for short transits.

The IVAN ROGOV during sea trials in the Baltic in the summer of 1978. The ROGOV is significantly larger, more capable, and more versatile than previous Soviet amphibious ships, being the first to have helicopter facilities and a docking well for landing craft. (1978). However, large-scale production has not been reported.

Design: These are the first Soviet amphibious ships to have a helicopter capability and docking well. There are helicopter landing areas aft and forward, with a control facility on the after end of the superstructure, adjacent to the hangar door. The hangar can accommodate four Hormone helicopters; they can be moved through the superstructure and down a ramp to the forward landing area. The funnel uptakes are split to allow the helicopter to pass through. The float-in docking well can hold three Lebed air-cushion landing craft.

The ship has a flat bottom and a large tank deck with bow doors to permit the unloading of amphibious vehicles into the water or across the beach. Ten light or medium tanks plus 30 armored personnel carriers can be transported.

The barrage rocket launcher is mounted atop a four-level structure, offset to starboard, forward of the main superstructure. The four Gatling guns are mounted alongside the pylon mast.

Designation: Soviet BDK type.

Names: Ivan Rogov was a senior political officer of the Soviet Navy.

A low-oblique bow view of the Ivan Rogov showing the forward doors to the "drive through" helicopter hangar.

The Ivan Rogov with a Ka-25 Hormone parked on the after landing area. The huge stern door swings out and down to reveal a docking well capable of accommodating three Lebed air-cushion landing craft. (1980, Royal Navy)

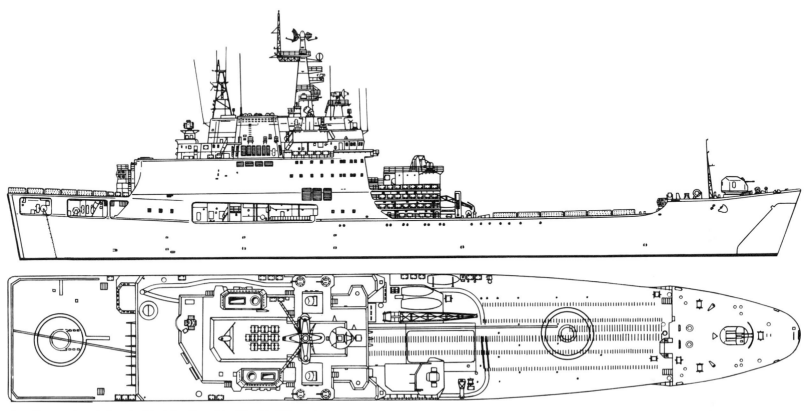

IVAN ROGOV-class helicopter/dock landing ship (Siegfried Breyer)

## 13 TANK LANDING SHIPS: ROPUCHA CLASS

| Name | Completed |
|------|-----------|
| . . . . . . | 1975–1978 |

| | |
|------|------|
| Builders: | Polnocny Shipyard, Gdansk |
| Displacement: | approx. 2,500 tons standard |
| | approx. 3,200 tons full load |
| Length: | 373 ft (113.0 m) |
| Beam: | 47 ft 10 in (14.5 m) |
| Draft: | 11 ft 11 in (3.6 m) aft |
| | 6 ft 8 in (2.0 m) forward |
| Propulsion: | 2 diesels; 10,000 bhp; 2 shafts |
| Speed: | 18 knots |
| Range: | 3,500 n.miles at 16 knots |
| | 6,000 n.miles at 12 knots |
| Complement: | approx. 70 |
| Troops: | approx. 230 |
| Helicopters: | no facilities |
| Missiles/Rockets: | 4 quad SA-N-5 Grail launchers (32) in some ships |
| Guns: | 4 57-mm/80-cal AA (2 twin) |
| Radars: | 1 Don-2 (navigation) |
| | 1 Muff Cob (fire control) |
| | 1 Strut Curve (air search) |
| EW systems: | IFF only |

Stern view of Ropucha LST. Note the stern door that provides access to the tank deck for amphibious tanks, which is similar to the arrangement in the U.S. Navy NEWPORT (LST 1179) class. (1975)

These ships are smaller than the previous, Soviet-built Alligator class. Of the 13 ships in Soviet service, 3 are in the Northern Fleet, 3 in the Baltic Fleet, and 7 in the Pacific Fleet.

Class: One ship of this class was transferred to South Yemen in 1980. No ships of this type are in Polish service.

Design: The Ropucha class has traditional LST lines with superstructure aft and bow and stern ramps for unloading vehicles. Cargo capacity is 450 tons with a usable deck space of 600 m². Up to 25 armored personnel carriers can be embarked. The superstructure is big and boxy, with large, side-by-side funnels. The Ropucha class, as well as the Polnocny class, has a long sliding hatch cover above the bow section to permit vehicles and cargo to be lowered into the tank deck by dockside cranes.

Several ships have been fitted with Grail short-range missiles. There are provisions for two barrage rocket launchers on the forecastle, but they have not been installed.

Designation: Soviet BDK type.

The Ropucha class is the latest Soviet LST design. In addition to the 57-mm twin AA mounts forward and aft of the superstructure, there is space forward of the bridge for a quad Grail missile launcher. Note the twin funnel arrangement abaft the tall lattice mast.

Ropucha LST pendant No. 108 under way at high speed (1982)

## 14 TANK LANDING SHIPS: ALLIGATOR CLASS

| Name | Name | Name | Completed |
|------|------|------|-----------|
| ALEKSANDR TORTSEV | NIKOLAY VILKOV | VORONEZHKIY KOM. | |
| DONETSKIY SHAKHTER | NIKOLAY OBYEKOV | 50 LET SHEFSTVA | |
| KRASNAYA PRESNYA | PETR IL'ICHYEV | V.L.K.S.M. | 1966–1977 |
| KRYMSKIY KOM. | SERGEI LAZO | . . . . . . (2 units) | |
| NIKOLAY FIL'CHENKOV | TOMSKIY KOM. | | |

| | |
|---|---|
| Builders: | Kaliningrad |
| Displacement: | 3,400 tons standard |
| | 4,700 tons full load |
| Length: | 372 ft 3 in (112.8 m) |
| Beam: | 50 ft 6 in (15.3 m) |
| Draft: | 14 ft 6 in (4.4 m) |
| Propulsion: | 2 diesels; 8,000 bhp; 2 shafts |
| Speed: | 18 knots |
| Range: | 9,000 n.miles at 16 knots |
| | 14,000 n.miles at 10 knots |
| Complement: | approx. 75 |
| Troops: | approx. 300 |
| Helicopters: | no facilities |
| Missiles/Rockets: | 1 40-tube 122-mm barrage rocket launcher in some ships |
| | 2 or 3 quad SA-N-5 Grail launchers (16 or 24) in some ships |

| | |
|---|---|
| Guns: | 2 57-mm/70-cal AA (1 twin) |
| | 4 25-mm/60-cal AA (2 twin) in some ships |
| Radars: | 2 Don-2 (navigation) and/or Spin Trough (search) |
| EW systems: | IFF only |

Built on traditional LST lines, these ships are less attractive than the later Ropucha class, but have a significantly larger cargo capacity. Two ships are assigned to the Northern Fleet, 2 to the Baltic Fleet, 5 to the Black Sea Fleet, and 5 to the Pacific Fleet.

Design: The Alligator class has a superstructure-aft configuration with bow and stern ramps for unloading vehicles. The arrangement of individual ships differs; early units have three cranes—one 15-ton capacity, two 5-ton capacity; later ships have one crane. There are two to four large hatches above the tank deck to permit vehicles and cargo to be lowered by ship or dockside cranes. Later ships have an enclosed bridge and a rocket launcher forward, and the last two ships have 25-mm guns.

About 25 to 30 armored personnel carriers or 1,500 tons of cargo can be carried.

Designation: Soviet BDK type.

Alligator-class LST

The Alligator lacks the streamlined appearance of the later Ropucha LST. This later-series ship has a single large crane for handling cargo and vehicles over the side. This ship, photographed in the Mediterranean, has heavy trucks on her main deck. (U.S. Navy, 1973)

## 55 MEDIUM LANDING SHIPS: POLNOCNY A/B/C CLASSES

| Name | Completed |
|------|-----------|
| . . . . . . (A class) | 1963–1967(?) |
| . . . . . (B class) | 1968–1970 |
| . . . . . (C class) | 1970–1973 |

### Polnocny A Class

| | |
|---|---|
| Builders: | Polnocny Shipyard, Gdansk |
| Displacement: | 770 tons full load |
| Length: | 241 ft (73.0 m) |
| Beam: | 28 ft 5 in (8.6 m) |
| Draft: | 6 ft 7 in (2.0 m) |
| Propulsion: | 2 diesels; 4,000 bhp; 2 shafts |
| Speed: | 19 knots |
| Range: | 900 n.miles at 18 knots |
| | 1,500 n.miles at 14 knots |
| Complement: | approx. 35 |
| Troops: | |
| Helicopters: | no facilities |
| Missiles/Rockets: | 2 18-tube 140-mm barrage rocket launchers |
| | 2 or 4 quad SA-N-5 Grail launchers (16 or 32) in most ships |
| Guns: | 2 30-mm/65-cal close-in (1 twin) in some ships |
| | 2 14.5-mm machine guns (1 twin) in some ships |
| Radars: | 1 Spin Trough (search) |
| EW systems: | IFF only |

### Polnocny B Class

| | |
|---|---|
| Builders: | Polnocny Shipyard, Gdansk |
| Displacement: | 800 tons full load |
| Length: | 244 ft 2 in (74.0 m) |
| Beam: | 28 ft 5 in (8.6 m) |
| Draft: | 6 ft 7 in (2.0 m) |
| Propulsion: | 2 diesels; 4,000 bhp; 2 shafts |
| Speed: | 19 knots |
| Range: | 900 n. miles at 18 knots |
| | 1,500 n.miles at 14 knots |
| Complement: | approx. 40 |
| Troops: | approx. 100 |
| Helicopters: | no facilities |
| Missiles/Rockets: | 2 18-tube 140-mm barrage rocket launchers |
| | 4 quad SA-N-5 Grail launchers (32) in most ships |
| Guns: | 2 or 4 30-mm/65-cal close-in (1 or 2 twin) in most ships |
| Radars: | 1 Drum Tilt (fire control) |
| | 1 Spin Trough (search) |
| EW systems: | IFF only |

### Polnocny C Class

| | |
|---|---|
| Builders: | Polnocny Shipyard, Gdansk |
| Displacement: | 1,150 tons full load |
| Length: | 268 ft 8 in (81.3 m) |
| Beam: | 33 ft 4 in (10.1 m) |
| Draft: | 7 ft (2.1 m) |
| Propulsion: | 2 diesels; 5,000 bhp; 2 shafts |
| Speed: | 18 knots |
| Range: | 900 n.miles at 17 knots |
| Complement: | approx. 40 |
| Troops: | approx. 180 |
| Helicopters: | no facilities |
| Missiles/Rockets: | 2 18-tube 140-mm barrage rocket launchers |
| | 4 quad SA-N-5 Grail launchers (32) |
| Guns: | 4 30-mm/65-cal close-in (2 twin) |
| Radars: | 1 Drum Tilt (fire control) |
| | 1 Spin Trough (search) |
| EW systems: | IFF only |

The Polnocny LSM series consists of three principal variants, with the design being enlarged and improved during its construction period. Most of the Soviet units are of the B variant. Of the 55 ships in Soviet service, about 5 are assigned to the Northern Fleet, 20 to the Baltic Fleet, 20 to the Black Sea Fleet, and 10 to the Pacific Fleet.

Class: Ships of this type have been transferred since 1966 to Angola (3 B class), Cuba (2), Egypt (3 A), Ethiopia (1 B), India (2 A/4 C), Iraq (3 C), Libya (3 C), and South Yemen (4 B). Some of the transferred ships have a platform for light helicopters installed immediately forward of the superstructure. Another 23 ships of this design were built at Polnocny for the Polish Navy (completed 1964–1971).

Design: The Polnocnys have a conventional landing ship appearance with bow doors. The A class has a convex bow while the later series have a concave bow. Superstructure and mast details differ among classes and individual ships. Cargo capacity is about 180 tons in the A and B classes and 250 tons in the C class. The earlier ships can carry 6 to 8 armored personnel carriers and the C class about eight.

Designation: Soviet SDK type. The NATO code name is derived from the Polnocny yard that constructed all of these ships. Initially NATO designated the Polnocny classes with Roman numerals vice the current A-B-C scheme.

Missiles: Some ships have been observed with SA-7 Grail shoulder-fired missile launchers.

Polnocny C-class landing ship; blast shields are fitted aft of the shore bombardment rocket launchers.

A Polnocny C-class landing ship in the eastern Mediterranean. This class can be identified by the lattice mast, lengthened deck house forward of the bridge, and short funnel.

The improved Polnocny B class has a second 30-mm gun mount aft of the taller, streamlined funnel. Note the shore bombardment rocket launchers and canisters for life rafts forward.

A Polnocny A-class landing ship. This design has a pole mast, short stack, and twin 30-mm gun mount forward of the bridge (in most ships). Life-raft canisters are mounted in tandem on the forward deck as well as around the after part of the superstructure.

**FEW MEDIUM LANDING SHIPS: MP 4 CLASS**

| | |
|---|---|
| Completed: | 1956–58 |
| Builders: | |
| Displacement: | 620 tons standard |
| | 780 tons full load |
| Length: | 184 ft 10 in (56.0 m) |
| Beam: | 26 ft 5 in (8.0 m) |
| Draft: | 8 ft 11 in (2.7 m) |
| Propulsion: | 1 diesel; 1,100 bhp; 1 shaft |
| Speed: | 10 knots |
| Range: | |
| Complement: | approx. 50 |
| Helicopters: | no facilities |
| Missiles: | none |
| Guns: | 4 25-mm/60-cal AA (2 twin) in some ships |
| Radars: | . . . . . . (navigation) |

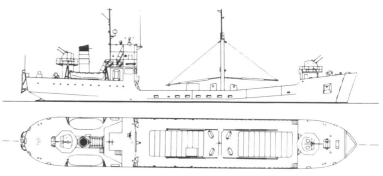

MP 4-class landing ship (Siegfried Breyer)

These ships resemble coastal merchant ships with bow doors and ramps. The few surviving units are in reserve. The other MP-series landing ships have been discarded or converted to auxiliaries.

Aist air-cushion landing craft; the engine pods are fitted with four-blade propellers.

# 20

# Landing Craft

### 10 + AIR-CUSHION LANDING CRAFT: LEBED CLASS

| | |
|---|---|
| Completed: | 1975– |
| Builders: | |
| Displacement: | 86 tons full load |
| Length: | 81 ft 10 in (24.8 m) |
| Beam: | 35 ft 8 in (10.8 m) |
| Draft: | |
| Propulsion: | 3 gas turbines; 2 aircraft-type propellers (tractor) + lift fans |
| Speed: | 70 knots on air cushion |
| Range: | 100 n.miles at 65 knots |
| | 250 n.miles at 60 knots |
| Complement: | |
| Troops: | approx. 120 |
| Guns: | 1 30-mm close-in (multibarrel) |
| Radars: | none |
| EW systems: | none |

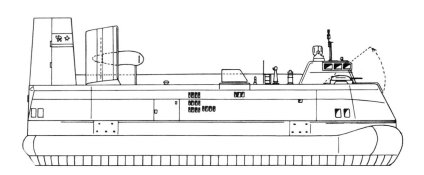

These landing craft are the type seen aboard the amphibious ship IVAN ROGOV. They can carry two PT-76 amphibious tanks or troops or cargo. Their control cabin is offset to starboard with the Gatling gun mounted on top.

### 12 + AIR-CUSHION LANDING CRAFT: AIST CLASS

| | |
|---|---|
| Completed: | 1972– |
| Builders: | |
| Displacement: | 250 tons full load |
| Length: | 156 ft (47.3 m) |
| Beam: | 58 ft 9 in (17.8 m) |
| Draft: | |
| Propulsion: | 2 gas turbines (NK-12MV); 4 aircraft-type propellers (2 pusher/ 2 tractor) + 2 lift fans |
| Speed: | 80 knots on air cushion |
| Range: | 100 n.miles at 70 knots |
| | 350 n.miles at 60 knots |
| Complement: | |
| Troops: | approx. 220 |
| Guns: | 4 30-mm/65-cal close-in (2 twin) |
| Radars: | 1 Drum Tilt (fire control) |
| | 1 Spin Trough (search) |
| EW systems: | IFF only |

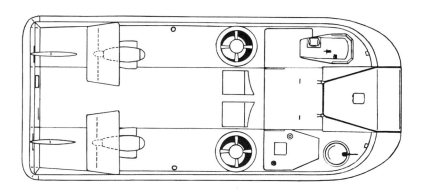

These are the world's largest military air-cushion vehicles. They can carry four PT-76 amphibious tanks or two medium tanks or some 220 troops or cargo. Bow and stern ramps are fitted to the "drive-through" cargo space. The twin Gatling guns are mounted forward.

Designation: Soviet DKVP type.

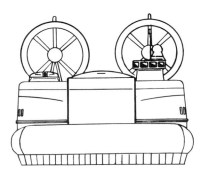

Lebed-class air-cushion landing craft (Siegfried Breyer)

An Aist air-cushion landing craft, showing the twin 30-mm gun mounts forward, the Drum Tilt fire-control radar atop the superstructure, and the distinctive tandem, fore-and-aft facing pairs of propellers.

Aist air-cushion landing craft

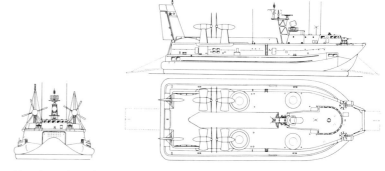

Aist-class air-cushion landing craft (Siegfried Breyer)

## 35 AIR-CUSHION LANDING CRAFT: GUS CLASS

| | |
|---|---|
| Completed: | 1969–(?) |
| Builders: | |
| Displacement: | 27 tons full load |
| Length: | 70 ft 4 in (21.3 m) |
| Beam: | 23 ft 5 in (7.1 m) |
| Draft: | |
| Propulsion: | 3 gas turbines; 2,340 shp; 2 aircraft-type propellers (tractor) + 1 lift fan |
| Speed: | 60 knots |
| Range: | 185 n.miles at 50 knots |
| | 200 n.miles at 43 knots |
| Complement: | |
| Troops: | approx. 25 |
| Guns: | none |
| Radars: | short-range navigation |
| EW systems: | none |

These were the first naval air-cushion landing craft to be produced in significant numbers. They cannot carry vehicles. There is a training variant with two control cabins.

The Gus is a naval version of the civilian Skate Air-Cushion Vehicle (ACV), reflecting the contribution of Soviet civilian ACVs to the craft listed above. The Soviet Union operates the world's largest fleet of commercial air-cushion vehicles.

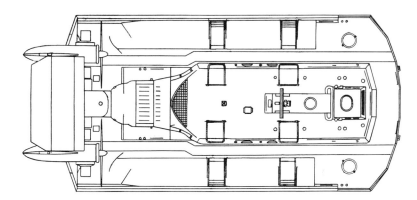

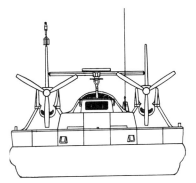

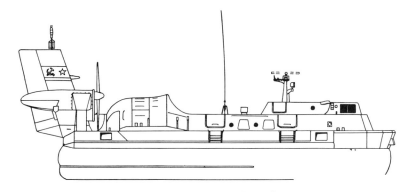

Gus-class air-cushion landing craft (Siegfried Breyer)

Gus air-cushion landing craft

## 15 UTILITY LANDING CRAFT: VYDRA CLASS

| | |
|---|---|
| Completed: | 1967–1969 |
| Builders: | |
| Displacement: | 425 tons standard |
| | 600 tons full load |
| Length: | 181 ft 2 in (54.9 m) |
| Beam: | 25 ft 1 in (7.6 m) |
| Draft: | 6 ft 7 in (2.0 m) |
| Propulsion: | 2 diesels; 800 bhp; 2 shafts |
| Speed: | 12 knots |
| Range: | 2,700 n.miles at 10 knots |
| | 3,500 n.miles at 9 knots |
| Complement: | approx. 20 |
| Troops: | approx. 100 |
| Missiles: | none |
| Guns: | none |
| Radars: | 1 Spin Trough (search) |
| EW systems: | IFF only |

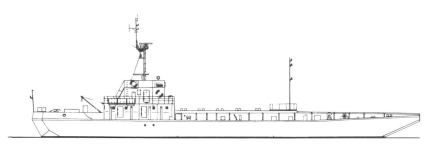

Vydra-class landing craft (Siegfried Breyer)

These are conventional LCU/LCT-type ships. Egypt received 10 ships in 1967–1969, and Bulgaria received 18 of them in 1970–1979.
Designation: Soviet DK type.

## SEVERAL LANDING CRAFT: ONDATRA CLASS

| | |
|---|---|
| Completed: | 1978– |
| Builders: | |
| Displacement: | 90 tons full load |
| Length: | 79 ft 2 in (24.0 m) |
| Beam: | 19 ft 10 in (6.0 m) |
| Draft: | |
| Propulsion: | 2 diesels; 600 bhp; 2 shafts |
| Speed: | 10 knots |
| Range: | |
| Complement: | |
| Guns: | none |

Small personnel/vehicle landing craft. One is embarked in the IVAN ROGOV for use as a tug for the Lebed air-cushion vehicles.

A T-4 landing craft carrying a PT-76 amphibious tank pulls into line behind a torpedo boat during a Navy Day review at Leningrad. (1967, Sovfoto)

## SEVERAL LANDING CRAFT: T-4 CLASS

| | |
|---|---|
| Completed: | 1954–1974 |
| Builders: | |
| Displacement: | 70 tons full load |
| Length: | 62 ft 7 in (19.0 m) |
| Beam: | 14 ft 2 in (4.3 m) |
| Draft: | 3 ft 4 in (1.0 m) |
| Propulsion: | 2 diesels; 600 bhp; 2 shafts |
| Speed: | 10 knots |
| Range: | |
| Complement: | approx. 5 |
| Guns: | none |

Small landing craft, some fitted with bow ramps to permit loading light and medium tanks.

A T-4 landing craft carrying a tank

# 21

# Naval Auxiliaries

## OILERS AND TANKERS

All of these ships are employed to carry fuels for Soviet naval forces. The terms "oiler" and "tanker" in the Western vernacular refer to ships that perform at-sea replenishment and point-to-point fuel transport, respectively. The ships listed here have the Soviet designations of military tanker (VT) except for the one-of-a-kind BEREZINA, which is a military transport (VTR). The latter designation is used for a number of naval dry-cargo ships as well as for other auxiliaries.

The Soviet Navy has long used merchant tankers for at-sea replenishment and continues to do so on a large scale. Until the mid-1960s even naval fuel ships refueled warships while dead in the water or over the stern while towing. Subsequently, several new classes were acquired in the 1960s and 1970s with an alongside Underway Replenishment (UNREP) capability, while older ships were refitted with a limited alongside capability.

The relatively high acquisition rate of fuel ships in the 1960s and 1970s apparently halted in early 1979 when the last of four DUBNA-class ships was acquired. Also, only one ship of the large BEREZINA-class UNREP ship has been built. (She is the only Soviet ship comparable to the U.S. Navy's large AOE/AOR ships.)

## 1 REPLENISHMENT OILER: "BEREZINA"

| Name | Completed |
|------|-----------|
| BEREZINA | 1977 |

| | |
|---|---|
| Builders: | 61 Kommuna Shipyard, Nikolayev |
| Displacement: | approx. 40,000 tons full load |
| Length: | 699 ft 7 in (212.0 m) |
| Beam: | 85 ft 10 in (26.0 m) |
| Draft: | 36 ft 7 in (12.0 m) |
| Propulsion: | 2 diesels; 54,000 bhp; 2 shafts |
| Speed: | 22 knots |
| Range: | 12,000 n.miles at 18 knots |
| Complement: | approx. 600 |
| Helicopters: | 2 Ka-25 Hormone-C |
| Missiles: | 1 twin SA-N-4 launcher (20) |
| Guns: | 4 57-mm/80-cal AA (2 twin) |
| | 4 30-mm close-in (4 multibarrel) |
| ASW weapons: | 2 RBU-1000 rocket launchers |
| Radars: | 2 Bass Tilt (fire control) |
| | 1 Don-2 (navigation) |
| | 2 Don Kay (navigation) |
| | 1 Muff Cob (fire control) |
| | 1 Pop Group (fire control) |
| | 1 Strut Curve (air search) |
| Sonars: | . . . . . . (hull mounted) |
| EW systems: | IFF |

The one-of-a-kind BEREZINA at anchor. Only the one ship of this type was constructed and no more are expected in the near future, possibly indicating a reallocation of resources previously intended for replenishment ships.

This is the Soviet Navy's largest and most capable replenishment ship. Only one unit has been built, and no others are reported to be under construction. The BEREZINA made her first operational deployment from the Black Sea into the Mediterranean in December 1978.

Design: The ship was designed from the outset for the underway replenishment of petroleum, munitions, and stores. The ship can carry an estimated 16,000 tons of fuels, 500 tons of fresh water, and 2,000 to 3,000 tons of munitions and provisions. She can transfer fuel stores to ships on either side and fuel over the stern. Special provisions are provided for replenishing submarines. There are four 10-ton-capacity cranes for loading stores and servicing ships alongside.

Of special significance is the ship's heavy armament, which includes ASW weapons. She is currently the only armed Soviet replenishment ship.

Designation: Soviet VTR type.

Name: The Berezina is a major river in Belorussia and the scene of a major battle in Napoleon's retreat from Moscow in 1812.

A later photo of the BEREZINA. In addition to her extensive anti-aircraft defenses, she may be the world's only auxiliary ship with ASW armament. (1982)

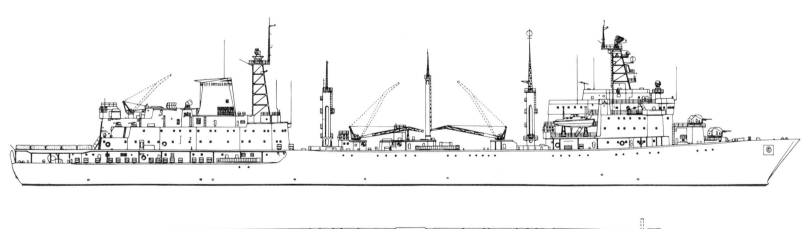

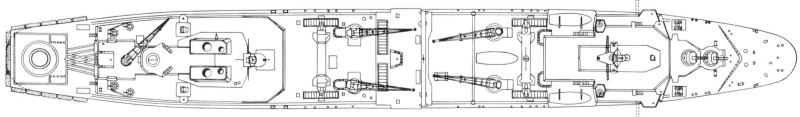

BEREZINA (Siegfried Breyer)

## 4 REPLENISHMENT OILERS: "DUBNA" CLASS

| Name | Completed |
| --- | --- |
| DUBNA | 1974 |
| IRKUT | 1975 |
| PECHENGA | 1979 |
| SVENTA | 1979 |

| | |
| --- | --- |
| Builders: | Rauma-Repola, Rauma (Finland) |
| Displacement: | approx. 4,300 tons light |
| | 13,500 tons full load |
| Tonnage: | 6,500 DWT |
| Length: | 429 ft 4 in (130.1 m) |
| Beam: | 66 ft (20.0 m) |
| Draft: | 23 ft 9 in (7.2 m) |
| Propulsion: | 1 diesel (8DRPH); 6,000 bhp; 1 shaft |
| Speed: | 16 knots |
| Range: | 8,000 n.miles at 15 knots |
| Complement: | approx. 60 |
| Helicopters: | no facilities |
| Missiles: | none |
| Guns: | none |
| Radars: | 1 Okean (navigation) |

These are small replenishment ships with at least the first two units, the DUBNA and IRKUT, having been employed initially to support the Soviet fishing fleet as well as naval forces.

Design: These ships can transfer fuel and dry stores to ships on either side and over the stern.

Designation: Soviet VT type.

Overhead view of the underway replenishment ship BEREZINA

The DUBNA-class replenishment oiler PECHENGA, one of a class of four highly capable, albeit small, underway replenishment ships in Soviet naval service. In addition to their relatively small capacity, they are slower and lack helicopter facilities in comparison to the more-modern U.S. Navy UNREP ships. (1982)

## 6 REPLENISHMENT OILERS: "BORIS CHILIKIN" CLASS

| Name | Name | Name | Completed |
|---|---|---|---|
| BORIS BUTOMA | DNESTR | IVAN BUBNOV | 1967–1978 |
| BORIS CHILIKIN | GENRIKH GASANOV | VLADIMIR KOLYACHITSKIY | |

| | |
|---|---|
| Builders: | Baltic Shipyard, Leningrad |
| Displacement: | 8,750 tons light |
| | 24,450 tons full load |
| Length: | 535 ft 3 in (162.2 m) |
| Beam: | 70 ft 8 in (21.4 m) |
| Draft: | 38 ft (11.5 m) |
| Propulsion: | 1 diesel; 9,600 bhp; 1 shaft |
| Speed: | 16.5 knots |
| Range: | 10,000 n.miles at 16.5 knots |
| Complement: | |
| Helicopters: | no facilities |
| Missiles: | none |
| Guns: | removed |
| Radars: | 2 Don Kay (navigation) (see notes) |

These are naval versions of the VELIKIY OKTYABR-class merchant tankers, a large number of which were constructed for Soviet and foreign merchant fleets. The merchant ships are 16,540 DWT.

Design: Cargo capacity is 13,500 tons of fuel and fresh water, 400 tons of munitions, and 800 tons of stores and provisions. These ships can transfer fuel to ships from either side and astern; the early units could transfer provisions from both sides, but the later ships only to starboard.

Four ships were completed with four 57-mm/80-cal AA in twin mounts forward as well as Muff Cob fire-control radar and Strut Curve air-search radar. Subsequently removed. The IVAN BUBNOV and GENRIKH GASANOV were completed in merchant configuration without these guns or naval radars.

Designation: Soviet VT type.

The BORIS CHILIKIN, still carrying her forward guns, while refueling the helicopter carrier MOSKVA. The ability to refuel while under way increases the mobility of Soviet naval forces and reduces their vulnerability during UNREP operations (Royal Air Force)

An early BORIS CHILIKIN-class replenishment oiler at sea, still mounting the two 57-mm twin AA mounts forward. Interestingly, the guns were deleted from this class at the same time as the BEREZINA was being built with her heavy armament. (U.S. Navy, 1974)

The Boris Chilikin-class replenishment oiler Ivan Bubnov while consolidating fuel with the larger Berezina (1982)

## 5 REPLENISHMENT OILERS: ALTAY CLASS

| Name | Name | Name | Completed |
|------|------|------|-----------|
| Ilim | Kola | Yel'nya | } 1968–1973 |
| Izhora | Yegorlik | | |

| | |
|------|------|
| Builders: | Rauma-Repola, Rauma |
| Displacement: | approx. 2,200 tons light |
| | 7,230 tons full load |
| Tonnage: | 5,045 DWT |
| Length: | 350 ft 2 in (106.1 m) |
| Beam: | 50 ft 10 in (15.4 m) |
| Draft: | 22 ft 1 in (6.7 m) |
| Propulsion: | 1 diesel (B&W-550 VTBN-110); 3,250 bhp; 1 shaft |
| Speed: | 14 knots |
| Range: | 5,000 n.miles at 13 knots |
| | 8,600 n.miles at 12 knots |
| Complement: | approx. 60 |
| Helicopters: | no facilities |
| Missiles: | none |
| Guns: | none |
| Radars: | 2 Don-2 (navigation) |
| EW systems: | IFF |

Some 60 ships of this type have been built, most for service with the Soviet fishing and merchant fleet, with most deliveries between 1968 and 1973.

Design: These ships can refuel one ship at a time from either side plus astern refueling. Their masts and details differ.

Designation: Soviet VT type.

The Altay-class replenishment oiler Yel'nya refueling a SAM Kotlin in the Mediterranean during the 1975 Okean exercises (1975)

The Altay-class replenishment oiler Izhora en route to the Indian Ocean

The Altay-class replenishment oiler Kola

A Pevek-class tanker

### 3 TANKERS: "OLEKHMA" AND "PEVEK" CLASSES

| Name | Completed |
|------|-----------|
| Olekhma | 1964 |
| Iman | 1966 |
| Zolotoi Rog | 1958 |

| | |
|---|---|
| Builders: | Rauma-Repola, Rauma |
| Displacement: | Olekhma 7,380 tons full load |
| | Pevek 7,280 tons full load |
| Tonnage: | Olekhma 4,400 DWT |
| | Pevek 4,320 DWT |
| Length: | Olekhma 347 ft 10 in (105.4 m) |
| | Pevek 346 ft 10 in (105.1 m) |
| Beam: | 48 ft 10 in (14.8 m) |
| Draft: | 22 ft 6 in (6.8 m) |
| Propulsion: | 1 diesel (B&W); 2,900 bhp; 1 shaft |
| Speed: | 13.5 knots |
| Range: | 10,000 n.miles at 13.5 knots |
| Complement: | approx. 40 |
| Helicopters: | no facilities |
| Missiles: | none |
| Guns: | none |
| Radars: | |

Fifty tankers of this design were built for the USSR. (Two similar tankers were built by Sweden for Soviet use.) The Zolotoi Rog belongs to the first series (delivered 1956–1960) and the other ships to the second series (1961–1967).

Design: These ships have a traditional "three-island" layout compared to the one- or two-island arrangement of most Soviet oilers and tankers. The Zolotoi Rog differs in detail from the two other ships.

One of more of these ships were modified from 1978 on with an A-frame aft of the bridge to facilitate underway refueling of one ship off either beam. In addition, as with essentially all Soviet naval and merchant tankers, they can refuel over the stern. Note the lack of a helicopter platform in these and most other Soviet replenishment ships compared to Western UNREP ships.

Designation: Soviet VT type.

PEVEK-class tanker IMAN

---

**1 TANKER: "SOFIA" CLASS**

| Name | Completed |
|------|-----------|
| AKHTUBA (ex-HANOI) | 1963 |

| | |
|------|------|
| Builders: | Leningrad |
| Displacement: | 62,600 tons full load |
| Tonnage: | 49,385 DWT |
| Length: | 760 ft 8 in (230.5 m) |
| Beam: | 102 ft 4 in (31.0 m) |
| Draft: | 39 ft (11.8 m) |
| Propulsion: | steam turbines; 19,000 shp; 1 shaft |
| Boilers: | 2 |
| Speed: | 17 knots |
| Range: | 21,000 n.miles at 17 knots |
| Complement: | approx. 70 |

| | |
|------|------|
| Helicopters: | no facilities |
| Missiles: | none |
| Guns: | none |
| Radars: | |

The AKHTUBA is the largest auxiliary in the Soviet Navy. More than 20 SOFIA-class tankers were delivered between 1963 and 1970, some for foreign merchant service. The AKHTUBA was taken over for naval service in 1969. They are the second largest merchant tanker design to be constructed in the Soviet Union.

Design: Cargo capacity is 44,500 tons of fuel. Can refuel only over the stern.

Designation: Soviet VT type.

The SOFIA-class fleet oiler AKHTUBA

## 6 TANKERS: UDA CLASS

| Name | Name | Name | Completed |
|------|------|------|-----------|
| DUNAY | LENA | TEREK | |
| KOIDA | SHEKSNA | VISHERA | 1962–1964 |

| | |
|------|------|
| Builders: | Vyborg |
| Displacement: | 7,100 tons full load |
| Length: | 402 ft 3 in (121.9 m) |
| Beam: | 52 ft 10 in (16.0 m) |
| Draft: | 20 ft 10 in (6.3 m) |
| Propulsion: | 2 diesels; 8,000 bhp; 1 shaft |
| Speed: | 17 knots |
| Range: | 4,000 n.miles at 17 knots |
| Complement: | approx. 85 |
| Helicopters: | no facilities |

| | |
|------|------|
| Missiles: | none |
| Guns: | see notes |
| Radars: | 1 or 2 Don-2 (navigation) |
| EW systems: | IFF only |

These are small tankers built for naval service. Three ships of this type were transferred to Indonesia.

Design: There are provisions for fitting eight 57-mm/70-cal AA guns in quad mounts (plus one Strut Curve and two Muff Cob radars). At least one ship was observed in the Baltic in 1962 with one 57-mm quad mount, apparently in a test role.

The LENA and VISHERA have a second A-frame, providing two amidships refueling positions.

Designation: Soviet VT type.

The Uda-class tanker LENA refuels the Krivak II-class frigate GORDELIVYY in the North Atlantic while both ships steam at relatively high speed. Although Soviet UNREP ships are smaller than their U.S. Navy counterparts, the integration of the Soviet merchant fleet in the naval support role provides a considerable replenishment capability. (1980)

The Uda-class tanker SHEKSNA; some units (as LENA) do not have the amidships replenishment mast fitted. (1977)

## 17 TANKERS: "KHOBI" CLASS

| Name | Name | Name | Completed |
|------|------|------|-----------|
| ALAZAN | LOVAT' | SOS'VA | |
| BAYMAK | METAN | SYSOLA | |
| CHEREMSHAN | ORSHA | TARTU | 1955–(?) |
| GORYN | SASHA | TITAN | |
| INDIGA | SEIMA | TUNGUSKA | |
| KHOBI | SHELON' | | |

| | |
|---|---|
| Builders: | Zhdanov Shipyard, Leningrad |
| Displacement: | 1,525 tons full load |
| Length: | 208 ft 6 in (63.2 m) |
| Beam: | 33 ft (10.0 m) |
| Draft: | 14 ft 10 in (4.5 m) |
| Propulsion: | 2 diesels; 1,600 bhp; 2 shafts |
| Speed: | 13 knots |
| Range: | 2,500 n.miles at 12.5 knots |
| Complement: | approx. 30 |
| Helicopters: | no facilities |
| Missiles: | none |
| Guns: | none |
| Radars: | 1 Don-2 (navigation) |
| | 1 Spin Trough (search) |
| EW systems: | IFF |

These are small tankers, similar to U.S. Navy gasoline tankers (AOG). They will probably be discarded in the near future. Two ships of this type have been transferred to Albania and three to Indonesia.

Design: Cargo capacity is approximately 1,500 tons of fuel. They generally refuel naval units over the bow.

Designation: Soviet VT type.

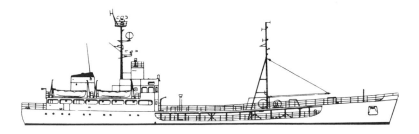

KHOBI-class tanker (Siegfried Breyer)

**4 TANKERS: "KONDA" CLASS**

| Name | Name | Name | Completed |
|------|------|------|-----------|
| Konda Rossoch' | Soyana | Yakhroma | 1954–1965 |

| | |
|---|---|
| Builders: | Turku (Finland) |
| Displacement: | 1,980 tons full load |
| Tonnage: | 1,265 DWT |
| Length: | 228 ft (69.1 m) |
| Beam: | 33 ft (10.0 m) |
| Draft: | 14 ft 6 in (4.4 m) |
| Propulsion: | 1 diesel; 1,600 bhp; 1 shaft |
| Speed: | 12.5 knots |
| Range: | 2,500 n.miles at 10 knots |
| Complement: | approx. 25 |
| Helicopters: | no facilities |
| Missiles: | none |
| Guns: | none |
| Radars: | 1 or 2 Don-2 (navigation) and/or Spin Trough (search) |

The Konda-class tanker Yakhroma

Small tankers. Cargo capacity is approximately 1,100 tons of fuel. Their naval designation is VT.

The Konda-class tanker Yakhroma

**3 TANKERS: "NERCHA" CLASS**

| Name | Name | Name | Completed |
|------|------|------|-----------|
| KLYAZMA | NARVA | NERCHA | 1952–1955 |

| | |
|---|---|
| Builders: | Crichton-Vulcan or Valmet, Abo (Finland) |
| Displacement: | 1,800 tons full load |
| Tonnage: | 1,300 DWT |
| Length: | 209 ft 6 in (63.5 m) |
| Beam: | 33 ft (10.0 m) |
| Draft: | 14 ft 10 in (4.5 m) |
| Propulsion: | 1 diesel; 1,000 bhp; 1 shaft |
| Speed: | 11 knots |
| Range: | 2,000 n.miles at 10 knots |
| Complement: | approx. 25 |
| Helicopters: | no facilities |
| Missiles: | none |
| Guns: | none |
| Radars: | 1 Don series (navigation) |

Small tankers. Several similar ships are in Soviet merchant service. They refuel over the stern. Soviet naval designation is VT.

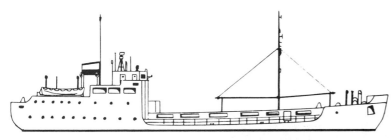

NERCHA-class tanker (Siegfried Breyer)

**3 TANKERS: "KAZBEK" CLASS**

| Name | Name | Name | Completed |
|------|------|------|-----------|
| ALATYR' | DESNA | VOLKHOV | 1951–(?) |

| | |
|---|---|
| Builders: | Kherson |
| Displacement: | 16,250 tons full load |
| Tonnage: | 11,800 DWT |
| Length: | 480 ft 2 in (145.5 m) |
| Beam: | 63 ft 4 in (19.2 m) |
| Draft: | 28 ft 9 in (8.7 m) |
| Propulsion: | 2 diesels; 4,000 bhp; 2 shafts |
| Speed: | 15 knots |
| Range: | 18,000 n.miles at 12.5 knots |
| Complement: | approx. 45 |
| Helicopters: | no facilities |
| Missiles: | none |
| Guns: | none |
| Radars: | 2 Don-2 (navigation) |
| EW systems: | IFF |

About 50 of these tankers were built at Kherson and the Admiralty yard in Leningrad between 1951 and 1958. Many remain in merchant service and are used periodically to refuel naval ships.

Design: These ships are similar in design to the United States T-2 type of the late 1930s. Kingposts and an A-frame are fitted to the naval units to carry refueling hoses. They can carry about 12,000 tons of fuel.

Designation: Soviet VT type.

The BORIS CHILIKIN-class replenishment oiler IVAN BUBNOV lies alongside the KAZBEK-class merchant tanker CHEBOKSARY during a consolidation of their fuel loads. The BUBNOV's forward 57-mm gun mounts have been removed. (1982)

The KAZBEK-class tanker DESNA refuels a Kara-class missile cruiser off her port side and a Kashin-class missile destroyer astern. Of conventional design, the KAZBEK class consists of some 50 ships built in the 1950s. There is a strong resemblance to the American T-2 design; note the tripod replenishment mast forward of the tanker's bridge. (Royal Air Force)

---

**1 TANKER: "POLYARNIK"**

| Name | Completed |
|---|---|
| POLYARNIK (ex-German KARNTEN, ex-Dutch TANKBOOT I) | 1942 |

| | |
|---|---|
| Builders: | C. av den Giessen, Krimpen (Netherlands) |
| Displacement: | 12,500 tons full load |
| Tonnage: | 6,640 DWT |
| Length: | 436 ft (132.1 m) |
| Beam: | 53 ft 6 in (16.2 m) |
| Draft: | 25 ft (7.6 m) |
| Propulsion: | 2 diesels (Werkspoor); 7,000 bhp; 1 shaft |
| Speed: | 15 knots |
| Range: | |
| Complement: | approx. 55 |
| Helicopters: | no facilities |
| Missiles: | none |
| Guns: | none |
| Radars: | |

This ship was laid down for the Dutch Navy in December 1939 and taken over by German troops while still on the ways in May 1941; subsequently launched on 3 May 1941 and commissioned by the Ger-

man Navy on 27 December 1941. She was taken over by the Soviets in December 1945. Still in active service, the POLYARNIK serves in the Pacific Fleet.

Design: Cargo capacity is 5,600 tons of fuel; she also carries dry stores and provisions.

Designation: Soviet VT type.

The POLYARNIK is the oldest and in many respects the most interesting tanker of the Soviet Navy. (1976)

## SPECIAL-PURPOSE TANKERS

### 1 NUCLEAR WASTE TANKER: "URAL"

| Name | Completed |
|------|-----------|
| URAL | 1969 |

| | |
|---|---|
| Builders: | Dalzavod Shipyard, Vladivostok |
| Displacement: | 2,600 tons full load |
| Length: | 297 ft (90.0 m) |
| Beam: | 33 ft (10.0 m) |
| Draft: | 12 ft 3 in (3.7 m) |
| Propulsion: | 2 diesels; 1,200 bhp; 1 shaft |
| Speed: | 10 knots |
| Range: | 3,000 n.miles at 9 knots |
| Complement: | |
| Helicopters: | no facilities |
| Missiles: | none |
| Guns: | none |
| Radars: | |

The URAL is a small, superstructure-aft tanker employed to carry nuclear waste. She has a high freeboard and a travelling crane.
Designation: Soviet TNT type.

### 9 SPECIAL CARGO TANKERS: LUZA CLASS

| Name | Name | Name | Completed |
|------|------|------|-----------|
| ALAMBAY | DON | SASIMA | |
| ARAGUY | KANA | SELENGA | 1960s |
| BARGUZIN | OKA | YENISEY | |

| | |
|---|---|
| Builders: | Middle Neva Shipyard, Kilpino |
| Displacement: | 1,900 tons full load |
| Length: | 206 ft 3 in (62.5 m) |

| | |
|---|---|
| Beam: | 35 ft 4 in (10.7 m) |
| Draft: | 14 ft 2 in (4.3 m) |
| Propulsion: | 1 diesel; 1,000 bhp; 1 shaft |
| Speed: | 12 knots |
| Range: | 2,000 n.miles at 11 knots |
| Complement: | |
| Helicopters: | no facilities |
| Missiles: | none |
| Guns: | none |
| Radars: | 1 Don-2 (navigation) |

These small tankers are used to transport volatile liquids, probably fuel for Soviet SLBMs.
Designation: Soviet TNT type.

### 5 NUCLEAR WASTE TANKERS: VALA CLASS

| | |
|---|---|
| Completed: | |
| Builders: | |
| Displacement: | 3,100 tons full load |
| Length: | 251 ft 6 in (76.2 m) |
| Beam: | 41 ft 3 in (12.5 m) |
| Draft: | 16 ft 6 in (5.0 m) |
| Propulsion: | 1 diesel; 1,000 bhp; 1 shaft |
| Speed: | 14 knots |
| Range: | 2,000 n.miles at 11 knots |
| Complement: | |
| Helicopters: | no facilities |
| Missiles: | none |
| Guns: | none |
| Radars: | |

This class of small tankers carries radioactive waste.
Designation: Soviet TNT type.

The Luza-class special tanker BARGUZIN is one of several specialized liquid-cargo carriers in Soviet service that transport missile fuels and other volatile liquids. The tops of the ship's special cargo tanks can be seen forward and aft of the bridge island structure. (1982)

## WATER TANKERS

### 2 WATER TANKERS: "MANYCH" CLASS

| Name | Completed |
| --- | --- |
| MANYCH | 1971 |
| TAYGIL | 1977 |

| | |
| --- | --- |
| Builders: | Vyborg |
| Displacement: | 7,800 tons full load |
| Length: | 379 ft 6 in (115.8 m) |
| Beam: | 52 ft 2 in (15.8 m) |
| Draft: | 22 ft 1 in (6.7 m) |
| Propulsion: | 2 diesels; 9,000 bhp; 2 shafts |
| Speed: | 18 knots |
| Range: | 7,500 n.miles at 16 knots |
| | 11,500 n.miles at 12 knots |
| Complement: | approx. 90 |
| Helicopters: | no facilities |
| Missiles: | none |
| Guns: | none (see notes) |
| Radars: | 2 Don Kay (navigation) |

These ships were designed as naval replenishment ships to provide diesel fuel and stores to submarines. However, the design was not operationally successful, and they became water carriers. Soviet water tankers provide water to submarines and surface ships for crew consumption and (in surface ships) for use in boilers.

Design: These ships have a conventional small tanker design with a single, heavy kingpost forward for handling UNREP equipment.

Designation: Soviet MVT type.

The MANYCH-class water tanker TAYGIL (1980)

Guns: The MANYCH was completed as an oiler with four 57-mm AA guns in twin mounts supported by two Muff Cob radars. Her armament was removed in 1975. However, the Muff Cob directors, fore and aft of the mast, were retained. The TAYGIL was completed without guns.

The MANYCH at sea, with her forward and after 57-mm AA twin gun mounts removed. The TAYGIL was completed without guns. These ships were designed as tankers–submarine support ships, but were unsuccessful in that role, and hence only two were built and employed as freshwater tankers. (1982, U.S. Navy)

## 14 WATER TANKERS: VODA CLASS

| Name | Name | Name | Completed |
|------|------|------|-----------|
| ABAKAN | MVT 9 | MVT 20 | |
| SURA | MVT 10 | MVT 21 | |
| VODOLEY-2 | MVT 16 | MVT 134 | 1956–? |
| VODOLEY-3 | MVT 17 | MVT 138 | |
| MVT 6 | MVT 18 | | |

Builders:
Displacement:          2,100 tons standard
                       3,100 tons full load
Length:                269 ft (81.5 m)

Beam:                  38 ft (11.5 m)
Draft:                 14 ft 2 in (4.3 m)
Propulsion:            2 diesels; 1,600 bhp; 2 shafts
Speed:                 12 knots
Range:                 3,000 n.miles at 10 knots
Complement:            approx. 40
Helicopters:           no facilities
Missiles:              none
Guns:                  none
Radars:                1 Neptune or Don-2 (navigation)

These ships are water-distilling-and-carrying ships.
Designation: Soviet MVT type.

VODA-class water tanker ABAKAN (1973, Royal Air Force)

## MISSILE TRANSPORT AND AMMUNITION SHIPS

### 3 MISSILE TRANSPORTS: "AMGA" CLASS

| Name | Completed |
| --- | --- |
| AMGA | 1972 |
| DAUGAVA | 1981 |
| VETLUGA | 1976 |

| | |
| --- | --- |
| Builders: | Krasnoye Sovmovo, Gor'kiy |
| Displacement: | 4,800 tons standard |
| | 5,500 tons full load except DAUGAVA 6,200 tons |
| Length: | AMGA 341 ft 10 in (103.6 m) |
| | VETLUGA 361 ft 8 in (109.6 m) |
| | DAUGAVA 372 ft 11 in (113.1 m) |
| Beam: | 58 ft 5 in (17.7 m) |
| Draft: | 14 ft 6 in (4.4 m) |
| Propulsion: | 2 diesels; 4,000 bhp; 2 shafts |
| Speed: | 16 knots |
| Range: | 4,500 n.miles at 14 knots |
| Complement: | approx. 200 |
| Helicopters: | none |
| Missiles: | none |
| Guns: | 4 25-mm/60-cal AA (2 twin) |
| Radars: | 1 Don-2 (navigation) |
| EW systems: | IFF only |

These ships transport missiles for Delta-class SSBNs.

Design:  Improved versions of the previous Lama class but with lighter armament. Propulsion machinery, accommodations, and controls are aft with missile stowage forward. Their hulls are ice strengthened. A 55-ton-capacity crane is fitted.

### 7 MISSILE TRANSPORT/TENDERS: LAMA CLASS

| Name | Name | Name | Completed |
| --- | --- | --- | --- |
| GENERAL RIYABAKOV (PB 155) | PM 93 | PB 625 | |
| VORONEZH | PM 131 | | 1963–1979 |
| PM 44 | PM 150 | | |

| | |
| --- | --- |
| Builders: | Black Sea Shipyard, Nikolayev |
| Displacement: | approx. 4,500 tons standard |
| | approx. 6,000 tons full load |
| Length: | 372 ft 4 in (112.8 m) |
| Beam: | 49 ft 2 in (14.9 m) |
| Draft: | 14 ft 6 in (4.4 m) |
| Propulsion: | 2 diesels; 4,000 bhp; 2 shafts |
| Speed: | 14 knots |
| Range: | 6,000 n.miles at 10 knots |
| Complement: | approx. 250 |
| Helicopters: | none |
| Missiles: | 4 quad SA-N-5 Grail launchers (32) in GENERAL RIYABAKOV |
| Guns: | 4 or 8 57-mm/70 cal AA (2 or 4 twin) except 2 57-mm/80-cal AA (1 twin) in GENERAL RIYABAKOV |
| | 4 25-mm/60-cal AA guns (2 twin) in ships with 4 57-mm guns |
| Radars: | 1 Don-2 (navigation) |
| | 1 Slim Net or Strut Curve (air search) |
| | 1 or 2 Hawk Screech or 2 Muff Cob in ships with 57-mm guns |
| EW systems: | IFF only |

These are missile transports that carry cruise missiles for surface ships and submarines.

Design:  Machinery, accommodations, and controls are aft with missile stowage forward. Details differ. Two ships (GENERAL RIYABAKOV and

The AMGA shortly after completion. The 55-ton-capacity crane dominates the appearance of the missile ship, intended to carry SLBMs for the Delta-class strategic missile submarines.

PB 625) have enlarged missile stowage, a smaller working deck forward, and modified armament. Reportedly, these two ships serve Nanuchka and Osa surface missile ships. Some of the other ships have larger superstructures. Five ships have 20-ton-capacity cranes and the two modified ships two 10-ton-capacity cranes.

Designation: Soviet PM type except GENERAL RIYABAKOV and PB 625 are designated PB.

The Lama-class missile transport/tender PM 93 at anchor. She has a standard Lama configuration with larger missile handling cranes, but smaller missile stowage and superstructure.

A modified Lama-class missile transport/tender. Note the smaller cranes, enlarged superstructure, and additional gun mount abaft the funnel. (1982, U.S. Navy)

Modified Lama-class missile transport/tender

## 2 MISSILE TRANSPORTS } MODIFIED "ANDIZHAN" CLASS
## 3 CARGO SHIPS

| Name | Type | Completed |
|------|------|-----------|
| ONDA | C | |
| POSET | C | |
| YEMETSK | C | 1958–1960 |
| VENTA (ex-LAKHTA) | M | |
| VILYUY (ex-POSYET) | M | |

| | |
|---|---|
| Builders: | Neptun Shipyard, Rostock |
| Displacement: | approx. 4,500 tons standard |
| | approx. 6,740 tons full load |
| Tonnage: | 4,375 DWT |
| Length: | 343 ft 10 in (104.2 m) |
| Beam: | 47 ft 6 in (14.4 m) |
| Draft: | 21 ft 9 in (6.6 m) |
| Propulsion: | 1 diesel (M.A.N.); 3,250 bhp; 1 shaft |
| Speed: | 14 knots |
| Range: | 6,000 n.miles at 13.5 knots |
| Complement: | approx. 100 |
| Helicopters: | landing platform |
| Missiles: | none |
| Guns: | none |
| Radars: | 2 Don-2 (navigation) |
| EW systems: | IFF only |

These ships are former merchant ships converted in the 1970s, two to transport missiles (M) and three to naval cargo ships (C).

Class: They are former ANDIZHAN/KOVEL-class dry-cargo ships, almost 50 of which were built by the Neptun yard. Most entered Soviet merchant service, including three as training ships. Three other ships were completed as naval oceanographic ships (POLYUS class).

Design: A single heavy-lift crane is fitted forward and a pole mast aft in place of the original A-frame cranes in the missile transports. Their forward holds can carry 10 SS-N-9 missiles and 20 SA-N-1 or SA-N-3 missiles. Cargo capacity is 3,950 tons.

Designation: Soviet VTR type.

ANDIZHAN-class cargo ship ONDA

The ANDIZHAN-class missile transport VILYUY. There is a missile handling crane forward between the four hatches to the missile magazines. A helicopter landing platform is fitted abaft the tripod mast. (1981)

| **2 MISSILE TRANSPORTS**<br>**3 CARGO SHIPS** } | **MP 6 CLASS** (Former Landing Ships) | |

| Name | Type | Completed |
| --- | --- | --- |
| BIRA | C | |
| BUREYA | M | |
| IRGIZ | C | 1958–1960 |
| KHOPER | M | |
| VOLOGDA | C | |

| | |
| --- | --- |
| Builders: | (Hungary) |
| Displacement: | 1,870 tons full load |
| Length: | 246 ft 6 in (74.7 m) |
| Beam: | 37 ft 3 in (11.3 m) |
| Draft: | 14 ft 6 in (4.4 m) |
| Propulsion: | 1 diesel; 1,000 bhp; 1 shaft |
| Speed: | 10.5 knots |
| Range: | 3,300 n.miles at 9 knots |
| Complement: | |
| Helicopters: | no facilities |
| Missiles: | none |
| Guns: | see notes |
| Radars: | Neptune (navigation) |

These are former MP 6-class landing ships, two of which have been modified to transport missiles (M) and three to naval cargo ships (C). They resemble small coastal freighters with their superstructure aft.

Class: About 10 landings ships of this design were built.
Designation: All believed to be Soviet VTR type.
Guns: No armament is fitted; there are provisions for six 37-mm/60-cal AA guns (3 twin mounts).

Modification: Their bow doors were welded shut and their bow ramps removed about 1960 to permit their use as missile transports. The missile transports carry SS-N-5 SLBMs for Hotel- and Golf-class submarines.

MP 6-class cargo ship IRGIZ

The BIRA alongside the cruiser-command ship ZHDANOV in the Mediterranean. Two of the BIRA's three hatches are open as she transfers supplies to the cruiser at a quiet anchorage. (1974, U.S. Navy)

The BIRA is one of several cargo and missile ships converted from MP 6 landing ships. They have merchant-ship lines with a tank deck and bow doors (welded shut).

**9 TORPEDO TRANSPORTS: MUNA CLASS**

| | |
|---|---|
| Completed: | |
| Builders: | Nakhodka |
| Displacement: | 680 tons full load |
| Length: | 168 ft 4 in (51.0 m) |
| Beam: | 28 ft (8.5 m) |
| Draft: | 8 ft 11 in (2.7 m) |
| Propulsion: | 1 diesel; 600 bhp; 1 shaft |
| Speed: | 11 knots |
| Range: | |
| Complement: | approx. 40 |
| Helicopters: | no facilities |
| Missiles: | none |
| Guns: | none |
| Radars: | 1 Spin Trough (search) |
| EW systems: | IFF only |

These are small, superstructure-aft, torpedo and missile transports.

Designation: They have the designation MBSS—*Morskaya Barzha Samokhodnaya Sukhogruznaya* (seagoing self-propelled dry-cargo lighters) when in Soviet home waters, and VTR when deployed.

Muna-class torpedo transport

## ACOUSTIC MONITORING SHIPS

The Soviet Navy uses several ships to deploy and monitor hydrophone arrays to measure the radiated sound levels of its own surface ships and submarines. (The U.S. Navy uses only fixed acoustic ranges for this information.)

### 3 + HYDROACOUSTIC MEASURING SHIPS: ONEGA CLASS

| Name | Name | Name | Completed |
|------|------|------|-----------|
| GKS 83 | SFP . . . . | . . . . . . | 1973– |
| GKS . . . | | | |

| | |
|---|---|
| Builders: | |
| Displacement: | approx. 2,000 tons standard |
| | approx. 2,500 tons full load |
| Length: | 283 ft 8 in (86.0 m) |
| Beam: | 34 ft 8 in (10.5 m) |
| Draft: | 14 ft 10 in (4.5 m) |
| Propulsion: | 1 gas turbine; 1 shaft |
| Speed: | 16 knots |
| Range: | |
| Complement: | approx. 45 |
| Helicopters: | landing deck aft |
| Missiles: | none |
| Guns: | none |
| Radars: | |

These are relatively large ships for the mission, with their gas turbine propulsion providing a very low self-generated noise signature.

Designation: The Soviet designation GKS stands for hydroacoustic monitoring ship. The meaning of SFP is not known.

### 19 HYDROACOUSTIC MONITORING SHIPS: MODIFIED T-43 CLASS

| Name | Name | Name | Completed |
|------|------|------|-----------|
| GKS 11 | GKS 18 | GKS 25 | |
| GKS 12 | GKS 19 | GKS 26 | |
| GKS 13 | GKS 20 | GKS 42 | |
| GKS 14 | GKS 21 | GKS 45 | 1950s |
| GKS 15 | GKS 22 | GKS 46 | |
| GKS 16 | GKS 23 | | |
| GKS 17 | GKS 24 | | |

| | |
|---|---|
| Builders: | Leningrad, Kerch´ |
| Displacement: | 500 tons standard |
| | 570 tons full load |
| Length: | 191 ft 5 in (58.0 m) |
| Beam: | 28 ft 5 in (8.6 m) |
| Draft: | 7 ft 7 in (2.3 m) |
| Propulsion: | 2 diesels (9D); 2,200 bhp; 2 shafts |
| Speed: | 14 knots |
| Range: | |
| Complement: | approx. 75 |
| Helicopters: | no facilities |
| Missiles: | none |
| Guns: | none |
| Radars: | 1 Neptune (navigation) or Spin Trough (search) |
| EW systems: | IFF only |

Based on the T-43 minesweeper design, these ships were built specifically for the monitoring role. There are provisions for fitting a single 37-mm AA gun mount.

Designation: Soviet GKS type.

Hydroacoustic monitoring ship GKS 14

## CARGO AND STORE SHIPS

### 4 + KGB SUPPLY SHIPS: "IVAN ANTONOV" CLASS

| Name | Name | Name | Completed |
|------|------|------|-----------|
| Ivan Antonov | Ivan Lednev | . . . . . . | } 1977– |
| Ivan Asdnev | Irbit | | |

| | |
|---|---|
| Builders: | (USSR) |
| Displacement: | 5,200 tons full load |
| Length: | 313 ft 10 in (95.1 m) |
| Beam: | 48 ft 6 in (14.7 m) |
| Draft: | 21 ft 6 in (6.5 m) |
| Propulsion: | 1 diesel; 1 shaft |
| Speed: | 16 knots |
| Range: | |
| Complement: | |
| Helicopters: | no facilities |
| Missiles: | none |
| Guns: | see notes |
| Radars: | 1 . . . (navigation) |

These are specialized supply ships employed to support KGB Border Troops in remote locations. Small landing craft are carried.

Guns: There are positions for light guns on the forecastle and amidships.

### 1 CARGO-PASSENGER SHIP: "AMGUEMA" CLASS

| Name | Completed |
|------|-----------|
| Yauza | 1975 |

| | |
|---|---|
| Builders: | (USSR) |
| Displacement: | 15,100 tons full load |
| Tonnage: | 9,045 DWT |
| Length: | 439 ft 3 in (133.1 m) |
| Beam: | 62 ft 4 in (18.9 m) |
| Draft: | 30 ft (9.1 m) |
| Propulsion: | DE: 4 diesel generators/electric motors; 7,200 bhp; 1 shaft |
| Speed: | 15 knots |
| Range: | approx. 10,000 n.miles at 10 knots |
| Complement: | |
| Helicopters: | no facilities |
| Missiles: | none |
| Guns: | none |
| Radars: | 2 Don-2 (navigation) |

One of a class of about 15 passenger-cargo ships designed for polar operations. One ship, the Mikhail Somov, is an Arctic research and supply ship.

Design: Cargo capacity is 6,600 tons. The ship has a limited icebreaking capability, recessed anchors, and other features for ice/cold-weather operations.

The Yauza is a combination passenger-cargo ship of a type widely used in the Soviet merchant fleet. The ship has an icebreaking bow and an ice-strengthened hull. (1976)

## 4 CARGO SHIPS: "YUNIY PARTIZAN" CLASS

| Name | Name | Name | Completed |
|---|---|---|---|
| Pechora<br>Pinega | Turgay | Ufa | } 1975–1978 |

| | |
|---|---|
| Builders: | Turnu-Severin Shipyard, Romania |
| Displacement: | 3,947 tons full load |
| Tonnage: | 2,150 DWT |
| Length: | 292 ft 10 in (88.75 m) |
| Beam: | 42 ft 3 in (12.8 m) |
| Draft: | 17 ft 2 in (5.2 m) |
| Propulsion: | 1 diesel (Sulzer); 2,080 bhp; 1 shaft |
| Speed: | 13 knots |
| Range: | 4,000 n.miles at 12 knots |
| Complement: | approx. 25 |
| Helicopters: | no facilities |
| Missiles: | none |
| Guns: | none |
| Radars: | 1 Don-2 (navigation) |
| EW systems: | IFF only |

These are small coastal container ships. About 25 were built for Soviet merchant service, including these four taken over for naval use; others fly the Romanian flag.

Design: Cargo capacity in merchant service is 58 standard freight containers. These are superstructure-aft ships with three 10-ton-capacity cranes, one of which can be rigged to lift up to 28 tons.

## 6 REFRIGERATED STORESHIPS: "MAYAK" CLASS

| Name | Name | Name | Conversion Completed |
|---|---|---|---|
| Bulzuluk<br>Ishim | Lama<br>Mius | Neman<br>Rioni | } 1971–1976 |

| | |
|---|---|
| Builders: | Dnepr Shipyard, Kiev |
| Displacement: | 1,050 tons full load |
| Length: | 180 ft 2 in (54.6 m) |
| Beam: | 30 ft 8 in (9.3 m) |
| Draft: | 11 ft 11 in (3.6 m) |
| Propulsion: | 1 diesel; 800 bhp; 1 shaft |
| Speed: | 11 knots |
| Range: | 9,400 n.miles at 11 knots |
| Complement: | approx. 30 |
| Helicopters: | no facilities |
| Missiles: | none |
| Guns: | none |
| Radars: | 1 Spin Trough (search) |

These are converted Mayak-class side trawlers. They have been modified to carry provisions for naval ships. A large number of these craft were completed from 1962 onward, with several others converted to naval intelligence ships (AGI).

Design: Small, superstructure-aft ships, built to trawl over the starboard side and fitted with freezer holds. Fisheries designation was SRTM—*Svedni Rybolovnyi Trauler Moroshechik* (medium-size fish trawler with freezer).

Designation: Soviet VTR type.

The Bulzuluk is one of the Mayak-class trawlers converted to refrigerated supply ships. Several sister ships serve in this role and as intelligence collection ships (see chapter 22). These ships are relatively small in comparison to Western naval store ships. (1980)

## 8 SUPPLY–SPACE SUPPORT SHIPS: "VYTEGRALES" CLASS

| Name | Name | Completed |
|---|---|---|
| APSHERON (ex-TOSNALES) | DONBASS (ex-KIRISHI) | |
| BASKUNCHAK (ex-VOSTOK-4) | SEVAN (ex-VYBORGLES) | 1964–1966 |
| DAURIYA (ex-SUZDAL) | TAMAN' (ex-VOSTOK-3) | |
| DIKSON (ex-VAGALES) | YAMAL (ex-SVIRLES) | |

| | |
|---|---|
| Builders: | Zhdanov Shipyard, Leningrad |
| Displacement: | 6,100 tons full load |
| Tonnage: | approx. 6,000 DWT |
| Length: | 402 ft 3 in (121.9 m) |
| Beam: | 55 ft 2 in (16.7 m) |
| Draft: | 23 ft 5 in (7.1 m) |
| Propulsion: | 1 diesel (B&W Bryansk); 5,200 bhp; 1 shaft |
| Speed: | 16 knots |
| Range: | 7,400 n.miles at 14.5 knots |
| Complement: | approx. 90 |

| | |
|---|---|
| Helicopters: | landing platform |
| Missiles: | none |
| Guns: | none |
| Radars: | 2 Don-2 (navigation) |
| | 1 Big Net (air search) in DONBASS |
| EW systems: | IFF only |

These are converted merchant timber carriers. They were originally converted to an SESS configuration with the addition of special communications and radar equipment plus a helicopter platform aft. Subsequently employed as fleet supply ships. Another six ships of this type were converted to civilian satellite tracking ships (under the aegis of the Soviet Academy of Sciences).

About 20 additional ships of this class remain is merchant service, some of which are fitted to carry containers.

Designation: Soviet VTR type.

The TAMAN' is one of eight VYTEGRALES- or VOSTOK-class timber carriers adopted for use as Space Event Support Ships (SESS) and subsequently employed as cargo ships. Details of the ships differ; the TAMAN' has a deckhouse of special equipment between her second mast and superstructure, and a Ka-25 Hormone rests on her helicopter platform.

The YAMAL (pennant number 201) while supporting Soviet spacecraft recovery operations in the Indian Ocean in 1982. She and some of her sister ships retain specialized missile-space support equipment. Note the helicopter control station, built-up deckhouse, and Ka-25 Hormone aft. (1982, Royal Australian Air Force)

## 9 CARGO SHIPS: "KEYLA" CLASS

| Name | Name | Name | Completed |
|------|------|------|-----------|
| MEZEN′ | RITSA | UNZHA | |
| ONEGA | TERIBERKA | USSURI | 1960–1966 |
| PONOY | TULOMA | YERUSLAN | |

| | |
|------|------|
| Builders: | (Hungary) |
| Displacement: | 2,400 tons full load |
| Tonnage: | 1,280 DWT |
| Length: | 260 ft (78.8 m) |
| Beam: | 34 ft 8 in (10.5 m) |
| Draft: | 15 ft 2 in (4.6 m) |
| Propulsion: | 1 diesel; 1,000 bhp; 1 shaft |
| Speed: | 11.4 knots |
| Range: | 3,000 n.miles at 11 knots |
| Complement: | approx. 25 |
| Helicopters: | no facilities |
| Missiles: | none |
| Guns: | none |
| Radars: | 1 Don-2 (navigation) or Spin Trough (search) |

Small cargo ships. The RITSA has special communications equipment installed.

Design: Cargo capacity is 1,100 tons.

Designation: Soviet VTR type.

## 4 CARGO SHIPS: "CHULYM" CLASS

| Name | Name | Completed |
|------|------|-----------|
| INSAR | LENINSK-KUZNETSKIY | |
| KAMCHATKA | SEVERODONETSK | 1953–1957 |

| | |
|------|------|
| Builders: | Warski Shipyard, Szczecin (Poland) |
| Displacement: | 4,600 tons full load |
| Tonnage: | 3,200 DWT |
| Length: | 312 ft 6 in (94.7 m) |
| Beam: | 44 ft 11 in (13.6 m) |
| Draft: | 19 ft 2 in (5.8 m) |
| Propulsion: | compound reciprocating with auxiliary turbine; 1,650 ihp; 1 shaft |
| Boilers: | 2 |
| Speed: | 11.5 knots |
| Range: | 8,500 n.miles at 11.5 knots |
| Complement: | approx. 40 |
| Helicopters: | no facilities |
| Missiles: | none |
| Guns: | none |
| Radars: | 1 Don-2 (navigation) |

These are small, amidships-superstructure cargo ships, among the few remaining from a class of 41 ships built at Szczecin. A few others are in Soviet merchant service, while others may remain in other communist merchant fleets.

Design: Cargo capacity 2,240 tons.

Designation: Soviet VTR type.

## 1 CARGO SHIP: "DONBASS" CLASS

| Name | Completed |
|------|-----------|
| SVIR | 1955 |

| | |
|------|------|
| Builders: | Warski Shipyard, Szczecin |
| Displacement: | 7,200 tons full load |
| Tonnage: | 4,865 DWT |
| Length: | 357 ft 3 in (108.2 m) |
| Beam: | 48 ft 2 in (14.6 m) |
| Draft: | 23 ft 9 in (7.2 m) |
| Propulsion: | compound reciprocating with low-pressure turbine; 2,300 ihp; 1 shaft |
| Boilers: | 2 |
| Speed: | 12 knots |
| Range: | 9,800 n.miles at 12 knots |
| Complement: | |
| Helicopters: | no facilities |
| Missiles: | none |
| Guns: | none |
| Radars: | 1 Neptune (navigation) |

The SVIR is the only ship of this large class in Soviet naval service. The DONBASS class were designed as colliers, with up to 50 serving as general (tramp) cargo ships in the Soviet merchant marine and several foreign merchant fleets. Three are in use by the Soviet Union as fish carriers.

Designation: Soviet VTR type.

Engineering: Originally a coal-burner; converted to oil.

## 3 CARGO SHIPS: "KOLOMNA" CLASS

| Name | Name | Name | Completed |
|------|------|------|-----------|
| KRASNOARMEYSK | MEGRA | SVANETIYA | 1952–1954 |

| | |
|------|------|
| Builders: | Neptun Shipyard, Rostock |
| Displacement: | 6,700 tons full load |
| Tonnage: | 4,355 DWT |
| Length: | 337 ft 11 in (102.4 m) |
| Beam: | 47 ft 6 in (14.4 m) |
| Draft: | 21 ft 9 in (6.6 m) |
| Propulsion: | 1 triple-expansion compound plus low-pressure turbine; 2,400 ihp; 1 shaft |
| Boilers: | 2 |
| Speed: | 14 knots |
| Range: | 6,900 n.miles at 13 knots |
| Complement: | approx. 45 |
| Helicopters: | none |
| Missiles: | none |
| Guns: | none |
| Radars: | 1 Neptune (navigation) |

These ships are former KOLOMNA-class merchant ships, some 30 of which were built by the Neptun yard. Another hull was completed as the Soviet research ship MIKHAIL LOMONOSOV, and six sister ships serve as the ATREK-class submarine tenders. The SVANETIYA is used for experimental work. The naval cargo ship KUZNETSK was discarded.

Design: The KOLOMNA configuration has an amidships superstructure with two cargo hatches forward and two aft, each pair served by kingpost cranes.

Designation: Soviet VTR type except SVANETIYA has OS designation.

The KOLOMNA-class cargo ship SVANETIYA (1982, U.S. Navy)

**3 CARGO SHIPS  
1 CABLE SHIP } "TELNOVSK" CLASS**

| Name | Name | Name | Completed |
|---|---|---|---|
| BUREVESTNIK | MANOMETER | KS 7 | } 1950s |
| LAG | | | |

| | |
|---|---|
| Builders: | Budapest (Hungary) |
| Displacement: | 1,700 tons full load |
| Tonnage: | 1,130 DWT |
| Length: | 231 ft (70.0 m) except KS 7 240 ft 11 in (73.0 m) |
| Beam: | 33 ft (10.0 m) |
| Draft: | 13 ft 10 in (4.2 m) |
| Propulsion: | 1 diesel (Karl Liebknecht); 800 bhp; 1 shaft |
| Speed: | 11 knots |
| Range: | 3,300 n.miles at 10 knots |
| Complement: | approx. 40 in cargo ships |
| Helicopters: | no facilities |
| Missiles: | none |
| Guns: | none |
| Radars: | |

**FEW CARGO SHIPS: KHABAROVSK CLASS**

| | |
|---|---|
| Completed: | 1950s |
| Builders: | (USSR) |
| Displacement: | 650 tons full load |
| Tonnage: | 400 DWT |
| Length: | 153 ft 2 in (46.4 m) |
| Beam: | 26 ft 4 in (8.0 m) |
| Draft: | 10 ft 11 in (3.3 m) |
| Propulsion: | 1 diesel; 600 bhp; 1 shaft |
| Speed: | 10 knots |
| Range: | 1,600 n.miles at 8 knots |
| Complement: | approx. 30 |
| Helicopters: | no facilities |
| Missiles: | none |
| Guns: | 2 14.5-mm machine guns (1 twin) in some ships |
| Radars: | 1 Neptune or Don (navigation) |

These are small, superstructure-aft cargo ships.

Small, superstructure-aft cargo ships with one ship modified to serve as a cable ship. About 100 ships of this type were built by the same yard with almost all being delivered to the USSR. (Many subsequently went to other nations.) Five other Soviet units are used as survey ships. The above ships are expected to be discarded in the near future.

Modification: The KS 7 has cable sheaves three meters long projecting from her bow and has other modifications to serve as a cable ship.

## SUBMARINE SUPPORT SHIPS

These ships are similar to Western submarine tenders and (British) depot ships. They provide specialized services to submarines in Soviet base areas, coastal waters, and on the high seas. However, the Soviet support ships of the Ugra and Don classes additionally provide extensive command-and-control capabilities and significant local self-defense.

In addition, the auxiliary ships of the EL'BRUS class, which appear to have the primary functions of submarine rescue and salvage, also may have some submarine support capabilities. (These ships are listed in this chapter under the heading Salvage and Rescue Ships.)

### 6 SUBMARINE SUPPORT SHIPS: UGRA CLASS

| Name | Name | Name | Completed |
|------|------|------|-----------|
| IVAN KOLYSHKIN | IVAN VAKHRAMEEV | VOLGA | 1963–1972 |
| IVAN KUCHERENKO | TOBOL | . . . . . . | |

| | |
|---|---|
| Builders: | Nikolayev |
| Displacement: | 6,750 tons standard |
| | 9,600 tons full load |
| Length: | 478 ft 6 in (145.0 m) |
| Beam: | 58 ft 5 in (17.7 m) |
| Draft: | 21 ft 2 in (6.4 m) |
| Propulsion: | 4 diesels; 8,000 bhp; 2 shafts |
| Speed: | 17 knots |
| Range: | 21,000 n.miles at 10 knots |
| Complement: | approx. 450 |
| Helicopters: | landing deck; hangar facilities for 1 Ka-25 Hormone-C in IVAN KOLYSHKIN |
| Missiles: | 2 quad SA-N-5 Grail launchers (16) being fitted to these ships |
| Guns: | 8 57-mm/80-cal AA (4 twin) |
| Radars: | 1 to 3 Don-2 (navigation) |
| | 2 Muff Cob (fire control) |
| | 1 Strut Curve (air search) |
| EW systems: | Watch Dog |

These are enlarged versions of the previous Don-class submarine support ships.

Class: One ship of this class was transferred to India in 1968; her armament and radars were changed before transfer, possibly to simplify logistics by the Indian Navy. Two other Soviet units are employed as training ships and are listed separately.

Design: These ships are larger than the previous Don class, with a larger forward superstructure and a shorter funnel. They are fitted with one 10-ton-capacity and two 6-ton-capacity cranes. Extensive modifications have changed the appearance of these ships from their original configuration and from each other. One ship has been fitted with a helicopter hangar; others have the after superstructure built up, and the VOLGA has a large after lattice mast topped by twin Vee Cone communication antennas (as found in the SVERDLOV cruiser command ships and some SESS).

These ships have extensive workshops and can provide submarines alongside with food, diesel fuel, fresh water, and torpedoes.

Designation: Soviet PB type.

IVAN KOLYSHKIN (1982)

The Ugra-class submarine tender IVAN KUCHERENKO. The ship has been fitted with a tall mast aft (to support Vee Cone satellite communication antennas) and a helicopter platform. The Ugra class is an improvement of the earlier Don design. (1982)

An Ugra-class submarine tender steaming off Puerto Rico during a cruise to the Caribbean in support of Soviet surface and submarine forces. She has a Muff Cob fire control radar on a short lattice mast aft and a second Muff Cob atop the bridge. (1971)

The Ivan Kolyshkin represents the third basic Ugra design, with a large helicopter hangar aft. (Courtesy *Flottes de Combat*)

---

**6 SUBMARINE SUPPORT SHIPS: DON CLASS**

| Name | Name | Completed |
|------|------|-----------|
| Dmitriy Galkin | Magadanskiy | |
| Fyodor Vidyaev | Komsomolets | 1958–1961 |
| Kamchatskiy | Magomed Gadziev | |
| Komsomolets | Viktor Kotel'nikov | |

| | |
|---|---|
| Builders: | Nikolayev |
| Displacement: | 6,730 tons standard |
| | approx. 9,000 tons full load |
| Length: | 461 ft 8 in (139.9 m) |
| Beam: | 58 ft 1 in (17.6 m) |
| Draft: | 17 ft 10 in (5.4 m) |
| Propulsion: | 4 diesels; 8,000 bhp; 2 shafts |
| Speed: | 17 knots |

| | |
|---|---|
| Range: | 21,000 n.miles at 10 knots |
| Complement: | approx. 450 |
| Helicopters: | landing deck in 2 ships |
| Missiles: | none |
| Guns: | 4 100-mm/56-cal DP (4 single); 2 guns in Viktor Kotel'nikov and none in Magadanskiy Komsomolets |
| | 8 57-mm/70-cal AA (4 twin) |
| | 8 25-mm/60-cal AA (4 twin) in Dmitriy Galkin and Fyodor Vidyaev |
| Radars: | 1 or 2 Don-2 (navigation) |
| | 2 Hawk Screech (fire control); none in Dmitriy Galkin and Fyodor Vidyaev |
| | 1 Slim Net (air search) |
| | 1 Sun Visor (fire control); deleted from Magadanskiy Komsomolets |
| EW systems: | Watch Dog |

The Don-class ships were the first modern Soviet submarine tenders comparable to their Western counterparts.

Class: An additional ship of this class was transferred to Indonesia in 1962.

Design: These are large submarine support ships and flagships. Details differ; the MAGADANSKIY KOMSOMOLETS was completed with a large helicopter platform and without 100-mm guns. The VIKTOR KOTEL'NIKOV had her after 100-mm guns replaced by a helicopter platform. At least two ships, the DMITRIY GALKIN and FYODOR VIDYAEV, have had Vee Cone antennas fitted to their after lattice masts.

They have a bow hook with a 100-ton lift capacity plus one 10-ton, two 5-ton, and two 1-ton cranes.

Designation: Soviet PB type.

A Tango-class diesel submarine is serviced by a Don-class tender. This is the "standard" Don configuration, with a "balanced" 100-mm and 57-mm gun arrangement, and a Slim Net long-range, air-search radar mounted on a tall lattice mast amidships. (1981)

The DMITRIY GALKIN, one of at least two Don-class tenders fitted with the Vee Cone antennas on an after lattice mast, with the Slim Net radar moved to a new lattice mast fitted forward in place of the original pole mast. The ships with 100-mm guns have a Wasp Head director above the bridge. (1980)

The VIKTOR KOTEL'NIKOV is one of two Don-class tenders fitted with a helicopter deck, in this ship relacing the two after 100-mm gun mounts.

## 6 SUBMARINE SUPPORT SHIPS: "ATREK" CLASS

| Name | Name | Name | Completed |
|------|------|------|-----------|
| ATREK | BAKHMUT | EVGENIY OSIPOV | |
| AYAT | DVINA | MURMAT | 1956–1957 |

| | |
|---|---|
| Builders: | Neptun Shipyard, Rostock (East Germany) |
| Displacement: | 3,413 tons standard |
| | 5,450 tons full load |
| Length: | 337 ft 11 in (102.4 m) |
| Beam: | 47 ft 6 in (14.4 m) |
| Draft: | 18 ft 2 in (5.5 m) |
| Propulsion: | 1 triple-expansion compound plus low-pressure turbine; 2,400 ihp; 1 shaft |
| Boilers: | 2 |
| Speed: | 14 knots |

| | |
|---|---|
| Range: | 6,900 n.miles at 13 knots |
| Complement: | |
| Helicopters: | none |
| Missiles: | none |
| Guns: | 6 37-mm/60-cal AA (3 twin) in some ships |
| Radars: | 1 Neptune (navigation) |

These ships were begun as civilian KOLOMNA merchant ships and completed as submarine tenders. Some 30 merchant ships of this type were built by the Neptun yard; another hull was completed as the Soviet research ship MIKHAIL LOMONOSOV, and three serve as naval cargo ships.

Design: The ships have two 5-ton-capacity cranes for handling torpedoes and supplies. The radar antenna is fitted to a small mast on the starboard side of the bridge.

Designation: Soviet PB type.

The ATREK-class submarine tender BAKHUMT riding at anchor in 1975. She and her sister ships were begun as merchant ships, but completed to this configuration to support submarines. Beyond their complement, they are reported to have temporary accommodations for up to 400 submarine crewmen. All later Soviet submarine tenders were built for that role.

## REPAIR SHIPS

### 21 REPAIR SHIPS: AMUR CLASS

| Name | Name | Name | Completed |
|------|------|------|-----------|
| PM 9 | PM 73 | PM 139 | |
| PM 34 | PM 75 | PM 140 | |
| PM 40 | PM 81 | PM 156 | |
| PM 49 | PM 82 | PM 161 | |
| PM 52 | PM 94 | PM 163 | 1969–1978 |
| PM 56 | PM 129 | PM 164 | 1981– |
| PM 64 | PM 138 | PM . . . | |

| | |
|------|------|
| Builders: | Warski Shipyard, Szczecin |
| Displacement: | 5,000 tons standard |
| | 6,500 tons full load |
| Length: | 401 ft 7 in (121.7 m) |
| Beam: | 56 ft (17.0 m) |
| Draft: | 18 ft 10 in (5.1 m) |
| Propulsion: | 2 diesels; 4,000 bhp; 1 shaft |
| Speed: | 12 knots |
| Range: | 13,200 n.miles at 8 knots |
| Complement: | approx. 220–300 |
| Helicopters: | no facilities |
| Missiles: | none |
| Guns: | none |
| Radars: | 1 Don-2 (navigation) |
| EW systems: | IFF only |

These are enlarged Oskol-class repair ships.

Design: They perform maintenance and repairs on surface ships and submarines. They have workshops and stock spare parts. Two 5-ton-capacity cranes are fitted. Increased complements in later ships.

Designation: Soviet PM type.

The PM 82 servicing a Foxtrot-class submarine in the Mediterranean (1980)

The Amur-class repair ship PM 138 at anchor

An Amur-class repair ship (1975)

## 12 REPAIR SHIPS: OSKOL I/II/III CLASSES

| Name | Name | Name | Completed |
|------|------|------|-----------|
| PM 20 | PM 28 | PM 148 | |
| PM 21 | PM 51 | PM 447 | 1964–1967 |
| PM 24 | PM 68 | PM . . . . | |
| PM 26 | PM 146 | PM . . . . | |

| | |
|---|---|
| Builders: | Warski Shipyard, Szczecin |
| Displacement: | 2,500 tons standard |
| | 3,000 tons full load |
| Length: | 301 ft 8 in (91.4 m) |
| Beam: | 40 ft 3 in (12.2 m) |
| Draft: | 13 ft 2 in (4.0 m) |
| Propulsion: | 2 diesels; 4,000 bhp; 1 shaft |
| Speed: | 12 knots |
| Range: | |
| Complement: | approx. 100 |
| Helicopters: | no facilities |
| Missiles: | none |
| Guns: | 2 57-mm/70-cal AA (1 twin) and 4 25-mm/60-cal AA (2 twin) in 1 ship |
| Radars: | 1 Don-2 (navigation) |
| EW systems: | IFF only |

These are small repair ships with limited capabilities. Each ship has one or two 3.4-ton-capacity cranes.

Design: Details differ—the last three ships being flush decked with higher bridges are known as Oskol III type. The Oskols differ from the Amurs by a deck structure forward and the absence of a crane aft.

Designation: Soviet PM type.

Guns: Only the PM 24 is armed (no fire control radar); known as Oskol II type.

Oskol-class repair ship PM 21

Oskol-class repair ship PM 26

---

**5 REPAIR SHIPS: DNEPR I/II CLASSES**

| Name | Name | Name | Completed |
|------|------|------|-----------|
| PM 17 | PM 30 | PM 135 | 1960–1964 |
| PM 22 | PM 130 | | |

| | |
|---|---|
| Builders: | Black Sea Shipyard, Nikolayev |
| Displacement: | 4,500 tons standard |
| | 5,300 tons full load |
| Length: | 373 ft 11 in (113.3 m) |
| Beam: | 54 ft 6 in (16.5 m) |
| Draft: | 14 ft 6 in (4.4 m) |
| Propulsion: | 1 diesel; 2,000 bhp; 1 shaft |
| Speed: | 11 knots |
| Range: | 6,000 n.miles at 8 knots |
| Complement: | approx. 420 |
| Helicopters: | no facilities |
| Missiles: | none |
| Guns: | none |
| Radars: | 1 Don or Don-2 (navigation) |
| EW systems: | IFF only |

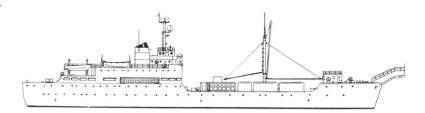

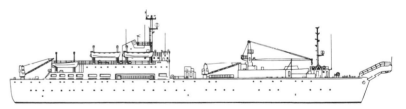

These repair ships have a distinctive, 150-ton-capacity bow hoist in addition to smaller cranes.

Design: Details and equipment varies. The last two ships are flush-decked (Dnepr II type).

Designation: Soviet PM type.

Guns: These ships are designed to be armed with a 57-mm AA twin gun mount.

Dnepr I- (top) and Dnepr II-class repair ships (Siegfried Breyer

## SALVAGE AND RESCUE SHIPS

In addition to the salvage ships listed below, the Navy operates a number of buoy and mooring tenders and lift ships that can be used for salvage operations.

### 1 + 1 SALVAGE AND RESCUE SHIPS: "EL'BRUS" CLASS

| Name | Completed |
|------|-----------|
| EL'BRUS | 1981 |
| . . . . . . | (1983) |

| | |
|------|-----------|
| Builders: | Northern Shipyard, Nikolayev |
| Displacement: | 15,000 + tons full load |
| Length: | |
| Beam: | |
| Draft: | |
| Propulsion: | diesel; 2 shafts |
| Speed: | |
| Range: | |
| Complement: | approx. 400 |
| Helicopters: | 1 or 2 Ka-25 Hormone-C |
| Missiles: | none |
| Guns: | none (see notes) |
| Radars: | |

The EL'BRUS-class ships are the world's largest submarine salvage and rescue ships, at least four times the displacement of the U.S. Navy's largest ships of this type, the PIGEON (ASR 21) and ORTOLAN (ASR 22). The EL'BRUS began her first deployment from the Black Sea into the Mediterranean in late December 1981.

Design: The EL'BRUS has a massive superstructure with a helicopter platform aft. There is a gantry-crane arrangement amidships for lowering submersibles over the side. A tall hangar is provided, with the "drawbridge" door forming a ramp down to the platform. The ships have extensive mooring, diving, and fire-fighting equipment.

At least two rescue submersibles are carried, apparently of the same type as carried aboard the India-class submarine. The EL'BRUS layout indicates that the submersibles are stowed and serviced inside hangars abaft the gantry cranes, in the outboard portion of the massive superstructure.

Designation: Soviet SS type.

Guns: The ship has provisions for mounting four 30-mm guns of either the twin-barrel or multi-barrel (Gatling) type.

Names: EL'BRUS is named for the highest peak in Europe, in the Caucasus Mountains.

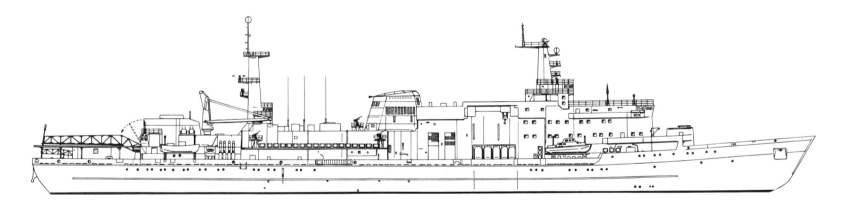

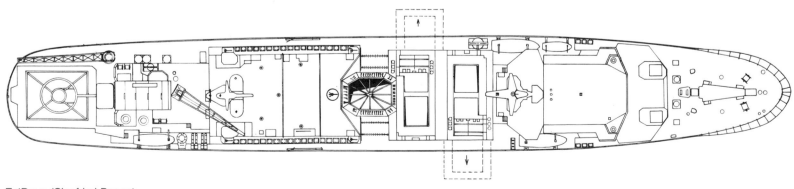

EL'BRUS (Siegfried Breyer)

The large salvage and rescue ship EL'BRUS under way in the North Atlantic. There are cranes between the bridge and funnel for handling submersibles over the side. There is a helicopter hangar and landing platform aft. (1982, U.S. Navy)

## 2 SALVAGE AND RESCUE SHIPS: "PIONER MOSKVYY" CLASS

| Name | Conversion Completed |
| --- | --- |
| GIORGIY KOZMIN | 1980 |
| MIKHAIL RUDNITSKIY | 1979 |

| | |
| --- | --- |
| Builders: | Vyborg |
| Displacement: | 10,700 tons full load |
| Length: | 430 ft (130.3 m) |
| Beam: | 57 ft 1 in (17.3 m) |
| Draft: | 24 ft 1 in (7.3 m) |
| Propulsion: | 1 diesel (B&W Bryansk); 6,100 bhp; 1 shaft |
| Speed: | 15.5 knots |
| Range: | 12,000 n.miles at 15.5 knots |

| | |
| --- | --- |
| Complement: | approx. 120 |
| Helicopters: | no facilities |
| Missiles: | none |
| Guns: | none |
| Radars: | 2 Don-2 (navigation) |

These are converted freight-container ships, more than 20 of which were built at Vyborg during the 1970s. The others are in Soviet merchant service, with 2 ships transferred to East Germany in 1979.

Design: Large, superstructure-aft ships, with two large kingposts and two 40-ton-capacity and two 20-ton-capacity booms.

Names: These ships are named for pioneers in submersible development.

PIONEER MOSKVYY-class salvage and rescue ship (1979)

PIONEER MOSKVYY-class salvage and rescue ship (1980)

**2 SALVAGE AND RESCUE SHIPS: INGUL CLASS**

| Name | Completed |
|------|-----------|
| MASHUK | 1974 |
| PAMIR | 1975 |

| | |
|---|---|
| Builders: | Admiralty Shipyard, Leningrad |
| Displacement: | 3,200 tons standard |
| | 4,050 tons full load |
| Length: | 305 ft 11 in (92.7 m) |
| Beam: | 50 ft 10 in (15.4 m) |
| Draft: | 19 ft 2 in (5.8 m) |
| Propulsion: | 2 diesels (58D-4R); 9,000 bhp; 2 shafts |
| Speed: | 20 knots |
| Range: | 9,000 n.miles at 19 knots |
| Complement: | approx. 120 |
| Helicopters: | no facilities |
| Missiles: | none |
| Guns: | none (see notes) |
| Radars: | 2 Don-2 (navigation) |
| EW systems: | IFF only |

Salvage tug PAMIR

These are powerful salvage tugs, fitted with submarine rescue, diving, salvage, and fire-fighting equipment. Two sister ships serve in the Soviet merchant fleet. These ships should not be confused with two (smaller) intelligence collection ships of the PAMIR class or the KLAZMA-class cable ship INGUL.

Design. The hull has a bulbous bow with thrusters fitted for precise maneuvering. Note the high horsepower of these ships.

Designation:  Soviet SS type.

Guns:  These ships have provisions for mounting one 57-mm AA twin gun amount and two 25-mm AA twin gun mounts.

Salvage tug PAMIR

## 1 SUBMARINE SALVAGE AND RESCUE SHIP: NEPA CLASS

| Name | Completed |
|------|-----------|
| KARPATY | 1968 |

| | |
|------|------|
| Builders: | Nikolayev |
| Displacement: | 9,800 tons full load |
| Length: | 427 ft 4 in (129.5 m) |
| Beam: | 63 ft 4 in (19.2 m) |
| Draft: | 21 ft 1 in (6.4 m) |
| Propulsion: | 2 or 4 diesels; 8,000 bhp; 2 shafts |
| Speed: | 16 knots |
| Range: | 8,000 n.miles at 14 knots |
| Complement: | approx. 270 |
| Helicopters: | no facilities |
| Missiles: | none |
| Guns: | none |
| Radars: | 2 Don-2 (navigation) |
| EW systems: | IFF only |

The KARPATY is a large, one-of-a kind submarine salvage and rescue ship. She has a 600-ton lift device mounted on the stern plus submarine rescue, fire-fighting, diving, and salvage equipment.

Designation: Soviet SS type.

Submarine rescue and salvage ship KARPATY. Diving bells are stowed on either side of the kingpost, and mooring buoys are stowed on deck below the kingpost. There is a large stern hoist for lifting submarines.

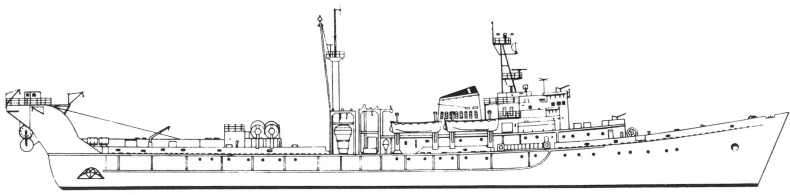

KARPATY (Siegfried Breyer)

## 9 SUBMARINE SALVAGE AND RESCUE SHIPS: PRUT CLASS

| Name | Name | Name | Completed |
|------|------|------|-----------|
| ALTAY | ZHIGULI | SS 26 | |
| BESHTAU | SS 21 | SS 44 | 1961–1968 |
| VLADIMIR TREFOLEV | SS 23 | SS 83 | |

| | |
|------|------|
| Builders: | Nikolayev |
| Displacement: | 3,300 tons full load |
| Length: | 297 ft 8 in (90.2 m) |
| Beam: | 47 ft 2 in (14.3 m) |
| Draft: | 18 ft 2 in (5.5 m) |
| Propulsion: | 4 diesels; 8,000 bhp; 2 shafts |
| Speed: | 20 knots |
| Range: | 10,000 n.miles at 16 knots |
| Complement: | approx. 120 |
| Helicopters: | no facilities |
| Missiles: | none |
| Guns: | none (see notes) |
| Radars: | 1 or 2 Don-2 or Don |

These are large tug-type ships fitted for submarine rescue and diving operations.

Designation: Soviet SS type.

Guns: These ships have provisions for a single 57-mm AA quad mounting and Muff Cob radar; one ship was armed in this manner.

The Prut-class submarine rescue ship BESHTAU, similar in design to the U.S. Navy's older ASR-type ships. This class has diving bells on the port and starboard side forward of the second mast and mooring buoys behind the mast. The ships are fitted for diving, salvage, submarine rescue, and towing operations.

Prut-class submarine rescue ship

## 2 SALVAGE TUGS: "PAMIR" CLASS

| Name | Completed |
|------|-----------|
| AGATAN | 1958 |
| ALDAN | 1958 |

| | |
|--|--|
| Builders: | Gavle (Sweden) |
| Displacement: | 2,030 tons full load |
| Length: | 257 ft 5 in (78.0 m) |
| Beam: | 42 ft 3 in (12.8 m) |
| Draft: | 13 ft 6 in (4.1 m) |
| Propulsion: | 2 diesels (M.A.N. G10V); 4,200 bhp; 2 shafts |
| Speed: | 17.5 knots |
| Range: | 15,200 n.miles at 17.5 knots |
| Complement: | |
| Helicopters: | no facilities |
| Missiles: | none |
| Guns: | none |
| Radars: | 1 or 2 Don-2 and/or Don (navigation) |

These tugs are fitted for diving, salvage, and fire-fighting. Two sister ships serve as intelligence collectors (AGI). Note their very long range.

Design: Salvage features include fire-fighting equipment, diver support gear, decompression chambers, and air compressors. Fitted with one 10-ton-capacity and two 1½-ton-capacity booms.

Designation: Soviet SS type.

Pamir-class salvage tug off the coast of California. This particular unit, at the time named Arban, was later converted to an AGI configuration and renamed Peleng. (1965, U.S. Navy)

---

### 13 SUBMARINE RESCUE SHIPS: CONVERTED T-58 MINESWEEPERS

| Name | Name | Name | Completed |
|------|------|------|-----------|
| Gidrolog | SS 30 | SS 50 | |
| Kazbek | SS 35 | SS 53 | late 1950s |
| Khibiny | SS 40 | SS . . . | |
| Valday | SS 47 | | |
| Zangezur | SS 48 | | |

| | |
|---|---|
| Builders: | Khabarovsk Leningrad |
| Displacement: | 930 tons full load |
| Length: | 236 ft 7 in (71.7 m) |
| Beam: | 31 ft 8 in (9.6 m) |
| Draft: | 8 ft 11 in (2.7 m) |
| Propulsion: | 2 diesels; 4,000 bhp; 2 shafts |
| Speed: | 17 knots |
| Range: | 2,500 n.miles at 12 knots |
| Complement: | approx. 60 |
| Helicopters: | no facilities |
| Missiles: | none |
| Guns: | none (see notes) |
| Radars: | 1 Don-2 (navigation) |
| | 1 Spin Trough (search) |
| Sonars: | Tamir high-frequency |
| EW systems: | Dead Duck |

These ships were modified while under construction and completed as submarine rescue ships with a rescue chamber fitted on the port side. Also fitted with diving equipment.

Class:  One ship of this type was transferred to India (1971). No ships of this class remain in the minesweeping role.

Designation:  Soviet SS type.

Guns:  In the minesweeping configuration two 57-mm AA twin mounts were fitted with Ball End or Muff Cob radars. It is believed that the rescue ships have never carried armament.

The T-58-class submarine rescue ship SS 40. She has a diving bell on the port side amidships and a heavy-lift system aft. (1978)

The heavy-lift system of a T-58 rescue ship; a one-man diving chamber is under the lift. (1978)

## 3 SALVAGE TUGS: "OREL" CLASS

| Name | Name | Name | Completed |
|------|------|------|-----------|
| SB 43 | . . . . . . | . . . . . . | late 1950s |

| | |
|---|---|
| Builders: | Valmet Shipyard, Turku (Finland) |
| Displacement: | 1,200 tons standard |
| | 1,760 tons full load |
| Length: | 202 ft 3 in (61.3 m) |
| Beam: | 39 ft 3 in (11.9 m) |
| Draft: | 14 ft 10 in (4.5 m) |
| Propulsion: | 1 diesel (M.A.N. G5Z52/70); 1,700 bhp; 1 shaft |
| Speed: | 15 knots |
| Range: | 14,000 n.miles at 13.5 knots |
| Complement: | approx. 35 |
| Helicopters: | no facilities |
| Missiles: | none |
| Guns: | none |
| Radars: | 1 Don-2 or Don (navigation) |

The OREL class consisted of about 25 large tugs built in Turku for the Soviet Navy and fishing fleet. Several naval units have been discarded. They are fitted for salvage.

Designation: Soviet SB type.

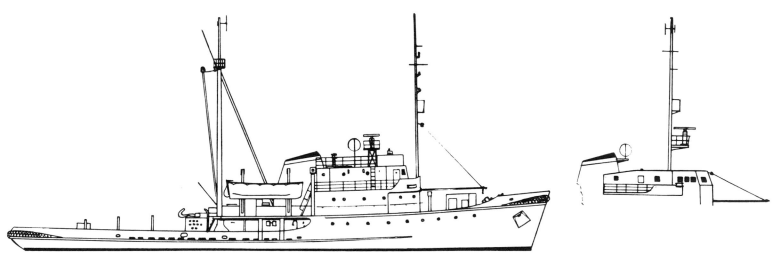

OREL-class salvage tug; inset shows bridge variation. (Siegfied Breyer)

## BUOY AND MOORING TENDERS AND LIFT SHIPS

These ships plant and maintain navigation buoys and undertake salvage tasks. The Soviet Navy's hydrographic survey ships listed in chapter 22 also plant and maintain navigation buoys.

### 10 MOORING TENDERS: SURA CLASS

| Name | Name | Name | Completed |
|------|------|------|-----------|
| KIL 1 | KIL 23 | KIL 32 | |
| KIL 2 | KIL 27 | KIL 33 | 1965–1972 |
| KIL 21 | KIL 29 | | |
| KIL 22 | KIL 31 | | |

| | |
|---|---|
| Builders: | Neptun Shipyard, Rostock |
| Displacement: | 2,370 tons standard |
| | 3,150 tons full load |
| Length: | 287 ft 2 in (87.0 m) |
| Beam: | 48 ft 10 in (14.8 m) |
| Draft: | 16 ft 6 in (5.0 m) |
| Propulsion: | DE: 4 diesels (Karl Liebknecht); 2,240 bhp; 4 generators connected to 2 electric motors; 2 shafts |
| Speed: | 12.5 knots |
| Range: | 2,000 n.miles at 10.5 knots |
| Complement: | |
| Helicopters: | no facilities |
| Missiles: | none |
| Guns: | none |
| Radars: | 2 Don-2 (navigation) |

These ships are employed as buoy tenders and salvage ships. Several additional ships of this type are operated by the Soviet merchant fleet.

Design: Propulsion machinery is forward in these ships, hence the use of the diesel-electric plant to alleviate the need for very long propeller shafts. Stern winch/lift gear is rated at 60-ton capacity. A smaller crane and boom are fitted amidships. Cargo capacity is 890 tons. In addition, the ships have a very large fuel capacity for transfer to other ships.

Designation: Soviet KIL type.

Mooring tender-lift ship KIL 22 during operations in the Caribbean area. (1970, U.S. Navy)

### 14 MOORING TENDERS: NEPTUN CLASS

| Name | Name | Name | Completed |
|------|------|------|-----------|
| KIL 3 | KIL 14 | KIL . . . | |
| KIL 5 | KIL 15 | KIL . . . | |
| KIL 6 | KIL 16 | KIL . . . | 1957–1960 |
| KIL 9 | KIL 17 | KIL . . . | |
| KIL 12 | KIL 18 | | |

| | |
|---|---|
| Builders: | Neptun Shipyard, Rostock |
| Displacement: | 700 tons standard |
| | 1,240 tons full load |
| Length: | 189 ft 1 in (57.3 m) |
| Beam: | 37 ft 8 in (11.4 m) |
| Draft: | 11 ft 3 in (3.4 m) |
| Propulsion: | 2 triple-expansion reciprocating; 1,000 ihp; 2 shafts |
| Boilers: | 2 |
| Speed: | 12 knots |
| Range: | 1,000 n.miles at 11 knots |
| Complement: | approx. 40 |
| Helicopters: | no facilities |
| Missiles: | none |
| Guns: | none |
| Radars: | |

These are small mooring tenders. They have an 80-ton-capacity bow lift for handling buoys and for salvage operations. All originally were coal burners; some have been converted to oil.

Designation: Soviet KIL type.

Sura-class mooring tender KIL 22

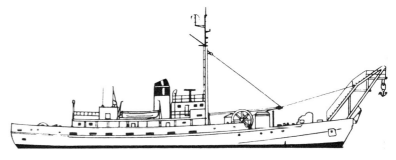

Neptun-class mooring tender (Siegfried Breyer)

## OCEANGOING TUGS

In addition to the tugs listed below, several tugs specially fitted for salvage and fire-fighting are listed under Salvage and Rescue Ships.

Goryn-class oceangoing tug in the Pacific with pendant No. MB 105 (1982, U.S. Navy)

### 4 OCEANGOING TUGS: GORYN CLASS

| Name | Name | Name | Completed |
|------|------|------|-----------|
| Baykalsk Berezinsk | Bilbino | Bolshevetsk | }1977–1978 |

| | |
|---|---|
| Builders: | Rauma-Repola, Rauma |
| Displacement: | approx. 2,600 tons full load |
| Length: | 209 ft 6 in (63.5 m) |
| Beam: | 47 ft 2 in (14.3 m) |
| Draft: | 16 ft 10 in (5.1 m) |
| Propulsion: | 1 diesel (67N); 3,500 bhp; 1 shaft |
| Speed: | 14.5 knots |
| Range: | |
| Complement: | |
| Missiles: | none |
| Guns: | none |
| Radars: | 1 Don-2 (navigation) |

These are oceangoing tugs with a salvage and fire-fighting capability.
Designation: Soviet MB type.

Oceangoing tug MB 105 (1981)

### 12 OCEANGOING TUGS AND PATROL CRAFT: SORUM CLASS

| Name | Name | Name | Completed |
|------|------|------|-----------|
| Amur | Primor'ye | MB 119 | |
| Brest | Sakhalin | MB . . . | }1973–1977 |
| Kamchatka | MB 105 | MB . . . | |
| Primorsk | MB 115 | MB . . . | |

| | |
|---|---|
| Builders: | (USSR) |
| Displacement: | 1,210 tons standard |
| | 1,655 tons full load |
| Length: | 192 ft 4 in (58.3 m) |
| Beam: | 41 ft 7 in (12.6 m) |
| Draft: | 15 ft 2 in (4.6 m) |
| Propulsion: | DE: 2 diesels (5-2D42); 1,500 bhp; 1 shaft |
| Speed: | 14 knots |
| Range: | 6,700 n.miles at 13 knots |
| Complement: | approx. 35 |
| Missiles: | none |
| Guns: | 4 30-mm/65-cal close-in (2 twin) in ships operated by KGB |
| Radars: | 2 Don-2 (navigation) |
| EW systems: | IFF only |

Several of these tugs are operated by the KGB Maritime Border Troops as patrol craft. Those units have had side-by-side 30-mm twin mounts installed forward of the bridge. Tugs of this class are also operated by the Soviet merchant fleet.

Designation: Naval units are designated MB; those operated by KGB are PSKR.

An armed Sorum-class patrol craft, pendant No. 599, operated by the KGB Maritime Border Troops.

Closeup of a civilian Sorum-class oceangoing tug with twin water cannon mounted. Note the unoccupied twin gun positions forward of the bridge.

Civilian Sorum-class oceangoing tug

## 8 + SEAGOING FIRE TUGS: KATUN I/II CLASSES

| Name | Name | Name | Completed |
|------|------|------|-----------|
| PZHS 64 | PZHS 124 | PZHS . . . | |
| PZHS 96 | PZHS 209 | PZHS . . . | 1969– |
| PZHS 123 | PZHS 282 | PZHS . . . | |

| | |
|---|---|
| Builders: | Middle Neva Shipyard, Kilpino |
| Displacement: | 1,016 tons standard |
| Length: | *Katun I*  206 ft 7 in (62.6 m) |
| | *Katun II*  216 ft 6 in (65.6 m) |
| Beam: | 33 ft 8 in (10.2 m) |
| Draft: | 11 ft 11 in (3.6 m) |
| Propulsion: | 2 diesels (40DM); 4,000 bhp; 2 shafts |
| Speed: | 17 knots |
| Range: | 2,200 n.miles at 16 knots |
| Complement: | approx. 30 |
| Helicopters: | no facilities |
| Missiles: | none |
| Guns: | none |
| Radars: | 1 Don-2 (navigation) |
| EW systems: | IFF only |

These ships are ocean-going fire-fighting and decontamination tugs. The Admiralty yard has built additional ships for civilian use.

Design: The later ships are slightly longer and have an additional bridge level; they are Katun II.

Designation: Original Soviet PDS type (fire-fighting and decontamination ship); subsequently changed to PZHS (fire-fighting ship).

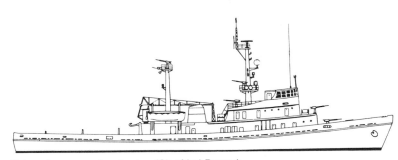

Katun-class seagoing fire tug (Siegfried Breyer)

## ~55 OCEANGOING TUGS AND PATROL CRAFT: OKHTENSKIY CLASS

| | |
|---|---|
| Completed: | late 1950s and 1960s |
| Builders: | Okhtenskiy |
| Displacement: | 700 tons standard |
| | 925 tons full load |
| Length: | 156 ft 1 in (47.3 m) |
| Beam: | 43 ft (10.3 m) |
| Draft: | 18 ft 2 in (5.5 m) |
| Propulsion: | 2 diesels; 1,500 bhp; 1 shaft |
| Speed: | 13 knots |
| Range: | 5,800 n.miles at 13 knots |
| Complement: | approx. 35 |
| Missiles: | none |
| Guns: | 2 57-mm/70-cal AA (1 twin) in ships operated by KGB |
| Radars: | 1 Don-2 (navigation) or Spin Trough (search) |
| EW systems: | IFF only |

Some of these tugs are specially configured for ocean-rescue operations and a few (armed) units are employed by the KGB Maritime Border Troops in the patrol role.

Designation: Naval units are MB with those used for ocean rescue SB; the KGB-operated units are PSKR.

Names: The Soviet class name is SIL'NYY.

OKHTENSKIY-class oceangoing tug SB 5 (indicating the tug is assigned to ocean rescue duties). (1981, Royal Air Force)

### ~10 OCEANGOING TUGS: ZENIT CLASS

| | |
|---|---|
| Completed: | 1948–1955 |
| Builders: | (Finland) |
| Displacement: | 800 tons full load |
| Length: | 158 ft 1 in (47.9 m) |
| Beam: | 33 ft (10.0 m) |
| Draft: | 14 ft 2 in (4.3 m) |
| Propulsion: | reciprocating; 800 ihp; 2 shafts |
| Boilers: | 2 |
| Speed: | 10 knots |
| Range: | 10,000 n.miles at 8 knots |
| Complement: | |
| Missiles: | none |
| Guns: | none |
| Radars: | |

More than 100 tugs of this type were built as war reparations for the USSR. The surviving naval units will probably be phased out in the near future.

### ~15 OCEANGOING TUGS: ROSLAVL CLASS

| | |
|---|---|
| Completed: | 1950s |
| Builders: | Galatz, Romania |
| Displacement: | 750 tons full load |
| Length: | 146 ft 10 in (44.5 m) |
| Beam: | 31 ft 4 in (9.5 m) |
| Draft: | 11 ft 3 in (3.4 m) |
| Propulsion: | DE: 2 diesels; 1,200 bhp; 2 shafts |
| Speed: | 12 knots |
| Range: | 6,000 n.miles at 11 knots |
| Complement: | approx. 28 |
| Missiles: | none |
| Guns: | none |
| Radars: | |

These are MB-series oceangoing tugs.

OKHENTSKIY-class oceangoing tug SERLETEY (19˙

Roslavl-class tug SB 11 (U.S. Navy, 1982)

## CABLE SHIPS

These ships lay and tend underwater cables for communications purposes and support Soviet sea-floor hydrophone arrays. They are supplemented in these roles by several civilian-operated cable ships (see chapter 22).

In addition to the ships listed below, the cable ship KS 7 is described under the heading Cargo and Store Ships.

### 3 CABLE SHIPS: "EMBA" CLASS

| Name | Completed |
| --- | --- |
| EMBA | 1980 |
| NEPRYADVA | 1981 |
| SETUN | 1981 |

| | |
| --- | --- |
| Builders: | Wärtsilä Shipyard, Turku |
| Displacement: | 2,050 tons full load |
| Length: | 250 ft 6 in (75.9 m) |
| Beam: | 41 ft 7 in (12.6 m) |
| Draft: | 10 ft (3.0 m) |
| Propulsion: | 2 diesels (Wärtsilä Vasa 6R22); 1,360 bhp; 1 shaft |
| Speed: | 11 knots |
| Range: | |
| Complement: | 38 |
| Helicopters: | no facilities |
| Missiles: | none |
| Guns: | none |
| Radars: | |

These are coastal cable ships.

Designation: Soviet KS type.

Engineering: Fitted with two propeller pods on the rudder and a bow-thruster for precise station keeping.

### 8 CABLE SHIPS: KLAZMA CLASS

| Name | Completed |
| --- | --- |
| DONETS | 1969 |
| INGUL | 1962 |
| INGURI | 1978 |
| KATYN | 1973 |
| TAVDA | 1977 |
| TSNA | 1968 |
| YANA | 1963 |
| ZEYA | 1970 |

| | |
| --- | --- |
| Builders: | Wärtsilä Shipyard, Turku |
| Displacement: | 6,920 tons full load except INGUL and YANA 6,810 tons and KATYN 7,885 tons |
| Length: | 430 ft 4 in (130.4 m) |
| Beam: | 52 ft 10 in (16.0 m) |
| Draft: | 17 ft 2 in (5.2 m) |
| Propulsion: | DE: 5 diesels (Wärtsilä 624TS); 4,950 bhp; driving 5 generators connected to 2 electric motors; 2 shafts (see notes) |
| Speed: | 16 knots |
| Range: | 10,000 n.miles at 14 knots |
| Complement: | approx. 110 |
| Helicopters: | no facilities |
| Missiles: | none |
| Guns: | none |
| Radars: | |

These are large cable ships, fitted with British-built cable equipment. Details vary.

Designation: Soviet KS type.

Engineering: The first two ships completed, INGUL and YANA, have four 2,436-bhp diesels (they also have a longer forecastle). A 550-hp active rudder and 650-hp bow-thruster are fitted for precise station keeping while handling cables.

Klazma-class cable ship TAVDA

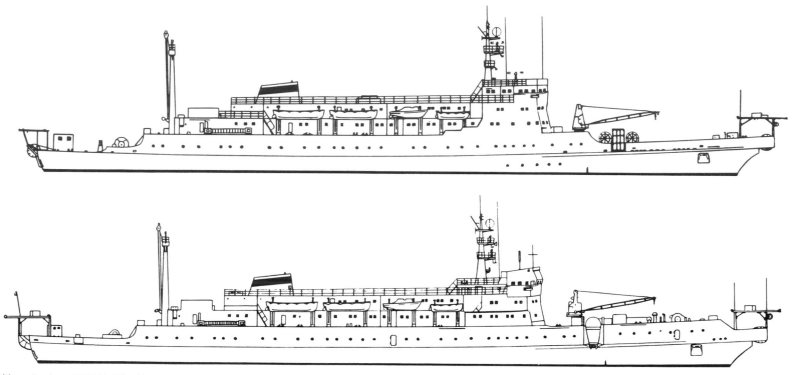

Yana (top) and TSNA (Siegfried Breyer)

Bow of Zeya, showing sheaves for handling cables over bow (1975)

## DEGAUSSING/DEPERMING SHIPS

### 1 + DEGAUSSING SHIPS: PELYM CLASS

| Name | Name | Completed |
|------|------|-----------|
| SR 409 | . . . . . .(?) | 1972– |

| | |
|---|---|
| Builders: | |
| Displacement: | 1,300 tons full load |
| Length: | 216 ft 2 in (65.5 m) |
| Beam: | 38 ft 3 in (11.6 m) |
| Draft: | 11 ft 3 in (3.4 m) |
| Propulsion: | 2 diesels; 2 shafts |
| Speed: | 16 knots |
| Range: | 4,500 n.miles at 12 knots |
| Complement: | |
| Helicopters: | no facilities |
| Missiles: | none |
| Guns: | none |
| Radars: | |

These are small, specialized degaussing/deperming ships.
Designation: Soviet SR type.

### SEVERAL DEGAUSSING SHIPS: SEKSTAN CLASS

| | |
|---|---|
| Completed: | 1950s |
| Builders: | (Finland) |
| Displacement: | 280 tons standard |
| | 400 tons full load |
| Length: | 135 ft 4 in (41.0 m) |
| Beam: | 30 ft 8 in (9.3 m) |
| Draft: | 13 ft 10 in (4.2 m) |
| Propulsion: | 1 diesel; 400 bhp; 1 shaft |
| Speed: | 10.5 knots |
| Range: | 1,200 n.miles at 10.5 knots |
| Complement: | approx. 25 |
| Helicopters: | no facilities |
| Missiles: | none |
| Guns: | none |
| Radars: | |

These are small, wooden-hulled cargo ships modified for the degaussing role. Others were modified for survey activities.
Designation: Soviet SR type.

### "FEW" DEGAUSSING SHIPS: KHABAROVSK CLASS

| | |
|---|---|
| Completed: | 1950s |
| Builders: | (USSR) |
| Displacement: | approx. 600 tons full load |
| Length: | 153 ft 2 in (46.4 m) |
| Beam: | 26 ft 4 in (8.0 m) |
| Draft: | 10 ft 11 in (3.3 m) |
| Propulsion: | 1 diesel; 600 bhp; 1 shaft |
| Speed: | 10 knots |
| Range: | 1,600 n.miles at 8 knots |
| Complement: | |
| Helicopters: | no facilities |
| Missiles: | none |
| Guns: | none |
| Radars: | |

One or more of these small cargo ships remain in use as degaussing
ships. There is a large deckhouse over the forward hold area.

## ELECTRIC GENERATOR SHIPS

### 4 ELECTRIC GENERATOR SHIPS: TOMBA CLASS

| Name | Name | Name | Completed |
|------|------|------|-----------|
| ENS 244 | ENS 348 | ENS 357 | 1974–1976 |
| ENS 254 | | | |

| | |
|---|---|
| Builders: | Warski Shipyard, Szczecin |
| Displacement: | approx. 4,000 tons standard |
| | 5,800 tons full load |
| Length: | 353 ft 1 in (107.0 m) |
| Beam: | 56 ft 1 in (17.0 m) |
| Draft: | 16 ft 6 in (5.0 m) |
| Propulsion: | 1 diesel; 4,500 bhp; 1 shaft |
| Speed: | 14 knots |
| Range: | 7,000 n.miles at 12 knots |
| Complement: | approx. 50 |
| Helicopters: | no facilities |
| Missiles: | none |
| Guns: | none |
| Radars: | 1 Don-2 (navigation) |
| EW systems: | IFF only |

These ships provide electric power in remote areas.
Designation: Soviet ENS type.

Electric generating ship ENS 244

## ICEBREAKERS

The KGB Maritime Border Troops are estimated to operate seven ice-breakers, and the Soviet Navy is believed to have eight similar ships, seven listed here as support icebreakers and one polar research ship (see chapter 22). The Soviet Union's nuclear icebreakers and additional conventional icebreakers are civilian operated (see chapter 23).

### 7 PATROL ICEBREAKERS: "IVAN SUSANIN" CLASS

| Name | Name | Completed |
|------|------|-----------|
| AYSBERG | NEVA | |
| DUNAY | RUSLAN | 1974–(?) |
| IMENI XXV SEZDA K.P.S.S. | . . . . . . | |
| IVAN SUSANIN | | |

| | |
|---|---|
| Builders: | Admiralty Shipyard, Leningrad |
| Displacement: | 3,800 tons full load |
| Length: | 231 ft (70.0 m) |
| Beam: | 60 ft 5 in (18.3 m) |
| Draft: | 21 ft 2 in (6.4 m) |
| Propulsion: | DE: 3 diesels (13D100) driving 3 generators connected to electric motors; 5,400 bhp; 3 shafts (1 forward) |
| Speed: | 14.5 knots |
| Range: | 5,500 n.miles at 12.5 knots |
| | 13,000 n.miles at 9.5 knots |
| Complement: | approx. 140 |
| Helicopters: | landing deck |
| Missiles: | positions for SA-7 Grail launcher in DUNAY and NEVA |
| Guns: | 2 76.2-mm/60-cal AA (1 twin) |
| | 2 30-mm close-in (2 multibarrel) |
| Radars: | 2 Don Kay (navigation) |
| | 1 Owl Screech (fire control) |
| | 1 Strut Curve (search) |
| EW systems: | IFF only |

All of these ships appear to be operated by the KGB as patrol ships along the Arctic and Northern Pacific coasts. Ships of a similar class are operated by the Navy (see below) and by the merchant fleet, with one ship modified for polar research (see chapter 23).

Designation: Soviet PSKR type.

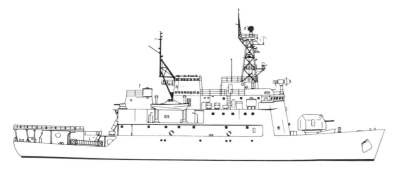

IVAN SUSANIN-class icebreaker (Siegfried Breyer)

A closeup of the IVAN SUSANIN's superstructure showing the back of the Owl Screech radar (above the bridge), the Strut Curve radar atop the lattice mast, and two Don Kay navigation radars stepped on the mast. There are two optical directors for the 30-mm Gatling guns on the small deckhouse aft of the funnel.

Stern view of AYSBERG, showing helicopter platform, control station, and two 30-mm Gatling guns.

Bow view of the IVAN SUSANIN, showing the twin 76.2-mm gun mount and—above the bridge—the Owl Screech fire control radar.

## 7 SUPPORT ICEBREAKERS: "DOBRYNYA NIKITICH" CLASS

| Name | Name | Completed |
|---|---|---|
| BURAN | PURGA | |
| DOBRYNYA NIKITICH | SADKA | 1959–1974 |
| IL'YA MUROMETS | VYUGA | |
| PERSEVET | | |

| | |
|---|---|
| Builders: | Admiralty Shipyard, Leningrad |
| Displacement: | 3,800 tons full load |
| Length: | 231 ft (70.0 m) |
| Beam: | 60 ft 5 in (18.3 m) |
| Draft: | 21 ft 2 in (6.4 m) |
| Propulsion: | DE: 3 diesels (13D100) driving 3 generators connected to electric motors; 5,400 bhp; 3 shafts (1 forward) |
| Speed: | 14.5 knots |
| Range: | 5,500 n.miles at 12.5 knots |
| | 13,000 n.miles at 9.5 knots |
| Complement: | approx. 100 |
| Helicopters: | no facilities |
| Missiles: | none |
| Guns: | 2 57-mm/70-cal AA (1 twin) in 4 ships |
| | 2 25-mm/60-cal AA (1 twin) in 4 ships |
| Radars: | 1 or 2 Don-2 (navigation) |
| EW systems: | IFF only |

These are Navy-manned icebreakers; at least four ships are armed. The Navy units can be distinguished from the similar KGB-operated IVAN SUSANIN class by their smaller superstructure, absence of 76.2-mm turret forward, and open fantail (KGB ships have helicopter platform).

Designation: Soviet LDK type.

DOBRYNYA NIKITICH-class icebreaker IL'YA MUROMETS is named for a Russian folk hero. The name was given to the world's first four-engine bombers, built in Russia by Igor Sikorsky and used extensively by the Russians in World War I. (1973)

## TRANSPORTS

### 1 TRANSPORT: "MIKHAIL KALININ" CLASS

| Name | Completed |
|---|---|
| KUBAN (ex-NADEZHDA KRUPSKAYA) | 1963 |

| | |
|---|---|
| Builders: | Mathias Thesen Shipyard, Wismar (East Germany) |
| Displacement: | 6,380 tons full load |
| Tonnage: | 1,355 DWT |
| Length: | 403 ft 3 in (122.2 m) |
| Beam: | 52 ft 10 in (16.0 m) |
| Draft: | 17 ft 6 in (5.3 m) |
| Propulsion: | 2 diesels (M.A.N.); 8,000 bhp; 2 shafts |
| Speed: | 18 knots |
| Range: | 8,100 n.miles at 17 knots |
| Complement: | |
| Troops: | 340 |
| Helicopters: | no facilities |
| Missiles: | none |
| Guns: | none |
| Radars: | 2 Don-2 (navigation) |

The KUBAN was transferred to the Navy in 1976 (renamed) for use as a transport to support naval forces in the Mediterranean. Another 18 ships are in Soviet merchant service. (Twenty-four ships were ordered but five were not built.)

Design: Cargo capacity is 1,000 tons.

Designation: Soviet VTR type.

## HOSPITAL SHIPS

### 2 HOSPITAL SHIPS: "OB'" CLASS

| Name | Completed |
|---|---|
| OB' | 1980 |
| YENISEY | 1981 |

| | |
|---|---|
| Builders: | Warski Shipyard, Szczecin |
| Displacement: | 11,000 tons full load |
| Length: | 508 ft 2 in (154.0 m) |
| Beam: | 67 ft 8 in (20.5 m) |
| Draft: | 17 ft 2 in (5.2 m) |
| Propulsion: | 2 diesels; 2 shafts |
| Speed: | 20 knots |
| Range: | |
| Complement: | approx. 80 + 200 medical staff |
| Helicopters: | 1 Ka-25 Hormone-C |
| Missiles: | none |
| Guns: | none |
| Radars: | 3 Don-2 (navigation) |

These ships are civilian manned but carry naval medical personnel. The commanding officers are believed to be Navy captains 3rd rank, and the medical personnel are commanded by lieutenant colonels of the Naval Medical Service. The OB' is assigned to the Pacific Fleet and the YENISEY to the Black Sea Fleet.

Design: These are believed to be the world's first built-for-the-purpose hospital ships. They have 7 operating rooms, 100 beds, and a hangar for a single Hormone-C helicopter for medical evacuation. A bow-thruster is fitted.

The ships are painted white with large red crosses on their sides.

Names: These ships are named for major rivers. The name OB' was previously carried by a scientific research ship.

The hospital ship OB' at sea. She is the first Soviet ship to be designed specifically for the hospital role. (Skyfotos Ltd., 1980)

Stern view of the Oʙ′, showing the ship's helicopter hangar and platform and large helicopter control station above the hangar door.

## TRAINING SHIPS

These ships primarily serve the Navy's higher naval schools (i.e., naval academies). The armament of the Smol′ny class can permit those ships to be employed in a combat role.

### 3 TRAINING SHIPS: "SMOL′NY" CLASS

| Name | Name | Name | Completed |
|------|------|------|-----------|
| Khasan | Perekop | Smol′ny | 1976–1978 |

| | |
|---|---|
| Builders: | Warski Shipyard, Szczecin |
| Displacement: | 8,500 tons full load |
| Length: | 455 ft 5 in (138.0 m) |
| Beam: | 59 ft 5 in (18.0 m) |
| Draft: | 20 ft 6 in (6.2 m) |
| Propulsion: | 4 diesels; 16,000 bhp; 2 shafts |
| Speed: | 20 knots |
| Range: | 12,000 n.miles at 15 knots |
| Complement: | . . . . + 270 trainees |
| Helicopters: | no facilities |
| Missiles: | none |
| Guns: | 4 76.2-mm/60-cal AA (2 twin) |
| | 4 30-mm/65-cal close in (2 twin) |
| ASW weapons: | 2 RBU-2500 rocket launchers |
| Radars: | 4 Don-2 (navigation) except 3 in Perekop |
| | 1 Don Kay in Perekop |
| | 1 Drum Tilt (fire control) |
| | 1 Head Net-C (air search) |
| | 1 Owl Screech (fire control) |
| Sonars: | medium frequency |
| EW systems: | Watch Dog |

These are large, graceful training ships of a type not employed in Western navies.

Designation: Soviet US type.

The training ship Smol′ny, lead ship for a class of three built-for-the-purpose, armed cadet training ships

The training ship SMOL'NY under way

---

## 2 TRAINING SHIPS: "WODNIK" CLASS

| Name | Name | Completed |
|------|------|-----------|
| LUGA | OKA | 1977 |

| | |
|---|---|
| Builders: | Polnocny Shipyard, Gdansk |
| Displacement: | 1,500 tons standard |
| | 1,800 tons full load |
| Length: | 237 ft 7 in (72.0 m) |
| Beam: | 36 ft 7 in (12.0 m) |
| Draft: | 13 ft 10 in (4.2 m) |
| Propulsion: | 2 diesels (Zgoda-Sulzer 6TD48); 3,600 bhp; 2 shafts |
| Speed: | 16.5 knots |
| Range: | 7,500 n.miles at 11 knots |
| Complement: | approx. 60 + 90 trainees |
| Helicopters: | no facilities |
| Missiles: | none |
| Guns: | none |
| Radars: | |

These are navigation training ships. Two similar ships serve in the Polish Navy and one in the East German Navy.

Design: The WODNIK design is based on the Moma class.

Designation: Soviet US type.

## 2 TRAINING SHIPS: UGRA CLASS

| Name | Completed |
|------|-----------|
| BORODINO | 1970 |
| GANGUT | 1971 |

| | |
|---|---|
| Builders: | Nikolayev |
| Displacement: | 6,750 tons standard |
| | 9,650 tons full load |
| Length: | 478 ft 6 in (145.0 m) |
| Beam: | 58 ft 5 in (17.7 m) |
| Draft: | 21 ft 2 in (6.4 m) |
| Propulsion: | 4 diesels; 8,000 bhp; 2 shafts |
| Speed: | 17 knots |
| Range: | 21,000 n.miles at 10 knots |
| Complement: | approx. 300 + 400 trainees |
| Helicopters: | no facilities |
| Missiles: | none |
| Guns: | 8 57-mm/80-cal AA (4 twin) |
| Radars: | 4 Don-2 (navigation) |
| | 2 Muff Cob (fire control) |
| | 1 Strut Curve (air search) |
| EW systems: | Watch Dog |

These ships were built as training ships with classrooms and training facilities in place of the workshops and storerooms of the Ugra-class submarine tenders.

Design: The ships' superstructures have been built up aft in comparison with the submarine tenders.

Designation: Soviet US type.

Training ship GANGUT (1981, Giorgio Arra)

Training ship BORODINO (1980)

## EXPERIMENTAL AND TRIALS SHIPS

In addition to the ships listed below, various other Soviet ships appear to be assigned the designation OS (experimental vessel) on a temporary and permanent basis. Among the ships believed to have this designation are the cargo ship SVANETIYA (KOLOMNA class) and the research ship RYBACHIY (Moma class). Also, a number of former minesweepers of the T-43 class are employed in experimental work.

### 4 + TRIALS SHIPS: POTOK CLASS

| Name | Name | Name | Completed |
|---|---|---|---|
| OS 100 | OS 145 | OS . . . | |
| OS 138 | OS 225 | | 1978– |

| | |
|---|---|
| Builders: | |
| Displacement: | 750 tons standard |
| | 860 tons full load |
| Length: | 234 ft 3 in (71.0 m) |
| Beam: | 30 ft (9.1 m) |
| Draft: | 8 ft 3 in (2.5 m) |
| Propulsion: | 2 diesels; 4,000 bhp; 2 shafts |
| Speed: | 18 knots |
| Range: | |
| Complement: | |
| Helicopters: | no facilities |
| Missiles: | none |
| Guns: | none |
| Torpedoes: | 1 21-in (533-mm) torpedo tube |
| | 1 16-in (406-mm) torpedo tube |
| Radars: | 1 Don-2 (navigation) |

These ships are used for torpedo trials and recovery activities.
Designation: Soviet OS type.

### 1 SHIPBUILDING RESEARCH SHIP: "IZUMRUD"

| Name | Completed |
|---|---|
| IZUMRUD | 1979 |

| | |
|---|---|
| Builders: | Nikolayev |
| Displacement: | 5,100 tons full load |
| Tonnage: | 2,640 DWT |
| Length: | 327 ft 11 in (99.4 m) |
| Beam: | 46 ft 2 in (14.0 m) |
| Draft: | 15 ft 6 in (4.7 m) |
| Propulsion: | DE: 4 diesels driving 4 generators connected to electric motors; 1 shaft |
| Speed: | 13.75 knots |
| Range: | |
| Complement: | (civilian) |
| Helicopters: | no facilities |
| Missiles: | none |
| Guns: | none |
| Radars: | |

This ship was constructed specifically to test ship structures and materials. The ship is civilian manned, but operated by the Krylov Naval Institute of Shipbuilding; she operates in the Black Sea.

Design: There are some similarities in appearance to the large AKADEMIK KRYLOV-class scientific ships. The IZUMRUD has Vee Cone antennas atop the forward (bridge) mast and a profusion of dipole antennas.

Part of the ship's superstructure is fiberglass. The ship is equipped with stands for subjecting materials to the marine environment and laboratories to measure the environment's effects. The ship also has laboratories for testing machinery, heat exchangers, piping, electrical, and communications equipment, etc.

Name: The ship is "civilian" with the name IZUMRUD used for a Grisha II-class corvette operated by the KGB Maritime Border Troops.

The shipbuilding and materials research ship IZUMRUD (Courtesy Ambrose Greenway)

Forward mast of Izumrud, as seen from bow, showing Vee Cone antenna (Courtesy Ambrose Greenway)

**1 OR 2 TRIALS SHIPS: DALDYN CLASS**

| | |
|---|---|
| Completed: | |
| Builders: | |
| Displacement: | 360 tons full load |
| Length: | 104 ft 7 in (31.7 m) |
| Beam: | 23 ft 9 in (7.2 m) |
| Draft: | 9 ft 3 in (2.8 m) |
| Propulsion: | 1 diesel (8NVD 36U); 300 bhp; 1 shaft |
| Speed: | 9 knots |
| Range: | |
| Complement: | approx. 15 |
| Helicopters: | no facilities |
| Missiles: | none |
| Guns: | none |
| Radars: | 1 Spin Trough (search) |

Modified seiners of the Kareliya class, used for experimental work.

## SERVICE AND TARGET CRAFT

The Soviet Navy operates a large number of service and target craft, the latter being primarily small craft—some discarded combat vessels that are radio controlled. The new Shelon-class torpedo retrievers are 270-ton, 135 ⅓-ft (41-m) craft capable of about 20 knots. There are several of these, and they may be the successors to the widely used Poluchat I class. The latter craft, which are also used for patrol, are described in chapter 17. Some 60 or more of the Poluchat I class are employed as torpedo retrievers. Both types of TL (*Torpedolov*) or torpedo retrievers can be armed with light machine guns.

A Shelon-class torpedo retriever picking up a torpedo in the Barents Sea. Note the stern ramp. These 240-ton craft are diesel powered and could be armed for use as patrol craft.

This view of a Shelon torpedo retriever shows the craft at high speed. Delivered since 1978, these craft will replace the 60 or more Poluchat-class craft still in use as torpedo retrievers.

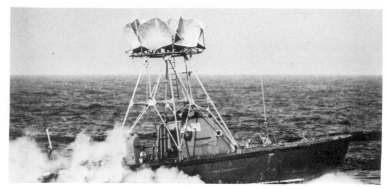

A Komar missile craft modified for use as a radio-controlled target. The boat has radar reflectors installed for radar-homing missiles.

This radio-controlled target craft has an Osa-type hull and machinery. The craft has been fitted with radar reflecting "corners" and two heat generators to attract homing missiles.

Poluchat I-class torpedo retriever recovering "fish" during an exercise; the patrol version is similar.

Also based on the Osa hull, this craft is fitted to direct radio-controlled target craft. A Square Tie radar is fitted on the forward lattice mast; elaborate communications equipment has been installed.

A Poluchat I torpedo recovery craft. This craft has the pendant number 841; some units have the prefix letters TR. Note the navigation radar antenna at the forward edge of the deckhouse. This unit does not have a radio direction-finding loop. (1982)

# 22

# Research and Intelligence Ships

All of the ships listed in this chapter are operated by naval personnel.

## INTELLIGENCE COLLECTION SHIPS

Most of the Soviet Navy's intelligence-collection ships (designated AGI by Western navies) are based on trawler designs, probably because of their availability, good seakeeping qualities, long endurance, and insulated fish storage holds that provide space for electronic equipment bays. The largest of the AGI classes—the Bal'zam—appears to have been designed from the outset specifically for intelligence collection and processing activities.

A large number of Al'pinist-class conversions may be undertaken to replace the aging Okean-class AGIs.

In addition to the weapons listed here, several AGIs have been observed with shoulder-fired SA-7 Grail missile launchers (the same missile as fired from the SA-N-5 launcher).

### 2+ INTELLIGENCE COLLECTION SHIPS: AL'PINIST CLASS

| Name | Completed |
| --- | --- |
| GS 7 | 1982 |
| GS 39 | 1981 |
| . . . . . . | |

| | |
| --- | --- |
| Builders: | (USSR) |
| Displacement: | 1,135 tons full load |
| Length: | 162 ft 4 in (49.2 m) |
| Beam: | 34 ft 8 in (10.5 m) |
| Draft: | 14 ft 10 in (4.5 m) |
| Propulsion: | 1 diesel; 1,320 bhp; 1 shaft |
| Speed: | 13 knots |
| Range: | 7,200 n.miles at 13 knots |
| Complement: | |
| Missiles: | none |
| Guns: | none |
| Radars: | |

This class is a converted stern trawler design. Possibly the second unit is a modified design, being slightly larger. They have controllable-pitch propellers.

Several hundred ships of this type are in commercial service, being rated at 322 DWT.

The converted stern trawler GS 39 of the new Al'pinist-class AGI. The "name" GS 39 appears on the bow with Cyrillic letters and on the bridge with English letters. The large production run of trawlers, their large insulated holds, and their excellent seakeeping and endurance features make them useful ships for conversion to the intelligence collection configuration. (1981, French Navy)

Al'pinist-class AGI GS 39 (1981)

## 2+ INTELLIGENCE COLLECTION SHIPS: BAL'ZAM CLASS

| Name | Completed |
|------|-----------|
| SSV 516 | ⎫ |
| . . . . . . | ⎬ 1980– |
|  | ⎭ |

| | |
|------|------|
| Builders: | Kaliningrad |
| Displacement: | 5,000 tons full load |
| Length: | 348 ft 2 in (105.5 m) |
| Beam: | 51 ft 2 in (15.5 m) |
| Draft: | 19 ft 2 in (5.8 m) |
| Propulsion: | 2 diesels; 9,000 bhp; 2 shafts |
| Speed: | 17 knots |
| Range: | |
| Complement: | approx. 180-200 |
| Missiles: | 2 quad SA-N-5 Grail launchers (16) |
| Guns: | 1 30-mm close-in (multibarrel) |
| Radars: | 2 Don Kay (navigation) |

This is the largest AGI in Soviet service and the first to be completed with armament.

Design: The Bal'zam class appears to have been designed specifically for the intelligence-collection role. They have elaborate at-sea replenishment facilities.

The SSV 516 is the lead ship of a new class of very large AGIs, given the NATO code name Bal'zam. This is also the first AGI class completed with defensive weapons and the first with extensive fittings for the underway replenishment of fuel and stores. The spherical radomes may house satellite communication antennas. The Bal'zam and PRIMOR'YE classes are among the few modern ships with three major masts. (1981)

Another view of the SSV 516. During the late 1970s the designation SSV (*Sudno Svyazyy*) or communication vessel was adopted by the Soviets for most AGIs. However, the designation GS (*Gidroficheskoye Sudno*) or hydrographic vessel is also used.

## 6 INTELLIGENCE COLLECTION SHIPS: "PRIMOR'YE" CLASS

| Name | Name | Name | Completed |
|------|------|------|-----------|
| KAVKAZ (591) | PRIMOR'YE (465) | ZAKARPAT'YE | |
| KRYM | ZABAYKAL'YE (454) | ZAPOROZH'YE | 1970–(?) |

| | |
|------|------|
| Builders: | (USSR) |
| Displacement: | 2,600 tons standard |
| | 3,700 tons full load |
| Length: | 279 ft 6 in (84.7 m) |
| Beam: | 46 ft 2 in (14.0 m) |
| Draft: | 18 ft 10 in (5.7 m) |
| Propulsion: | 1 diesel; 2,000 bhp; 1 shaft |
| Speed: | 13 knots |
| Range: | 12,000 n.miles at 13 knots |
| | 18,000 n.miles at 12 knots |
| Complement: | approx. 160 |
| Missiles: | 2 quad SA-N-5 Grail launchers (16) in some ships |
| Guns: | none |
| Radars: | 2 Don Kay or Don-2 (navigation) |

These AGIs have large, distinctive "box" structures forward and aft on their superstructures to house electronic equipment.

Design: These ships are based on a highly successful, Soviet-built series of stern trawler–factory ships. Almost 300 units have been built as the MAYAKOVSKIY (1958), LUCHEGORSK (1969), and KRONSHTADT (1974) classes; several were transferred to other nations and almost a score modified to fisheries research ships. Their fisheries designation is BMRT.

In their AGI configuration the ships have a distinctive superstructure with three antenna masts, while some ships retain the trawler kingpost aft. Details differ.

Designation: Soviet SSV type (with pendant numbers indicated above).

PRIMOR'YE-class AGI ZAKARPAT'YE

PRIMOR'YE-class AGI SSV 501 (1982, U.S. Navy)

The PRIMOR'YE-class AGI ZAKARPAT'YE, photographed in the Atlantic while shadowing a U.S. aircraft carrier. The configuration of units within AGI classes differs with respect to masts and antennas, as shown in these photos of the PRIMOR'YE class. The PRIMOR'YE (SSV 465) has a small third mast and no kingpost aft. The light-colored deck structures also vary. These ships bear little resemblance to the MAYAKOVSKIY-class factory trawlers from which the design is derived. (1973, U.S. Navy)

PRIMOR'YE-class AGI SSV 501 (1982, U.S. Navy)

PRIMOR'YE (SSV 465) (1982)

## 9 INTELLIGENCE COLLECTION SHIPS: MOMA CLASS

| Name | Name | Name | Completed |
|---|---|---|---|
| ARKHIPELAG (512) | KIL'DIN | SELIGER (514) | |
| EKVATOR | NAKHODKA (506) | VEGA (501) | 1969–1974 |
| IL'MEN (117) | PELORUS | YUPITER | |

| | |
|---|---|
| Builders: | Polnocny Shipyard, Gdansk |
| Displacement: | 1,260 tons standard |
| | 1,530 tons full load |
| Length: | 241 ft 11 in (73.3 m) |
| Beam: | 37 ft (11.2 m) |
| Draft: | 12 ft 11 in (3.9 m) |
| Propulsion: | 2 diesels (Zgoda-Sulzer 6TD48); 3,600 bhp; 2 shafts |
| Speed: | 17 knots |
| Range: | 8,000 n.miles at 11 knots |
| Complement: | approx. 80-120 |
| Missiles: | 2 quad SA-N-5 Grail launchers (16) in SELIGER and YUPITER |
| Guns: | none |
| Radars | 2 Don-2 (navigation) |

These are converted survey ships/buoy tenders; about 40 ships were built to this design. The SELIGER was assigned to monitor the first missile launch tests from the first U.S. Trident submarine, the OHIO (SSBN 726), off the Florida coast in January 1982.

Design: The ships vary considerably in details. Some retain their buoy-handling cranes; others have a low deckhouse of varying length between the forward mast and superstructure; forward mast positions (in some ships) vary in height and configuration. There is a deck area abaft the funnel, and there are boat davits for carrying vans with electronic equipment.

Designation: Eight ships are designated SSV with the IL'MEN designated GS.

Moma-class AGI ARKHIPELAG (deckhouse and electronic mast forward)

Moma-class AGI (deckhouse above bridge) (1980)

The SELIGER of the Moma class on the U.S. Eastern Test Range as a U.S. strategic missile submarine is about to launch a Poseidon SLBM. These craft regularly observe ship trials and missile tests off the U.S. coasts. Some Moma-class AGIs have had the forward crane removed and the deckhouse extended forward to house electronic gear. The SELIGER has her name displayed on the bridge in English. (1971, U.S. Air Force)

## 8 INTELLIGENCE COLLECTION SHIPS: MAYAK CLASS

| Name | Name | Name | Completed |
|---|---|---|---|
| ANEROYD | KURS | GS 239 | |
| GIRORULEVOY (536) | KURSOGRAF | GS 242 | 1968–1970 |
| KHERSONES | LADOGA | | |

| | |
|---|---|
| Builders: | Dnepr Shipyard, Kiev |
| Displacement: | 1,050 tons full load |
| Length: | 179 ft 2 in (54.3 m) |
| Beam: | 30 ft 8 in (9.3 m) |
| Draft: | 11 ft 11 in (3.6 m) |
| Propulsion: | 1 diesel (8NVD48); 800 bhp; 1 shaft |
| Speed: | 12 knots |
| Range: | 9,400 n.miles at 11 knots |
| | 11,000 n.miles at 7.5 knots |
| Complement: | approx. 60 |
| Missiles: | 2 quad SA-N-5 Grail launchers (16) in all except KURS and GS 239 |
| Guns: | 4 14.5-mm machine guns (2 twin) in KURSOGRAF |
| Radars: | 1 or 2 Don-2 (navigation) and /or Spin Trough (search) |

These ships are former side trawlers that have been converted to the AGI role. More than 100 Mayak-class ships were built in the 1960s at several shipyards.

Design: Details vary, with the GIRORULEVOY having a flat-topped radome fitted above the bridge, the KHERSONES has a wider main deckhouse, the LADOGA has a separate structure forward of the bridge and a third lattice mast, and the KURS a tall deckhouse on the stern. The deckhouse forward of the bridge varies in length, and mast configurations vary. One ship was fitted with two twin machine gun mounts in 1980.

Designation: Fisheries designation was SRTM. The Soviet naval designation for this class is GS.

Mayak-class AGI KURSOGRAF (deckhouse forward and lattice mast above bridge) (1982)

Mayak-class AGI KHERSONES (small deckhouse above bridge) (1973)

Mayak-class AGI (with deckhouse above bridge) (1982)

Mayak-class AGI KURS (with higher deckhouse aft)

Mayak-class AGI GS 242 (1974)

## 2 INTELLIGENCE COLLECTION SHIPS: "PAMIR" CLASS

| Name | Completed | Conversion Completed |
|---|---|---|
| GIDROGRAF (ex-ARBAN) (480) | 1958 | 1967 |
| PELENG (ex-PAMIR) (477) | 1958 | |

| | |
|---|---|
| Builders: | Gavle (Sweden) |
| Displacement: | 2,030 tons full load |
| Length: | 257 ft 5 in (78.0 m) |
| Beam: | 42 ft 3 in (12.8 m) |
| Draft: | 13 ft 10 in (4.2 m) |
| Propulsion: | 2 diesels (M.A.N. G10V); 4,200 bhp; 2 shafts |
| Speed: | 17.5 knots |
| Range: | 15,200 n.miles at 17.5 knots |
| | 21,800 n.miles at 12 knots |
| Complement: | approx. 120 |
| Missiles: | none (see notes) |
| Guns: | none |
| Radars: | 2 Don-2 (navigation) |

These ships are converted salvage tugs (with two ships remaining in that role; see chapter 21). Their superstructures have been enlarged and antennas fitted for the AGI role. There are positions in these ships for three quad SA-N-5 Grail launchers (24 missiles). They have a very long range.

Designation: Soviet SSV type.

The PAMIR-class AGI GIDROGRAF just before she was classified as SSV 480. The bridge structure has been built up. She and her sister ship, PELENG, are former long-range salvage and rescue tugs. (1978)

PAMIR-class AGI PELENG

## 3 INTELLIGENCE COLLECTION SHIPS: "NIKOLAY ZUBOV" CLASS

| Name | Completed |
|---|---|
| GAVRIL SARYCHEV (468) | |
| KHARITON LAPTEV (503) | 1964–(?) |
| SEMYEN CHELYUSHKIN (469) | |

| | |
|---|---|
| Builders: | Warski Shipyard, Szczecin |
| Displacement: | 2,200 tons standard |
| | 3,100 tons full load |
| Length: | 297 ft (90.0 m) |
| Beam: | 42 ft 11 in (13.0 m) |
| Draft: | 15 ft 6 in (4.7 m) |
| Propulsion: | 2 diesels (Zgoda 85D48); 4,800 bhp; 2 shafts |
| Speed: | 16.5 knots |
| Range: | 11,000 n.miles at 14 knots |
| Complement: | approx. 100 |
| Missiles: | see notes |
| Guns: | none |
| Radars: | 2 Don-2 (navigation) |
| | 1 Strut Curve (search) in SEMYEN CHELYUSHKIN |

These are former oceanographic ships (completion dates above) converted to AGIs. The GAVRIL SARYCHEV has been extensively rebuilt with her forecastle deck extended to the stern and an additional level added to the superstructure. Positions for three quad SA-N-5 Grail launchers (24 missiles) have been provided on the SARYCHEV.

Designation: Soviet SSV type.

The AGI KHARITON LAPTEV waits for a U.S. missile submarine to fire a Poseidon SLBM on the Eastern Test Range. The ship's electronic surveillance/intercept equipment is housed in the dome atop the bridge and in the container on the fantail as well as within the ship. Compare these ships with the ZUBOV-class units configured for oceanographic research. (1970)

Nikolay Zubov-class AGI Gavril Sarychev

## 4 INTELLIGENCE COLLECTION SHIPS: MIRNYY CLASS

| Name | Name | Name | Completed |
|------|------|------|-----------|
| Bakan | Val | Vertikal | 1964–(?) |
| Lotsman | | | |

| | |
|---|---|
| Builders: | Northern Shipyard, Nikolayev |
| Displacement: | 850 tons standard |
| | 1,300 tons full load |
| Length: | 207 ft 11 in (63.0 m) |
| Beam: | 31 ft 4 in (9.5 m) |
| Draft: | 14 ft 10 in (4.5 m) |
| Propulsion: | DE: 4 diesels; 4,000 bhp; 1 shaft |
| Speed: | 17.5 knots |
| Range: | 8,700 n.miles at 11 knots |
| Complement: | approx. 60 |
| Missiles: | none |
| Guns: | none |
| Radars: | 2 Don-2 (navigation) |

These ships are converted whale hunter/catcher ships, easily identified by their high, "notched" bows. Details vary. New deckhouses were fitted between the superstructure and forward mast in the early 1970s.

Mirnyy-class AGI Lotsman (1979)

## 15 INTELLIGENCE COLLECTION SHIPS: OKEAN CLASS

| Name | Name | Name | Completed |
|------|------|------|-----------|
| Alidada | Ekholot | Redukto | |
| Ampermetr | Gidrofon | Repiter | |
| Barograf | Krenometr | Teodolit | 1965–(?) |
| Barometr | Linza | Travers | |
| Deflektor | Lotlin' (GS) | Zond | |

| | |
|---|---|
| Builders: | Volks Shipyard (East Germany) |
| Displacement: | 760 tons full load |
| Length: | 167 ft 8 in (50.8 m) |
| Beam: | 29 ft 4 in (8.9 m) |
| Draft: | 12 ft 3 in (3.7 m) |
| Propulsion: | 1 diesel; 540 bhp; 1 shaft |
| Speed: | 11 knots |
| Range: | 7,900 n.miles at 11 knots |
| Complement: | approx. 60 |
| Missiles: | see notes |
| Guns: | 4 14.5-mm machine guns (2 twin) in Barograf |
| Radars: | 1 or 2 Don-2 (navigation) |

The original lines of the Mirnyy-class whale catchers converted to AGIs have been marred by the extension of the forward deckhouse and the additions to the bridge structure, as seen here with the Bakan. She was photographed in the Mediterranean by a U.S. Navy P-3 Orion aircraft.

The Okean-class AGIs are the most numerous intelligence collection ships in Soviet naval service. Again, their antenna arrays differ considerably, and some units have extended deckhouses to increase work and equipment spaces. This class is easily identified by the forward mast's twin supports.

This is the largest and hence probably most observed class of AGIs. They are converted side trawlers. Details differ. They retain their trawler arrangement of a tripod mast well forward and a pole mast well aft.

There are provisions in most ships for two quad SA-N-5 Grail launchers (16 missiles). One ship has been fitted with MGs.

Designation: Soviet GS type.

## 2 INTELLIGENCE COLLECTION SHIPS: DNEPR CLASS

| Name | Name | Completed |
|------|------|-----------|
| IZERMETEL | PROTRAKTOR | 1959 |

| | |
|---|---|
| Builders: | Ishikawa Hajima, Tokyo |
| Displacement: | 750 tons full load |
| Length: | 173 ft 11 in (52.7 m) |
| Beam: | 29 ft 8 in (9.0 m) |
| Draft: | 11 ft 7 in (3.5 m) |
| Propulsion: | 2 diesel (Burmeister & Wain); 1,210 bhp; 1 shaft |
| Speed: | 14 knots |
| Range: | 7,500 n.miles at 13 knots |
| Complement: | |
| Missiles: | none |
| Guns: | 2 14.5-mm machine guns (1 twin) in PROTRAKTOR |
| Radars: | |

These AGIs were built as tuna fishing–research ships. Their conversion to intelligence ships included adding a small deckhouse abaft the funnel.

Okean-class AGI LINZA (extended deckhouse and built up superstructure) (1974)

Okean-class AGI DEFLEKTOR (extended deckhouse and built up superstructure)

Okean-class AGI BAROGRAF (1974)

Dnepr-class AGI PROTRAKTOR (1979)

Dnepr-class AGI (1982)

## COMMUNICATIONS SHIPS

### SEVERAL COMMUNICATIONS SHIPS: CONVERTED T-43 CLASS

| | |
|---|---|
| Completed: | 1950s |
| Builders: | Leningrad, Kerch' |
| Displacement: | 590 tons full load |
| Length: | 198 ft (60.0 m) |
| Beam: | 28 ft 5 in (8.6 m) |
| Draft: | 7 ft 7 in (2.3 m) |
| Propulsion: | 2 diesels (2/9D); 2,200 bhp; 2 shafts |
| Speed: | 14 knots |
| Range: | 2,000 n.miles at 14 knots |
| | 3,200 n.miles at 10 knots |
| Complement: | |
| Guns: | removed |
| ASW weapons: | removed |
| Radars: | 1 Don-2 (navigation) or Spin Trough (search) |
| Sonars: | Tamir high frequency |
| EW systems: | IFF only |

Several T-43-class minesweepers have been converted to communications relay ships to support ship-to-ship and ship-to-shore radio traffic. They replaced the smaller Libau-class ships.

Their minesweeper armament has been removed. They could be rearmed in wartime. See chapter 18 for additional details.

Designation: Soviet SSV type.

A T-43 minesweeper as a communications ship carrying the SSV designation. There are whip antennas forward of the bridge and attached to the short funnel.

## RESEARCH SHIPS

### 10 OCEANOGRAPHIC RESEARCH SHIPS: "YUG" CLASS

| Name | Name | Name | Completed |
|---|---|---|---|
| Gidrolog | Seimesh | Yug | |
| Pegas | Senezh | Zodiak | 1978–1979 |
| Persey | Strelets | | |
| Pluton | Tayga | | |

| | |
|---|---|
| Builders: | Polnocny Shipyard, Gdansk |
| Displacement: | 2,500 tons full load |
| Length: | 272 ft 3 in (82.5 m) |
| Beam: | 44 ft 7 in (13.5 m) |
| Draft: | 12 ft 10 in (3.9 m) |
| Propulsion: | 2 diesels (Zgoda-Sulzer 6TD48); 4,400 bhp; 2 shafts |
| Speed: | 17 knots |
| Range: | 11,000 n.miles at 12 knots |
| Complement: | approx. 45 + 20 scientists |
| Helicopters: | no facilities |
| Missiles: | none |
| Guns: | see notes |
| Radars: | 2 Don-2 (navigation) |
| EW systems: | IFF only |

Built specifically for the oceanographic research role with facilities for hydrographic surveys. They have provisions for the installation of three 25-mm AA twin gun mounts.

Design: These ships are fitted with two 100-kw electric motors for quiet, slow-speed operations and a 300-hp bow-thruster for precise station keeping. They have two 5-ton-capacity booms. Six laboratories.

Designation: Soviet EHOS type.

Yug-class oceanographic research ship Gidrolog

**6 OCEANOGRAPHIC RESEARCH SHIPS: "AKADEMIK KRYLOV" CLASS**

| Name | Name | Completed |
|------|------|-----------|
| ADMIRAL VLADIMIRSKY | LEONID DEMIN | |
| AKADEMIK KRYLOV | LEONID SOBELYEV | 1974–1979 |
| IVAN KRUZENSHTERN | MIKHAIL KRUSKIY | |

| | |
|--|--|
| Builders: | Warski Shipyard, Szczecin |
| Displacement: | 6,600 tons standard |
| | 9,200 tons full load |
| Length: | 485 ft 1 in (147.0 m) except LEONID DEMIN and MIKHAIL KRUSKIY 488 ft |
| | 5 in (148.0 m) |
| Beam: | 61 ft 5 in (18.6 m) |
| Draft: | 21 ft 1 in (6.4 m) |
| Propulsion: | 4 diesels; 16,000 bhp; 2 shafts |
| Speed: | 20.4 knots |
| Range: | 23,000 n.miles at 15.3 knots |
| Complement: | approx. 90 |
| Helicopters: | 1 utility helicopter |
| Missiles: | none |
| Guns: | none |
| Radars: | 3 Don-2 (navigation) |
| EW systems: | IFF only |

These are the largest oceanographic research ships in Soviet service.

Design: This class has graceful, liner-like lines with a crane on the long forecastle. There are 20 to 26 laboratories in each ship. There is a helicopter hangar and flight deck aft. The last two ships, the DEMIN (1978) and KRUSKIY (1979), have pointed sterns, slightly increasing their length.

Designation: Soviet EHOS type.

The oceanographic research ships of the AKADEMIK KRYLOV class, as the LEONID DEMIN, shown here, are the world's largest ships of this type. They have large superstructures and a helicopter hangar and landing deck aft.

AKADEMIK KRYLOV-class oceanographic research ship LEONID SOBELYEV. (1975)

## 1 OCEANOGRAPHIC RESEARCH SHIP: "DOBRYNYA NIKITICH" CLASS

| Name | Completed |
| --- | --- |
| Vladimir Kavrayskiy | 1973 |

| | |
| --- | --- |
| Builders: | Admiralty Shipyard, Leningrad |
| Displacement: | 3,800 tons full load |
| Length: | 231 ft (70.0 m) |
| Beam: | 60 ft 5 in (18.3 m) |
| Draft: | 21 ft 2 in (6.4 m) |
| Propulsion: | DE: 3 diesels (13D100) driving 3 generators connected to electric motors; 5,400 bhp; 3 shafts (1 forward) |
| Speed: | 14.5 knots |
| Range: | 5,500 n.miles at 12.5 knots |
| | 13,000 n.miles at 9.5 knots |
| Complement: | |
| Helicopters: | landing deck |
| Missiles: | none |
| Guns: | none |
| Radars: | 2 Don-2 (navigation) |

This ship is a Navy-manned icebreaker extensively modified for polar research. She is painted white. (Sister ships serve as Navy and civilian icebreakers.)

Design: The ship has a helicopter deck aft but no hangar; a helicopter control station is prominent at the after end of the superstructure. She is fitted with nine laboratories and has one 8-ton crane and two 3-ton booms.

The Vladimir Kavrayskiy is more extensively modified for Arctic research than the three civilian Dobrynya Nikitich-class icebreakers employed in polar research. (1974)

## 4 OCEANOGRAPHIC RESEARCH SHIPS: "AKADEMIK KURCHATOV" CLASS

| Name | Name | Completed |
| --- | --- | --- |
| Abkhaziya | Bashkiriya | 1972–1973 |
| Adzhariya | Moldaviya | |

| | |
| --- | --- |
| Builders: | Mathias Thesen Shipyard, Wismar (East Germany) |
| Displacement: | 5,460 tons standard |
| | 7,500 tons full load |
| Length: | 409 ft 10 in (124.2 m) |
| Beam: | 56 ft 1 in (17.0 m) |
| Draft: | 21 ft 6 in (6.5 m) |
| Propulsion: | 2 diesels (Halberstadt-M.A.N. K6Z 57/80); 8,000 bhp; 2 shafts |
| Speed: | 19 knots |
| Range: | 20,000 n.miles at 16 knots |
| Complement: | approx. 85 |
| Helicopters: | 1 utility helicopter |
| Missiles: | none |
| Guns: | none |
| Radars: | 3 Don-2 (navigation) |

These are Navy-manned research ships, similar to seven ships operated by the Academy of Sciences (see chapter 23).

Design: Built with graceful, liner lines, these ships have a helicopter deck and telescoping hangar. There are 27 laboratories and extensive communications equipment (including Vee Cone antennas). Two 190-hp bow-thrusters are fitted along with a 300-hp active rudder for precise station keeping.

Designation: Soviet EHOS type.

Akademik Kurchatov-class oceanographic research ship (1977)

The ABKHAZIYA is one of the naval versions of the AKADEMIK KURCHATOV-class oceanographic research ships. Vee Cone communication antennas are fitted on the mast abaft the funnel in some units; there is a helicopter deck aft and a telescoping hangar. (1980)

AKADEMIK KURCHATOV-class oceanographic research ship BASHKIRIYA under way in the South China Sea (1974, U.S. Navy)

## 8 OCEANOGRAPHIC RESEARCH SHIPS: "NIKOLAY ZUBOV" CLASS

| Name | Name | Completed |
|------|------|-----------|
| ALEKSEY CHIRIKOV | FYODOR LITKE | |
| ANDREY VIL'KITSKIY | NIKOLAY ZUBOV | 1964–1968 |
| BORIS DAVYDOV | SEMEN DEZHNEY | |
| FADDEY BELLINGSGAUZEN | VASILIY GOLOVNIN | |

| | |
|---|---|
| Builders: | Warski Shipyard, Szczecin |
| Displacement: | 2,200 tons standard |
| | 3,100 tons full load |
| Length: | 296 ft (89.7 m) |
| Beam: | 42 ft 11 in (13.0 m) |
| Draft: | 15 ft 6 in (4.7 m) |
| Propulsion: | 2 diesels (Zgoda-Sulzer 8TD48); 4,800 bhp; 2 shafts |
| Speed: | 16.5 knots |
| Range: | 11,000 n.miles at 14 knots |

| | |
|---|---|
| Complement: | approx. 50 |
| Helicopters: | no facilities |
| Missiles: | none |
| Guns: | none |
| Radars: | 2 Don-2 (navigation) |
| EW systems: | IFF only |

Eight of these ships are configured for oceanographic research, and three, listed separately, are AGIs. The lead ship, the NIKOLAY ZUBOV, was placed in commission on 1 April 1964.

Design: These ships are designed for polar operations. They have two 7-ton and two 5-ton booms; they are fitted with nine laboratories. Details of the ships vary. The ZUBOV and possibly others have more elaborate communications equipment, including Vee Cone antennas.

Designation: Soviet EHOS type.

NIKOLAY ZUBOV-class oceanographic research ship VASILIY GOLOVNIN (1974)

NIKOLAY ZUBOV-class oceanographic research ship ALEKSEY CHIRIKOV off the island of Hawaii. The ship shows the effect of a long and arduous research cruise. The array of signal flags are in celebration of the USSR Armed Forces Day, 23 February. (1975, U.S. Navy)

**3 OCEANOGRAPHIC RESEARCH SHIPS: "POLYUS" CLASS**

| Name | Name | Name | Completed |
|------|------|------|-----------|
| BAYKAL | BALKHASH | POLYUS | 1962–1964 |

| | |
|---|---|
| Builders: | Neptun Shipyard, Rostock |
| Displacement: | approx. 4,500 tons standard |
| | 6,700 tons full load |
| Length: | 368 ft 3 in (111.6 m) |
| Beam: | 47 ft 6 in (14.4 m) |
| Draft: | 19 ft 10 in (6.0 m) |
| Propulsion: | DE: 4 diesels driving 4 generators connected to two electric motors; |
| | 4,000 bhp; 1 shaft |
| Speed: | 16 knots |

| | |
|---|---|
| Range: | 25,000 n.miles at 12 knots |
| Complement: | |
| Helicopters: | no facilities |
| Missiles: | none |
| Guns: | none |
| Radars: | 2 Don-2 (navigation) |

These ships were built on ANDIZHAN/KOVEL cargo hulls for the oceanographic research role.

Design: Details and masts vary (the POLYUS has her bridge mast abaft the funnel; others are forward). The ships have an active rudder and bow-thruster for station keeping. There are 17 laboratories.

Designation: Soviet EHOS type.

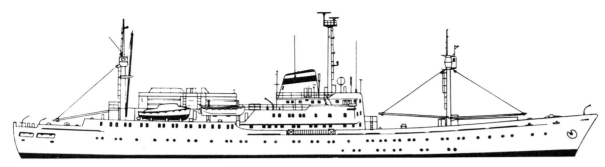

POLYUS-class research ship BAYKAL (1979)

---

**1 OCEANOGRAPHIC RESEARCH SHIP: "NEVEL'SKOY"**

| Name | Completed |
|------|-----------|
| NEVEL'SKOY | 1961 |

| | |
|---|---|
| Builders: | Nikolayev |
| Displacement: | 2,500 tons full load |
| Length: | 276 ft 6 in (83.8 m) |
| Beam: | 50 ft 2 in (15.2 m) |
| Draft: | 12 ft 6 in (3.8 m) |
| Propulsion: | 2 diesels; 4,000 bhp; 2 shafts |
| Speed: | 17 knots |

| | |
|---|---|
| Range: | 10,000 n.miles at 11 knots |
| Complement: | approx. 45 |
| Helicopters: | no facilities |
| Missiles: | none |
| Guns: | none |
| Radars: | 2 Don-2 (navigation) |

A one-of-a-kind ship, probably the prototype for the NIKOLAY ZUBOV class.

Designation: Soviet EHOS type.

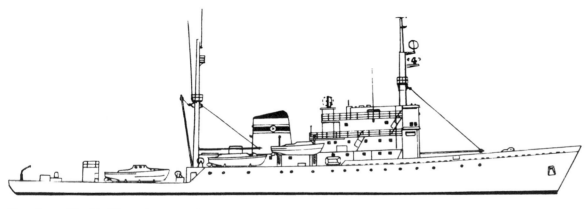

NEVEL'SKOY (Siegfried Breyer)

## HYDROGRAPHIC SURVEY SHIPS

### 13 HYDROGRAPHIC SURVEY SHIPS: FENIK CLASS

| Name | Name | Name | Completed |
|------|------|------|-----------|
| GS 44 | GS 280 | GS 401 | |
| GS 47 | GS 388 | GS 402 | |
| GS 270 | GS 392 | GS 403 | 1978–1981 |
| GS 272 | GS 397 | | |
| GS 278 | GS 398 | | |

| | |
|---|---|
| Builders: | Polnocny Shipyard, Gdansk |
| Displacement: | 1,100 tons full load |
| Length: | 203 ft (61.5 m) |
| Beam: | 39 ft (11.8 m) |
| Draft: | 10 ft (3.0 m) |
| Propulsion: | 2 diesels (Cegielski-Sulzer); 1,920 bhp; 2 shafts |
| Speed: | 13 knots |
| Range: | |
| Complement: | approx. 28 |
| Missiles: | none |
| Guns: | none |
| Radars: | 2 Don-2 (navigation) |
| EW systems: | IFF only |

Like most ships of this type, these are combination hydrographic survey and buoy-tending ships with a 7-ton-capacity crane. Electric motors provide quiet, low-speed operations.

Fenik-class hydrographic survey ship GS 402 (1980, French Navy, courtesy *Combat Fleets*)

Fenik-class hydrographic survey ship GS 47 (1980)

Fenik-class hydrographic survey ship GS 397 (1980)

### 12 HYDROGRAPHIC SURVEY SHIPS: BIYA CLASS

| Name | Name | Name | Completed |
|------|------|------|-----------|
| GS 193 | GS 204 | GS 214 | |
| GS 194 | GS 206 | GS 271 | |
| GS 198 | GS 208 | GS 273 | 1971–1976 |
| GS 202 | GS 210 | GS 275 | |

| | |
|---|---|
| Builders: | Polnocny Shipyard, Gdansk |
| Displacement: | 750 tons full load |
| Length: | 181 ft 6 in (55.0 m) |
| Beam: | 30 ft 4 in (9.2 m) |
| Draft: | 8 ft 7 in (2.6 m) |
| Propulsion: | 2 diesels; 1,200 bhp; 2 shafts |
| Speed: | 13 knots |
| Range: | 4,700 n.miles at 11 knots |
| Complement: | approx. 25 |
| Missiles: | none |
| Guns: | none |
| Radars: | 1 Don-2 (navigation) |

These ships are of an improved Kamenka design with a longer superstructure at the expense of buoy-handling capability. They have a 5-ton-capacity crane.

One unit was transferred to Cuba (1980) and one to Cape Verde (1981).

Biya-class hydrographic research ship (Siegfried Breyer)

## 10 HYDROGRAPHIC SURVEY SHIPS: KAMENKA CLASS

| Name | Name | Name | Completed |
|------|------|------|-----------|
| BEL'BEK | GS 74 | GS 203 | |
| SIMA | GS 82 | GS 207 | |
| VERNIER | GS 107 | | 1969–1972 |
| GS 66 | GS 108 | | |

| | |
|---|---|
| Builders: | Polnocny Shipyard, Gdansk |
| Displacement: | 703 tons full load |
| Length: | 176 ft 7 in (53.5 m) |
| Beam: | 30 ft (9.1 m) |
| Draft: | 8 ft 7 in (2.6 m) |
| Propulsion: | 2 diesels (Zgoda-Sulzer); 1,765 bhp; 2 shafts |
| Speed: | 13.7 knots |
| Range: | 4,000 n.miles at 10 knots |
| Complement: | approx. 40 |
| Missiles: | none |
| Guns: | none |
| Radars: | 1 Don-2 (navigation) |

These ships have a 5-ton-capacity crane. One ship of this class was transferred to East Germany (1972).

Designation: All Soviet GS type.

Kamenka-class hydrographic survey ship GS 108

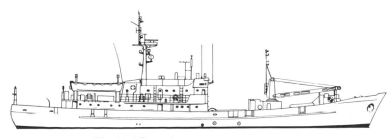

Kamenka-class (Siegfried Breyer)

## 19 HYDROGRAPHIC SURVEY SHIPS: MOMA CLASS

| Name | Name | Name | Completed |
|------|------|------|-----------|
| ALTAYR | CHELEKEN | OKEAN | |
| ANADYR' | ELTON | RYBACHIY (ex- | |
| ANDROMEDA | KOLGUEV | ODOGRAF) | |
| ANTARES | KRIL'ON | SEVER | 1967–1974 |
| ANTARTIKA | LIMAN | TAYMRY | |
| ARTIKA | MARS | ZAPOLAR'E | |
| ASKOL'D | MORZHOVETS | | |

| | |
|---|---|
| Builders: | Polnocny Shipyard, Gdansk |
| Displacement: | 1,260 tons standard |
| | 1,530 tons full load |
| Length: | 241 ft 11 in (73.3 m) |
| Beam: | 37 ft (11.2 m) |
| Draft: | 12 ft 11 in (3.9 m) |
| Propulsion: | 2 diesels (Zgoda-Sulzer 6TD48); 3,600 bhp; 2 shafts |
| Speed: | 17 knots |
| Range: | 8,000 n.miles at 11 knots |
| Complement: | approx. 55 |
| Missiles: | none |
| Guns: | none |
| Radars: | 2 Don-2 (navigation) |
| EW systems: | IFF only |

The Momas were built for the hydrographic survey/buoy tender role, with nine additional ships serving as AGIs (of which one is designated GS). Two ships of this class were transferred to Poland (1975–1976) and one to Yugoslavia (1977).

Design: There is a 7-ton-capacity crane forward except in the RYBACHIY, which has a deckhouse forward.

Designation: All Soviet GS type.

Moma-class hydrographic survey ship RYBACHIY (with deckhouse extended forward). (1982, U.S. Navy)

Moma-class hydrographic survey ship ELTON (1982, U.S. Navy)

Samara-class hydrographic research ship VAYGACH (1982, U.S. Navy)

Moma-class hydrographic survey ship RYBACHIY (with deckhouse extended forward) (1982, U.S. Navy)

Samara-class hydrographic research ship KOMPAS (1978)

## 15 HYDROGRAPHIC RESEARCH SHIPS: SAMARA CLASS

| Name | Name | Name | Completed |
|------|------|------|-----------|
| AZIMUT | GRADUS | TURA (ex-GLOBUS) | |
| DEVIATOR | KOMPAS | VAYGACH | |
| GIGROMETR | PAMYAT'MERKURIYA | VOSTOK | 1962–1964 |
| GLUBOMETR | RUMB (GS 118) | ZENIT | |
| GORIZONT | TROPIK | GS 275 (ex-YUG) | |

| | |
|---|---|
| Builders: | Polnocny Shipyard, Gdansk |
| Displacement: | 1,050 tons standard |
| | 1,275 tons full load |
| Length: | 194 ft 8 in (59.0 m) |
| Beam: | 34 ft 4 in (10.4 m) |
| Draft: | 14 ft 2 in (4.3 m) |
| Propulsion: | 2 diesels (Zgoda 5TD48); 3,000 bhp; 2 shafts |
| Speed: | 15 knots |
| Range: | 6,200 n.miles at 10 knots |
| Complement: | approx. 45 |
| Missiles: | none |
| Guns: | none |
| Radars: | 2 Don-2 (navigation) |

These were the first of several classes of small, efficient combination hydrographic ships and buoy tenders. A 7-ton-capacity crane is fitted. Details vary. The TURA was modified in 1978; her forecastle was extended to her superstructure and her crane deleted.

Designation: All Soviet GS type, except that the TURA may have been redesignated. The RUMB is GS 118.

Melitopol-class hydrographic survey ship

## 3 HYDROGRAPHIC SURVEY SHIPS: MELITOPOL CLASS

| Name | Name | Name | Completed |
|------|------|------|-----------|
| MAYAK | NIVILER | PRIZMA | 1952–1955 |

| | |
|---|---|
| Builders: | (USSR) |
| Displacement: | 1,200 tons full load |
| Length: | 189 ft 9 in (57.5 m) |
| Beam: | 29 ft 8 in (9.0 m) |
| Draft: | 14 ft 2 in (4.3 m) |
| Propulsion: | 1 diesel (6DR30/40); 600 bhp; 1 shaft |
| Speed: | 11 knots |
| Range: | 2,500 n.miles at 10.5 knots |
| Complement: | |
| Missiles: | none |
| Guns: | none |
| Radars: | 1 Don (navigation) |

These are converted small cargo ships.

## 5 HYDROGRAPHIC SHIPS: "TELNOVSK" CLASS

| Name | Name | Name | Completed |
|------|------|------|-----------|
| AYTODOR | STVOR | ULYANA GROMOVA | 1949–1957 |
| SIRENA | SVIYAGA | | |

| | |
|---|---|
| Builders: | (Hungary) |
| Displacement: | 1,300 tons standard |
| | 1,900 tons full load |
| Length: | 231 ft 8 in (70.2 m) |
| Beam: | 33 ft 4 in (10.1 m) |
| Draft: | 13 ft 10 in (4.2 m) |
| Propulsion: | 1 diesel (Ganz); 800 bhp; 1 shaft |
| Speed: | 11 knots |
| Range: | 3,000 n.miles at 9.7 knots |
| Complement: | approx. 50 |
| Missiles: | none |
| Guns: | none |
| Radars: | 1 Neptune or Don or Don-2 |
| | (navigation) |

These are former cargo ships. Details vary. The STVOR has been employed as a training ship.

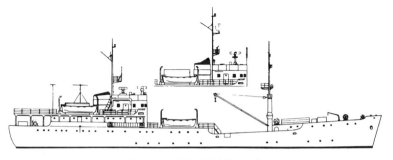

Telnovsk-class training ship STVOR (Siegfried Breyer)

## INSHORE SURVEY CRAFT

Several smaller survey craft are in service, principally of a 95-ft 8-in (29-m) type and a 36-ft 4-in (11-m) type, the latter being carried aboard the larger survey and oceanographic ships.

## MISSILE RANGE INSTRUMENTATION SHIPS

These Navy-manned ships support the Soviet test firings of Soviet long-range ballistic missiles (ICBMs and SLBMs). These ships have a different role than the civilian-manned Space Event Support Ships (SESS) listed in chapter 23.

## 2 MISSILE RANGE INSTRUMENTATION SHIPS: DESNA CLASS

| Name | Completed |
|------|-----------|
| CHAZHMA (ex-DANGERA) | 1963 |
| CHUMIKAN (ex-DOLGESCHTCHEL'YE) | |

| | |
|---|---|
| Builders: | Warnow Shipyard, Warnemünde (East Germany) |
| Displacement: | 13,500 tons full load |
| Length: | 461 ft 8 in (139.9 m) |
| Beam: | 59 ft 5 in (18.0 m) |
| Draft: | 26 ft 1 in (7.9 m) |
| Propulsion: | 1 diesel (M.A.N.); 5,400 bhp; 1 shaft |
| Speed: | 15 knots |
| Range: | 12,000 n.miles at 13 knots |
| Complement: | |
| Helicopter: | 1 or 2 Ka-25 Hormone-C |
| Missiles: | none |
| Guns: | none |
| Radars: | 2 Don-2 (navigation) |
| | 1 Head Net-B (air search) |
| | 1 Ship Globe (tracking) |
| EW systems: | Watch Dog |

Converted from the DZANKOY-class ore/coal ships, these are the largest naval-manned missile range instrumentation ships.

The Desna-class missile range instrumentation ship CHUMIKAN with a Ka-25 Hormone helicopter (1978)

Design: These ships have a distinctive arrangement, with two island structures. Three tracking directors are mounted forward with the Ship Globe radome mounted above the forward island structure. The after structure consists of the funnel, with a faired-in mast mounting two Vee Cone antennas, and a helicopter hangar on each side of the funnel. There is a large helicopter landing area aft.

Designation: Soviet OS type.

Desna-class missile range instrumentation ship CHUMIKAN (1981)

---

### 4 MISSILE RANGE INSTRUMENTATION SHIPS: "SIBIR'" CLASS

| Name | Name | Completed |
|------|------|-----------|
| CHUKOTA | SIBIR' | |
| SAKHALIN | SPASSK (ex-SUCHAN) | 1960 |

| | |
|---|---|
| Builders: | Warski Shipyard, Szczecin |
| Displacement: | 8,400 tons full load |
| Length: | 357 ft 1 in (108.2 m) |
| Beam: | 48 ft 6 in (14.7 m) |
| Draft: | 22 ft 1 in (6.7 m) |
| Propulsion: | compound piston with low-pressure turbine; 2,500 ihp; 1 shaft |
| Boilers: | 2 |
| Speed: | 12 knots |
| Range: | 9,800 n.miles at 12 knots |
| | 11,800 n.miles at 11 knots |
| Complement: | |
| Helicopters: | 1 Ka-25 Hormone-C |
| Missiles: | none |
| Guns: | none |
| Radars: | 1 Big Net or Head Net-C (3-D air search) |
| | 2 Don-2 (navigation) |
| | . . . . . . (tracking) |

These ships were converted during construction from DONBASS-class cargo ships. They were Polish built but completed in Leningrad.

Design: The CHUKOTA is flush-decked; the others have a well deck forward. They have an impressive appearance, with large, antenna-bearing kingposts forward and abaft the central superstructure. Two or three tracking radars are mounted forward of the bridge. A large helicopter platform is fitted aft. One Hormone-C is normally embarked, although the ships do not have a hangar.

Designation: Soviet OS type.

Superstructure of CHUKOTA (1982)

The Sɪʙɪʀ'-class missile range instrumentation ship Cʜᴜᴋᴏᴛᴀ with a Ka-25 Hormone helicopter; note that she is a flush-deck ship compared to the Sᴘᴀssᴋ. Antenna arrays and arrangements differ on these ships. (1981)

Sɪʙɪʀ'-class missile range instrumentation ship Sᴘᴀssᴋ

# Civilian Auxiliary Ships

Although the entire Soviet Merchant Marine is available to support the nation's military establishment, the Space Event Support Ships (SESS), research ships, icebreakers, and some of the training ships regularly appear to support military and naval activities.

In addition to the ships listed here, there are more than 50 fisheries research ships in service.

None of these ships are armed.

## SPACE EVENT SUPPORT SHIPS

These ships support Soviet civilian and military space activities as well as upper-atmosphere research and communications research programs.

### (1) SPACE CONTROL–MONITORING SHIP: "MARSHAL NEDELIN"

| Name | Completed |
| --- | --- |
| MARSHAL NEDELIN | 1983 |

| Builders: | Admiralty Shipyard, Leningrad |
| --- | --- |

This is the largest Soviet SESS yet constructed, built specifically for this role.

Name: Chief Marshal of Artillery M.I. Nedelin was the first commander in chief of the Soviet Strategic Rocket Forces. He assumed the post in 1959 and was killed in October of the following year in the accidental explosion of an ICBM.

### 4 SPACE CONTROL–MONITORING SHIPS: "KOSMONAUT PAVEL BELYAYEV"

| Name | Completed | Conversion Completed |
| --- | --- | --- |
| KOSMONAUT GEORGIY DOBROVOLSKIY (ex-SEMYON KOSINOV) | 1968 | 1978 |
| KOSMONAUT PAVEL BELYAYEV (ex-VYTEGRALES) | 1963 | 1977 |
| KOSMONAUT VIKTOR PATSAYEV (ex-NAZAR GUBIN) | 1968 | 1978 |
| KOSMONAUT VLADILAV VOLKOV (ex-YENISEILES) | 1964 | 1977 |

| | |
| --- | --- |
| Builders: | Zhdanov Shipyard, Leningrad |
| Displacement: | approx. 5,500 tons full load |
| Tonnage: | 2,590 DWT |
| Length: | 402 ft 6 in (122.0 m) |
| Beam: | 55 ft 3 in (16.75 m) |
| Draft: | 23 ft 1 in (7.0 m) |
| Propulsion: | diesel (Burmeister & Wain Bryansk); 5,200 bhp; 1 shaft |
| Speed: | 15.5 knots |
| Range: | |
| Complement: | approx. 100 |
| Helicopters: | no facilities |
| Radars: | |

The KOSMONAUT VLADILAV VOLKOV is one of several large space control–monitoring ships operated by the USSR in support of civilian and military space programs. These ships have a secondary capability of intelligence collection and communications relay. (Courtesy *Flottes de Combat*)

These ships were converted from VYTEGRALES-class merchant ships. Their conversion permitted two ships, the BEZHITSA and RISTNA, temporarily employed in this role, to return to merchant cargo service. All four ships were built and subsequently converted at the Zhdanov yard.

The KOSMONAUT GEORGI DOBROVLSKIY in the Indian Ocean. (1982, Royal Australian Air Force)

**1 SPACE CONTROL–MONITORING SHIP: "KOSMONAUT YURI GAGARIN"**

| Name | Completed |
| --- | --- |
| KOSMONAUT YURI GAGARIN | Dec 1971 |

| | |
| --- | --- |
| Builders: | Baltic Shipyard, Leningrad |
| Displacement: | 37,500 tons standard |
| | 45,000 tons full load |
| Tonnage: | 31,300 DWT |
| Length: | 764 ft 11 in (231.8 m) |
| Beam: | 102 ft 4 in (31.0 m) |
| Draft: | 33 ft 8 in (10.7 m) |
| Propulsion: | TE: 2 steam turbines; 19,000 shp; 2 shafts |
| Boilers: | |
| Speed: | 17.5 knots |

| | |
| --- | --- |
| Range: | |
| Complement: | approx. 300 (including scientists) |
| Helicopters: | no facilities |
| Radars: | 2 Don Kay (navigation) |
| | 2 Ship Globe (tracking) |
| | . . . . . . (tracking) |

The GAGARIN is the world's largest ship fitted for scientific activities and the largest ship in service with turbo-electric propulsion. The ship was built for the purpose with a SOFIA-class tanker hull.

Recreation facilities include three swimming pools and a theater seating 300 persons plus a sports hall.

Names: The ship is named for the world's first astronaut/kosmonaut, who died in a 1968 plane crash.

Named for the first man to fly in space, the KOSMONAUT YURI GAGARIN is the world's largest scientific research/support ship. She is home-ported in Odessa on the Black Sea. (1980)

Space control–monitoring ship KOSMONAUT YURI GAGARIN (1976)

## 1 SPACE CONTROL–MONITORING SHIP: "AKADEMIK SERGEI KOROLEV"

| Name | Completed |
|------|-----------|
| AKADEMIK SERGEI KOROLEV | Dec 1970 |

| | |
|------|------|
| Builders: | Black Sea Shipyard, Nikolayev |
| Displacement: | 17,115 tons standard |
| | 21,250 tons full load |
| Tonnage: | 7,180 DWT |
| Length: | 600 ft 3 in (181.9 m) |
| Beam: | 82 ft 9 in (25.1 m) |
| Draft: | 26 ft 1 in (7.9 m) |
| Propulsion: | diesel (Burmeister & Wain Byransk); 12,000 bhp; 1 shaft |
| Speed: | 17.5 knots |
| Range: | 22,500 n.miles at 16 knots |
| Complement: | approx. 300 including scientists |
| Helicopters: | no facilities |
| Radars: | 2 Don Kay (navigation) |
| | 2 Ship Globe (tracking) |
| | . . . . . . (tracking) |

Although smaller than the GAGARIN, this is still a large and imposing SESS. The KOROLEV was built from the keel up for this role. The ship is flagship of the Soviet Union's Far East civilian research fleet.

## 1 SPACE CONTROL–MONITORING SHIP: "KOSMONAUT VLADIMIR KOMAROV"

| Name | Completed |
|------|-----------|
| KOSMONAUT VLADIMIR KOMAROV (ex-GENICHESK) | 1967 |

| | |
|------|------|
| Builders: | Nikolayev |
| Displacement: | 11,090 tons standard |
| | 17,500 tons full load |
| Tonnage: | 6,650 DWT |
| Length: | 513 ft 11 in (155.7 m) |
| Beam: | 76 ft 11 in (23.3 m) |
| Draft: | 30 ft (9.1 m) |
| Propulsion: | diesel (Burmeister & Wain Bryansk); 9,000 bhp; 2 shafts |
| Speed: | 17.5 knots |
| Range: | |
| Complement: | approx. 115 + 125 scientists |
| Helicopters: | no facilities |
| Radars: | 2 Don Kay (navigation) |
| | . . . . . . (tracking) |
| | . . . . . . (tracking) |

The KOMAROV was converted during construction from a POLTAVA-class dry cargo ship, being completed in Leningrad.

Space control–monitoring ship Aκαδεμικ Sεργει Κοroλεv

Κοsmonaut Vladimir Komarov

Space control–monitoring ship KOSMONAUT VLADIMIR KOMAROV

Stern of KOSMONAUT VLADIMIR KOMAROV showing two sets of Vee Cone communications antennas, the second set mounted above the ship's funnel.

## 4 SPACE CONTROL–MONITORING SHIPS: "BOROVICHI" CLASS

| Name | Completed |
|------|-----------|
| BOROVICHI | 1965 |
| KEGOSTROV | 1966 |
| MORZHOVETS | 1966 |
| NEVEL | 1966 |

| | |
|---|---|
| Builders: | Zhdanov Shipyard, Leningrad |
| Displacement: | |
| Tonnage: | 1,835 DWT |
| Length: | 402 ft 6 in (122.0 m) |
| Beam: | 55 ft 3 in (16.75 m) |
| Draft: | 22 ft 5 in (6.8 m) |
| Propulsion: | diesel (Burmeister & Wain Bryansk); 5,200 bhp; 1 shaft |
| Speed: | 15.5 knots |
| Range: | |
| Complement: | |
| Helicopters: | no facilities |
| Radars: | |

Laid down as VYTEGRALES-type cargo ships but completed to an SESS configuration. These ships differ in configuration from the BELYAYEV class, which were converted after service as cargo ships.

Borovichi-class space control–monitoring ship Kegostrov (Courtesy *Flottes de Combat*)

Borovichi-class space control–monitoring ship Nevel in Leningrad (1975, U.S. Navy)

## RESEARCH SHIPS

### 5 HYDROGRAPHIC-METEOROLOGICAL RESEARCH SHIPS: "AKADEMIK SHULEYKIN" CLASS

| Name | Name | Completed |
|------|------|-----------|
| AKADEMIK SHULEYKIN | PROFESSOR MOLCHANOV | |
| AKADEMIK SHOKAL'SKIY | PROFESSOR MUL'TANOVSKIY | 1982– |
| PROFESSOR KHROMOV | | |

| | |
|---|---|
| Builders: | Laivateollisuus Shipyard, Turku (Finland) |
| Displacement: | 2,000 tons full load |
| Length: | |
| Beam: | |
| Draft: | |
| Propulsion: | 2 diesels; 3,000 bhp; 1 shaft |
| Speed: | |
| Range: | |
| Complement: | 38 + 38 scientists |
| Helicopters: | no facilities |
| Radars: | |

These ships are specially designed for arctic operations. The lead ship, AKADEMIK SHULEYKIN, began her first scientific cruise on 18 July 1982.

### 1 HYDROGRAPHIC RESEARCH SHIP: "AKADEMIK MSTISLAV KELDYSH"

| Name | Completed |
|------|-----------|
| AKADEMIK MSTISLAV KELDYSH | Feb 1981 |

| | |
|---|---|
| Builders: | Hollming Shipyard, Rauma (Finland) |
| Displacement: | |
| Length: | 403 ft 3 in (122.2 m) |
| Beam: | 58 ft 9 in (17.8 m) |
| Draft: | 19 ft 6 in (5.9 m) |
| Propulsion: | 4 diesels (Wärtsilä Vasa 824TS); 5,820 bhp; 2 shafts |
| Speed: | 16 knots |
| Range: | |
| Complement: | approx. 50 + 80 scientists |
| Helicopters: | no facilities |
| Radars: | |

The AKADEMIK MSTILAV KELDYSH is listed by the Soviet Union as the flagship of the nation's oceanographic fleet. The ship is based at Kaliningrad.

Design: The ship has 15 separate laboratories and can carry and support PISCES-type research submersibles. A bow-thruster and a stern auxiliary propulsion unit are fitted for precise station keeping during research activities. The latter is an Aquamaster unit with thrust provided through a Z-drive arrangement, can be rotated 360°, and is fully retractable.

The flagship of the Soviet oceanographic fleet, the AKADEMIK MSTISLAV KELDYSH, under way in mid-1982 while on her first series of scientific cruises. (1982, U.S. Navy)

## 3 HYDROGRAPHIC–METEOROLOGICAL RESEARCH SHIPS: "VITYAZ'" CLASS

| Name | Completed |
| --- | --- |
| Akademik Aleksandr Nesmeyanov | 1982 |
| Vityaz' | 1981 |
| . . . . . . | 1982 |

| | |
| --- | --- |
| Builders: | Warski Shipyard, Szczecin |
| Displacement: | approx. 6,000 tons full load |
| Tonnage: | 1,800 DWT |
| Length: | 359 ft 8 in (109.0 m) |
| Beam: | 53 ft 6 in (16.2 m) |
| Draft: | 17 ft 10 in (5.4 m) |
| Propulsion: | diesel (Sulzer Zgoda); 6,400 bhp; t shaft |
| Speed: | 17 knots |
| Range: | |
| Complement: | . . . . . . + 60 scientists |
| Helicopters: | |
| Radars: | |

These ships are the Polish B86 design. Fitted with 20 to 26 laboratories and provisions for deep-sea "saturation" diving to depths of 850 ft (250 m). They can also carry manned research submersibles of the Argus type and the unmanned Zvuk-type submersibles. The Vityaz' was launched on 5 Sep. 1980, and the Nesmeyanov in Feb. 1981.

## 1 POLAR RESEARCH SHIP: "MIKHAIL SOMOV" CLASS

| Name | Completed |
| --- | --- |
| Mikhail Somov | 1975 |

| | |
| --- | --- |
| Builders: | Kherson |
| Displacement: | |
| Tonnage: | 8,445 DWT |
| Length: | 441 ft 7 in (133.8 m) |
| Beam: | 66 ft (20.0 m) |
| Draft: | |
| Propulsion: | DE: 2 diesels driving generator connected to 1 electric motor; 7,200 bhp; 1 shaft |
| Speed: | 15.5 knots |
| Range: | |
| Complement: | |
| Helicopters: | landing area |
| Radars: | |

The Somov is a modification of the Amguema-class cargo design. The ship is operated by the Arctic and Antarctic Research Institute as a research and logistic support ship.

Hydrographic-meteorological research ship Vityaz' (1982)

**9 HYDROGRAPHIC–METEOROLOGICAL RESEARCH SHIPS: "VALERIAN URYVAYEV" CLASS**

| Name | Name | Name | Completed |
|---|---|---|---|
| DALNIYE ZELYENTSY | MORSKOY GEOFIZIK | VSEVLOD BERYOZKIN | |
| ISKATEL | RUDOLF SAMOYLOVICH | VULKANOLOG | 1974–1978 |
| ISSLEDOVATEL | VALERIAN URYVAYEV | YAKOV GAKKEL | |

| | |
|---|---|
| Builders: | Khabarovsk |
| Displacement: | |
| Tonnage: | 350 DWT |
| Length: | 181 ft 2 in (54.9 m) |
| Beam: | 31 ft 2 in (9.5 m) |
| Draft: | |
| Propulsion: | diesel (Karl Liebknecht); 875 bhp in early ships, 1,320 bhp in later ships; 1 shaft |
| Speed: | 11.5 knots in early ships, 12.5 knots in later ships |
| Range: | |
| Complement: | |
| Helicopters: | no facilities |
| Radars: | |

These ships have with a bow-thruster for precision station keeping.

The MIKHAIL SOMOV is a modification of the AMGUEMA-class cargo design operated as a research and logistic support ship by the Arctic and Antarctic Research Institute. Note the icebreaking prow. (L. & L. Van Ginderen, 1982)

**9 HYDROGRAPHIC RESEARCH SHIPS: MODIFIED "DMITRIY OVTSYN" CLASS**

| Name | Name | Completed |
|---|---|---|
| FEDOR MATISEN | PROFESSOR BOGOROV | |
| GEORGIY MAKSIMOV | PROFESSOR KURENTSOV | |
| IVAN KIREYEV | PROFESSOR SHTOKMAN | 1976–1983 |
| PAVEL BASHMAKOV | PROFESSOR VODYANITSKIY | |
| YAKOV SMIRNITSKIY | | |

| | |
|---|---|
| Builders: | Laivateollisuus Shipyard, Turku |
| Displacement: | 1,600 tons full load |
| Tonnage: | 600 DWT |
| Length: | 220 ft 6 in (66.8 m) |
| Beam: | 39 ft 3 in (11.9 m) |
| Draft: | |
| Propulsion: | diesel (Klockner-Humboldt-Deutz); 2,200 bhp; 1 shaft |
| Speed: | 13.5 knots |
| Range: | |
| Complement: | |
| Helicopters: | no facilities |
| Radars: | |

These research ships are improved versions of the DMITRIY OVTSYN design. They have cranes forward and an open working deck aft. Bow-thrusters are fitted.

**12 HYDROGRAPHIC RESEARCH SHIPS: "DMITRIY OVTSYN" CLASS**

| Name | Name | Name | Completed |
|---|---|---|---|
| DMITRIY LAPTEV | NIKOLAY KOLOMEYTSYEV | VALERIAN ALBANOV | |
| DMITRIY OVTSYN | NIKOLAY YEVGENOV | VLADIMIR | |
| DMITRIY STERLIGOV | SERGEY KRAVKOV | SUKHOTKIY | 1970–1974 |
| EDUARD TOLL | STEPHAN MALYGIN | | |

| | |
|---|---|
| Builders: | Laivateollisuus Shipyard, Turku (Finland) |
| Displacement: | |
| Tonnage: | 640 DWT |
| Length: | 227 ft 4 in (68.9 m) |
| Beam: | 41 ft (12.4 m) |
| Draft: | |
| Propulsion: | diesel (Klockner-Humboldt-Deutz); 2,200 bhp; 1 shaft |
| Speed: | 13.5 knots |
| Range: | |
| Complement: | |
| Helicopters: | no facilities |
| Radars: | |

These ships can be distinguished by their stub mast on the forecastle. Fitted with bow-thruster.

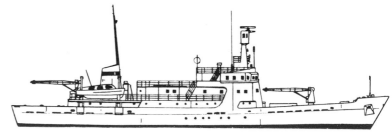

DMITRIYI OVTSYN-class hydrographic research ship (Siegfried Breyer)

**3 HYDROGRAPHIC–METEOROLOGICAL RESEARCH SHIPS: MOD. "PASSAT" CLASS**

| Name | Completed |
|---|---|
| ERNST KRENKEL (ex-VIKHR) | 1971 |
| GEORGIY USHAKOV (ex-SHKVAL) | 1971 |
| VIKTOR BUGAEV (ex-PORYV) | 1971 |

| | |
|---|---|
| Builders: | Warski Shipyard, Szczecin |
| Displacement: | |
| Tonnage: | 1,500 DWT |
| Length: | 300 ft 4 in (100.1 m) |
| Beam: | 48 ft 10 in (14.8 m) |
| Draft: | |
| Propulsion: | 2 diesels (Sulzer or Zgoda); 4,800 bhp; 2 shafts |
| Speed: | 16 knots |
| Range: | |
| Complement: | |
| Helicopters: | no facilities |
| Radars: | 2 Don-2 (navigation) |

Modified PASSAT-class ships.

**6 HYDROGRAPHIC–METEOROLOGICAL RESEARCH SHIPS: "PASSAT" CLASS**

| Name | Name | Name | Completed |
|---|---|---|---|
| MUSSON | PASSAT | PRIBOY | 1968–1970 |
| OKEAN | PRILIV | VOLNA | |

| | |
|---|---|
| Builders: | Warski Shipyard, Szczecin |
| Displacement: | |
| Tonnage: | 1,170 DWT |
| Length: | 320 ft 5 in (97.1 m) |
| Beam: | 45 ft 8 in (13.8 m) |
| Draft: | 17 ft 2 in (5.2 m) |
| Propulsion: | 2 diesels (Sulzer or Cegielski); 4,800 bhp; 2 shafts |
| Speed: | 16 knots |
| Range: | |
| Complement: | approx. 50 + 60 scientists |
| Helicopters: | no facilities |
| Radars: | 2 Don-2 (navigation) |

These ships are Polish B88 design with 23 laboratories provided.

Modified PASSAT-class hydrographic-meteorological research ship GEORGIY USHA-KOV (1977, di Carlo Martinelli)

PASSAT-class hydrographic-meteorological research ship PRIBOY (1981, L. & L. Van Ginderen)

**7 OCEANOGRAPHIC RESEARCH SHIPS: "AKADEMIK KURCHATOV" CLASS**

| Name | Name | Completed |
|---|---|---|
| AKADEMIK KOROLOYOV | AKADEMIK VERNADSKIY | |
| AKADEMIK KURCHATOV | AKADEMIK VIZE | 1966–1968 |
| AKADEMIK MENDELEYEV | AKADEMIK ZUBOV | |
| AKADEMIK SHIRSHOV | | |

| | |
|---|---|
| Builders: | Mathias Thesen Shipyard, Wismar (East Germany) |
| Displacement: | 5,460 tons standard |
| | 7,500 tons full load |
| Length: | 409 ft 10 in (124.2 m) |
| Beam: | 56 ft 1 in (17.0 m) |
| Draft: | 21 ft 6 in (6.5 m) |
| Propulsion: | 2 diesels (Halberstadt-M.A.N. K6Z 57/80); 8,000 bhp; 2 shafts |
| Speed: | 19 knots |
| Range: | 20,000 n. miles at 16 knots |
| Complement: | approx. 85 + 80 scientists |
| Helicopters: | 1 utility helicopter |
| Radars: | 2 or 3 Don-2 (navigation) |

These are similar to four ships operated by the Soviet Navy. They have graceful, liner-like lines, with a helicopter deck and telescoping hangar. There are 27 laboratories. They are also fitted with two 190-hp bow-thrusters and an active 300-hp rudder for precise station keeping.

**1 NONMAGNETIC SAILING SCHOONER: "ZARYA"**

| Name | Completed |
|---|---|
| ZARYA | 1956 |

| | |
|---|---|
| Builders: | (Finland) |
| Displacement: | 580 tons light |
| Length: | 131 ft (39.7 m) |
| Beam: | 32 ft 6 in (9.8 m) |
| Draft: | |
| Propulsion: | diesel; 300 bhp; 1 shaft |
| Speed: | 6.5 knots with sails |
| | 9 knots with auxiliary engine |
| Complement: | approx. 25 + 9 scientists |
| Radars: | |

The ZARYA is a three-masted schooner with a wooden hull and minimum built-in iron and steel, with brass and copper-bronze alloys used where possible. The ship is employed in surveys of the earth's magnetic field. Several other three-masted schooners are believed being used for training and research, the survivors of a class built in Finland shortly after World War II.

AKADEMIK KURCHATOV-class oceanographic research ship AKADEMIK SHIRSHOV (1980)

The nonmagnetic sailing schooner ZARYA during a port call in Hobart, Tasmania. The ship provides Soviet scientists with an essentially nonmagnetic platform for studies in remote ocean areas.

## ICEBREAKERS

There are several river and inland icebreakers in service in addition to the ships listed here.

### 4 ICEBREAKERS: "KAPITAN SOROKIN" CLASS

| Name | Completed |
| --- | --- |
| KAPITAN DRANITSYN | 1980 |
| KAPITAN KLEBNIKOV | 1981 |
| KAPITAN NIKOLAYEV | 1978 |
| KAPITAN SOROKIN | 1977 |

| | |
| --- | --- |
| Builders: | Wärtsilä Shipyard, Helsinki |
| Displacement: | 14,900 tons full load |
| Tonnage: | 4,225 DWT |
| Length: | 435 ft 3 in (131.9 m) |
| Beam: | 88 ft 1 in (26.7 m) |
| Draft: | 28 ft (8.5 m) |
| Propulsion: | DE: 6 diesels (Wärtsilä/Sulzer ZH40) 24,840 bhp driving 6 generators 48 connected to 3 electric motors, 10,000 shp; 3 shafts |
| Speed: | 19 knots |
| Range: | |
| Complement: | 185 |
| Helicopters: | 1 or 2 utility helicopters |
| Radars: | |

These are shallow-draft polar icebreakers. They have a massive superstructure with a helicopter hangar and landing deck. They have especially elaborate accommodations, including a swimming pool, gymnasium, library, and cinema seating 54 persons.

### 2 + 1 NUCLEAR–PROPELLED ICEBREAKERS: "ARKTIKA" CLASS

| Name | Launched | Completed |
| --- | --- | --- |
| LEONID BREZHNEV (ex-ARKTIKA) | Oct 1973 | 1 May 1975 |
| SIBIR' | 23 Feb 1976 | 27 Dec 1977 |
| ROSSIYA | | (1983)(?) |

| | |
| --- | --- |
| Builders: | Baltic Shipyard, Leningrad |
| Displacement: | approx. 25,000 tons full load |
| Length: | 488 ft 5 in (148.0 m) |
| Beam: | 99 ft (30.0 m) |
| Draft: | |
| Propulsion: | TE: 2 steam turbines (Kirov), 75,000 shp driving 3 generators (Elektrosila); 3 shafts |
| Reactors: | 2 pressurized-water type |
| Speed: | 21 knots |
| Range: | see below |
| Complement: | |
| Helicopters: | 2 utility helicopters |
| Radars: | |
| EW systems: | 1 Head Net-C IFF only |

These are the world's most powerful icebreakers. The lead ship was originally named ARKTIKA; the ship was renamed LEONID BREZHNEV in honor of the late Soviet president and party chief, L. I. Brezhnev, who died in November 1982. The ARKTIKA began sea trials on 3 November 1974 and the SIBIR' on 22 October 1977. Construction of the ROSSIYA began in 1981.

The ARKTIKA was the first surface ship to reach the geographic North Pole, doing so on 17 August 1977. (The U.S. Coast Guard icebreaker WESTWIND [WAGB 281] came within 375 n.miles of the North Pole in 1979.) The ARKTIKA spent 15 hours at the North Pole; her round trip from Murmansk took 13 days.

The design provides for a large helicopter deck aft and helicopter hangar. Vee Cone antennas are on the aftermast/exhaust stack.

The ARKTIKA is reported to have been armed during her initial sea trials, carrying two 76-mm twin mounts, four 30-mm Gatling guns, and associated fire control systems; they were subsequently removed.

The ships' nuclear cores are expected to have a five-year service life.

The SIBIR' breaking ice in the Kara Sea. (1978, Sovfoto)

The LEONID BREZHNEV (formerly ARKTIKA) in the Kola Gulf. Note her icebreaking bow, massive superstructure, high freeboard, and Vee Cone antenna aft. She has Head Net-C radar on her forward mast.

## 3 ICEBREAKERS: "YERMAK" CLASS

| Name | Completed |
|------|-----------|
| ADMIRAL MAKAROV | 12 June 1975 |
| KRASIN | 1976 |
| YERMAK | 1973 |

| | |
|---|---|
| Builders: | Wärtsilä Shipyard, Helsinki |
| Displacement: | 20,240 tons full load |
| Tonnage: | 7,560 DWT |
| Length: | 445 ft 6 in (135.0 m) |
| Beam: | 85 ft 10 in (26.0 m) |
| Draft: | 36 ft 3 in (11.0 m) |
| Propulsion: | DE: 9 diesels (Wärtsilä/Sulzer 12ZH40/48) 41,400 bhp driving 9 generators connected to 3 electric motors, 36,000 hp; 3 shafts |
| Speed: | 19.5 knots |
| Range: | 40,000 n.miles at 15 knots |
| Complement: | 118 |
| Helicopters: | 1 or 2 utility helicopters |
| Radars: | |

These ships are improved and enlarged versions of the MOSKVA class. They have a helicopter hangar and landing platform. There are spare accommodations for 28 passengers. Accommodations include a theater seating 100, swimming pool, sauna, and gymnasium.

## 3 RESEARCH ICEBREAKERS: MODIFIED "DOBRYNYA NIKITICH" CLASS

| Name | Completed |
|------|-----------|
| GEORGIY SEDOV | 1967 |
| OTTO SCHMIDT | 1979 |
| PETR PASHTUSOV (ex-LEDOKOL 10) | 1966 |

| | |
|---|---|
| Builders: | Admiralty Shipyard, Leningrad |
| Displacement: | 3,800 tons full load |
| Length: | 223 ft 5 in (67.7 m) |
| Beam: | 59 ft 9 in (18.1 m) |
| Draft: | |
| Propulsion: | DE: 3 diesels (13D100) driving 3 generators connected to 3 electric motors, 5,400 bhp; 3 shafts (1 forward) |
| Speed: | 14.5 knots |
| Range: | 5,500 n. miles at 12.5 knots |
| | 13,000 n. miles at 9.5 knots |
| Complement: | . . . . . . + 30 scientists |
| Helicopters: | platform fitted |
| Radars: | . . . Don Kay (navigation) |

These icebreakers are specially configured for polar research. They have a kingpost aft and a taller funnel compared to the numerous other ships of this basic design. Fourteen laboratories are provided.

YERMAK (U.S. Navy)

## 12 ICEBREAKERS: "DOBRYNYA NIKITICH" CLASS

| Name | Name | Completed |
|------|------|-----------|
| AFANASIY NIKITIN | SEMYEN CHELYUSHKIN | |
| FYODOR LITKE | SEMYEN DEZHNEV | |
| IVAN KRUZENSHTERN | VASILIY POYARKOV | 1961–1971 |
| IVAN MOSKVITIN | VASILIY PRONCHISHCHEV | |
| KHARITON LAPTEV | YURIY LIYANSKIY | |

| | |
|---|---|
| Builders: | Admiralty Shipyard, Leningrad |
| Displacement: | 3,800 tons full load |
| Length: | 231 ft (70.0 m) |
| Beam: | 60 ft 5 in (18.3 m) |
| Draft: | 21 ft 2 in (6.4 m) |
| Propulsion: | DE: 3 diesels (13D100) driving 3 generators connected to electric motors; 5,400 bhp; 3 shafts (1 forward) |
| Speed: | 14.5 knots |
| Range: | 5,500 n. miles at 12.5 knots |
| | 13,000 n. miles at 9.5 knots |
| Complement: | |
| Helicopters: | no facilities |
| Radars: | . . . Don-2 (navigation) |

Icebreakers of this class are also operated by the Soviet Navy and similar ships by the KGB (see chapter 21), and four ships of a modified configuration for polar research are listed separately. One additional ship of this design was delivered to East Germany in 1968.

Names: These ships were originally designated LEDOKOL (icebreaker) in a numeral series.

DOBRYNYA NIKITICH-class icebreaker IVAN MOSKVITIN

DOBRYNYA NIKITICH-class icebreaker IVAN KRUZENSHTERN

## 5 ICEBREAKERS: "MOSKVA" CLASS

| Name | Name | Name | Completed |
|------|------|------|-----------|
| KIEV | MOSKVA | VLADIVOSTOK | 1960–1968 |
| LENINGRAD | MURMANSK | | |

| | |
|---|---|
| Builders: | Wärtsilä Shipyard, Helsinki |
| Displacement: | |
| Tonnage: | 5,610 DWT |
| Length: | 403 ft 3 in (122.2 m) |
| Beam: | 81 ft 2 in (24.6 m) |
| Draft: | 31 ft 4 in (9.5 m) |
| Propulsion: | DE: 8 diesels (Wärtsilä/Sulzer), 26,000 bhp driving 8 generators connected to 4 electric motors, 22,000 hp; 3 shafts |
| Speed: | 18.25 knots |
| Range: | 20,000 n.miles at 12 knots |
| Complement: | approx. 110 |
| Helicopters: | 1 utility helicopter |
| Radars: | |

These ships have a helicopter hangar and landing platform.

MOSKVA-class icebreaker MURMANSK (Sovfoto)

The MOSKVA-class icebreaker KIEV, like most of the Soviet Union's larger, non-nuclear icebreakers, was built in Finland. The Finnish shipbuilding industry has specialized in this type of ship. (Wärtsilä Shipyard)

## 1 NUCLEAR–PROPELLED ICEBREAKER: "LENIN"

| Name | Launched | Completed |
|---|---|---|
| LENIN | 5 December 1957 | September 1959 |

| | |
|---|---|
| Builders: | Admiralty Shipyard, Leningrad |
| Displacement: | 17,280 tons full load |
| Tonnage: | 3,850 DWT |
| Length: | 442 ft 3 in (134.0 m) |
| Beam: | 91 ft 1 in (27.6 m) |
| Draft: | 31 ft 8 in (9.6 m) |
| Propulsion: | TE: 4 steam turbines (Kirov), 44,000 shp driving 4 generators connected to 3 electric motors (Elektrosila), 39,200 hp; 3 shafts |
| Reactors: | 2 pressurized-water type |
| Speed: | 18 knots |
| Range: | see below |
| Complement: | approx. 150 |
| Helicopters: | 1 utility helicopter |
| Radars: | |

The LENIN was the world's first nuclear-propelled surface ship. The ship's keel was laid down on 25 August 1956; the ship left the shipyard for the first time on 12 September 1959 and anchored in the Neva River until beginning sea trials on 15 September 1959. The LENIN arrived at Murmansk to begin operations in the Arctic in May 1960.

The LENIN began Arctic operations on 15 July 1960, with the ship's first navigation season on the Northern Sea route lasting to 24 October.

There was a 16-year interval between completion of the LENIN and the next Soviet nuclear surface ship, the icebreaker ARKTIKA.

Design: The ship has a conventional icebreaker design. As built, the shielding for the three-reactor plant weighed more than 3,000 tons. The ship introduced a high degree of habitability to Soviet icebreakers, with one- or two-man cabins, a movie theater, library, music salon, and an extensive medical facility.

Engineering: The ship was built with three reactors, two being sufficient to propel the ship at full speed, with the third reactor available for maintenance and research. The ship suffered a major nuclear radiation accident in the late 1960s and was abandoned for more than a year; she was rebuilt and a two-reactor plant installed. The ship's fuel cores have a service life of 18 months.

## 3 ICEBREAKERS: "KAPITAN BELOUSOV" CLASS

| Name | Name | Name | Completed |
|---|---|---|---|
| KAPITAN BELOUSOV | KAPITAL MELEKHOV | KAPITAN VORONIN | 1955–1956 |

| | |
|---|---|
| Builders: | Wärtsilä Shipyard, Helsinki |
| Displacement: | 4,500 tons full load |
| Tonnage: | 1,445 DWT |
| Length: | 274 ft 7 in (83.2 m) |
| Beam: | 64 ft (19.4 m) |
| Draft: | 20 ft 6 in (6.2 m) |
| Propulsion: | DE: 6 diesels (Polar), 10,500 bhp driving 6 generators connected to electric motors; 4 shafts (2 forward and 2 aft) |
| Speed: | 16.5 knots |
| Range: | |
| Complement: | approx. 85 |
| Helicopters: | no facilities |
| Radars: | |

One additional icebreaker of this class was built for Sweden and one for Finland.

KAPITAN BELOUSOV-class icebreaker

The nuclear icebreaker LENIN in her natural Arctic environment. (Sovfoto)

## TRAINING SHIPS

The following ships provide at-sea instruction for Soviet Merchant Marine personnel, mainly in engineering, seamanship, and cargo handling. Some of these ships are believed to be used for training naval personnel. There are also several smaller merchant training ships as well as a number of fisheries training ships.

### 9 TRAINING SHIPS: PROFESSOR CLASS

| Name | Name | Completed |
|------|------|-----------|
| PROFESSOR ANICHKOV | PROFESSOR RYBALTOVSKIY | |
| PROFESSOR KHLYUSTIN | PROFESSOR SHCHYOGOLEV | |
| PROFESSOR KUDREVICH | PROFESSOR UKHOV | 1970–1973 |
| PROFESSOR MINYAYEV | PROFESSOR YUSHCHENKO | |
| PROFESSOR PAVLENKO | | |

| | |
|---|---|
| Builders: | Warski Shipyard, Szczecin |
| Displacement: | |
| Tonnage: | 5,385–5,455 DWT |
| Length: | 402 ft 10 in–405 ft 8 in (122.1 m–122.9 m) |
| Beam: | 56 ft 2 in (17.0 m) |
| Draft: | |
| Propulsion: | diesels (Burmeister & Wain Cegielski); 4,900 bhp; 1 shaft, except KHLYUSTIN and PAVLENKO have Sulzer diesels; 5,500 bhp |
| Speed: | 15.25 knots, except KHLYUSTIN and PAVLENKO 15.75 knots |
| Range: | |
| Complement: | |
| Helicopters: | no facilities |
| Radars: | |

These are Polish B80-design ships employed in cadet training. Details vary. A similar ship was built for Bulgaria, two for Poland, and one for Romania.

Professor-class training ship PROFESSOR UKHOV (1975)

### 3 TRAINING SHIPS: MODIFIED "KOVEL" CLASS

| Name | Name | Name | Completed |
|------|------|------|-----------|
| GORIZONT | MERIDIAN | ZENIT | 1961–1962 |

| | |
|---|---|
| Builders: | Neptune Shipyard, Rostock |
| Displacement: | |
| Tonnage: | 3,085 DWT |
| Length: | 343 ft 2 in (104.0 m) |
| Beam: | 47 ft 7 in (14.4 m) |
| Draft: | |
| Propulsion: | diesel (M.A.N.); 3,250 bhp; 1 shaft |
| Speed: | 14 knots |
| Range: | |
| Complement: | |
| Helicopters: | no facilities |
| Radars: | |

These ships were completed as cadet training ships, being converted during construction from KOVEL-class dry cargo ships. (Three other ships of this class are civilian research ships.)

### 1 TRAINING SHIP: CONVERTED CARGO SHIP

| Name | Completed |
|------|-----------|
| EQUATOR (ex-MERIDIAN, ex-EMPIRE NEATH, ex-German CATANIA) | 1935 |

| | |
|---|---|
| Builders: | Rostock |
| Displacement: | |
| Length: | 323 ft 7 in (98.1 m) |
| Beam: | 43 ft 9 in (13.3 m) |
| Draft: | |
| Propulsion: | compound with low-pressure turbine |
| Boilers: | |
| Speed: | |
| Range: | |
| Complement: | |
| Helicopters: | no facilities |
| Radars: | |

Converted in 1949 from a dry cargo ship.

## 1 SAIL TRAINING BARK: "TOVARISCH"

| Name | Completed |
| --- | --- |
| TOVARISCH (ex-German GORCH FOCK) | 1933 |

| | |
| --- | --- |
| Builders: | Blohm & Voss, Hamburg (Germany) |
| Displacement: | 1,350 tons standard |
| | 1,500 tons full load |
| Length: | 269 ft 6 in (81.7 m) |
| Beam: | 39 ft 4 in (11.9 m) |
| Draft: | 17 ft (5.2 m) |
| Propulsion: | 1 auxiliary diesel; 520 bhp; 1 shaft |
| Speed: | 8 knots on diesel |
| Range: | |
| Complement: | approx. 50 + 120 cadets |
| Radars: | |

The ship was built as the training ship GORCH FOCK for the German Navy, one of four similar sail training vessels (the MIRCEA built for Romania and the HORST WESSEL and ALBERT LEO SCHLAGETER for Germany). The GORCH FOCK served as a naval training ship until scuttled on 1 May 1945 near Stralsund. The ship was salvaged by Soviet forces in 1948 and placed in service in 1951 as the TOVARISCH. She is home-ported in Kherson as a training ship for the Soviet merchant marine.

The HORST WESSEL now serves as the U.S. Coast Guard training bark EAGLE (WIX 327) and the ex-ALFRED LEO SCHLAGETER, after briefly being held by the U.S. Navy, serves in the Portuguese Navy. The TOVARISCH and KRUZENSHTERN participated in Operational Sail during the American Bicentennial celebrations in U.S. ports in July 1976.

She is rigged as a bark with approximately 18,400 ft$^2$ of sail area.

Sail training bark TOVARISCH (1975, Archiv Koop)

## 1 SAIL TRAINING BARK: "KRUZENSHTERN"

| Name | Completed |
| --- | --- |
| KRUZENSHTERN (ex-German PADUA) | 1926 |

| | |
| --- | --- |
| Builders: | Tecklenborg, Wesermünde (Germany) |
| Displacement: | 3,065 tons standard |
| | 3,570 tons full load |
| Length: | 375 ft 4 in (113.7 m) |
| Beam: | 46 ft (13.9 m) |
| Draft: | 25 ft 7 in (7.75 m) |
| Propulsion: | 2 auxiliary diesels; 1,600 bhp; 1 shaft |
| Speed: | |
| Range: | |
| Complement: | approx. 70 + 200 cadets |
| Radars: | |

The ship was the last cargo-carrying, four-masted bark to be built. Named PADUA, she sailed for the Hamburg firm of L. Laeisz until being laid up in 1932. She sailed again briefly before World War II and was taken over by the USSR in 1945 and subsequently employed as a sail training ship. She is home-ported in Riga as a training ship for the fishing industry.

She is a four-masted bark with approximately 36,600 ft$^2$ of sail area.

The Soviet sail training bark TOVARISCH while participating in Operation Sail, part of the American bicentennial celebrations in New York Harbor on 4 July 1976. Just behind the ship (to left) are the buildings of Ellis Island, the arrival point for millions of Russians who immigrated to the United States prior to the revolution of 1917. (U.S. Navy)

Sail training bark KRUZENSHTERN (1976, U.S. Navy)

### 1 SAIL TRAINING BARK: "SEDOV"

| Name | Completed |
|---|---|
| SEDOV (ex-German KOMMODORE JOHNSON, ex-MAGDALENE VINNEN) | 1922 |

| | |
|---|---|
| Builders: | Germania Shipyard, Kiel (Germany) |
| Displacement: | 3,065 tons standard |
| | 3,570 tons full load |
| Length: | 387 ft 5 in (117.4 m) |
| Beam: | 47 ft 10 in (14.5 m) |
| Draft: | 24 ft 1 in (7.3 m) |
| Propulsion: | 2 auxiliary diesels; 1 shaft |
| Speed: | |
| Range: | |
| Complement: | . . . . . . + 130 cadets |
| Radars: | |

This ship was built as a training ship for the North German Lloyd line. She was acquired by the Soviet Union in 1945 and employed as a sail training ship. She was laid up from 1967 to January 1981 and subsequently employed as a merchant marine and fisheries training ship. Home-ported in Riga.

She is a four-masted bark with a sail area of approximately 37,000 ft².

The sail training bark KRUZENSHTERN also participated in the American bicentennial celebrations, where both of these photos were taken. She is significantly larger than the TOVARISCH and four-masted although still with a bark rig. (1976, U.S. Navy)

# 24
# Naval Aircraft

The Blackjack-A is shown in flight with its variable-geometry wings extended in this artist's concept of the new Soviet strike aircraft. The Blackjack began flight tests in 1982 and could be operational as early as 1986–1987. The plane's unrefuelled strike range is estimated (on the basis of aircraft size) to be equal to that of the Backfire-B with one in-flight refueling. (U.S. Department of Defense)

This chapter describes the principal aircraft currently flown by Soviet Naval Aviation (SNA).[1]

## DESIGNATIONS

Contemporary Soviet aircraft are given designations in two schemes: The first uses a NATO code name that indicates the aircraft type and the specific aircraft, and the other the Soviet method of identifying the aircraft design bureau and sequence of the aircraft.

The NATO scheme now in use was adopted in 1954 with name assignments being made by the Air Standards Coordinating Committee. The following categories are applicable to SNA aircraft:

B = Bomber (one-syllable names for propeller aircraft and two-syllable names for jet aircraft)
C = Cargo
F = Fighter
H = Helicopter
M = Miscellaneous fixed-wing (including maritime patrol aircraft)

Suffix letters are appended to the NATO code names to indicate variants of a basic aircraft. The addition of these variant suffix letters to the *Soviet* designations, as Tu-20D, is incorrect.

Soviet design-bureau designations applicable to naval aircraft are based on the following code, derived from the names of the founders of the specific bureaus:

Be = Beriev
Il = Ilyushin
Ka = Kamov
Mi = Mil´
Su = Sukhoi
Tu = Tupolev
Yak = Yakovlev

This basic scheme was adopted by the Soviet government in 1940 (although aircraft designs supervised by Andrei N. Tupolev carried the bureau prefix ANT until 1947). The numbers used in conjunction with these bureau designations indicate the sequence of the aircraft, with two numerical series in use for some aircraft, one indicating the bureau design and one the (later) military designation.

Suffixes are used with these bureau designations, the most common ones being *bis* for later variants, M for *Modifikatsirovanny* (modification), R for *Razvedchik* (reconnaissance), and U for *Uchebno* (instructional—for trainer version).

## TECHNICAL DATA

Performance data is approximate, based on the best available public sources. Radius generally indicates a majority of the flight to and from the target at optimum speed and altitude, with a low-level, high-speed "dash" to and from the target, except that missile launching aircraft will generally release their weapons at a medium altitude (approximately 20,000 ft/6,000 m).

[1]More detailed descriptions of Soviet aircraft will be found in the monthly journal *Air International* and the annual *Jane's All the World's Aircraft*. In addition, an excellent discussion of contemporary Soviet naval aircraft is provided in Bill Sweetman, *Soviet Military Aircraft* (Novato, Calif.: Presidio Press, 1981).

## AIRCRAFT TYPES

The aircraft listed in table 24-1 are currently operated by Soviet Naval Aviation and are described in this chapter. Variants of bomber-type aircraft flown by Soviet strategic aviation are also noted for completeness and because of their ability to support naval missions. Aircraft are listed in the chapter by type and then alphabetically by NATO code name.

**TABLE 24-1. SOVIET NAVAL AIRCRAFT**

| Soviet Designation | NATO Name | Variant | SNA | Strategic Aviation | Role |
|---|---|---|---|---|---|
| | | Bomber-type Aircraft | | | |
| Tu-22M | Backfire | A | | | (pre-production aircraft) |
| | | B | • | • | missile strike |
| Tu-16 | Badger | A | • | • | bomber or tanker |
| | | B | | | (out of service) |
| | | C | • | | missile strike |
| | | D | • | • | ELINT/electronic recon |
| | | E | • | • | photo recon |
| | | F | • | • | electronic/photo recon |
| | | G | • | • | missile strike |
| | | H | • | • | EW/strike escort |
| | | J | • | • | EW/strike escort |
| | | K | • | • | ELINT/electronic recon |
| Tu-20 | Bear | A | | • | bomber |
| | | B | | • | missile strike |
| | | C | | • | missile strike |
| | | D | • | | recon/targeting |
| | | E | | • | ELINT/photo recon |
| | | F | • | | ASW |
| Tu-22 | Blinder | A | • | • | bomber |
| | | B | | • | missile strike |
| | | C | • | • | photo recon |
| | | D | • | • | trainer |
| | | Other Aircraft | | | |
| Il-18 | Coot | A | | | ELINT/electronic recon |
| An-12 | Cub | B | | | ELINT/electronic recon |
| | | C | | | ECM |
| | | — | | | ASW test bed |
| Su-17 | Fitter | C/D | | | fighter/attack |
| Yak-36 | Forger | A | | | fighter/attack |
| | | B | | | fighter/attack-trainer |
| Mi-14 | Haze | A | | | ASW |
| Ka-32 | Helix | — | | | ASW |
| Mi-8 | Hip | — | | | transport |
| | | — | | | mine countermeasure |
| Ka-25 | Hormone | A | | | ASW |
| | | B | | | missile targeting |
| | | C | | | utility/transport |
| Be-12 | Mail | — | | | reconnaissance/ASW |
| Il-38 | May | — | | | reconnaissance/ASW |

## BOMBER AIRCRAFT

### Tu-22M Backfire (Tupolev)

The Tu-22M Backfire is a long-range, high-performance bomber flown by Soviet strategic aviation and Soviet Naval Aviation. In the former service the Backfire appears to be assigned to the theater strike role and is not intended for strategic attacks against the United States; SNA employs the Backfire in the anti-ship missile role. Backfires have been assigned to the two Soviet air services in approximately equal numbers since the start of production, with some 200 built by 1982.

The prototype Backfire-A aircraft underwent extensive redesign to produce the definitive -B version. In particular, the wings and landing gear were thoroughly changed. The Backfire is a variable-geometry aircraft with the outer wing sections extending for takeoff, landing, and cruise flight, and sweeping back for high speed flight. Two large turbofan engines are buried in the wing roots. The huge tail fin is fitted with fuel tanks and ECM equipment as well as with the tail-gun mounting. A fixed refueling probe can be installed in the nose. A twin 23-mm, remote-control gun mounting is provided in the tail. Offensive ordnance consists of one AS-4 or possibly AS-6 missile semirecessed under the fuselage or two missiles carried on pylons under the forward portion of the very long engine housings. The aircraft also carries ECM pods and possibly decoys. An internal weapons bay is provided for carrying bombs, but cannot be used when a missile is fitted in the semirecessed configuration. The aircraft's EW/ECM capabilities may alleviate the need to have jammer aircraft operate with the strike planes.

Designation: The M suffix indicates that the Backfire evolved from an extensive modification of the Tu-22 Blinder (see below). The designation

This SNA Backfire-B strike aircraft with wings extended over the Baltic Sea. The aircraft has the nose refueling probe installed; it is deleted in the aircraft shown with wings swept back. (Swedish Air Force)

An SNA Backfire-B strike aircraft photographed with its wings swept back for high-speed flight. The plane's huge tail fin appears to house electronic countermeasures equipment and fuel. The internal ECM suite has been estimated by some Western analysts as being comparable to that of the specialized Badger ECM aircraft. Note the remote-control tail turret.

Tu-26 has been used for the Backfire in the Western press. The Backfire-A was a pre-production development aircraft with different wing and landing-gear arrangements and other features.

Status: Western military leaders announced the existence of the Backfire in 1969. Flight tests began in 1969 with the Backfire-A prototypes, the Backfire-B entering service in 1975. It is flown by Soviet strategic aviation and SNA.

Backfire-B data:

| | |
|---|---|
| Crew: | 4 |
| Engines: | 2 Kuznetsov NK-144 derivative turbofans with afterburner; approx. 45,000 lbst (20,500 kgst) |
| Weights: | empty 110,000 lbs (50,000 kg) |
| | maximum T/O 270,000 lbs (121,500 kg) |
| Dimensions: | span 113 ft (34.5 m) fully extended |
| | span 86 ft (26.2 m) fully swept |
| | length 132 ft (40.2 m) |
| | height 30 ft (9.1 m) |
| Speed: | cruise 560 mph (1,900 kmh) at 33,000 ft (11,000 m); 500 mph (800 kmh) at sea level |
| | maximum 1,200–1,320 mph (1,930–2,120 kmh) at 36,000 ft (11,000 m) (Mach 1.8–2.0); 650 mph (1,050 kmh) at sea level |
| Ceiling: | service 55,000 ft (17,000 m) |
| Range: | approx. 2,875 mi (4,625 km) radius with missile |
| | approx. 3,400 mi (5,470 km) radius with bombs/mines |
| Armament: | 2 AS-4 Kitchen air-to-surface missiles or 26,400 lbs (12,000 kg) ordnance in weapons bay |
| | 2 23-mm cannon (remote-control tail turret) |
| Radar: | Down Beat (bombnav) |
| | Fan Tail (gunfire control) |

## Tu-16 Badger (Tupolev)

The Tu-16 Badger is a turbojet-powered medium bomber that has been in wide use by the Soviet Union for three decades. It serves in the conventional bomber, anti-ship missile, reconnaissance, ELINT, ECM, and tanker roles with Soviet strategic aviation and SNA.

The Badger has a swept wing with two large turbojet engines housed in nacelles faired into the fuselage at the wing roots. The engines have been updated during the aircraft's long production run, culminating in the engines listed below. When employed in the tanker role, the Badger has fuel tanks fitted in the weapons bay and trails a drogue from the starboard wing-tip; the receiving probe is fitted in the port wing-tip. The -A variant carries gravity bombs in an internal weapons bay; the -C and -G strike aircraft carry air-to-surface missiles under the fuselage or on wing pylons. Most aircraft have two 23-mm cannon in dorsal, ventral, and tail mounts, with bombers not having a large radome able to mount a seventh cannon fixed on the starboard side of the nose.

Designation: The Tupolev bureau's design designation for the Badger was Tu-88. The Tu-98 Backfin was a Badger airframe flown in 1955 in the research role. The Tu-104 Camel civil airliner was a derivative of the Badger, the prototype of which flew for the first time in June 1955.

Status: The Badger's first flight took place in late 1952; production began the following year with Air Forces squadron delivery from 1954–1955 and Navy deliveries beginning in the late 1950s. Approximately 2,000 Badgers were built in the Soviet Union through the mid-1960s, and more than 80 were produced in China. SNA currently flies some 275 Badgers in the missile-strike role; 80 Badger-A aircraft in the tanker role;

A Badger-B/G strike aircraft in flight. The shaped wing fuel tanks and twin rails on the wings for air-to-surface missiles are readily visible as are the twin 23-mm tail turrets, above which are the gunner's position and fire control radome.

Badger-D maritime reconnaissance aircraft

A Badger-A tanker (lower), with its refueling hose stowage fitted to the starboard wingtip, refuels another Badger. SNA and Soviet strategic aviation (the latter with some 35 Mya-4 Bison and 10 Tu-16 Badger tankers) are both in need of improved tanker capabilities; however, the range of the new Blackjack strike aircraft reduces this requirement.

A Badger-F aircraft configured for electronic warfare. There are electronic pods on wing pylons as well as ventral and dorsal antennas along the fuselage. In addition to its tactical number "23" on the tail fin, this Badger has its serial number visible on the nose and tail fin—1883313. (U.S. Navy)

perhaps 80 Badgers in the reconnaissance, ELINT, and ECM roles; and a few Badgers in the conventional bomber and trainer configurations.

Transfers: Badgers have been transferred to China, Egypt, Indonesia, Iraq, and Libya.

Naval variants:

Badger-A    bomber, tanker, trainer; flown by SNA and strategic aviation; can carry 8,360 lbs (3,800 kg) bombs with 2,975 n.mile (4,800 km) radius; IOC 1954-1955.

Badger-C    missile strike; 2 AS-2 Kipper or 2 AS-5 Kelt missiles; Puff Ball radar with AS-2; Short Horn radar with AS-5; IOC 1960.

Badger-D    electronic reconnaissance; Puff Ball radar.

Badger-E    photo reconnaissance; cameras in weapons bay.

Badger-F    electronic and photo reconnaissance.

Badger-G    missile strike; 2 AS-5 Kelt or 2 AS-6 Kingfish missiles; 1,985 + n.mile (3,200 + km) radius; Short Horn radar; IOC 1965.

Badger-H    EW/strike escort.

Badger-J    EW/strike escort.

Badger-K    ELINT/electronic reconnaissance.

Badger C/G data

| | |
|---|---|
| Crew: | 6 |
| Engines: | 2 Mikulin AM-3M turbojets; 20,950 lbst (9,425 kg) each in later aircraft |
| Weights: | empty 80,000 lbs (36,000 kg) |
| | loaded 115,742 lbs (52,500 kg) |
| | maximum T/O 169,756 lbs (77,000 kg) |
| Dimensions: | span 113 ft 3 in (34.5 m) |
| | length 120 ft (36.5 m) |
| | height 35 ft 6 in (10.8 m) |
| Speed: | cruise 530 mph (850 kmh) (Mach 0.8) |
| | maximum 620 mph (1,000 kmh) (Mach 0.91) |
| Ceiling: | service 46,000 ft (14,000 m) |
| Range: | approx. 1,400 mi (2,250 km) radius with missiles |
| | approx. 1,780 mi (2,865 km) radius with bombs/mines |
| Armament: | 18,000 lbs (8,100 kg) in weapons bay in Badger-A |
| | 2 AS-2 Kelt or AS-4 Kitchen missiles in Badger-C |
| | 2 AS-4 Kitchen or 2 AS-6 Kingfish missiles in Badger-G |
| | up to 7 23-mm cannon |
| Radar: | see above for bombnav radars |
| | Bee Hind (gunfire control) |

Badger-G strike aircraft

A Badger-G with two AS-5 Kelt anti-ship missiles under its wings. Note the glazed nose and the single 23-mm cannon faired into the starboard side of the nose. The Badger-C/D variants have "solid" noses; the others have glazed noses.

## Tu-20 Bear (Tupolev)

The Tu-20 Bear was developed as a strategic bomber and has been in Soviet first-line service for almost three decades. It continues in operation with Soviet strategic aviation and SNA, in the latter air arm being flown in the reconnaissance-ship targeting and ASW roles. The Bear is the largest aircraft flown by the Soviet Navy.

The only turboprop-propelled strategic bomber to enter service with any air force, the Bear is a large, swept-wing aircraft with four turboprop engines turning contra-rotating, four-bladed propellers. The plane's long range can be further extended through in-flight refueling with a fixed receiving probe fitted to the nose. Defensive armament can consist of one 23-mm fixed cannon in the nose and up to three 23-mm twin gun turrets (dorsal, ventral, and tail). The Bear-D is a naval reconnaissance and targeting version; it carries no offensive weapons, but is fitted with a large surface search radar and a Video Data Link (VDL) for transmitting target data to missile-launching units. The Bear-F ASW variant carries expendable sonobuoys as well as radar for detecting submarines and can attack with a large payload of ASW homing torpedoes and depth bombs. Some Bear-D aircraft have been observed with the tail turret replaced by an extended tailcone, possibly housing a low-frequency wire antenna.

The Bear's genealogy began with the Tupelov Tu-4 Bull, a direct copy of the U.S. B-29 Superfortress. A larger aircraft of this type was begun, the Tu-88, but abandoned by Tupolev in favor of a still larger aircraft that evolved into the Tu-95 design.

Designation: Tu-95 is the Tupolev design bureau designation; this is sometimes used (incorrectly) in the West to indicate military versions of the aircraft, which the Soviets at least initially designated Tu-20. The Bear-F has the bureau designation Tu-142. The Tu-114 *Rossiya* (NATO Cleat), the world's largest civilian passenger aircraft before the Boeing 747, uses the engines, wing, tail assembly, and other components of the Bear. The Tu-114D Moss, a Soviet AWACS (Airborne Warning and Control System) aircraft, in turn is a derivative of the Cleat.

Status: First flight 1954; the aircraft entered LRA service in 1955 and SNA in the early 1960s. Approximately 250 to 300 Bear aircraft were built, production of the Bear-F continuing at least into the early 1980s, probably a world record for continuous production of a major military aircraft. The aircraft remains in service with Soviet strategic aviation as a bomber while SNA flies some 45 Bear-D reconnaissance-targeting aircraft and some 50 Bear-F ASW aircraft.

(Soviet strategic aviation flies the A/B/C/E variants, the last being a reconnaissance aircraft; the Bear-A has an unrefuelled combat *radius* estimated at 3,360 miles/5,425 km with a 25,000-lb/11,350-kg bomb load or 4,500 miles/7,240 km with an 11,000-lb/5,000-kg load; the Bear-B and -C aircraft, carrying the AS-3 Kangaroo missile, are capable of attacking naval targets.)

Naval variants:

Bear-D    reconnaissance/anti-ship targeting aircraft.
Bear-F    reconnaissance/ASW aircraft.

| | |
|---|---|
| Crew: | |
| Engines: | 4 Kuznetsov NK-12MV turboprops; 15,000 shp each |
| Weights: | empty approx. 165,000 lbs (75,000 kg) |
| | Bear-D maximum T/O 356,000 lbs (160,200 kg) |
| | Bear-F maximum T/O 380,000 lbs (171,000 kg) |
| Dimensions: | Bear-D span 159 ft (48.5 m) |
| | Bear-F span 167 ft 8 in (51.1 m) |
| | Bear-D length 155 ft 10 in (47.5 m) |
| | Bear-F length 162 ft 5 in (49.5 m) |
| | Bear-D height 38 ft 8 in (11.8 m) |
| | Bear-F height 39 ft 9 in (12.1 m) |
| Speed: | cruise 465 mph (750 kmh) |
| | maximum 550 mph (880 kmh) |
| Ceiling: | service 41,000 ft (12,500 m) |
| Range: | Bear D: approx. 9,000 mi (14,480 km) |
| Armament: | up to 7 23-mm NR-23 cannon |
| | 17,600+ lbs (8,000+ kg) torpedoes, depth bombs in Bear-F |
| Radar: | Big Bulge-A (surface search) in Bear-D |
| | Wet Eye (surface search) in Bear-F |
| | gunfire control |

Closeup of a Bear-D; note the contra-rotating propellers, radomes, and the tactical number "10" on the nosewheel doors.

A Bear-D maritime reconnaissance/targeting aircraft in flight. Note the aircraft's four large, turboprop engines with contra-rotating propellers, swept wings and horizontal tail surfaces. The approximately 45 Bear-D aircraft vary in detail, especially with respect to antennas. All have a small "chin" radome plus the large Big Bulge radar under the ventral position. (U.S. Navy)

A Bear-F anti-submarine aircraft in flight, with an unusual antenna housing atop the aircraft's tail fin. The plane has a smaller ventral radar than the Bear-D's Big Bulge and no "chin" radome. This Bear-F's weapons bay is open. Like the Bear-D, this variant also has an in-flight refueling capability with a rigid probe projecting from the nose.

Closeup of Bear-D tail showing the tail gunner, 23-mm twin gun turret, and gunfire control radar. (U.S. Air Force)

This Bear-D is fitted with an extended tail cone in place of the 23-mm gun turret; it apparently houses a very long, low-frequency wire antenna.

## Tu-22 Blinder (Tupolev)

The Tu-22 Blinder was the first supersonic bomber to enter Soviet service. The twin-turbojet aircraft is in service with Soviet strategic aviation and SNA. However, it has been less than fully successful and did not enter large-scale production to replace the Badger as once planned. The Blinder was the last bomber-type aircraft to be produced in the Soviet Union until the debut of the Tu-22M Backfire. In SNA service the Blinder is used to deliver free-fall bombs, with a few aircraft configured for reconnaissance and training.

The Blinder is a swept-wing aircraft with two turbojet engines mounted in pods at the base of the tail fin. Most aircraft have a partially retractable in-flight refuelling probe in the nose, a nose radome, and tandem seating for the crew of three. External fuel tanks are faired into the trailing edges of the wings. The Blinder-A carries bombs internally in tandem weapon bays, while the Blinder-B can carry an AS-4 Kitchen missile. Defensive armament consists of a remote-control single NR-23 23-mm tail gun. The Blinder-D trainer has a raised rear cockpit with dual controls for an instructor (replacing the radar observer's position). The aircraft has a supersonic dash capability.

Designation: The Tupolev design bureau designation for the aircraft was Tu-105. The Blinder was apparently developed as a competitive supersonic bomber with the Myasishchev M-52 Bounder, which did not enter squadron service.

Status: About 50 Blinder-A bombers are in SNA service, plus a few Blinder-C reconnaissance and Blinder-D training aircraft.

Transfers: Iraq, Libya.

Naval variants:

Blinder-A    bomber carrying gravity bombs.
Blinder-C    photoreconnaissance.
Blinder-D    trainer (Tu-22U) with modified cockpit.

| | |
|---|---|
| Crew: | 3 |
| Engines: | 2 Kolesov VD-7 turbojets with afterburner; approx. 31,000 lbst (14,000 kgst) |
| Weights: | empty 90,000 lbs (40,000 kg) |
| | maximum T/O 190,000 lbs (85,000 kg) |
| Dimensions: | span 94 ft 6 in (28.8 m) |
| | length 136 ft 9 in (41.7 m) |
| | height 28 ft 2 in (8.6 m) |
| Speed: | cruise 560 mph (900 kmh) at 36,000 ft (11,000 m) (Mach 0.85) |
| | maximum 1,000 mph (1,600 kmh) at 36,000 ft (11,000 m) (Mach 1.5) |
| Ceiling: | service 60,000 ft (18,000 m) |
| Range: | approx. 950 mi (1,530 km) radius with bombs/mines |
| Armament: | 1 23-mm NR-23 cannon |
| | 17,500 lbs (8,000 kg) bombs |
| Radar: | Down Beat (bombnav) |
| | Bee Hind (gunfire control) |

An overhead view of a Blinder-A showing the unusual side-by-side engine arrangement, swept wings, auxiliary tanks faired into the trailing edges of the wings, and narrow cockpit with tandem seating for the three-man crew. The Blinder-A is flown mostly as a conventional bomber aircraft.

A Blinder-C photoreconnaissance aircraft in a "dirty" configuration about to touch down. In addition to a battery of six cameras in the weapons bay, this Tu-22 appears to have a modified nose fitted with electronic intercept equipment. The plane's unusual features include downward ejection seats for two crew members and a conventional ejection seat for the pilot.

Mechanics work on the twin turbojet engines of a Blinder. The plane's tail position for a single 23-mm gun is open.

## CARGO AIRCRAFT

### Il-18 Coot (Ilyushin)

The Il-18 is a turboprop-powered transport that was in wide use during the 1960s and early 1970s with *Aeroflot*, the Soviet national airline, on both domestic and international routes. The basic Il-18 airframe and engines became the basis of the Il-38 May maritime patrol/ASW aircraft flown by the Soviet naval air arm (see below). In the late 1970s a modified version of the Il-18 was observed flying in the ELINT role, designated Coot-A by NATO.

The Il-18 is a low-wing, four-turboprop aircraft of conventional design. The improved Il-18D civilian variant (Soviet designation) carries up to 122 passengers. Several aircraft have been configured for research projects, the Il-18D aircraft for polar research operating in the Antarctic and from Arctic drift stations.

The ELINT version has a large, side-looking radar beneath the forward fuselage in a "canoe" housing about 10.25 m long and 1.15 m in diameter; other antennas are faired into the fuselage, including a large "hump" on the left forward side of the fuselage (approximately 4.4 m long and 0.88 m in diameter).

Status: In operational service as a civilian airliner and, in limited numbers, as a research and ELINT aircraft. First flight July 1957 with estimates of total production ranging from 600 to 900 aircraft. The ELINT versions are probably conversions of civilian or military passenger aircraft, with the first Coot-A being observed in early 1978. While being phased out of *Aeroflot*, it is still flown by several Eastern European nations as well as by North Korea and Vietnam.

Il-18D/E transport data:

| | |
|---|---|
| Crew: | 5 + 122 passengers |
| Engines: | 4 Ivshenko AI-20M turboprops; 4,250-ehp each |
| Weights: | empty 77,000 lbs (35,000 kg) |
| | maximum T/O 141,000 lbs (64,000 kg) |
| Dimensions: | span 122 ft 8½ in (37.4 m) |
| | length 117 ft 9½ in (35.9 m) |
| | height 33 ft 4 in (10.2 m) |
| Speed: | cruise 380–390 mph (610–625 kmh) at 26,250 ft (8,000 m) |
| Ceiling: | service 26,250–32,800 ft (8,000–10,000 m) |
| Range: | 2,480 mi (4,000 km) with 30,000-lb (13,500-kg) payload; 4,030 mi (6,500 km) with 14,330 lbs (6,500 kg) |
| Armament: | none |
| Radar: | |

Coot-A electronic collection aircraft

The Coot-A intelligence collection aircraft is easily recognized by its assortment of pods, blisters, and fins housing various antennas, plus the large antenna "canoe" mounted under the forward fuselage. The "standard" Il-18 fuselage and ports indicate the plane is a modification of the commercial aircraft and not the Il-38 May ASW variant.

## An-12 Cub (Antonov)

The An-12 Cub is a cargo–transport aircraft, one of the most important aircraft of this category in Soviet military and civilian operation. Several planes have been configured for the ECM and ELINT roles, and, more recently, the Cub has been seen as an ASW systems test bed. The Soviet designation for the basic cargo/transport aircraft is An-12BP.

The Cub evolved as a militarized version of the An-10 Cat transport. The aircraft has a high-wing configuration to provide clear cargo space and has four turboprop engines. Similarly, the main landing gear is housed in pods on the fuselage to avoid cutting into floor space. The sharply upswept rear fuselage incorporates an underside rear-loading ramp. A tail-gun position for twin 23-mm cannon is provided in most aircraft (even some with civilian markings), although there is no fire-control radar. In the cargo role up to 44,090 lbs (20,015 kg) of material can be lifted.

A variety of military electronic configurations of the Cub have been observed since 1970. The Cub-B designation covers ECM aircraft, with antenna domes faired into the fuselage and tail (no tail turret); the Cub-C design is used for ELINT configurations, with ventral antenna housings and other features indicating the capability of "ferreting" electronic intelligence. In the early 1980s a Cub was identified in the ASW role, probably as a systems test bed.

Status: First flight in fall of 1955; the first flight of the military variant (An-12PB) took place in 1958. About 850 aircraft were produced. In the cargo/transport role the Cub is widely used by the Soviet Air Forces as well as those of other Warsaw Pact air arms and Third World services. Some aircraft—civilian and military—fly with *Aeroflot* markings.

Transfers (Cub-C): Egypt.

Cub-A transport data:

| | |
|---|---|
| Crew: | 6 (including tail gunner) + 100 troops |
| Engines: | 4 Ivchenko AI-20K turboprops; 4,000 shp each |
| Weights: | empty 75,000 lbs (35,000 kg) |
| | maximum T/O 134,500 lbs (61,000 kg) |
| Dimensions: | span 124 ft 7 in (38.0 m) |
| | length 108 ft 6 in (33.1 m) |
| | height 32 ft 3 in (9.8 m) |
| Speed: | cruise 360 mph (580 kmh) |
| | maximum cruise 400 mph (640 kmh) |
| Ceiling: | service 33,500 ft (10,200 m) |
| Range: | 2,100 mi (3,400 km) with 22,000 lbs (10,000 kg) payload |
| Armament: | 2 × 23-mm NR-23 cannon in some aircraft (tail turret) |
| Radar: | Toad Stool (I-band) navigation radar |

Flying with an *Aeroflot* serial number (SSSR-11916), this Cub was photographed in 1981 configured as a testbed for an advanced anti-submarine system. Note the aircraft's extended nose and tail cones.

This Cub is one of several -C variants configured for electronic warfare (ECM). The aircraft is fitted with extensive electronic intercept and jamming equipment. It can be distinguished from other Cubs by the larger radome in the "chin" position, various pods and blisters, and solid tail cone. This plane operated out of Egypt with Egyptian markings prior to 1973.

Still another Cub variant (with *Aeroflot* serial number SSR-11417), this EW-configured aircraft was photographed in 1982 with large blisters/pods on the lower side of the fuselage abaft the cockpit, under the tail ramp, and under the tail-gun position.

A Cub "transport" aircraft wearing commercial *Aeroflot* insignia while on a reconnaissance flight over the Indian Ocean. Note the Cub's tail gun position (sans weapons) and small ventral electronic pods. (U.S. Navy)

## FIGHTER/ATTACK AIRCRAFT

### Su-17 Fitter-C/D (Sukhoi)

This is a ground-support fighter with variable-sweep wings that evolved from the Su-7 fixed-wing strike fighter. It is flown by the Soviet Air Forces and several foreign nations, the Soviet Navy having one regiment of these aircraft in the Baltic Fleet, with a second regiment being established in the Pacific in the early 1980s.

The Fitter-C and later variants are swept-wing, variable-geometry aircraft, with a streamlined configuration based on a single, high-powered AL-21F engine. The outer wing sections, fitted with slates and trailing-edge flaps, are used primarily to aid STOL takeoff and landing. The aircraft suffers from limited internal fuel, and is generally seen with two large drop tanks (294 gal/1,130 litre each) on twin fuselage pylons. It has an advanced weapon-aiming system and six or eight weapon (or drop tank) pylons plus two 30-mm cannon in the wing roots. The D variant has improved avionics and an electro-optical or laser weapon guidance system. (Fitter-E through -H variants have also been identified.)

Status: A modified Su-7 served as a test bed for the variable-sweep aircraft, and was first observed publicly in 1967 (code named Fitter-B). The definitive Su-17/Fitter-C was first seen in 1970 and the Fitter-D in 1977. It is flown by the Soviet Air Forces and SNA as well as by the air forces of Egypt, Peru, Poland, and Syria.

Crew:          1
Engines:       1 Lyulka AL-21F turbojet with afterburner; 24,500 lbst (11,000 kgst)
Weights:       empty 22,000 lbs (10,000 kg)
               maximum T/O 37,500 lbs (17,000 kg)

Dimensions:    span 45 ft (14.0 m) fully extended
               span 34 ft 6 in (10.5 m) fully swept
               length 58 ft (17.6 m) over nose probe
               height 15 ft (4.6 m)
Speed:         maximum 1,200 mph (1,925 kmh) at 36,000 ft (11,000 m) (Mach 1.8); 830 mph (1,340 kmh) at sea level (clean) (Mach 1.1); maximum with external stores approx. 650 mph (1,050 kmh) (Mach 0.88) at sea level
Ceiling:       service 55,000 ft (17,000 m)
Range:         300-mi (480-km) strike radius
Armament:      2 30-mm NR-30 cannon
               7,500 lbs (3,500 kg) external stores (bombs, rockets, missiles, including AA-2 Atoll air-to-air missiles)
Radar:

### Yak-36 Forger (Yakovlev)

The Forger is a Vertical Take-Off and Landing (VTOL) aircraft developed for operation from the KIEV-class aircraft carriers. The plane is believed intended for the fighter-attack roles.

The Forger has a lift-plus-lift-cruise configuration using two forward lift engines that are mounted vertically and an aft-mounted vectored thrust engine for both vertical lift and propulsion. This configuration enhances VTOL payload compared to the British-U.S. Harrier VSTOL aircraft, the Forger having a 64 percent VTOL payload advantage over the AV-8A model and 25 percent over the AV-8B model. The Soviet plane has no STOL capability. Thus, the Harrier has relatively more thrust available for forward flight. The Forger has a swept-wing configuration, the outer

A Fitter-C/D fighter-attack aircraft of the type flown by Soviet Naval Aviation. The aircraft was developed from the straight-wing Su-7, with variable-sweep outer-wing panels, which have slats and trailing-edge flaps, for enhanced performance, including a STOL capability. The plane also serves with Soviet Frontal (tactical) Aviation and the Polish Air Force.

Yak-36 Forger-A fighter/attack aircraft on the deck of the carrier MINSK. Their outer wing sections are folded for carrier stowage, and canvas covers their cockpits. There are air-to-air missiles on pylons under the fixed sections of the wings. Two lift-jet engines are mounted, in tandem, immediately aft of the cockpit.

panels folding upward for shipboard handling, and the wing area is relatively small (approximately 170 ft²/15.8 m²). Single-seat (A) and tandem-seat (B) versions have been observed, the latter a combat trainer. Four wing pylons can accommodate a variety of weapons or fuel tanks.

Steps in the Forger development included the MiG-21PFM Fishbed-G lift-engine test bed, a high-performance fighter with two lift engines buried in its fuselage, and the Yakovlev Freehand, a VSTOL technology demonstration aircraft, twin-engined with vectorable nozzles. The Freehand, first seen publicly in 1967, was reported to have flown VTOL sea trials aboard the helicopter carrier MOSKVA. The Soviet designation for the Forger is Yak-36MP.

Status: First deployed aboard the KIEV in 1976 and subsequently aboard the other ships of the class. Operational only in SNA.

Forger-A data:

| | |
|---|---|
| Crew: | 1 in Forger-A |
| | 2 in Forger-B |
| Engines: | 1 Lyulka AL-21(?) turbojet cruise engine; approx. 17,500 lbst (7,650 kgst) |
| | 2 Kolesov turbojet lift engines; approx. 8,000 lbst (3,600 kgst) each |
| Weights: | maximum T/O 22,000 lbs (9,900 kg) |
| Dimensions: | span 23 ft (7.0 m) |
| | Forger-A length 49 ft 2 in (15.0 m) |
| | Forger-B length 58 ft (17.7 m) |
| | height 10 ft 6 in (3.2 m) |
| Speed: | maximum 800 mph (1,280 kmh) at 36,000 ft (11,000 m) |
| | (Mach 1.2); 650 mph (1,050 kmh) at sea level (Mach 0.85) |
| Ceiling: | service 46,000 ft (14,000 m) |
| Range: | 175-mi (280-km) radius as deck-launched interceptor |
| | 100-mi (160-km) strike radius with 2,000 lbs (900 kg) weapons (hi-lo-hi strike mission) |
| Armament: | 2,200 lbs (1,000 kg) external stores (bombs, rockets, missiles, gun pods, including AA-8 Aphid air-to-air missiles) |
| Radar: | small ranging radar |

A Forger-A from the KIEV with wheels down and lift engines operating (note open hatch for air intake abaft the cockpit). (West German Navy)

A two-seat Forger-B (aircraft No. 30) aboard a KIEV-class carrier

A Forger-A landing aboard the carrier KIEV in the Mediterranean; its markings include the aircraft's tactical number (14) and the Soviet Navy's ensign on each side of the fuselage.

## MARITIME PATROL AIRCRAFT

### Be-12 Mail (Beriev)

The Mail is one of the two remaining flying boats in first-line naval service (the other being the Japanese PS-1 *Shin Meiwa*). SNA has about 100 of these amphibians for maritime patrol, ASW, and search-and-rescue operations. The Soviet designation for this aircraft is M-12 and its popular Russian name is *Tchaika* (seagull).

This is the last aircraft in a long line of Beriev flying boats produced in the USSR. The Mail has distinctive gull-shaped wings, twin tail, and other features of the earlier, piston-engine Be-6 Madge.[2] The Mail has an elongated nose radome protruding from a glazed nose, and a Magnetic Anomaly Detector (MAD) boom mounted in the tail. Twin turboprop engines are mounted high on the wings. The main landing gear and tail wheel retract fully into the boat hull. A variety of torpedoes, mines, and depth bombs can be carried on a pylon under each wing and in an internal weapons bay fitted in the after section of the hull. Expendable sonobuoys can also be carried.

Status: First flight in 1960. Operational only in SNA.

---

[2]The principal intermediate design between the Be-6 and Be-12 was the swept-wing, turbojet Be-10 Mallow, which, like its contemporary U.S. P6M Seamaster, did not enter operational service.

This Mail ASW amphibian is from the Baltic Fleet's air arm. Along with the newer Japanese PS-1 *Shin Meiwa*, the Mail is the only naval flying boat remaining in service. The U.S. Navy's last patrol flying boat, the P5M/PBM Mariner, was discarded in 1966.

Crew:          5
Engines:       2 Ivchenko AL-20D turboprops; 4,190 shp each
Weights:       empty 47,850 lbs (21,700 kg)
               maximum T/O 66,140 lbs (30,000 kg)
Dimensions:    span 97 ft 6 in (29.7 m)
               length 99 ft (30.2 m)
               height 23 ft (7.0 m) on undercarriage
Speed:         cruise 200 mph (320 kmh)
               maximum 380 mph (610 kmh)
Ceiling:       service 37,000 ft (11,300 m)
Range:         2,500 mi (4,000 km)
Armament:      ASW torpedoes, mines, depth bombs
Radar:

A Mail sits on a runway with engines running; the main landing gear folds into the boat hull, and the tail wheel fully retracts.

## Il-38 May

Generally resembling the P-3 Orion patrol aircraft in appearance and role, the May is the first Soviet land-based aircraft designed from the outset for the maritime patrol/ASW mission. The aircraft was adopted from Il-18 Coot transport (much the same as the Orion was adapted from the commercial Lockheed Electra).

The May is a large, low-wing aircraft with four turboprop engines. The fuselage is lengthened from the original Il-18 design, and the wings have been strengthened and mounted farther forward. A radome is fitted under the forward fuselage, a MAD antenna boom extends from the tail, and there is an internal weapons bay for torpedoes, mines, or depth bombs. Expendable sonobuoys and nonacoustic sensors are also carried, and the plane has a computerized tactical evaluation system. No defensive armament is fitted. Endurance is about 12 hours at cruise speed.

The Il-18 Coot ELINT and ECM aircraft are variants of the original passenger configuration, and not of the Il-38 May.

Status: The aircraft apparently flew in prototype form in 1967–1968 and entered squadron service in 1970. Several aircraft have been transferred to India. Some Mays were flown with Egyptian markings in 1972, but were subsequently removed from Egypt.

Crew:          12
Engines:       4 Ivchenko AI-20M turboprops; 5,200 shp each
Weights:       empty 90,000 lbs (40,000 kg)
               maximum T/O 150,000 lbs (68,000 kg)
Dimensions:    span 122 ft 9 in (37.4 m)
               length 129 ft 10 in (36.9 m) over MAD boom
               height 33 ft 4 in (10.3 m)
Speed:         cruise 290 mph (460 kmh)
               maximum 400 mph (640 kmh)
Ceiling:
Range:         5,150 mi (8,300 km)
Armament:      ASW torpedoes, mines, depth bombs
Radar:

Closeup of Mail with mechanics checking both turboprop engines

A modified May with a second radome abaft the standard radome

The May maritime patrol/ASW aircraft's clean fuselage lines and turboprop engines reveal its origins in the commercial Il-18 airliner. There is a strong superficial resemblance to the Lockheed P-3 Orion aircraft, also derived from a commercial airliner (the Electra).

## HELICOPTERS

### Mi-14 Haze (Mil')

This is a land-based ASW helicopter, developed as a replacement for the less-capable and outdated ASW configuration of the Mi-4 Hound. The Haze is too large to fit the elevators of the helicopter ships of the MOSKVA class or aircraft carriers of the KIEV class.

The Haze is an ASW derivative of the Mi-8 helicopter (see below), using the power plant and dynamic components of the Hip-C. The two aircraft differ primarily in the fuselage configuration and in the equipment installed. The ASW configuration provides for an amphibious hull with stabilizing sponsons on each side that house the main wheels of the tricycle undercarriage. A surface-search radar is fitted in the "chin"

With its dipping sonar extended, a land-based Haze amphibious helicopter flies low over the sea. The helicopter's sensors also include radar in a dome faired into the forward boat hull and a towed MAD device, shown here stowed at the rear of the Haze's cabin. (West German Navy)

Haze anti-submarine helicopter

position, with the dome projecting beneath the hull. The Haze also has MAD gear (towed), expendable sonobuoys, and probably a dipping sonar, and can carry ASW homing torpedoes. During the *Zapad* 81 exercises in the Baltic Sea, Haze helicopters were reported to be employed in the aerial minesweeping role along with Hip helicopters.

Status: The first flight of the Haze occurred about 1973, and it entered service with SNA in 1975. These helicopters have also been transferred to East Germany and Poland.

| | |
|---|---|
| Crew: | approx. 6 |
| Engines: | 2 Isotov TV2-117A turboshafts; 1,500 shp each |
| Weights: | loaded approx. 24,000 lbs (10,900 kg) |
| Dimensions: | length 60 ft (10.8 m) |
| | rotor diameter approx. 70 ft (21.0 m) |
| Speed: | maximum 115 mph (250 kmh) |
| Ceiling: | |
| Range: | |
| Armament: | ASW torpedoes |
| Radar: | |

### Ka-27 Helix (Kamov)

The Kamov-designed Helix is successor to the Ka-25 Hormone as a ship-based ASW helicopter.

The aircraft has the familiar contra-rotating rotors of Kamov helicopters of the past 35 years and generally resembles the Hormone. However, the Helix is larger and the empennage has a horizontal stabilizer with twin fins (the Hormone has three fins).

Status: The Helix was first observed at sea aboard the ASW destroyer UDALOY in September 1981. (Two helicopters were embarked, one in standard Soviet naval markings and one in *Aeroflot* colors.)

Detailed characteristics were not available when this volume went to press.

| | |
|---|---|
| Crew: | 4-5 |
| Engines: | 2 turboshafts |
| Weights: | |
| Dimensions: | length 39 ft 6 in (12 m) |
| | rotor diameter 55 ft 3 in (16.75 m) |
| Speed: | |
| Ceiling: | |
| Range: | |
| Armament: | |
| Radar: | |

A Helix anti-submarine helicopter on board the destroyer UDALOY during the ship's 1981 trials in the Baltic Sea. The Kamov-designed Helix is larger than its predecessor, the Ka-25 Hormone, and has only two tail fins vice three in the earlier helicopter. Kamov helicopters are distinguished by their contra-rotating main rotors which alleviate the need for tail booms and rotors.

## Mi-8 Hip (Mil')

The Hip is the primary transport helicopter of the Soviet armed forces and has been flown by almost 30 other nations. SNA has employed the Hip in the transport and minesweeping roles.

The basic Hip design provides for an all-metal, five-blade main rotor and three-blade tail rotor driven by two turboshaft engines. The fuselage is an all-metal, semi-monocoque pod; the tail boom mounts the smaller rotor on the starboard side of a small vertical stabilizer with a small horizontal stabilizer near the end of the tailboom. A fixed tricycle landing gear is fitted. There are clamshell doors at the rear of the cabin. Up to 8,820 lbs (4,000 kg) of cargo can be carried internally. External fuel tanks can be fitted.

The Hip-C is the production version, the A/B having been prototypes; the E/F models are assault helicopter/gunships fitted with anti-tank missiles. The helicopter was observed flying from the helicopter carrier LENINGRAD in 1974 in mine-clearing operations at the southern end of the Suez Canal. However, the helicopter was too large to be accommodated on the ship's twin elevators.

Status: The first flight of the Mi-8 occurred in 1962, and it was introduced into Soviet service in 1967.

Hip-C data:

| | |
|---|---|
| Crew: | 2 + 24 troops |
| Engines: | 2 Isotov TV2-117A turboshafts; 1,500 shp each |
| Weights: | empty 15,000 lbs (6,816 kg) |
| | loaded 26,400 lbs (12,000 kg) |
| Dimensions: | length 60 ft ¾ in (18.3 m) |
| | rotor diameter 68 ft 10½ in (21.0 m) |
| Speed: | cruise 139.5 mph (225 kmh) |
| | maximum 161 mph (260 kmh) |
| Ceiling: | hover OGE 2,625 ft (800 m) |
| | hover IGE 6,233 ft (1,900 m) |
| | service 14,760 ft (4,500 m) |
| Range: | 300 mi (480 km) |
| Armament: | none |
| Radar: | |

The Hip is the most widely flown helicopter in the Soviet armed forces and in the Warsaw Pact military services (a troop carrier in Czech markings is shown here). Soviet Naval Aviation flies a small number of Hip-type helicopters in the amphibious assault, minesweeping, and utility roles.

These Hormone helicopters on a MOSKVA-class carrier have their rotors folded back for shipboard storage. The Hormone at left rests on a net-like device to retard its movement as the ship rolls, while the helicopter at right is being lowered on one of the ship's two elevators. The elevators are too narrow for the Haze ASW helicopter.

## Ka-25 Hormone

The Hormone is the principal Soviet ship-based ASW and missile targeting helicopter, being found on board the KIEV and MOSKVA carriers, as well as on various cruiser classes and auxiliary ships.

The Ka-20 Harp was the prototype for the Hormone, the earlier aircraft being publicly seen for the first time in July 1961 flying at a Soviet aviation display with two dummy missiles fitted on its fuselage. The Hormone has a distinctive configuration with a compact fuselage, two contra-rotating rotors driven by twin turboshaft engines, a short tail boom supporting a multi-fin empennage, and a quadricycle landing gear. The rotor arrangement alleviates the need for a tail boom, facilitating shipboard handling. The main rotors also fold. Some helicopters have inflatable flotation bags attached to the landing gear in the event the helicopter has to come down at sea.

The Hormone-A ASW configuration has surface-search radar, expendable sonobuoys, dipping sonar that can be lowered while the helicopter is in a hover, and an internal weapons bay for ASW homing torpedoes or depth bombs. An electro-optical sensor has been seen on some helicopters. The Hormone-B is fitted with the larger Big Bulge-B radar for surface surveillance and can transmit targeting data via VDL to surface ships and submarines armed with anti-ship missiles. The Hormone-C is a utility/passenger variant that can carry 12 passengers. None has been observed armed with air-to-surface missiles, as indicated by the Ka-20 prototype.

The helicopter is used as a civilian flying crane in the Ka-25K version.

| | |
|---|---|
| Crew: | 4-5 |
| Engines: | 2 Glushenkov GTD-3F turboshafts; 900 shp each |
| Weights:[3] | empty 9,680 lbs (4,400 kg) |
| | loaded 16,060 lbs (7,300 kg) |
| Dimensions:[3] | length 32 ft 3 in (9.8 m) |
| | rotor diameter 51 ft 8 in (15.7 m) |
| Speed: | cruise 120 mph (193 kmh) |
| | maximum 136 mph (220 kmh) |
| Ceiling: | service 11,500 ft (3,500 m) |
| Range: | 400 mi (650 km) |
| Armament: | ASW torpedoes, depth bombs |
| Radar: | |

[3]Dimensions and weights are given for the civilian Ka-25K; the naval version is believed similar, but with military equipment.

Yagi-type antennas are fitted to some Hormones, as shown here; this helicopter also has auxiliary fuel tanks mounted on each side, between the forward and main wheels. (U.S. Navy)

This Hormone-A anti-submarine helicopter was photographed while observing the U.S. aircraft carrier NIMITZ (CVN 68). The Hormone has an internal weapons bay. (U.S. Navy)

A MINSK-based Hormone-A helicopter shown almost head-on. There is a sonobuoy dispenser mounted on starboard side as well as two small cylindrical containers.

# 25
# Naval Weapons

These Soviet sailors on board a Kresta II-class missile cruiser were working on a 30-mm ADMG-630 Gatling gun when they stopped for a look at a Western aircraft looking at them. Just above them are two of the ship's eight Side Globe ECM domes and the optical sight for the Gatling guns, and forward are four of the ship's eight SS-N-14 missile tubes. Soviet warships generally carry more weapons per displacement ton than do their Western counterparts.

**ANTI-SUBMARINE WEAPONS**

The following Soviet anti-submarine weapons are believed to be in current use. They are arranged by launch platform. Missiles, mines, and torpedoes are discussed in subsequent sections of this chapter.

*Air Launched.* Soviet fixed-wing ASW aircraft and helicopters carry depth bombs, torpedoes, and mines.

*Surface Launched.* The older Soviet ASW ship and some smaller craft carry depth charges, generally launched from rails over the stern. Most Soviet surface combatants and ASW craft have torpedo tubes that can launch ASW torpedoes, while mine rails are also fitted in most cruisers and destroyers, including ships of the new UDALOY and SOVREMENNYY classes.

Soviet frigates and larger warships (including aircraft carriers) are fitted with multiple rocket launchers.[1] These weapons have the Soviet designation RBU for *Raketnaya Bombometnaya Ustanovka*. All are multibarrel rocket launchers developed from the ahead-firing "hedgehog" principle. They can fire high-explosive charges with either depth or influence fuzing. Most can be trained in azimuth and elevation. The charges are immune to torpedo countermeasures, and if influence fuzing is used, they will not affect sonar performance as they will not detonate unless they make contact with a submarine's magnetic signature.

The following are Soviet RBU designations. Characteristics are approximate.

**RBU-6000**

A twelve-barrel launcher arranged in a horseshoe and fired in paired sequence; can be trained and elevated. Elevates to vertical position for rapid, automatic reloading. Formerly given the NATO designation MBU-2500-A.

| | |
|---|---|
| Maximum range: | 6,600 yds (6,000 m) |
| Barrel length: | 5.28 ft (1.6 m) |
| Projectile diameter: | 250 mm |
| Projectile weight: | |
| Warhead weight: | 46 lbs (21 kg) |
| IOC: | 1962 |
| Platforms: | *carriers*  KIEV, MOSKVA |
| | *cruisers*  Kara, KIROV, Kresta I/II, Kynda |
| | *destroyers*  Kanin, Kashin, Kotlin, SAM Kotlin, UDALOY |
| | *frigates*  Grisha, Krivak, Petya |
| | *corvettes*  Poti |

**RBU-2500**

Sixteen-barrel launcher arranged in two rows of eight; can be trained and elevated. Manual reloading. Formerly designated MBU-2500.

| | |
|---|---|
| Maximum range: | 2,750 yds (2,500 m) |
| Barrel length: | 5.28 ft (1.6 m) |
| Projectile diameter: | 250 mm |
| Projectile weight: | |
| Warhead weight: | 46 lbs (21 kg) |
| IOC: | 1957 |
| Platforms: | *destroyers*  Kildin, Kotlin, SAM Kotlin, SKORYY (Mod) |
| | *frigates*  Riga |
| | *corvettes*  Poti |

[1]The underway replenishment ship BEREZINA is fitted with two RBU-1000 launchers.

RBU-6000 launcher on Kashin (Royal Navy)

RBU-6000 launchers on East German PARCHIM-class corvette with port launcher in the vertical position for reloading

RBU-2500 launcher being manually loaded

RBU-2500 launchers on stern of Petya I-class frigate.

## RBU-1200

Five barrels, with three mounted over two; tubes elevate but do not train. Manual reloading. Formerly designated MBU-1800.

| | |
|---|---|
| Maximum range: | 1,320 yds (1,200 m) |
| Barrel length: | 4.6 ft (1.4 m) |
| Projectile diameter: | 250 mm |
| Projectile weight: | 154 lbs (70 kg) |
| Warhead weight: | 75 lbs (34 kg) |
| IOC: | 1958 |
| Platforms: | *small combatants* S.O.-1 |
| | *minesweepers* Natya, T-58 |

RBU-1200 launchers on S.O.-1

## RBU-1000

Six barrels in two vertical rows of three; can be trained and elevated. Automatic reloading. Formerly designated MBU-4500.

| | | |
|---|---|---|
| Maximum range: | 1,100 yds (1,000 m) | |
| Barrel length: | | |
| Projectile diameter: | 300 mm | |
| Projectile weight: | 198 lbs (90 kg) | |
| Warhead weight: | 121 lbs (55 kg) | |
| IOC: | 1962 | |
| Platforms: | *cruisers* | Kara, KIROV, Kresta I/II |
| | *destroyers* | Kashin |
| | *auxiliaries* | BEREZINA |

RBU-1000 launcher (U.S. Navy)

## RBU-600

Two rows of three barrels in the horizontal position; rockets are fired in salvo only. Manual reloading.

| | |
|---|---|
| Maximum range: | 660 yds (600 m) |
| Barrel length: | 5 ft (1.5 m) |
| Projectile diameter: | 300 mm |
| Projectile weight: | 198 lbs (90 kg) |
| Warhead weight: | 121 lbs (55 kg) |
| IOC: | 1960 |
| Platforms: | *destroyers* Kotlin |

The major ASW ships (Krivak-class frigates and larger) have SS-N-14 launchers for rocket-propelled torpedoes. These are somewhat similar in concept to the French Malafon and Anglo-Australian Ikara torpedo-carrying missiles. The aircraft carriers of the Moskva and Kiev classes do not have the SS-N-14, instead mount the SUW-N-1 missile launcher that fires the FRAS-1, a nuclear-only, ballistic weapon.

A few of the older ASW craft retain earlier ASW weapons. See individual ship listings.

Depth-charge racks fitted to mine rails on East German Koni-class frigate Ro-stock (Towed torpedo decoys are between the DC racks.)

*Submarine Launched.* Soviet submarines all have 533-mm bow torpedo tubes that can launch ASW weapons, and most have 533-mm or 400-mm stern tubes. Since the late 1960s Soviet submarines have also been fitted with the SS-N-15 and SS-N-16 ASW missiles, carrying a nuclear warhead and homing torpedo, respectively. (See Missiles section.)

Most submarines can also carry tube-launched mines, normally in the ratio of two mines per torpedo space.

## NAVAL GUNS

### 152-mm/57-caliber limited DP (triple)[2]

These are the largest naval guns in service today with any navy except for the 16-inch (406-mm) guns aboard U.S. Iowa (BB 61)-class battleships. The 152-mm guns are of prewar design and are fitted in triple mounts in the Sverdlov-class cruisers, including the two command ship conversions and the one Sverdlov missile-ship conversion. The barrels within the turrets can be individually elevated and loaded. They have a limited AA capability with barrage fire.

| | |
|---|---|
| Muzzle velocity: | 915 m/sec |
| Rate of fire: | 4 to 5 rounds per minute per barrel |
| Maximum range: | 29,700 yds (27,000 m) |
| Effective range: | 19,800 yds (18,000 m) |
| Elevation: | −5° to +50° |
| Projectile weight: | 110 lbs (50 kg) |
| Fire control radar: | Egg Cup-A, Top Bow |
| Platforms: | *cruisers* Adm. Senyavin, Dzerzhinskiy, Sverdlov |

### 130-mm/70-caliber DP (twin)

These are fully automatic guns fitted in new cruiser and destroyer classes. They have water cooling jackets. Note that the range of the gun exceeds the earlier 152-mm weapon. The barrels are mounted close together and probably share a common cradle.

| | |
|---|---|
| Muzzle velocity: | |
| Rate of fire: | 65 rounds per minute per barrel |
| Maximum range: | 30,800 yds (28,000 m) |
| Effective range: | |
| Elevation: | −5° to +80° |
| Projectile weight: | |
| Fire control radar: | Kite Screech |
| Platforms: | *destroyers* Sovremennyy |
| | *cruisers* Krasina |

### 130-mm/58-caliber DP (twin)

Developed as the main battery for destoyers, these are semiautomatic guns introduced into service about 1953.

| | |
|---|---|
| Muzzle velocity: | 900 m/sec |
| Rate of fire: | 10 rounds per minute per barrel |
| Maximum range: | anti-surface 30,800 yds (28,000 m) |
| | anti-air 14,300 yds (13,000 m) |
| Effective range: | anti-surface 17,600–19,800 yds (16,000–18,000 m) |
| Elevation: | −5° to +80° |
| Projectile weight: | 59 lbs (27 kg) |
| Fire control radar: | Wasp Head director with Sun Visor; Egg Cup-B |
| Platforms: | *destroyers* Kotlin, SAM Kotlin |

### 130-mm/50-caliber SP (twin)

These are semiautomatic guns of 1930s design deployed as the main battery for destroyers. They have insufficient elevation for dual-purpose use.

| | |
|---|---|
| Muzzle velocity: | 875 m/sec |
| Rate of fire: | 10 rounds per minute per barrel |

[2]Gun barrel length is determined by multiplying the inner diameter of the barrel by the caliber. Thus, the 152-mm/57 gun has a length of 8,664 mm or approximately 28.9 ft.

Maximum range:     26,400 yds (24,000 m)
Effective range:    15,400–16,500 yds (14,000–15,000 m)
Elevation:          −5° to +45°
Projectile weight:  59 lbs (27 kg)
Fire control radar: Four Eyes director with Top Bow or Post Lamp
Platforms:          *destroyers* SKORYY

Triple 152-mm turrets on SVERDLOV-class cruiser ALEKSANDR SUVOROV; the second mount has an Egg Cup-A GFC radar. (U.S. Navy)

Twin 130-mm gun turret on destroyer SOVREMENNYY; in center is an SA-N-7 missile launcher and at right quad anti-ship missile launchers. (U.S. Navy)

Twin 130-mm gun turret on Kotlin-class destroyer

Twin 130-mm gun turret on SKORYY-class destroyer

## 100-mm/. . .-caliber DP (single)

Rapid-fire, water-cooled gun fitted in Soviet warships from mid-1970s.

| | |
|---|---|
| Muzzle velocity: | |
| Rate of fire: | 80 rounds per minute |
| Maximum range: | 16,500 yds (15,000 m) |
| Effective range: | 8,800 yds (8,000 m) |
| Elevation: | |
| Projectile weight: | |
| Fire control radar: | Kite Screech |
| Platforms: | *cruisers*   KIROV |
| | *destroyers*   UDALOY |
| | *frigates*   Krivak II |

## 100-mm/50-caliber DP (twin)

Secondary gun battery in SVERDLOV cruisers. Available from the late 1940s onward.

| | |
|---|---|
| Muzzle velocity: | 900 m/sec |
| Rate of fire: | 15 rounds per minute per barrel |
| Maximum range: | anti-surface 22,000 yds (20,000 m) |
| | anti-air 16,500 yds (15,000 m) |
| Effective range: | anti-surface 11,000–13,200 yds (10,000–12,000 m) |
| | anti-air 8,800–9,900 yds (8,000–9,000 m) |
| Elevation: | −15° to +85° |
| Projectile weight: | 35 lbs (16 kg) |
| Fire control radar: | Round Top director with Sun Visor and/or Top Bow or Post Lamp; Egg Cup-B |
| Platforms: | *cruisers*   ADM. SENYAVIN, DZERZHINSKIY, SVERDLOV |

## 100-mm/56-caliber SP (single)

Dual-purpose gun fitted in shield rather than in fully enclosed mount. Elevation limits AA effectiveness. They were developed in the 1930s and updated for installation from the later 1940s.

| | |
|---|---|
| Muzzle velocity: | 850 m/sec |
| Rate of fire: | 15 rounds per minute |
| Maximum range: | 17,600 yds (16,000 m) |
| Effective range: | 11,000 yds (10,000 m) |
| Elevation: | −5° to +40° |
| Projectile weight: | 30 lbs (13.5 kg) |
| Fire control radar: | Wasp Head director with Sun Visor; Top Bow |
| Platforms: | *frigates*   Riga |
| | *tenders*   Don |

Single 100-mm gun on UDALOY-class destroyer

### 85-mm/50-caliber AA (twin)

Obsolescent anti-aircraft weapon available from about 1943.

| | |
|---|---|
| Muzzle velocity: | 850 m/sec |
| Rate of fire: | 10 rounds per minute per barrel |
| Maximum range: | anti-surface 16,500 yds (15,000 m) |
| Effective range: | anti-surface 8,800–9,900 yds (8,000–9,000 m) |
| | anti-air 6,600 yds (6,000 m) |
| Elevation: | −5° to +70° |
| Projectile weight: | 26 lbs (12 kg) |
| Fire control radar: | Cylinder Head director (no radar) |
| Platforms: | *destroyers* SKORYY |

### 76.2-mm/60-caliber AA (twin)

Rapid-fire mounting in Soviet surface warships and auxiliary ships. Fitted in ships completed from the early 1960s.

| | | |
|---|---|---|
| Muzzle velocity: | 900 m/sec | |
| Rate of fire: | 45 rounds per minute per barrel | |
| Maximum range: | anti-air 11,000 yds (10,000 m) | |
| Effective range: | anti-air 6,600–7,700 yds (6,000–7,000 m) | |
| Elevation: | 0° to +80° | |
| Projectile weight: | 13 lbs (6 kg) | |
| Fire control radar: | Hawk Screech or Owl Screech | |
| Platforms: | *carriers* | KIEV |
| | *cruisers* | Kara, Kynda |
| | *destroyers* | Kashin |
| | *frigates* | Koni, Krivak I, Mirka, Petya |
| | *auxiliaries* | IVAN SUSANIN, SMOL'NYY |

### 76.2-mm/60-caliber DP (single)

Fully automatic gun installed in corvettes and small combatants from about 1960.

| | | |
|---|---|---|
| Muzzle velocity: | | |
| Rate of fire: | 120 rounds per minute | |
| Maximum range: | anti-surface 15,400 yds (14,000 m) | |
| | anti-air 11,000 yds (10,000 m) | |
| Effective range: | anti-air 6,600–7,700 yds (6,000–7,000 m) | |
| Elevation: | (?) to +85° | |
| Projectile weight: | 13 lbs (6 kg) | |
| Fire control radar: | Bass Tilt | |
| Platforms: | *corvettes* | Nanuchka III, Pauk, Tarantul |
| | *small combatants* | Matka, Slepen |

Twin 76.2-mm guns on Krivak I-class destroyer

### 57-mm/80-caliber AA (twin)

This is a fully automatic weapon installed in a variety of ships of various sizes. The barrels are water cooled. In service from the early 1960s.

| | | |
|---|---|---|
| Muzzle velocity: | 1,000 m/sec | |
| Rate of fire: | 110 to 120 rounds per minute per barrel | |
| Maximum range: | anti-surface 13,200 yds (12,000 m) | |
| | anti-air 7,370 yds (6,700 m) | |
| Effective range: | anti-air 5,500–6,600 yds (5,000–6,000 m) | |
| Elevation: | (?) to +85° | |
| Projectile weight: | 6 lbs (2.8 kg) | |
| Fire control radar: | Bass Tilt or Muff Cob | |
| Platforms: | *carriers* | MOSKVA |
| | *cruisers* | Kresta I, Kresta II |
| | *corvettes* | Grisha, Nanuchka I, Poti |
| | *small combatants* | Turya |
| | *amphibious* | Ropucha |
| | *auxiliaries* | BEREZINA, BORIS CHILIKIN, MANYCH, Ugra |

### 57-mm/70-caliber AA (single, twin, quad)

This is a widely used weapon, installed in a variety of ships since the late 1950s.

| | | |
|---|---|---|
| Muzzle velocity: | 900 to 1,000 m/sec | |
| Rate of fire: | 120 rounds per minute per barrel | |
| Maximum range: | anti-surface 9,900 yds (9,000 m) | |
| | anti-air 6,600 yds (6,000 m) | |
| Effective range: | anti-surface 8,800 yds (8,000 m) | |
| | anti-air 4,950 yds (4,500 m) | |
| Elevation: | 0° to +90° | |
| Projectile weight: | 6 lbs (2.8 kg) | |
| Fire control radar: | Hawk Screech or Muff Cob | |
| Platforms: | *destroyers* | Kanin, Kildin, SKORYY (Mod) |
| | *minelayers* | Alesha |
| | *minesweepers* | Sasha, T-58 |
| | *amphibious* | Alligator |
| | *auxiliaries* | Don, Lama |

Quad 57-mm gun mounts on Kildin-class destroyer (U.S. Navy)

Twin 57-mm gun mount on Nanuchka II-class corvette; Muff Cob GFC radar at right. (U.S. Navy)

Quad 45-mm gun mount on Kotlin-class destroyer (U.S. Navy)

## 45-mm/85-caliber AA (single, quad)

This semi-automatic weapon is mounted principally in destroyers.

| | |
|---|---|
| Muzzle velocity: | 900 m/sec |
| Rate of fire: | 75 rounds per minute per barrel |
| Maximum range: | anti-surface 9,900 yds (9,000 m) |
| | anti-air 7,700 yds (7,000 m) |
| Effective range: | anti-surface 4,400 yds (4,000 m) |
| | anti-air 4,180 yds (3,800 m) |
| Elevation: | 0° to +90° |
| Projectile weight: | 4.8 lbs (2.2 kg) |
| Fire control radar: | Hawk Screech (in destroyers) |
| Platforms: | *destroyers*  Kildin (1 unit), Kotlin, SAM Kotlin |
| | *minesweepers*  Sasha (single mounting) |

## 37-mm/60-caliber AA (twin)

| | |
|---|---|
| Muzzle velocity: | 900 m/sec |
| Rate of fire: | 160 rounds per minute per barrel |
| Maximum range: | anti-surface 10,230 yds (9,300 m) |
| | anti-air 6,160 yds (5,600 m) |
| Effective range: | anti-surface 4,400 yds (4,000 m) |
| | anti-air 3,300 yds (3,000 m) |
| Elevation: | 0° to +80° |
| Projectile weight: | 1.5 lbs (0.7 kg) |
| Fire control radar: | none |
| Platforms: | *cruisers*  ADM. SENYAVIN, DZERZHINSKIY, SVERDLOV |
| | *destroyers*  SKORYY |
| | *frigates*  Riga |
| | *minesweepers*  T-43 |

Twin 37-mm gun mount

## 30-mm Gatling AA (multibarrel "Gatling")

This is a close-in weapon intended to defeat incoming anti-ship missiles introduced in the late 1960s. The mounting has six 30-mm barrels within a larger barrel-like cylinder. It is similar in concept to the U.S. Navy's 20-mm/76-caliber Mk 15 Phalanx Close-In Weapon System (CIWS). The Soviet weapon was originally reported to have a 23-mm barrel diameter. The Soviet designation is ADMG-630.

| | |
|---|---|
| Muzzle velocity: | |
| Rate of fire: | 3,000 rounds per minute per mount |
| Maximum range: | |
| Effective range: | |
| Elevation: | |
| Projectile weight: | |
| Fire control radar: | Bass Tilt |

| Platforms: | | |
|---|---|---|
| | *carriers* | KIEV |
| | *cruisers* | KARA, KIROV, ADM. SENYAVIN, Kresta II, Kynda |
| | *destroyers* | Kashin, SOVREMENNYY, UDALOY |
| | *frigates* | Grisha III |
| | *corvettes* | Nanuchka III, Pauk, Tarantul |
| | *small combatants* | Babochka, Matka, Sarancha |
| | *amphibious* | IVAN ROGOV |
| | *auxiliaries* | BAL'ZAM, BEREZINA, Ivan SUSANIN |

Twin 30-mm close-in gun systems on Kotlin-class destroyer SKRYTNYY; a Drum Tilt GFC radar is at upper left. (U.S. Navy)

### 30-mm/60-caliber AA (twin)

These are fully automatic, close-in defense weapons introduced into the Soviet Navy about 1960. The *theoretical* rate of fire is 1,050 rounds per minute per barrel, but 200-240 rounds is the maximum realistic rate. There is a backup optical director.

| | |
|---|---|
| Velocity: | 1,000 m/sec |
| Rate of fire: | 200 to 240 rounds per barrel per minute |
| Maximum range: | anti-surface 4,400 yds (4,000 m) |
| | anti-air 5,500 yds (5,000 m) |
| Effective range: | anti-surface 2,750 yds (2,500 m) |
| | anti-air 2,750–3,300 yds (2,500–3,000 m) |
| Elevation: | (?) to +85° |
| Projectile weight: | 1.2 lbs (0.54 kg) |
| Fire control radar: | Drum Tilt |

| Platforms: | | |
|---|---|---|
| | *cruisers* | ADM. SENYAVIN, SVERDLOV |
| | *destroyers* | Kanin, SAM Kotlin |
| | *small combatants* | Osa, Shershen, Stenka |
| | *minesweepers* | various classes |
| | *amphibious* | Polnocny |
| | *auxiliaries* | various classes |

### 25-mm/60-caliber AA (twin)

| | |
|---|---|
| Muzzle velocity: | 900 m/sec |
| Rate of fire: | 150–200 rounds per minute per barrel |
| Maximum range: | anti-surface 4,400 yds (4,000 m) |
| Effective range: | anti-surface 2,530 yds (2,300 m) |
| | anti-air 3,300 yds (3,000 m) |
| Elevation: | (?) to +85° |
| Projectile weight: | 0.75 lbs (0.34 kg) |
| Fire control radar: | none |
| Platforms: | various ships and small craft |

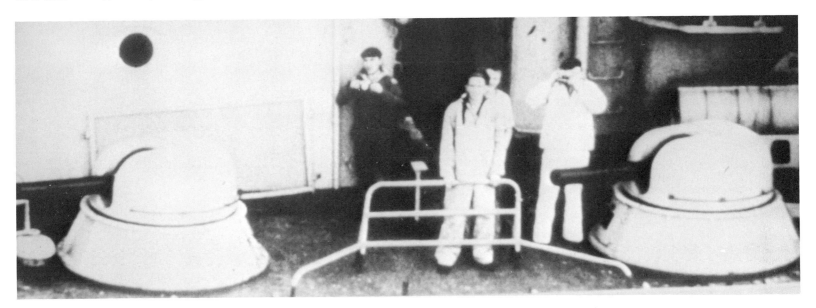

30-mm Gatling guns on Soviet cruiser

## NAVAL MINES

The Soviet Navy is estimated to maintain a stock of between 300,000 and 400,000 naval mines, several times the number available to the U.S. Navy. Many of these mines date to World War II. However, most are newer weapons, including mines given the NATO code names Cluster Bay and Cluster Gulf. These appear to be deep-water mines, probably with a capability of being planted in depths to 3,000 feet (910 m). These mines are fitted with passive acoustic detection and, like the U.S. Navy's Mk-60 CAPTOR mine, release an anti-submarine weapon that homes on submarine targets.

Analyses of Soviet literature indicate that the Soviet Navy has developed influence mines of all types—homing mines, rising mines, remotely controlled mines, and mines capable of being planted in virtually any water depth. Minelaying is exercised by naval aircraft, surface ships, and submarines. Many classes of cruisers, destroyers, and frigates as well as small combatants have mine rails, while most submarines can carry mines in place of torpedoes at the ratio of one or two mines per torpedo, depending upon the type of mine.

(The intense Soviet interest in mine warfare is also demonstrated by the Navy's large coastal and ocean-going mine countermeasures forces; see chapter 18.)

## MISSILES

Missiles in use with the Soviet Navy are described below. Some of the air-launched missiles are also used by Soviet strategic aviation. All weapons in the missile designation scheme are listed to provide continuity.

According to official U.S. government statements, the Soviets currently have more than 1,200 anti-ship cruise missile launchers—i.e., launchers on surface ships and submarines, and launch rails on aircraft. Of these, more than 500 have ranges less than 100 n.miles (185 km), and more than 700 have ranges in excess of 100 n.miles. During the next few years these numbers are predicted to change significantly. The number of shorter-range missiles will decline, to about 400, while the longer-range weapons will increase to more than 1,000, for a total of more than 1,400 anti-ship missiles.

The most significant shifts will be an increase in anti-ship missile launchers of both categories in Soviet surface ships, and a decline in the short-range air-launched missiles in favor of a net increase of perhaps 250 long-range air-launched missiles. The surface ship numbers address Soviet aircraft carriers, cruisers, and destroyers, but not missile corvettes and smaller craft. The increase in air-launched missiles predates the anticipated service introduction of the Blackjack strike aircraft in 1986 or 1987 at the earliest.

Designations: Soviet missiles are given designations in two NATO schemes, one of which assigns an alphanumeric serial and the other a code name. The serial number indicates the launch platform and target with the following primary designations:

AS    = Air-to-Surface
SA    = Surface-to-Air
SS    = Surface-to-Surface (also underwater-to-surface)
SUW = Surface-to-Underwater (Weapon)

The additional letter N is added to the designation of all missiles except air-launched weapons to indicate naval use; NX is used to indicate naval missiles under development; and the letter C is added to surface-to-surface missiles to indicate land-launched versions used for coastal defense.

The NATO code names, which are not assigned to all missiles, indicate the launch platform and target and have the initial letters listed below:

G = surface-to-air
K = air-to-surface
S = surface-to-surface (also underwater-to-surface)

Soviet strategic aviation also has the AS-3, -4, -5, and possibly -6 missiles, mainly for use against ground targets, but probably with a secondary capability against surface ships.

Characteristics: Characteristics are approximate, based mainly on published U.S. Department of Defense estimates.

Platforms: Only missile-armed platforms currently in naval service are listed.

## AIR-TO-SURFACE MISSILES

### AS-1 Kennel

This appears to have been the first fully operational Soviet air-to-surface missile, designated "Komet" in Soviet service. Development started in 1946 and possibly earlier, being developed intitally for use with the Tu-4 Bull, a Soviet copy of the Boeing B-29 Superfortress. Admiral Gorshkov has implied that the missile was developed for use aboard surface ships, but limitations of the engine dictated that it be used only from aircraft.[3] The land-launched SS-C-2b Samlet was a variant of this weapon. The missile, with a range of over 50 n. miles (92.5 km), was operational from 1958–1959, but is no longer used by the Soviet armed forces.

### AS-2 Kipper

| | |
|---|---|
| Weight: | 9,260 lbs (4,200 kg) |
| Length: | 31 ft (9.5 m) |
| Span: | 16 ft (4.9 m) |
| Propulsion: | turbojet |
| Range: | 100+ n.miles (185+ km) |
| Guidance: | inertial or autopilot with radar homing |
| Warhead: | nuclear or conventional (2,200 lbs/1,000 kg) |
| Platforms: | Badger-C/G |
| IOC: | 1961 |

### AS-3 Kangaroo

This is a strategic attack missile fitted with a nuclear warhead carried by the Bear-B/C bombers of Soviet strategic aviation. Range is estimated at more than 200 n.miles (370 km). It is *not* believed to have an effective anti-ship homing system; nuclear warhead only.

[3]See Admiral Gorshkov, *The Sea Power of the State*, p. 204.

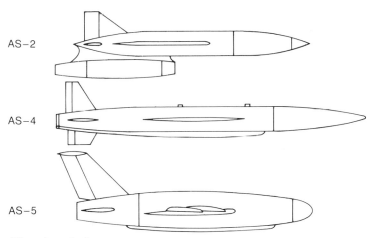

AS-2

AS-4

AS-5

AS- series missiles

## AS-4 Kitchen

The AS-4 was developed as a stand-off, anti-ship missile for the Bear and Blinder bombers, being first seen in 1961 on the Blinder-B of the strategic air arm. It has been subsequently adopted for the Backfire-B, and the Bear-B/C of Soviet strategic aviation. (SNA Blinders and Bears do not carry missiles.) The ventral fin of the AS-4 folds to starboard while carried under the launching aircraft. After launch from medium altitude (approximately 20,000 ft/6,090 m), the missile climbs steeply to achieve cruise altitude and speeds estimated at between Mach 2.5 to 3.5, and then dives steeply at its target.

| | |
|---|---|
| Weight: | 14,330 lbs (6,500 kg) |
| Length: | 37 ft (11.3 m) |
| Span: | 11 ft (3.35 m) |
| Propulsion: | turbojet |
| Range: | 150–250 n.miles (278–463 km) |
| Guidance: | inertial or autopilot with terminal radar (J-band) or infrared homing |
| Warhead: | nuclear or conventional (2,200 lbs/1,000 kg) |
| Platforms: | Backfire-B, Bear-B/C, Blinder |
| IOC: | 1967 |

## AS-5 Kelt

Improved anti-ship missile.

| | |
|---|---|
| Weight: | approx. 10,500 lbs (4,725 kg) |
| Length: | 31 ft (9.45 m) |
| Span: | 15 ft (4.6 m) |
| Propulsion: | liquid-fuel rocket |
| Range: | 100 + n.miles (185 + km) |
| Guidance: | inertial or autopilot with radar homing (J-band) |
| Warhead: | nuclear or conventional (2,200 lbs/1,000 kg) |
| Platforms: | Badger-C/G |
| IOC: | 1965–1966 |

## AS-6 Kingfish

This is an advanced anti-ship missile, believed to have been developed for use from the Backfire bomber. However, up to press time of this edition the AS-6 has been observed only on Badger aircraft. A flight profile similar to the AS-4 is estimated with maximum speeds of between Mach 2.5 to 3.5.

AS-4 Kitchen on centerline of Backfire-B

| | |
|---|---|
| Weight: | approx. 11,000 lbs (4,950 kg) |
| Length: | 34 ft 7 in (10.5 m) |
| Span: | 8 ft 2 in (2.5 m) |
| Propulsion: | turbojet |
| Range: | 150–250 n.miles (278–463 km) |
| Guidance: | inertial with terminal active radar homing (J-band) |
| Warhead: | nuclear or conventional (1,100 lbs/500 kg) |
| Platforms: | Badger-C/G |
| IOC: | 1970 |

## AS- . . .

In early 1983 the U.S. Secretary of Defense announced that at least one long-range, air-launched cruise missile was under development in the USSR. The weapon has an estimated range of some 1,620 n.miles (3,000 km). The missile is expected to be carried by the Backfire and Blackjack, and possibly the older Bear aircraft. Although a land attack missile, its uses could include strikes against ports and other naval targets by naval aircraft.

## SURFACE-TO-AIR MISSILES

### SA-N-1 Goa

This was the first surface-to-air missile to be widely fitted in Soviet warships and is considered effective at low to medium altitudes and in the surface-to-surface mode. It is fired from a single twin-arm launcher in destroyers and one or two launchers in cruisers, with the missiles loaded with the launcher at 90° elevation from a below-deck magazine. The four square-shaped tail fins are folded until the missile leaves the launcher. The missile system is derived from the land-based SA-3 system, which became operational in 1964. Maximum speed is approximately Mach 2.0. The Peel Group fire control radar is used with the SA-N-1.

| | |
|---|---|
| Weight: | 882 lbs (400 kg) |
| Length: | 22 ft (6.6 m) |
| Span: | 4 ft 11 in (1.5 m) |
| Diameter: | missile 18.1 in (460 mm) |
| | booster 27.6 in (701 mm) |
| Propulsion: | solid-fuel rocket with tandem solid-fuel boosters |
| Range: | approx. 17 n.miles (31.5 km) |
| Guidance: | radio command |
| Warhead: | conventional (132 lbs/60 kg) |
| Platforms: | *cruisers*    Kresta I, Kynda |
| | *destroyers*   Kanin, Kashin, SAM Kotlin |
| IOC: | 1961 |

SA-N-1 Goa

### SA-N-2 Guideline

The SA-N-2 was adopted from the land-based SA-2 missile system and is considered a medium-altitude weapon. Only one cruiser of the SVERD-LOV class has been fitted with the sea-based version, indicating a lack of success in that mode, although the land-based missile is used by a large number of nations. The Fan Song-E fire control radar and High Lune height-finding radar are associated with the system. Maximum speed is approximately Mach 2.5. The land-based SA-2 became operational in 1957. The DZERZHINSKIY system is not operational.

| | |
|---|---|
| Weight: | 5,070 lbs (2,300 kg) |
| Length: | 35 ft 2 in (10.7 m) |
| Span: | 7 ft 2.2 in (2.2 m) |
| Diameter: | |
| Propulsion: | solid-fuel rocket with liquid-fuel booster |
| Range: | approx. 25 n.miles (44 km) |
| Guidance: | radio command |
| Warhead: | conventional (287 lbs/130 kg) |
| Platforms: | *cruisers*   DZERZHINSKIY |
| IOC: | 1961 (limited basis) |

### SA-N-3 Goblet

This missile system went to sea in the "second generation" of warships that went to sea during the Gorshkov regime, beginning with the MOSKVA-class helicopter carrier-cruisers and Kresta II cruisers. It is a low- to medium-altitude missile with improved capabilities over the SA-N-1, which it succeeds. Like most other Soviet naval surface-to-air missiles, it is derived from a land-based system, the SA-6 Gainful which became operational in 1967. The SA-N-3 is reported to have an effective surface-to-surface as well as anti-aircraft capability. Maximum speed is approximately Mach 2.5. It is employed with the Head Light fire control radar.

| | |
|---|---|
| Weight: | 1,213 lbs (550 kg) |
| Length: | 20 ft 4 in (6.2 m) |
| Span: | 5 ft (1.5 m) |
| Diameter: | 13.2 in (335 mm) |
| Propulsion: | ramjet with solid-fuel booster |
| Range: | approx. 30 n.miles (55.5 km) |
| Guidance: | semiactive homing |
| Warhead: | conventional (176 lbs/80 kg) |
| Platforms: | *carriers*   MOSKVA, KIEV |
| | *cruisers*   Kresta II, Kara |
| IOC: | 1967 |

SA-N-1 Goa launcher on SAM Kotlin

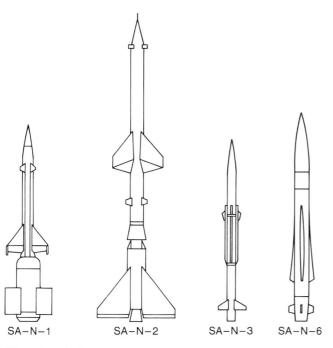

SA- series missiles

## SA-N-4

The SA-N-4 system has a fully retractable, twin-arm launcher for point-defense of large ships as well as small combatants. The SA-N-4 uses the Pop Group missile-control radar, which is similar to the radar associated with the land-based SA-8 Grechko surface-to-air missile.

| | |
|---|---|
| Weight: | approx. 420 lbs (190 kg) |
| Length: | 10 ft 6 in (3.2 m) |
| Span: | 2 ft 1.2 in (0.64 m) |
| Diameter: | 8.25 in (210 mm) |
| Propulsion: | solid-fuel rocket |
| Range: | approx. 8 n.miles (14.8 m) |
| Guidance: | semiactive homing |
| Warhead: | conventional (110 lbs/50 kg) |
| Platforms: | *carriers*  KIEV |
| | *cruisers*  KIROV, SVERDLOV (command ships), Kara |
| | *frigates*  Krivak, Koni |
| | *small combatants*  Nanuchka, Grisha, Sarancha |
| | *amphibious ships*  IVAN ROGOV |
| | *auxiliary ships*  BEREZINA |
| IOC: | early 1970s |

SA-N-3 Goblet launcher on Kara-class cruiser (Royal Air Force)

Forward SA-N-4 launcher on Krivak I-class frigate

SA-N-4 launcher on converted SVERDLOV-class command ship

## SA-N-5

This is a small, shipborne form of the SA-7 Grail (formerly Strela) missile and is fitted in various small combatants and amphibious and auxiliary ships. It is fired from a four-missile launch rack or a single, shoulder-held launch tube. The missile became operational in Soviet Ground Forces in 1966.

| | |
|---|---|
| Weight: | 20.3 lbs (9.2 kg) |
| Length: | 2 ft 5.25 in (0.76 m) |
| Span: | (small canard stabilizing fins) |
| Diameter: | 2.75 in (69.9 mm) |
| Propulsion: | solid-fuel rocket |
| Range: | 5.6 n.miles (10.36 km) |
| Guidance: | infrared homing |
| Warhead: | conventional (5.5 lbs/2.5 kg) |
| Platforms: | *corvettes*  Pauk, Tarantul |
| | *small combatants*  Osa |
| | *amphibious ships*  Polnocny, Ropocha |
| | *auxiliary ships*  various AGIs |
| IOC: | |

## SA-N-6

This is an advanced surface-to-air missile with anti-cruise missile capabilities. The SA-N-6 is vertically launched from a below-deck rotary magazine, with eight missiles per launcher. Guidance provides for track-via-missile, with the missile in flight providing radar data to the launching ship. Initially fitted in one Kara-class cruiser and subsequently in the KIROV-class nuclear cruisers. It appears to be adopted from the SA-10 missile. Uses Top Dome radar.

| | |
|---|---|
| Weight: | |
| Length: | 23 ft (7 m) |
| Span: | |
| Propulsion: | solid-fuel rocket |
| Range: | 30 + n.miles (55.5 + m) |
| Guidance: | |
| Warhead: | conventional |
| Platforms: | *cruisers*  Kara (1 ship), KIROV, Krasina |
| IOC: | 1977–1978 |

## SA-N-7

This is a shipboard version of the land-based SA-11 missile that went to sea in 1981 aboard the Kashin-class destroyer PROVORNYY and in the new SOVREMENNYY-class destroyers. The PROVORNYY was extensively modified with eight directors for the SA-N-7, but only one single-arm launcher, installed aft. There appear to be provisions forward for two more launchers. The SOVREMENNYY-class ships have two launchers and six Front Dome radar directors.

| | |
|---|---|
| Weight: | |
| Length: | |
| Span: | |
| Diameter: | |
| Propulsion: | solid-fuel rocket |
| Range: | approx. 15 n.miles (28 m) |
| Guidance: | |
| Warhead: | conventional |
| Platforms: | *destroyers*  Kashin (1 unit), SOVREMENNYY |
| IOC: | 1981 |

An advanced surface-to-air missile system employing vertical launch techniques will be fitted in the UDALOY-class destroyers. The missile is probably a successor to the short-range SA-N-4 system. See UDALOY-class listing in chapter 14 for details of arrangement.

SA-7 launcher held by Polish marine

## SA-N-...

The Soviet Navy is developing a submarine-to-air missile, according to comments by U.S. Secretary of the Navy John Lehman. A possible mockup of this weapon was observed on a Tango-class submarine in the Adriatic Sea. The submarine carried a twin ramp for a weapon similar in size to the SA-N-4. It is not known if the weapon would be launched while the submarine is submerged or surfaced.

A submerged submarine can detect aircraft with a towed passive sonar array.

The forward missile batteries of cruiser KIROV showing, from left, the SS-N-14 twin launcher, hatches for 12 SA-N-6 vertical/rotary launchers, and hatches for SS-N-19 vertical-launch missiles. The SA-N-6 hatch arrangement reflects the 12 rotary magazines, each with eight missiles, arranged with the magazines for the port and starboard rows outboard and the magazine for the center row to port, providing the unbalanced arrangement. The SS-N-14 tubes are reloaded from a magazine forward of the launcher.

Forward vertical launch missile position on destroyer UDALOY

Fittings for short-range surface-to-air missile system in destroyer UDALOY; there are four circular cover plates two meters (approximately six and a half feet) in diameter on a raised portion of the forecastle. Two sets of similar cover plates are located amidships for a total of eight such fittings.

**SURFACE-TO-SURFACE MISSILES**

## SS-N-1 Scrubber/Strela

The Scrubber was the first surface-to-surface missile to be deployed by the Soviet Navy, going to sea from 1959 in four destroyers of the Kildin class (1 launcher) and from 1960 in eight destroyers of the Krupnyy (2 launcher) class. The missile had a maximum range of approximately 100 n.miles (185 km), but had several limitations and was awkward to handle aboard ship. By the late 1960s the Scrubber-armed ships were being discarded or converted. Scrubber was the NATO code name, but American intelligence agencies tended to use the name Strela.

## SS-N-2 Styx

The Styx was developed to provide an anti-ship missile capability for small combat craft in the coastal defense role. It is a subsonic missile that has undergone several developmental stages, the designation SS-N-11 being used briefly to indicate the SS-N-2c version. Soviet doctrine appears to call for launching the SS-N-2a/b versions at a range of some 10 to 13 n.miles (18 to 24 km), or about one-half their maximum range. Maximum speed is approximately Mach 0.9. The Square Tie radar is used to detect targets. Once launched, there is no data link to the SS-N-2a/b version, with the terminal radar seeker being automatically switched on some five miles from the estimated target position. The missile will home on the largest target.

The SS-N-2a was first deployed aboard Soviet Komar-class missile boats and subsequently in the Osa I. The -2b was initially used in the Osa II and was followed by the improved -2c version, the -2a/b also being fitted in later small combatants. Including Third World sales, the Styx was the world's most widely used anti-ship missile prior to the French Exocet becoming operational in 1973 and the U.S. Harpoon in 1977. The Styx gained international attention after Egyptian Komar boats, from the safety of Alexandria Harbor, sank the Israeli destroyer ELATH steaming 12 miles offshore on 25 October 1967. The weapon was subsequently used by the Indian Navy to sink a number of Pakistani ships in the 1971 Indo-Pakistani conflict and by the Egyptian and Syrian navies without effect in the 1973 war with Israel.

| | |
|---|---|
| Weight: | SS-N-2a/b approx. 5,500 lbs (2,500 kg) |
| Length: | SS-N-2a/b 19 ft (5.8 m) |
| | SS-N-2c 21 ft 6 in (6.55 m) |
| Span: | 9 ft 2 in (2.8 m) |
| Diameter: | SS-N-2a/b 29.5 in (750 mm) |
| | SS-N-2c 31 in (788 mm) |
| Propulsion: | turbojet with solid-fuel booster |
| Range: | SS-N-2a approx. 25 n.miles (46 km) |
| | SS-N-2b approx. 27 n.miles (50 km) |
| | SS-N-2c approx. 40–45 n.miles (74–83 km) |
| Guidance: | active radar homing (plus infrared homing in SS-N-2c); additional inertial in SS-N-2c version |
| Warhead: | conventional (1,100 lbs/500 kg) |
| Platforms: | *destroyers* Kashin, Kildin |
| | *small combatants* Osa, Matka, Tarantul; in Nanuchkas for foreign transfer |
| IOC: | SS-N-2a 1958 |
| | SS-N-2b 1964 |
| | SS-N-2c 1967 |

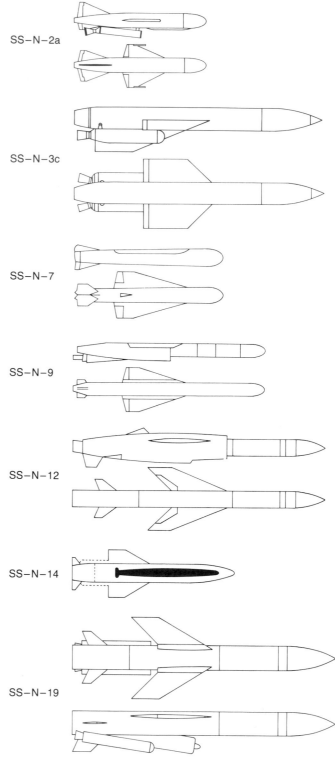

SS-N-2a

SS-N-3c

SS-N-7

SS-N-9

SS-N-12

SS-N-14

SS-N-19

SS-N- series

SS-N-2 Styx tubes (partially open) on Egyptian Osa I-class missile boat

Twin SS-N-3 Shaddock tubes on Kresta I-class cruiser

SS-N-2 Styx anti-ship missiles on parade

## SS-N-3 Shaddock

The Shaddock is a large, air-breathing cruise missile originally developed for the strategic attack role in the SS-N-3c variant (a contemporary of the U.S. Regulus missile, which was operational from 1954, on a limited basis, to 1964). When submarine launched it is fired from the surface. The land-launched SS-C-1 Sepal missile is similar (see chapter 7/ Coastal Artillery). The SS-N-3b was also assigned the NATO code name Sepal, but all ship-launched versions are generally referred to as Shaddock. The SS-N-12 is an improved version and has replaced the SS-N-3 in some Echo II submarines. (The five Echo I SSGNs that originally carried the SS-N-3 have been converted to attack submarines, and most of the earlier Whiskey SSG conversions have been discarded.) The Scoop Pair radar is used for fire control in surface ships and the Front Door or Front Piece radar in submarines.

The missile requires mid-course guidance for over-the-horizon use. This is sent as a radar picture via Video Data Link (VDL) from the targeting ship or aircraft to the launching ship and then relayed—with target indicated—to the missile in flight. The launching submarine is thus required to remain on the surface after launch, for as long as 25 minutes when firing against targets at a range of some 250 n.miles.

| | |
|---|---|
| Weight: | approx. 12,000 lbs (5,400 kg) |
| Length: | SS-N-3c 38 ft 6 in (11.75 m) |
| | SS-N-3a/b 33 ft 6 in (10.2 m) |
| Span: | approx. 6 ft 10 in (2.1 m) |
| Diameter: | approx. 39 in (975 mm) |
| Propulsion: | turbojet + 2 solid-fuel boosters |
| Range: | SS-N-3c 400+ n.miles (740+ km) |
| | SS-N-3a/b 250 n.miles (463 km) |
| Guidance: | inertial with mid-course correction; active radar for terminal phase |
| Warhead: | nuclear or conventional (2,200 lbs/1,000 kg) |
| Platforms: | SS-N-3a *submarines*  Juliett, Echo II |
| | SS-N-3b *cruisers*   Kynda, Kresta I |
| | SS-N-3c *submarines*  Whiskey (mod.), Juliett, Echo II |
| IOC: | SS-N-3a 1962 |
| | SS-N-3b 1962 |
| | SS-N-3c 1960 |

## SS-N-4 Sark

The SS-N-4 was the Soviet Navy's first operational SLBM, being a surface-launched weapon originally fitted in the Zulu-V, Golf, and Hotel submarine classes. The Zulu-V craft (2 missiles) have been discarded, while 13 of the Golf class and 7 of the nuclear-powered Hotel class were converted to fire the SS-N-5 missile (3 missiles per submarine).

| | |
|---|---|
| Weight: | approx. 44,000 lbs (19,800 kg) |
| Length: | approx. 46 ft (14 m) |
| Span: | (ballistic) |
| Diameter: | 71 in (1,800 mm) |
| Propulsion: | liquid-fuel rocket |
| Range: | approx. 350 n.miles (650 km) |
| Guidance: | inertial |
| Warhead: | nuclear (approx. 1 MT; 1 RV) |
| Platforms: | *submarines*  Golf I |
| IOC: | 1959–1960 |

SS-N-4 Sark at Moscow parade honoring October Revolution. (UPI)

## SS-N-5 Serb

The SS-N-5 was an improved SLBM, featuring underwater launch and a greater range compared to the previous SS-N-4. It replaced the SS-N-4 in 13 of the Golf class submarines and 7 of the Hotel-class SSBNs with 3 missiles per submarine. The range is believed to have been increased during service life from approximately 700 n.miles (1,300 km) to the distance indicated below.

Weight:      approx. 37,000 lbs (16,650 kg)
Length:      approx. 43 ft (13 m)
Span:        (ballistic)
Diameter:    approx. 48 in (1,217 mm)
Propulsion:  liquid-fuel rocket
Range:       900 n.miles (1,650 km)
Guidance:    inertial
Warhead:     nuclear (approx. 800 KT; 1 RV)
Platforms:   *submarines*  Golf II, Hotel II
IOC:         1963

## SS-N-6

This strategic missile was deployed in the Yankee-class submarines, the first modern Soviet SSBN class. It is a single-stage, liquid-fuel, underwater-launch missile. All Yankee SSBNs originally carried the S-N-6; one has subsequently been rearmed with the SS-N-17, and some have had their missile tube sections removed in conversion to an SSN configuration. A single Golf-class SSB was fitted to fire the SS-N-6. The SLBM given the NATO code name Sawfly was apparently a competitive prototype to the SS-N-6 and not the same missile.

Weight:      approx. 42,000 lbs (18,900 kg)
Length:      approx. 33 ft (10 m)
Span:        (ballistic)
Diameter:    approx. 71 in (1,800 mm)
Propulsion:  liquid-fuel rocket
Range:       Mod 1 1,300 n.miles (2,400 km)
             Mod 2 1,600 n.miles (2,950 km)
             Mod 3 1,600 n.miles (2,950 km)
Guidance:    inertial
Warhead:     nuclear (approx. 1 MT; 1 RV in Mod 1 and 2; 2 MRV in Mod 3);
             approx. 750 kiloton per RV
Platforms:   *submarines*  Yankee I, Golf IV
IOC:         Mod 1 1968
             Mod 2/3 1972–1973

## SS-N-7

The SS-N-7 is the Soviet Navy's first underwater-launched, anti-ship cruise missile. Maximum speed is approximately Mach 0.9. It has been succeeded in later Charlie-class SSGNs by the SS-N-9, which has about double the earlier missile's range.

Weight:      approx. 7,500 lbs (3,375 kg)
Length:      23 ft (7 m)
Span:
Propulsion:  solid-fuel rocket
Range:       30–35 n.miles (55–64 km)
Guidance:    radar homing (J-band)
Warhead:     nuclear or conventional (1,100 lbs/500 kg)
Platforms:   *submarines*  Charlie I
IOC:         1971

## SS-N-8

This SLBM was developed for the Delta-class strategic missile submarines. It is the first two-stage submarine missile, being significantly larger than the SS-N-6 used in the previous Yankee-class SSBNs, indicating it was developed from the SS-N-4/5 SLBM series. One Golf-class SSBN was modified as a test bed to launch the SS-N-8.

Weight:      approx. 45,000 lbs (20,450 kg)
Length:      approx. 43 ft (13 m)
Span:        (ballistic)
Propulsion:  liquid-fuel rocket
Range:       Mod 1 4,240 n.miles (7,800 km)
             Mod 2 4,950 n.miles (9,100 km)
Guidance:    inertial
Warhead:     nuclear (approx. 0.8–1.5 MT; 1 RV)
Platforms:   *submarines*  Delta I, II, Golf III (1 unit)
IOC:         Mod 1 1973
             Mod 2 1977

## SS-N-9 Siren

This is a supersonic anti-ship missile, launched initially from surface ships and reported to have been subsequently fitted in the later Charlie-class SSGNs for underwater launch. Maximum speed is approximately Mach 0.9. The Band Stand radar is used on surface ships for search and fire control. The Nanuchka-class missile corvettes transferred to Algeria, India, and Libya have the SS-N-2c missile in place of the SS-N-9.

Weight:      approx. 6,500 lbs (2,950 kg)
Length:      29 ft (8.84 m)
Span:
Propulsion:  solid-fuel rocket
Range:       60 n.miles (111 km)
Guidance:    infrared and active radar homing; mid-course guidance required for maximum range
Warhead:     nuclear or conventional (1,100 lbs/500 kg)
Platforms:   *small combatants*  Nanuchka, Sarancha
             *submarines*  Charlie II, Papa
IOC:         1968–1969

## SS-N-10

The SS-N-14 anti-submarine missile was originally assigned this designation at the time Western intelligence evaluated it as an anti-ship missile.

Triple SS-N-9 on Nanuchka I-class corvette (U.S. Navy)

## SS-N-11

This designation was initially assigned to an improved version of the Styx, which was subsequently redesignated SS-N-2c.

## SS-N-12 Sandbox

This missile is an advanced version of the SS-N-3 Shaddock being fitted to the aircraft carriers of the KIEV class, Krasina-class, and the Echo II-class SSGNs. It is used with the Trap Door radar in the KIEV. This missile is approximately twice as fast as the SS-N-3.

| | |
|---|---|
| Weight: | |
| Length: | 38 ft 6 in (11.7 m) |
| Span: | |
| Propulsion: | turbojet |
| Range: | 300 n.miles (555 km) |
| Guidance: | radio command and active radar homing |
| Warhead: | nuclear or conventional (2,200 lbs/1,000 kg) |
| Platforms: | *carriers*   KIEV |
| | *cruisers*   Krasina |
| | *submarines*   Echo II |
| IOC: | 1973 |

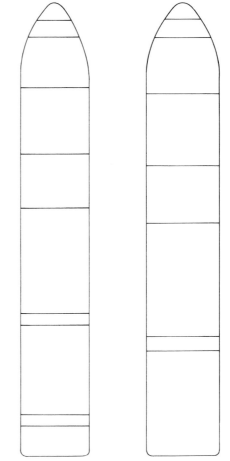

SS–N–5     SS–N–6     SS–N–8     SS–N–17     SS–N–18     SS–N–20

SS-N- series

## SS-NX-13

This is a *tactical* ballistic missile intended for the anti-carrier role. It apparently was developed for launch from the Yankee-class SSBNs, possibly with satellite targeting at launch and a terminal radar-homing system. It was flight-tested in the USSR from the late 1960s until November 1973. The missile has not been deployed. Range was approximately 370 n.miles (685 km) with a terminal maneuvering capability of some 30 n.miles (55 km). A nuclear warhead would have been used with the operational missile.

## SS-N-14 Silex

This is a rocket-propelled anti-submarine weapon, carrying a homing torpedo out to the first sonar convergence zone. Water entry is slowed by a parachute. Minimum effective range is estimated at four n.miles (7.4 km). It could probably be employed against surface ships as well. Of the five warship classes armed with the missile, only the nuclear-powered Kirov has an on-board reload capability. The SS-N-14 was initially evaluated by Western intelligence as an anti-ship weapon and designated SS-N-10.

| | |
|---|---|
| Weight: | |
| Length: | approx. 25 ft (7.6 m) |
| Span: | |
| Propulsion: | solid-fuel rocket |
| Range: | 30 n.miles (55 km) |
| Guidance: | inertial |
| Warhead: | acoustic ASW homing torpedo (conventional) |
| Platforms: | *cruisers*    Kara, Kirov, Kresta II |
| | *destroyers*    Udaloy |
| | *frigates*    Krivak |
| IOC: | 1968 |

SS-N-14 Silex launchers on Kresta II-class cruiser (U.S. Navy)

## SS-N-15

An ASW weapon similar to the U.S. Navy's SUBROC (Submarine Rocket), the SS-N-15 is fired from standard submarine torpedo tubes and carries a nuclear warhead.

The weapon is fired with range and bearing derived from the launching submarine's sonar.

| | |
|---|---|
| Weight: | |
| Length: | |
| Span: | |
| Diameter: | 21 in (533 mm) (maximum) |
| Propulsion: | solid-fuel rocket |
| Range: | 20 n.miles (37 km) |
| Guidance: | inertial |
| Warhead: | nuclear |
| Platforms: | *submarines*    Alfa, Victor |
| IOC: | 1972 |

## SS-N-16

A further development of the SS-N-15, this missile carries an anti-submarine homing torpedo in lieu of the nuclear warhead. A parachute lowers the torpedo into the water, and a protective nosecap separates upon water entry, and when the torpedo reaches a prescribed depth, a programmed search maneuver is begun, with the torpedo homing on any target detected during the search. The weapon is launched from tubes larger than the standard 533-mm torpedo tubes.

| | |
|---|---|
| Weight: | |
| Length: | |
| Span: | |
| Propulsion: | solid-fuel rocket |
| Range: | 30–50 n.miles (55–92 km) |
| Guidance: | inertial (to torpedo release point) |
| Warhead: | ASW homing torpedo (conventional) |
| Platforms: | *submarines*    Alfa (?), Victor II/III |
| IOC: | early 1970s |

## SS-N-17

A single Yankee-class SSBN has been fitted with the SS-N-17 missile. This missile was the first Soviet solid-propellant SLBM and the first to employ a Post Boost Vehicle (PBV) or "bus" to aim the single reentry vehicle. It has greater accuracy than previous Soviet SLBMs, but has not been deployed beyond replacing the SS-N-6 in a single submarine. Flight testing began in 1975.

| | |
|---|---|
| Weight: | |
| Length: | approx. 35 ft (10.6 m) |
| Span: | (ballistic) |
| Propulsion: | solid-fuel rocket |
| Range: | 2,000 + n.miles (3,700 + km) |
| Guidance: | inertial |
| Warhead: | nuclear (approx. 1 MT; 1 RV) |
| Platforms: | *submarines*    Yankee II |
| IOC: | approx. 1977 |

## SS-N-18

One variant of the SS-N-18 is the first Soviet SLBM to have a MIRV warhead (initially two reentry vehicles). This is a two-stage weapon. Flight testing began in 1975. The Soviet designation for this missile is

RSM-50. The Circular Error of Probability (CEP) has been estimated in the Western press as 0.76 n.miles for the MIRV version.

Weight:        approx. 44,500 lbs (20,250 kg)
Length:        approx. 45 ft (13.6 m)
Span:          (ballistic)
Propulsion:    liquid-fuel rocket
Range:         Mod 1 3,530 n.miles (6,500 km)
               Mod 2 4,350 n.miles (8,000 km)
               Mod 3 3,530 n.miles (6,500 km)
Guidance:      inertial
Warhead:       nuclear (approx. 750 KT for single warhead, approx. 500 KT for each multi-
               ple warhead; Mod 1 3 MIRV; Mod 2 1 RV; Mod 3 7 MIRV)
Platforms:     *submarines*  Delta III
IOC:           1978

## SS-N-19

This is an improved long-range, anti-ship cruise missile that evolved from the SS-N-3/12 designs. The high speed of the SS-N-19 (Mach 1+) alleviates the need for mid-course guidance because of the limited distance that the target ship could travel during the missile's time of flight. It is carried in the large KIROV-class nuclear cruisers and submerged-launched from the large Oscar-class SSGNs.

Weight:
Length:
Span:
Propulsion:    turbojet
Range:         240+ n.miles (445+ km)
Guidance:      inertial with terminal radar homing
Warhead:       conventional or nuclear
Platforms:     *cruisers*    KIROV
               *submarines*  Oscar
IOC:           1971

## SS-N-20

The largest Soviet SLBM yet produced, the three-stage SS-N-20 was developed for launch from the Typhoon-class SSBN, the largest submarine yet constructed by any nation. It is presumed to have a greater payload and more accuracy than any previous SLBM and is the first solid-propellant SLBM to be produced in quantity. The missile was reported to have experienced significant development problems, but there have been Western press stories citing a successful series of tests in December 1981.

Weight:
Length:
Span:          (ballistic)
Propulsion:    solid-fuel rocket
Range:         4,500 n.miles (8,300 km)
Guidance:      inertial
Warhead:       nuclear (6–9 MIRV); approx. 100 kiloton per RV
Platforms:     *submarines*  Typhoon
IOC:           1982–1983

## SS-N-21

Development has been reported of an anti-ship cruise missile launched from standard submarine torpedo tubes in a manner similar to the U.S. Harpoon and Tomahawk weapons. However, the Soviet weapon may also be suitable for launching from surface ship torpedo tubes. The weapon is expected to enter service in the mid-1980s. Range is estimated at approximately 1,620 n.miles (3,000 km)

## SS-N-22

Reported to be an improved and much higher speed version of the SS-N-9 anti-ship cruise missile, the SS-N-22 is carried in the triple launch tubes of the SOVREMENNYY-class destroyers.

Weight:
Length:
Span:
Propulsion:    solid-fuel rocket
Range:         approx. 60 n.miles (111 km)
Guidance:      mid-course guidance with terminal radar homing
Warhead:       conventional or nuclear
Platforms:     *destroyers*  SOVREMENNYY
IOC:           1981

## SURFACE-TO-UNDERWATER MISSILES

## SUW-N-1

This is a short-range ASW missile system found on the two Soviet carrier classes built to date, apparently in place of the SS-N-14 found in other modern Soviet warships. However, this is a ballistic weapon with a shorter range, and carries only a nuclear warhead. The projectile itself is designated FRAS-1, for Free Rocket Anti-Submarine. The SUW-N-1 is a twin-arm launcher similar in design to the SA-N-1/3 launchers. The rocket was developed from the FROG-7 artillery rocket (Free Rocket Over Ground) and is unguided after being launched on a ballistic trajectory.

Weight:
Length:
Span:          (ballistic)
Propulsion:    solid-fuel rocket
Range:         16 n.miles (29.6 km)
Guidance:      unguided (inertial)
Warhead:       nuclear
Platforms:     *carriers*  KIEV, MOSKVA
IOC:           1967

FRAS-1 missile on SUW-N-1 launcher on the helicopter carrier MOSKVA

## NUCLEAR WEAPONS

The Soviet Navy has a large number and variety of nuclear weapons available. Such weapons have been in the Soviet Fleet since the 1950s when nuclear torpedoes were deployed. According to some sources, these were intended for "strategic" attacks against Western coastal cities.

Subsequently, the Soviets deployed nuclear weapons at sea and in naval aircraft for the anti-air, anti-submarine, anti-surface, and land-attack roles. The reported detection of nuclear torpedoes in the Whiskey-class submarine that ran aground in Swedish waters in October 1981 tends to indicate the proliferation of these weapons in the fleet. The Whiskey was at least 25 years old, operating in waters close to the Soviet Union, in a noncrisis period, and on an intelligence-collection mission against a neutral nation.

Naval weapon systems indicated in the press to have a nuclear capability are listed in table 25-1. (Current U.S. naval systems are indicated for comparative purposes.)

### TABLE 25-1. NUCLEAR WEAPONS

| Launch Platform | Weapon | Role | U.S. Naval System |
|---|---|---|---|
| Surface Ships | SA-N-1 (?) | anti-aircraft | Terrier BTN* |
| | SA-N-3 | anti-aircraft/anti-ship | Standard-ER/SM-2 (in development) |
| | SS-N-3† | anti-ship | |
| | SS-N-9† | anti-ship | |
| | SS-N-12† | anti-ship | |
| | SS-N-19† | anti-ship | |
| | SS-N-21 (?) | anti-ship | |
| | SS-N-22† | anti-ship | T-LAM‡ (in development) |
| | 152-mm gun | anti-ship | |
| | torpedoes (?) | anti-ship/ASW | |
| | SUW-N-1/FRAS-1 | anti-submarine | ASROC |
| Attack Submarines | torpedoes | anti-ship/ASW | |
| | SS-N-15 | anti-submarine | SUBROC |
| Strategic Submarines | SS-N-4 | land attack | |
| | SS-N-5 | land attack | |
| | SS-N-6 | land attack | |
| | SS-N-8 | land attack | Poseidon C-3 Trident D-4 |
| | SS-N-17 | land attack | |
| | SS-N-18 | land attack | |
| | SS-N-20 | land attack | |
| Aircraft | bombs | anti-ship/land-attack | B-57 B-61 |
| | depth bomb | ASW | B-57 |
| | AS-2 | anti-ship | |
| | AS-4 | anti-ship | |
| | AS-5 | anti-ship | |
| | AS-6 | anti-ship | |
| Coastal Defense | SS-C-1 (?) | anti-ship | |

*BTN = Beam-riding, Terrier, Nuclear.
†Also carried by attack submarines.
‡T-LAM = Tomahawk Land-Attack Missile.

## TORPEDOES

The Soviet Navy employs primarily torpedoes of 533-mm (21-inch) and 406-mm (16-inch diameter). In addition, there have been reports of a significantly larger torpedo entering service in the early 1980s, possibly some 600 mm (24 inches) or larger in diameter.[4]

### 533-mm torpedoes

These torpedoes are launched from trainable tubes in surface warships and fixed tubes in submarines for use against surface and submarine targets. Propulsion is provided by steam or electric motors (batteries) with speeds from 28 up to approximately 45 knots and effective ranges from two miles (3.2 km) up to possibly ten miles (16 km). Guidance is both preset (straight- or pattern-running) and acoustic homing.

Warheads are both high explosive and nuclear, with torpedoes having been the first Soviet naval weapon with a nuclear capability. The Soviet

[4] In this century the only torpedoes with a larger diameter than 21 inches (533 mm) were the German Type H-8 (23.6 in/600 mm) and British Mk I (24.5 in/622 mm) of World War I, and the famed Japanese Type-93 "Long Lance" (24 in/610 mm) of World War II.

A 533-mm (21-inch) torpedo is eased through the forward loading hatch of a Foxtrot-class submarine.

Three 533-mm (21-inch) torpedoes partially exposed in the starboard quadruple torpedo bank of a Krivak I-class frigate. Frigates and larger Soviet warships retain "long" torpedo tubes while all U.S. and most large NATO surface ships have only "short" tubes for Mk-44 and Mk-46 324-mm (12.75-inch) torpedoes.

53 VA torpedo, which has been exported to Warsaw Pact and Third World nations for use with Soviet-built small combatants, has a high-explosive warhead of 1,250 lbs (562.5 kg) with an electromagnetic exploder.

### 406-mm torpedoes

These are anti-submarine weapons, launched from small ASW ships and craft, and from stern submarine tubes. They are also dropped from ASW fixed-wing aircraft and helicopters with a parachute fitted to slow water entry. These torpedoes apparently have electric (battery) propulsion, acoustic homing guidance, and high-explosive warheads.

# 26

# Naval Electronics

## ELECTRONIC WARFARE

Soviet combat aircraft, surface ships, and submarines have electronic warfare equipment to (1) detect threats, (2) collect Electronic Intelligence (ELINT), (3) identify friendly forces (IFF), and (4) counter threats (ECM). Few details of these systems are available for publication.

Soviet EW systems are assigned NATO code names that generally reflect their antenna appearance and not their function.

The following are the identified EW systems fitted in Soviet surface ships and submarines. In addition, surface ships (as well as some aircraft) have chaff and decoy launchers, and surface ships and submarines have some other IFF sets.

| | | |
|---|---|---|
| Bell Bash | Bell Tap | Rum Tub |
| Bell Clout | Bell Thump | Side Globe |
| Bell Shroud | Cage Pot | Square Head (IFF) |
| Bell Slam | Dead Duck (IFF) | Top Hat |
| Bell Squat | High Pole-A/B (IFF) | Watch Dog |

Modern Soviet warships, as the destroyer UDALOY shown here, carry a forest of electronic antennas. When this photo was taken in the Barents Sea, the ball-and-diamond shapes flying from the UDALOY's starboard yardarm indicated that she was towing her variable-depth sonar.

## RADARS

Soviet naval radars are identified by NATO code names, which are generally derived from antenna appearance. The names do not indicate type or purpose of radar.[1]

Several specialized space and missile-tracking radars are in use by Soviet SESS, with the Ship Globe being the best known. Also, some naval auxiliaries and civilian auxiliaries that support naval activities have commercial radars of the Neptune and Okean series.

The radars listed below are categorized by platform—aircraft and ships (including submarines), with the latter subdivided into purpose—gun control, missile control, and search.

### AIRCRAFT RADARS

#### Bee Hind

Tail warning radar generally fitted in bomber aircraft. I-band.

Aircraft:     Badger
              Bear
              Blinder

#### Big Bulge

Surface search and targeting radar; used with Video Data Link (VDL). The -A mod is used in the Bear-D aircraft and the -B mod in the Hormone-B helicopter. I/J-band.

Aircraft:     Bear-D
              Hormone-B

#### Down Beat

Surface search and targeting radar for AS-4 missile. J-band.

Aircraft:     Backfire-B
              Blinder

#### Fan Tail

Gunfire control radar for remote-controlled tail turret.

Aircraft:     Backfire-B

#### High Fix

Range-only air intercept radar in fighter-type aircraft. Range approx. 5 miles (8 km). I-band.

Aircraft:     Fitter-C/D

#### Puff Ball

Surface search and targeting radar for AS-2 missile. I-band.

Aircraft:     Badger-C/D/G

#### Short Horn

Surface search and targeting radar for AS-5 and AS-6 missiles. J-band.

Aircraft:     Blinder

---

[1]A limited open-source description of Soviet radars is found in Norman Friedman, *Naval Radar* (Annapolis, Md.: Naval Institute Press, 1981). A fascinating discussion of the initial, pre–World War II radar development in the USSR is in John Erickson, "Radio-location and the Air Defense Problem: The Design and Development of Soviet Radar 1934–1940," *Science Studies*, no. 2, 1972, pp. 241–68.

#### Wet Eye

Surface search radar; may have sufficient target definition for locating submarine periscopes and snorkel masts. J-band.

Aircraft:     Bear-F

### GUNFIRE CONTROL RADARS

#### Bass Tilt

Primarily the fire control radar for 30-mm Gatling gun; similar to Drum Tilt and Muff Cobb radars. In the Nanuchka III, Tarantul, and Pauk corvettes, the Bass Tilt is also used to control the 76-mm guns, and in the Grisha III the 57-mm guns. Fitted in various warships, amphibious ships, and auxiliary ships.

The destroyer SOVREMENNYY showing Top Steer (top), Palm Frond (on mast extensions), Front Dome (atop bridge), and Bass Tilt (lower) radars. An HF/DF loop is mounted forward of the Front Dome radars.

## Bow series

Target designation radars found on older surface combatants. Half Bow is associated with torpedoes; Top Bow is used for 152-mm gun control. I-band.

Platforms:    *cruisers*    SVERDLOV
              *destroyers*    Kildin, SKORYY

## Drum Tilt

Acquisition and tracking radar for twin 25-mm and 30-mm AA guns. First of the drum-shaped weapon-control radars. Can track only one target at a time. Introduced in 1961. H/I bands. The Soviet designation is *Rys.*

Platforms:    *cruisers*    SVERDLOV
              *destroyers*    Kanin, Kotlin
              *frigates*    Koni
              *various small combatants*
              *amphibious*    Aist (ACV), Polnocny

## Egg Cup

Modified Skin Head radar used for gunfire spotting for 130-mm and 152-mm guns. Provides range-only data. E-band.

Platforms:    *cruisers*    SVERDLOV
              *destroyers*    Kotlin, SAM Kotlin, SKORYY

## Hawk Screech

Widely used fire control director for 45-mm, 57-mm, 76-mm, and 100-mm AA guns. Circular dish antenna with feedhorn supported by four legs and large housing for transmitter and receiver abaft antenna. Introduced in 1954. Similar to Owl Screech; operates in I-band.

Platforms:    *destroyers*    Kanin, Kildin, Kotlin, SAM Kotlin
              *frigates*    Koni, Mirka, Petya
              *auxiliaries*    Don, Lama

## Kite Screech

Fire control radar for 100-mm and new 130-mm guns. First seen in 1976–1977 on Krivak II class.

Platforms:    *cruisers*    Krasina
              *destroyers*    SOVREMENNYY, UDALOY
              *frigates*    Krivak II

Top Bow radar immediately above the Long Ears GFC director on a SVERDLOV-class light cruiser

## Muff Cobb

Fire control radar for 57-mm AA guns; similar to Drum Tilt but improved stabilization. First seen in 1962. H-band.

Platforms:    *carriers*    MOSKVA
              *cruisers*    Kresta I, II
              *frigates*    Grisha
              *corvettes*    Nanuchka
              *small combatants*
              *auxiliaries*    BEREZINA, Lama, Manych, Ugra

## Owl Screech

An improved version of Hawk Screech used for 76-mm AA guns. Operational from about 1961. I-band.

Platforms:    *carriers*    KIEV
              *cruisers*    Kara, Kynda
              *destroyers*    Kashin, Kildin
              *frigates*    Krivak I
              *amphibious*    IVAN ROGOV
              *auxiliaries*    IVAN SUSANIN

## Post Lamp

Torpedo fire-control radar. I-band.

Platforms:    *destroyers*    SKORYY

## Pot Drum

Torpedo search and fire-control radar in Shershen torpedo boats. Identical to Square Tie radar in Osa missile boats (see below), except that antenna is in a plastic dome. The Soviet designation is *Baklan.*

Drum Tilt radar on East German Koni-class frigate

## Sun Visor

Gunfire control radar with solid parabolic antenna. Fitted to Round Top and Wasp Head fire control directors in older ships (completed from 1953 onward) for use with 130-mm and 100-mm guns. Sun Visor is I-band with Round Top and Wasp Head fitted with H-band radar.

| Platforms: | *cruisers* | SVERDLOV |
| | *destroyers* | Kanin, Kotlin, SAM Kotlin |
| | *frigates* | Riga |
| | *auxiliaries* | Don |

## Top Bow

Fire control radar associated with 152-mm guns.

| Platforms: | *cruisers* | SVERDLOV |

Kite Screech radar on UDALOY-class destroyer

Egg Cup-B radars on 100-mm gun mounts on SVERDLOV-class cruiser

Hawk Screech radar on East German Koni-class frigate

Muff Cob radar on Ropucha-class landing ship

Pot Drum radome, Square Head IFF interrogator antenna, and Drum Tilt radar on East German Shershen-class torpedo boat

## MISSILE FIRE-CONTROL RADARS

### Band Stand

Missile tracking and control radar for SS-N-9 anti-ship missile mounted in large radome.

Platforms:    *destroyers*    SOVREMENNYY
              *corvettes*    Nanuchka, Sarancha, Tarantul II
              *small combatants*  Sarancha

### Cheese Cake

Missile targeting radar for SS-N-2c Styx missiles. Installed from late 1970s.

Platforms:    *small combatants*  Matka

### Eye Bowl

Fire control radar for the SS-N-14 ASW missile in ships without larger Head Lights radar. F-band.

Platforms:    *cruisers*    KIROV, Krasina
              *destroyers*    UDALOY
              *frigates*    Krivak

Sun Visor-B radar mounted on Wasp Head GFC director with Head Net-C radar on mast of SAM Kotlin-class destroyer

Band Stand radome on Nanuchka I-class missile corvette

## Fan Song-E

Fire control radar for SA-N-2 missile. There are three parabolic dish antennas coupled with vertical and horizontal Lewis-type scanners; one dish is for missile command-guidance and two for tracking the missile. G-band.

Platforms:   *cruisers*   DZERSHINSKIY

## Front series

The Front Door and Front Piece are submarine sail-mounted radars for mid-course guidance of the SS-N-3 Shaddock and SS-N-12 anti-ship missiles. The forward edge of the sail structure swings open for radar operation. A version of this radar is also mounted at the bow on the KIEV-class carriers; see Trap Door.

Platforms:   *submarines*   Echo II, Juliett

## Front Dome

Multiple radomes for target illumination and missile tracking of SA-N-7 system. Resembles Bass Tilt gun control radar.

Platforms:   *destroyers*   Kashin (1 unit), SOVREMENNYY

Head Net-C radar on mast and two Eye Bowl radars stepped above bridge of Krivak I-class frigate

## Head Lights series

This radar is associated with the SA-N-3 anti-aircraft missile system and in cruisers may additionally provide guidance for the SS-N-14 ASW missile. The antenna consists of two large (almost four-meter diameter) dishes, somewhat resembling headlights, with two smaller dishes above. The main dishes are balanced by vanes at their rear. The entire array can elevate and rotate 360°. Head Light-A is mounted in the carriers and the -B model in cruisers. Operates in D/F/G/H-bands.

Platforms:   *carriers*   KIEV, MOSKVA
             *cruisers*   Kara, Kresta II

## Peel Group

Missile control radar for SA-N-1 missile system. This is an awkward-looking grouping consisting of four antennas with elliptical and solid reflectors; two large and two small antennas are mounted in the horizontal and vertical positions to provide tracking (I-band) and missile guidance (E-band), respectively. Range is approximately 30–40 n.miles (55–74 km).

Platforms:   *cruisers*   Kresta I, Kynda
             *destroyers*   Kashin, SAM Kotlin

## Pop Group

Fire control radar for SA-N-4 low-altitude missile system. F/H/I-bands.

Platforms:   *carriers*          KIEV
             *cruisers*          Kara, KIROV, Krasina
             *frigates*          Grisha, Koni, Krivak
             *corvettes*         Nanuchka
             *small combatants*  Sarancha
             *amphibious*        IVAN ROGOV
             *auxiliaries*       BEREZINA

## Scoop Pair

Fire control radar for mid-course guidance of the SS-N-3 (Shaddock) surface-to-surface missile. The "pair" consists of top-and-bottom antennas, each with a double feedhorn. I-band.

Platforms:   *cruisers*   Kresta I, Kynda

## Square Tie

Search radar and target designation radar in small combatants for SS-N-2 Styx missile. Range to detect a destroyer is up to 25 n.miles (40 km) and a small combatant up to 10 n.miles (16 km).

Platforms:   *small combatants*   Osa

## Top Dome

Missile guidance radar for SA-N-6 consisting of 4-meter hemispheric radome, fixed in elevation and mechanically steered in azimuth. It is installed with a series of smaller radomes for tracking multiple targets.

Platforms:   *cruisers*   KIROV, Krasina

## Trap Door

Retractable-antenna radar for mid-course guidance of the SS-N-12 anti-ship missile. The Front-series radars in submarines are similar.

Platforms:   *carriers*   KIEV

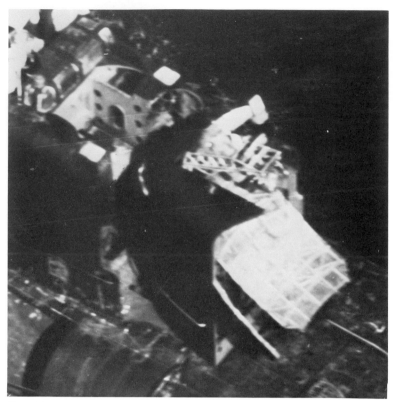

Front Door/Front Piece radars exposed on front of sail structure of Echo II-class cruise missile submarine

Peel Group radar on SAM Kotlin destroyer

Two of the eight Front Dome directors for the SA-N-7 missile system on the modified Kashin-class destroyer PROVORNYY are visible forward of the bridge (above RBU-6000 launchers). (*Bibliothek fur Zeitgeschichfe*)

Pop Group radar on East German Koni-class frigate

Peel Group radar on SAM Kotlin destroyer

Top Dome radar (right), Top Steer radar, and Vee Tube communications antennas on cruiser KIROV

Square Tie antenna on radio-controlled target craft

Trap Door radar in retracted position on bow of aircraft carrier MINSK (U.S. Navy)

## SEARCH AND NAVIGATION RADARS

### Ball End

Navigation radar found in several ship types. I-band.

### Band Stand

Search and missile launch radar for SS-N-9 missile.

Platforms:    *corvettes*    Nanuchka

### Big Net

This is a long-range, air-surveillance radar, generally found in larger ships with the SA-N-1 missile and the one cruiser fitted with the SA-N-2. The antenna has an elliptical parabolic form with a thin outline. There is a large, curved feedhorn and twin balancing vanes. Range is over 100 n.miles (184 km). The Big Net antenna is mounted back-to-back with the Top Sail to form Top Pair. C-band. First mounted on the SIBIR′-class missile range ships in 1960.

Platforms:    *cruisers*       DZERSHINSKIY, KRESTA I, SVERDLOV
              *destroyers*    Kashin
              *radar pickets*  T-43, T-58
              *auxiliaries*    SIBIR′

### Boat Sail

Long-range search radar fitted in Whiskey-class submarines modified to radar pickets (NATO code name Canvas Bag, derived from the covering sometimes seen on the folded Boat Sail radar). E/F-band.

### Cross Bird

Long-range air-search radar adopted from British World War II-era radar designated Type 291. Fitted in early postwar Soviet warships. Antenna consists of X-shaped structure supporting dipoles. The Soviet designation is GUIS-2. P-band.

Platforms:    *destroyers*    SKORYY

Head Net-A (left) and Big Net radars on Kashin-class destroyer

### Don series

These are primarily navigation radars, but probably have a target-designation function as well. They are installed in a variety of ship types. They are horizontally polarized I-band radars. Series includes Don and Don-2 (9250–9500 MHz) and Don Kay (9350–9500 MHz). The Palm Frond radar is being installed in their place in newer Soviet ships.

### Flat Spin

Air-surveillance radar for smaller surface warships. Similar to Head Net-A.

Platforms:    *destroyers*    Kotlin
              *frigates*      Riga

### Hair Net

Medium-range search radar; being phased out. Previously fitted in older cruisers and Kotlin and Tallinn destroyers. E-band.

Platforms:    *frigates*    Riga

### Head Net-A

Air-search radar with two identical sets mounted in some ships. Fitted with large balancing vanes. C-band.

Platforms:    *cruisers*      Kynda
              *destroyers*    Kashin

### Head Net-B

Back-to-back installation of two Head Net-A antennas with one angled 15° in elevation to provide both high and low coverage.

Platforms:    *auxiliaries*    DESNA-class missile range ships

### Head Net-C

Back-to-back installation of two Head Net-A antennas with one angled 30° in elevation for simultaneous use as air-search and height-finding radar. First observed in 1963, Head Net-C is widely used on missile-armed ships, in company with Top Sail on larger units. Range is approximately 60–70 n.miles (110–129 km).

Platforms:    *carriers*      MOSKVA
              *cruisers*      Kara, Kresta I, II
              *destroyers*    Kashin, Kanin, Krupnyy, SAM Kotlin
              *frigates*      Krivak
              *amphibious*    IVAN ROGOV

### High Lune

This is a "nodding" height-finding radar associated with SA-N-2 missile system; used in conjunction with Fan Song-E missile control radar on the cruiser DZERSHINSKIY. Removed in 1976.

### High Sieve

Air- and surface-search radar.

Platforms:    *cruisers*      SVERDLOV
              *destroyers*    SKORYY

## Knife Rest-A/B

Early-warning radar also mounted on ground vehicles (Soviet designations are P-8 and P-10). Range of the land version is estimated at 190 n.miles (350 km). Originally mounted in SVERDLOV-class cruisers and destroyers, but removed in late 1950s and early 1960s. A-band.

Platforms:    *radar pickets*   T-43

## Low Sieve

Surface-search radar found on some cruisers. Being phased out.

Platforms:    *cruisers*   SVERDLOV

## Neptune

Navigation radar found in older ships. I-band.

Platforms:    *cruisers*     SVERDLOV
              *destroyers*   Kotlin

## Okean

Search and navigation radar on auxiliary ships.

## Palm Frond

Small search-navigation radar mounted in a variety of ship types; replacing the Don-series radars. I-band.

## Peel Pair

Small surface-search and navigation radar.

Platforms:    *corvettes*   Nanuchka

## Plinth Net

Medium-range search radar, possibly associated with the SS-N-3 Shaddock missile system.

Platforms:    *cruisers*   Kresta I, Kynda

## Pot Head

Surface-search radar for small combatants housed in drum-shaped radome with a diameter of about 1.5 meters. I-band.

## Punch Bowl

Mast-mounted submarine radome.

## Sea Gull

Surface search evolved from Cross Bird (i.e., British Type 291). Found on a few older ships. Soviet designation GUIS-2M. Consists of a curved mesh reflector fed by a pair of attached Yagi structures.

## Sheet Bend

Small navigation radar found on coastal and river craft.

## Ship Globe

Large tracking radar for use with long-range missile tests and satellites. The parabolic reflector is about 16 meters in diameter. In use since 1964-1965 on missile tracking and Space Event Support Ships (SESS).

## Slim Net

High-definition (i.e., narrow-beam), air- and surface-search radar. Open lattice antenna with multi-leg feedhorn and two, large balancing vanes. In service from 1957. E/F-band.

Platforms:    *destroyers*    Kildin, Kotlin
              *frigates*      Petya, Riga
              *auxiliaries*   Don, Lama

## Spin Trough

Search and navigation radar installed as alternative to Don-series radars in surface ships and small craft. I-band.

## Snoop series

These are mast-mounted, surface-search radars found in various nuclear and conventionally powered submarines; types are: Snoop Plate, Snoop Slab, and Snoop Tray.

Krivak-class frigates are typical of modern, antenna-laden Soviet warships.

## Spoon Rest

An early-warning radar, apparently developed as a successor to Knife Rest. The naval version is adopted from the land-based P-12 (Soviet designation), which is generally used with the SA-2 missile. The Spoon Rest antenna consists of six vertical pairs of yagi arrays with a peak power of 350 kw. Range is credited at about 150 n.miles (276 km).

Platforms:   *cruisers* SVERDLOV

## Strut Curve

Small air- and surface-search radar fitted in smaller warships and auxiliaries. F-band.

Platforms:   *frigates*   Koni, Mirka, Petya
*corvettes*   Grisha, Poti
*amphibious*   Ropucha
*various small combatants*
*auxiliaries*   IVAN SUSANIN, Lama, Ugra

## Strut Pair

Air-search radar with antenna formed by two Strut Curve antennas mounted back-to-back.

Platforms:   *destroyers*   Kashin (1 unit), Kildin (1 unit), UDALOY

Pot Head radome on S.O.-1 patrol craft; Pot Drum is similar, but slightly larger and more streamlined.

Slim Net radar on Petya I-class frigate. Note the balancing vanes in this rear view.

## Top Knot

Spherical aircraft navigation/control radar.

Platforms:   *carriers* KIEV

## Top Pair

See Top Sail listing for details.

Platforms:   *cruisers* KIROV

## Top Sail

Large, 3-dimensional air-search and early-warning radar fitted in aircraft carriers and larger cruisers. The antenna consists of a large lattice scanner that has a cylindrical cross section with the axis tilted back about 20° from the vertical. The reflector is illuminated by a linear radiating element located parallel to the cylindrical axis. It uses frequency scan in elevation. Two large balancing vanes are fitted. The Top Sail is used in conjunction with the Head Net-C search radar and Head Light missile fire-control radar. Top Sail is mounted back-to-back with Big Net to form the Top Pair radar. C-band.

Platforms:   *carriers*   KIEV, MOSKVA
*cruisers*   Kara, Kresta II, Krasina

## Top Steer

Medium-size, 3-dimension air-search radar, somewhat similar in appearance to the larger Top Sail. Fitted back-to-back with the Strut Pair radar antenna with common feed. The Top Steer uses frequency scan in elevation. F-band.

Platforms:   *carriers*     KIEV
*cruisers*     Krasina
*destroyers*   Kashin (1 unit), SOVREMENNYY

## Top Trough

This surveillance radar has a bar-like antenna with a slotted waveguide that feeds a curved reflector. In service since 1960, it is located on the second mast of most SVERDLOV-class cruisers. Top Trough is used for target discrimination for the ships' 100-mm and 152-mm guns. The radar was installed in the 1970s. C-band.

Platforms:   *cruisers*     SVERDLOV
*destroyers*   SKORYY

Spoon Rest radar with Long Ears GFC director in SVERDLOV-class cruiser ALEKSANDR SUVOROV (U.S. Navy)

Strut Curve radar on Ropucha-class landing ship

Strut Pair radar on UDALOY-class destroyer VITSE ADMIRAL KULAKOV

Strut Curve radar on East German Koni-class frigate

Top Trough radar on second mast of SVERDLOV-class cruiser (U.S. Navy)

Top Sail-B radar (left) and Head Lights (right) on Kresta II-class cruiser

Rear of new air-search radar on Pauk-class corvettes

Head Lights radar on Kara-class cruiser

## SONARS

The Soviet Navy began major efforts in the early 1960s to put high-performance sonars to sea. The initial postwar surface ships mostly had the Tamir-5 series of high-frequency, hull-mounted sonars. They were succeeded by the Pegasus-2 series from the mid-1950s, and the Herkules series from the late 1950s. The contemporary submarines were fitted with the Tamir-5L sonar.

Subsequently, a variety of improved sonars were developed for the Soviet warships that began joining the fleet in the 1960s.

The following types of sonars are installed in contemporary Soviet ships, several classes having multiple sonars. In particular, there has been a recent effort to reduce frequencies, and during the past two decades they have been reduced from the 20–30 KHz range to about 2–15 KHz. In addition, Variable Depth Sonars (VDS), dipping sonars (from helicopters and surface ships), and directional systems have been introduced. The Soviets do not appear to be using narrow-band processors, towed arrays, or long-range moored systems beyond coastal waters on an operational basis. (There are some moored systems in coastal and regional seas.)

Details of their official NATO or Soviet designations are not available, nor is information on their performance.

### High-frequency/Hull-mounted (Tamir series)

Platforms:    *small combatants*  S.O.-1

### High-frequency/Hull-mounted (Herkules or Pegas)

Platforms:    *destroyers*  Kildin, Kotlin, SKORYY
              *frigates*    Mirka, Petya, Riga

ASW destroyer UDALOY trailing variable-depth sonar during exercises in the Barents Sea in 1982

### Medium-frequency/Hull- or bow-mounted

Platforms:  *cruisers*     Kresta II
            *destroyers*   Kanin
            *frigates*     Krivak
            *corvettes*    Grisha

### Medium-frequency/VDS

Platforms:  *carriers*     KIEV, MOSKVA
            *cruisers*     Kara
            *destroyers*   Kashin
            *frigates*     Krivak

### Low-frequency/Hull- or bow-mounted

Platforms:  *carriers*     KIEV, MOSKVA
            *cruisers*     KIROV
            *destroyers*   UDALOY

### Low-frequency/VDS

Platforms:  *carriers*     KIEV
            *cruisers*     KIROV

### Helicopter dipping

Platforms:  *helicopters*       Haze, Helix, Hormone-A
            *frigates*          Mirka, Petya
            *small combatants*  Pchela, Poti, Stenka, Turya

The older Soviet submarines have active-passive Herkules and passive Fenks sonars; the newer undersea craft are fitted with low-frequency sonars.

Air-dropped, expendable sonobuoys are carried by Soviet ASW aircraft and helicopters.

Herkules and Feniks sonar installations in Foxtrot-class submarine

Variable-depth sonar deployed from modified Petya I-class frigate

Variable-depth sonar housing on UDALOY

# 27

# Bases and Ports

Break-bulk cargo ships at Il´ichevsk, near Odessa on the Black Sea. Il´ichevsk is a relatively new port, built during the past two decades. The nearby port of Yuzhnyy is now under development and eventually will have a cargo-handling capacity about as great as Il´ichevsk and Odessa combined, evidence of the continuing Soviet effort to increase maritime trade.

The Soviet Union's very long coastlines are dotted with military bases and commercial ports.[1]

During the past decade there has been a massive effort to enlarge the commercial port capacity and increase cargo-handling facilities. In an extensive containerization program, container ships have been constructed in large numbers (see chapter 29), ports have been built or refitted to handle cargo containers, and special rail services have been established. One of these is the Japan-Nakhodka-Trans-Siberian-Western route, reducing by half the transit time of the traditional sea route from Japan to Western Europe, which normally takes about 40 days. The first special trans-Siberian container train travelling east to west departed the Siberian port of Nakhodka in November 1973, with regular service beginning in 1975. About 120,000 standard containers per year now pass through the USSR on this route.

The Soviets joined an international convention to permit the transit of such containers free of import duties and taxes. Of course, the Soviets collect rail-freight tariffs and handling costs from the shippers who, in turn, save perhaps 20 days in transit time.

The Soviet port expansion also included facilities for more rapidly handling coal, ore, lumber, and petroleum products. Since the USSR has become a petroleum exporter (although most via pipeline to Eastern Europe), there are also provisions for the handling of large tankers.

[1]The major Soviet coastlines are:

| Region | length (n.miles) |
| --- | --- |
| Arctic | 8,166 |
| Baltic | 988 |
| Black Sea | 867 |
| Pacific | 6,075 |
| Total | 16,096 |

By comparison, U.S coastlines total 10,985 n.miles, of which 6,544 are in Alaska.

Naval base facilities have also been expanded, primarily to service the increasing number of nuclear-powered submarines and the larger surface warships of the Soviet fleet, especially the KIROV-class nuclear battle cruisers and the KIEV-class aircraft carriers. In order to dock the latter ships in the Northern Fleet (Arctic) and Pacific Fleet base areas, the Soviets have purchased large floating docks. A Swedish-built floating dock was provided for the naval base at Murmansk and a Japanese-built floating dock for the base at Vladivostok, both capable of accommodating a KIEV-class aircraft carrier.

The following are the major Soviet bases and ports, listed by geographic area.

## ARCTIC[2]

Arkhangel'sk is the oldest seaport of the country—a major port, provincial capital, and the largest city on the Soviet Arctic coast. Although it is blocked by ice for up to 190 days per year, the extensive use of icebreakers keeps the port open almost continuously. During the past few years the port's facilities—along 32 miles (51.5 km) of waterways—have been greatly enlarged, and container and fuel-handling facilities have been added. Arkhangel'sk, on the delta of the Dvina River as it enters the White Sea, can be reached by ship from Leningrad via the lake-canal route between Leningrad and the White Sea. The White Sea Canal (formerly the Stalin Canal), is iced over five or six months of the year, as is the White Sea itself. The canal is 140 miles (227 km) long and was built in

[2]See Robert E. Athay, "The Sea and Soviet Domestic Transportation," Naval Institute *Proceedings* (Naval Review), May 1972, pp. 158–77, and Gerald E. Synhorst, "Soviet Strategic Interest in the Maritime Arctic," Naval Institute *Proceedings* (Naval Review), May 1973, pp. 88–111.

Arctic coast of the USSR

The recent Soviet ship construction has led to a shortfall of base facilities in the Arctic and Pacific to support some of the new warships. As a result, a large floating dry dock was purchased from Sweden to support KIEV-class carriers at Murmansk in the Arctic and from Japan to support such ships at Vladivostok. This is the Japanese-built dock, 1,105 feet (335 m) long with an 80,000-ton capacity, under tow to Vladivostok in 1978.

just 20 months in the early 1930s as Stalin's first major slave-labor project.[3]

About 25 miles (40 km) west of Arkhangel'sk is the major shipyard complex of Severodvinsk, known as Molotovsk until 1957. A railway line ties the two cities together and links them with the main rail systems. Severodvinsk was founded in the late 1903s as Stalin sought to develop major naval support facilities in the Arctic. Today Severodvinsk rivals Arkhangel'sk in size. It has a small port, but its principal importance is as a shipbuilding and industrial center.

Northwest of Severodvinsk-Arkhangel'sk on the Kola Peninsula are the sprawling port of Murmansk and the satellite ports of Pechenga and Polyarnyy. About 155 miles (250 km) of the Kola coast east of the border with Norway, including Murmansk, are free of ice year around, kept open by the North Cape Gulf Stream, a continuation of the Gulf Stream.

Well-known in Western naval annals because of the "Murmansk run" for Allied merchant ships in World War II, Murmansk is some 125 miles (200 km) north of the Arctic Circle. (Arkhangel'sk was also a key port for the Murmansk run.) The port is the western terminus for the commercial Northern Sea Route. It has recently been modernized to handle freight containers. It is also a focal point of the fishing and fish-processing industries, has two building yards for commercial ships, and has intermediate and higher maritime schools. The town of Severomorsk (formerly Vayenga), about ten miles (16 km) northeast of Murmansk, is the headquarters of the Northern Fleet.

A 900-mile (1,450-km) rail line connects Murmansk with Leningrad, with goods being transshipped at Leningrad for the North Sea Route. From Murmansk ships also sail westward, to Europe and the Americas, especially during the winter months when the eastern Baltic is partially blocked by ice.

The port of Polyarnyy (formerly Aleksandrovsk), north of Murmansk on the Kola fjord, is a major base for Northern Fleet surface ships and submarines. Pechenga is northwest of Murmansk and only 18.5 miles (30 km) from the Norwegian border. Pechenga, formerly Finnish Pet-

[3]Several hundred thousand slave laborers died in constructing the canal. A graphic and terrifying description of their efforts and privations in building this inland waterway is given in Aleksandr I. Solzhenitsyn, *The Gulag Archipelago—Two* (New York: Harper & Row, 1975), pp. 86–100.

A container port at work. Although the Soviet merchant marine stresses break-bulk cargo ships, recent ship construction and hence Soviet port development have also stressed bulk cargoes and containers. One aspect of Soviet container efforts has been to develop Pacific and Baltic coast container ports served through rail links to capture part of the inter-ocean trade.

samo, is both a naval and fishing port. There are many other bases on the Kola Peninsula, which is estimated to have 40 military airfields as well as bases for two army motorized rifle divisions and the Northern Fleet's marine regiment. Other major naval bases supporting the Northern Fleet are Iokanga, Savdaguba, Litsaguba, and Olenyaguba.

There are a number of smaller but still significant ports along the Arctic coast. Several are transshipment points for the intensive river traffic that plies the long Siberian rivers. South of the Novaya Zemlya Islands in the Kara Sea are the ports of Khabarov and Amderma. These ports on the Yugorskiy Peninsula are used to ship coal from mines on the mainland, and have provided logistic support for the huge slave-labor camp established on Novaya Zemlya in the 1930s and later for the early Soviet missile test site on those islands.

Farther east are the ports of Dikson at the mouth of the Yenisey River, Komsomolskaya on Pravda Island off the northern coast of the Taymyr Peninsula, Nordvik on Khatanga Bay, Tiksi at the delta of the Lena River, Ambarchik near the mouth of the Kolyma River, Pevek at Chaunskaya Bay, and Uelen on the Bering Strait at the eastern tip of Siberia.

## BALTIC SEA[4]

Leningrad is the second largest city of the Soviet Union and the shipping and shipbuilding center of the Soviet Baltic coast with five major shipyards, several lesser yards, and a large commercial port. The city is at the eastern end of the Gulf of Finland, built on the delta of the Neva River, and is laced with rivers and canals. The city is also the Baltic entrance to the lake-canal route to the White Sea. The Gulf of Finland is iced over about half the year, but here, too, the use of modern icebreakers significantly extends the shipping season and provides continuous access for naval units.

The large commercial port is on the southern side of the city. Although there are a great number of naval shipyards and training activities in the city, the Baltic Fleet headquarters are not at Leningrad nor are many

[4]Rear Admiral Edward Wegener, FGN, "A Strategic Analysis of the Baltic Sea and the Danish Straits," *Naval Review 1969* (Annapolis, Md.: U.S. Naval Institute, 1969), pp. 2–23.

warships based there. There are always naval units there for trials, training, and overhaul.

Some 15 miles (24 km) west of Leningrad in the Gulf of Finland is Kotlin Island. In its old port city of Kronshtadt are a commercial port, a naval base, and ship repair yards. Oranienbaum, south of Kronshtadt on the mainland, is believed to be a base for light naval forces.

Farther west, at the southern entrance to the Gulf, is the port of Tallinn (formerly Reval), capital of the Estonian Soviet Socialist Republic (SSR). Estonia, Latvia, and Lithuania comprise the Baltic states. They were Russian before World War I, then independent from 1918–1920 until 1939, when at the outset of World War II, they were seized by Soviet troops and incorporated into the Soviet Union.

At Tallinn are naval and commercial ports that are ice-free most of the year, and numerous warships up to cruiser size are home-ported there. Nearby are air bases and army installations. A new port was to be started in 1982 on the Bay of Muuga near Tallinn. It will accommodate ships up to 100,000 deadweight tons and may become the largest commercial port on the Baltic Sea.

Almost directly south of Tallinn on the Gulf of Riga is the city of Riga, capital of the Latvian SSR and a major seaport. Riga's history as a port dates more than a thousand years, when it was a crossroads for trade

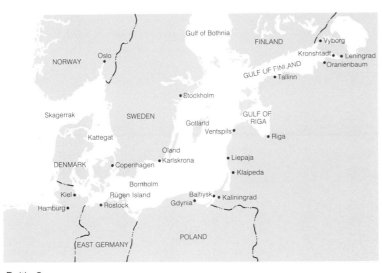

Baltic Sea

Leningrad is a center of naval and maritime activity. Sometimes called the Venice of Russia because of the numerous branches of the Neva River, there are naval and maritime activities scattered throughout the city. In this view from the Neva are the Naikhimov secondary naval training school and the cruiser Avrora, which has been preserved as a museum since 1948. (C.P. Lemieux)

between Scandinavian tribes and Greece. Actually situated on the Daugava River, Riga has several shipyards, and extensive container-handling facilities have been added. A Soviet naval base has been reported under development in the area.

West of Riga is the newer commercial port of Ventspils (formerly Windau), at the mouth of the Venta River. This port has several times the cargo-handling capacity of Riga, and a new oil export facility can accommodate supertankers of more than 100,000 deadweight tons. American firms have assisted in the construction of a large loading complex for ammonia and other chemicals at the port. While the Gulf of Riga is iced over 80 to 90 days per year, Ventspils is almost always ice-free.

The next significant Baltic port is Liepaja (formerly Libau) on a narrow sandspit between the Baltic and Lake Libau. There are protected naval and commercial harbors.

Klaipeda (formerly Memel) in the Lithuanian SSR at the mouth of the Memel River is the republic's capital city. It has long been a shipbuilding center and has commercial and naval harbors and a petroleum-loading port.

South of Klaipeda the cities of Baltiysk (formerly Pillau) and Kaliningrad (Königsberg) are of major importance to Soviet naval operations in the Baltic. Both are located in what formerly was East Prussia, which after being overrun by Soviet troops in World War II was incorporated into the Soviet Union after the war.

Kaliningrad is headquarters for the Baltic Fleet while Baltiysk is home port for most of the fleet's major warships. There is also a fishing port. And being near the Polish border, it also has a flotilla of KGB Maritime Border Troops. Kaliningrad, on the Pregolya River, is connected to Baltiysk by canal. It is a major commercial port and contains a large shipyard. A number of naval activities are located in the area, in part because these are the westernmost ports of the Soviet Union.

## BLACK SEA

The Black Sea is a major trading and shipbuilding region of the Soviet Union. The newest of the major ports is at the western end of the sea, near Vilkovo, at the northernmost mouth of the Danube River. Named Ust'-Dunaysk, it was developed in the late 1970s to handle ships of the international association Interlikhter (whose members are Bulgaria, Czechoslovakia, Hungary, and the USSR), especially SEABEE barge-carrying ships as the JULIUS FUCIK and TIBOR SZAMUELI (see chapter 29) and bulk cargo ships.

Odessa is the westernmost of the older Soviet ports on the Black Sea. It is probably the nation's largest, handling over 20 million tons of cargo annually, almost twice the amount handled by Leningrad. Unlike most Soviet ports, Odessa is not located on a river but on the Black Sea coast a few miles east of the mouth of the Dniester River. One of Russia's oldest cities, Odessa is also a major passenger/tourist terminal in an area of historical and cultural importance. Odessa's commercial port has more than five miles (eight km) of quays, with facilities for handling specialized cargoes such as grain and sugar. Because Odessa's port area is surrounded by the city proper and cannot be expanded, two large, new ports are being built nearby. In addition, Odessa city officials fear that dust and

Black Sea

air pollution from the ships and dry cargoes may discourage the tourist trade and damage historic structures. (The city was founded in the fourteenth century around a Tatar fortress.)

Twelve miles (19 km) southwest of Odessa is the new commercial port of Il'ichevsk, construction of which began in 1957. It also has specialized facilities for handling containers and grain, as well as iron ore and coal. Nearby Yuzhnyy is also being developed as a major port, the ammonia tanker BALDURY being the first ship to sail from there in August 1978. Pipelines running from a large mineral fertilizer plant in Odessa directly to the harbor permit the loading of ammonia into specialized tankers. Loading complexes for containers, lumber, coal, and ore are also being developed, with a goal of handling some 25 million tons of cargo per year. Eventually the Yuzhnyy port should be about as large as Odessa and Il'ichevsk combined (the latter port handling about 16 million tons of cargo in 1982).

These ports and others along this portion of the Black Sea coast are frozen for about three months of the year, but are kept open for ship traffic by icebreakers.

The largest shipbuilding and industrial center as well as the major port of the Black Sea is Nikolayev. Located at the junction of the Bug and Ingul rivers, the city has two major and several lesser shipyards and ship-repair facilities. The commercial port has more than two miles (3.2 km) of quays.

A short distance to the east is Kherson on the Dnepr River, about 20 miles (32 km) from where that long and important waterway enters the Black Sea. There are several industries and a major shipyard in the city in addition to the large commercial port.

Historic Sevastopol' on the Crimean Peninsula is headquarters for the Black Sea Fleet and the main base area for naval units that operate in the Black Sea and Mediterranean. Small craft and submarines are based in Sevastopol' and its southeastern suburb of Balaklava. Several small shipyards as well as extensive naval storage and other support facilities are located in and around Sevastopol'. Also in the Crimea is the smaller port of Feodosiya, used mainly by submarines and escorts. Most of the Black Sea Fleet's air bases are located in the Crimea.

Odessa currently handles more cargo than any other Soviet port, although this situation is rapidly changing with the development of new ports. It is also a passenger center for river and Black Sea traffic. The passenger ship RUSSIA (ROSSIYA) is shown here with two of the numerous passenger-carrying river hydrofoils in the foreground.

Northeast of the Crimea is the Sea of Azov, entered through the narrow Kerch′ Strait between the Kerch′ and Taman peninsulas. Most of the Sea of Azov is frozen from the end of November until mid-April. About 180 miles (290 km) northeast of the Kerch′ Strait and 30 miles (48 km) north of where the Don River enters the Sea of Azov is Rostov. Rostov is the meeting point for cargo from the Don and Volga rivers, the latter being connected by canal to the Don. Through these rivers and canals, there is a flow of goods and materials to and from Black Sea and Caspian Sea ports and to many inland ports of European Russia.

Zhdanov (formerly Mariupol) on the western coast of the Sea of Azov is the second major port of that sea after Rostov. It is an industrial city, being a major steel center. Also shipped through Zhdanov's commercial port are grain, coal, and petroleum.

Novorossiysk, on the Black Sea to the east of the Kerch′ Strait, is another major industrial city with a commercial port and a naval harbor for light forces. There are repair yards in the area, but no significant shipbuilding facility.

Lesser ports along the northern coast of the Black Sea include Kerch′ and Tuapse, which are naval and commercial ports (Kerch′ is the location of the Kamysh-Burun shipyard); Ochamchire, a commercial port and possibly a submarine facility; Poti, at the mouth of the Rioni River, with commercial and naval sections in its port, destroyers being based there; and Batumi, near the Turkish border and the starting point of the Trans-Caucasian Railway. Batumi is also the coastal terminal for the oil pipeline from Baku and handles both commercial and naval ships up to escort size.

## PACIFIC[5]

Vladivostok, "Ruler of the East," is the major Soviet port complex on the Pacific coast. Located at the southern end of the Muraiev Peninsula, Vladivostok is at the head of Golden Horn Bay, an arm of Peter the Great Bay. It was the original eastern port terminus of the Trans-Siberian Railway. The port city is only ten miles (16 km) from the Chinese border and less than 100 miles (160 km) from North Korea, making it extremely vulnerable.

The city houses the headquarters of the Pacific Fleet and is home port for much of the fleet's surface and submarine forces, including the aircraft carrier MINSK. Naval installations include logistic and training centers for the fleet, some located on adjacent Russian Island, which is connected to Vladivostok by several sea-floor tunnels. A submarine school is also reported on Russian Island. Other military bases in Peter the Great Bay include Novgoradsky, Possiet, Shkotovo, and Tynkin. Accordingly, Vladivostok is closed to most foreign ships. Westerners did obtain a limited look at the city in November 1974 when President Gerald Ford and Party Secretary Brezhnev held a summit meeting there with considerable press coverage.

There is a major fishing base and fish-processing complex at Vladivostok as well as shipyards and repair facilities. A new fishing port at Troitsa, on Peter the Great Bay near Vladivostok, was built in the late 1970s.

Sixty miles (96.5 km) east of Vladivostok lies Nakhodka on the Gulf of Amerika, formerly Wrangel Bay. This is the principal commercial port of Siberia. Named "the find" because of its excellent location, the port's development as a major shipping center began in 1960, and the Soviet Union's first mechanized container-handling facility opened there in late

1973. Within a few months it was in full operation, handling 1,000 freight containers per day as the Siberian transfer point on the trans-Soviet express container run. Nakhodka is also being developed as a major passenger and fishing port.

However, Nakhodka cannot handle the increasing flow of foreign and domestic trade. Thus, only nine miles (15 km) away, also on the Gulf of Amerika, Vostochnyy has been under development as a major port since 1970. The port was designed in conjunction with the new Siberian railway, the Baykal-Amur Mainline (BAM), which stretches from the Lena River to the Pacific coast.

Within a decade of the start of construction of Vostochnyy, some two million tons of cargo per year were being handled. Soviet officials plan for Vostochnyy to have an "eventual" capacity of handling 30 to 40 million tons of cargo annually over its planned 66 wharves, making it the largest port in the USSR. Called the "Japanese port" because of Japanese technical assistance and credit used in its development, Vostochnyy loads large amounts of Siberian timber being shipped to Japan. It is also being provided with container- and coal-handling facilities, the first container ship having sailed from Vostochnyy in May 1976.

(An automated ship-tracking system is being set up for the Gulf of Amerika, using radar to locate ships and a computer to keep track of the status of 200 vessels using the area's ports.)

Farther up the coast, on the Tatar Strait, is Sovetskaya Gavan', formerly Imperatorhafen, and the port of Nikolayevsk at the mouth of the Amur River, just below the Sea of Okhotsk. Sovetskaya Gavan' is a commercial port, handling mostly timber, and home of one of the three most important naval bases of the Pacific Fleet (the others being Vladivostok and Petropavlovsk). A submarine base and school are also reported to be located there, and it serves as well as a home port for warships up to destroyer size. Nikolayevsk is a fishing center.

To the north, Anadyr', at the mouth of the river of that name, is important as a coal port and for Arctic shipping. Major improvements were made at the commercial port in the late 1970s. Light naval forces are believed to be based there, also. Neither Anadyr', Magadan on the Sea of Okhotsk, nor Petropavlovsk on the Kamchatka Peninsula are connected to railway systems; rather, they are totally dependent upon sea and air transport. Magadan is a base for submarines and light forces.

Petropavlovsk is a domestic commercial shipping and fishing port, but adjacent Talinskaia Bay is the principal base for submarines of the Pacific Fleet, with two shipyards located there. "Petro" has direct access to the Pacific, the only major Pacific Fleet port with this advantage. However, the naval and civilian populations of the peninsula (there are 220,000 inhabitants in the city), as well as the troops stationed in the area, must be supplied entirely by sea and air.

The Kamchatka Peninsula and the Soviet-controlled Kuril Islands form a protective barrier for the Sea of Okhotsk. The Soviets have tried hard through both legal arguments and practice to make the Sea of Okhotsk an "inland sea," forbidden to foreign military and commercial shipping.[6]

[5]Also see P'an Hsi-t'ang, "Expansion of Soviet Naval Power in the Far East," *Issues & Studies* (A Journal of China Studies and International Affairs), October 1981, pp. 38–50.

[6]See Deam W. Given, "The Sea of Okhotsk—USSR's Great Lake?" Naval Institute *Proceedings*, September 1970, pp. 46–51. Mr. Given was on the staff of the U.S. Director of Naval Intelligence at the time.

Pacific coast of the USSR

The Pacific coast, like the Arctic coast and, to a lesser extent, the Baltic and Black Sea coasts, are plagued much of the time by ice. Here the tug MB-11 stands by to assist a Golf I-class missile submarine in the Sea of Okhotsk. The Soviets have largely overcome the problems of their environment, and naval and merchant ships have essentially free use of all major ports year-around.

On Sakhalin Island, held by Japan from 1905 to 1945, are the naval bases of Korsakov (formerly Otomari) and Aleksandrovsk.[7] Another port was developed at Kholmsk in the 1970s for handling cargo and supporting fish factory ships, and Vostochnyy at the northern end of Sakhalin is a commercial port that began container operations in 1976.

Most Siberian ports are iced over for up to half the year. At Vladivos-tok, the southernmost port, snow lies on the ground for more than three months of the year, and Peter the Great Bay is greatly hampered by ice during much of the winter. The entire Sea of Okhotsk is covered by thin ice from October to June, but again, the large fleet of Soviet coastal and ocean-going icebreakers keep the Far Eastern ports operating around the year.

The coastal area contains a large number of air and ground bases in support of the many troops deployed in Siberia to counter U.S., Japanese, and Chinese forces.

[7] The island was taken by Japan after the Russo-Japanese War of 1904–1905 and retaken by the USSR at the end of World War II.

The Soviet Navy stresses close ties between ships, units, and naval bases and the local communities. Here Communist youth groups participate in ceremonies aboard a Kynda-class cruiser. Note the photograph of Lenin in the center background; pictures of the leader of the Bolshevik Revolution and the current leader of the USSR are generally on display at all ceremonies. (Soviet Navy)

## INLAND

On the Amur River inland from the Pacific coast are the shipbuilding centers of Komsomol'sk and Khabarovsk. The latter is one of the largest cities in Siberia. Both have major military and commercial industries and are rail and river transportation crossroads. Their waterfronts are frozen over from November through June.

The Soviet Union has several major inland river and canal routes, some of which provide passage for small and some even medium-sized ships between the Arctic, Baltic, and Black Sea ports. In Siberia the Lena, Ob', and Yenisey rivers all are navigable for more than 2,000 miles (3,200 km), permitting river craft to carry raw materials north to the Arctic coast and return manufactured goods and other products from European Russia.

Major inland ports on these rivers include Narym, Tomsk, Turukhansk, Verkholensk, Yakutsk, and Yeniseysk.

In European Russia the Volga River runs some 2,300 miles (3,700 km), and most of it, from north of Moscow south to the Caspian Sea, is navigable. The Volga-Don Canal, completed in 1952, links the Volga to the Don River and the Sea of Azov and hence to the Black Sea. There are numerous ports along this route. Among the more significant ones are Gor'kiy, with its submarine and river craft building yards, Kazan', Volgograd (formerly Stalingrad and before that Tsaritsyn), and Astrakhan', near the Volga's entrance into the Caspian Sea.

On the inland Caspian Sea, Baku is the largest city and chief port. Smaller port facilities are found at Astrakhan', Gur'yev, and Krasnovodsk. These ports played a major role in the transshipment of U.S. lend-lease war material sent to the Soviet Union through Iran during World War II.

# 28

# Shipyards

The Soviet Union has a large, modern industry that has produced and maintained large numbers of advanced warships and commercial ships since World War II. In addition, Soviet yards have built many ships for other nations.[1]

There are 19 major shipyards in the USSR, measured on the basis of having 2,000 or more full-time employees.[2] Of these yards, 3 are believed to build only warships, 11 build both warships and commercial ships, and 4 only commercial ships. (See table 28-1)

There are several hundred lesser shipyards that build and repair both naval and commercial ships, including the large number of craft that operate on Soviet rivers, lakes, and inland seas. Collectively, these large and small yards aggregate the world's largest shipbuilding industry, ably supported by research institutes and design bureaus.

*History.* The first effort at shipbuilding by the Moscow (Muscovite) government came in 1570 when Tsar Ivan IV ordered vessels built on the Arctic coast. When Peter I became tsar in 1682, the port of Arkhangel'sk on the frigid northern coast was Russia's only outlet to sea. There barges and coastal craft were constructed for coastal and river trade. At Peter's direction, the first small but ocean-going ships were constructed there from 1693, the first being his 12-gun "yacht" named St. Peter.[3]

The next Russian shipbuilding effort, in support of Peter's quest to wrest the inland Sea of Azov from the Turks, was much more ambitious. Peter chose the town of Voronezh, at the junction of the Voronezh and Don Rivers, some 300 miles below Moscow and 300 miles north of the Sea of Azov, as the site for his shipyards. The local lords were commanded to send almost 28,000 laborers to work in the yards. Peter

[1]This chapter is based in part on "Technical Assessment of Current Soviet Shipbuilding Capabilities (U)," prepared by Mr. Joel Bloom of the Naval Intelligence Support Center (24 February 1975). The most detailed description in English of Soviet shipyard development appears in David R. Jones (ed.), *The Military-Naval Encyclopedia of Russia and the Soviet Union*, vol. 3 (Gulf Breeze, Fla.: Academic International Press), 1981, pp. 74–139, 158–241. Also see N. Polmar, "Soviet Shipbuilding and Shipyards," Naval Institute *Proceedings*, (Naval Review) May 1972, pp. 272–80.

[2]By these criteria the United States has 23 major shipyards—eight government-owned naval facilities and 15 private yards—and all other nations about 75.

[3]An interesting account of Peter's early days at Arkhangel'sk and his naval interests is found in Robert K. Massie, *Peter the Great* (New York: Alfred A. Knopf, 1981).

## TABLE 28-1. MAJOR SOVIET SHIPYARDS

| Yard | Location | Current Types of Construction |
|---|---|---|
| Severodvinsk (ex-Molotovsk) | Arctic | naval only (submarines) |
| Admiralty | Baltic | naval and commercial (including submarines)* |
| Baltic (ex-Ordzhonikidze) | Baltic | naval and commercial |
| Kaliningrad | Baltic | naval and commercial |
| Klaipeda | Baltic | commercial only |
| Petrovskiy | Baltic | naval only |
| Sudomekh | Baltic | naval only (submarines) |
| Vyborg | Baltic | commercial only |
| Zhdanov | Baltic | naval and commercial |
| Black Sea (ex-Nikolayev Nosenko) | Black Sea | naval and commercial |
| Kamysh-Burun/B. Ye. Butoma, Kerch' | Black Sea | naval and commercial |
| Kherson (Kerch') | Black Sea | commercial only |
| Nikolayev Northern | Black Sea | naval and commercial |
| Oktyabr'skoye | Black Sea | commercial only |
| Khabarovsk | Pacific | naval and commercial |
| Komsomol'sk | Pacific | naval and commercial (including submarines) |
| Vladivostok | Pacific | naval and commercial |
| Krasnoye Sormovo (Gor'kiy) | Inland | naval and commercial (including submarines) |
| Zelenodolsk | Inland | naval and commercial |

*Commercial includes merchant, fishing, fish factory, and research scientific ships.

brought Russian and foreign artisans from Arkhangel'sk, appealed to Venice to send him shipbuilding experts, and had a galley, newly arrived at Arkhangel'sk from Holland, cut into sections and transported to Moscow to serve as a model for his new ships. Smaller craft were built inland in pieces and dragged on sledges to Voronezh for final assembly. Peter (with no real technical training in shipbuilding) took personal charge of the effort at Voronezh, at times working himself as a shipbuilding apprentice on the ships. By the summer of 1696, the yards had produced 28 galleys and several hundred barges. With these ships, manned mostly by Greeks and commanded by a Swiss officer, Peter was able to gain control of the Sea of Azov and hence an outlet to the Black Sea through the Kerch' Strait.

Now that he had control of this sea whose waters were open to navigation more of the year than those of the frigid Arctic coast, Peter

The Soviet Union has a large, modern shipbuilding industry with a surprising amount of flexibility for a component of Soviet society. Series production of ships is carried out in some yards, as the one shown here, while others emphasize "custom" construction of a small number of large or highly specialized ships. (TASS)

ordered a huge fleet constructed. In addition to ships built by the state, each major landowner was to finance the building of a ship as was each large monastery. The state would provide the timber, but landowners or church officials would provide the cannon, fittings, ropes, sails, and all else needed. The *ukaz*, as decrees from the tsar were known, was rigidly enforced, with harsh penalties for failure.

This effort was assisted again by the importation of Western European workers and ships. And some 50 Russians, mostly sons of the nobility, were to be sent to England, Holland, and Venice to study shipbuilding, seamanship, and navigation. In the following years more Russians were sent abroad to study naval and maritime matters, and the most distinguished student would be Peter himself.

In the spring of 1697, he departed for the West. Working under the alias Peter Mikhailoff, but readily known to all, Peter actually studied and labored in shipyards in England and Holland. (More formal visits were made to other countries.) One workman at the Royal Dockyard at Deptford alleged, "The Tzar of Muscovy worked with his own hands as hard as any man in the yard."[4] After these visits to Western Europe, Peter enlisted some 700 English officers and artisans to help him build a fleet, mainly for the Baltic, where he planned a campaign against the Swedes.

When Peter built his new capital city of St. Petersburg (now Leningrad) on the Baltic, he gave shipbuilding a high priority, and Russian peasants and Western artisans, under the supervision of English and some Dutch shipwrights, began building his Baltic fleet. At first construction was carried out on the shores of Lake Ladoga, connected to the Baltic by the Neva River. But by November 1704, storms on the lake and problems in navigating the river led Peter to establish a new yard on the left bank of the Neva, across the river and downstream from his new Peter and Paul Fortress (Petropavlovsk), whose guns could help protect the new yard.[5] From 1805 to 1840 the Admiralty was the most important Russian shipbuilding facility on the Baltic. As late as 1714 the tsar worked at the yard in various roles, using his alias Peter Mikhailoff. As other yards were given the name Admiralty, the original yard was known as the Main Admiralty from 1723 on.

Nearby, where the Moika River flowed into the Neva, from 1709 there were timber storage sheds and other ancillary functions of the Admiralty yard. Known as Galley Court, by 1713 small ships were being built there, and a major thoroughfare was built to connect the new yard to the Admiralty (originally named Galernaia Street and now known as Krasnaia). The yard was renamed Galerniy Island, although at times the area, on an island formed by the Neva and Moika rivers, was called Admiralty Island. When the older Admiralty yard ceased building ships, the Galerniy Island facility became known as the Admiralty yard. (A New Admiralty yard was begun in 1800 under Tsar Paul I on the left bank of the Neva.)

Under Peter's reign other yards were begun in the area of his new capital city, including one on Kotlin Island, in the Gulf of Riga. Originally called Kronshlot and now Kronshtadt, this yard had a dry dock as early as 1705 and began constructing ships in 1716. (By the early twentieth century all construction had stopped at the yard when Kronshtadt became a fleet base and repair yard.)

When Peter died in 1725, his Baltic Fleet consisted of 48 ships of the line and almost 800 minor warships crewed by 28,000 sailors. Virtually all of this fleet had been built in Russian yards.

Leningrad has continued as the center of Russian shipbuilding. And two major characteristics of Peter's shipbuilding industry survived into the Soviet era: the use of foreign technicians and the outright acquisition of foreign ships, components, and technologies.

The shipbuilding industry continued to develop and spread as Peter's successors pushed Russia's borders to the Black Sea and Pacific coasts. In 1780 a Russian city was established at Sevastopol' near the southern end of the Crimean Peninsula, site of settlements since a Greek colony founded in the late sixth century B.C. A naval base and shipyard were started in 1784, and Sevastopol' became the main base and shipyard for the Russian fleet on the Black Sea. But the base declined after the Crimean War (1854–1855). Subsequently, the government yard that had been started in 1798 at Nikolayev, near the mouth of the Bug River, became the major Russian shipbuilding center of the Black Sea. This naval (southern) yard at Nikolayev was followed by a private shipyard, with the former's facilities also being taken over by a private firm in 1911.

In Siberia a primitive yard was started in 1714 at Okhotsk, on the sea of that name, with Swedish prisoners serving as laborers. This yard became the base of the Siberian naval flotilla. Okhotsk was followed by yards at Petropavlovsk on barren Kamchatka Peninsula, Nikolayevsk near the mouth of the Amur River, and finally Vladivostok. The last was established as a Russian military post in 1860 with a shipyard dating from 1869. Two years later Vladivostok became the principal base of the Siberian flotilla.

Indigenous construction and foreign purchases resulted in a Russian fleet at the beginning of the twentieth century that stood third in strength after Britain and France, and ahead of Germany, Italy, Japan, and the United States. The scale of the Soviet shipbuilding industry could be seen in the 18 battleships that were completed between 1900 and 1917 at six Russian yards, three in St. Petersburg and three on the Black Sea:[6]

3 ships at New Admiralty Shipyard, St. Petersburg
7 ships at Baltic Shipyard, St. Petersburg
2 ships at Galerniy Island, St. Petersburg
4 ships at Nikolayev Factories Company, Nikolayev ("north" yard— now the Nikolayev Northern shipyard)
1 ship at Russian Shipbuilding Company, Nikolayev ("south"—now the Black Sea shipyard)
1 ship at Sevastopol'

[4]Nathan Dews, *The History of Deptford* (London: Conway Maritime Press, 1971 [a new impression of the 1884 edition]), p. 183.

[5]The yard's offices soon became headquarters for the Russian fleet. Above them rose a tall wooden spire, topped by a weathervane in the shape of a ship, completed in 1721. Through rebuilding, the central spire was retained and remains a dominant feature of Leningrad's skyline.

[6]Five other battleships were launched in 1915–1916, but not completed. The Galerniy Island shipyard merged with New Admiralty in 1908 to form the Admiralty shipyard.

This is a SVERDLOV-class cruiser in the late 1950s probably built at the Marti (now Admiralty) shipyard in Leningrad, prior to being scrapped. Alongside is the Belgium-built Soviet merchant ship STANISLAVSKY.

Russian warships produced in this period were the equal and some even superior to comparable ships of other maritime powers. (Commercial shipbuilding was largely ignored in this period, with only eight merchant ships being built in Russian yards from 1905 to 1917.) However, the Russians continued to be heavily dependent upon other nations for design talent and, to a lesser extent, for ship construction. Battleship construction at the New Admiralty yard in St. Petersburg and at the northern yard at Nikolayev were under the technical management of John Brown and Company; at the southern yard at Nikolayev construction was under Vickers, both British companies. There was also strong Italian influence; for example, the largest ships built in tsarist Russia—the four 23,360-ton battleships of the PETROPAVLOVSK class, laid down in 1909—were based on the designs of Italy's Vittorio Cuniberti, pioneer in the development of all-big-gun battleships.

Major Russian ships were also built in foreign yards in this period, among them the battleship TSESAREVITCH, launched in France in 1901; the battleship RETVIZAN, launched in the United States (the William Cramp yard in Philadelphia) in 1900; and the armored cruiser RURIK, launched in England in 1906. Similarly, the Russian Navy bought Lake and Holland submarines built in America in the early 1900s and three German submarines completed about 1907. When the First World War began, two light cruisers were under construction in German yards for the Russians. Lesser naval units were built for the Russian fleet in these countries as well as in Denmark and Sweden.

The chaos of the Russian Revolution and Civil War brought shipbuilding to a virtual halt. The new Communist government gave emphasis to merchant ship construction from the mid-1920s in an effort to enhance domestic transportation and foreign trade. Four timber carriers and a tanker were laid down in 1925, which was the start of the rehabilitation of the shipyards and merchant fleet. Limited efforts were also undertaken to rebuild the fleet, mostly modernizing the existing, tsarist-era warships. The first five-year economic plan (1929–1932) visualized the construction of 216 merchant ships, only a few of which were actually completed. The principal naval units built under the first five-year plan were the six DEKABRIST-class submarines, completed 1930–1931, three of which were built at the Ordzhonikidze (now Baltic) yard in Leningrad and three at the southern or Marti (now Black Sea) yard in Nikolayev.

Between the world wars there was a particularly strong Italian influence on Soviet naval ship design, and in the 1930s there was a remarkable American-Soviet liaison as American designs and components were sought for aircraft carriers and battleships. The latter would have been the largest such ships afloat, with some designed to carry aircraft. Nothing resulted from these efforts, however, mostly because of intentional foot-dragging by U.S. naval officers. Just before World War II erupted, there was an increase in German technical assistance to the Soviet Navy, culminating in the German sale of the unfinished heavy cruiser LÜTZOW to the Soviets in 1940.[7]

During the war there was an influx of U.S. and British naval ships of various types, and after the war several German and Italian warships were transferred to the Soviet Navy. These ships and their systems, plus German engineers and technicians, provided a technical basis for the postwar Soviet shipbuilding industry. After the war the rehabilitation of shipyards and their supporting industries was given very high priority by Stalin. The contemporary Soviet fleet is based in large part on this immediate postwar effort to provide the industrial base for a large navy.

The current Soviet shipyards date from three periods: the tsarist era, the Stalin era, and the Khrushchev period. Particularly significant were the yards built under Stalin's regime (1922–1953). His drive to industrialize the country led to the construction of seven major and many lesser shipyards. Large yards were built on the Arctic and Pacific coasts as well as along the Baltic and Black Seas, and inland. The Arctic and Pacific yards were intended to increase the independence of those flotillas. Stalin's approach to shipbuilding was to build the same classes of ships in two or more fleet areas at the same time.

During World War II the Soviets significantly enlarged the inland yards at Gor'kiy and Zelenodolsk on the Volga River. At the same time several of the major yards on the Baltic and Black Sea coasts were severely damaged in battle and by Russian and then German sappers who destroyed facilities as their troops withdrew from them.

During Khrushchev's tenure, several yards were shifted from naval to merchant construction, and five new major yards were established, all but one of which were intended for commercial shipbuilding. Also in the Khrushchev era the construction of nuclear surface ships and submarines began in the USSR. The Admiralty yard in Leningrad built the nuclear icebreaker LENIN, which first got under way on nuclear power in

---

[7] The LÜTZOW was a sister ship to the better-known PRINZ EUGEN, which displaced 14,800 tons standard and mounted eight 8-inch guns. The LUETZOW was never completed, but served as a floating gun battery (renamed TALLINN in 1942 and PETROPAVLOVSK in 1944). The unfinished SEYDLITZ of the same class was taken by the Soviets after the war (renamed POLTAVA), but she too was never finished. Both ships are believed to have been scrapped in the 1950s.

September 1959, predating the U.S. nuclear merchant ship SAVANNAH and the nuclear missile cruiser LONG BEACH (CGN 9). Almost simultaneously, the Severodvinsk yard in the Arctic began building nuclear submarines, the first being completed in 1958. Two years later the Komsomol'sk yard in Siberia completed its first nuclear submarine.

The Krasnoye Sormovo yard at Gor'kiy, one of the major inland shipyards, became the third nuclear submarine yard, completing its first such craft in 1967. Several years after building the LENIN, the Admiralty yard in Leningrad began constructing nuclear submarines, with its first completion also in 1967. The adjacent Sudomekh yard completed the first of the advanced Alfa-class nuclear submarines about 1967, bringing to five the number of nuclear submarine yards. (The Admiralty and Sudomekh yards were subsequently merged administratively as the United Admiralty shipyard.)

These five submarine yards are currently producing about eight nuclear submarines and three diesel-electric boats annually. This is about double the U.S. nuclear construction rate planned during the 1980s (with no U.S. diesel boats being built).[8] The five Soviet yards have an estimated capability of producing about 20 nuclear submarines per year on a triple shift basis. All of their submarine building facilities are covered and heated to permit year-round construction. Although the Admiralty yard had built the first nuclear icebreaker, beginning in the 1970s the Baltic

[8] The two U.S. submarine yards engaged in nuclear submarine construction did produce eight units in 1981—one Trident SSBN and seven SSNs—a situation brought about because of previous program delays and larger authorizations in the 1970s. The General Dynamics/Electric Boat yard and Newport News Shipbuilding yard have a combined construction capability of 1½ Trident SSBNs and five SSNs per year.

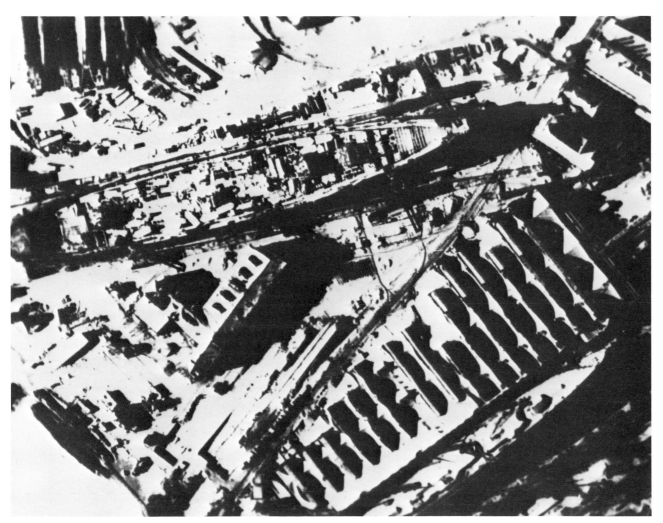

This is the Baltic Shipyard as seen from a German reconnaissance aircraft on 8 June 1942, during the Germans' three-year seige of Leningrad. The never-finished battleship SOVIETSKII SOYUZ is on the building ways at the top of the photo, the Neva River is at the lower left, and the CHAPAYEV-class light cruiser CHKALOV is on the ways in the lower right.

Schoolchildren leave the LENIN as the nuclear icebreaker was being fitted out at a wharf in Leningrad's Admiralty shipyard. The ship's icebreaking stem is clearly visible in this view. While the Admiralty and Baltic yards have built the nation's nuclear icebreakers, Finland has built the large conventional icebreakers in accord with the Soviet scheme of relying on foreign technology when appropriate—a concept that dates back to Tsar Peter I. (Sovfoto)

**TABLE 28-2. SOVIET SUBMARINE CONSTRUCTION (1973–1983 PROGRAMS)**

| | Nuclear Submarines | | | Diesel-electric Submarines | |
|---|---|---|---|---|---|
| Shipyard | SSBN | SSGN | SSN | SS | SSAG |
| Admiralty Sudomekh | | | Victor Alfa (new) | Foxtrot* | Lima |
| Krasnoye Sormovo (Gor'kiy) | | Charlie Papa | | Tango | |
| Komsomol'sk | Yankee Delta I | | Victor | Kilo | India |
| Severodvinsk | Yankee Delta I/II/III Typhoon | Oscar | Alfa(?) (new) | | |

*Recent units constructed for foreign transfer.

shipyard in Leningrad has built the improved ARKTIKA icebreakers and the KIROV-class nuclear battle cruisers.

Today the Soviet Union's shipbuilding industry is large, modern, and versatile. All major shipbuilding programs—naval and commercial—are directed by a central Ministry of Shipbuilding. Created in 1939, the shipbuilding ministry is directed by a civilian official working in close coordination with the naval, merchant, and fishing fleets.

According to Western intelligence estimates, there are some 215,000 shipyard workers in the Soviet Union:

| | |
|---|---|
| Arctic coast yards | 50,000 |
| Baltic coast yards | 54,000 |
| Black Sea yards | 63,000 |
| Pacific coast yards | 30,000 |
| Inland yards | 18,000 |

"The Soviet shipbuilding industry has a corps of well-trained and efficient workers at all skill levels. Training continues after the worker joins a shipyard, as night school and correspondence school courses are offered in most disciplines," according to a U.S. Navy report.[9] Shipyard workers are paid on the basis of longevity and for upgrading their technical competence. In addition, there are cost-of-living allowances based on the location of the yard. Workers on the Arctic coast receive 50 to 70 percent additional pay, those on the Pacific coast 20 to 40 percent, and those at inland yards 10 to 20 percent.

Approximately 75 design bureaus and research institutes are also part of the shipbuilding industry. Among the latter is the Krylov Institute in Leningrad, described by the U.S. Navy as "the world's foremost shipbuilding research and development center."[10] The Krylov Institute operates several research ships, including the unique systems/materials research ship IZUMRUD. The Institute, a part of the Grechko Naval Academy (i.e., war college), has a staff of approximately 5,000 personnel, including 1,700 professionals.

The smaller, specialized shipbuilding and ship repair facilities in the USSR are under the control of the Ministries of Merchant Marine, River Fleet, and Fishing Fleet.

Soviet shipyards use a number of advanced construction techniques, including modular assembly, horizontal or level construction positions with indirect launching, numerically controlled equipment, and semi-automatic or automatic welding. The USSR is the world leader in the last technique. The construction of the titanium-hull Alfa SSN demonstrates an ability to work this advanced metal in large sections, an ability that does not now exist in the West.

The quality of Soviet shipyard work can be gauged, in part, by the sales of naval units and merchant ships to other countries. Such traditional seafaring nations as Great Britain, Norway, and Sweden are among the customers for recent Soviet-built merchant ships. Nevertheless, some Soviet ships have had major problems that could be attributed to their construction. A large fish factory ship built at the Admiralty yard in Leningrad required more than a year of additional work after her sea trials; the poor workmanship was cited in the Soviet press.

The Soviets also purchase numerous naval and commercial ships from foreign yards. Landing ships, research-surveying ships, intelligence collectors (AGIs) and other auxiliary ships are built in East German and Polish yards (see chapter 31), while commercial ships have been purchased from those countries as well as Denmark, Finland, Great Britain, and Japan. The USSR buys Western-built ships and components to acquire technology or to avoid having to develop a specialized or difficult design. For example, Finland's shipyards have provided numerous conventionally powered icebreakers as well as large SEABEE-type cargo ships for the USSR.

The principal shipyards of the Soviet Union are listed below, in alphabetical order under geographic area.

[9]Bloom, op. cit., p. 14.

[10]Alexei H. Krylov was the principal designer of Russian battleships of the SEVASTOPOL' and SOVIETSKII SOYUZ classes.

## ARCTIC SHIPYARDS

### Severodvinsk (Shipyard No. 402)

The Severodvinsk yard is the world's only major shipbuilding facility above the Arctic circle and ranks as the world's largest submarine, if not ship, construction yard. It was formerly known as the Molotovsk yard.

The yard is located on the Dvina Gulf, about 30 miles (48 km) across the delta of the Northern Dvina River from the city of Arkangel'sk. The gulf opens onto the White Sea. The yard is connected to Leningrad by the White Sea-Baltic Canal system (completed in 1933) as well as by rail lines.

*History.* An estimated 120,000 political and criminal prisoners were brought to the area in 1938–1939 to start construction of the shipyard. Stalin envisioned the yard as the largest in the world, capable of building ships up to battleship size and making the Northern Fleet independent of Baltic shipyards. The eventual work force when the yard was completed was projected to be 35,000–40,000.

The main building dock was erected under cover to permit work to be carried on year around. This dock measures some 1,100 feet (335 m) in length and 452 feet (137 m) in width, having been intended to permit side-by-side construction of two SOVIETSKII SOYUZ-class battleships (to have had a full-load displacement of 64,000 tons). Two of these ships were laid down at Severodvinsk in 1940, but all work on capital ships in the USSR ceased that October and the ships were never finished. Components and materials for these ships were brought to the yard from Leningrad and Nikolayev. During World War II the yard had a peak work force of about 5,000 and produced destroyers and S-class submarines, most of the destroyers actually being completed after the war.

Subsequently, the yard began construction of the postwar surface warship classes—two SVERDLOV-class light cruisers and 18 SKORYY-class destroyers. More significant, the Severodvinsk yard made prep-

This is the huge enclosed battleship construction dock at Severodvinsk, large enough for two battleships to be built side-by-side. This photo was taken in 1944 when components of two SOVIETSKII SOYUZ-class battleships were still in place. The structure and a still larger enclosed dock at Severodvinsk are now used for nuclear submarine construction. There have been recent increases in the yard's work area, probably making it the world's largest shipyard. (U.S. Navy)

arations for advanced submarine construction and in 1953 completed the first of eight Zulu-class diesel attack submarines built at the yard. It then shifted to producing the Golf ballistic missile submarine (SSB) and two nuclear classes, the November SSN and the Hotel SSBN.

Some commercial work was done at the yard into the 1950s.

Since the mid-1950s Severodvinsk has constructed only nuclear-powered submarines of the following classes and during the past two decades has concentrated on cruise and ballistic missile submarines.

| SSN | November | SSBN | Yankee |
|---|---|---|---|
| SSGN | Echo II | SSBN | Delta |
| SSGN | Oscar | SSBN | Typhoon |

The yard may also be building Alfa and an improved SSN design in the early 1980s.

The battleship-building hall begun in 1937–1938 has been supplemented by an even larger submarine construction hall in which the Oscars and Typhoons are being built. All building facilities are covered and heated, permitting year-round work, and all permit horizontal construction. Admiral H.G. Rickover, at the time head of the U.S. nuclear propulsion program, stated in the late 1960s that Severodvinsk had "several times the area and facilities of all of the U.S. submarine yards combined." The statement is indicative of the size of the yard, and there have been subsequent increases in its size.

## Arkhangel'sk Yards

The smaller Krasnaya Kuznitsa and Arkhangel'sk ship repair yards are located in Arkhangel'sk and do commercial work. They build small coastal and inland craft and ships, with the Arkhangel'sk yard building small air-cushion vessels.

### BALTIC SHIPYARDS

### Admiralty (Shipyard No. 194)

Admiralty is one of the four major shipyards in Leningrad. Recent programs have consisted of merchant and fisheries support ships, naval auxiliaries, and nuclear-powered submarines. Since the early 1970s the Admiralty and adjacent Sudomekh yards have been consolidated into a single administrative entity, the United Admiralty Shipyard.

The Admiralty yard is located on Galerniy Island, at the intersection of the "large" Neva River and the Fontanka Canal. The Sudomekh yard is adjacent to the northeast, separated from Admiralty by the small Moika and Proshka rivers.

*History.* Tsar Paul I established the New Admiralty yard on the left bank of the Neva in 1800, as the Main Admiralty was unsuitable for continued expansion because of the city growing up around it. Battleships were begun at the New Admiralty in the early 1800s as the facility became one of the major Russian shipyards.

In 1908 the New Admiralty yard was merged with the Galerniy Island Admiralty, which had been building naval ships since 1713. (The Galerniy yard had been called the Société Franco-Russe yard from about 1884 to

Leningrad

1891.) After the merger that yard was called simply Admiralty. Among the more famous ships built at the yard were the first Russian steamship, the ELIZAVETA and the historic cruiser AVRORA. From 1921 to 1956 the yard was named Marti for the French sailor-revolutionary André Marti. Also, from 1921 to 1926 the yard was administratively merged with the Baltic shipyard.

During the between-war period Shch-class submarines and then large K classes were built at the yard. Large surface warship construction began in 1938 with the keel laying for a CHAPAYEV-class light cruiser (not completed until 1949). The following year the keel was laid for the lead ship of the KRONSHTADT-class battle cruisers (which were never finished).

Virtually all ship work halted at the Leningrad yards during World War II as the city was beseiged by German forces for three years. After the war, in addition to completing the light cruiser ZHELEZNIAKOV, the yard geared up for participation in the SVERDLOV cruiser program. However, only three of these ships were completed before the yard ceased building surface warships. Similarly, reported plans to produce the STALINGRAD-class battle cruisers at the yard were halted (see below).

From the mid-1950s onward the Admiralty yard has specialized in noncombatant construction, including merchant ships, conventional icebreakers, large rescue and salvage ships, fish factory ships, floating dry docks, and some naval auxiliaries. The yard is also building the giant SESS MARSHAL NEDELIN.

The yard built the nuclear-powered icebreaker LENIN, launched in late 1957, but no additional nuclear ships were produced at the Admiralty yard for a decade. (The later Soviet nuclear icebreakers were built at the Baltic shipyard.) Admiralty subsequently became the fifth yard in the USSR to produce nuclear submarines, with the first Victor SSNs being launched in 1967.

Leningrad has been a shipbuilding center since Peter the Great established his capital in the Neva marshes almost three centuries ago. This view of the Petrovskiy shipyard taken a few years ago shows a Nanuchka-class missile corvette and other small combatants being fitted out. (N. Polmar)

## Baltic (Shipyard No. 189)

The large Baltic or Baltiysk shipyard mainly produces merchant and research ships, with the notable exception of the large, ARKTIKA-class nuclear icebreakers and the KIROV-class nuclear battle cruisers. Known as the Baltic Shipyard and Engineering Works before the Revolution, after 1918 the yard was renamed Ordzhonikidze, and subsequently it was renamed the Baltic Shipyard.

This yard is at the lower end of Leningrad's large Vasilevsky Island, near the mouth of the Neva River.

*History.* The yard was established in 1856 as a major ship construction facility to build merchant ships. However, there also was naval shipbuilding directed by the government at the yard, and in 1864 it launched two monitors designed by Johann (John) Ericksson of American Civil War fame, in 1892 launched the famed armored cruiser RURIK,

and later built the first Russian submarines as well as early steel battleships.

During the 1930s the yard was extensively modernized and began the construction of cruisers, destroyers, and several classes of submarines. On the eve of World War II the yard began building SOVIETSKII SOYUZ-class battleships. Shipbuilding stopped during the seige of Leningrad, and the yard was severely damaged.

After the war the yard built six SVERDLOV-class cruisers, and series production of the Whiskey-class submarine began. The first Whiskeys built at the Baltic yard were completed in 1955. Only 14 of these submarines were completed before the yard shifted primarily to merchant and special-purpose ships.

A variety of merchant ships have been built at the Baltic yard during the past two and a half decades—tankers, refrigerated cargo ships, dry bulk cargo ships—as well as icebreakers and trawlers. Some of these ships have been for foreign customers. The yard has also built the large Space Event Support Ship (SESS) KOSMONAUT YURI GAGARIN.

Although the Baltic yard is one of four large tsarist-era shipyards, it demonstrates how older facilities can be adapted to modern techniques. For example, sectional construction methods were used in building the SOFIA-class tankers (61,000 tons deadweight), with the result that time on the building ways was reduced from six months to three and a half months for the first ship built by the new method. A variety of merchant ship types are built at the Baltic shipyard for Soviet and foreign use.

The yard began constructing nuclear surface ships in the late 1960s, the icebreaker ARKTIKA being launched in 1973 followed by her sister ships SIBIR' and ROSSIYA. These ships were joined on the building ways by the KIROV-class battle cruisers.

## Kaliningrad (Shipyard No. 820)

The Kaliningrad yard builds surface warships and amphibious ships. It is the ex-German Schichau shipyard.

The yard is located at the Lithuanian port of Kaliningrad, formerly the German city of Königsberg. Adjacent to the large Soviet fleet base at Baltiysk (formerly Pillau), the yard covers almost 200 acres.

*History.* The yard became a major German shipbuilding facility in the 1880s constructing torpedo boats. After World War II the Soviets rebuilt the yard to produce small commercial and naval ships, among them frigates of the Kola, Riga, and Petya classes.

In the 1960s the Kaliningrad yard began producing the larger Krivak-class frigates and the Alligator-class landing ships. The complexity of the Krivak indicates a considerable increase in the yard's capabilities. Subsequently, the yard has produced the UDALOY-class missile destroyers, which at 8,200 tons are the largest as well as the most complex warships yet built at Kaliningrad.

In addition to new construction, the yard modernizes escort ships and performs overhaul and maintenance for the Baltic Fleet. There has been only limited commercial construction work at Kaliningrad since 1960 (e.g., ferries in the 1970s).

## Klaipeda

Merchant ships are produced at this yard, which is also a former German shipyard, known as the Lindenau yard prior to Soviet takeover of the area at the end of World War II. Klaipeda reached major yard status in the 1950s, and since about 1960 has built only merchant ships. Recent production has included fish factory ships, trawlers, and floating dry docks.

The yard is located at Klaipeda in Lithuania and was previously known as Memel. It is north of Kaliningrad on the Baltic coast.

## Petrovskiy

This Leningrad yard constructs small combatants. It is located on Petrovskiy Island, in the small Neva, north of Vasilevsky Island. It became a major shipbuilding facility in the 1930s. Various mine, patrol, torpedo, and missile boats have been built at Petrovskiy, the largest to date being the 930-ton Nanuchka-class missile corvettes.

## Sudomekh

The Sudomekh yard is a specialized submarine construction facility in Leningrad. It is located in downtown Leningrad between the Neva and Moika rivers. Sudomekh is adjacent to the Admiralty yard, and the yards are administratively joined as the United Admiralty Shipyard.

*History.* The yard became a major shipbuilding facility in the 1930s at which time it built submarines of the Shch and M or *Malyuka* ("baby") classes. The yard was damaged extensively during the war but was rapidly rebuilt in the late 1940s for submarine construction. Submarines of the Shch and M-V classes were completed through 1952.

Equipment removed from German submarine yards was installed in Sudomekh, and with the help of German scientists and technicians, advanced submarine designs and propulsion systems were developed. Long-range Zulu-class diesel submarines were launched at Sudomekh from 1952 on, and smaller Quebec-class submarines, developed for closed-cycle propulsion, were launched from 1954. (Sudomekh built all 30 of the Quebec class.)

Subsequently, from the late 1950s Sudomekh produced the long-range Foxtrot class, successor to the Zulu. Foxtrots were built at a steady rate of five or six units per year during the 1960s, with construction continuing into the 1980s for foreign transfer.

Sudomekh completed the first Alfa-class SSN about 1967, marking the debut of a submarine significantly faster and deeper diving than any previous combat submarine. After lengthy trials and extensive modification, the Alfa entered series production at Sudomekh. There are reports of a "next-generation" SSN under development at the yard based on Alfa technology.

## Vyborg

As its name implies, Vyborg is located in former Finnish territory. It builds only merchant ships. Becoming a major shipyard in the 1960s, Vyborg almost exclusively builds dry cargo ships, including large container carriers.

Vyborg is northwest of Leningrad, in the area ceded by Finland to the Soviet Union after the 1939–1940 "winter war."

## Zhdanov (Shipyard No. 190)

The large Zhdanov shipyard in Leningrad constructs both commercial and naval ships, the latter mostly missile cruisers and destroyers. From about 1855 it was known as the Putilov Marine Engine Works and briefly as the Northern Shipyard before being named for A.A. Zhdanov in 1935.

The yard is located in the commercial port area, in the southern environs of Leningrad. The yard covers more than 200 acres.

*History.* The Putilov yard built destroyers and had laid down light cruisers prior to the Revolution. Zhdanov again began building naval ships in 1936. Ships up to destroyer size were begun prior to World

War II. Extensively damaged during the war, the yard was rehabilitated and became the leading surface combatant builder in the late 1940s. Initially, destroyers were built at Zhdanov (SKORYY, Tallinn, Kotlin, Krupnyy, Kanin, Kashin classes) and then all of the missile cruisers of the Kynda and Kresta I/II classes.

The yard is currently building missile destroyers of the SOVREMENNYY and UDALOY classes, Krivak-class missile frigates, and a variety of merchant ships, with about one-third of the yard currently allocated to commercial work. The latter includes the construction of roll-on/roll-off, dry cargo, and passenger ships. The yard has both open and covered building facilities.

Other significant but smaller Baltic-area yards include the Riga ship repair yard in Riga; the Order of Lenin naval shipyard on Kronshtadt Island; and the Kolpino Ust, Izhora, Kanonerskiy, Petrozavodsk, and Dekabristov yards in Leningrad. The last produces air-cushion vehicles.

## BLACK SEA SHIPYARDS

### Black Sea (Shipyard No. 444)

Often referred to as the Nikolayev south yard, this is the largest shipyard on the Black Sea. Aircraft carriers are constructed at the yard as well as commercial ships and naval auxiliaries. The yard is located south of the city of Nikolayev, at the mouth of the southern Bug River. The yard currently covers almost 500 acres.

*History.* The yard was built in 1895–1899 as a Belgian-owned enterprise, the Nikolayev Shipbuilding, Mechanical, and Iron Works. It began building naval ships in 1901, constructing surface ships up to battleship size as well as submarines. After the Revolution the yard was renamed for André Marti (Marti south).

In the 1930s construction was reinitiated on surface warships and submarines. Destroyer construction was followed by the keel laying in 1940 of a battleship of the SOVIETSKII SOYUZ class. Reportedly, the water depth at the yard was limited, and the battleship would have had to be towed to Sevastopol' after launching for completion. Work on the ship stopped in October 1940, but considerable progress had already been made. Prewar submarines built at the yard were of the S and M classes.

The yard was occupied by German troops in August 1941 and was not recaptured by the Russians until March 1944. As German troops approached Nikolayev, several unfinished cruiser and destroyer hulls were towed from the Marti and 61 Kommuna yards to Black Sea ports farther east, but only one destroyer, launched in 1940 at the 61 Kommuna yard, was finished at Batum before the end of the war. Extensive damage was inflicted on both Nikolayev yards by fighting and German demolition. The Marti (south) yard was rebuilt and was able to undertake the construction of surface ships and submarines in a relatively short period of

Northern Black Sea area

This view of cargo ships being series produced on a horizontal assembly facility at Kherson, on the Black Sea at the mouth of the Dnepr River, is similar to the scene at several other Soviet yards. Despite the large amount of Soviet naval construction, Kherson and several other yards build only merchant ships. (TASS)

time. Several small M-V type submarines were completed from 1947 to 1950, and the yard started launching Whiskey-class submarines. Submarine construction continued only to the late 1950s, with an estimated 65 being built at the yard.

More impressive were the yard's surface warship programs. The keel for the first STALINGRAD-class battle cruiser was laid down on the rejuvenated battleship ways at Nikolayev south in 1949. Work proceeded rapidly, and the ship is said to have been about 60 percent complete and ready for launching in early 1953 when Stalin died. All work on the project ceased, and the hull was later launched and probably expended in weapon tests. (A second ship was to have been built on the ways vacated by the first hull; the Admiralty yard was also reported to have been gearing up to build ships of this class.)

The yard also built three SVERDLOV-class light cruisers before the mid-1950s cutback in naval construction. The yard then concentrated on merchant construction for the remainder of the decade.

Since the early 1960s the Black Sea shipyard has undertaken the construction of aviation ships for the Soviet Navy: first, the two 18,000-ton MOSKVA-class helicopter carrier–missile cruisers, followed by the four

KIEV-class VTOL aircraft carriers of some 38,000 tons, and subsequently the reported 60,000-ton nuclear carrier. Naval auxiliaries are also constructed at the yard.

The Black Sea shipyard also produces large commercial ships—primarily dry cargo ships, fish factory ships, and large trawlers.

The yard has two shipbuilding areas—one for naval projects, with end-launch building ways and building docks, and one for commercial projects with a horizontal, dock-launching facility.

### Kamysh-Burun/B. Ye. Butoma

This yard constructs warships up to frigate size and also large commercial ships, including the Soviet merchant marine's supertankers. The yard was named in 1981 for B.Ye. Butoma, the late head of the shipbuilding ministry.

The yard is located at Kerch', on the Crimean Peninsula near the entrance to the Sea of Azov. It occupies some 150 acres of land.

*History.* The Kerch' yard became a major shipbuilding facility in the 1930s. In the postwar period the yard built small combatants as well as merchant ships. There was a major expansion of facilities beginning in the mid-1960s, at which time construction of frigates of the Krivak class was begun. (Previously the Poti-class corvettes were the largest combat vessels built at Kerch'.)

The merchant ships built at the yard range up to the KRYM-class supertankers, the largest merchant ships built in the USSR. All six ships of the class were built at Kamysh-Burun.

Modular construction methods are used at the yard, fabricated sections being built in the construction halls and then moved onto the ways for assembly. The completed hull then passes to a transverser for launching. The KRYM-class tankers were built in a large graving dock constructed during the expansion of the 1960s.

Nikolayev is one of several shipbuilding centers in the Soviet Union. This large fish factory ship is shown under construction at one of the three large yards at the Black Sea city. This ship is also being built on a horizontal construction way, a highly efficient method of producing ships, especially in series production. (TASS)

## Kherson

The yard at Kherson builds merchant ships exclusively. It is located at the mouth of the Dnepr River. Kherson achieved the status of a major shipyard in the 1950s. Dry cargo ships and tankers are constructed at the yard, some for foreign transfer.

## Nikolayev Northern (Shipyard No. 445)

This yard produces the Kara-class guided missile cruisers and the successor class, the Krasina missile cruiser, as well as merchant ships. The yard is located at Nikolayev, at the mouth of the southern Bug River. It covers almost 200 acres.

*History.* The yard was begun as an admiralty shipyard in 1789 and could be ranked as a major shipyard from about 1800. After a century of operation the yard was closed down in 1910 and reopened the following year as a commercial venture, the Russian Shipbuilding Corporation (Russud). The yard built warships up to battleship size during the tsarist era. After the revolution it became the Marti north yard and then the 61 Kommuna yard. During the 1930s the yard built CHAPAYEV-class light cruisers, destroyers, and submarines of the Shch class. The second battle cruiser of the KRONSHTADT class was laid down at the 61 Kommuna yard in 1938–1939. The unfinished hull was captured by the Germans in August 1941, having been partially wrecked by Russian demolitions. (The ship was never finished, but was cut up for scrap after the war.) The yard was heavily damaged during the war.

After being rebuilt, the yard produced Riga-class frigates, destroyers of the SKORYY, Kotlin, Krupnyy, Kildin, Kanin, and Kashin classes, and then the large, all-gas-turbine cruisers of the Kara class, as well as undertaking the modernization of destroyer-type ships (Kashin and Kildin).

The yard has built all seven ships of the Kara class and is now building the Kara's successor, the Krasina.

Refrigerated cargo ships are also built at the yard.

It is one of the few shipyards in the Soviet Union that has only inclined end-launch building ways and no covered construction halls.

## Oktyabr'skoye

This yard constructs dry cargo and refrigerated cargo ships. The yard became a major shipbuilding center in the 1950s.

Also located in the Black Sea area are the yard at Feodosiya, on the Black Sea coast of the Crimea, which builds small combatants; the Ordzhonikidze Maritime yard at Poti, near Sevastopol'; and the Okean shipyard in the Korabel'nyy district of Nikolayev, the third construction yard in that city. The Ordzhonikidze yard (not to be confused with the Baltic Shipyard) builds commercial craft, especially hydrofoils. The Okean yard builds the large oil/ore carriers of the BORIS BUTOMA type (130,000 deadweight tons) as well as other merchant ships and large trawlers. The ship repair yard at Il'ichevsk is a major producer of freight containers, having produced more than 25,000 through 1982.

## PACIFIC COAST SHIPYARDS

### Khabarovsk

This yard, at the junction of the Amur and Ussuri rivers in eastern Siberia, produces small combatants and merchant and research ships. Khabarovsk is some 435 miles (695 km) south of the mouth of the Amur River where it enters the Tatar Strait.

The yard became a major shipbuilding facility in the 1950s. It produces patrol craft, small combatants, and minesweepers. Some commercial ships are also built at the yard, including scientific research vessels.

### Komsomol'sk (Shipyard No. 199)

This is a major submarine construction yard with some merchant work being undertaken. The Komsomol'sk yard is about 280 miles (455 km) south of the mouth of the Amur River in Siberia. The depth of water prevented the yard from completing the large Delta I-class SSBNs, which are fitted out at a coastal yard after being launched.

*History*. The Komsomol'sk yard was constructed in 1932–1937 to provide a major shipyard for the planned expansion of the Pacific Fleet. The yard built two heavy cruisers of the older KIROV class (completed 1946–1947) as well as destroyers and submarines (Shch class) during World War II. Smaller surface combatants and naval auxiliaries as well as some merchant ships were also built at this Siberian yard.

In the postwar period the yard has been primarily engaged in submarine construction. During the 1950s the yard constructed 11 Whiskey-class diesel attack submarines and 7 Golf-class diesel ballistic missile submarines.

Komsomol'sk was the second yard in the USSR to construct nuclear-powered submarines. The first of five Echo I-class SSGNs was finished in 1960, followed by 11 of the larger Echo II SSGNs. (The yard subsequently converted the Echo I submarines to an SSN configuration.) The yard has since constructed submarines of the Yankee and Delta I classes, sharing these SSBN projects with Severodvinsk. The later Soviet SSBNs appear to be too large to travel the Amur River. The yard has shifted to the construction of the Victor III SSN.

The Maritime Shipyard at Nakhodka is the largest facility in the Soviet Far East supporting the nation's massive fishing fleet. This view shows several trawlers under construction and undergoing repairs. The yard was begun in the late 1950s, a period of expansion of the Soviet Union's merchant and fishing fleets. (Sovfoto)

The Komsomol'sk yard has also continued to develop advanced diesel-electric submarines, sharing this effort with Gor'kiy and Sudo-mekh in Leningrad. In the 1960s Komsomol'sk built four Bravo target and training submarines (SST), followed by two India salvage and rescue craft (AGSS) and the Kilo attack submarines (SS).

## Vladivostok

Vladivostok is a major maritime center. The shipyards construct merchant and fishing ships, but apparently they overhaul naval units as well. Vladivostok is located in Peter the Great Bay on the Sea of Japan.

There are several yards in the city, the principal building yard being formerly known as the Dalzavod yard. During the 1930s this yard constructed destroyers and submarines (L, Shch, and S classes). In recent years the yard has constructed merchant and fishing ships.

There are numerous other shipyards on the Pacific coast. The yard at Slavyanka Bay near Vladivostok was built in the 1970s as a ship repair facility. There are also large ship and submarine repair yards at Petropavlovsk on the Kamchatka Peninsula—the Freza ship repair yard and V.I. Lenin shipyard.

## INLAND SHIPYARDS

### Krasnoye Sormovo (Shipyard No. 112)

Located at the large industrial city of Gor'kiy, this is one of five Soviet shipyards currently building submarines. In addition, river and inland craft are constructed, including hydrofoils and air-cushion vehicles.

This yard is located some 200 miles (320 km) east of Moscow on the Volga River at its confluence with the Oka River. Submarines built here generally transit down the Volga River to the Black Sea, most for subsequent assignment to other fleet areas.

*History.* Krasnoye Sormovo is credited with being the oldest major shipbuilding location in the country.[11] The first "modern" shipbuilding effort was the Nizhegorodskaya Machine Plant, which started producing river boats and barges in 1849. The facility became one of the major shipyards of the Soviet Union in the early 1940s. At that time the yard built M-class submarines that were fabricated in sections and then taken by

[11]Prior to 1932 Gor'kiy was known as Nizhny Novgorod, which was founded in the early thirteenth century and became a major trading center.

barge to various coastal yards for assembly. The larger S-class submarines were also built at Gor'kiy.

After the war Gor'kiy became the principal Whiskey-class submarine yard, completing 146 units from 1950 to 1957—with 40 submarines completed in the peak year 1955. The yard then built all 20 of the Romeo-class attack submarines and the 16 Juliett-class guided missile submarines.

Krasnoye Sormovo became the fourth Soviet shipyard to construct nuclear submarines, completing the first Charlie SSGN in 1967. While continuing Charlie construction, in the 1970s the yard initiated the Tango-class diesel attack submarine (SS), successor to the Foxtrot class as a long-range diesel attack submarine. The single advanced Papa-class SSGN was built at Gor'kiy, but the subsequent, series-produced Oscar SSGN is being constructed at the larger Severodvinsk yard.

Large numbers of commercial inland and river craft are also built at Gor'kiy.

### Zelenodolsk (Shipyard No. 340)

This yard produces mainly small combatants, trawlers, and hydrofoils. Among its naval products were the Kronshtadt, S.O.-1, Poti, and Grisha classes. In the mid-1970s construction began on the Koni-class frigates, the largest naval units yet built at the yard.

This yard is located near Kazan', some 200 miles (320 km) east of Gor'kiy, on the Volga River. It was built in 1945–1946.

There are numerous smaller inland yards on the many lakes and rivers of the USSR. These include the Dnepr shipyard (also known as Leninskaya Kusnica) near Kiev on the Dnepr River; the Kama shipbuilding yard at Perm' on the Kama River; the yard at Krasnoyarsk on the Yenisey River in central Siberia; the Moryakovskiy shipbuilding yard at Tomsk, on the Tom River near its junction with the Ob', in Siberia; the Maritime and Uritskiy yards at Astrakhan' at the mouth of the Volga on the Caspian Sea; the Navashinskiy shipyard at Rostov on the Don River; the Oka shipyard in Navashino near Gor'kiy; the yard at Rybinsk, on the man-made lake of that name, just north of Moscow (with access to the Volga River); the Kiev shipbuilding yard in the capital city of the Ukraine on the Dnepr River; the Volgograd shipyard at Volgograd (formerly Stalingrad) on the Volga; and the yard at Yaroslavl, on the Volga northeast of Moscow.

# 29

# Merchant Marine

The Soviet Union has a large, modern, and highly competitive merchant marine. The merchant fleet initially developed slowly in the post–World War II period, mainly to carry the large coastal trade of the nation.

The Khrushchev period brought a massive expansion of this fleet, initially to support overseas clients and then to help trade with other Third World nations. Khrushchev's interest in developing a strong Soviet merchant fleet was further reinforced by the Cuban missile crisis, which demonstrated the need for shipping to support long-range military operations. The ranking of the Soviet fleet rose from twenty-sixth place in the late 1950s to twelfth place in 1962, and to seventh place in 1964 (although since then it has periodically slipped to eighth place, as there have been spurts in U.S. merchant fleet strength). In the 1970s there was another phase of fleet expansion as merchant ships became a major earner of "hard" Western currency.

Today this merchant fleet carries cargo and passengers on more than 70 international trade routes, calling at ports in over 125 countries throughout the world. However, when this book went to press there were virtually no Soviet merchant ships calling at U.S. ports.

Regular Soviet cargo service to the United States began in late 1970 after an absence of almost two decades. Soviet passenger ships began calling at New York and other U.S. cities in June of 1973, initiating a service that would extend briefly to the Caribbean cruise route before ending a few years later. Soviet merchant ships called increasingly at almost 60 U.S. ports, reaching a peak of some 1,700 port arrivals per year. (Some of these were multiple U.S. port calls, as this figure includes the same ship calling at different ports.) Soviet merchant service to U.S. ports was halted abruptly in 1979 by U.S. longshoremen who refused to offload the ships in protest against the Soviet assault on Afghanistan.

Soviet merchant ships compete effectively with Western shipping on virtually all major trade routes in the world except for those that include calls on U.S. ports. The Soviets practice rate cutting to ensure a share of those markets in which they have an interest. For example, when the

Ports in the United States saw a large number of Soviet merchant ships during the 1970s as the Soviets sought to capture some of the lucrative American trade. The Soviet-U.S. grain sale agreements stipulated that a large amount of the grain had to be carried on Soviet ships, such as the KRASNOGRAD, lead ship of a Finnish-built class, shown here at Houston, Texas. (Port of Houston)

The KOMSOMOL'SK, one of the world's largest and fastest roll-on/roll-off ships, is typical of the modern Soviet merchant fleet. Like much of that merchant fleet, the KOMSOMOL'SK is foreign built (the Valmet yard in Helsinki) and provides a viable commercial capability as well as a potential military capability. She is shown here riding high in the water shortly after completion in 1976. In addition to vehicles, the KOMSOMOL'SK can carry 1,368 standard containers (including 390 on deck, as shown here).

Soviet Baltic Shipping Company began container service in 1974 to New York, Baltimore, and Philadelphia, the line announced that the service would be 10 percent below regular rates to make sure a certain amount of cargo would be carried. But the Soviet emphasis seems to be on carrying cargoes to and from the Third World, even on routes that do not include Soviet ports. These efforts have both economic and political motives. Because Soviet ships are largely built in Soviet and Eastern Bloc shipyards with "cheap" rubles—which have no exchange value outside of the country—and their operating costs and crews are paid for in rubles, the hard Western currency earned by the merchant fleet is a profit for the government.

The economic-political goals of these practices were candidly linked by V. Kudryavtsev, a political observer for the Soviet newspaper *Izvestiya*, who wrote on 15 February 1972 that: "The Soviet Union does not conceal the fact that economic relations with the developing countries are an integral part of the struggle between two world systems, socialism and capitalism. These relations undermine the imperialist powers of economic and trade ties with the developing countries and force the capitalist states to make concessions."

Soviet merchant ships have also supported Soviet military goals. This became evident to the West in the early 1960s, when Soviet and Eastern Bloc merchant ships carried a variety of arms, including long-range missiles and strike aircraft to Cuba. Subsequently, during much of the Vietnam War an average of more than one Soviet ship per day entered North Vietnamese ports carrying equipment, food, building materials, and other supplies from the USSR. (Most of the weapons and munitions provided by the Soviet Union apparently were transferred by rail through China, possibly because of the fear that the United States would blockade Vietnamese ports.)

Similarly, Soviet ships have carried weapons and other supplies in support of Soviet political-economic-military goals to Third World nations throughout the world.

The Soviet maritime effort has several unique features. There is major continued emphasis on break-bulk cargo ships, small tankers, roll-on/roll-off vehicle-carrying ships, SEABEE barge-carrying ships, and passenger ships, all of which are useful in merchant service but also have great military utility. The Soviets have built some supertankers and large container ships, but they began these efforts later than the major Western maritime nations and were thus not caught with as many ships as some nations were when the crude petroleum shipping situation changed radically in the 1970s, resulting in a world glut of large tankers.

In terms of numbers of ships, the USSR probably has the second largest fleet if certain ships assigned to support the fishing industry, training ships, and icebreakers are included (approximately 2,500 ships). However, if only merchant ships that operate on Soviet domestic and foreign shipping routes are counted, the USSR ranks fifth in number of ships (the United States is tenth) and eighth in carrying capacity (the United States is seventh).

There are several methods of measuring merchant ships. The most common methods are Gross Register Tonnage (GRT) and Deadweight Tonnage (DWT).[1] Table 29-1 below, based on U.S. Navy data, addresses active merchant ships over 1,000 GRT and their tonnage; ships that support the fishing industry, training ships, and icebreakers are not included. (Because merchant ship sizes vary greatly, some merchant

[1]Gross Register Tonnage is the cubic contents of a vessel expressed in units of 100 cubic feet (2.83 cubic meters); Deadweight Tonnage is the vessel's lift capacity when loaded in salt water (based on long tons of 2,240 lbs/1,000 kg).

**TABLE 29-1. WORLD MERCHANT FLEETS, MID-1982**

| Number of Ships | | Gross Tonnage* | | Deadweight Tonnage* | |
|---|---|---|---|---|---|
| Panama | 2,803 | Liberia | 72,731 | Liberia | 140,730 |
| Greece | 2,698 | Greece | 41,014 | Greece | 70,481 |
| Liberia | 2,122 | Japan | 37,310 | Japan | 63,278 |
| Japan | 1,843 | Panama | 30,682 | Panama | 51,094 |
| USSR | 1,723 | Britain | 21,979 | Norway | 37,689 |
| Britain | 949 | Norway | 20,851 | Britain | 35,929 |
| China | 926 | USSR | 13,980 | USA | 21,248 |
| Italy | 631 | USA | 13,374 | USSR | 19,271 |
| Norway | 603 | France | 10,168 | France | 18,141 |
| USA | 564 | Italy | 9,672 | Italy | 16,259 |

*Tonnage in thousands.

fleets appear in one or two columns but not all three. For example, mainland China has the seventh largest fleet in terms of numbers of ships, but because of their small individual size, China is not within either of the top ten tonnage categories.)

These numbers are very close to Soviet-provided data. For example, in early 1981 the Soviet Minister of Merchant Marine listed 1,748 ships with a capacity of 18.6 million DWT in the Soviet merchant fleet. Soviet officials have indicated that there will be no further growth in the size of the Soviet merchant marine during the next few years, but rather an emphasis on modernization of the existing fleet.

The Soviet merchant fleet has supported Third World allies with weapons and military supplies as these ships were doing when they carried vehicles and supplies to North Vietnam. The MITSENEK (top), her decks and holds crowded with cargo, was photographed in the Gulf of Tonkin in 1968 en route to Haiphong, and her sister ship MICHURIN—the photo annotated by intelligence experts—was headed for the same port with a deckload of military trucks in 1972. (U.S. Navy)

The Soviet merchant fleet especially seeks trade with the West and Third World to earn hard currency for the Soviet economy. While the reduction of trade to and from the United States has hurt Soviet efforts in this regard, extensive trade with American allies continues. Here the Soviet-built BALASHIKHA is pushed to a pier in Nantes, France. (U.S. Navy, C.E. Fritz)

Soviet merchant ships are smaller than the average ships of the major maritime powers. One reason for this is that many Soviet ports are relatively small, and a large percentage of the Soviet merchant fleet are assigned to intra-country routes.[2] However, these smaller ships are also more suitable for serving Third World nations, which have few if any ports that can accommodate some of the large Western merchant ships and insufficient trade to make it "profitable" for Western shipping lines.

A final merchant fleet measure is ship age. The large and continuing deliveries of merchant ships during the past two decades have provided the USSR with a relatively modern fleet. The average age of the Soviet fleet is about 12 years, with approximately 90 percent of the ships having had less than 20 years of service.

The Soviet merchant fleet has been expanding at an annual rate of about 750,000 DWT during the past few years. This rate of growth can be expected to continue, since 250 ships are being acquired in the current (1981–1985) five-year plan. (Some of these ships are icebreakers and other noncargo types, and some older ships will be retired—thus the net growth will be slightly less.)

## ORGANIZATION

The Soviet merchant fleet is directed by the Ministry of Merchant Marine. Within the ministry there are regional organizations to administer each ocean area, with headquarters at Murmansk, Leningrad, Odessa, and Vladivostok. In Moscow and at each regional headquarters there is a computing center by which administrators can keep track of all shipping and help plan schedules, port calls, overhauls, and future operations.

Merchant ship operations on both the intra-Soviet and international routes are under the jurisdiction of 17 shipping lines. Those lines that have operated most of the ships calling at U.S. ports in the 1960s were the Baltic Shipping Co. of Leningrad and the Far East Shipping Co. (FESCO) of Vladivostok.[3]

---

[2] See Robert E. Athay, "The Sea and Soviet Domestic Transportation," Naval Institute *Proceedings* (Naval Review), May 1972, pp. 158–77.

[3] The other shipping companies are: the Azov, Black Sea, Caspian, Danube, Estonian, Georgian, Kamchatka, Latvian, Lithuanian, Murmansk, Northern, Novorossiysk, Primorsk, Sakhalin, and Sorfract.

The Ministry of Merchant Marine also operates Soviet ports, ship repair facilities, research institutes, schools for various levels and types of merchant training, and several school ships, as well as most of the Soviet Union's large fleet of icebreakers. The merchant schools train ships' officers and crewmen as well as certain specialists to operate shore equipment. Among the more noted schools is the Admiral Makarov Higher Marine Engineering School in Leningrad, which educates merchant marine engineers.

Details of the relationship between the large Ministry of Merchant Marine and the Soviet Navy are not altogether clear from published material. The merchant fleet transfers most of the fuel to Soviet warships on the high seas. The Navy's specialized Boris Chilikin and Berezina classes, as well as the Navy-manned oilers, are taking an increasing share of the replenishment load. However, the development of the Kiev-class aircraft carriers has created heavy demands for Underway Replenishment (UNREP) ships, and thus merchant tankers are still important for the long-range operations of the Soviet Navy.

There are some naval officers assigned to the merchant fleet, and many merchant officers are known to be naval reservists. Finally, the coordination of naval and merchant ship construction by a single Ministry of Shipbuilding has facilitated the incorporation of advanced features in both types of ships, with some commonality of parts and components.

Also, many Soviet merchant ships have military features, such as CBR "washdown" systems to help clean off the effects of chemical, biological, and radiological (nuclear) weapons.

## MERCHANT SHIPS

About half of the current Soviet merchant fleet has been built in Soviet shipyards and almost half in Eastern Europe—in Bulgarian, East German, Finnish, Polish, and Yugoslav shipyards (see chapter 31). The latter ships are purchased with "soft" rubles or obtained through various trade and aid agreements. A few merchant ships have been purchased from the Western nations, including Austria, Britain, France, Italy, and Norway.

It is beyond the scope of this volume to discuss specific characteristics of Soviet merchant ships.[4] The remainder of this chapter discusses some of the more significant categories and types of ships in the Soviet merchant fleet.

*General Cargo Ships.* About half of the merchant fleet consists of general or break-bulk cargo ships. These ships are particularly suited for carrying military cargoes, while their generally small size permits them to call on relatively minor ports. During the past few years the USSR has been the world's largest contractor of general cargo ships and should continue to procure this type of ship.

[4]Detailed characteristics are provided in Jeffery Curtis and Ambrose Greenway, *Soviet Merchant Ships* (Havant, Hampshire: Kenneth Mason, 1980), and Bruno Bock and Klaus Bock, *Soviet Bloc Merchant Ships* (Annapolis, Md.: Naval Institute Press, 1981). The former book is in a loose-leaf format and periodically updated; the Bock volume was originally published in German in 1977, but was partially updated in 1980.

The Pridneprovsk is typical of the general or break-bulk cargo ships that make up about half of the Soviet merchant fleet. The ships of this type, the Soviet-built Poltava class, all have one 60-ton-capacity derrick plus several 5-ton-capacity cranes as shown here. (U.S. Navy)

*Container Ships.* The Soviet merchant fleet has a large number of container and partial container ships, and combination container-RO/RO ships (see below). The largest all-container ships are the German-built modified MERCUR type, delivered from 1975 onward. These ships are 559¾ ft (169.6 m) overall, have a capacity of 14,490 DWT and can carry 729 standard containers. Diesel engines drive the ships at 20 knots.

Apparently the Soviet government felt the need for a small number of faster container ships, and the Nikolayev south yard built the KAPITAN SMIRNOV class of combination container-RO/RO ships. These are 716-ft (217-m), 20,175-DWT ships that can carry vehicles or up to 1,200 stan-dard containers. They have two gas turbines that provide a maximum speed of 25 knots, while bow- and stern-thrusters provide a high degree of maneuverability in port.

*Roll-On/Roll-Off Ships.* The USSR has the largest fleet of RO/RO ships of any nation, with more than 50 in service. Again, these ships are particularly valuable for military operations. While they require piers to unload their vehicles, their rapid unloading capability and large vehicle capacity are most useful.

The KHUDOZHNIK PROROKOV is one of the East German-built container ships of the MERCUR class. With a capacity of 729 standard freight containers, these are the largest "cellular" container carriers in Soviet service. These ships have limited military capability compared to the RO/RO and break-bulk cargo ships.

The Finnish-built INZHENIR MACHULSKIY-class RO/RO ships have large stern ramps fitted to square transoms, one shown here in the raised position on the lead ship of the class. There are two internal decks for vehicles, with a ramp (forward of bridge) leading to the deck space available for vehicles or containers.

*SEABEE Ships.* There are merchant designs that permit the carrying of large, fully loaded barges or lighters that can be floated or lifted on and off the ship. This scheme speeds up loading and unloading and allows cargo to be handled without the need for piers or wharves. The two principal barge-carrying designs are known as LASH (Lighter Aboard Ship) and SEABEE (Sea Barge); the former use cranes to lift barges to the cargo decks, and the latter employ elevators.

During the 1970s the Soviets purchased the plans from a U.S. firm for the SEABEE design and contracted with the Finnish shipyard Valmet to construct two 36,383-DWT ships, larger than any barge carriers that had been built until that time. These ships, the JULIUS FUCIK (delivered in 1978) and TIBOR SZAMUELI (1979), are 880 ft (266.5 m) long and diesel propelled to provide a sea speed of 20 knots. They can carry 26 barges, each 125½ × 36⅓ ft (38 × 11 m) and displacing up to 1,300 tons. To load ship the barges are floated in pairs to the stern of the ship; an elevator lifts them up to one of three cargo decks where trolleys move them to stowage positions. A ship of this type can offload up to 25,000 tons of cargo in 13 hours without the need for piers.

Soviet spokesmen have stated that construction is under way on a nuclear-propelled version of the LASH design, especially configured for Arctic operations. The nuclear ships are being built in the Baltic Shipyard (Leningrad) where the ARKTIKA nuclear icebreakers and the KIROV nuclear battle cruisers are constructed. The LASH ships are reported to be about 858 ft (260 m) long and have a capacity of 32,000 deadweight tons. They will carry up to 75 barges. These ships will be used for year-around operations in the Soviet Arctic.

Another class of large LASH vessels is under construction at Kherson. These will each carry an estimated 82 lighters and are intended for Arctic operation as well as on routes between the Soviet Union and South America.

*Ore-Bulk-Oil Ships.* The OBO ships transport large quantities of liquid fuel, grain, or ore. The first Soviet ship of this type, the MARSHAL BUDENNYY, 810 ft (245.5 m) long with a capacity of 105,000 deadweight tons, was delivered by the Paris Kommuna shipyard in Poland in 1975. Six additional ships (the last three 116,283 DWT) followed from Poland, and another six of 109,640 DWT have been built at the Okean shipyard in Nikolayev. Several smaller bulk carriers are also in Soviet service (and a large number have been built by Soviet yards for other nations).

*Tankers.* The Soviet merchant fleet operates approximately 465 tankers of all types with a capacity of just over seven million DWT. This figure includes about 80 tankers subordinated to the Ministry of Fishing to support worldwide fishing activities. There are also a number of special-cargo tankers, especially liquified gas and ammonia gas carriers.

The Soviet Union lagged behind the Western maritime nations in the construction of supertankers (i.e., over 100,000 DWT). The first Soviet supertanker was the KRYM, a 974-ft (295.2 m), 150,000-DWT ship launched on 9 April 1974 at the Kamysh-Burun shipyard in Kerch'. The KRYM and her sister ships, all built at Kerch', are highly automated with a number of advanced features. The ships' pumps can unload a full cargo of 150,000 tons of oil in ten hours.

Even as the KRYM class was being built, the merchant-ship design bureau in Leningrad began plans for a tanker 1,135 ft (344 m) long with a capacity of some 300,000 to 370,000 tons. However, the larger ships were never built because of the reduced need for supertankers in the late 1970s.

Again, most Soviet merchant tankers are smaller than the average tankers in major Western merchant fleets, making them more useful for naval and Third World operations than the larger ships would be.

The TIBOR SZAMUELI moving at high speed has seven barges on her upper deck. Built to the American-developed SEABEE design, the ship has three cargo decks served by the large stern elevator. Note the bridge that straddles the upper cargo deck and the twin funnels amidships. (U.S. Navy)

The Soviets periodically purchase merchant ships from Japan and the West, as this Japanese-built medium tanker of the LISICHANSK class illustrates. Ten ships of this design were built by Ishikawajima-Harima at Aio specifically for Soviet service. (U.S. Navy)

Long a familiar sight on the world's oceans: A Soviet merchant tanker, this one the ZHITOMIR of the large KOSTROMA/KAZBEK class, dead in the water while astern refueling a Krupnyy-class missile destroyer. Based partially on the U.S. T-2 design, the ZHITOMIR was completed in 1957. Like many of her sister ships, she still has a merchant role as well as the ability to back up modern Soviet naval oilers. (U.S. Navy)

*Specialized Cargo Ships.* There are a number of specialized cargo ships in Soviet service, among them heavy lift ships, timber carriers, and cable layers. Among the most interesting are the three heavy lift ships of the STAKHANOVETS KOTOV class. They can carry heavy, outsize loads, and have two 350-ton-capacity gantry cranes. The cable ships primarily support military programs and are described in chapter 22.

Two recent classes of merchant ships have been built with special features to permit them to service Arctic ports that are normally icebound. These are the 14,500-DWT NORILSK ships, built in Finland, and the 19,600-DWT bulk carrier-container ships of the DMITRIY DONSKOY class, built in East Germany. The former are particularly versatile ships, able to carry heavy-lift items, vehicles, containers, and bulk cargoes.

Among the more interesting ships of the Soviet merchant fleet are the three heavy-lift units of the Stakhanovets Kotov class. The unusual, Finnish-built ships have docking wells and are provided with two heavy-lift gantry cranes. In this view one crane is positioned amidships and one all the way aft; note the funnels on each side of the docking well, amidships.

In this view of the Stakhanovets Kotov-class freighter Stakhanovets Yermolenko, taken in the Bay of Cadiz in 1982, two Osa II-class missile craft are being carried in the ship's docking well. The availability of a large, specialized merchant fleet, including ships of this type, provides the USSR with a major military lift capability. (U.S. Navy)

*Passenger Ships.* The Soviet Union operates the world's largest fleet of passenger ships and currently operates some 70 such ships.[5] They sail on scheduled routes and in cruise service. More than 50 million passengers per year are carried in them.

The largest of the Soviet passenger ships is the MAKSIM GOR'KIY, built in West Germany in 1968. The ship was operated by a German line until

1974 when, found unprofitable to operate, was purchased by the USSR. The ship carries almost 800 passengers. Other ships with almost that capacity are also in operation as are many smaller passenger ships. The Soviet merchant fleet is continuing to acquire passenger ships.

Again, these ships earn hard currencies for the Soviet Union, help to "capture" trade routes, provide an opportunity for political influence, and offer the potential for moving large numbers of troops by sea.

[5]The United States has two all-passenger ships in service.

The Soviet Union is the only nation with a large fleet of modern passenger ships. This is the KARELIYA, one of five medium-size cruise liners built by the Finnish yard of Wärtsilä in the mid-1970s. These ships can berth 500 passengers and can carry another 500 for day cruises and have a RO/RO capability for cars and trucks. (L. & L. Van Ginderen)

Another oft-seen class of Soviet passenger ships are the IVAN FRANKO class. This ship, the MIKHAIL LERMONTON, and four similar ships were built at the Mathias Thesen yard in East Germany. Their normal capacity is 700-750 passengers. This photo shows the ship at Malaga, Spain, in 1981. (U.S. Navy, Douglas P. Tesner)

The ALEKSANDR FADEYEV, shown here laden with CTI containers, is a Kherson-built Soviet merchant ship of the type regularly plying the seas, carrying a substantial share of Western and Third World trade.

Soviet merchant marine cadets (U.S. Navy)

*Training Ships.* The Soviet merchant marine has a number of training schools and educational institutions. Several training ships support these activities, the best-known being the sail-training ships KRUZENSHTERN, SEDOV, and TOVARISCH (see chapter 23). These ships train cadets from merchant marine and fisheries training schools. All German-built, they are the largest sailing vessels in the world, displacing more than 3,000 tons and carrying up to 200 cadets on their far-ranging cruises.

*Icebreakers.* The Soviet Union has the world's largest and most powerful icebreaker fleet. These ships are vital for keeping ports open for naval and commercial operations. Most are civilian operated, with a few having naval crews. The major civilian ships are also described in chapter 23.

In addition to their icebreaking functions, these ships are invaluable for Arctic research, which is important for both military and commercial operations. The newer nuclear icebreakers LEONID BREZHNEV (formerly ARKTIKA) and SIBIR' have been especially useful.

# 30
# Fishing Fleet

A familiar sight on the high seas: A Soviet stern trawler-factory ship at high speed en route to a lucrative fishing area. The LESKOV—with the designation RT 401—is one of more than 60 B26-type ships built in Poland during the 1960s, almost all for the Soviet fishing fleet. Several have been converted to fisheries research vessels. The ship's deadweight tonnage is about 1,400 tons with an overall length of 274 feet (83.1 meters). (U.S. Navy)

With some 4,000 ocean-going fishing and support vessels, the Soviet Union operates the world's largest fishing fleet. This fleet's annual fish catch exceeds 10 million tons, placing the USSR in second place behind Japan.[1]

Considerable resources have been invested in the fishing industry in the postwar period, with emphasis on the construction of high-technology fishing and support vessels, and high-capacity processing plants ashore and afloat.

The Soviets' large flotillas of ships exploit fishing grounds throughout the world. Flotillas of up to 100 and 200 trawlers are not unusual, and on occasion even larger formations have been observed. Some of these trawlers can handle more than 50 tons of fish per day and are equipped to filet, salt, and can or freeze the catch on board. Smaller trawlers transfer their catch directly to factory or "mother" ships, which process and can or freeze the fish. In many cases, refrigerated cargo ships take off the catch and carry it to market in the USSR or other nations, while the trawlers and mother ships remain in the operating area. Fishing flotillas in remote areas are often supported by specialized repair ships, tugs, tankers, and fresh-water carriers.

Most of the fish caught by these vessels—over 90 percent—are for human consumption, being consumed by Soviets or given or sold to other nations. It is estimated that 20 percent of Soviet protein consumption consists of seafood. Seafood exports include such delicacies as caviar from the Caspian Sea and king crab caught off the coast of Alaska. That part of the catch that is not used as food is usually processed into fish meal for fertilizer. Fish oil is also produced. There is little waste from this industry.

Soviet fishing operations off U.S. territory have created confrontations between the United States and USSR. The establishment of a 200-mile (322-km) economic zone around the United States in 1977 was, in part, an effort to restrict Soviet fishing activities. Periodically the U.S. Coast Guard has arrested masters of Soviet fishing vessels for violating this zone. Increasingly the Soviet fishing industry is being faced with protection policies in many areas of the world, which restrict their fishing and force them to exploit new and more remote areas.

At the same time, the Soviet Union is using its expertise in fishing and fish processing to assist other countries, particularly Third World nations, to improve their fishing industries. By sharing area catches and profits, and by exporting Soviet fishing equipment and technical assistance, the USSR hopes to increase influence with those nations. Among the countries that have received Soviet assistance in this field are Bangladesh, Cuba, Egypt, Ghana, Guinea, India, Indonesia, Nicaragua, Senegal, Sri Lanka, Sudan, Tanzania, Vietnam, and South Yemen.

The Soviets need to increase their catch for both domestic and foreign economic reasons. Modernization of the fishing fleet and continued advances in technology are expected and should result in the USSR becoming the leading harvester of the world's marine life.

[1]See Commander Richard T. Ackley, U.S. Navy (Ret.), "The Fishing Fleet and Soviet Strategy," Naval Institute *Proceedings*, July 1975, pp. 30–38; and I.P. Moskovoj, "Soviet Sea-Fisheries 1970–75," *Navy International* [England], June 1976, pp. 6–10.

This view of the Soviet fishing fleet on the high seas shows the stern trawler GURIYA loading her cargo of fish aboard the refrigerated cargo ship MUSSON. The GURIYA, a TROPIK-class stern trawler of some 1,200 deadweight tons, was built in East Germany, while the MUSSON, at 3,480 deadweight tons, is one of six similar "reefers" purchased from West Germany in 1963–1964. (TASS)

## ORGANIZATION AND PERSONNEL

As with other Soviet industries, the fishing industry is highly centralized. The Ministry of Fish Production directs overall operations and fleet development, and has a computer control center in Moscow that keeps track of the worldwide activities of the fleet.

Under the ministry are specialized port facilities (see chapter 27), processing plants, the fishing fleet itself, fisheries research ships (and previously submarines!), and the various support ships. Personnel to man these ships are trained at several schools and on board special ships. There are different types of fisheries schools. The first is available after graduation from eighth grade of normal school and produces skilled workers without a secondary school diploma. The next school level trains officers for the coastal and inland fishing fleets and provides a secondary school diploma. Separate schools similarly train officers for the high-seas fishing and support ships. The six higher technical and engineering institutes are college-level schools, with four-and-a-half year courses. Their admission standards are rigorous, and their graduates become economists, planners, and managers within the fishing industry.

In 1975 the U.S. government estimated that there were 61,000 students studying in the 31 Soviet secondary and higher fishery schools and institutes. The graduates of these schools enter an industry in which salaries are twice, and in some instances three times, as high as those paid to ordinary workers, in part to compensate for arduous duty at sea and for being based on the Arctic and Pacific coasts when ashore. Quite often crews for an entire flotilla of fishing ships are flown out from the Soviet Union to a Third World port to relieve men who have been at sea for several months, thus alleviating the loss of time for the ships to return to the USSR to change crews and replenish supplies. For example, in 1981–1982 special passenger flights carrying Soviet fishing crewmen to the Peruvian port of Callao for this purpose reached a rate of five flights per week.

The larger ships, like naval and merchant ships, are produced under the direction of the Ministry of Shipbuilding. And like the merchant fleet, many ship captains and masters are naval reserve officers. Obviously, the fishing fleet—like the merchant fleet—provides intelligence for naval operations. In the past, the tankers supporting the fishing fleet, which is diesel propelled, provided fuel to diesel-electric submarines in remote areas. While there have not been publicized reports of this activity in recent years, fishing support ships have on occasion rendered emergency services to Soviet submarines.

## SHIPS

As with merchant and research-scientific ships, many Soviet fishing vessels are built abroad, mainly in East German and Polish shipyards. During the 1960s a number of trawler factory ships were built for the Soviet fleet in Danish, Dutch, and Japanese yards (and in the 1950s several were built in West Germany). A few of these ships have also been built in France for the USSR.[2]

*Trawlers.* Soviet trawlers come in a variety of sizes and configurations. The largest ships in the trawler category are three French-built ships of the NATALIA KOVHOVA class, delivered in 1965. These are

[2] The major fishing and support ships are described in the previously referenced Curtis-Greenway and Bock-Bock books (fn 5, chapter 29).

The Soviet fishing fleet includes several hundred oceangoing stern trawler–factory ships. More than 100 ships were built in Soviet yards to the MAYAKOVSKIY design, the TURGENEV shown here being a typical example. The ships of this class are 1,250 deadweight tons and 277 feet (83.9 meters) long.

Soviet trawlers come in various sizes and shapes. This is a small SRT or *Svedni Rybolovnyi Trauler* or side trawler type (the Cyrillic letters on the bridge are CPT, shown with the craft's registration number 4500). (U.S. Navy)

421-ft (127.7-m) ships with a tonnage of 4,710 DWT; they can both harvest and process fish. Only slightly smaller, but more significant because of the larger number, are the Polish-built trawlers of the Sprut class (Polish B400 design). In production since 1978, the Spruts are 392½ feet (119.0 m) long with a tonnage of 3,550 DWT. These are handsome ships and well equipped for sustained, long-range fishing operations.

*Factory Ships.* The Soviet Union's largest factory ships are the Sovietskaya Ukrainia and Sovietskaya Rossia, approximately 26,000 DWT ships completed in 1959 and 1961, respectively. These giants, built at Nikolayev, are approximately 718 ft (217.5 m) overall and have crews of more than 500 men and women who specialize in processing whales. About 65 whales per day can be processed, producing 1,000 tons of whale oil in addition to meat. The factory ships operate with flotillas of smaller whale-catching ships.

Only slightly smaller is the Vostok, built at Leningrad's Admiralty yard. The 22,110-DWT ship (43,000 displacement tons) was delivered in 1971 after some technical difficulties. She was intended to carry 14 fishing craft of 60-tons each plus helicopters and was designed to process more than 300 tons of fish daily. Even after completion the Vostok has not been fully successful, and instead of operating as a small-craft carrier and factory, she has been employed only in the latter role. No additional ships of the class have been built.

Instead, the Vostok was followed on the ways at the Admiralty yard by four smaller factory ships of the 50 Letiye SSR ("50 years of the USSR") class. These are 13,040-DWT ships of a more conventional factory design and with diesel propulsion (as in the Sovietskaya-type ships; the Vostok has four steam turbines). These four ships, completed between 1972 and 1980, are very efficient, and with their crews of more than 500 are reported to be able to process more than 800 tons of fish per day.

The Vostok was an unsuccessful effort by the Soviet fishing fleet to develop a fishing craft carrier-factory ship. There have been several such failures in Soviet naval-maritime development efforts, but the magnitude of the Soviet thrust to the sea can permit such mistakes as different concepts and designs are tried.

The fish factory–mother ship Baltiyskaya Slava operating off Cape Hatteras, North Carolina. Built in West Germany, the ship provides full support to deployed fishing craft and can fully process their catches. She is one of eight ships with a 10,000 to 11,100 DWT, and is 552 feet (167.3 meters) long; note the stern chute for taking floating catches from trawlers; the ship can process about 400 tons of raw fish daily. Another ship of this class is shown off the coast of Virginia transferring canned fish to a refrigerated cargo ship for transport to market. (U.S. Navy)

More than 100 smaller factory ships are also in service (in addition to the trawler factory vessels). The factory ships also provide logistic support, maintenance services, and medical facilities to the trawlers in their working area.

*Support Ships.* The Soviet merchant marine operates a large number of refrigerated cargo ships, fuel tankers, water carriers, repair ships, and ocean-going tugs in support of the fishing fleet.

*Training Ships.* There are several fisheries training ships in service, mostly trawlers modified with student accommodations and classrooms.

*Research Ships and Submarines.* The fishing industry has several trawlers modified to conduct research into fish hunting and catching techniques. At least two, the 1,070-DWT IKHTIANDR and ODISSEY, have been modified to carry research submersibles.

Also, in the 1960s two diesel-electric submarines of the Whiskey class were converted to oceanographic–fisheries research submarines. Renamed SEVERYANKA and SLAVYANKA, their forward torpedo rooms were converted into laboratories, observation stations were installed to permit scientists to view the water outside, exterior lights were fitted, and provisions were made to recover sea-floor samples. About six to eight scientists were assigned to these missions. The two undersea craft operated in the research role for several years before being discarded.

Several small submersibles are operated in support of fisheries activities.

*Aircraft.* Aircraft are employed periodically to support the fishing industry. Helicopters have been based aboard the larger ships to help track down schools of fish. In addition, land-based aircraft have been used, especially Il-14 Crate twin-engine aircraft and Il-18D Coot four-engine aircraft. The decision to use the longer-range Coot was made, in part, because of farther-ranging fishing areas brought about by the 200-mile economic zones. The initial Coot flights in 1980–1981 were sponsored by the Polar Institute of Marine Fishing and Oceanography and the State Scientific Research Institute of Civil Aviation.

A large number of refrigerated cargo ships (reefers), water ships, and tankers support the Soviet fishing fleet. This fully loaded small tanker of the Finnish-built NERCHA class is off Halifax, Nova Scotia, supporting fishing activities in the western Atlantic. (U.S. Navy)

The EKVATOR is one of several MAYAKOVSKIY-class trawlers modified for fisheries research. The Soviets have invested considerable manpower, ships, and facilities in obtaining the knowledge necessary to reap the harvests of the world's oceans efficiently. The EKVATOR is based at the fisheries research complex in Vladivostok. (U.S. Navy)

The ODISSEY has also been modified from a MAYAKOVSKIY-class trawler for research. Her more-extensive changes include the large structure amidships to house research submersibles. Although the USSR is behind the United States in manned submersible vehicle technology, their use in civilian research appears to be more extensive. She is based at Murmansk.

Soviet fishing activities frequently intrude into territorial waters of other nations. Here the LAMUT, flagship of the Soviet Bering Sea fishing force, is detained near St. Matthew Island, Alaska, by the U.S. Coast Guard Cutter STORIS (WMEC 38). The LAMUT is a Japanese-built herring factory ship, with a 3,320 DWT and length of 364 feet (110.3 m). (U.S. Coast Guard)

# 31
# Warsaw Pact Navies

Poland's guided missile destroyer WASZAWA is the largest warship in the non-Soviet navies of the Warsaw Pact. The smaller Pact navies provide significant small combatants and amphibious forces for use in the Baltic Sea and, to a lesser extent, in the Black Sea. These fleets use mostly Soviet-type ships and equipment, and closely follow Soviet doctrine and tactics.

The Soviet Union and seven "satellite" nations in Eastern Europe signed the Treaty of Friendship and Mutual Assistance in Warsaw on 14 May 1955. The treaty was in part a response to the establishment of the North Atlantic Treaty Organization (NATO) in 1949. The Warsaw Pact signatories, in addition to the USSR, were Albania, Bulgaria, Czechoslovakia, East Germany, Hungary, Poland, and Romania.

The Albanian government broke relations with Moscow for ideological reasons in 1961 and thus effectively withdrew from the Warsaw Pact. This withdrawal was made official in 1968. Albania's loss to the USSR was significant from a naval point of view, because the small country, with a coastline on the Adriatic Sea, had provided the Soviets with Mediterranean bases. In 1960 a Soviet submarine tender and eight submarines had been sent to the Albanian island of Saseno (Sazan) in the Gulf of Valona. This base was abandoned by the Soviets in 1961, with Albania seizing two of the Whiskey-class submarines by refusing them permission to leave at the time of the Soviet withdrawal. (Two other Whiskey submarines had been transferred to Albania in 1960.)

In addition to the Soviet Union, only Bulgaria, East Germany, Poland, and Romania have naval forces. Of the non-Soviet navies, only those of East Germany and Poland have offensive capabilities. Both of these navies are intended primarily for employment in the Baltic and cannot be realistically considered effective opponents for NATO forces beyond those important, but restricted, waters.[1]

Since 1957 the Soviet, East German, and Polish navies have conducted joint exercises on a regular basis in the Baltic, and in 1980 and again in 1981 the three navies conducted exercises in the North Sea. However, these operations seem to have been for political and military reasons. In 1981, for the first time, the operation was under the command of an East German admiral.

As noted in chapter 5 (Baltic Sea Fleet), in wartime the East German and Polish navies would join with Soviet naval forces to provide support for ground operations along the southern Baltic coast, would deny use of the Baltic to NATO naval forces, and would seize control of the Danish straits. Amphibious landings would probably be carried out in support of these activities, including the capture of the Danish island of Bornholm, which lies north of Poland, and probably some of the Danish coastline. (Soviet troops occupied Bornholm from 1945 to 1947.)

Table 31-1 provides a summary of the four non-Soviet navies. In the Baltic region the East German and Polish navies have large numbers of missile, patrol, and torpedo boats to operate against Western forces and to escort their own amphibious forces. East Germany and Poland have amphibious ships, and East Germany has minesweepers to carry out landings. Poland also has a naval division—i.e., marines—and East Germany has army units, both of whom train in amphibious operations.

Poland, with four Whiskey-class submarines, also has a very limited offensive capability.

[1]See Milan N. Vego, "East European Navies," Naval Institute *Proceedings*, March 1981, pp. 34–39. This was the first annual review of foreign navies by the *Proceedings*. Dr. Vego provided an update of his original survey in the issue of March 1982, pp. 43–47 and March 1983, pp. 42–46.

**TABLE 31-1. WARSAW PACT NAVIES**

| | Baltic Sea | | Black Sea | | |
|---|---|---|---|---|---|
| | East Germany | Poland | Bulgaria | Romania | Total |
| Attack Submarines | — | 4 | 2 | — | 6 |
| Guided Missile Destroyers | — | 1 | — | — | 1 |
| Frigates | 2 | — | 2 | — | 4 |
| Corvettes | 17 | — | 3 | 3 | 23 |
| Missile Craft | 15 | 13 | 4 | 5 | 37 |
| Torpedo Boats | 49 | 10 | 6 | 30 | 95 |
| Patrol Boats | 18* | 34* | 6 | 22* | 80 |
| Minesweepers | 47 | 26 | 10 | 5 | 88 |
| Amphibious Ships | 12 | 23 | — | — | 35 |

*Some operated by border guards.

In the Black Sea, the Bulgarian and Romanian navies are used primarily for coastal defense. Bulgaria, which shares a border with NATO member Turkey, has a large number of torpedo and patrol boats, plus two Romeo-class submarines.

The military activities of the Warsaw Pact nations are directed totally by the Soviet Union, with a Soviet marshal in the post of commander in chief. Numerous other Soviet officers—some naval—are assigned to key staff positions. In peacetime the Warsaw Pact high command directs the Groups of Soviet Forces in Czechoslovakia, East Germany, Hungary, and Poland, certain Soviet forces in the three western military districts of the USSR, and all East German military forces. In contrast to the East German forces, those of the five smaller Warsaw Pact nations are subordinate to the Warsaw Pact high command only during periods of external threat. Efforts by the Soviet Union to establish standing Warsaw Pact armies were attempted in 1956–1957 and again in 1967–1968, but were rejected by the member nations.

The air, ground, and naval forces of the non-Soviet nations use mainly Soviet-type equipment, Soviet tactical and hence training doctrine, Soviet communications procedures, and so forth. East Germany and Poland have made significant developments in equipment, especially in the naval areas, but this equipment is intended to fit into the Soviet "style" of warfare and often has Soviet components. This rigidity within the Warsaw Pact is in strong contrast to the NATO nations, who tend to use significant amounts of American equipment only for economic reasons, and most of the nations have their own tactical doctrine and mostly their own equipment. Although some U.S. and other NATO ships have weapons and electronics developed by other nations, virtually all NATO navies operate fleets built entirely in their own shipyards.

A final factor of major importance to the Soviet Navy is the shipbuilding capability of the Warsaw Pact nations—East Germany, Poland, and to a lesser extent Bulgaria and Romania being major suppliers of ships to the USSR. Most of this Eastern European shipbuilding effort consists of merchant ships, which are significant to Soviet naval operations in peace and war. However, the East German and Polish yards provide the Soviet Navy with large numbers of amphibious, intelligence collection, research, and auxiliary ships.

## BULGARIA

Bulgaria borders on the Black Sea, between Romania to the north and the European portion of Turkey to the south. Bulgaria has a small navy by NATO standards, consisting primarily of coastal forces and river craft that serve on the Danube River.

Two Romeo-class submarines were transferred from the USSR in 1971–1972, replacing two older Whiskey submarines. These craft can provide limited ASW training and can serve in the coastal defense role.

Significantly, the Navy's two Riga-class frigates and its small oiler did deploy to the Mediterranean during the summer of 1980 for exercises with the Soviet Navy, the joint exercises being repeated in July 1981. The replenishment ship ANLENE, built in Bulgaria in 1980, is thus the harbinger of more extended training operations for the diminutive Bulgarian fleet.

*Naval command.* Vice Admiral V.G. Yanakiev is CinC of the Navy.

*Naval personnel.* The Bulgarian Navy has some 8,800 uniformed personnel of whom 1,900 are assigned to ships and craft, about 2,100 to coastal defenses, 1,800 to training activities, and some 2,500 to shore support. A naval air arm estimated at 480 officers and enlisted men fly 24 helicopters—12 Mi-14 Haze ASW helicopters and 12 utility-rescue helicopters. There are about 5,000–6,000 conscripts in the Navy on three years' obligatory service.

*Bases and ports.* The principal bases and ports on the Black Sea are Sozopol; Varna at the mouth of the Provadiya River, which has commercial and naval facilities; and Burgas, the nation's most important harbor and the center of its fishing industry.

*Shipyards.* The major Bulgarian shipbuilding facilities are the George Dimitrov shipyard at Varna and yards at Burgas and Ruse (on the Danube, near the Romanian border). The principal customer of these

### TABLE 31-2. BULGARIAN NAVY

| Number | Type | Class | Builder |
|---|---|---|---|
| 2 | Attack Submarines | Romeo | USSR |
| 2 | Frigates | Riga | USSR |
| 3 | Corvettes | Poti | USSR |
| 4 | Missile Craft | Osa I/II | USSR |
| 6 | Torpedo Boats | Shershen | USSR |
| 6 | Patrol Boats | S.O.-1 | USSR |
| 4 | Minesweepers | Vanya | USSR |
| 2 | Minesweepers | T-43 | USSR |
| few | Inshore/Coastal Minesweepers | (various) | USSR |
| 18 | Landing Craft | Vydra | USSR |
| 10 | Landing Craft | MFP-D3 | East Germany |
| 1 | Oiler | ALENE | Bulgaria |
| 1 | Survey Ship/Tender | Moma | Poland |
| 1 | Salvage Tug | Type 700 | East Germany |

yards has been the USSR—the Ruse yard building a series of 3,000-DWT tankers and the Dimitrov yard container ships for the Soviet Union during the 1980s. Recent deliveries to the USSR have included bulk carriers up to 38,000 tons. (In return, Bulgaria has been receiving Soviet-built fishing vessels.)

*Merchant marine.*[2] 108 ships are reported in the Bulgarian merchant fleet, consisting of 2 combination passenger ships, 50 freighters, 39 bulk carriers, and 17 tankers. Total tonnage is 1,620,000 DWT. These ships are operated by the Bulgarian Maritime Shipping Line.

[2]Merchant Marine data from "Merchant Fleets of the World," U.S. Maritime Administration, 1 January 1981.

The Bulgarian training ship NIKOLA VAPTZAROV visited Antwerp in 1982, reflecting the increasing range of operations by Warsaw Pact forces. (1982, L. & L. van Ginderen)

## CZECHOSLOVAKIA

Czechoslovakia has no coastline, but army personnel operate several armed motor launches on the Danube River. The government owns a large number of river craft.

*Shipyards.* There is a major shipyard in Komárno, the Gabor Steiner yard, for building and maintaining river craft, as well as lesser facilities along the Danube. The Komárno yard has built more than 250 river and coastal ships for the USSR since the late 1940s.

*Merchant marine.* The Czechoslovak International Maritime Company (founded in 1959) operates 16 ships totalling 229,000 DWT. These consist of 11 cargo ships and 5 bulk carriers operated by the Czechoslovak Ocean Shipping and Czechoslovak Danube Shipping lines.

## EAST GERMANY (GERMAN DEMOCRATIC REPUBLIC)

East Germany, toward the western end of the Baltic, is of considerable naval significance to the Soviet Union because of its proximity to Denmark and the Danish straits. The East German Navy ranks after the Polish fleet and is characterized by large numbers of small combatants with significant missile (Styx), minesweeper, and amphibious capabilities. This force apparently has the twofold mission of helping to control the western Baltic and of conducting amphibious operations against the West German and Danish coasts.

During the past few years the Navy has been undergoing a modernization program. Among the more recent acquisitions are two new, Soviet-built frigates of the Koni class, transferred in 1978–1979, to replace two ineffective ships of the Riga class. Similarly, a new class of 1,200-ton PARCHIM corvettes are being built in East Germany. These ships were earlier designated Bal-Com-4 (Baltic Combatant) by NATO, with the name of one unit, the KORALLE, sometimes being cited by the

### TABLE 31-3. EAST GERMAN NAVY

| Number | Type | Class | Builder |
|---|---|---|---|
| 2 | Frigates | Koni | USSR |
| 5* | Corvettes | PARCHIM | East Germany |
| 12+ | Corvettes | Hai III | East Germany |
| 15 | Missile Craft | Osa I | USSR |
| 18 | Torpedo Boats | Shershen | USSR |
| 31 | Torpedo Boats | Libelle | East Germany |
| 18† | Patrol Boats | (various) | East Germany |
| 26 | Minesweepers | Kondor II | East Germany |
| 21 | Inshore Minesweepers | Kondor I | East Germany |
| 12 | Landing Ships | Frosch | East Germany |
| 2 | Tenders | Frosch | East Germany |
| 3 | Intelligence Ships | (various) | USSR-East Germany |
| 6 | Survey Ships | (various) | Poland, East Germany |
| 8 | Buoy Tenders | (various) | East Germany |
| 5 | Oilers | (various) | USSR-East Germany |
| 1 | Training Ship | Wodnik | Poland |
| 1 | Salvage Ship | Piast | Poland |
| 1 | Diving Ship | Havel | East Germany |
| 10 | Miscellaneous Ships | | |

*At least seven additional units under construction.
†Several operated by the East German border guards.

press as a class name. Additional small combatants are expected to be procured. Some of the smaller units are operated by the Coastal Frontier Brigade (GBK).

The German army's 29th motorized rifle regiment is especially trained in amphibious operations.

*Naval command.* The Navy commander is Vice Admiral Willi Ehm. (Dr. Ehm was appointed CinC of naval forces with the rank of rear admiral in August 1959.)

The East German Navy is being modernized by the transfer of Koni-class frigates from the USSR and the construction of PARCHIM-class corvettes (formerly Bal-Com-4) at the Peenewerft yard at Wolgast, shown here.

The Baltic Sea is an excellent operating area for small combatants. Here the East German Shershen-class torpedo boat JOSEPH ROEMER (852) closes on the Osa I-class missile craft RUDOLF EGELHOFER (752). (West German Navy)

An East German Frosch-class medium landing ship under way at high speed in the Baltic. These German-built ships are generally similar to the Soviet Ropucha class, but smaller and more heavily armed. While the satellite navies use mainly Soviet-type ships, the 14 Frosch-class ships are an example of several national designs.

*Naval personnel.* The East German Navy has an estimated 14,700 men. Of these, 5,100 are assigned afloat, 2,700 to coastal defense, 1,600 to training activities, and 5,100 to shore support. A naval air arm of 260 men flies about 15 utility helicopters, which have minimal ASW capability. However, Mi-14 Haze ASW helicopters are probably being transferred to Germany. About 10,000 of the men are conscripts with two years required service in the Navy.

*Bases and ports.* Rostock is the largest and most important port in East Germany, being located on the Warnow River near where it enters the Baltic Sea. Among the commercial and naval activities at Rostock are the Navy's headquarters, a major oil terminal, and a large fishing center. Under an expansion plan the port's cargo handling is being increased from 15.3 million tons in 1980 to 24 million tons by 1985.

Warnemünde, the outer port of Rostock, is a seaside resort with naval and commercial facilities. Wismar, on the gulf of that name, is mainly a commercial port; Stralsund, on the Strelasund, is a naval base and commercial port, as is Sassnitz on the opposite side of Rügen Island; Wolgast, near the mouth of the Peene River, appears also to be a naval and commercial port; and nearby Peenemünde, former center for German missile development, is a major naval facility.

*Shipyards.* There are several shipyards in East Germany, most being

These Polish naval officers and sailors aboard an Osa I are exchanging greetings with a NATO ship passing close aboard. The level of training in the Polish fleet is reported to be high.

The non-Soviet merchant ships of the Warsaw Pact provide the USSR with some flexibility in trading with other nations, especially those that the Soviet Union does not officially recognize. The MANSFIELD is one of six similar grain carriers built in East Germany in the early 1960s. The ship is 13,150 DWT with a length of 501 feet (151.8 meters). (U.S. Navy)

employed to construct and repair fishing, coastal, and river craft. There are five major shipyards: the Warnow yard at Warnemünde; the Matthias-Thesen yard at Wismar; the Neptune yard at Rostock; the Volks yard at Stralsund; and the Peenewerft yard at Wolgast. All build commercial ships, while Peenewerft builds small combatants and the Frosch-class landing ships for the East German Navy, and Wolgast is constructing the PARCHIM-class corvettes. During 1981 the East German yards built 59 ships (455,897 DWT), of which 42 were for the Soviet Union. The USSR has received over 1,300 of the merchant and fishing ships built in East Germany since 1946. This represents 60 percent of the ships built by the country.

Recent commercial shipbuilding programs of these yards include the ATLANTIK-class supertrawlers, improved MERCUR-class container ships, and the 19,885-DWT Arctic freighters for the USSR.

*Merchant marine.* The East German merchant fleet has 158 merchant ships of 1,776,000 DWT. These consist of 2 passenger-cargo ships, 129 cargo ships, 19 bulk carriers, and 8 tankers. The firm of VEB Deutfracht/Seereederei operates East Germany's merchant ships.

The proximity of East Germany to West Germany and Denmark, including the Baltic island of Bornholm, makes intelligence collection a primary activity of the East German armed forces. The HYDROGRAPH, a modified Okean-class trawler, is one of three East German AGIs.

The East German Koni-class frigate Rostock

## HUNGARY

Hungary, like Czechoslovakia, has no coastline, but operates river patrol craft under army command on the Danube River. The army also has a few small landing craft. The smaller of these craft have been built and are maintained at minor shipyards and repair facilities along the Danube. Some of these yards have built large numbers of river tugs and other small craft for the Soviet Union.

*Merchant marine:* Twenty-one ships totalling 101,000 DWT are registered to Hungary, all freighters operated by the Mabart line.

## POLAND

The Polish Navy is the largest of the non-Soviet Warsaw Pact forces in terms of ship size, ship tonnage, and naval personnel. The Navy is relatively "balanced" in the sense of having four submarines, a missile destroyer, a large force of missile-torpedo craft, and a significant amphibious and mine countermeasure capability. However, the submarines are outdated Whiskey-class boats, transferred in 1962–1965,

and the destroyer is the Warszawa, a SAM Kotlin transferred to Poland in 1970, but having been built—like the Whiskeys—more than 30 years ago. Still, the ships are maintained in excellent condition, and the navy has long been a source of pride to the nation.[3]

In the immediate postwar period the Polish Navy was built up with considerable Soviet support, including the assignment of Soviet officers of Polish origin. In 1956 Poland became the first satellite nation to receive Soviet submarines (M class), and in 1957 the first to be given Soviet-built destroyers (Skoryy class), which have since been discarded. It is anticipated that Poland will receive replacements for the submarines and the destroyer in the near future, with probably one or more frigates taking the

[3]A Polish Navy was established between the World Wars. After the fall of Poland in 1939 a Polish Navy-in-exile was established, with headquarters in England. At war's end the Polish Navy had one light cruiser, six destroyers, six submarines, and several smaller craft. Another cruiser, four destroyers, and two submarines were lost during the war.

**TABLE 31-4. POLISH NAVY**

| Number | Type | Class | Builder |
|---|---|---|---|
| 4 | Attack Submarines | Whiskey | USSR |
| 1 | Missile Destroyer | SAM Kotlin | USSR |
| 13 | Missile Craft | Osa I | USSR |
| 10 | Torpedo Boats | Wisla | Poland |
| 5 | Patrol Boats | Pilica | Poland |
| 12 | Patrol Boats | Wisloka | Poland |
| 8* | Patrol Boats | Obluze | Poland |
| 9* | Patrol Boats | Gdansk | Poland |
| 12 | Minesweepers | KROGULEC | Poland |
| 12 | Minesweepers | T-43 | Poland |
| 2† | Coastal Minesweepers | (new) | Poland |
| 28 | Inshore Minesweepers | K-8 | Poland |
| 23 | Landing Ships | Polnocny | Poland |
| 4 | Landing Craft | Marabut | Poland |
| 2 | Intelligence Ships | Moma | Poland |
| 1 | Intelligence Ship | B-1 (trawler) | Poland |
| 6 | Coastal Oiler | (various) | Poland |
| 2 | Salvage Ships | Piast | Poland |
| 2 | Training Ships | WODNIK | Poland |
| 4 | Training Ships | BRYZA | Poland |
| 2 | Hydrographic Ships | ZODIAK | Poland |

*Operated by Polish border guards.
†Additional units under construction.

place of the WARSZAWA. However, their replacement may be delayed because of the political problems in Poland during the early 1980s.

Poland has the only satellite navy with a significant air arm. There is a reconnaissance-bomber squadron with 10 Il-28 Beagle turbojet light bombers, three attack squadrons with 40 MiG-17 Fresco turbojet fighters, and two helicopter squadrons with 25 Mi-2 Hoplite/Mi-4 Hound/Mi-8 Hip helicopters. There are also several training aircraft. These aircraft are all outdated and in need of replacement.

The Polish Army's 7th Amphibious Landing Division regularly exercises with the Navy's amphibious ships.

*Naval command.* Admiral Ludwik Janczyszyn commands the Polish Navy.

*Naval personnel.* There are a reported 21,800 men in the Polish Navy, with 5,600 afloat, 2,100 with the naval air arm, 5,600 assigned to coastal defense, 2,300 involved in training activities, and 6,200 in shore support billets. Of this force, about 6,000 are conscripts, drafted for 18 months.

*Bases and ports.* Most Polish ports and naval bases are in territory that was German through World War II, and all were heavily damaged during the war and then stripped by the Russians of their useful equipment and other material.

The principal Polish commercial port and naval base are at Gdynia, known as Götenhafen from 1939 to 1945. It was a small fishing village until the mid-1920s when there was a period of rapid growth and development, making it a major port. It is the main base of the Polish Navy, a large commercial port (especially for the shipment of coal from Upper Silesia), and a major shipbuilding center.

Just south of Gdynia, also on the Gulf of Danzig, is the city of Gdańsk, which is also a major commercial port, with some naval activities and three major shipyards.

There are smaller naval bases at Hel (formerly Hela) on the Pólwysep Hel Peninsula, and at Świnoujście (Swinemünde) on the Polish-East

The Polish salvage and rescue ships of the PIAST class are a variation of the Moma-design, used extensively by the Soviet Navy in the survey and AGI roles. The Polish ships, one of which is shown here, and one East German ship of this type have diving bells as well as diving, salvage, and fire-fighting equipment.

The Polish cargo ship STOCZNIOWIEC, her decks loaded with heavy vehicles, steams through the Gulf of Tonkin en route to North Vietnam in 1970, passing the U.S. aircraft carrier CORAL SEA (CVA 43). Poland has a large, modern merchant fleet. The STOCZNIOWIEC and her sister ships are 14,250 DWT with a length of 517 feet (156.7 meters). (U.S. Navy, H.M. Thomas)

German border. Nearby Szczecin (Stettin), on the Oder River, is a commercial port.

*Shipyards.* Poland has one of the world's most advanced shipbuilding industries, ship construction being one of the nation's largest sources of foreign currency. The Polish and former German shipyards, which were devastated in World War II, were totally rebuilt from the late 1940s onward with Soviet assistance.

Since the first oceangoing ship was laid down in 1948, the Polish yards have produced commercial ships for some two dozen nations, sending more than half of their total output to the USSR. Polish yards have also produced almost 80 landing ships of the Polnocny class and 14 of the Ropucha class as well as large numbers of intelligence collection ships, survey ships, and other naval units for the Soviet Navy and for transfer to Soviet allies. Although large naval ships are not built in Poland, the shipyards do produce supertankers and large bulk carriers as well as specialized merchant ships.

There are four major shipyards and several smaller building and repair

facilities. The major yards are the Lenin (ex-Schichau) and Polnocny (ex-Danziger) in Gdańsk, the Paris Kommuna in Gdynia, and the Adolf Warski (ex-Vulcan) yard in Szczecin. All build commercial ships and some naval auxiliaries.

The Lenin yard is the pride of the Polish shipbuilding industry. It is the oldest and largest shipyard in Poland, employing some 15,000 workers. The yard's 900-ton capacity crane, standing 348 ft (105.5 m) high, dominates the Gdańsk skyline. During the past few years the yard has delivered large numbers of fish factory ships and oceangoing trawlers for the Soviet fishing fleet.

On 6 March 1982 the Lenin yard launched the 340-ton sail-training barkentine ISKRA II for use by the Polish Navy. Another sail training ship, the DAR MOLODIEZY, was built at the Lenin yard for the Polish merchant marine academy (replacing the famous DAR POMORZA, retired after 70 years of service). Additional ships of this type are being built for the Soviet Union.

Near the Lenin yard is the Polnocny yard, also known as the Northern

The Polish Navy's 23 landing ships of the Polnocny classes represent a major amphibious lift force in the Baltic region, supplementing the large Soviet amphibious capability. This Polish Polnocny-A can be distinguished from the B series by the lower bridge and mast-mounted Drum Tilt GFC radar.

The Orzel is one of the four Whiskey-class submarines operated by the Polish Navy. These undersea craft are in need of replacement and, with the reestablishment of a Soviet-controlled government in Poland, the Whiskeys may be exchanged for newer submarines, most likely of the Kilo class.

yard. This facility produces amphibious ships for the Soviet and Polish navies (with many being transferred to the Third World), various classes of survey and research ships, the WODNIK-class training ships, trawlers, and other types of fishing craft.

(Also in Gdańsk is the smaller Wisla yard, which built the BRYZA-class small training ships that are used extensively by Poland and the USSR for training merchant marine and fisheries employees.)

At Gydnia is the Paris Kommuna ("Commune") yard, which produces many of the advanced merchant ships flying the Soviet flag. These include the large "Marshal"-class ore-bulk-oil carriers and the "Skulptor"-series roll-on/roll-off ships, as well as numerous smaller merchant ships of various types and, with the Lenin yard in Gdańsk, the numerous B26-type stern trawler–factory ships. The Paris Kommuna yard has also built minesweepers and other craft for the Polish Navy.

The fourth major yard is the Adolf Warski facility in Szczecin. This yard has built numerous cargo and passenger ships as well as specialized ships. The last includes ocean research ships, training ships, and hospital ships for the Soviet Navy.

Another large shipyard is being built in the port of Ustka (formerly Stolpmünde). This yard currently builds fishing craft, but will be expanded to build 100,000-deadweight-ton merchant ships. It will employ some 11,000 workers out of a total national shipyard work force likely to number more than 100,000 in this decade.

(Shipyard workers have generally been among the leaders of political unrest in postwar Poland. The political crises of the early 1980s began in August 1980 when 15,000 workers at the Lenin shipyard went on strike. One of their key demands was for the construction of a monument to shipyard workers killed by police in 1970 during the riots that toppled the government of Wladyslaw Gomulka and brought in the government in power when the 1980 unrest began. The workers also sought major labor and union reforms.)

*Merchant fleet.* The Polish merchant marine has a reported 318 ships of 4,686,000 DWT. This consists of 4 passenger-cargo ships, 220 freighters, 81 bulk carriers, and 13 tankers. The most recent acquisitions (not included in these totals) are four French-built combination container-and-RO/RO ships of 22,709 DWT, which are able to carry 1,100 containers plus vehicles. Several additional RO/RO and container ships are on order from Polish and Spanish yards as part of an ongoing expansion of the Polish merchant marine.

The three shipping lines—the Polish Steamship Company, the Polish Baltic Ship Company, and the Polish Ocean Lines—have suffered a large number of desertions in the early 1980s, as has the large Polish fishing fleet, because of the political unrest in the country.

## ROMANIA

On the western coast of the Black Sea between Bulgaria and the Soviet Union lies Romania. Romania's naval forces consist mainly of coastal torpedo and patrol boats. The largest units are three Poti-class corvettes. Some of the more recent acquisitions are of Chinese design (built in Romania) with a few units having been transferred from China. Many of the patrol craft serve with the border guards.

**TABLE 31-5. ROMANIAN NAVY**

| Number | Type | Class | Builder |
|---|---|---|---|
| 3 | Corvettes | Poti | USSR |
| 5 | Missile Craft | Osa I | USSR |
| 10 | Torpedo Boats | Epitrop | Romania |
| 20* | Torpedo Boats | Huchuan | Romania |
| 19† | Patrol Boats | Shanghai II | China-Romania† |
| 3 | Patrol Boats | Kronshtadt | USSR |
| 5 | Minesweepers | T-301 | USSR |
| 1 | MCM Support Ship | Cosar | Romania |
| 1 | Research Ship | Mod. Cosar | Romania |
| 1 | Tender | Croitor | Romania |
| 3 | Coastal Tankers | (various) | Romania |
| 4 | Ocean Tugs | Roslavl | USSR |
| 1 | Training Ship | MIRCEA | Germany (1938) |
| 3 | Training Ships | FRIPONNE | France (1916) |

*Some operated by Romanian border guards.
†3 units built in China and the remainder in Romania.

*Naval command.* Rear Admiral Ioan Musat is commander of the Romanian Navy.

*Naval personnel.* The Navy has an estimated 6,800 men—2,300 assigned afloat, 600 assigned to training, 1,500 to shore support activities, 2,300 to coastal defense, and almost 100 to a small air arm that has a few helicopters.

*Bases and ports.* Romania, with the shortest coastline of those Warsaw Pact nations that border on seas, has two major seaports. Constanta handles most of the country's overseas trade, is the terminal point for the Ploeşti oil pipeline, and the country's major naval base. A port at Vilovo at the mouth of the Danube—called Ust'-Dunaysk—was opened in 1980 to handle bulk cargoes. Mangalia to the south has recently been enlarged to handle ships up to 55,000 DWT.

Sulina at the central mouth of the Danube, and Tulcea and Brăila on the Danube, have limited port facilities. A new port has been built at Călăraşi, an industrial center. It is connected with the Danube through a canal.

*Shipyards.* The country has four shipyards that build mostly coastal and small seagoing ships, and also has several minor facilities. The significant yards are at Brăila, Constanta, Galaţi, Mangalia, and Sulina.

The Constanta yard builds large bulk ore carriers as well as supertankers of 150,000 DWT. The Galaţi yard, located on the Danube, built two submarines at the beginning of World War II, but subsequent naval construction has been limited to smaller units.[4] Mangalia has been constructing Shanghai II-class patrol boats of Chinese design. The Soviet Union is a major customer for these yards, while several merchant ships have also been built for Cuba during the past few years.

*Merchant marine.* Romania has a reported 191 merchant ships in service of 2,408,000 DWT. There are reported to be four passenger ships, 220 freighters, 81 bulk carriers, and 13 tankers flying the Romanian flag for the Navrom line.

[4]These submarines joined an Italian-built submarine in Romanian service. Submarines are no longer operated by the Romanian Navy.

# A

# Soviet Flag Officers, 1983

## MINISTRY OF DEFENSE[1]

| Position | Rank | Name | Year |
|---|---|---|---|
| Deputy Minister of Defense | Adm. Fleet SU | S.G. Gorshkov | 1956 |
| General Staff | | | |
|   Deputy Chief | Adm. | N.N. Amel'ko | 1978 |
|   External Relations Directorate | | | |
|     Deputy Chief | Rear Adm. | V.Z. Khuzhokov | 1978 |
| Main Political Directorate | | | |
|   1st Deputy Chief | Adm. | A.I. Sorokin | 1981 |
| Main Directorate of Navigation and Oceanography | | | |
|   Chief | Adm. | A.I. Rassokho | 1963 |
|   Deputy Chief | Rear Adm. | A.N. Motrokhov | 1973 |
|   Deputy Chief | Rear Adm. | A.G. Yevlanov | 1977 |
| Lenin Political-Military Academy | | | |
|   Head of Faculty | Rear Adm. | G.G. Kostev | |
| Sports Committee Chairman | Vice Adm. | N.A. Shashkov | 1975 |

## JOINT ARMED FORCES OF THE WARSAW PACT

| Position | Rank | Name | Year |
|---|---|---|---|
| Deputy CinC for Naval Forces | Adm. | V.V. Mikhaylin | 1980 |
| Deputy Chief of Staff | Vice Adm. | F.I. Savel'yev | 1975 |

## NAVY

| Position | Rank | Name | Year |
|---|---|---|---|
| Commander in Chief | Adm. Fleet SU | S.G. Gorshkov | 1956 |
| 1st Deputy Commander in Chief | Adm. Fleet | N.I. Smirnov | 1974 |
| Deputy CinC for Combat Training | Adm. | G.A. Bondarenko | 1973 |
|   Deputy | Rear Adm. | I.F. Uskov | 1978 |
| Deputy CinC for Rear Services | Adm. | L.B. Mizin | 1974 |
|   Deputy and Chief of Staff | Maj. Gen. Quartermaster | N.I. Kobelev | 1977 |
|   Chief Navy Finance Service | Maj. Gen. Quartermaster | V. Belov | 1977 |
|   Chief Navy Medical Service | Maj. Gen. Medical Serv. | N. Potemkin | 1981 |
| Deputy CinC for Shipbuilding and Armaments | Engr. Adm. | P.G. Kotov | 1966 |
|   Deputy | Engr. Vice Adm. | I.I. Tynyankin | 1980 |
|   Chief Main Directorate of Ship Repair Plants | Engr. Rear Adm. | A.M. Gevorkov | 1975 |
| Deputy CinC for Naval Educational Institutions | Vice Adm. | A.M. Kosov | 1978 |
| Deputy | Engr. Rear Adm. | V.S. Yefremov | 1981 |
| Deputy CinC | Engr. Adm. | V.G. Novikov | 1970 |
| Chief Navigator | Rear Adm. | R. Zubkov | |
| Chief Naval Air Defense[2] | Rear Adm. | S. Tegler | 1982(?) |
| Chief Inventions Bureau | Engr. Rear Adm. | N. Popov | 1980 |

## Main Naval Staff

| Position | Rank | Name | Year |
|---|---|---|---|
| Chief[3] | Adm. | V.N. Chernavin | 1982 |
| 1st Deputy Chief | Adm. | P.N. Navoystev | 1976 |
| Deputy Chief | Vice Adm. | Y.P. Kovel' | 1968 |
| Deputy Chief | Rear Adm. | O.M. Kalinin | 1981 |
| Chief Observation Directorate | Rear Adm. | M.M. Krylov | 1977 |

## Political Directorate

| Position | Rank | Name | Year |
|---|---|---|---|
| Chief | Adm. | P.N. Medvedev | 1981 |
| 1st Deputy Chief | Rear Adm. | S.P. Vargin | 1981 |
| Deputy Chief | Rear Adm. | Ya. Grechko | 1978 |
| Deputy Chief for Agitation and Propaganda | Rear Adm. | E.Yu. Zimin | 1980 |
| Chief Organizational Party Work Department | Rear Adm. | S.M. Yefimov | 1979 |
| Party Commission Secretary | Rear Adm. | A. Kolchin | 1982 |

## Auxiliary Fleet and Salvage—Sea Rescue Service

| Position | Rank | Name | Year |
|---|---|---|---|
| Chief | Rear Adm. | S.P. Zuyenko | 1975 |

## Naval Aviation

| Position | Rank | Name | Year |
|---|---|---|---|
| Commander | Col. Gen. Aviation | A.A. Mironenko | 1975 |
| Deputy Commander | Col. Gen. Aviation | A.N. Tomashevskiy | 1972 |
| Deputy Commander for Political Affairs | Maj. Gen. Aviation | I.M. Tropynin | 1978 |
| Chief of Staff | Col. Gen. Aviation | G.A. Kuznetsov | 1975 |

## Naval Infantry and Coastal Artillery Force

| Position | Rank | Name | Year |
|---|---|---|---|
| Commander | . . . . . . | | |

[1]Rank abbreviations are listed at the end of the appendix; dates indicate year position was assumed.

[2]This is a relatively new position, probably established in the early 1980s, in conjunction with the reorganization of Soviet air defense activities.

[3]Also a first deputy CinC of the Soviet Navy.

## NORTHERN FLEET

| | | | |
|---|---|---|---|
| Commander in Chief | Adm. | A.P. Mikhaylovskiy | 1982 |
| 1st Deputy | Vice Adm. | V.S. Kruglyakov | 1976 |
| Deputy for Training & Chief of Combat Training | Rear Adm. | V. Ryabov | 1981 |
| Deputy for Rear Services | Vice Adm. | V.M. Petrov | 1978 |
| Chief of Staff | Rear Adm. | V. Denisov | 1981 |
| Chief of Finance Department | Maj. Gen. Quartermaster | I. Burnayev | 1978 |
| Chief of Staff | Vice Adm. | V. Korobov | 1981 |
| 1st Deputy | Rear Adm. | M.D. Iskanderov | 1979 |
| Chief Political Directorate | Vice Adm. | N.V. Usenko | 1980 |
| 1st Deputy | Rear Adm. | V.T. Polivanov | 1976 |
| Deputy Chief | Rear Adm. | V. Losikov | 1978 |
| Commander Naval Aviation | Maj. Gen. Aviation | V.P. Potapov | 1981 |
| Chief Political Department | Maj. Gen. Aviation | M.S. Mamay | 1969 |
| Chairman Military Tribunal | Maj. Gen. Justice | V. Bobkov | 1981 |
| Chief Personnel Department | Rear Adm. | V. Zuyev | 1977 |

## BALTIC FLEET

| | | | |
|---|---|---|---|
| Commander in Chief | Adm. | I.M. Kapitanents | 1981 |
| 1st Deputy & Chief of Staff | Vice Adm. | K. Makarov | |
| Deputy for Rear Services | Rear Adm. | P.P. Belous | 1976 |
| Chief Political Department | Rear Adm. | V. Kabanov | |
| Deputy for Construction | Maj. Gen. Engr. | O. Anikanov | 1979 |
| Chief Political Directorate | Vice Adm. | I.F. Alikov | 1980 |
| Commander Naval Aviation | Lt. Gen. Aviation | A.I. Pavlovskiy | 1977 |
| Chief of Staff | Maj. Gen. Aviation | V. Budeyev | 1981 |
| Chief Political Department | Maj. Gen. | B.I. Grekov | 1976 |
| Commander Riga Naval Base | Rear Adm. | I.I. Verenikin | 1975 |
| Commander Tallinn Naval Base | Rear Adm. | L.K. Zarubin | 1974 |

## LENINGRAD NAVAL BASE

| | | | |
|---|---|---|---|
| Commander | Vice Adm. | V.A. Samoylov | 1982 |
| 1st Deputy | Rear Adm. | Ye V. Butuzov | 1978 |
| Deputy | Rear Adm. | I.M. Kolchin | 1974 |
| Deputy for Rear Services | Rear Adm. | V.N. Bashkin | 1982 |
| Chief Political Department | Rear Adm. | A. Korniyenko | |
| Deputy Chief | Rear Adm. | A.P. Prosvernitsyn | 1978 |

## BLACK SEA FLEET

| | | | |
|---|---|---|---|
| Commander in Chief | Adm. | N.I. Khovrin | 1974 |
| 1st Deputy | Vice Adm. | V.I. Akimov | 1978 |
| Deputy | Rear Adm. | P.T. Zenchenko | 1978 |
| Deputy for Rear Services | Rear Adm. | N.A. Yermakov | 1979 |
| Chief of Staff | Rear Adm. | L.Y. Dvidenko | 1981 |
| Chief Political Department | Rear Adm. | A. Morozov | |
| Chief of Staff | Rear Adm. | N.G. Klitnyy | 1981 |

| | | | |
|---|---|---|---|
| Deputy | Rear Adm. | A. Gorshkolepov | |
| Chief Political Directorate | Vice Adm. | R.N. Likhvonin | 1981 |
| 1st Deputy | Rear Adm. | V.I. Popov | 1980 |
| Deputy | Rear Adm. | S. Rybak | 1981 |
| Commander Naval Aviation | Col. Gen. Aviation | V.I. Voronov | 1971 |
| Chief of Staff | Lt. Gen. Aviation | F.G. Nefedov | 1973 |
| Chief Political Department | Maj. Gen. Aviation | Yu. Sinyakov | 1975 |
| Chief Hydrographic Directorate | Rear Adm. | L. Mitin | 1979 |
| Task Force Commander[4] | Vice Adm. | N.I. Ryabinskiy | |
| Task Force Commander[4] | Vice Adm. | G.I. Shalygin | |

## CASPIAN SEA FLOTILLA

| | | | |
|---|---|---|---|
| Commander | Vice Adm. | G.G. Kasumbekov | 1977 |
| Chief of Staff | Rear Adm. | V. Tolkachev | |
| Chief Political Directorate | Rear Adm. | V.P. Nekrasov | 1981 |

## PACIFIC FLEET

| | | | |
|---|---|---|---|
| Commander in Chief | Adm. Fleet | V.V. Sidorov | 1981 |
| 1st Deputy | Vice Adm. | N.Ya. Yasakov | 1979 |
| Deputy for Rear Services | Vice Adm. | M.A. Kosyachenko | 1977 |
| Chief Finance Service | Maj. Gen. Quartermaster | V. Novikov | 1976 |
| Deputy for Construction | Maj. Gen. Engr. | V. Skuratov | 1980 |
| Chief of Staff | Vice Adm. | Ya.M. Kudel'kin | 1976 |
| Deputy Chief | Rear Adm. | V.N. Perelygin | 1978 |
| Chief Observation & Communications Directorate | Rear Adm. | A. Morev | 1981 |
| Chief Political Directorate | Vice Adm. | N.P. D'yakonskiy | 1981 |
| 1st Deputy | Rear Adm. | A.M. Slavskiy | 1980 |
| Deputy Chief | Rear Adm. | V.V. Abramov | 1976 |
| Deputy Chief | Rear Adm. | V.G. Semiletenko | 1978 |
| Commander Naval Aviation | . . . . . . | | |
| Deputy Commander | Maj. Gen. Aviation | P. Ryzhkov | 1979 |
| Chief Construction Directorate | Maj. Gen. Engr. | V. Skuratov | 1980 |
| Chief Auxiliary Fleet | Rear Adm. | A. E. Yakimchik | 1981 |
| Task Force Commander | Rear Adm. | G.I. Semenov | |

## NAVAL EDUCATIONAL INSTITUTIONS

| | | | |
|---|---|---|---|
| Grechko Naval Academy | Adm. | V.S. Sysoyev | 1974 |
| Dzerzhinskiy HNS (Engineering) | Vice Adm. | N.K. Yegorov | 1975 |
| Frunze HNS | Rear Adm. | N.K. Fedorov | 1980 |
| Kaliningrad HNS | Vice Adm. | V.S. Pilipenko | 1970 |
| Kiev HNS (Political) | Vice Adm. | N.S. Kaplunov | 1980 |
| Kirov Caspian HNS | Vice Adm. | V.A. Arkhipov | 1976 |
| Lenin HNS (Engineering) | Engr. Vice Adm. | B.A. Lapshin | 1975 |
| Leninsky Komsomol HNS (Submarine Warfare) | Vice Adm. | G.L. Nevolin | 1974 |
| Makarov Pacific HNS | Rear Adm. | I. Karmadonov | 1982 |
| Nakhimov Black Sea HNS | Rear Adm. | P. Sokolan | |
| Popov HNS (Radio-Electronics) | Vice Adm. | A.A. Rulyuk | 1975 |
| Sevastopol' HNS (Engineering) | Engr. Vice Adm. | A.A. Sarkisov | 1972 |

[4]Both men have recently commanded Soviet naval forces in the Mediterranean.

## MISCELLANEOUS ASSIGNMENTS

| | | | |
|---|---|---|---|
| Chairman Central Committee DOSAAF | Adm. Fleet | G.M. Yegorov | 1982 |
| Military Attaché, German Democratic Republic | Vice Adm. | M.N. Lyshchin | 1979 |
| Editor, *Morskoy Sbornik* | Rear Adm. | A. Pushkin | |
| Military Correspondent, *Pravda* | Rear Adm. | T.A. Gaydar | 1973 |
| Institute of U.S. Studies, Academy of Sciences | Rear Adm. (Ret.) | B. Yashin | |
| Commanding Officer, SSBN | Rear Adm. | O. Chefonov | |
| Commanding Officer, SSBN | Rear Adm. | V.V. Naumov | |
| Commanding Officer, SSBN | Rear Adm. | V. Frolov | |

Abbreviations:
| | | | |
|---|---|---|---|
| Adm. | = Admiral | Gen. | = General |
| Col. | = Colonel | HNS | = Higher Naval School |
| Engr. | = Engineer | Lt. | = Lieutenant |
| Flt. | = Fleet | Maj. | = Major |
| | | SU | = Soviet Union |

In many respects the Soviet Navy has watched Western naval activity more intensively than the West has watched the Soviets. To aid them in their observations, these Soviet officers and sailors have silhouettes of Western aircraft painted on the superstructure.

A Bear-F with weapons bay open while releasing sonobuoys (one with parachute open is visible between the right-wing engine nacelles). First seen in the West in 1973, the Bear-F, as well as a missile-carrying version, are reported in production. (Ministry of Defence)

# B

# Soviet Naval Order of Battle, 1945–1982

This appendix lists the major ships of the Soviet Navy in active service at five-year intervals since the end of World War II. Sources vary as to the numbers because of differing methodologies of keeping track of Soviet warships, different dates for data in the various categories, and other counting problems. The last column reflects late 1982 Western intelligence estimates.

| | 1945 | 1950 | 1955 | 1960 | 1965 | 1970 | 1975 | 1980 | 1982 |
|---|---|---|---|---|---|---|---|---|---|
| **Submarines—Nuclear** | | | | | | | | | |
| SSBN | — | — | — | 1 | 9 | 31 | 60 | 70 | 69 |
| SSGN | — | — | — | — | 20 | 36 | 40 | 45 | 50 |
| SSN | — | — | — | 3 | 15 | 23 | 40 | 55 | 65 |
| **Submarines—Diesel** | | | | | | | | | |
| SSB | — | — | — | 13 | 29 | 25 | 23 | 17 | 15 |
| SSG | — | — | — | 1 | 25 | 33 | 25 | 25 | 18 |
| SS/SSQ/SSR | — | — | 117 | 285 | 259 | 208 | 143 | 155 | 145 |
| SST/AGSS | — | — | — | — | — | 4 | 4 | few | few |
| Pre-1950 Designs | 241 | 286 | 249 | 131 | | | | | |
| (Total Submarines) | (241) | (286) | (366) | (434) | (357) | (360) | (335) | (372) | (367) |
| | | | | | | | | | |
| Aircraft Carriers | — | — | — | — | — | — | 1 | 2 | 3 |
| Helicopter Carriers | — | — | — | — | — | 2 | 2 | 2 | 2 |
| Battleships | 3 | 2 | 2 | — | — | — | — | — | — |
| Heavy Cruisers (180 mm guns) | 7 | 7 | 7 | 5 | 2 | 2 | — | — | — |
| Light Cruisers (150–152 mm guns) | 2 | 6 | 21 | 20 | 12 | 9 | 11 | 11 | 9 |
| Guided Missile Cruisers | — | — | — | — | 6 | 10 | 19 | 24 | 27 |
| Destroyers | 41 | 52 | 115 | 120 | 81 | 44 | 36 | 30 | 25 |
| Guided Missile Destroyers | — | — | — | — | 6 | 26 | 35 | 36 | 39 |
| Guided Missile Destroyers (SSM only) | — | — | — | 6 | 12 | 10 | 1 | 1 | 1 |
| Guided Missile Frigates (Krivak class) | — | — | — | — | — | 1 | 10 | 27 | 31 |
| Frigates/Ocean Escorts | 19 | 29 | 67 | 88 | 56 | 45 | } 106 | } 135 | } 145 |
| Light Frigates | — | — | — | — | 34 | 64 | | | |

The VTOL aircraft carrier KIEV demonstrates the complexity of modern Soviet warships. About a score of the ship's weapon, fire control, radar, electronic warfare, and communication systems are visible in this view. Hormone helicopters, with rotors spread, rest on her flight deck.

The Kashin-class missile destroyer PROVORNYY, test ship for the SA-N-7 system, appears to have two positions for SA-N-7 launchers forward. The bridge structure mounts Front Dome, Top Steer, and Owl Screech radars as well as two RBU-1000 rocket launchers.

# C
# Suggested Reading

The following is a guide to the English-language writings that address Soviet and Russian naval and related maritime subjects.

## BOOKS

For the first two decades of the post–World War II era there was a dearth of English-language writings on the Soviet Navy. Little of what was happening behind the "iron curtain" was known in the West, and in the opinion of many of the contemporary observers, little was happening. That judgment was based more on the indications of the quality of Stalin's fleet-building program and not the quantity, which was, in some respects, remarkable for any country in peacetime.

Marin Mitchell's *The Maritime History of Russia 848-1948* (London: Sidgwick and Jackson Limited, 1949) obviously stressed the first eleven hundred years of the book's coverage. However, there are several useful discussions on naval and shipbuilding matters, and on the personalities that affected postwar developments.

More useful was M.G. Saunders's *The Soviet Navy* (New York: Praeger Publishers, 1958), which comprised a set of essays by Western naval officers, analysts, and journalists. Saunders, a commander in the Royal Navy, provided a most valuable overview in his introduction to the book.

The first American effort of note was Robert Waring Herrick's *Soviet Naval Strategy* (Annapolis, Md.: U.S. Naval Institute, 1968). With the subtitle "Fifty Years of Theory and Practice," Herrick's heavily annotated work suggested that the Soviet Navy was defensively oriented. Herrick, a retired U.S. naval intelligence officer had, like Saunders, served in Moscow as an assistant attaché.

A steady flow of books on Soviet naval and maritime subjects began in the 1960s, and the flow continues unabated. In addition to the specific books listed below, the so-called "Dalhousie papers" are recommended reading. These are the published collections of papers presented at a series of conferences on the Soviet Navy chaired by Michael MccGwire, a formal Royal Navy intelligence officer, at Dalhousie University, Halifax. (Mr. MccGwire also served as an assistant naval attaché in Moscow.) The papers are by many of the leading Western analysts of Soviet naval developments and published as *Soviet Naval Developments: Capability and Context* (1973), *Soviet Naval Policy: Objectives and Constraints* (1975), and *Soviet Naval Influence: Domestic and Foreign Dimensions* (1977), all by Praeger Publishers, New York. Together, these volumes cover almost all aspects of the Soviet Navy, most of them in a scholarly manner.

One other set of conference papers, while now somewhat dated, made a significant contribution to the understanding of Soviet naval issues. Published as *The Soviet Union in Europe and the Near East: Her Capabilities and Intentions* (London: Royal United Service Institution), this was the result of a seminar sponsored by Southampton University and the RUSI at Milford-on-Sea in March 1970.

Bathurst, Robert B. *Understanding the Soviet Navy: A Handbook.* Newport, R.I.: Naval War College Press, 1979. An effort to put the modern Soviet Navy into perspective as a navy and an institution, this soft-cover book is by a retired U.S. Navy captain and intelligence specialist.

Boyd, Alexander. *The Soviet Air Force Since 1918.* London: Macdonald and Jane's, 1977. This is possibly the best of several books on the Soviet air force; the subject is significant because of the position of Soviet naval aviation within the overall scheme of Soviet "air power."

Cable, James. *Gunboat Diplomacy.* New York: Praeger Publishers, 1971. An excellent analysis of this subject with appropriate coverage of Soviet efforts; a revised edition appeared in 1981 (New York: St. Martin's Press).

Erickson, John. *The Soviet High Command 1918–1941.* London: Macmillan, 1962. Professor Erickson, the dean of analysts of the Soviet defense establishment, the world's largest, covers the development of that establishment and the Soviet military philosophy behind it that continues to prevail today.

———. *Soviet Military Power.* Washington, D.C.: United States Strategic Institute, 1973. This soft-cover volume contains an invaluable overview of the Soviet armed forces. It is an updated version of the author's *Soviet Military Power* published by the RUSI in 1971.

Fairhall, David. *Russian Sea Power.* Boston: Gambit, 1971. Fairhall, an English journalist, provides a highly readable account stressing Soviet commercial activities at sea. (The English edition's title, *Russia Looks to the Sea*, was closer to the mark; the American cover shows a Soviet SLBM streaking skyward—an example of a misreading of the coverage of the book by the publisher.)

Gorshkov, Sergei G. *Red Star Rising.* Annapolis, Md.: Naval Institute Press, 1974. This is the compilation of Admiral Gorshkov's 11 essays originally published in *Morskoy Sbornik* and republished, in English, by the Naval Institute *Proceedings.* This soft-cover volume features comments on each essay by U.S. Navy flag officers.

————. *The Sea Power of the State*. Annapolis, Md.: Naval Institute Press, 1979. Admiral Gorshkov's "second" book, this volume expands his views of the importance of sea power to a nation, arguing that the Navy should have a dominant role in all areas of the world except Europe.

Higham, Robin, and Jacob W. Kipp, eds. *Soviet Aviation and Air Power*. Boulder, Colo.: Westview Press, 1977. A collection of essays on Soviet aviation, albeit mostly historical.

Jones, David R., ed. *The Military-Naval Encyclopedia of Russia and The Soviet Union*. Gulf Breeze, Fla.: Academic International Press. This ambitious project, relying extensively on Russian-language sources, is historically oriented, but covers the post–World War II period quite extensively. Three volumes (through ADP-TAIL) had been published through 1982, with the articles mostly by members of the academic community.

Jordan, John. *Soviet Surface Fleet*. London: Arms and Armour Press, 1983. A detailed and particularly well illustrated discussion of modern Soviet aircraft carriers, cruisers, and destroyers.

[Khrushchev, Nikita.] *Khrushchev Remembers, The Last Testament*. Boston: Little, Brown & Company, 1974. This second volume of Khrushchev's memoirs provides major coverage of military developments during his tenure as First Secretary of the Communist Party (1953–1964), especially the chapter "The Navy," which gives his perspective of "The Fall of Admiral Kuznetsov" and "The Rise of Admiral Gorshkov."

Polmar, Norman. *Soviet Naval Power—Challenge for the 1970s*. New York: Crane, Russak & Company, 1972. The second edition of a college text describing and explaining Soviet naval developments since World War II.

Scott, Harriet Fast, and William F. *The Armed Forces of the USSR*. Boulder, Colo.: Westview Press, 1979. A detailed and highly annotated description of the structure of the Soviet military establishment. They both served in the U.S. embassy in Moscow, he for two tours as Air Force attaché.

Seaton, Albert. *Stalin as a Military Commander*. New York: Praeger Publishers, 1976. This book ends with the Japanese surrender, but it has importance in understanding Stalin's attitudes and the environment that led to the postwar Soviet military establishment.

Sokolovskiy, V.D. *Soviet Military Strategy*. Stanford, Calif: Stanford Research Institute, 1975. This is the third edition of Marshal Sokolovskiy's modern classic, edited and with a commentary and analysis of differences in the three editions by Harriet Fast Scott.

Sweetman, Bill. *Soviet Military Aircraft*. Novato, Calif.: Presidio Press, 1981. An excellent review of modern Soviet military aircraft.

Theberge, James D. *Soviet Seapower in the Caribbean: Political and Strategic Implications*. New York: Praeger Publishers, 1972. This volume is limited in scope and to some extent overtaken by events, but still explains Soviet naval efforts in this area and their significance.

Warner, Edward L., III. *The Military in Contemporary Soviet Politics*. New York: Praeger Publishers, 1977. This "institutional analysis" is more philosophical than the Scotts' work, and covers more of the institutional factors. However, it is useful and heavily annotated.

U.S. Department of Defense. *Soviet Military Power*. Washington, D.C.: Government Printing Office, 1981. A graphic and imposing exposi-

tion by the Secretary of Defense on the Soviet "threat." Produced to help support the Reagan Administration's defense program, this soft-cover volume provides significant data on Soviet naval issues.

Watson, Bruce W. *Red Navy at Sea*. Boulder, Colo.: Westview Press, 1982. Subtitled "Soviet Naval Operations on the High Seas, 1956–1980," this is an excellent description and assessment of Soviet fleet operations, with emphasis on port visits and their political-military significance.

## REFERENCE WORKS

During the past few years *Combat Fleets of the World* has emerged as probably the best reference volume of the world's navies, especially the Soviet and other Warsaw Pact fleets. The book is adapted from the French-language *Flottes de Combat*, being published in alternate years by the Naval Institute Press (Annapolis, Md.).

*Weyer's Warships of the World* is similarly published in English in alternate years by the Nautical & Aviation Publishing Company (Annapolis, Md.). While this is a highly "abbreviated" pocket book, it is a handy and relatively inexpensive volume.

*Jane's Fighting Ships* continues as the largest and most expensive naval reference work, being published annually by Jane's Publishing Company (London). Unfortunately, of late *Jane's* appears to be declining in quality while increasing in cost.

Valuable for contemporary descriptions of Soviet naval aircraft is *Jane's All the World's Aircraft* (London: Jane's Publishing Company), edited by J.W.R. Taylor.

Two contemporary reference volumes address Soviet merchant ships. Ambrose Greenway's *Soviet Merchant Ships* (Havant, Hampshire: 1980) is a very useful, loose-leaf book updated every few years. It provides brief discussions and characteristics of Soviet merchant, fishing, research ships, and icebreakers.

*Soviet Bloc Merchant Ships* by Bruno Bock and Klaus Bock is the English-language edition (Annapolis, Md.: Naval Institute Press, 1981) of a German-language listing of Eastern Bloc merchant ships. There are useful discussions, but the ship listings are particularly austere with only small line drawings for illustration.

Finally, *Understanding Soviet Naval Developments* is a U.S. Navy publication that has been updated three times since its first appearance in 1974. This book was originally written for use by U.S. naval officers. A soft-cover book, it provides a good overview of Soviet naval activities and is heavily illustrated. The latest Navy (soft-cover) edition was published in January 1981; it is available through the Government Printing Office, Washington, D.C., and is commercially published in a hard-cover edition by the Nautical & Aviation Publishing Company (Annapolis, Md.).

## CONGRESSIONAL HEARINGS

The U.S. Congress annually publishes the hearings held by the various committees that consider defense programs. These include periodic briefings from the Director of Naval Intelligence on Soviet naval matters as well as limited discussions of Soviet naval matters by other senior U.S. officers. Of particular value during the 1960s and 1970s were the statements of Admiral H.G. Rickover, at the time head of the U.S. Navy's

# Soviet Maritime Flags

National Flag

Naval Ensign

Fleet Commander

DEP. Min. DEF

Nav. Aux

Squad Commander

Red Banner

Salv & Rescue

Form CDR

Guards

Hydro. Serv.

Form CDR

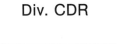

Div. CDR

Senior CDR

Commissioning Pennant of an Auxiliary

KGB

Jack

Combat

Aux.

# Combat Efficiency Awards

The Soviets conduct regular operational readiness inspections of their ships and those rated as outstanding are allowed to display the appropriate emblem.
Below are depicted the various awards–there will usually be painted on the bridge, except the individual gun or combat action stations award which is printed on the winning station.

Outstanding Ship of the Soviet Navy

Outstanding Ship of a Fleet

Outstanding Ship

Stern Emblem (Larger Ships)

Individual Guns or Combat Stations

Artillery

Minelaying

Rockets (AAW) and Radar

Torpedoes

Rockets (SSM)

Propulsion

Minesweeping

Air Defense/AAW

Rocket and Radar Technology
(Gold border indicates three or more awards)

ASW
(circles indicate awarded by Fleet Commander)

Artillery
(Gold circle indicates awarded by CINC of the Soviet Navy)

# Line Officers Insignia—Full Dress and Dress Uniforms

## (Service Uniforms and Dress Overcoats Have Black Shoulderboards Vice Gold)

**Higher Officers**

  *

Admiral of the Fleet
of the Soviet Union
(Admiral Flota Sovetskogo Soyuza)

Admiral
(Admiral)

Vice Admiral
(Vitse-Admiral)

Rear Admiral
(Kontr-Admiral)

**Senior Officers**

'Scrambled Eggs' and
Gold Chin Strap on Dress Service
Caps of Officers
and Service Caps
of Senior Officers

Captain, 1st Rank
(Kapitan Pervogo Ranga)

Captain, 2nd Rank
(Kapitan Vtorogo Ranga)

Captain, 3rd Rank
(Kapitan Tretyego Ranga)

**Junior Officers**

Captain-Lieutenant
(Kapitan-Leytenant)

Senior Lieutenant
(Starshiy-Leytenant)

Lieutenant
(Lelytenant)

Junior Lieutenant
(Miadshiy-Leytenant)

**Ornamentation on Collars of the
Full Dress and Dress Coats**

Fleet
Admiral

Admirals
and Generals

Other Officers

Line Engineering Officer Wear The Same Insignia but with the Silver Engineering Device Mounted on Shoulderboards.

*Fleet Admiral (Not Shown) Insignia 15 similar to FASU except Shoulderboard has only the large star and sleeve has 3½ bars above broad stripe.

# Enlisted Shoulderboards

## Afloat

| Senior Chief Petty Officer | Chief Petty Officer | Petty Officer 1st Class | Petty Officer 2d Class | Senior Seaman | Seaman |

## Shore-Based Units and Naval Aviation

| Master Sergeants | Senior Sergeants | Sergeants | Junior Sergeants | Senior Seaman | Seaman |

## Naval Infantry

| Master Sergeant | Senior Sergeant | Sergeant | Junior Sergeant | Corporal | Private |

## Cap Devices

| Hat Ribbon (With Name of Fleet) | On Winter Cap | On Service Cap | On Service Cap of Naval Infantry | Unit Citation Hat Ribbon Worn by Enlisted Personnel Serving In Units or Vessels Honored by "Guards" Designation |

nuclear propulsion program, before various committees of the House and Senate and, especially, the Joint Committee on Atomic Energy.

Also, during the 1970s the Congressional Research Service prepared a series of compendiums entitled *Soviet Oceans Development* that were published by the Committee on Commerce, Senate. These included essays on a variety of Soviet naval and maritime subjects.

## JOURNALS AND MAGAZINES

Excellent articles on Soviet naval subjects appear on a regular basis in the U.S. Naval Institute *Proceedings* (monthly), the U.S. *Naval War College Review* (bimonthly), the British journal *Naval International* (monthly), and the Swiss-published *International Defense Review* (bimonthly). Of particular interest is the November 1982 issue of the *Proceedings*, which was devoted to Soviet naval matters.

The British magazine *Defence* (monthly) has carried a series of excellent articles the past few years by Mr. John Jordan on Soviet warship classes.

Probably the best periodicals describing Soviet naval aircraft—past and present—are *Air International* and *Flight International*, both published in England. "News" of Soviet naval air and missile developments, although sometimes of questionable accuracy, is found in the American magazine *Aviation Week*.

Also available in English is the monthly Soviet journal *Military Review* (monthly). Although published in several languages and intended for non-Soviet consumption, it contains articles that are reprinted from professional Soviet military magazines. (*Military Review* is also published in Russian.)

# General Index*

*Ranks are the highest used in text.

# Ship Name and Class Index[*]

[*]Brit. = British, Bul. = Bulgarian, E.Ger. = East German, Ger. = German, Pol. = Polish, Rom. = Romanian, U.S. = United States

Norman Polmar is an internationally known naval analyst and writer. He has directed analytical and historical studies for the U.S. Navy, various agencies of the Department of Defense, the Maritime Administration, and American and foreign shipbuilding and aerospace firms.

Mr. Polmar is a member of the Secretary of the Navy's naval research advisory committee and serves on an advisory panel of the Center for Naval Analyses.

The author of a dozen books on naval, aviation, and strategic subjects, Mr. Polmar most recently coauthored the best-selling biography *Rickover: Controversy and Genius*. He is the editor of the eleventh and twelfth editions of *The Ships and Aircraft of the U.S. Fleet* and coauthor of the reference work *Military Helicopters of the World*, both published by the Naval Institute Press. Mr. Polmar's articles appear frequently in U.S. and foreign military journals, and he writes a regular column—"The U.S. Navy"—for the Naval Institute *Proceedings*.

As a defense consultant and journalist he has travelled throughout Europe and to North Africa and the Middle East, and has visited the Soviet Union as a guest of the Soviet Institute of U.S. Studies and Soviet Navy.

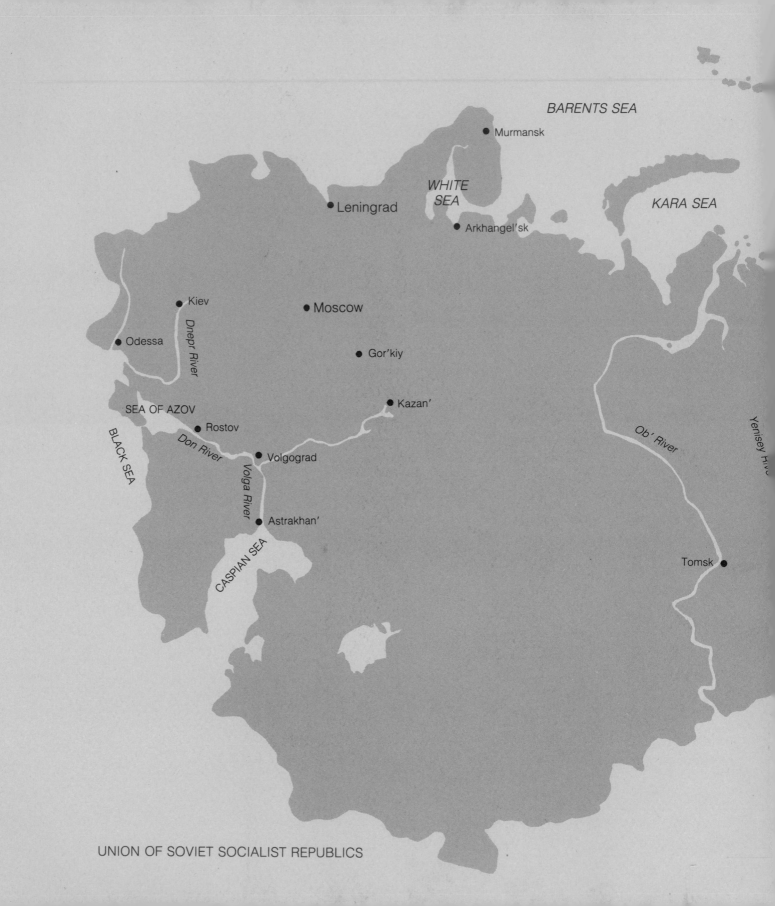

BARENTS SEA

● Murmansk

WHITE
SEA

KARA SEA

● Leningrad

● Arkhangel'sk

● Kiev

● Moscow

*Dnepr River*

● Odessa

● Gor'kiy

*Ob' River*

*Yenisey River*

● Kazan'

SEA OF AZOV

● Rostov

*Don River*

● Volgograd

*Volga River*

BLACK SEA

● Astrakhan'

CASPIAN SEA

● Tomsk

UNION OF SOVIET SOCIALIST REPUBLICS